Professional WebObjects 5.0 with Java

Michael DeMan
Josh Flowers
Gustavo Frederico
Ben Galbraith
John Hopkins
Pero Maric
Max Muller
Jim Roepcke
Bernhard Scholz
Daniel H. Steinberg
Thomas Termini
Pierce Wetter

with

Douglas Bergère

Wrox Press Ltd. ®

Professional WebObjects 5.0 with Java

© 2001 Wrox Press

All rights reserved. No part of this book may be reproduced, stored in a retrieval system or transmitted in any form or by any means, without the prior written permission of the publisher, except in the case of brief quotations embodied in critical articles or reviews.

The author and publisher have made every effort in the preparation of this book to ensure the accuracy of the information. However, the information contained in this book is sold without warranty, either express or implied. Neither the authors, Wrox Press nor its dealers or distributors will be held liable for any damages caused or alleged to be caused either directly or indirectly by this book.

Published by Wrox Press Ltd,
Arden House, 1102 Warwick Road, Acocks Green,
Birmingham, B27 6BH, UK
Printed in the United States
ISBN 1861004311

Trademark Acknowledgements

Wrox has endeavored to provide trademark information about all the companies and products mentioned in this book by the appropriate use of capitals. However, Wrox cannot guarantee the accuracy of this information.

Credits

Authors
Michael DeMan
Josh Flowers
Gustavo Frederico
Ben Galbraith
John Hopkins
Pero Maric
Max Muller
Jim Roepcke
Bernhard Scholz
Daniel H. Steinberg
Thomas Termini
Pierce Wetter

Contributing Author
Douglas Bergère

Technical Architect
Chanoch Wiggers

Technical Editors
John R. Chapman
Tabasam Haseen
Christian Peak
Mohammed Rfaquat

Category Manager
Louay Fatoohi

Author Agent
Velimir Ilic
Nicola Phillips

Project Administrators
Simon Brand

Technical Reviewers
John Paul Ashenfelter
Michael Boerner
Oliver Breidenbach
Bill Bumgarner
Robert Burns
Patrice Collardez
David A. Coyle
Dave Every
Hang Lau
Paul Lynch
Phil Powers-deGeorge
Patrick Robinson

Production Manager
Liz Toy

Production Coordinator
Pip Wonson

Production Assistants
Abbie Forletta
Paul Grove
Natalie O'Donnell

Indexers
Adrian Axinte

Proofreader
Agnes Wiggers

Cover Design
Dawn Chellingworth
Chris Morris

We would also like to thank mmalcolm Crawford for his continued support with the making of this book.

About the Authors

Michael DeMan

Michael DeMan is a senior consulting engineer specializing in enterprise software development and systems integration using WebObjects and J2EE technologies. He has been developing scalable multi-tier Internet applications since 1996, and has worked with object-oriented technologies since 1990.

Michael is the founder of Gemini Solutions, Inc., a software services and solutions company, and also co-founded the Pattern Research Foundation, a non-profit organization that provides technical assistance to other non-profit organizations.

Michael graduated with his Bachelor's degree in Philosophy from Western Washington University (WWU) in 1994. He also attended the computer science graduate program at WWU before beginning work in the commercial sector.

Michael can be reached at michael@geminisolutions.com.

Gustavo Frederico

After nine years trying to learn how to play the violin, Gustavo Frederico started studying Computer Science at Universidade Federal do Rio Grande do Sul (Brazil) in 1992, where he graduated.

Gustavo now lives in Ottawa, Canada, and has survived four winters, so far. He develops web-based solutions in Java for e-commerce projects at MONTAGE.DMC eBusiness Services, a division of AT&T Canada.

To my wife, Louise.

Ben Galbraith

Ben Galbraith first started programming when he was eight years old. He spent a considerable amount of his youth as a hobby programmer. In his late teens, he was hired by a Silicon Valley computer manufacturer to develop Windows-based client-server applications. In 1995, Ben began developing for the web and fell in love with Unix, VI, and Perl.

After some years as an Internet consultant, Ben now leads the Java development team at an insurance company in Salt Lake City. He regularly lectures, evangelizes, and gives classes on Java technology.

To my wife Jessica.

John Hopkins

Native of Fort Worth, Texas, I earned my B.S. in Mathematics at Texas Christian University, then started my programming career in the local aircraft industry at General Dynamics, where I met my wife. From there, we worked together in the electronic music industry in Australia, for Fairlight Instruments, Pty Ltd. on a music printing system. After a year of tutoring college-level mathematics, I moved on to desktop applications for the Mac OS, first with Data Tailor, then The SU5 Group, helping with the creation of Trapeze, Persuasion, DeltaGraph, FaxSTF Network and Meeting Maestro, and products for VariLite's theatrical lighting systems.

For the millennium, I helped scour UNIX system code for Y2K bugs. Then, I helped implement web sites, using WebObjects and J2EE technologies and Tensor Information Systems. I also taught classes in Java and XML, wrote for the company newsletter on programming and mathematics, and wrote a case study for Java Report. I am studying current and upcoming XML and peer-to-peer computing technologies for virtual supercomputing and cycle selling projects.

In my spare time, I help Dr Laurence Furr with Trinity Lutheran Church's music activities: singing, playing piano, organ, violin and hand bells, composing and arranging. I also play violin in the Fort Worth Civic Orchestra. Occasionally, I get a jazz piano gig, either live performance or recording session (check out the Paul Warren CD "Sweet Deliverance"). I try to keep up with developments in physics with the help of my friend, Dr Bruce Miller at TCU. Most of all, I enjoy spending time with my wife, Darlene – a fellow software engineer and musician, and my daughter, Elise – a fellow author and musician.

Pero Maric

Pero has been working with WebObjects since version 4.0 and has been developing Java applications since 1997. Currently he is a Technical Support Lead at MONTAGE.DMC (a Division of AT&T Canada), where he mentors and assists team members in providing support for WebObjects applications at Nortel Networks.

Pero's interests include application servers, long Ultimate games, cycling and squash.

> *Thanks to all the editors, authors and reviewers at Wrox Press for making this book possible. Also, a big thanks goes out to Samantha for her support.*

Max Muller

Max Muller was raised in the Midwest and first discovered the joys of programming while attending the Oklahoma High School for Science and Mathematics. Being a chronic overachiever, in four years at Georgetown University Max completed both a Bachelor of Science, majoring in Computer Science and Economics, and a Masters in Economics, focusing on mathematical modeling. At Georgetown, Max competed on various mathematical modeling and ACM competitions.

It was also at university that Max first started working with WebObjects in his spare time, before taking an internship on a large Department of Defense WebObjects project in his junior year. After graduating, Max moved to the Bay area and worked for several dotcoms before finding the perfect combination in NetStruxr, a corporate real estate procurement and transaction platform. Since starting at NetStruxr and learning the secrets of DirectToWeb from the original author and CTO of NetStruxr, Patrice Gautier, Max has become an outspoken advocate of building template- and rule-based user interfaces with WebObjects.

Max has written articles for online publication Stepwise, as well as giving presentations at the Bay Area NeXT Group. In his spare time Max enjoys writing, reading, sailing and traveling.

Max lives in San Jose, California, with his wife, and fellow WebObjects developer, Angela and their two hybrid Serval cats.

Jim Roepcke

Jim Roepcke is an experienced WebObjects developer from Canada currently experiencing WO nirvana at NetStruxr in San Francisco. Having lost much hair fighting with Active Server Pages in his early years developing web applications, Jim appreciates the refreshingly sane approach WebObjects takes.

Jim is a life-long Edmonton Oilers hockey fan, and a lover of silly British comedy – Red Dwarf and Black Adder are his favorites.

Jim wants to thank his daughter Cyan and wife Cheryl for putting up with his neglect as he toiled on this book, and WROX for not asking for a full-body shot for the cover. ;-)

Bernhard Scholz

I am currently working as a Consulting Engineer for Apple Germany, specializing in WebObjects and networking technologies.

After studying Computer Science at the Technische Universität München I signed a contract with the biggest WebObjects company in Germany, joining the team for two years before I finally joined Apple. Before this time I was also supporting the NeXT community by administrating the Peanuts-FTP-Server, which I'm told is still of high value for many people who love their black NeXT-boxes.

I've used Amiga, Windows32, X11R6, NEXTSTEP, OpenStep, WebObjects, Linux, Solaris, HP-UX, VMS and other technologies trying to learn the best from them. Currently I'm focusing on OO Design, project management, WebObjects and Mac OS X (especially server versions). I have used WebObjects from its early development and I believe it is one of the most beautiful pieces of software currently available.

> *For this book I want to thank my parents for giving me all the support and freedom to form my life as I wanted it to be. I hope they are happy with the current result.*

Daniel H. Steinberg

Daniel Steinberg is the Director of Java Offerings for Dim Sum Thinking in Cleveland, Ohio. He has covered Java on the Mac for the last five years for JavaWorld magazine, writes a monthly column for the O'Reilly Mac DevCenter, and is a regular contributor for IBM's developerWorks.

Daniel is a recovering Mathematician who runs seminars in the latest interest areas in Computer Science for area colleges trying to stay current. He is a non-apologetic Mac fan who curses whenever he has to spend too much time on his Windows box. His favorite moments are cooking for and with his wife and kids.

Thomas Termini

Tom Termini is a founder and managing director of BlueDog Inc. (www.bluedog.net), the premier WebObjects application service provider. Tom has been a NeXT and Apple developer since 1990, with clients from the World Bank, the U.S. Government, Volkswagen of America, Lockheed Martin, Allied Irish Banks, Philip Morris Companies, among others.

Tom processes with an eye towards innovative user interfaces. His ongoing goal: find new ways for information technology to serve business needs. In the 1980s he trail-blazed multimedia application design with database integration, and founded the new-media firm Enigma Concepts Inc.

Tom was born in Washington, DC; graduated in 1986 with a degree in Pre-17th Century English Literature from the University of Maryland, and was awarded an M.B.A. in 1993 from Loyola College of Baltimore.

When not pushing a mouse, Tom explores the backcountry on his mountain bike with Indy, the Australian Cattle Dog mascot of BlueDog.

Pierce Wetter

Pierce Wetter lives in beautiful Flagstaff, Arizona surrounded by one billion pine trees. When not shoveling snow, visiting the nearby Grand Canyon, making fun of "flatlanders", or reassuring people that Arizona does get snow (at least at 7,300 feet it does); Pierce works at Marketocracy (www.marketocracy.com) doing WebObjects programming.

Prior to trying to take over Wall Street, Pierce worked as a WebObjects consultant for companies like Apple and Time/Warner. He was very excited about contributing to this book, because he feels that WebObjects is the best web application platform, but the Apple documentation stopped just short of demonstrating how powerful WebObjects can be.

WEB

Table of Contents

Introduction   1

What is WebObjects?   1
Who Is This Book for?   3
The History of WebObjects   3
Why Should I Choose WebObjects?   4
Installing WebObjects 5.0   6
Conventions Used In This Book   8
Customer Support   8
How To Download the Sample Code for the Book   8
Errata   9
E-Mail Support   9
p2p.wrox.com   9

Chapter 1: WebObjects Architecture   13

The Request-Response Cycle   14
WebObjects Architecture   15
Benefits of Multi-Tier Architecture   16
    Scaling   16
    Performance   16
    Security   17
A Closer Look At WebObjects Architecture   17
The Enterprise Objects Framework   19
The Advantages of Using EOF   19
EOF Layers and Classes   21
    EOAccess   21
    EOControl   22
    EOInterface   23
    EODistribution and EOGeneration   23
Advanced WebObjects   23
Java Client   24
Rules-Based Rapid Application Development (RBRAD)   25
Documentation   26
Developer Help Center   26
WOInfoCenter   27
JavaBrowser   27
Apple Developer Connection   28
Summary   29

Table of Contents

Chapter 2: Introducing WebObjects Tools — 31

WebObjects Development Tools — 31

Project Builder — 32
- Organization of Files in a Project — 35
- Changing Preferences — 36
- Creating a Hello World Application — 37
- Java IDE Integration — 40

Summary — 41

Chapter 3: WebObjects Builder — 43

A Brief Tour of WebObjects Builder — 44
- Launching WebObjects Builder — 44
- The HTML Editor — 45
  - The Inspector — 46
  - Source View — 48
  - Other Tools — 49
  - Path View — 49
- The Object Browser — 50
  - Binding — 50
  - Dynamic Inspector — 55
- What Have We Learnt So Far? — 56

Creating Variables — 56
- A Personalized HelloWorld Application Using Swing — 56
- Creating and Reading from a Variable — 58
  - Creating Variable by Editing the Source File — 58
  - Creating a Variable Using WebObjects Builder — 59

Creating Methods — 60
- Constructing the WOForm — 60
- Binding the Form — 61
  - The Source Code for the Method — 62

A Closer Look At HTML Templates and Bindings — 62
- The HTML Template File — 63
- The Binding File — 63

Using Conditional Code — 64
- Adding Conditionals To the HTML — 65
- Changes To the Template and Binding Files — 67

Sending Information To Other Components — 68
- Creating the Project — 69
- Linking To the New Component — 69

Adding Hyperlinks — 71

Working with Lists — 72
- Adding Variables and Methods To the Session — 72
- Displaying Lists — 73

Summary — 75

Chapter 4: WebObjects Framework Classes — 77

Introducing The WebObjects Framework — 78
- Request Level Classes — 78
  - WOMessage — 79
  - WORequest — 79
  - WOResponse — 79
- Server and Application Level Classes — 79
  - WOAdaptor — 79
  - WOApplication — 80
- Session Level Classes — 80
  - WOSession — 81
- Page Level Classes — 82
  - WOElement — 82
  - WOComponent — 82
  - WODynamicElement — 83
- Database Integration Level Objects — 83
  - WODisplayGroup — 83
- Using Context — 84
  - WOContext — 84

A Closer Look At the Request-Response Cycle — 84
- Methods Important To the Request-Response Cycle — 84
- Phases of the Request-Response Cycle — 86
- Demonstrating the Request-Response Cycle — 87
  - What's in the URL for a WebObjects Page? — 90

Summary — 91

Chapter 5: Introducing EOModeler — 93

Basic Concepts — 94
- Database Concepts Reviewed — 94
- The EOModeler Tool — 96
- The Requirements of Our Sample Application — 97

Modeling Requirements — 97
- The Application Database Schema — 98
- Setting Up the Database — 101

JDBC — 102
- JDBC Drivers, Adaptors, and Plugins — 102

Using the EOModeler Tool — 108

Creating Entities — 111

Attributes — 113
- Attribute Inspector — 113
- Prototype — 118

Completing the Model — 118

Relationships — 121

Modeling an Existing Database — 123

Summary — 124

Table of Contents

Chapter 6: Advanced EOModeler — 127
Transforming the Model into Java Code — 127
- Generating EO Classes — 128

Some Database Topics — 130
- The Generated SQL Script — 130
- Synchronization — 132
- Multiple Databases — 133

Runtime Connections To the Database — 134

Advanced Modeling Concepts — 136
- Advanced Entity Properties — 136
- Advanced Attribute Properties — 138
- Advanced Relationship Properties — 140
  - Flattening Many-to-Many Relationships — 142

Display Groups — 144

Stored Procedures and Functions — 147

Summary — 151

Chapter 7: Components — 153
What Is a Component? — 154
- Creating Components — 154
- Why and When To Use Components? — 155

The Components — 155
- LoginCheck — 156
  - LoginCheck and LoginForm in Action — 163
  - An Aside — 164
- Building Components with Components — 165
  - Navigation Menus — 165
  - Testing MenuBar So Far — 171
  - Adding Direct Actions — 173
  - Stateless Components — 178
  - Automatic Bindings — 180
- The Finished Components — 185

Summary — 187

Chapter 8: Writing Fetch Specifications — 189
EOF – an Intermediate Lens On Our Database — 190
The Editing Context: Keeping Track of Changes — 190
What is a Fetch Specification? — 191
- Qualified vs. Unqualified Fetching — 192

Advanced Fetching Concepts — 192
- Ordering During the Initial Fetch — 192
- In-Memory Ordering — 192
- Fetching Raw Rows — 193

Improving Performance — 193
- Prefetching — 193
- Caching — 194
- Sharing — 194

Two Ways To Create and Use a Fetch Specification — 194
- Manually Creating a Fetch Specification — 194
  - Step One: Gathering What We Need — 195
  - Step Two: Creating the Interface in WebObjects Builder — 195
  - Step Three: Adding Custom Code in Project Builder — 198
- Creating a Fetch Specification Using EOModeler — 202
  - Step One: Starting with EOModeler — 202
  - Step Two: Creating the Interface in WebObjects Builder — 206
  - Step Three: Adding Custom Code in Project Builder — 209

Chapter 9: Advanced EOF — 215

Key-Value Coding — 215
- General Key-Value Coding: NSKeyValueCoding — 216
  - The Default Implementation — 219
  - Generalizing the Usage of Key-Value Coding — 220

The Value of Dictionaries — 221
- Special Key-Value Coding with EOF: EOKeyValueCoding — 223
  - How It Works — 223
  - Implementing EOF's Key-Value Coding — 225
  - Type Checking, Type Conversion and Null Values — 227
  - How To Use Package Access Instance Variables — 228

Validation and Exception Handling — 229
- Property Validation: NSValidation — 229
  - The Default Implementation — 230
  - Generalizing the Usage of Property Validation — 231
  - Writing Property Validation Methods — 231
- Special Validation with EOF: EOValidation — 233
  - How It Works — 233
  - The Default Implementation for Operation Validation — 234
  - Handling Validation Errors — 235
- Alternative Validation Strategies — 237
  - Working with Database Constraints — 237
  - Working with JavaScript — 238
  - Working with Formatters — 239
  - Handling the GUI — 240

Locking — 240
- Optimistic Locking — 241
- Pessimistic Locking — 242
  - Lock on Select — 243
  - Lock on Update — 244
  - Lock on Demand — 244
- Locking a Column — 245
- Locking By Application Logic — 246

Summary — 247

Table of Contents

Chapter 10: Direct To Web and Templating — 249

What is Direct To Web? — 249
Why Use Direct To Web? — 250
When Should You Use Direct To Web? — 250
Where Is Direct To Web? — 250
Direct To Web Documentation — 251
The Architecture of Direct To Web Applications — 251
D2W Factory — 252
Direct To Web Apps Are WebObjects Apps — 252
What Are Templates? — 253
Creating a Direct To Web Application — 254
The Elements of a Web Component — 255
Comparing the Default Looks — 255
    The Basic Look — 255
    The Neutral Look — 256
    The WebObjects Look — 256
Changing the Look — 257
Inside Main.java — 257
Direct To Web Tasks — 259
Direct To Web Page Interfaces — 262
    Single Object pages — 262
    Multiple Object Pages — 264
    Message Pages — 266
The Generated Web Components — 267
The Main Component — 268
The MenuHeader Component — 269
The PageWrapper Component — 272
Common Elements in a Web Application — 273
Creating the PageWrapper — 274
The Code in Session.java — 274
Finishing the PageWrapper — 275
Redesigning Main — 276
PersonalizedGreeting — 277
Modifying Templates Using WebAssistant — 278
Creating and Using a Custom Template — 280
Summary — 281

Table of Contents

Chapter 11: Direct To Web and Rules — 283

D2WContext: Bridging Two Worlds — 283
- Basic and Derived D2WContext Keys — 285
- The Rule System — 286
- When Does the Rule System Come Into Play? — 287
  - A Real Direct To Web Example — 287
- Rules: Cause and Effect — 288
  - Assignments: The Effect — 289
  - Conditions: The Cause — 291
- Rule Firing Is Cached — 295
- Customizing D2W Factory Using Rules — 296
- NetStruxr's ERDirectToWeb Framework — 297
- RuleEditor Traits — 297
  - Custom Assignment Packages — 297
  - RuleEditor and CVS — 297
  - A Note About Data Entry in Rule Editor — 298

Page Configurations — 298
- PageConfigurations and the like Qualifier Operator — 299
- Make Your Life Easier: Use Page Configurations — 301

Property Level Components — 302

Custom Property-Level Components — 302

NextPageDelegates — 305

D2W Embedded Components — 306

Direct To Web Techniques — 309

Summary — 310

Chapter 12: JavaClient/DirectToJavaClient — 313

The One Week Scenario — 314
- Creating the Application On Mac OS X — 314
- Creating the Application On Windows — 314

The One Day Scenario — 326
- Creating the Application — 326

The One Hour Scenario — 328
- Creating the Application — 329

Summary — 331

Table of Contents

Chapter 13: Managing Data — 333

Data Design — 334
- Repeatable Steps in the Design Process — 334
- Create a Model Vocabulary — 335
  - Related Data Items — 336
- Data Restriction — 336
  - Permissible Values — 336
  - Counts and Existence — 336
  - Access and Modification Rights — 336
- Use Cases — 337
  - Describe the Use Cases — 337
  - Write a Story — 337
  - Be Complete — 338
  - Maintenance — 338
- Separate the Constant and Variable Data — 338
  - Constants — 338
  - Editor Versus Auditor — 339
  - Anything Can Stay the Same — 340
- Class Design — 340
- Understand the Available Data Types — 341
  - Java 1.3.1 Types — 341
  - Java Collections — 343
  - WebObjects Foundation Collections — 343

Designing the Methods — 344

Designing the User Interface — 344
- Data Storage Considerations — 345
  - Where Are the Possibilities? — 346
  - What Makes Each Location Different from the Others? — 346
  - Databases — 346
  - The URL — 350
  - The File System — 350
  - Enterprise Objects — 351
  - Application Member Variables — 351
  - The Session — 352
  - The Cookie — 353
  - Other Locations — 354

Summary — 355

Chapter 14: Managing the Deployment Environment — 357

From Development To Deployment — 357

Installing WebObjects for Deployment — 358

Installing Patches — 359

Building and Installing the Application — 359
- Structure of the Build Directory — 360
- How to Select the Right Platform — 360
- Transferring Application To Deployment Environment — 361
- Monitoring Application Performance — 361

Table of Contents

JavaMonitor — **361**
- Location of JavaMonitor — 362
- Setting Up a Host within Monitor — 363
- Adding Applications — 364
  - Configuring Applications — 365
  - Adding Application Instances — 367
  - When Should Monitor Be Running? — 368
  - Scheduling — 369
  - Debugging Tip — 370

WOTASKD — **370**
- Accessing wotaskd Configuration — 371
- Password Protection — 372

HTTP Adaptors — **372**
- Types of Adaptors — 373
- Supported Platforms — 374
- Source Code — 374
- Configuring Adaptor Settings — 374
- WebObjects URL Format — 375
- Load Balancing — 376
- Adaptors and Configuration Information — 377
- Obtaining Configuration Information — 377
  - Available Applications — 378

Web Servers — **378**
- WebServerResources — 379
  - Split Installations — 379

WebObjects Deployment Files — **379**
- WebServerConfig.plist — 380
- JavaConfig.plist — 380
- SiteConfig.xml — 381
- Instance Logfile — 381
- Makefiles — 381
- License.key — 382

Frameworks — **382**
- Installing Frameworks — 382

Important WebObjects Services — **383**

Deployment Architecture — **384**
- Simple Web Application — 384
- Small Database Intensive Applications — 384
- Medium-Sized Web Applications — 385
- Large Web Applications — 385
- Many Deployment Scenarios — 386

Scaling WebObjects Applications — **386**

How Many Instances To Deploy — **386**

Database Connections — **387**
- Instance Connections — 388

Deployment Checklist — **388**

Summary — **389**

ix

Table of Contents

Chapter 15: Corporate Real Estate Case Study — 391
- The Example Application — 392

The Solution — 393

Framework Architecture — 394

Rapid Turnaround Development — 397
- Developer Setup — 397
- Rapid Turnaround Development with ProjectBuilderWO — 397
- Log4j — 399
- File Notification Center — 405
- Template Based Approach To Thrown Validation Exceptions — 406

DirectToWeb Template-Based Approach — 407
- Template Extensions — 407
- Skinnable Applications — 409

Patterns and Techniques — 411
- Handling Exceptions — 412
- LoginRequiredDirectAction — 414
- User Preferences — 418
  - The Goal — 418
  - The Problems — 420
  - Getting the Preferences from the User To the WODisplayGroup — 420
  - Propagating the Changes Made To the WODisplayGroup Back To the User — 427

Summary — 429

Appendix A: The EOUtilities Class — 431

Locking Editing Contexts — 432

Primary Keys — 432

Raw Rows — 432

Exceptions — 433

Database Connections — 434

Useful EOUtilities Methods — 434
- Creating New EOs — 434
- Fetching Multiple Objects — 434
- Fetching Single Objects — 436
- Accessing Object Information — 439
- Dealing with Raw Rows — 440
- Accessing the EOF Stack — 443
- Accessing EOModel Information — 444

Index — 447

Table of Contents

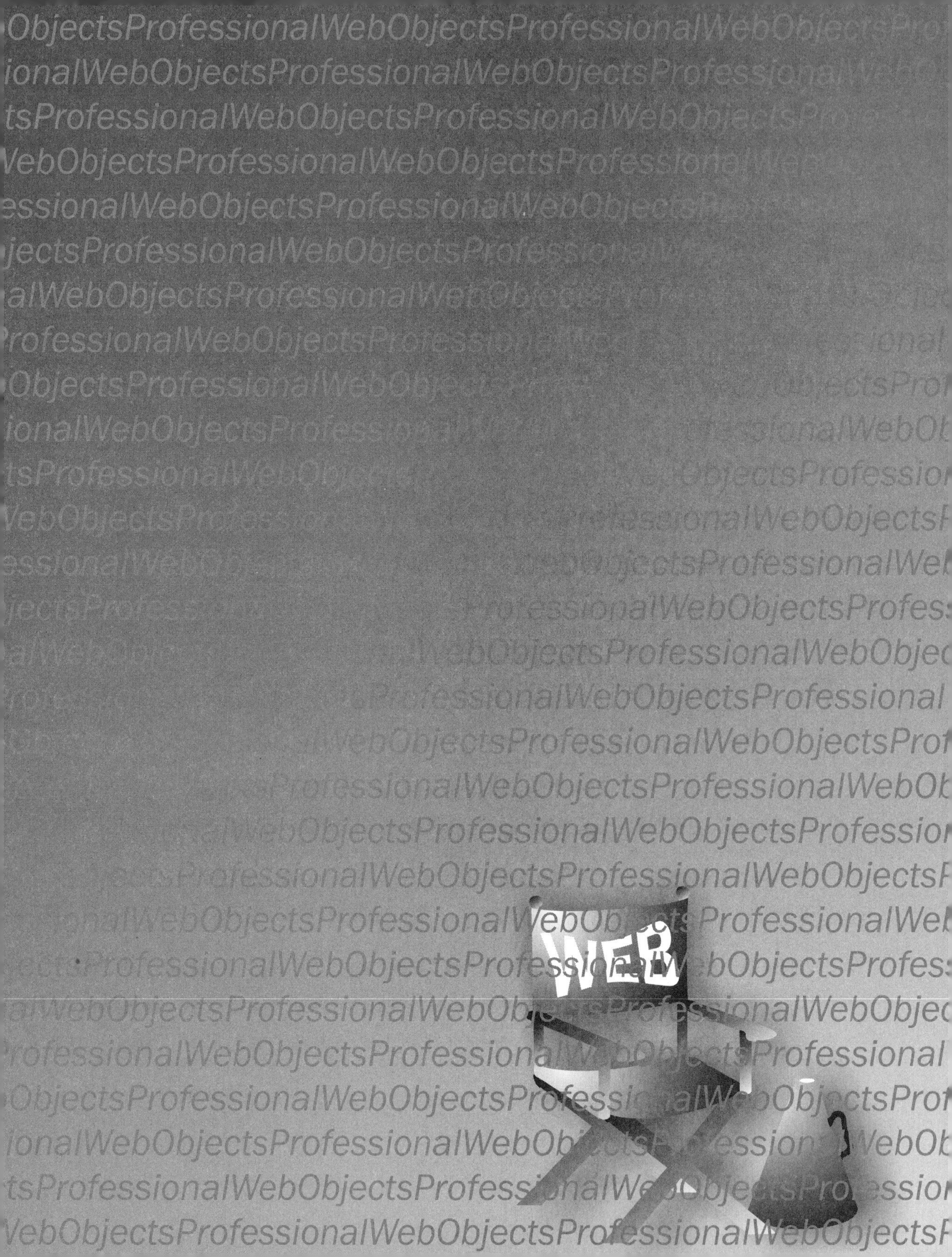
WEB

Introduction

What is WebObjects?

WebObjects 5 is the powerful new release of Apple's award-winning application server, built from the ground up in Java. WebObjects was the first object-oriented application server, and year on year remains the top application environment for many developers, offering a suite of tools for developing scalable three-tier web and stand-alone applications.

This mature product offers easy to develop and deploy distributed Java applications, and has powerful and simple data access, templating capabilities, and session management that allow the developer to get on with the task of writing business logic.

In addition, as WebObjects is based on Java, it can now run on virtually any server making it easily accessible to millions of Java programmers. In addition, WebObjects application development is in Java and WebObjects also integrates with other Java-based solutions such as EJB containers, servlets, and web services.

The combination of a Java runtime with advanced native tools for Mac OS X and Windows 2000 makes WebObjects an obvious environment for customers needing rapid development of flexible, scalable web applications.

It's an Application Server

Static web sites store all their content, presentation, and navigation in HTML files. Not only does this make it very difficult for web masters to do rapid and complex updates, it also means that every visitor sees exactly the same information in exactly the same way. Some rising new standards such as XML help address some shortcomings, but a different approach has been around since the early days of the Web – the application server. Evolving beyond client-server architecture developed in the 1980s, application serving addresses how to create, maintain, and distribute dynamic information.

Introduction

An application server typically stores content in a database and employs some form of scripting to create web pages dynamically. While this approach allows web developers to create sites that have easily updated content, flexibility comes at the price of greater complexity. This complexity increases development time and makes a web site harder to maintain.

WebObjects improves on the traditional application server architecture by cleanly separating the database access layer, the application-specific Java code, and the web page presentation layer. Supported by rich object-oriented frameworks and an object-relational mapping engine, this architecture is the foundation of the powerful technologies in WebObjects. Web components enable the efficient generation of HTML, XML, or SMIL from reusable templates. WebObjects provides an abstracted layer for database access via Enterprise Objects. When an HTML interface just won't do, Java applets or multi-tier Java client applications are supported.

It's a Development Environment

WebObjects provides an integrated suite of graphical tools to speed application development. Unlike other graphical tools that generate hard-to-read code, WebObjects dynamically binds application components with XML-like data structures, greatly simplifying application maintenance. Application components can be reused, and incremental development is easy – reducing total cost of ownership over the life cycle of an application.

At the heart of the WebObjects development process is Project Builder, a multi-language integrated development environment used extensively by Mac OS X developers. In addition to helping edit, compile, and debug WebObjects applications, Project Builder organizes all your components (including localized resources for multiple languages); provides templates and assistants covering the common application types; and, on Mac OS X, integrates with source code repositories such as CVS.

Perhaps the most powerful tool, EOModeler manages the object-relational mappings used by the data access layer, and can even help you organize your business logic. It can also be used to manage your database schema, either by reverse engineering a model from the schema or by using a new model to create the schema. In EOModeler, graphical entity-relationship diagrams represent the object relationships created and maintained by data access frameworks.

Although WebObjects uses standard HTML that can be edited with any text editing tool, a comprehensive layout tool called WebObjects Builder is also included that can manage the associated mapping files. WebObjects Builder can be used for general HTML layout and provides the usual preview mode and drag-and-drop palettes common in such tools. A developer can also drag a dynamic element into the web page, specify the mappings, and set the properties.

WebObjects Builder automatically generates the appropriate HTML and mapping information. One widely used technique that takes advantage of Apple's integrated development environment is to have a web designer focus on the aesthetics of the user interface design as represented in dynamic HTML, JavaScript, and Flash, while letting a programmer focus on writing the associated Java code to implement the mapped methods.

Who Uses WebObjects?

Many organizations are using WebObjects for both global internet and corporate intranet applications, including reservation systems, virtual catalogs, customer services, groupware, and several migration projects from Windows applications to the web.

Introduction

A combination of outstanding technology and innovative partners has attracted some of the best-known brands in the world to WebObjects. Fortune 500 companies have trusted it for years for Intranet application development, personalized Internet content delivery, and e-commerce. WebObjects-based solutions in this market include cutting-edge Internet sites such as the BBC, AAA, and MCI/WorldComm. WebObjects is also being used in powerful online applications for asset management or customer services, including tracking United Parcel Service packages and providing online services to US Postal Service customers. FannieMae and other financial institutions have built large, complex, and mission-critical applications with WebObjects.

In higher education, WebObjects is used by universities to create portals, labs, and administrative solutions, such as a student information site at the University of Michigan. Many universities are looking to use WebObjects as the basis of their web development courses, allowing students (or continuing education professionals) to create complete web applications in a single semester.

WebObjects is the basis of some of the most important publishing solutions for creative markets. Most notable is Adobe's InScope software for publishing workflows, which is built entirely around WebObjects.

Who Is This Book for?

Read this book if you want to develop and manage WebObjects applications. You'll need to have a beginning-to-intermediate understanding of Java. It also helps to have an understanding of HTML, JavaScript, and the workings of relational databases. WebObjects handles much of the work for you, but sometimes you need to get your hands dirty – for example, writing some original SQL code for a database search, although this is rare.

This book is meant to supplement the excellent on-line documentation that accompanies the development suite. Having a Java reference handy is a good idea as well: try Wrox's *Beginning Java 2* by Ivor Horton, *Thinking in Java* by Bruce Eckel (published by Prentice Hall) or O'Reilly's *Java in a Nutshell* by David Flanagan.

This book is a roadmap because as you follow the examples paired with explanations of theory, you will come to understand how to navigate application development and serving with WebObjects. When you are finished, you will be able to create dynamic applications that allow users to find, view, and modify data from back-end databases, accessible in any browser.

The History of WebObjects

When Tim Berners-Lee invented the World Wide Web using NeXTSTEP development tools while working at CERN (the European Organization for Nuclear Research, the world's largest particle physics center), the idea was to create a vast network of information and hypertext that would be an easy but powerful global information system.

NeXTSTEP employed a number of powerful design patterns that greatly simplified the creation of rich, graphical applications. This ease of use led to its adoption by a number of large enterprises that wanted to rapidly create sophisticated database applications.

To better serve this market, NeXT created a technology known as Enterprise Objects, the first commercially successful object-relational modeling framework. Because Enterprise Objects abstracted away all the work of database access, it quickly became the technology of choice for financial institutions creating sophisticated client/server applications.

Introduction

In 1995, NeXT realized that the World Wide Web would soon become the dominant format for client/server applications. Therefore, NeXT programmers applied that same object-oriented know-how to create a sophisticated set of frameworks for managing HTTP requests and HTML generation. In January 1996, NeXT announced WebObjects 1.0, the world's first object-oriented web application server. The power of WebObjects, leveraging the strengths of Enterprise Objects, quickly made it the dominant product in NeXT's portfolio.

In 1997, NeXT was acquired by Apple, primarily for its engineering talent and the UNIX-based operating system technology that eventually became the core of Mac OS X. WebObjects played a key role at Apple during this time, driving Apple's public Internet efforts such as the Apple Store and iTools. A combination of direct sales and a high price (up to $50,000 for a multi-CPU deployment license) kept WebObjects out of the reach of the vast majority of Apple developers. Apple announced in May 2000 a reduction of the price of WebObjects to less than $700 for both developer tools and a full deployment license, which would be sold via both the Apple Store and traditional retail channels.

Why Should I Choose WebObjects?

There are several competing products similar to WebObjects. Most offer similar-in-scope system-level services, web site creation tools, integrated development environments, and datasource conductivity features. Most notable are SilverStream, WebSphere, and Bluestone Software's Sapphire/Web. According to Network Computing magazine, if developers are going to spend most of their time with the integrated development environment, good tools and a clean, efficient process will pay for themselves a hundred times over in improved productivity and reduced development, deployment and maintenance costs.

WebObjects Uses Java

In its first several releases, WebObjects was written in Objective-C, one of the original object-oriented languages that provided much of the inspiration for Java. As Java became more important for server-side development, ongoing iterations of WebObjects added Java APIs.

With this version, the power of WebObjects is now fully accessible to Java programmers. The WebObjects runtime is written to the Java 2 Platform, allowing it to run virtually anywhere. Now that WebObjects is available on Java, it is instantly familiar and accessible to the millions of programmers who prefer that language. The use of standard Java also makes it easy for WebObjects to interoperate with other Java solutions, such as EJB containers, servlets, ORBS, and web services.

Apple chose a programming language that is of general purpose, easily available, and widely used. Java fits these requirements quite well: it is a relatively simple language supporting most aspects of object-oriented design. Java also has several modern technologies designed into the language (memory management, for example); and the high demand for Java programmers indicates the success people have with the language.

Why Should We Use Object-Oriented Programming?

Simplify and streamline. That's why object-oriented programming makes sense. Key to the concept of object-oriented software development is the definition of classes and methods. This process is independent a specific programming language – object-oriented design deals with general techniques and notations about how to derive the software components that best model a given problem. A simple rule of thumb might help: Write a quick and dirty problem specification. Nouns are candidates for classes, while verbs are candidates for methods. WebObjects provides an easy-to-use environment to implement object-oriented coding with Java.

Introduction

WebObjects efficiently generates HTML, XML, or SMIL output from reusable templates separating the presentation layer from business logic and the data model, allowing each piece to evolve independently.

WebObject's object-relational mapping engine means the developer writes all the business logic using objects. WebObjects automatically fetches, caches, and updates data from any JDBC 2.0 database or XML stream, even saving the developer from writing SQL statements. In a sense, WebObjects can extend the concept of the model-view-controller paradigm.

WebObjects Is Well-Designed

In a review of the top application servers, Network Computing magazine said:

> "The best enterprise-class product is Apple's WebObjects, a true powerhouse with its elegant interface and architecture. It's well designed from top to bottom, and full of useful architectural and design features that make it the best of breed in this fast-changing arena. Its IDE is clean and consistent, and encourages true code reuse and good object-oriented design."

Here are some of the reasons that the WebObjects architecture gets such rave reviews:

Friendly Development Tools

WebObjects incorporates a family of user-friendly project development and management tools. One of the tools available is Monitor, itself a WebObjects application that manages all the different WebObjects applications and the servers on which they are running. Monitor is used to start and stop instances, generate statistics, and configure how applications are run. Other tools enable you to record and play back sessions for both functional and stress testing.

Plethora of Deployment Options

WebObjects deploys on any Java 2 Platform, Standard Edition version 1.3 runtime environment, using JDBC 2.0 for universal database connectivity. WebObjects applications run on Mac OS X Server, Windows 2000 Pro, Solaris 8, even Linux. WebObjects applications are designed to use JDBC 2.0 for universal database connectivity, and are widely used with Oracle 8i, FrontBase, OpenBase, and MySQL.

With Monitor, you easily add servers using a variety of prebuilt scheduling mechanisms. In your system design, you can add more web servers to handle more static web connections. You can add more application servers to handle more instances. You can also add more memory to application servers to add more instances on that processor. You can also add multiple database servers to off load processor-intensive actions. This means that WebObjects is **scalable**.

WebObjects is also **robust**. WebObjects Monitor automatically restarts instances and connections as needed. Larger application size and better response can be addressed easily by adding more memory to the server.

Standards-Based

WebObjects incorporates the latest standards. For example, WebObjects has the Xerces parser from the Apache Software Foundation integrated directly. This allows developers to import and export XML datastreams as well as supporting SMIL for multimedia applications.

Wide Development Community

WebObjects development and deployment is cross-platform-enabling development on both Mac OS X and Windows 2000 and deployment on any Java 2 Platform, Standard Edition v1.3 system. But WebObjects 5 is especially designed to take full advantage of the power of Mac OS X, and is bundled as part of the newest release of Mac OS X Server.

Competitive Pricing

WebObjects also packs a powerful price-to-power ratio, with deployment costing less than $700 per processor. Coupled with the ease of development for quicker coding and easier maintenance, developers will realize a lower total cost of ownership.

Installing WebObjects 5.0

Given that WebObjects 5 is a great environment to develop dynamic web applications in, hopefully you'll want to install it and give it a try.

The first installation step is to choose whether you wish to simply develop WebObjects applications, or if you want to deploy them for use on the World Wide Web as well. Apple implement this choice as two installation options:

- WebObjects Developer
- WebObjects Deployment

As we mentioned before, you also have the luxury of being able to develop and deploy WebObjects on Mac, Windows 2000, and to deploy on Solaris too.

Installing On a Mac

To use WebObjects 5 on a Power Macintosh running Mac OS X, you will need at least 128 MB of RAM and 500MB of available hard disk space. Although not essential if you are simply developing applications, a web server (such as Mac OS X Server) would be pretty handy too, so that you can learn how to deploy your applications.

The first step for installation is to insert the *WebObjects 5 for Mac OS X* CD-ROM into the appropriate drive of your Mac. You should navigate to the Developer folder on the disk. Click on either the `WebObjectsDeveloper.pkg` or `WebObjectsDeployment.pkg` depending on your preference. This starts up the installer.

If you haven't logged on as the administrator (root) on the machine then you will have to click on the padlock icon. A window will pop up asking for the administrator username and password, then press **Continue**. The next screen is the license which you read, on pressing **Continue** another window will appear and you have a choice whether to accept the license agreement or not.

Assuming you have agreed to the license, you will be given the choice of which volume on your hard drive you want to install WebObjects on; after choosing click **Continue**. You can then choose to have the default **Easy** install, which is recommended, or by clicking on the **Custom** button, you can decide on installing only parts of WebObjects.

Introduction

The **Install** button will take you to the next stage where you enter the license key; this is on the front of your CD-ROM envelope. You then click **Install** and then **OK** on the new window that appears. The installation will start; after WebObjects has installed you will have to restart your computer.

Installing On Windows

To install in the Windows environment you'll need Windows 2000 with at least 500MB of available disk space. As with developing on the Mac, you would be strongly advised to have a web server such as Microsoft's IIS installed as well, in order to test application deployment.

Before you start the installation, make sure that you are logged into an account that has Administrative privileges, otherwise you will not be allowed to install new software. Pop the *WebObjects 5 for Windows and Solaris* CD into your computer's CD-ROM drive, and navigate to the Developer or Deployment folder on the disk (depending on your preference).

You should see a Windows folder inside this, which contains a `SetUp.exe` icon. Click on this; the WebObjects installer should start up.

Click on **Next** and read the subsequent license agreement. Provided you agree with its terms, click **Yes**. In the subsequent dialog box you will be asked to enter your name and the name of your company, as well as a valid license key (which can be found on the CD-ROM envelope). When you have entered this information, click **Next**.

The next choice to be made is whether you require a **Typical** installation or a **Custom** installation. As usual, a typical installation is strongly recommended unless you really need to customize.

When you click on **Next**, you will be asked to **Choose Destination Location**. This is where you get to specify the WebObjects root directory... you can either accept the default or click on **Browse** and specify a different (or new) folder.

> A few words of warning: don't install WebObjects into a system-related folder such as WinNT, and make sure the path to the root directory doesn't exceed twelve characters in length, or you may encounter problems with the software.

Next you will be asked for the path to your web server's CGI Bin (or Scripts) folder, and then the path to the root directory of the web server (for example `wwwroot` for IIS). The final option to specify is the program group for the WebObjects software.

When you have specified these options, the installer should install the WebObjects Developer components; this process will take a few minutes. Once installation is complete, you should restart your computer.

After Installation

You will probably want to use a database with your applications too. WebObjects comes with the OpenBase Lite relational database system, although Oracle 8i is the data source that is officially supported for WebObjects.

Before beginning, you should install and test WebObjects on your development platform. Run the 'Hello World' example to ensure everything installed properly. Keep an eye on permissions settings for the directories containing your work, as well as those containing the WebObjects application and framework files.

Introduction

Conventions Used In This Book

To help you get the most from the text and keep track of what's happening, we've used a number of conventions throughout the book. For instance:

> These boxes hold important, not-to-be forgotten information, which is directly relevant to the surrounding text.

While this background style is used for asides to the current discussion.

As for styles in the text:

- When we introduce them, we **highlight** important words.
- We show keyboard strokes like this: *Ctrl-A*.
- We show filenames and code within the text like so: `doGet()`
- Text on user interfaces and URLs are shown as: **Menu**.

We present code in three different ways. Definitions of methods and properties are shown as follows:

```
protected void doGet(HttpServletRequest req, HttpServletResponse resp)
                   throws ServletException, IOException
```

Example code is shown like this:

```
In our code examples, the code foreground style shows new, important,
   pertinent code
while code background shows code that is less important in the present context,
   or has been seen before.
```

Customer Support

We always value hearing from our readers, and we want to know what you think about this book: what you liked, what you didn't like, and what you think we can do better next time. You can send us your comments, either by returning the reply card in the back of the book, or by e-mail to feedback@wrox.com. Please be sure to mention the book title in your message.

How To Download the Sample Code for the Book

When you visit the Wrox site, http://www.wrox.com/, simply locate the title through our **Search** facility or by using one of the title lists. Click on **Download** in the **Code** column, or on **Download Code** on the book's detail page.

The files that are available for download from our site have been archived using WinZip. When you have saved the attachments to a folder on your hard-drive, you need to extract the files using a de-compression program such as WinZip or PKUnzip. When you extract the files, the code is usually extracted into chapter folders. When you start the extraction process, ensure your software (WinZip, PKUnzip, etc.) is set to use folder names.

Errata

We've made every effort to make sure that there are no errors in the text or in the code. However, no one is perfect and mistakes do occur. If you find an error in one of our books, like a spelling mistake or a faulty piece of code, we would be very grateful for feedback. By sending in errata you may save another reader hours of frustration, and of course, you will be helping us provide even higher quality information. Simply e-mail the information to support@wrox.com; your information will be checked and if correct, posted to the errata page for that title, or used in subsequent editions of the book.

To find errata on the web site, go to http://www.wrox.com/, and simply locate the title through our Advanced Search or title list. Click on the Book Errata link, which is below the cover graphic on the book's detail page.

E-Mail Support

If you wish to directly query a problem in the book with an expert who knows the book in detail then e-mail support@wrox.com, with the title of the book and the last four numbers of the ISBN in the subject field of the e-mail. A typical e-mail should include the following things:

- The **title of the book, last four digits of the ISBN**, and **page number** of the problem in the Subject field.
- Your **name, contact information**, and the **problem** in the body of the message.

We *won't* send you junk mail. We need the details to save your time and ours. When you send an e-mail message, it will go through the following chain of support:

- Customer Support – Your message is delivered to our customer support staff, who are the first people to read it. They have files on most frequently asked questions and will answer anything general about the book or the web site immediately.
- Editorial – Deeper queries are forwarded to the technical editor responsible for that book. They have experience with the programming language or particular product, and are able to answer detailed technical questions on the subject.
- The Authors – Finally, in the unlikely event that the editor cannot answer your problem, he or she will forward the request to the author. We do try to protect the author from any distractions to their writing; however, we are quite happy to forward specific requests to them. All Wrox authors help with the support on their books. They will e-mail the customer and the editor with their response, and again all readers should benefit.

The Wrox Support process can only offer support on issues that are directly pertinent to the content of our published title. Support for questions that fall outside the scope of normal book support, is provided via the community lists of our http://p2p.wrox.com/ forum.

p2p.wrox.com

For author and peer discussion join the P2P mailing lists. Our unique system provides **programmer to programmer**™ contact on mailing lists, forums, and newsgroups, all in addition to our one-to-one e-mail support system. If you post a query to P2P, you can be confident that it is being examined by the many Wrox authors and other industry experts who are present on our mailing lists. At p2p.wrox.com you will find a number of different lists that will help you, not only while you read this book, but also as you develop your own applications. Particularly appropriate to this book is the pro_webobjects list.
To subscribe to a mailing list just follow these steps:

Introduction

1. Go to http://p2p.wrox.com/.

2. Choose the **Web Apps** category from the left menu bar.

3. Click on the **pro_webobjects** mailing list you wish to join.

4. Follow the instructions to subscribe and fill in your e-mail address and password.

5. Reply to the confirmation e-mail you receive.

6. Use the subscription manager to join more lists and set your e-mail preferences.

Why This System Offers the Best Support

You can choose to join the mailing lists or you can receive them as a weekly digest. If you don't have the time, or facility, to receive the mailing list, then you can search our online archives. Junk and spam mails are deleted, and your own e-mail address is protected by the unique Lyris system. Queries about joining or leaving lists, and any other general queries about lists, should be sent to listsupport@p2p.wrox.com.

Introduction

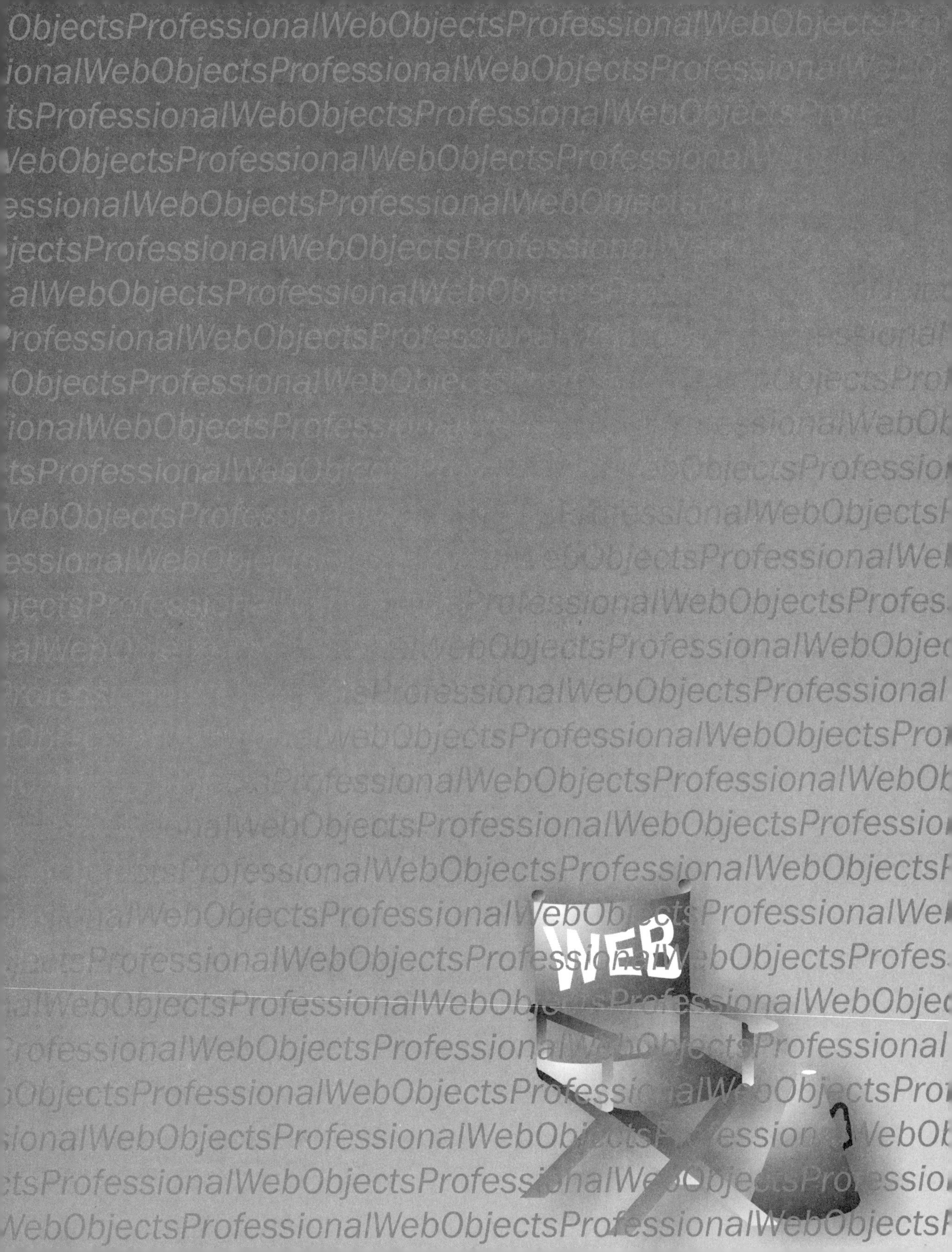
WEB

WebObjects Architecture

WebObjects and its associated frameworks are an extremely powerful and flexible way to design, develop and deploy a variety of applications. First and foremost WebObjects is an application server. As an application server, WebObjects can not only deliver applications through to a traditional HTML-based presentation layer, but also to Java clients distributed either as downloadable applets to be executed in the client browser or as full-blown Java desktop applications.

A "classic" WebObjects application is one that only uses the core functionality that WebObjects was intended to deliver when it was first released in 1996: database-driven dynamic HTML. More recent versions of WebObjects have built upon this core functionality, and introduced more advanced features.

In this chapter we will discuss key architectural concepts that apply to all WebObjects applications. This will provide you with a foundation for understanding WebObjects as a whole. We will also briefly introduce you to some of the more advanced features for WebObjects 5.0, in preparation for later chapters where we will cover these features in depth.

In the first part of the chapter, we will review the general architecture of WebObjects by covering the following subjects:

- WebObjects and the Request-Response Cycle
- Multi-Tier WebObjects Architecture

Then we will turn our attention to data persistence in WebObjects, which is handled by a group of classes called the Enterprise Objects Framework (EOF). In particular, we will discuss the following aspects of EOF:

- Advantages of Using EOF
- EOF Architecture and Layers
- EOF Classes

Chapter 1

Towards the end of the chapter we will briefly review advanced WebObjects topics, such as:

- Direct To Web
- Java Client
- Direct To Java Client

We will finish off by looking at the sources of WebObjects documentation available to us, and other tools that we can turn to for help when we are developing in WebObjects.

Let's begin, then, by looking at the process of sending a client request to a WebObjects application and receiving a response back from the application, which will allow us to get a useful overview of the WebObjects architecture.

The Request-Response Cycle

In this section we will briefly cover the request-response cycle, and how this applies to WebObjects applications.

Fundamentally the WebObjects request-response loop provides an event-driven programming model, except that the events are HTTP requests rather than mouse clicks, keyboard strokes or other more traditional IO. A client passes a bundle of data to an application via a web page, expecting the application to process this data in some way. This is known as a client **request**. The application processes this information and passes the processed data back to the client. This is known as the **response**. Therefore we say that this whole loop is the *request-response cycle*. In WebObjects the client request and the response to the client are usually passed using the HTTP protocol.

A simple example of how the request-response loop fits into a typical WebObjects application is given in the figure below. In WebObjects we often refer to the complete processing of a request-response cycle as a **transaction**.

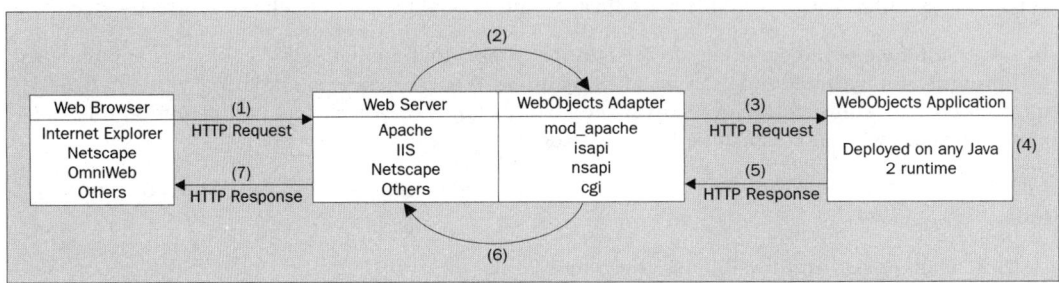

The steps in the figure above are as follows:

1. The user initiates an HTTP request with their web browser by entering a URL, clicking a hyperlink or some other type of activity. This HTTP request is sent like any other to the web server defined in the host portion of the URL. Note that this request may also be an SSL-encrypted HTTPS request.

2. The web server receives the HTTP request and forwards it to the **WebObjects Adaptor**, which executes on the same host as the web server. The simplest way to do it is through the default CGI adaptor installed during WebObjects installation, and Apple provides the source code for this adaptor so you can compile it to run on a wide variety of platforms. However, if you are using Apache, Netscape or Microsoft IIS for your web server you can configure it to communicate through their native APIs, which improves performance quite a bit compared to CGI.

Once the WebObjects Adaptor has received the HTTP request from the web server it parses it and determines which WebObjects application the request is destined for. For high traffic sites we typically run many instances of each application to improve performance, and these may be spread across multiple servers. In this case, the adaptor also makes the determination of which application instance the request is destined for. In the case of brand-new requests (from a new user entering a site for example) the instance is chosen randomly or round robin.

Once the adaptor has determined which application you wish to access, it then consults a configuration file to find out which host that application is running on and which TCP/IP socket it is listening on.

3. The adaptor then opens up a TCP/IP socket to the location WebObjects Application is listening on and forwards the request via HTTP to the WebObjects Application as a **request object** (of class WORequest).

4. The WebObjects Application receives the WORequest object from the adaptor, processes it and generates a **response object** (of class WOResponse). This response object usually contains HTML content but may be anything, such as a PDF document, an XML document or a QuickTime movie. It also contains the HTTP information required to send the response back to the client. We will look at the internals of how an application handles the request-response loop in Chapter 4.

5. The WebObjects Application then passes the WOResponse back to the WebObjects Adaptor via HTTP and the socket connection is closed.

6. The WebObjects Adaptor then passes the (HTTP) response to the web server.

7. The web server forwards the HTTP response to the client, and the client web browser displays the HTML (or whatever form the content of the response takes).

We will come back to the subject of the WebObjects request-response cycle in Chapter 4, and look at it in far more detail.

WebObjects Architecture

We can see from the previous diagram showing the request-response cycle that the architecture of WebObjects can be split into three "tiers":

- The Web Browser Tier
- Web Server/Adaptor Tier
- Application Logic Tier

In other words, there is an intermediate layer between the user's web browser and the WebObjects Application itself. This layer consists of the web server and the WebObjects Adaptor that the web server uses to communicate with the application. You should note that it is possible to run in direct mode without a web server by having the web browser make its request directly to the host and TCP/IP socket of the WebObjects Application itself. This is convenient for development, but is generally not suitable for deployment for several reasons that we will examine in the next section.

Benefits of Multi-Tier Architecture

There are several reasons that it is useful to divide up the WebObjects architecture into tiers.

Scaling

The first reason to use a multi-tier architecture is that it allows you to **scale** the application. Receiving HTTP requests and returning HTML is a relatively lightweight activity compared to talking to databases, making complex business-logic decisions and rendering dynamic HTML. The architecture above allows you to use a single web server to handle traffic and have many application servers behind it doing the hard work. Of course, for ultra-high volume sites you will still need a server farm even for your web servers, but it is amazing how much traffic you can handle with a single powerful web server and the WebObjects architecture described above.

Performance

Another reason to operate a separate web server is for **performance**. This is not just scaling the application as we discussed above, but providing higher performance for other HTML resources not directly generated by the application. For instance, many WebObjects applications will also have reference to static elements, such as images. By placing those images directly on the web server and making static rather than dynamic references to them, we decrease the amount of work the WebObjects application has to do. Also, since the images are located on the web server it can vend them out directly and as a final bonus both the client browsers and the numerous caching servers run by Internet Service Providers (ISPs) all around the globe will be able to cache them locally. This provides a great improvement in performance on the client side and further reduces the load on your servers.

Adjusting for these additional concepts, we can see an updated version of the request-response loop in the figure below:

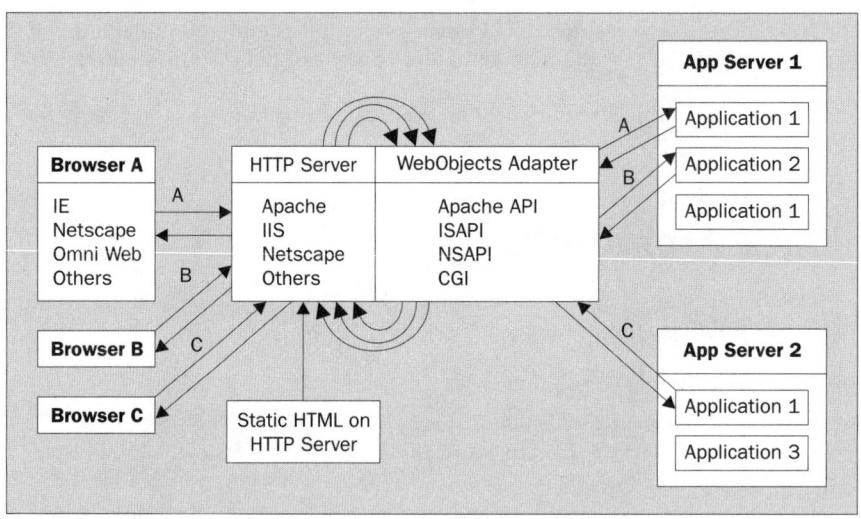

WebObjects Architecture

In the figure we can see that we have three different clients making requests – A, B, and C. For purposes of the figure, browsers A and C are using Application 1 while browser B is using Application 2. We can see on the far right that we now have two independent application servers. The first server is running two instances of Application 1, and one instance of Application 2. The second server is running one instance of Application 1 and one instance of Application 3.

The request-response loop is shown in each of its seven steps as before, except now there are three independent loops – one for each browser. Note that all the browsers connect to the same web server, but they are each serviced by different application servers on the back end. In particular, even though browsers A and C are both using Application 1, browser A is serviced by the application running on the first machine while application C is serviced by the second machine.

Finally, we have put another box near the HTTP server to show that static resources such as images are served directly by the server to the client(s). One item missing from this diagram is the effect of internet caching on the overall system. Requests to the application servers that require computation will not be cached, but any of the resources from the 'STATIC HTML' box may be cached out on the internet by the client's ISP.

Security

A third reason to operate a separate web server processing client requests and passing them on to the application server is for **security**. A typical deployment for security is with the web server operating behind a first firewall layer in what is often referred to as a DMZ (demilitarized zone). The actual application runs behind a second firewall for even more safety.

If you are new to internet security issues there are numerous good books on the topic, and once you become familiar with the concepts you will see the additional security given by this architecture.

A Closer Look At WebObjects Architecture

As we mentioned earlier, WebObjects also contains powerful mechanisms to interact with a wide variety of relational databases and can also act as a client or server for XML-based business-to-business (B2B) services. With this in mind, a more detailed architectural diagram is shown below:

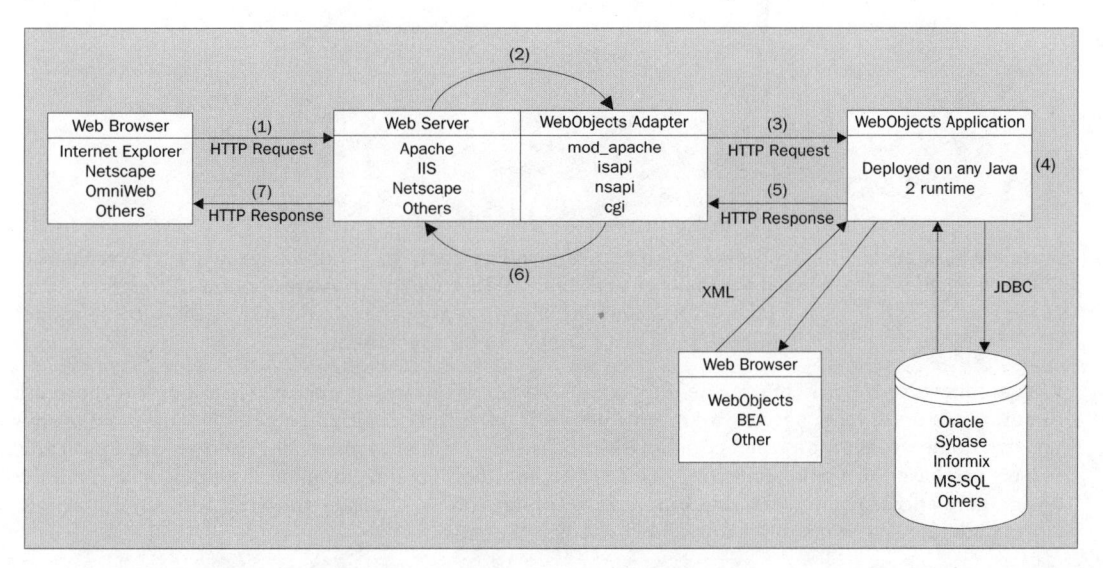

As you can see from the figure above, with WebObjects 5 all database access is performed with JDBC. In this example, the WebObjects Application is shown as a client to an XML business service. This XML service can be provided by any kind of application server.

A typical example for the architecture above might be for an airline reservation system. The client accesses the WebObjects application to query flights, perhaps with their personal preferences and customer profile information stored in your company's relational database while information on flight scheduling and reservations are made by sending XML requests to a third-party server.

But we haven't finished there. After we add in the firewalls and other security measures we discussed earlier, accounting for the fact that we can scale our application quickly by running multiple application servers, we end up with the final architecture as given in the figure below:

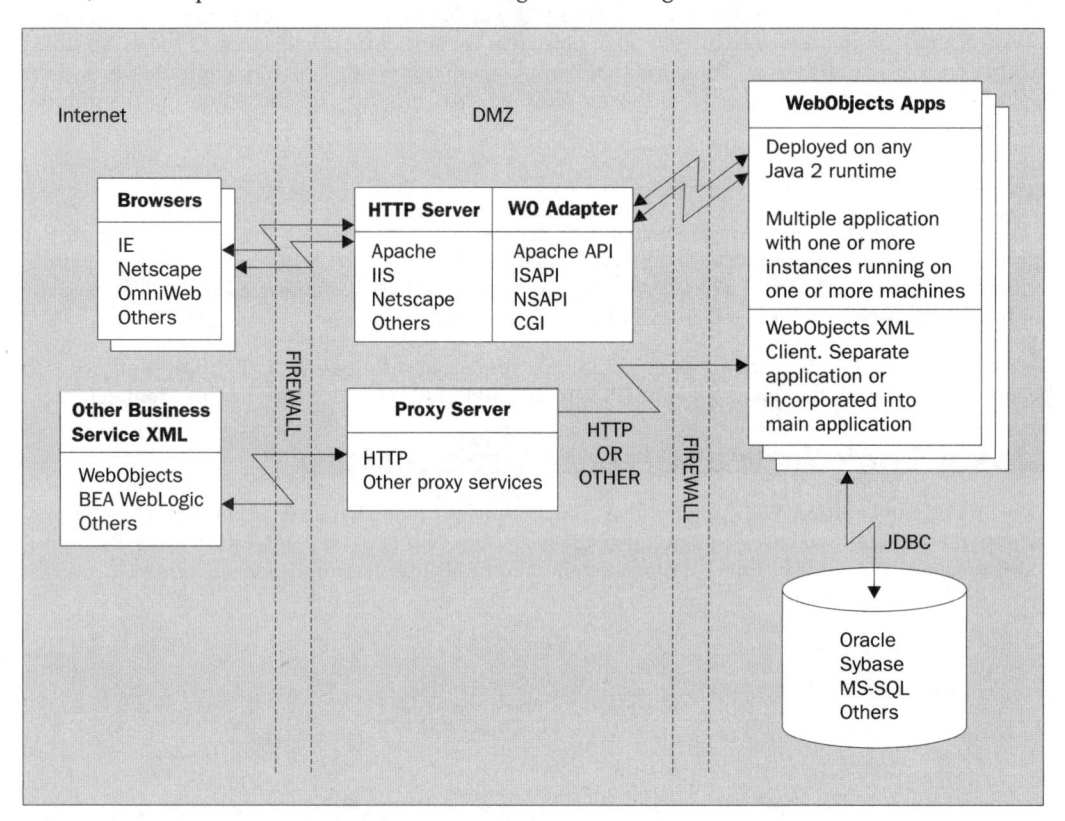

Here we have placed the web server behind a firewall in the DMZ, and the application server and our database further back behind another firewall. Our XML client queries are sent out through the DMZ again with an HTTP proxy server. Of course there is no reason that we need to send all these requests and responses over HTTP on port 80, it just happens to be convenient.

This architecture is by no means the only possibility for WebObjects deployment; rather it represents the more common case that you may come across. Your actual deployment will depend greatly on what you are doing. Often for a small company it is possible to run all the services (web server, application server, database) on a single machine. This is also common for development. The power of the *n*-tier design here allows you to scale that exact same application up to a very powerful web site by simply adding additional servers in whatever area needs it the most.

The Enterprise Objects Framework

In the previous section we noted that WebObjects allows us to connect our applications to a variety of relational databases. This is very important, because it allows us to persist data important to our applications across request-response transactions.

The Enterprise Objects Framework (EOF) defines how WebObjects handles this data persistence. The framework is a set of classes that enables us to map data in relational database tables to objects (called **Enterprise Objects**, or "EOs") that represent the same data. This technique is known as *object-relational mapping*. Therefore, in terms of WebObjects Architecture, EOF is a layer between the application and the relational database (also known as a *data source*).

For object-relational mapping to work, we must define how the database data maps to the objects. In WebObjects this map is called the EOModel (or simply "the Model"), and we create EOModels using a tool called EOModeler that we will cover in depth in Chapters 5 and 6.

The Advantages of Using EOF

At this point, you may be asking why we should want to hold database data in objects, and then access these EOs from applications, instead of just going directly to the database. It seems needlessly complex, right?

A key concept in WebObjects is the separation of the application's business logic from its presentation logic, which is what we achieve by creating the EOF layer. This separation of business logic (handled by EOF classes) from presentation logic has its roots in the Model-View-Controller paradigm of SmallTalk and the NeXTStep object-oriented development environment. Placing all of the business logic in the EOF layer in this way has many benefits.

Reuse

We can write our business logic in EOs once, and then all applications that need to use these Enterprise Objects gain from reusing that code. This means once you have developed your business logic to support an HTML-based application, that same code base can be leveraged to build a different HTML application.

Maintainability

Since the business logic is written in one place and reused, it is also easier to make changes to that logic later. You need only update the Enterprise Objects that require changes and every application that uses them will pick up the new changes upon redeployment.

Furthermore, it is easy to incorporate changes in the relational database schema, since only the Enterprise Objects that are affected need to be updated and not every application uses them.

Database Independence

Database independence is provided because EOF uses database adaptors to perform all low-level communication with the database. The developer programs directly against the EOF APIs in Java, *not* against a particular database. Issues such as variations in database data types and SQL syntax, and the writing of stored procedures, are entirely abstracted. Often, the transition from one database vendor to another can be done in a matter of hours, and EOF can even be leveraged to migrate the data itself in a reliable manner.

Multiple Database Support

Multiple database support refers to the ability to pull data from several databases. In this case, we create an EOModel for each database, and we can then utilize EOs containing data from both databases in our application without too much concern about the database the data came from. We can even map joins across the database. Because we have database independence these databases can be from different vendors – we could have a join from an `employee` table in a Sybase database to a `department` table in an Oracle database.

Support for Object Inheritance

Support for object inheritance means that you can continue to use one of the most powerful features of object-oriented programming with your persistent objects. There are several ways that inheritance can be modeled, including the ability to model it across multiple tables.

Automatic Primary and Foreign Key Generation

We do not have to worry about creating new primary or foreign keys, because EOF does it for you. There are several ways to create primary keys, including support to use stored procedures or custom code. Foreign keys 'just work'. We assign the instance variable of one Enterprise Object to be a destination Enterprise Object, and when the data is saved back to the database the foreign key will automatically be set correctly.

Transaction Management

When we modify persistent objects in EOF, we do all the work in a local area called an editing context. This editing context is a kind of sandbox for us to make our changes in; it keeps track of what objects have been created, updated or deleted, and even allows you to do things like revert all our objects back to how they were before you began changing them. Once we have finished with all our changes we can tell the editing context to save the changes to the database. EOF will write all the changes at one time, so if one update fails we do not leave the database in an inconsistent state.

Referential Integrity Enforcement

Referential integrity enforcement is handled automatically, based on definitions you provide in your EOModel, but can also be enhanced at the code level. Here, as in so many other places, the engineers at Apple provide us with 'hooks' to override default referential integrity and data validation rules.

EOF enforces referential integrity automatically and has an effective way to handle custom data and object validation for creation, insertion, updating and deletion. Since this is handled at the EOF layer, if a particular application has an error, any potential problem data will be caught at the EOF layer and not corrupt your database.

Furthermore, since EOF enables your application to be database independent, the data integrity and validation logic you write will be applied no matter what backend database you use and you do not need to rewrite it if you change database vendors (unlike stored procedures).

Object Faulting and Uniquing

Object faulting enables us to fetch one EO without having to pull lots of other EOs too. This problem occurs when you have a tightly coupled database with many joins between tables; fetching one EO and all of its appropriate relationships (joins) implies fetching more EOs. Since these EOs may also be joined to others, we can quickly reach a situation where we have the entire database in memory, which is very memory intensive.

Uniquing refers to the idea that if we perform several fetches that return the same row, we will have only one copy of that object in our application.

EOF Layers and Classes

While EOF provides an important layer within the WebObjects architecture, EOF itself also contains several layers. These layers are:

- `EOAccess`
- `EOControl`
- `EOInterface`
- `EODistribution` and `EOGeneration`

Here's an illustration of how these layers fit together:

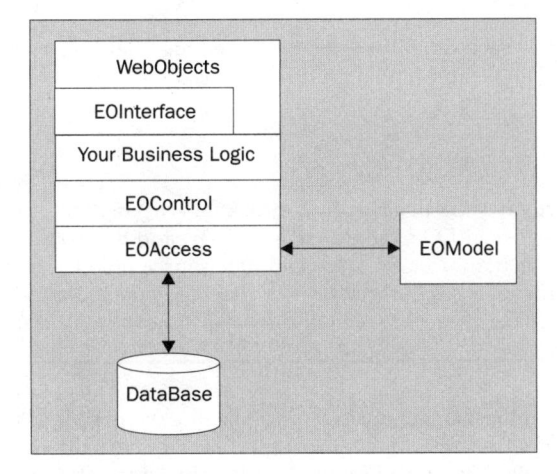

```
┌─────────────────────────────────────────┐
│         ┌─────────────────┐             │
│         │   WebObjects    │             │
│         ├─────────────────┤             │
│         │   EOInterface   │             │
│         ├─────────────────┤             │
│         │Your Business Logic│           │
│         ├─────────────────┤             │
│         │    EOControl    │             │
│         ├─────────────────┤   ┌───────┐ │
│         │    EOAccess     │◄─►│EOModel│ │
│         └────────┬────────┘   └───────┘ │
│                  ▲                      │
│                  ▼                      │
│              ╭───────╮                  │
│              │DataBase│                 │
│              ╰───────╯                  │
└─────────────────────────────────────────┘
```

The EOAccess and EOControl layers are particularly important, but let's now take a closer look at all of these layers.

EOAccess

The `EOAccess` layer provides classes that allow you to interact with database servers in an abstract way. It is further split into the `EODatabase` and `EOAdaptor` layers. The `EOAdaptor` layer provides server-independent database access, managing database rows packaged in dictionary form. The `EODatabase` layer is where EOs are created from these dictionaries.

The `EOAccess` layer contains a multitude of classes. Let's now discuss two of the most important.

EOEntity

An **entity** is a mapping between an enterprise object and a table (or multiple tables) in the database. In WebObjects, an entity is represented by an `EOEntity` object. Every `EOEntity` has a `className` and an `externalName`, which correspond to the name of the class that the EO belongs to and the name of the table in the database respectively. If there is no `className` for a given `EOEntity` then an `EOGenericRecord` (see below) is used by default as the EO.

As you might expect, `EOEntity` objects also contain information about primary keys, foreign keys, and row and column level locking. An `EOEntity` maintains a group of properties called **attributes** and **relationships**, represented by `EOAttribute` and `EORelationship` objects respectively. An `EOAttribute` represents database column or field, while an `EORelationship` object describes an association between two entities based on their attributes.

EOModel

The `EOModel` supports all the mappings we discussed earlier between your EOs and database data. When your application starts, all the `EOModels` for it are parsed and an `EOModel` class instantiated for each of them.

Each `EOModel` contains `EOEntity` objects, which as we have just noted represent database tables. You should note that an `EOModel` is database server-specific, so it stores connection information such as the name of the database adaptor to load, and other mapping information such as information about stored procedures and pre-defined fetch specifications. `EOModel` objects are loaded from model files created using the EOModeler tool.

`EOModels` can be related to each other, and so aggregated together into *model groups* (represented by an `EOModelGroup` object). The default model group contains all of the models for an application; this is created automatically.

EOControl

The `EOControl` layer provides the primary framework for working with Enterprise Objects directly. It manages the interaction between EOs, the `EOAccess` layer, and the `EOInterface` layer, providing an environment for EOs that is both user interface and data source independent. Its tasks include: tracking changes to EOs, prompting changes in the UI or the database when changes to objects are made, and managing uniquing. Let's have a look at some of this layer's most useful classes.

EOEditingContext

The `EOEditingContext` object is responsible for managing the **graph** of EOs in an application. A graph of objects is a group of related objects that represent an internally consistent view of an external data source. Each of the objects managed by the `EOEditingContext` is assigned a unique global identifier (`EOGlobalID`). The `EOEditingContext` functions as a local working area for the application to perform operations on persistent objects. We can fetch objects from the database into the `EOEditingContext`, perform modifications on them such as changing their attributes or deleting them, and even insert new EOs into it. All of the time the `EOEditingContext` keeps noting any changes made to the objects. When the operations on the objects are completed, the `EOEditingContext` can then save the changes or, if you wish, have them all undone.

EOEnterpriseObject

`EOEnterpriseObject` is an interface that defines the basic behavior for EOs. This behavior includes **key-value coding** as well as notification behavior to let other objects, in particular the `EOEditingContext`, know when its properties have been modified. In key-value coding, the properties of an object are accessed directly by name (key) not by calling a getter method on the object. We will learn more about key-value coding in Chapter 9.

EOCustomObject

`EOCustomObject` is the class you will typically inherit from to write your custom Enterprise Objects; it provides a default implementation of the `EOEnterpriseObject` interface, as well as other numerous interfaces such as `NSKeyValueCoding` and `EOKeyValueCoding` to support all the behavior EOF requires for an Enterprise Object to function properly.

EOGenericRecord

`EOGenericRecord` inherits directly from `EOCustomObject` and is useful when you have Enterprise Objects that do not require custom behavior. Since it inherits from `EOCustomObject`, it has all the required behavior to operate correctly in EOF. An `EOGenericRecord` determines what properties it should have by looking at the `EOModel`.

EOInterface

The `EOInterface` layer manages the presentation of Enterprise Objects through a user interface. In practicality there are three versions of this layer:

- HTML
- Swing
- Cocoa

The HTML version is what is used for a WebObjects Classic application, while Swing is used for Java Client and Cocoa for Mac OSX desktop applications. The `EOInterface` layer contains a wide variety of widgets that display Enterprise Objects as well as classes to manage communication between the UI widgets and the Enterprise Objects they represent. WebObjects tools such as WebObjects Builder allow these widgets to be laid out graphically, and the appropriate associations to Enterprise Objects to be set up such that little or no actual Java code needs to be written.

It is worth noting that many WebObjects Classic applications are written entirely without the use of the `EOInterface` layer. The advantage to this is that much more precise control over both the UI layout and the database interactions can be achieved. This is because we are directly managing the actual dynamic elements in the UI and their associations with the EOs they represent, as well as working directly with the `EOControl` layer to manage the database.

EODistribution and EOGeneration

At this point it is worth mentioning that there are two additional layers that are used for advanced WebObjects Applications, `EODistribution` and `EOGeneration`. `EODistribution` is used in Java Client applications to distribute and synchronize EOs between the WebObjects Application Server and the Java Client. The `EOGeneration` layer is used by Direct to Java Client to actually build the user interface dynamically at runtime based on developer-defined rules.

We will be encountering many of these EOF classes later in the book, when we start implementing database access in our WebObjects applications. For now, however, we will turn our attention to some of the more advanced features associated with WebObjects 5.0.

Advanced WebObjects

In this section we will give you a taste of the advanced WebObjects topics we will be covering in the book, and how they fit into the WebObjects architecture. These topics are:

Chapter 1

- Direct to Web
- Java Client and Direct To Java Client

Each of the technologies here is different from the classic WebObjects product in one or more ways. In some cases, such as Java Client, the entire HTML presentation is swapped out for a new technology (Swing) and in other cases, incremental improvements are made in the development tools and the way that development is done (Direct-To-Web).

The scope of this section is to provide an overview of each of the newer technologies with brief examples of how they can be used to deliver a wide variety of services in the internet economy.

Each of these technologies is as sophisticated, if not more sophisticated, than the classic WebObjects frameworks they are built on. Subsequent chapters in this book will discuss these technologies in more detail.

Java Client

WebObject's Java Client technology replaces the standard HTML browser based interface with a Java based one. The benefits of this approach include:

- Richer user interface
- Deployable as a Web Application or a Desktop Application
- Intelligent Object Distribution
- Partitioned Business Logic

Let's consider each of these benefits in more detail.

Richer User Interface

The user interface for Java Client applications is based on the Java Swing classes. WebObjects class applications are limited to the controls available in HTML such as forms and links. Java Client applications however have the full set of controls available from the Java Swing classes including modal windows, dropdown menus and numerous other items we have come to expect in a traditional desktop application.

Deployable As a Web Application Or a Desktop Application

You can deploy your Java Client either as an applet to be downloaded and executed over the internet, or as a desktop application. When you deploy over the internet you gain easier use of your application because no installation is necessary, and clients always get the latest version of the client code. Distributing as a desktop application however has performance advantages since it is executing directly in the Java runtime on the client rather than in the browser, and also has greater interactivity with the local system since it is not subject to the security criteria of applets (such as accessing the local hard drive).

Intelligent Object Distribution

Java Client uses an additional layer of WebObjects framework on both the client and the server called `EODistribution`. This layer provides an intelligent way to distribute business objects from the server to the client. Traditional distributed technologies that rely on CORBA or JavaRMI incur heavy performance penalties as they need to send messages to the server frequently to access variables. For example, if you wish to scroll down a list of last names for people in a database, CORBA and RMI techniques require that you send a request to the server for the last name of each object every time you scroll up or down the list. To improve performance with these technologies you may decide to store the last names in an array, but that requires a lot of coding... and how do you handle new objects inserted into the database, or changes made to a person's last name by another user?

Java Client, on the other hand, intelligently distributes the business objects directly to the client. When you fetch the list of people to display in your list, the EODistribution layer instantiates local copies of the objects on the client. This means that when you scroll up and down the list of last names all the data is present on the client, with no coding needed by you. WebObjects is also extremely smart about keeping your client-side data synchronized with updates that occur on the server, so if another user changes a person's last name your application will pick up that change.

Partitioned Business Logic

One problem with distributing business logic from the server to the client is security. For instance you may have data (such as a credit card number) and business logic (such as charging a credit card) that have high security requirements. Java Client allows you to partition your business logic, specifying data that is not distributed to the client, and specifying different classes to be instantiated for a given business object depending on whether it resides on the client or the server. There is also additional security that can be specified on server-side code when methods are invoked by client (and hence possibly modified) applications.

Rules-Based Rapid Application Development (RBRAD)

RBRAD encompasses both the **Direct-to-Web** and **Direct-to-JavaClient** technologies. The distinguishing feature of these two technologies is that they both use a rules-based system to generate the client user interface on the fly. Direct-to-Web delivers the application via HTML, while Direct-to-Java delivers it via the Java Client technology mentioned above. The primary benefits of rules-based development are:

- Extremely rapid development cycle
- Rules-based UI generation
- Intelligent default rules
- Customization of the rules
- Freezing of a specific UI element

Rapid Development Cycle

RBRAD technologies have an extremely rapid development cycle. This is because the tedious aspects of designing and coding the user interface are greatly reduced or entirely absent. Instead, the UI is generated automatically allowing the developer to focus on the data modeling and business logic for the application. In cases where the data modeling and business logic for a company's systems have already been built, the development cycle for a new HTML or Java Client application can be measured in days.

Chapter 1

Rules-Based UI Generation

Both Direct-to-Web and Direct-to-Java generate their UI based on a rule set. This rule set contains elements that say things like 'If the current object being viewed is a `Person`, and we are looking at the `firstName` property and we are editing the `Person` then use a `WOTextField` element to display the `firstName`'.

Since the UI is rules based, you never need to layout the HTML at all. Standard elements such as String, date and numbers are simply displayed using the appropriate `WOComponent` class. If we wish to edit an object, a `FORM` element is created and the properties are displayed with the corresponding HTML INPUT elements. We are given a choice of how to display to-one and to-many relationships, including simply with a hyperlink or displayed in-place. Editing for these relationships is done through automatically generated pick pages, where you are allowed to specify or add destination objects to relationships.

Intelligent Default Rules

The default rules for UI generation are extremely functional. If you have an EOModel already created for a database, you can have a completely usable HTML or Java Client application running against that database in under an hour.

Customization of the Rules

Of course, default rules are just that. If your application is to be used by the public, or requires security based on who is logged in then you will want to customize your rules. For instance, you may have a custom WebObjects component used in other applications at your company to display credit card numbers with digits hidden as in XXXX-XXXX-XXXX-1234. You could then add this component, say `MyCreditCardComponent`, to your project and add a rule that says something like 'If the name of the current property we are viewing is `creditCard` then use `MyCreditCardComponent` to display it'. Any time that `creditCard` property shows up in a web page then this custom component will be used to display it instead of a normal string output element.

Documentation

There are several documentation tools you can use to answer additional questions you may have, as well as view the various classes and APIs provided by WebObjects. The tools provided are:

- Developer Help Center (on Mac OS X)
- WOInfoCenter (on Windows)
- JavaBrowser Application
- Apple Developer Connection

Let's review each of these in turn.

Developer Help Center

In Mac OS X with WebObjects 5, you can access the Developer Help Center. to activate this, you need to be in the Project Builder tool (Developer|Applications|Project Builder on Mac OS X or Start|Programs|WebObjects|Project Builder in Windows 2000). Open up ProjectBuilder, go to the Help menu dropdown menu and choose Developer Help Center. In here you will see WebObjects listed as one of the choices:

WOInfoCenter

The equivalent of the Developer Help Center on Windows 2000 is the WebObjects InfoCenter (found in Start|Programs|WebObjects|WebObjects Info Centre). If you are developing on Mac OS X with WebObjects 4.5.1 you will also find the WOInfoCenter. This is because WOF 4.5.1 and WOF5 on Windows use an older version of ProjectBuilder that does not have the Developer Help Center built in. WOInfoCenter is itself a WebObjects application and will bring up a browser window when you run it. It allows you to query the documentation, sample code and other material just like the Developer Help Center.

JavaBrowser

JavaBrowser is a Java class library browser tool that ships with WebObjects for both MacOSX and Windows 2000. On OSX it is located under Developer/Applications, on Windows 2000 it is under Start|WebObjects|JavaBrowser. There are quite a few developer tools in here; you should spend a few minutes with each one just to get an idea of what they are, so that if you need them later you will know they are already there.

JavaBrowser by default parses only the Java classes in the class path. To get access to all the WebObjects classes you will want to add them to JavaBrowser. To do this, start up JavaBrowser now.

If you look through the various Java classes present you will see that all the packages and classes in your classpath are present, but under com|webobjects you will find only the _jdbcadaptor package, as shown below:

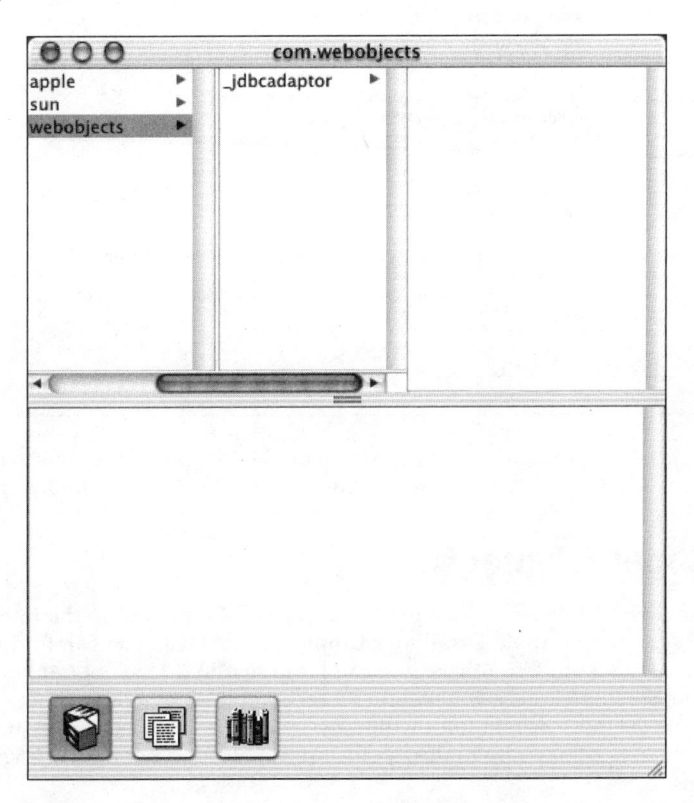

To add additional classes we wish to browse for WebObjects development, you must add the .jar files that contain those files. Let's say we want to add class files from a Framework. These are located under System/Library/Frameworks on Mac OS X (Apple\Library\Frameworks on Windows 2000).

From the **Browser** menu item, choose **Add Classes,** and go to the System/Library/Frameworks directory. Here you will find numerous frameworks for all the Java development supported on Mac OS X. The WebObjects frameworks are typically prefixed with the word 'Java'. We will want to add those to our class path. Continue by selecting JavaWebObjects.framework/Resources/Java and choose javawebobjects.jar.

Now you will see a com.apple.webobjects.appserver package appear in the JavaBrowser, and going down through it you will see the following:

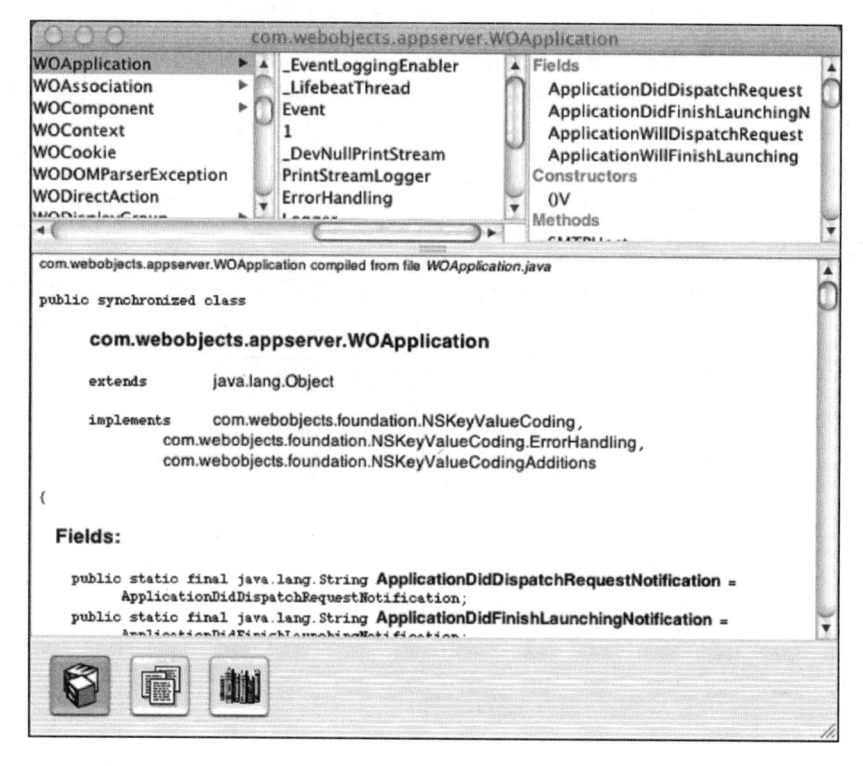

The ability to quickly review classes and their APIs with the JavaBrowser tool is very handy during development, and you may find it a useful tool while reading through this book as well.

Apple Developer Connection

The final resource for questions and documentation on WebObjects is on the internet at Apple's web site for developers called the Apple Developer Connection (ADC). You can find the ADC main page at http://developer.apple.com. From here you can jump to http://developer.apple.com/techpubs/ webobjects/webobjects.html, where you will find a section on WebObjects. Since this site is maintained by Apple is contains the most current information for new released documentation, sample code and other items. There are also links here to the **AppleCare Knowledge Base,** which you can query for technical questions.

Summary

In this chapter we gained an overview of the WebObjects architecture. We noted that the architecture has many tiers, which, although at first sight makes the architecture appear unnecessarily complicated, actually brings many benefits to us when we build WebObjects applications.

For example, by grouping objects together by the roles they perform within the application, we can increase the reusability, portability and maintainability of our application. In WebObjects, this is achieved by grouping all of the business logic classes together in the Enterprise Objects Framework (EOF) layer.

As well as providing the business logic, the objects in the EOF layer are also used for object-relational mapping to relational databases. This means that objects in the EOF data are used to store data from the database. The advantages of storing database data in objects are similar to those we saw from dividing up the presentation and business logic. By allowing our application to retrieve data from objects rather than the database, we abstract database connection code away from our application, which makes the application more reusable and portable.

We ended the chapter with a brief discussion of advanced WebObjects features such as Java Client and Direct To Web, and reviewed the help documentation available to WebObjects developers.

In the next few chapters we will get down to more practical matters, by taking you on a tour of the Builder tools that are provided by WebObjects for developing applications.

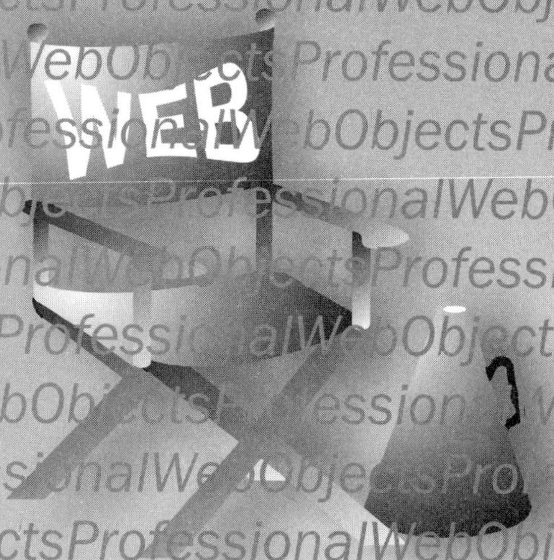
WEB

Introducing WebObjects Tools

In this chapter we'll introduce you to the three primary WebObjects development tools that will enable us to construct WebObjects applications: Project Builder, WebObjects Builder, and EOModeler. We will focus mainly on **Project Builder**, and illustrate its use by constructing and running an extremely simple WebObjects application. Building this application will provide a taste of many of the issues involved in constructing a WebObjects application that we will cover in far more depth in the next chapter. We will also discuss the organization of files within a WebObjects project.

WebObjects Development Tools

All of the elements of a WebObjects application (HTML files, bindings files, and Java code) are stored in plain text, which means that developers are free to modify them using a text editor at any time. However, WebObjects comes with several development tools to aid the development of an application. The main tools you will encounter are **Project Builder**, **WebObjects Builder** and **EOModeler**.

EOModeler is used to create the relationships (or mappings) between a relational database and Enterprise Objects. This mapping is referred to as an EOModel, or sometimes simply a "model". EOModeler is also used to configure various settings for the EOModel. It can create or modify the underlying relational database itself, although this is not recommended for anything but the simplest of applications.

WebObjects Builder is used to edit components, which consists of editing the HTML in a graphical environment and creating bindings between the HTML and Java code (the aforementioned `<WEBOBJECT>` tags).

Project Builder is used to maintain the entire application and write Java code. Project Builder can launch WebObjects Builder and EOModeler as appropriate. You can also compile, execute, and debug WebObjects applications from within Project Builder.

Project Builder can also be used to develop many other types of applications, including Carbon, Cocoa, and Java applications. It is Apple's generic IDE for creating OS X applications.

Project Builder

We've talked about a WebObjects application, now let's create one. In the process of doing so, we'll familiarize ourselves with the Project Builder tool. We will be giving details on how to access the IDE for both Mac and Windows users.

Mac Users

If you are using the Mac, you can access Project Builder by opening the `/Developer/Applications` directories. You may find an application called **ProjectBuilderWO**. This tool is from WebObjects 4.5 and you should use the Project Builder tool instead, as shown:

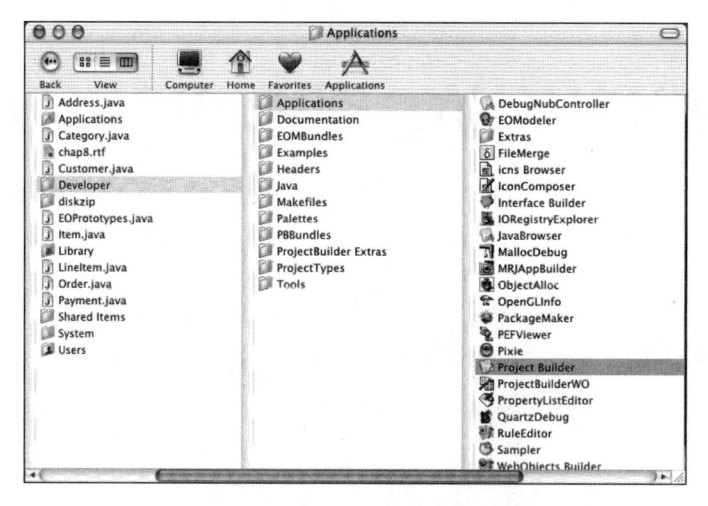

If this is your first time using Project Builder, you should see the following screen on the Mac:

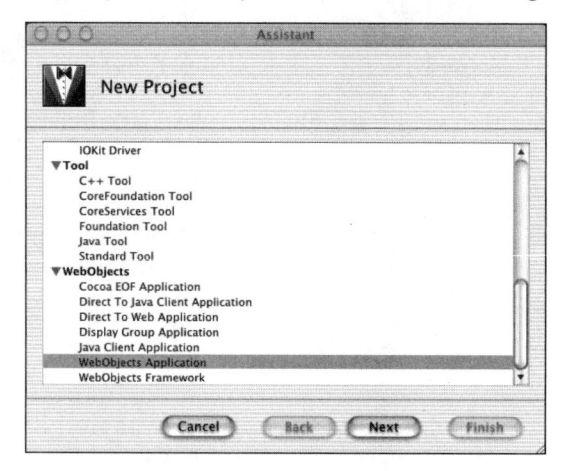

Introducing WebObjects Tools

If you don't see this screen, don't panic, just click on **File | New Project...** from the pull-down menu. Now, scroll down to the option **WebObjects Application** as shown in the above screenshot. Once you've highlighted it, click **Next**.

This next screen will prompt you to name your project and give it a location. Name your project **HelloWorld**. Now hit *Tab* and Project Builder will automatically generate a location based on the name; accept this location and then click **Finish**.

You should now see the main Project Builder IDE:

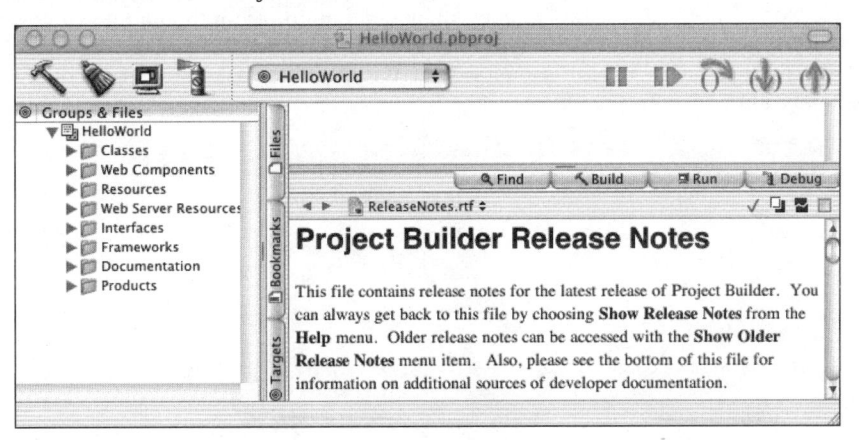

Windows Users

If you are using Windows you can access Project Builder from the Programs option:

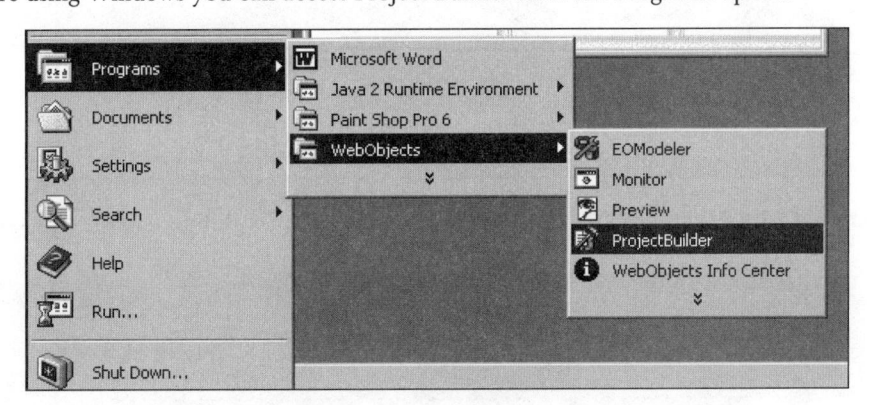

You will then see the following window:

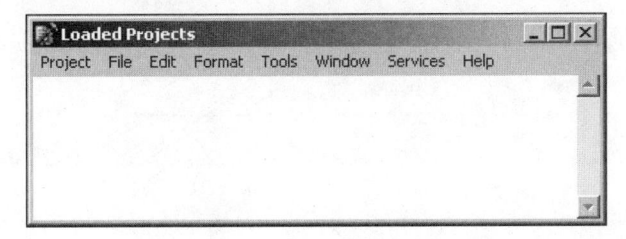

Chapter 2

Click on the **Project** option and select **New**. A dialog box will appear asking you to stipulate what type of application you want to develop and its location:

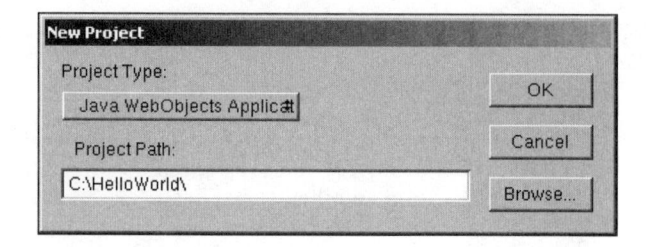

For **Project Type**, select the **JavaWebObjects Application** option from the pull down menu and in the **Project Path** choose a location for your application. Once you have entered this information, click **OK**. The WebObjects Application Wizard is then activated and you are asked to choose the type of assistance you require for your project:

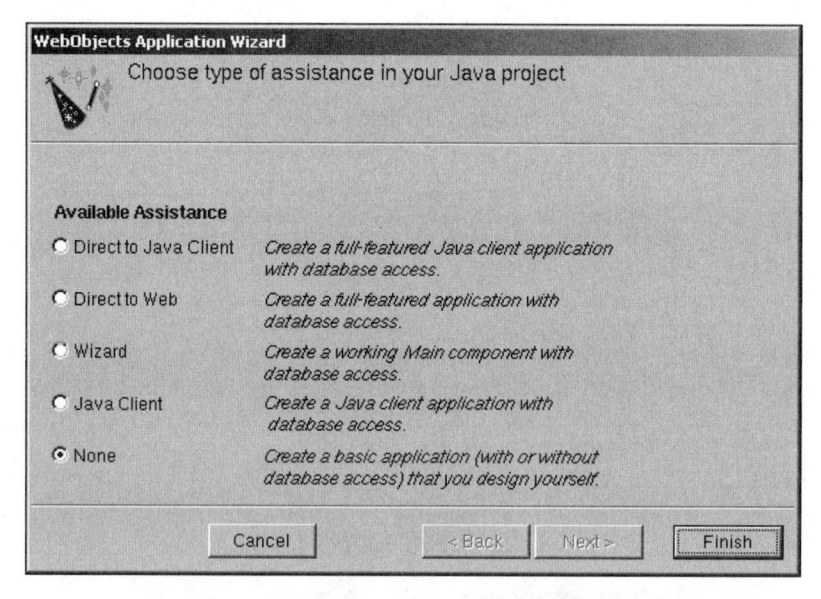

Select **None** and click **Finish**. You will then see the Windows Project Builder IDE:

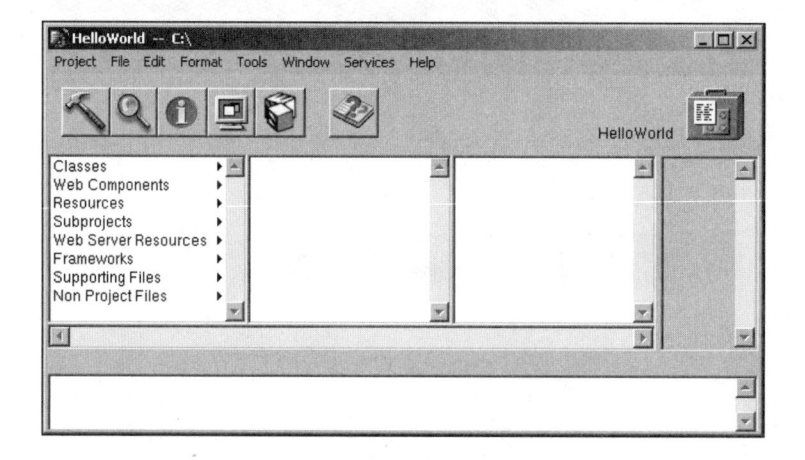

Organization of Files in a Project

Once you have activated Project Builder, you will see a list of directories. These contain all of the various files that make up your application. On the Mac these are entitled **Groups & Files** and the contents of these directories are displayed vertically, while on Windows these contents are displayed horizontally. If we expand some of the folders and take a closer look at them on the Mac, we can see something like the window pane shown to the right.

We see the project's name listed at the top, which in this case is `HelloWorld`. The **Classes** folder contains the core WebObjects objects: `Application.java` and `Session.java`, which represents the aforementioned application and session objects. The third file, `DirectAction.java`, is a container for various **direct action** methods which are accessed directly by the application's users (we will discuss direct actions in later chapters). These three classes are generated by Project Builder specifically for your project, and you can edit them directly. In addition to these three classes, you'll place your custom Java classes for your application here as well.

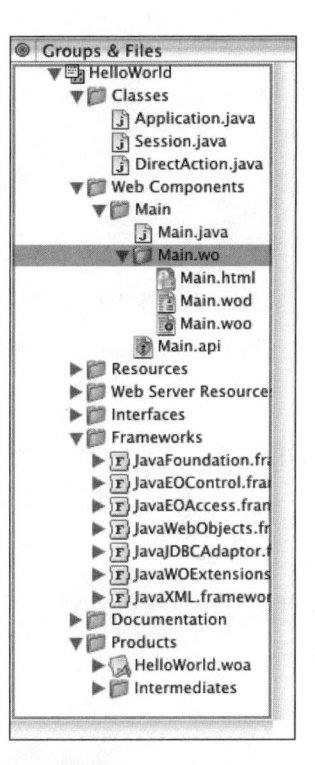

The **Web Components** directory contains the files for all of your components. Notice that the **Main** folder is in the **Web Components** folder. This folder represents a component named **Main** and contains all of its underlying files. WebObjects automatically created this component, which functions as the starting point of your application. Inside the **Main** folder are the following files:

File Name	Description
`Main.java`	Contains the component's programmatic logic.
`Main.wo`	Contains several additional files relating to the component.
`Main.html`	The component's HTML file.
`Main.wod`	The **bindings** between the `Main.html` and `Main.java`.
`Main.woo`	Stores information specific to **display groups**; this formats groups of data for display in the user interface. We don't need to worry about this file, because WO maintains it for us.
`Main.api`	Documents the parameters that your custom component requires.

Don't worry too much about what we mean by "bindings" or "display groups" – we will discuss these concepts in far more detail in subsequent chapters.

You should note that the organization of files is slightly different on Windows: here the `Main.java` file is under the **Classes** folder, and there is no **Main** folder beneath **Web Components**, only **Main.wo**.

35

The **Resources** folder contains external resources that your application may require that should **not** be publicly visible, such as localization strings, configuration files, etc.

The **Web Server Resources** directory contains any static elements that the web server may need to serve up to support your application, such as GIF or JPG files. These resources will be moved to a location that static HTML pages on your web server can access as well.

The **Interfaces** folder is used for storing the GUI interface files associated with a Java client application.

Inside the **Frameworks** directory we have all of the code libraries made available to your application. You should become familiar with these libraries; they contain some very useful classes. If you create your own reusable frameworks, they will be added to this folder.

The **Documentation** folder contains relevant documentation and **Products** contains all of those files generated by compiling your project.

Changing Preferences

Project Builder also provides us with the option to change many of its preferences. To view the options on a Mac, we need to select **Project Builder | Preferences**. This is what we can see:

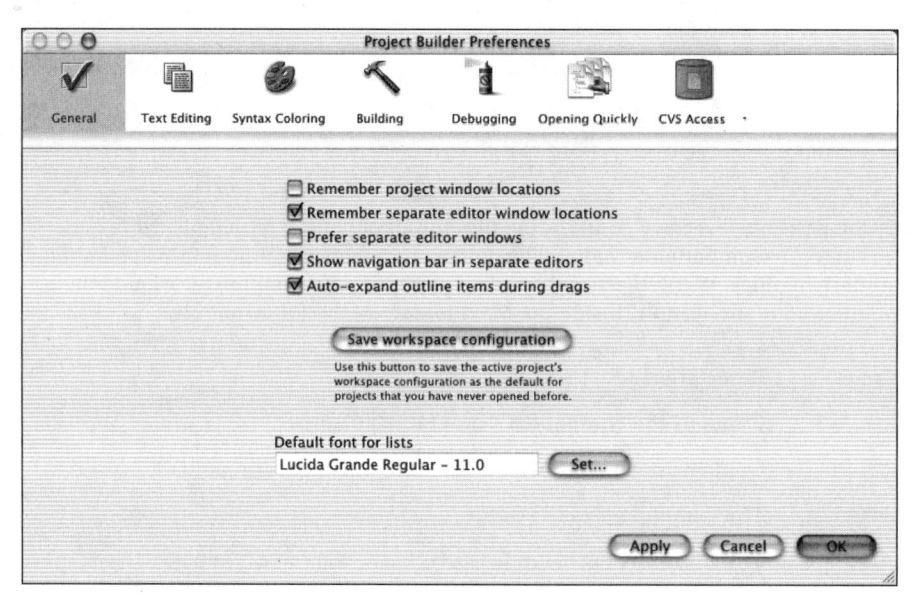

On a Windows machine, the corresponding window can be invoked in Project Builder through **Edit | Preferences** instead.

When we open the **Preferences** window, the default tab we are presented with is the **General** tab. However, the options presented to us by this tab differ between Mac and Windows. On the Mac, we are presented with lots of window configuration options, including the ability to save the workspace configuration of the active project as the default. Instead, on Windows we can specify the view where documentation files will be opened, as well as other options such as whether to prompt when quitting or closing a project.

Both platforms allow the user to configure basic text editing properties such as line wrapping, tabs, and indentation. On the Mac these options are available in the **Text Editing** tab; on Windows they are located in the **Editing** and **Indentation** tabs. Using these options we make sure all of the code in the project will be formatted just how we want it.

We can also configure the font colors and styles of different syntax in our code, such as comments, keywords, and constants, using the **Syntax Coloring** tab on the Mac or the **Syntax** tab on Windows. Using this option can help make the project's code easier to follow and debug. Actually, there also is a **Debugging** tab on both Windows and Mac versions, although they provide different debugging options (on the Mac we can choose the font style for the debugger and the color of the debug pointer; on Windows we can specify higher-level options such as whether to use the GDB debugger or not).

The **Build** tab is also present on both Mac and Windows, although (as with the **General** tab) the build configuration options available are different between platforms. For instance, on the Mac, we can specify where the products from building an application are placed; this option is not available on Windows.

There are many more **Preference** tabs available, some of which are platform-specific. It's worthwhile taking some time to review them so that you know the options available to you.

Creating a Hello World Application

Let's now continue with the creation of our sample application. We're going to create a simple web application that displays the words "Hello World" and today's date. The next step for us is to edit our HTML file. While we can do this textually through Project Builder, let's use the WebObjects Builder. Launch it by double-clicking on `Main.wo` (which is in the **Web components** directory).

Click on the upper portion of the screen and enter the words **Hello world! The present time is:** " as seen here:

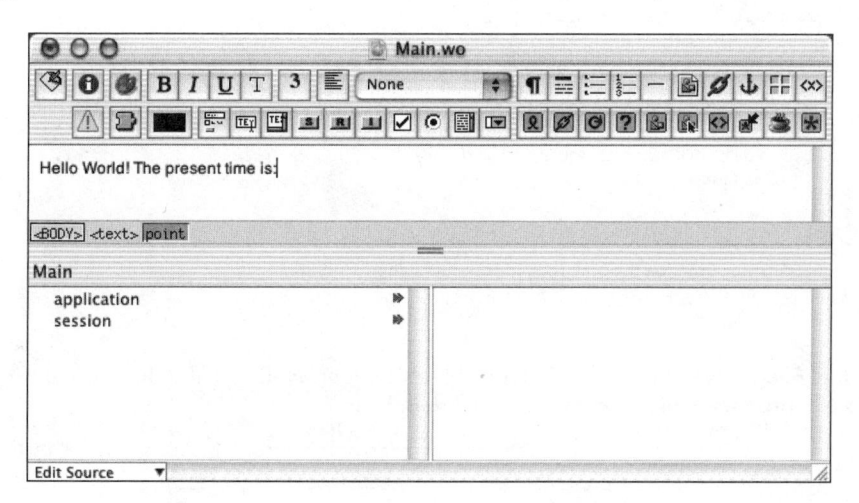

Now we need to add a Java method that will return the current time. Go back to the Project Builder and click on `Main.java`. This will display the source code in the editor pane of Project Builder, as seen here:

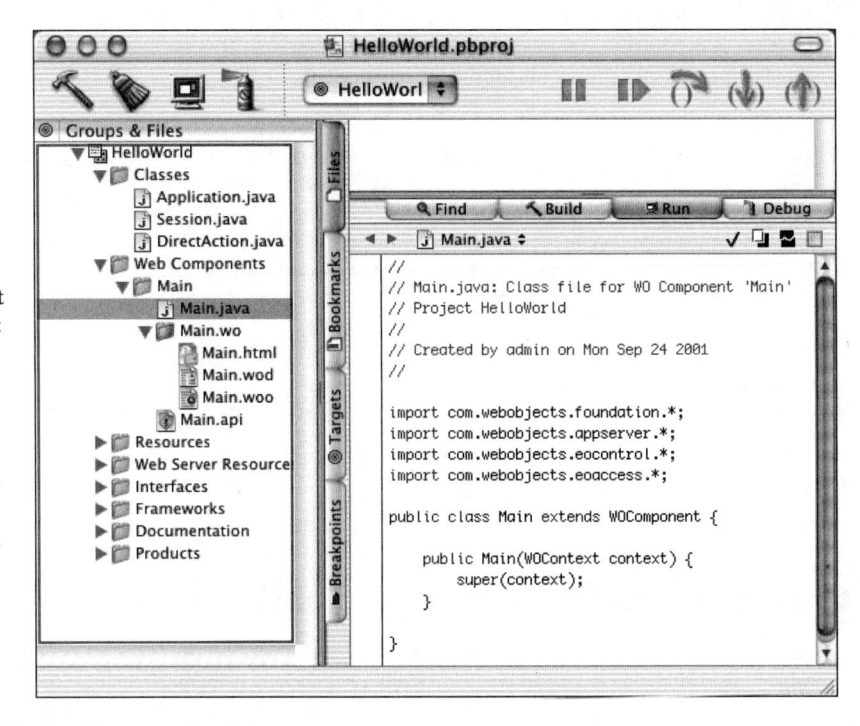

Add the following highlighted lines to the code:

```
import com.webobjects.foundation.*;
import com.webobjects.appserver.*;
import com.webobjects.eocontrol.*;
import com.webobjects.eoaccess.*;
import java.util.*;   // required for Date class

public class Main extends WOComponent {

    public Main(WOContext context) {
        super(context);
    }

    public Date getDate() {
        return new Date();
    }
}
```

Save the file (File | Save) and return to WebObjects Builder. Notice that **date** now appears as an option in the Objects browser which is in the lower left-hand corner:

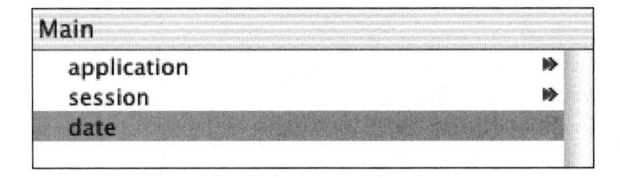

Introducing WebObjects Tools

WebObjects Builder has detected the new method and has made it available for inclusion as a dynamic datum in our component. Notice that WebObjects recognizes that `getDate()` is a "getter" method – it returns a property value; in this case the method name indicates that it returns the `date` property.

Now we need to create a placeholder in the HTML and link the placeholder to the date property. This linking is the "binding" that we referred to earlier. To do so, position the cursor to the right of the **Hello world! The present time is:** line, and click on the highlighted icon as shown below:

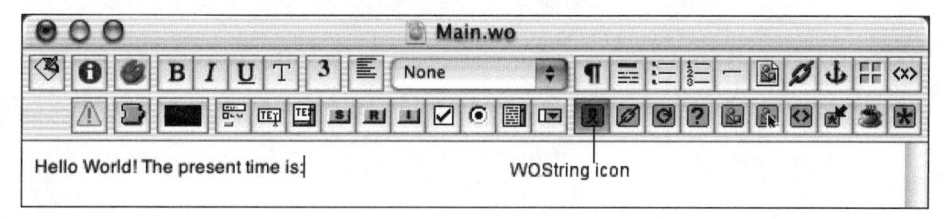

You've now inserted a `WOString` object into your HTML page. `WOString` can represent any dynamic datum that can be converted into a String value. Our date property is such an item. To link the date property to the `WOString` object, click and hold on **date**, and drag it to the `WOString` object as shown overleaf:

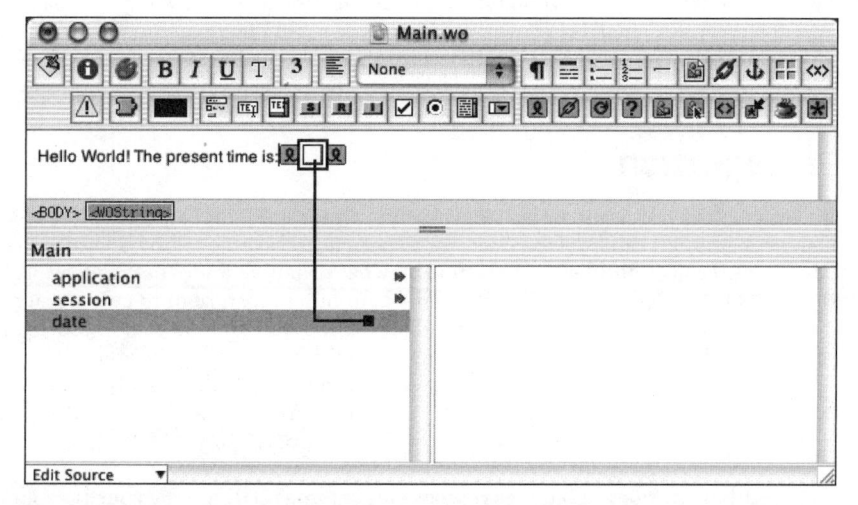

Now we're ready to run our application. Click on **File | Save All** and return to the Project Builder. Compile your project by clicking on the hammer icon in the upper left-hand corner. For Windows clicking on the hammer icon opens up another window and you must click on the hammer icon in the upper left corner of this new window to begin compilation. After the compilation has finished, run your project by clicking on the Monitor icon. For Windows clicking on the Monitor icon opens up a separate panel and you must click on the Monitor icon in this panel to launch your project. Eventually, your default web browser should automatically appear with a page similar to the following:

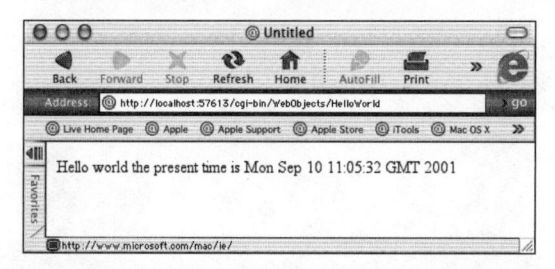

39

If your browser does not open automatically, you need to open your browser yourself and enter your application's URL. WebObjects changes your application's URL every time you launch it, so you'll need to copy it from Project Builder's output window, highlighted here:

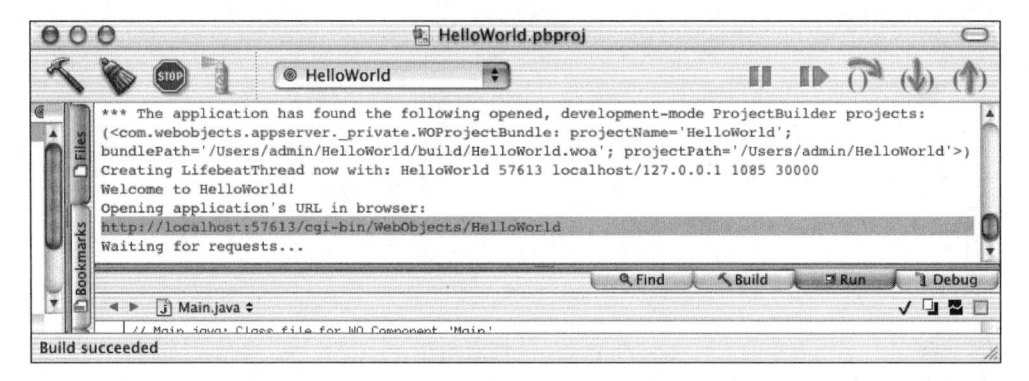

Congratulations! You've written your first WebObjects application. Now is a good time to further explore Project Builder on your own. It's pretty straightforward, and on-line help is always just a click away (Windows users: check out the WOInfoCenter). However, one thing you should not experiment with are the "targets" that Project Builder uses. These are fairly complicated configuration settings that determine where and how your WebObjects project gets compiled and executed, so it's best to leave them alone for now.

Java IDE Integration

Project Builder isn't a bad Java code editor. It provides some support for syntax coloring and indentation features amongst others. However, for experienced Java developers familiar with tools such as Forte or NetBeans, Project Builder may seem somewhat primitive and what features it does have don't compare well to other editors. Project Builder's auto-indent feature only indents subsequent lines to the same level as the previous line; it doesn't indent the first line of a new code block automatically. Project Builder's **show matching brace** feature shows you the matching curly brace for a code block but it only briefly blinks the matching brace, which limits its usefulness. Additionally Project Builder does not have code-insight features that indicate the expected parameters of a method, or automatic JavaDoc generation.

Fortunately, Project Builder does make it easy to use an external IDE to edit your Java code; it automatically detects when any source file has been modified and reloads it. One Java IDE you could use is the open-source jEdit editor (http://www.jedit.org). jEdit is an IDE written purely in Java. In the following screenshot we can see jEdit editing the **Main** component's Java source:

Introducing WebObjects Tools

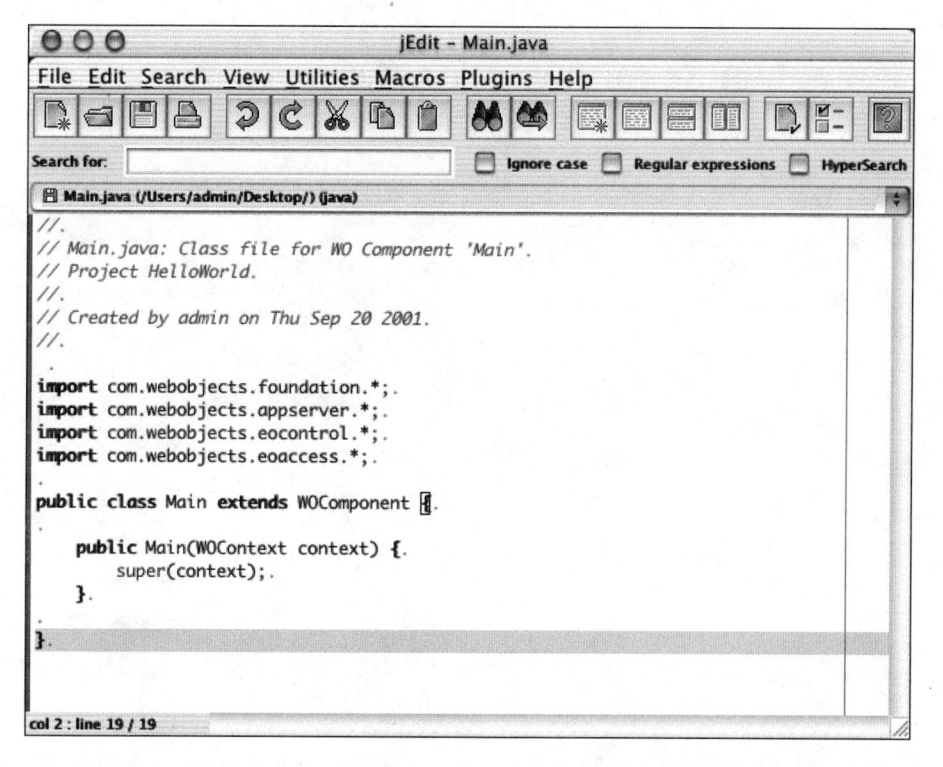

```
//.
// Main.java: Class file for WO Component 'Main'.
// Project HelloWorld.
//.
// Created by admin on Thu Sep 20 2001.
//.

import com.webobjects.foundation.*;.
import com.webobjects.appserver.*;.
import com.webobjects.eocontrol.*;.
import com.webobjects.eoaccess.*;.

public class Main extends WOComponent {.

    public Main(WOContext context) {.
        super(context);.
    }.

}.
```

Feel free to install any 100% Pure Java IDE you desire and experiment with it and WebObjects. It is also worth mentioning that Apple has promised the OS X development community that it will add more code editing features to future versions of Project Builder.

Summary

In this chapter we introduced you to the practicalities of WebObjects application creation. In particular we learned that:

- Project Builder is Apple's generic IDE which can be used to manage WebObject application projects.
- Project Builder can also be used to access the other two WebObjects development tools, WebObjects Builder and EOModeler.

We also learned how files in a WebObjects Project are organized, the tool configuration options available to us, and how to build and run a WebObjects application. In the next chapter we will focus on WebObjects Builder in much more detail.

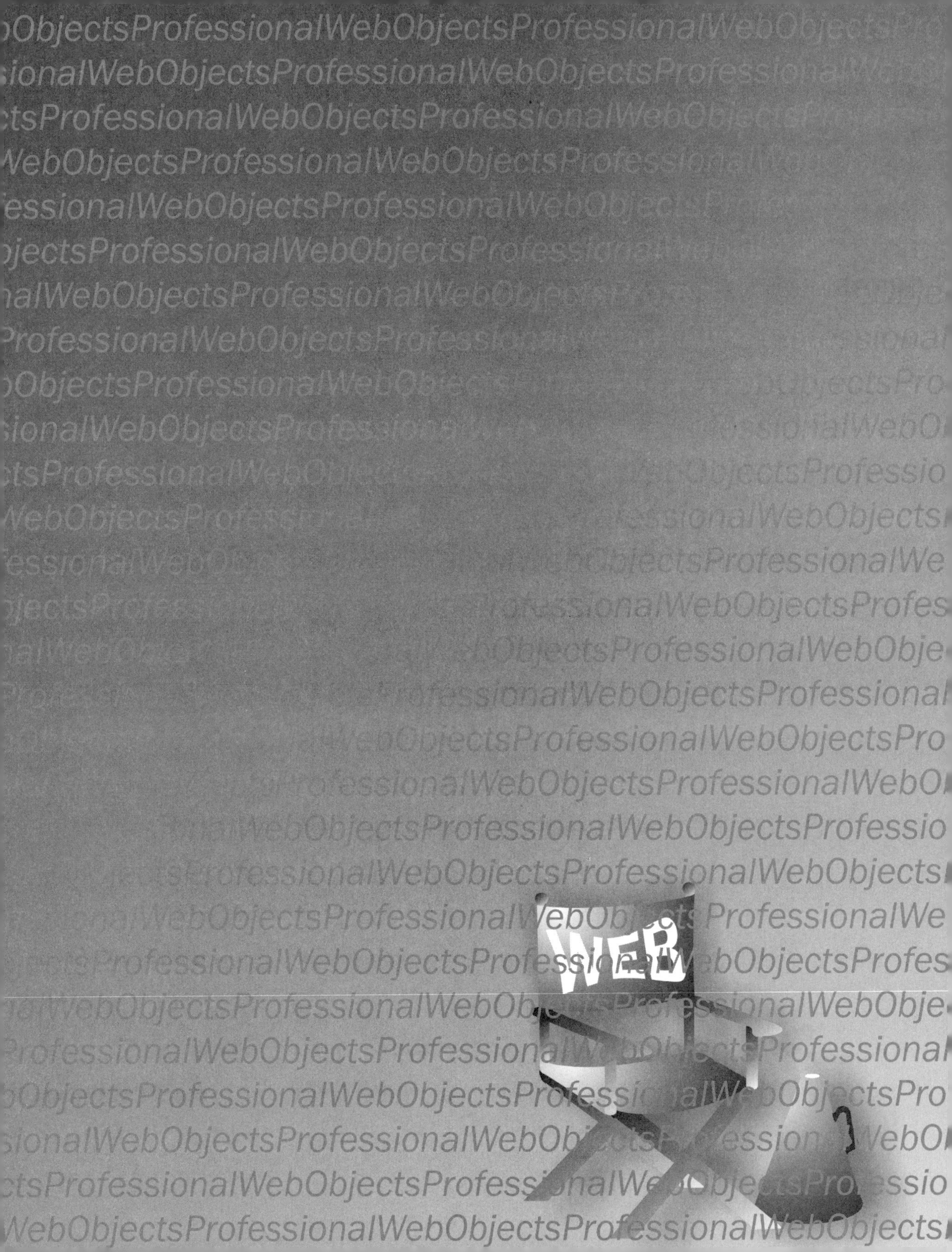
WEB

WebObjects Builder

In the previous chapter we saw that a WebObjects application consists principally of Java source code and WebObjects components, and that in this way WebObjects provides a natural separation of presentation and logic code. We've also seen that the Project Builder tool is used to manage these files in your WebObjects application. Project Builder is also the default editor for the Java source code. However, a different tool, WebObjects Builder, is used specifically for editing WebObjects components.

WebObjects Builder provides a user-friendly, feature-rich GUI for both editing HTML and binding Java code to your HTML. In this chapter, we'll examine WebObjects Builder and its most compelling features.

We'll begin this chapter by diving in and building a simple application using WebObjects Builder. In the process we will get a brief tour of many of the features that WebObjects Builder UI provides.

For the rest of the chapter we'll look more closely at the features that we introduced in the first section, and introduce a few more. We'll discuss the following topics:

- Creating variables and working with them in WebObjects Builder
- Adding dynamic elements to our site with methods
- Using conditionals to regulate what is displayed on a page
- Calling other pages while passing on information
- Making and displaying lists in tables using the `Session` object

By the end of the chapter we will have built an application that uses all of these features.

For the example in the first section, we will add variables while we are working on the look of our WebObjects component, and the variables are added to the associated Java file for us. In most applications, the flow will actually tend to work in the other direction, and this is the approach we will take for the example we build for the rest of the chapter. The variables and methods that you design in your source code will be available to the web designers to use in their pages. For experienced JSP developers this is refreshing: the tools support the separate roles of programmer and designer in ways that benefit each. The web designers can't put Java code in the middle of their web page.

Anyway, let's start simple, with a quick tour of the WebObjects Builder UI.

A Brief Tour of WebObjects Builder

In this first section we will get acquainted with the WebObjects Builder UI by building a simple application and then running it. In the process we will introduce several key features of WebObjects that we will discuss in more depth later in the chapter.

Launching WebObjects Builder

WebObjects Builder is located in the `/Developer/Applications` directory on the Mac OS along with Project Builder, but we saw in the previous chapter that it can be launched from within Project Builder itself. To demonstrate, run Project Builder and load the **HelloWorld** project that we created in Chapter 2 (to do this on Windows you'll need to select **File | Open** and then navigate to the `HelloWorld` project folder and open the `PB.project` file in this folder). Double-click on the folder named `Main.wo` in the Web Components folder of Project Builder. This folder contains the HTML file and bindings file that make up your component; double-clicking on it will launch WebObjects Builder with the Main component loaded. On the Mac you should see the following window:

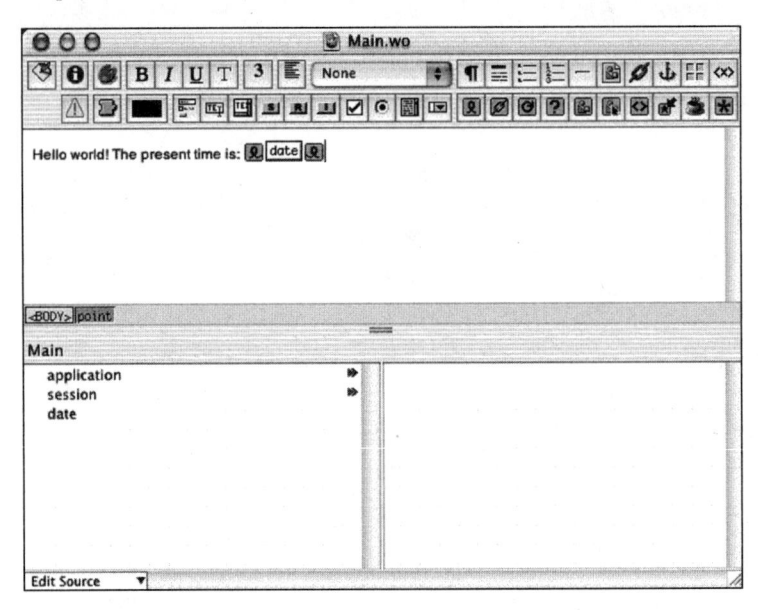

WebObjects Builder's interface is divided into two main sections: the HTML editor at the top, and the object browser below, which is split into two areas and displays variables and methods from your Java code. Let's take a look at each one separately, and then examine how they interoperate.

The HTML Editor

The upper portion of the interface is the HTML editor. Take a look at the toolbar; if you're familiar with HTML, you should recognize some of the icons. The top row contains static HTML elements; that is, those elements that cannot be directly bound to any values from your application's code. It contains icons representing common elements like a table, a hyperlink, a horizontal rule, and so on (as you move the mouse cursor over the icon, a "tool tip" will appear, telling you what each icon does).

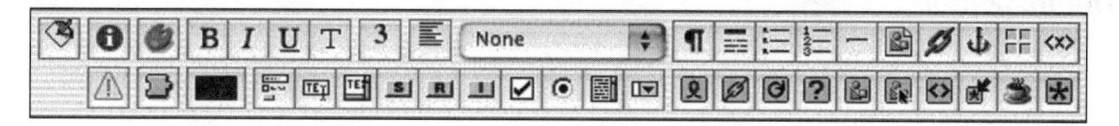

As you move the mouse across the bottom row of the toolbar, you'll see that for the most part their name starts with "WO". These are special WebObjects-specific elements that can be bound to your application's code to display dynamic data from your application. You should recall one of these elements, **WOString**, from the sample **HelloWorld** application in chapter 2.

Let's add a static element to our simple **Main** component. Position the cursor in the content area at the end of the text that already exists and click on the table icon:

You should see a table configuration dialog box like the following appear:

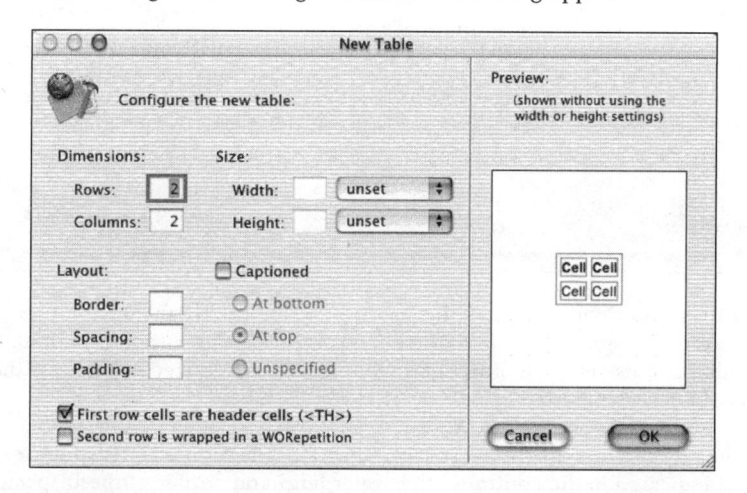

Set the number of rows and columns to 2 as shown above, and make sure that the **First row cells are header cells (<TH>)** checkbox is selected as shown above. Finally, click on OK. You should now see a visual representation of the table in the content area. You can click on the individual cells to change their contents. Your content area should look something like this:

Chapter 3

Hello world! The present time is: [Q] [date] [Q]
Cell Cell
Cell Cell

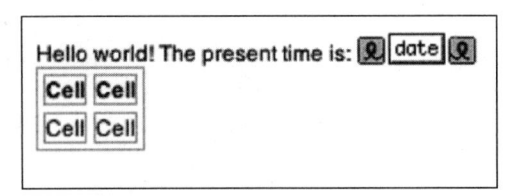

The Inspector

Once you create an HTML element, you are still free to modify it. You modify HTML elements using the Inspector window. Let's take a closer look.

Static Inspector

To use the Inspector, click anywhere in the table that you just created and then click on the Inspector icon:

Inspector icon

The Inspector window will now appear, which looks like this:

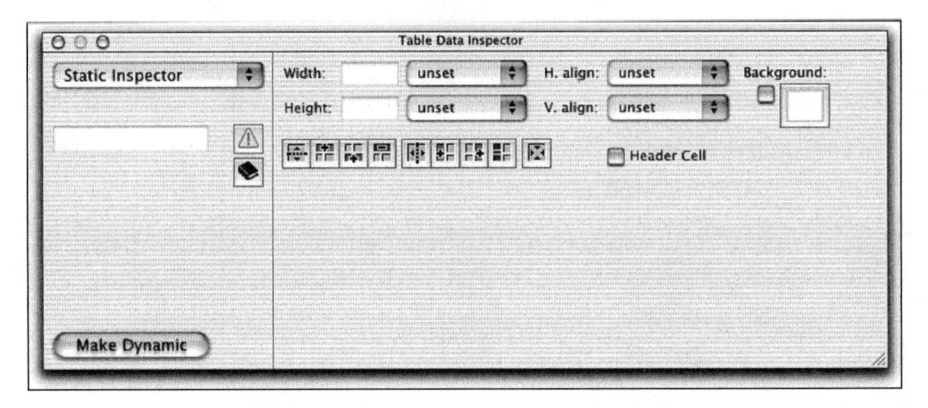

Table Data Inspector — Static Inspector: Width, Height, H. align, V. align, Background, Header Cell, Make Dynamic

This is the **Static Inspector**. With the Static Inspector you can modify the attributes of your HTML elements. In this example, you can see individual icons representing various manipulations you can perform on the table and its cells. The Inspector will present customized options for the various HTML elements that WebObjects supports.

There are two other Inspectors: the **Generic Inspector** and the **Dynamic Inspector**. The current mode of the Inspector is indicated in the control in the upper left-hand corner of the Inspector window; in this case, it's the Static Inspector. We'll look at the Dynamic Inspector a little later in the chapter, but first let's take a look at the Generic Inspector.

Generic Inspector

The Generic Inspector lets you add custom attribute/value pairs to any HTML elements. To demonstrate, select the entire table that you just added. This is a little tricky; don't click on any of the table cells but rather somewhere on the table border until you see the table outlined and shaded as shown:

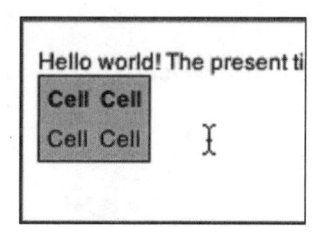

There is an alternative way of highlighting that we shall explore later. Now click on the Inspector again, and select "Generic Inspector" from the control in the upper left-hand corner. Your Inspector dialog should look like this:

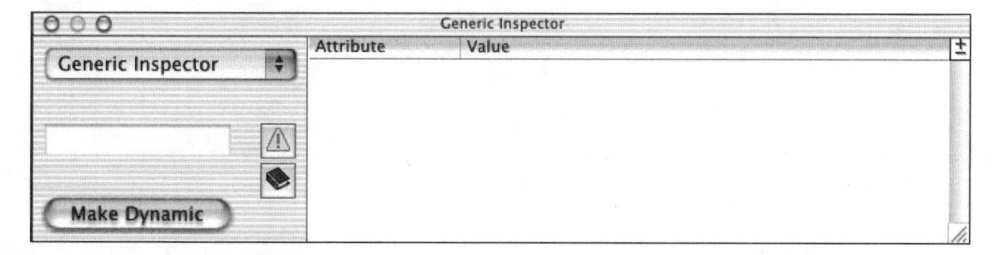

Click on the **Add / delete attributes** button (represented top right by the addition sign above the minus sign) and select **Add attribute**. A generic entry will be added. Double-click on the **Attribute** column and change it to **width**. Likewise double-click on the **value** column and enter 100%. You should see an immediate change to the table in the content area, which should now look like this:

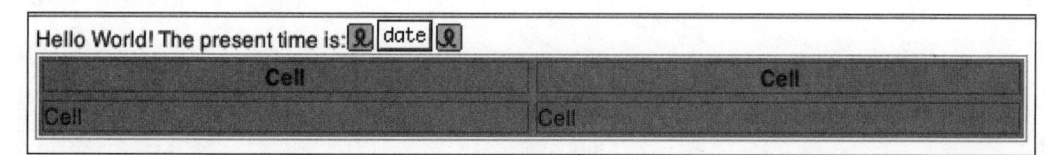

Note that the table header cells (the <TH> tags) that we used when we created the table are automatically centered.

While you'll typically use the Static Inspector to modify your HTML elements, at times the Static Inspector won't have icons representing the attributes or tags you want to add or modify. This scenario is somewhat likely because the Static Inspector is based on the tags and attributes found in the HTML 3.2 Specification, meaning newer HTML 4.0+ plus tags and attributes aren't included. When this occurs, you can use the Generic Inspector to add the desired tags or attributes to your component.

Chapter 3

Source View

For those who prefer to manually edit their HTML, WebObjects lets you get at the HTML source with ease. The view icon lets you switch between *preview*, *layout*, and *source view* modes. Up to this point, we've been working in the layout mode. Click on the view icon and select the source view icon (represented by two pages):

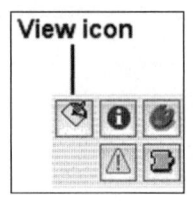

You should now see a screen like the following:

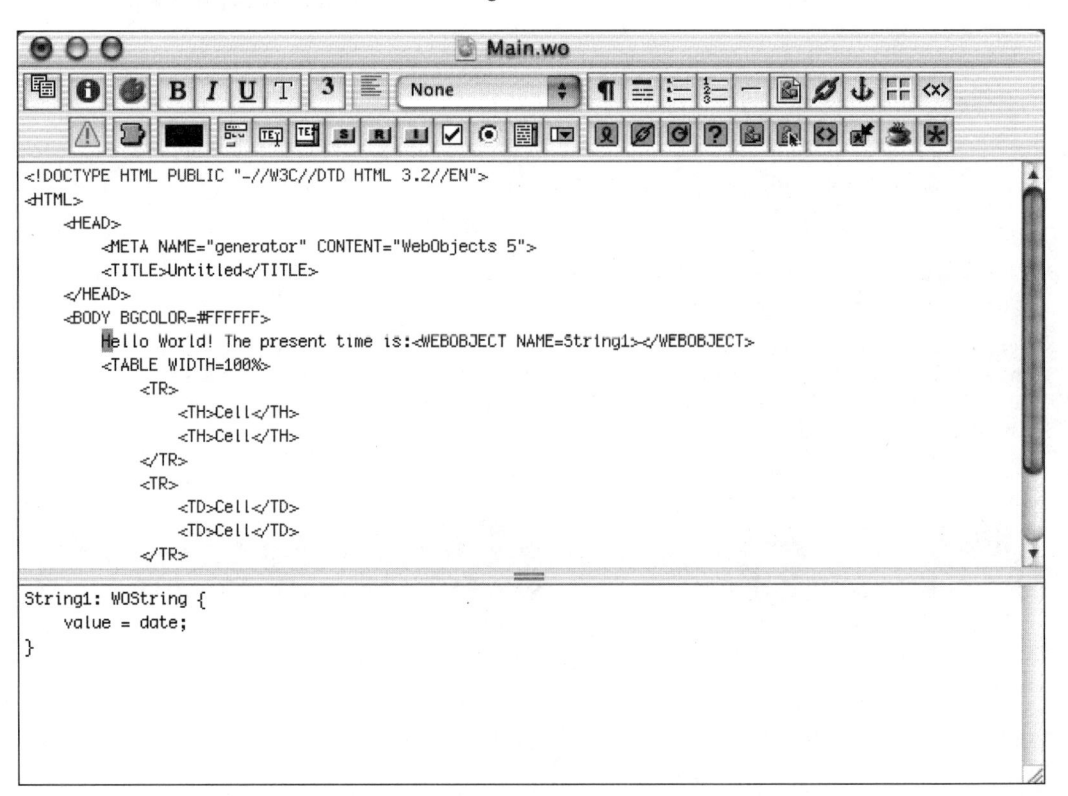

Go ahead and do all the hand-coding you like. You can also use the icons from the toolbar to add HTML elements just like you did in the layout view. WebObjects will add the source for those elements to the current text insertion point.

As you look at the source, you'll see the table that we recently created, as well as a `<WEBOJECT>` tag named `String1`. That's the `WOString` that we added in the previous chapter that's used to display the date. Notice the area of the screen below the HTML source. This is the binding source. We'll examine binding files more closely later in the chapter.

Cleaning Up HTML

If you're like me, you're really bothered by HTML that isn't formatted properly. Uneven or improper indents really bug you. Should the formatting of your HTML source be dirtied up by WebObjects or other coders – or even yourself on a bad day – you can use the **Reformat HTML** feature to pretty it back up. This feature is accessible from the **Format** pull-down menu.

Other Tools

The toolbar also contains links to three other common tools:

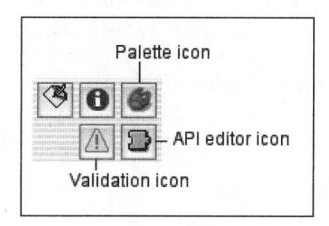

The **Palette** is a repository for additional HTML elements that can be incorporated into your components. You can also create your own palettes that store your own custom elements or components.

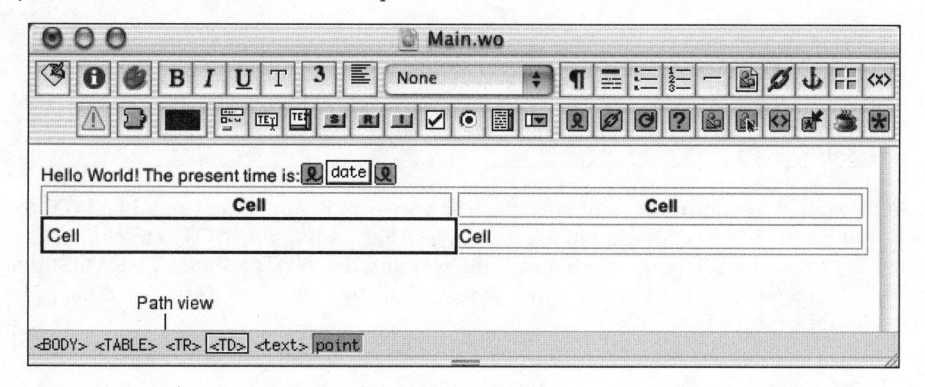

The **Validation Warning** icon shows you any errors that have been detected in your HTML syntax. You should note that WebObject's HTML validation is not perfect: it detects major errors like a malformed tag (like `<table` instead of `<table>`), but it smiles away happily if you have container tags (like `<table>`) missing their closing tag (in other words it doesn't mind HTML that is not *well-formed*). It also fails to complain about made-up or misspelled tags, such as `<hello>` or `<tabl>`.

However, the HTML Validation feature can also be used to validate custom rules that you define for the components that you create. As you distribute components for reuse, or build a large library for your own projects, that's a feature that can come in handy.

The **API Editor** lets you document how your component works for the benefit of others using it. It also lets you create the validation rules mentioned in the previous paragraph and further requires that certain bindings be made.

Path View

Directly beneath the HTML editor is the path view:

Chapter 3

The path view indicates the hierarchy of the currently selected item. You can see those tags that immediately precede the item you have selected, and you can click on them in the path view to select them. As stated earlier, there is an alternative way of highlighting and this is provided by the path view. For example, you can select an entire table by clicking on any of the table's cells and then clicking on the <TABLE> tag in the path view.

The Object Browser

Beneath the HTML editor is the object browser. The object browser allows you to bind so-called **keys** and **actions** to the special "WO" elements in your HTML page. Keys are either instance variables or methods that return values; in the object browser both types of keys are bound to HTML elements in exactly the same way. Actions are methods that return an object that is sent to the user, such as a **component** object (WOComponent) that will be displayed as a dynamic HTML page, a file contained in a response object (WOResponse) that can be downloaded, or a redirect object (WORedirect) that sends the user to a different URL.

Binding

To demonstrate binding, let's make some changes to our sample HelloWorld application. Change the view back to the layout view if you haven't already done so. Delete all the current content from the HTML editor. Now, add a WOForm element to your HTML. You can do this by either clicking on the appropriate icon in the toolbar or by selecting Forms | WOForm from the pull-down menu. A new WOForm element should appear in your HTML. Delete the word Form and replace it with **Please enter your name:** Your screen should look something like this:

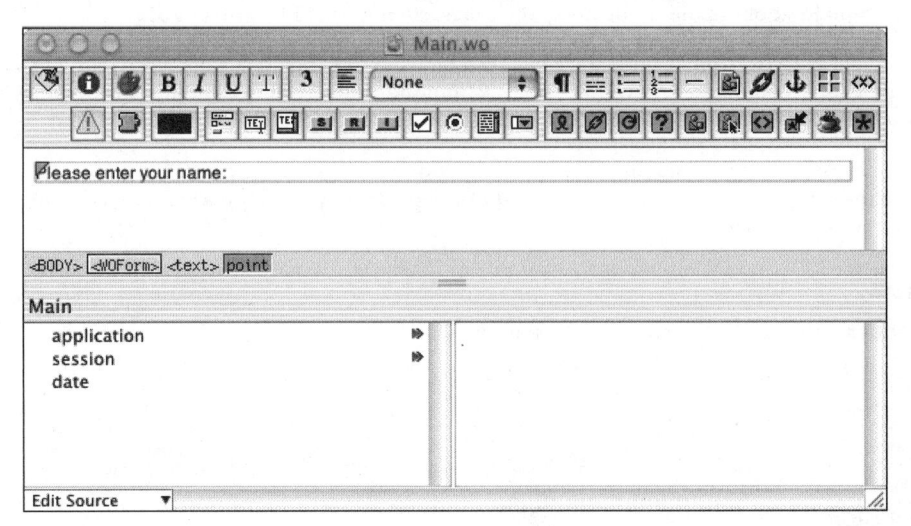

Add a WOTextField to your form right after the text you just entered. You can add a WOTextField via its icon or the Forms | WOTextField pull-down menu. After adding the WOTextField, add a WOSubmitButton to the WOForm just beneath the text and the WOTextField. The WOSubmitButton can be added via an icon or menu just as with the previous two elements. If you've done everything right, you should now see this:

WebObjects Builder

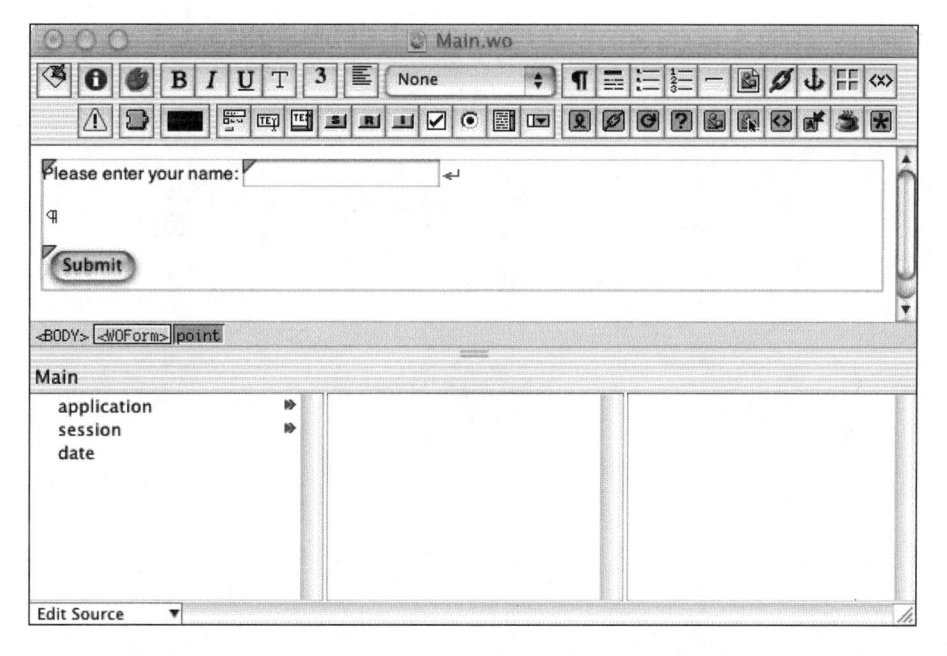

These new WO elements you've added now need to be bound to objects in your code. We're going to bind the **WOTextField** to a key so that the value entered will be copied into a variable, and we're going to bind the **WOSubmitButton** to an action so that it will return a new page to the user.

Let's create a key that we can bind to the **WOTextField**. In the lower left-hand corner of the object browser is an area labeled "**Edit Source**". When you click on it, a pop-up menu will appear, as shown here:

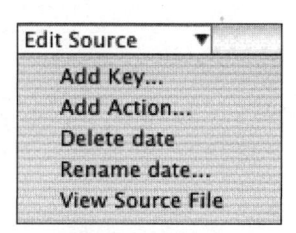

Select **Add Key**.... Name the key "**userName**", select "**String**" as the type, and make sure only the "**An instance variable**" checkbox is selected, as shown here:

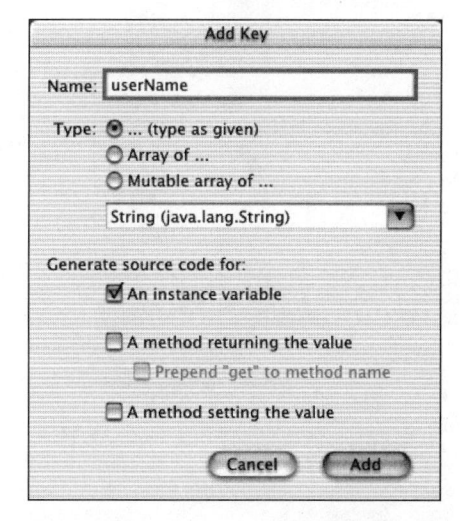

Chapter 3

Click on **Add** and you have a new key. WebObjects Builder automatically created an instance variable in the source code associated with this component (`Main.java`). Now, bind the **userName** key to the **WOTextField** just as you bound the **date** key to the **WOString** in the previous chapter: click on **userName** and drag to the **WOTextField**, and select **value** from the popup menu, as shown:

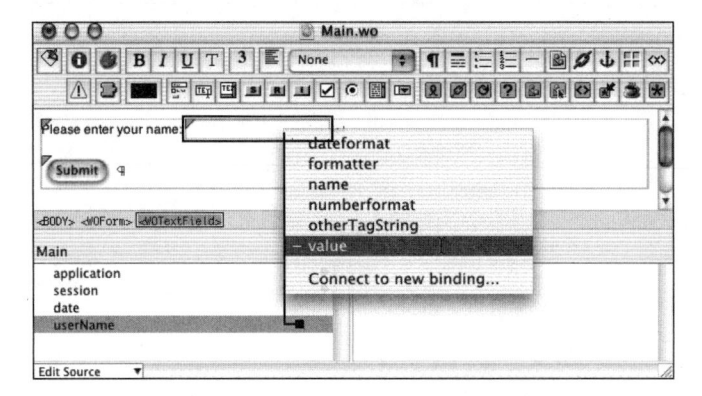

Now we're going to create a new component that will be used to display the value of **userName** after it is entered. Go back to Project Builder. Click on **Web Components** in the **Groups & Files** area and **Select File | New File** from the pull-down menu. In the new dialog box that is displayed, select **Component** from under the **WebObjects** header.

Click **Next** and you'll be taken to the **New Component** screen. Enter **ShowName** as the filename, and ensure that **Application Server** is selected as the target, as shown:

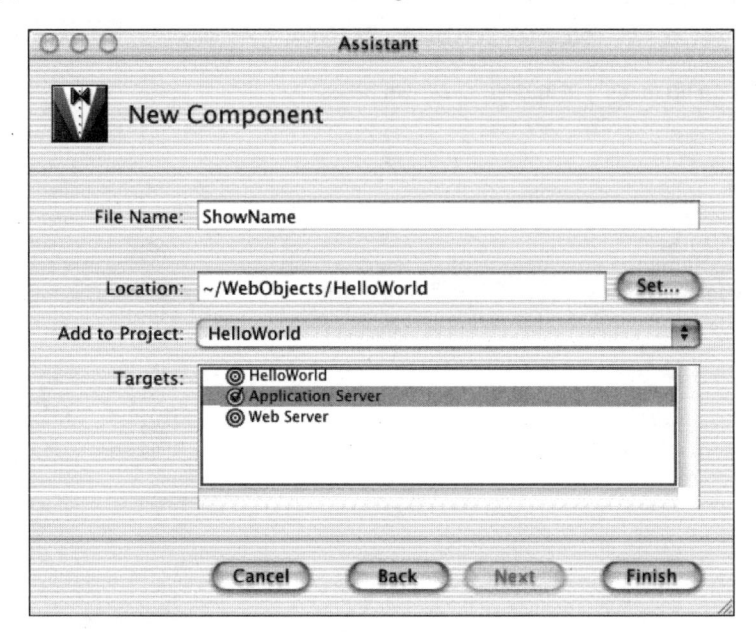

WebObjects Builder

A new component will appear in **Groups & Files**. Double-click on **ShowName.wo** to launch it in WebObjects Builder. Add text to your HTML file that says **Your name is:** and add a **WOString** after the text. Below the newly-added text add a **WOString**, and a **WOHyperlink**. Replace the default **Hyperlink** text with **Try Again**. Your WebObjects Builder screen should now look something like this:

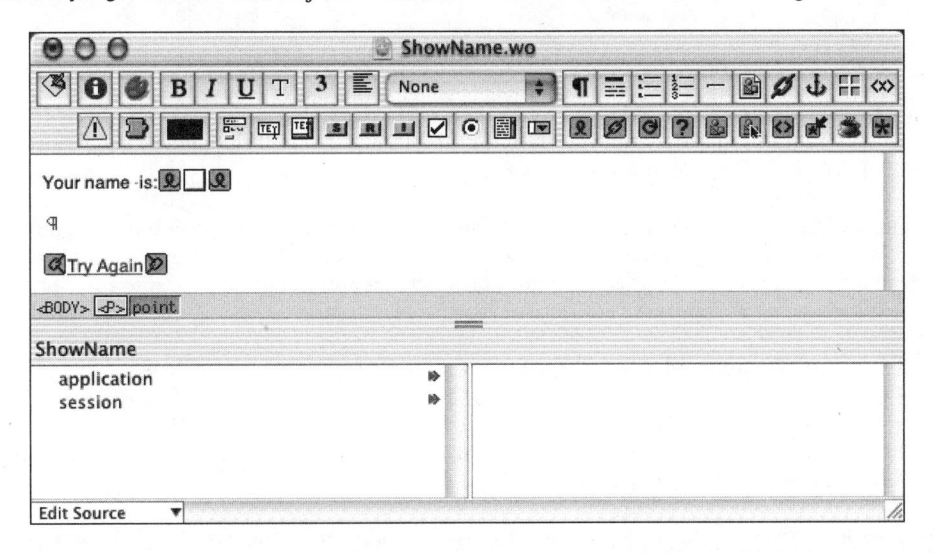

Now, add a new key to **ShowName** called **userName** just as you did to the **Main** component, but this time make sure all three checkboxes in the **Add Key** window are selected, as shown:

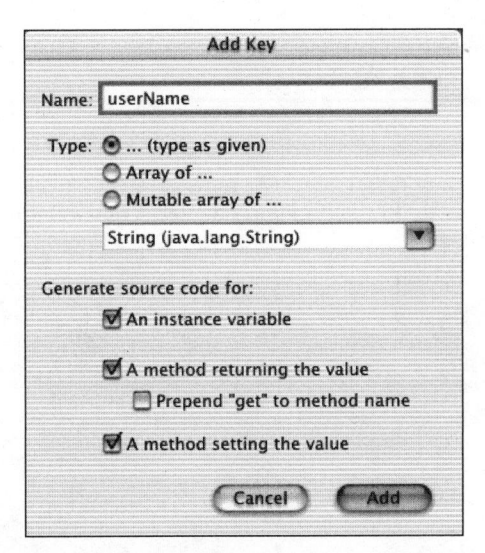

Add a new action to **ShowName** called **showMain**. For **Page returned**, select **Main** from the pull-down list. Here's what the **Add Action** dialog box looks like:

53

Chapter 3

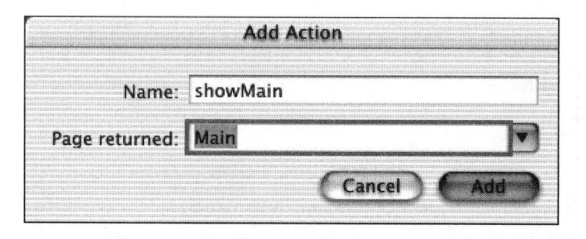

Bind the **userName** key to the **value** property of the **WOString**. Bind the **showMain** action to the **action** property of **WOHyperlink**. Then save your work.

Return to the **Main** component in WebObjects Builder. It should still be open but if it's not, just double-click on **Main.wo** from Project Builder. Add a new action to **Main**. Call it **showTest** and select **ShowName** as the page to be returned. After adding the action, bind the action to the **Submit** button by clicking and dragging as before.

Now click on **Edit Source** and select **View Source File**. You should now be back in Project Builder viewing the Java source for the Main component. You should see a new method in the code named `showTest()`. This method was added to the code by WebObjects Builder when you added the **showTest** action to the component. You should also see a variable declaration for `userName`; this corresponds to the **userName** key that you added to the component.

To pass the user's value to the component we need to modify the contents of the `showTest()` method as follows:

```
public ShowName showTest() {
    ShowName nextPage = (ShowName)pageWithName("ShowName");
    nextPage.setUserName(userName);
    return nextPage;
}
```

We'll examine this code in more detail later. For now, save your work in Project Builder, build the project, and run it just as you did in the previous chapter. Your web browser should display a page more or less like the following:

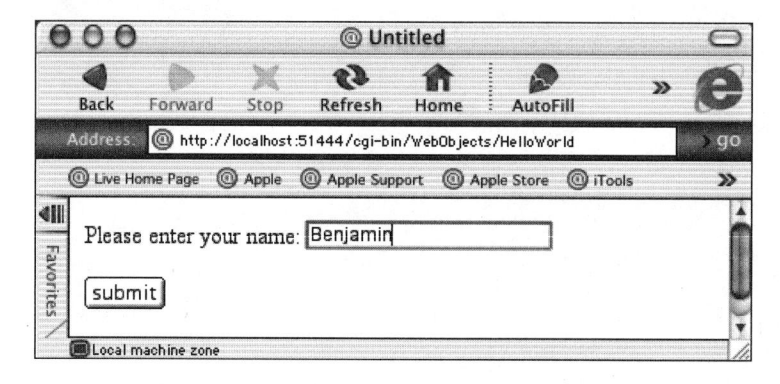

Enter a name, and click on **Submit**. The next page should look like this:

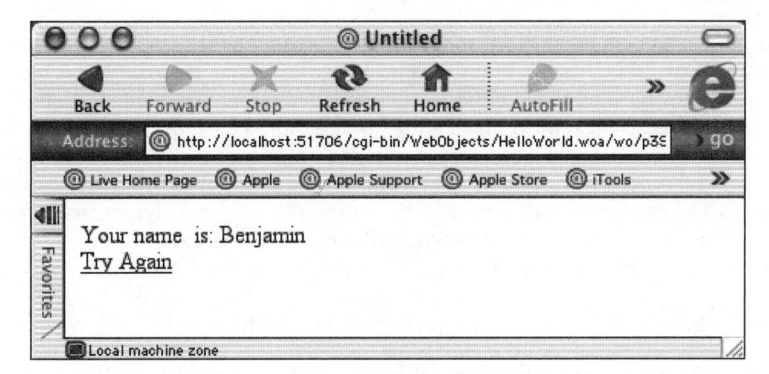

There you go! A more functional WebObjects application than our first example. WebObjects excels at taking care of the plumbing elements of web applications. In our sample application, we were able to automatically populate variables in our application with values from the HTML with trivial effort. The only coding we did involved what to do with the data once we retrieved it, which in our case was simply passing it along to another page.

Dynamic Inspector

I promised I'd come back to the Dynamic Inspector. We performed our bindings in this sample application using point-and-click mechanisms. The Dynamic Inspector can be used to set or modify bindings in a different fashion. When used on a bindable element, the Dynamic Inspector displays all the properties that accept bindings and allow you to select which key/action to bind to the element. An example of the Dynamic Inspector used on a **WOString** is shown below:

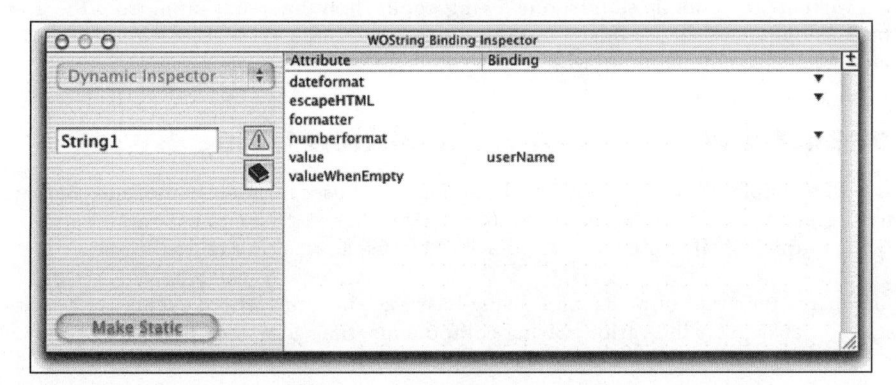

In the left-hand part of the screen, the text **String1** denotes the name of the element. You can name your element something else by typing it in here. It's good practice to name all of your elements something meaningful, as it will help you as you debug and develop your application, and it will help you and others maintain it.

The **Make Static** button will change your element from a dynamic <WEBOBJECT> element into the static equivalent. For example, a WOHyperlink element, which is a dynamic hyperlink, is converted into an anchor tag (<A>) when you click on the **Make Static** button.

55

Chapter 3

What Have We Learnt So Far?

WebObjects Builder is an easy-to-use GUI tool for editing components. It allows you to create your HTML layout and easily add dynamic WebObjects elements to your HTML. WebObjects Builder also provides an easy way for binding the WebObjects elements to your component's code. While a component can be created from start to finish with a text editor, WebObjects Builder makes it a lot easier.

Before moving on to the next section, you may want to take some time to further explore WebObjects Builder on your own. You can experiment with the other WebObjects elements, binding in different ways, and so on. On-line help with WebObjects Builder provides great reference material. For additional reference material, you can also check out the Apple documentation at:

http://developer.apple.com/techpubs/webobjects/webobjects.html

We touched upon many new concepts in this tour, such as keys, actions, bindings, and components, that we need to discuss in more depth than we've done so far. In the next section we will do that by looking inside the Java code that WebObjects Builder uses and manipulates. We will also introduce more advanced functionality accessible from WebObjects Builder. We will concentrate on adding functionality to applications by editing source code rather than creating it using the WebObjects Builder UI; this will help in our understanding of these features.

Creating Variables

The Java class associated with a WebObject web component fundamentally consists of what the component knows and what the component does. These variables and methods are then used by the HTML template part of the component to display the information to the user and to get user input. In this section we'll create a simple stand-alone Swing application that reads input from the user and then sends it back as output. We'll use this as a starting point to build a WebObjects application with similar functionality, and then compare the two.

A Personalized HelloWorld Application Using Swing

Let's start with a simple version of HelloWorld that asks the user for their name, and then prints back a personalized greeting based on that input. We'll use two `JLabels`: one to prompt the user and the other to display the output. We'll also need a `JTextField` to use to read in the user input.

Start by importing the usual suspects for a Swing-based applications where events are generated: the `javax.swing` package for the various Swing components; the `java.awt` package for the layout manager; and the `java.awt.event` package to respond to the user input:

```
import javax.swing.*;
import java.awt.event.*;
import java.awt.*;

public class SwingGreeting extends JFrame {
```

We will call our class `SwingGreeting` (so we should save this class in a file called `SwingGreeting.java`). Next declare the Swing components we'll need in this application, and then configure them inside the constructor:

```
    public JLabel inputRequestLabel, outputLabel;
    public JTextField inputTextField;

    public SwingGreeting() {
      // initialize JFrame and components
      super("SwingGreeting");
      inputRequestLabel = new JLabel("Please enter your name:");
      outputLabel = new JLabel();
      inputTextField = new JTextField("", 20);
      inputTextField.addActionListener( new InputListener());
```

The next section of the constructor sets up the look of our application. So that we don't have to spend too much time deciding where things should go, let's just use a `FlowLayout`:

```
      // sets up the appearance of the JFrame
      setSize(400,350);
      getContentPane ().setLayout(new FlowLayout());
      getContentPane().add(inputRequestLabel);
      getContentPane().add(inputTextField);
      getContentPane().add(outputLabel);
      setVisible(true);
      setDefaultCloseOperation(JFrame.EXIT_ON_CLOSE);
    } //end of constructor
```

We make the application responsive to user inputs with an inner class derived from `ActionListener`. This one is fairly generic. It waits until the user presses the *Enter* key after completing their input and updates the greeting:

```
    public class InputListener implements ActionListener {
      // outputs greeting when enter is pressed
      public void actionPerformed( ActionEvent e) {
        outputLabel.setText("Hello " + inputTextField.getText());
      }
    }
```

All that remains is to start up the application. We can either create a separate class that contains `main()` or just include the following inside `SwingGreeting.java`:

```
    // main creates the SwingGreeting
    public static void main( String[] args) {
      new SwingGreeting();
    }
  } //end of class SwingGreeting
```

Compile and run the application. The result looks something like this on a Mac:

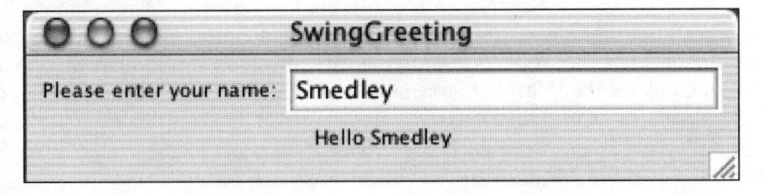

Chapter 3

Creating and Reading from a Variable

In the Swing version, the variables were used to get and display `Strings`. Really we only need to keep track of a single `String` representing the user's name. In this section we'll create a variable in our Java source code and will be able to immediately use it in our HTML template. We'll also be able to create variables from WebObject builder. In either case the variables will be instance variables in the Java file.

Start up ProjectBuilder, and create a new WebObjects Application called `WOGreeting`.

> In general it is not a good idea to name applications or components that begin with the prefix "WO" as Apple uses this convention for their own classes. We've used this name for this application in this case to distinguish the WebObjects version of the Greeting application from the Swing version.

If we take a look inside the file `Main.java`, we can see this:

```java
import com.webobjects.foundation.*;
import com.webobjects.appserver.*;
import com.webobjects.eocontrol.*;
import com.webobjects.eoaccess.*;

public class Main extends WOComponent {

  public Main(WOContext context) {
    super(context);
  }
}
```

This is the default `main` class we get when we create a new application. Our next step is to add some instance variables to this class.

Creating Variable by Editing the Source File

Let's add in an instance variable named `userName` of type `String`. In fact, to begin with, we will set it to the value `"Smedley"`:

```java
public class Main extends WOComponent {
    String userName = "Smedley";
    public Main(WOContext context) {
        super(context);
    }
}
```

Save the file, and then open up the WebObjects Builder by double-clicking on `Main.wo`. In the lower left corner we can see the variable **userName** is available for our use. Using what we learned in the previous chapter, quickly build a web page that displays **Hello Smedley**. Type the word **Hello** on the screen and then add a `WOString` object either using the button on the toolbar or selecting from the **WebObjects** menu. Click on the **userName** variable and drag a connection up to the `WOString` object. The object builder should now look like this:

WebObjects Builder

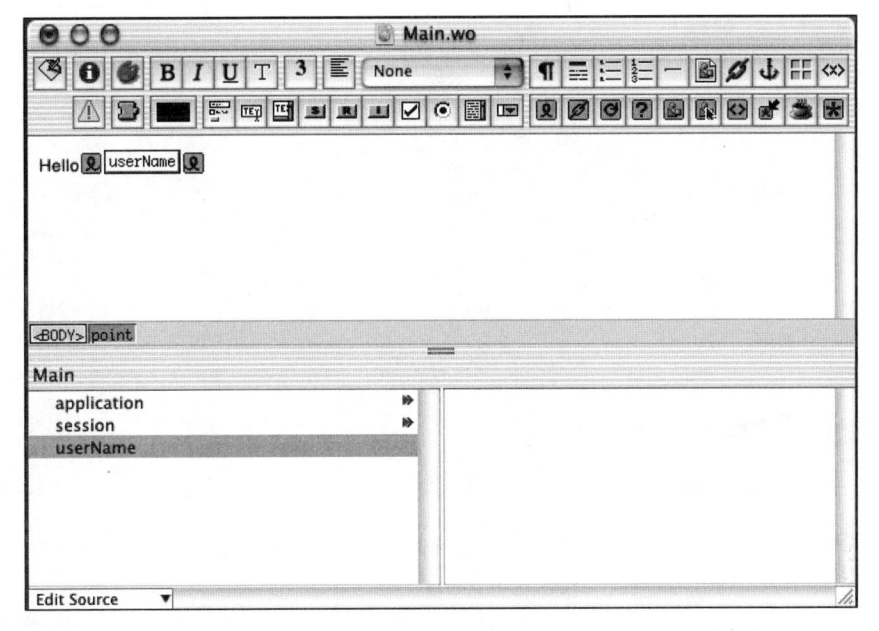

Build and run the application and the browser will open with **Hello Smedley** proudly displayed on the screen. As always with these kind of examples, there's a lot of infrastructure involved in displaying this limited application.

Creating a Variable Using WebObjects Builder

You just saw that changes you make to the source file are immediately visible in the WebObjects Builder. Now let's go in the opposite direction, and add a variable using WebObjects Builder, as we did in our quick tour earlier in the chapter. First, return to `Main.java` and delete the following line.

```
String userName = "Smedley";
```

If we return to WebObjects Builder, we can now see **application** and **session** listed, but **userName** no longer appears. Click on **Edit Source** and select **Add Key**. We'll use this panel to name our variable as well as choose its type and decide whether or not we want getters and setters for it:

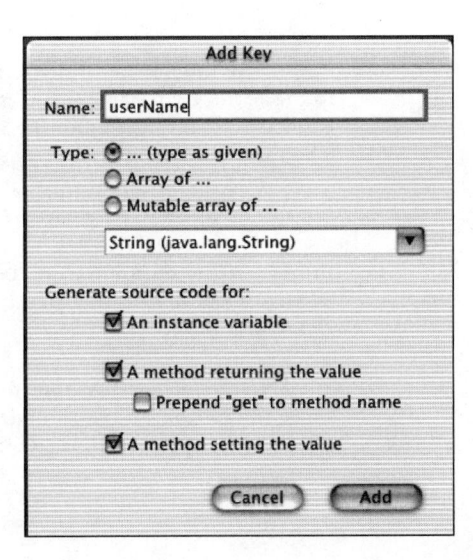

In this case we only need to create an instance variable, so deselect the choices regarding the getter and setter methods and then click **Add**. If we open up the `Main.java` source file now, it looks like this:

```
public class Main extends WOComponent {
    protected String userName;
    public Main(WOContext context) {
        super(context);
    }
}
```

In other words WebObjects Builder has edited the source file for us. All that's left for us to do now is to once again initialize the `String` to "Smedley", save, build, and run the project.

Creating Methods

So far the WebObjects version of the greeting doesn't do very much. That's not very surprising as there aren't any methods in our code. In this section, we'll add a simple method using the WebObjects Builder. We will also need to make some changes in our web page, and to know when the user is done submitting their input. Finally, we need to display the personalized greeting back to them. For our first attempt, we can do all this within the same form.

Constructing the WOForm

Open up WebObjects Builder by double-clicking on `Main.wo`. It is probably easiest for now just to remove all of the items in the object builder. Then create the form using the following steps:

1. Insert a `WOForm` into the visual designer using the button in the toolbar, and rename it (using the Inspector) to something more meaningful than the default name. Call it **NameEntryForm**.

2. Click inside the `WOForm` and type **Please enter your name** in place of the word **Form**.

3. Either use the button in the toolbar or the item in the **Forms** menu to add a `WOTextField` to the form. By default this is given the name **TextField1**. Double click on the `WOTextField` to bring up the inspector and change the name to **UserNameTextField**. Then close the inspector.

4. On the next line type **Hello**.

5. Either use the button on the toolbar or the item in the **WebObjects** menu to add a `WOString` to the form. Open the inspector for this element, and change its name to **UserNameString**.

6. Hit *Shift* and *Return* together to add whitespace, and then add a **Submit** button to the form using the button on the toolbar or by selecting **WOSubmitButton** from the **Forms** menu. Using the Inspector, change the name of this submit button to **NameSubmitButton**.

WebObjects Builder

The completed form should look like this.

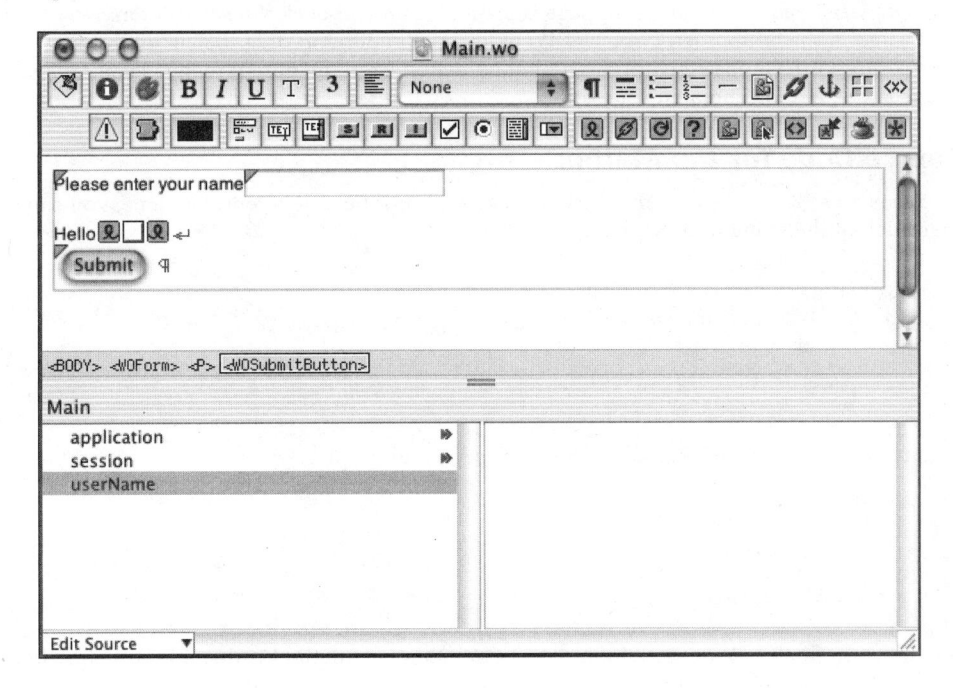

[Screenshot of Main.wo window in WebObjects Builder showing a form with "Please enter your name" text field, "Hello" with WOString placeholders, and a Submit button. The tag path shows `<BODY> <WOForm> <P> <WOSubmitButton>`. Below, the Main outline shows application, session, and userName (highlighted).]

Binding the Form

We want to read the user's name from the WOTextField and then, after the form has been submitted, output that name in the WOString. To do this, we need to define the bindings. Click so that the **userName** key is highlighted (as shown in the previous screenshot) and then drag the mouse until the cursor is inside the WOTextField. Release the mouse and choose to bind by value by clicking on the word **value** in the popup menu. Similarly, bind **userName** by value to the WOString.

Now take the application for a test drive. You'll see that it doesn't really do anything yet. This is because we need to be listening for an event that indicates when the user has entered their name. Unlike the Swing example, the user entry may be occurring on a different machine.

We can use the pressing of the **Submit** button as a signal that the information entered by the user is ready to be bundled up and sent to the server. The server will then generate a response that the client will render. In other words, we still have to wire up the **Submit** button. Click on **Edit Source**, but this time select **Add Action**. The following dialog box will appear:

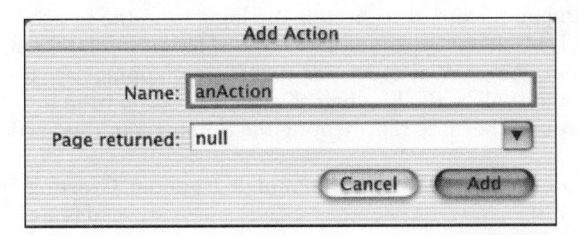

[Dialog box titled "Add Action" with Name: anAction, Page returned: null, and Cancel / Add buttons.]

61

Name the action **submitName**. Leave the value for **Page returned** as **null** so that when the response is generated by this request, the current page is loaded again and click the **Add** button. Now click on **submitName** in the bottom left corner of WebObjects Builder and drag the cursor to the `WOSubmitButton`. Choose the option to bind by **action** from the popup menu. Then save your work and take a look at the generated source.

The Source Code for the Method

Take a look at `Main.java` now. Because the user will now be able to enter a name, you can remove the initialization of the string `userName`:

```
public class Main extends WOComponent {
  protected String userName;
    public Main(WOContext context) {
        super(context);
    }
```

The generated method `submitName()` looks deceptively simple:

```
    public WOComponent submitName() {
      return null;
    }
}//end of class Main
```

The reason you don't have to do a lot in the `submitName()` method is that a lot is being done for you. We'll take a look at this in chapter 4.

Even though this is the default behavior generated by the WebObjects tool, there is a better way to reload the same page. Instead of returning `null`, we can return `context().page()` to maximize the reuse of the component and also to ensure that WebObjects stops searching for an action method when this particular `submitName()` action method completes execution. This technique will become more clear when we see how to call other components from `Main`. For now, just note that we are sending a request that results in the same page being requested with new information. Notice that `Main` extends `WOComponent`. We will return other `WOComponents` to request their corresponding pages.

A Closer Look At HTML Templates and Bindings

It looks as if the WebObjects version of the Java code is much simpler than the Swing version. Although it is true that the logic is a bit simpler, some of the work is being done by other files. The `Main.html` file contains all of the presentation code. That's where we define how the form should look in the browser.

However, to achieve the noble aim of separating the logic from the presentation, we must declare how the dynamic elements from the presentation layer (the HTML template) map to the methods and variables in the logic tier. We have already seen that these mappings are usually called the **bindings**. The `Main.wod` file contains all of the bindings that tie the `Main.java` and `Main.html` files together. So far we've danced around the code representing the bindings; in this section we'll take a closer look.

Let's start, however, by examining the HTML template from our Greeting application.

The HTML Template File

If you've worked with ASPs or JSPs then this HTML file should highlight some of the benefits of WebObjects for you. The code is clean – there is no programming logic mixed in with the HTML. You might think of this as being similar to programming with JSPs but you are forced to use custom tags. The HTML tags are parsed normally and the WebObjects tags are easily read by a web designer. The web designer often doesn't need to touch the actual HTML because a lot can be done using the visual tools. Here's the file `Main.html` in the `Main.wo` folder:

```html
<!DOCTYPE HTML PUBLIC "-//W3C//DTD HTML 3.2//EN">
<HTML>
  <HEAD>
    <META NAME="generator" CONTENT="WebObjects 5">
    <TITLE>Untitled</TITLE>
  </HEAD>
  <BODY BGCOLOR=#FFFFFF>
    <WEBOBJECT NAME=NameEntryForm>
      Please enter your name
      <WEBOBJECT NAME=UserNameTextField></WEBOBJECT>
      <P>
        Hello
        <WEBOBJECT NAME=UserNameString></WEBOBJECT><BR>
        <WEBOBJECT NAME=NameSubmitButton></WEBOBJECT>
      </P>
    </WEBOBJECT>
  </BODY>
</HTML>
```

The highlighted portion shows the composition of the form. It's some text followed by a text field, and then on the next line there's more text followed by a string. The remaining element is a submit button. We really don't even know that these are text fields, but the naming convention allows us to infer that `UserNameTextField` is a `WOTextField`, `UserNameString` is a `WOString`, and `NameSubmitButton` is a `WOSubmitButton`. The information about what these elements do and which variables and methods they are bound to is not contained in the HTML file. The logic remains in `Main.java` and the binding is in `Main.wod`.

The Binding File

The file `Main.wod` is a declarations file containing the bindings that you set using WebObjects Builder. Each element has an entry with the following syntax:

```
ElementName:ElementType{
  boundattribute1=key;
  ...
  boundattributeN=keyN;
}
```

To illustrate this, here is the `Main.wod` file from our sample application:

```
NameEntryForm: WOForm {
}

UserNameString: WOString {
  value=userName;
}
```

```
NameSubmitButton: WOSubmitButton {
  action=submitName;
}

UserNameTextField: WOTextField {
  value=userName;
}
```

We can see that both the `WOString UserNameString` and the `WOTextField UserNameTextField` have the value bound to the variable `userName`. The `WOSubmitButton SubmitButton` has the action bound to the method `submitName()`.

Even though it's pretty easy to understand the binding file that WebObjects creates, you'll probably use the layout view to perform all of your bindings, as it's quite a bit handier to use.

Using Conditional Code

Currently our web application looks a little messy. The user enters their name, pushes a button, and moments later the page looks like this:

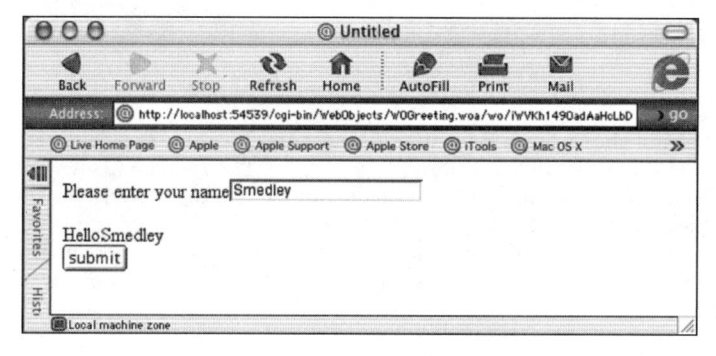

It would be nice to hide a little bit of the magic. On the first screen we could have the user enter their name and on the second screen we could greet them by name.

WebObjects provides `WOConditionals` for accomplishing this on one page. A `WOConditional` tests for a particular condition, and the result of the test determines if the contents of the conditional are displayed.

Look at the elements in the browser. We would like the textbox and submit button to be visible until the user enters a valid name, and then we would like just the second line to be visible. Therefore we'll create a method called `isNameEntered()` that returns a `boolean` indicating whether or not an acceptable name has been entered. You'll then tie the display of the form elements to the value of this `boolean` using `WOConditionals`.

The question could arise, "who does what?". Writing the code for the method `isNameEntered()` is clearly the job of the programmer. The code resides entirely within the file `Main.java`. Deciding what to display should be left to the web designer. The code for these conditionals will end up being shared by the `Main.html` and `Main.wod` files. Also, these decisions are design decisions. This code being generated will strictly deal with presentation logic.

You can generate the stub for the method `isNameEntered()` using WebObjects Builder or directly in the source file `Main.java`. You've probably had plenty of experience writing methods directly in Java files already, so let's use WebObjects Builder.

Start by opening up `Main.wo` in WebObjects Builder. Then click on **Edit Source** and select **Add Key**. This time you're going to add a method but not an instance variable. When the **Add Key** dialog box pops up, enter the method name and choose **boolean** from the drop down list for the return type. Make sure that the options for creating an instance variable and a setter method are both deselected, and that you have chosen to create a getter method without prepending the word **get** to the name, as shown below:

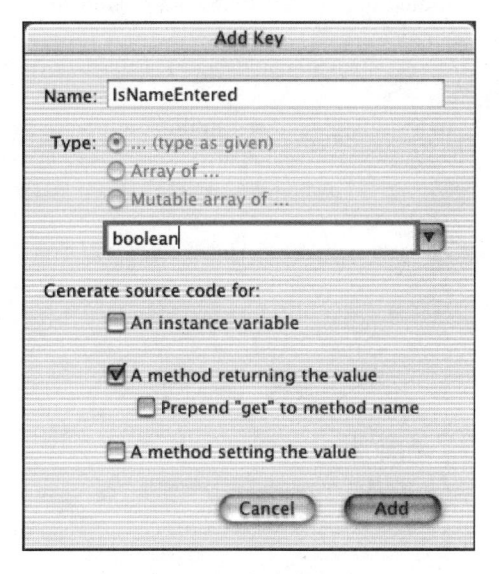

Now go back to the source code and edit the method, so that it returns `false` when `userName` has either a `null` or an empty string as its value, but `true` otherwise:

```
public boolean isNameEntered() {
    if (userName==null || userName=="") return false;
    else return true;
}
```

That's all of the application logic needed to determine whether or not an adequate username has been entered. We can now go back to the presentation logic.

Adding Conditionals To the HTML

Return to WebObjects Builder and select the text **Please enter your name** along with the `WOTextField UserNameTextField`. Either press the button with the question mark on it in the tool bar or select the menu item **WOConditional** from the **WebObjects** menu. The two elements you selected are now surrounded by a conditional. Add another `WOConditional` that surrounds the text "Hello " and the `WOString String1`. Add a third `WOConditional` that surrounds the `WOSubmitButton SubmitButton1`. Use the Inspector to name these conditionals **GetNameEntry**, **GreetByName**, and **SubmitName** respectively.

Now click bottom-left on the key **isNameEntered**, and drag your cursor up to the empty box following the question mark and the addition sign at the end of the first conditional. You should see **isNameEntered** appear in boxes on either side of the first conditional. Repeat the process to bind **isNameEntered** to the second and third conditionals as well.

Chapter 3

We want the first and third lines to appear when the condition is `false`, so click on the addition sign on either side of each of the elements to turn them into minus signs. The second line should appear when the condition is `true` so leave the addition sign alone. We can think of the second conditional as saying something like the following pseudocode:

```
if (isNameEntered()) then display this block
```

In a similar way, we can think of the first and third conditionals as saying something like this:

```
if (! isNameEntered()) then display this block
```

The finished WebObjects Builder screen should look like this:

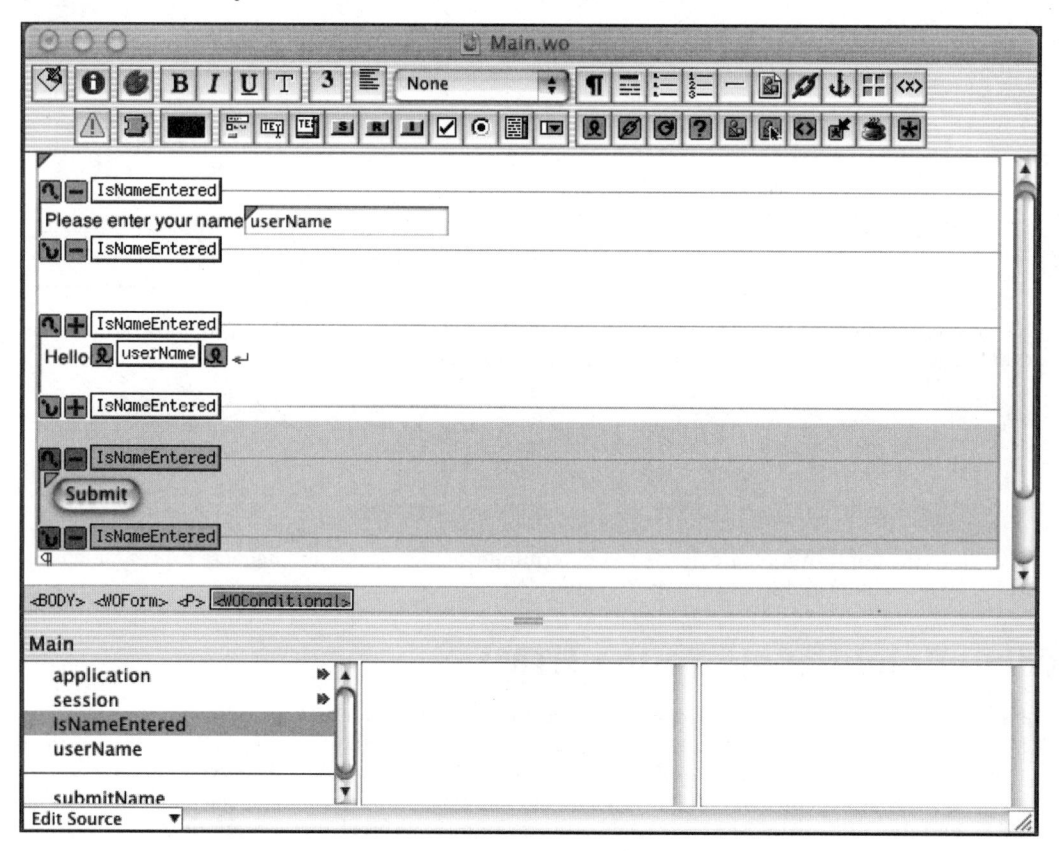

Save this file, then build and run the project. The user will be prompted to enter their name:

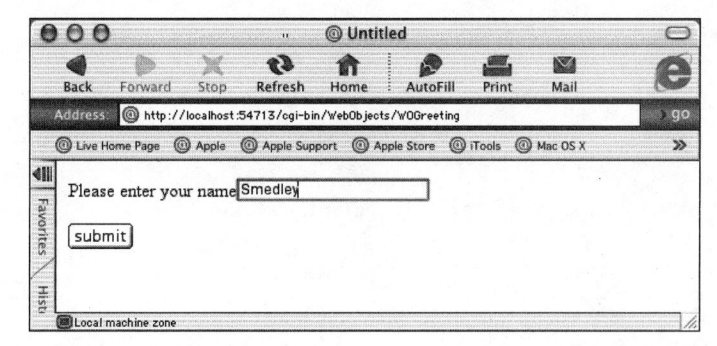

When the **Submit** button is clicked, the user is then taken to what appears to be a separate component that greets them by name:

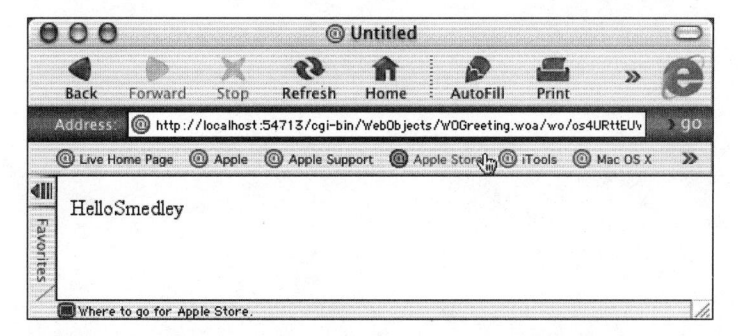

Changes To the Template and Binding Files

As with the last version of this project, we've actually made very few changes to `Main.java`. It is instructive to take a quick look at what has changed in the `Main.html` and `Main.wod` files too.

In `Main.html` there are three new `<WEBOBJECT>` conditional elements that contain the form elements to which the condition is being applied:

```
<!DOCTYPE HTML PUBLIC "-//W3C//DTD HTML 3.2//EN">
<HTML>
  <HEAD>
  <META NAME="generator" CONTENT="WebObjects 5">
  <TITLE>Untitled</TITLE>
  </HEAD>
  <BODY BGCOLOR=#FFFFFF>
    <WEBOBJECT NAME=NameEntryForm>
      <WEBOBJECT NAME=GetNameEntry>
        Please enter your name
        <WEBOBJECT NAME=UserNameTextField></WEBOBJECT>
      </WEBOBJECT>
      <P>
      <WEBOBJECT NAME=GreetByName>
        Hello
        <WEBOBJECT NAME=UserNameString></WEBOBJECT><BR>
```

```
            </WEBOBJECT>
            <WEBOBJECT NAME=SubmitName>
              <WEBOBJECT NAME=NameSubmitButton></WEBOBJECT>
            </WEBOBJECT>
          </P>
        </WEBOBJECT>
      </BODY>
</HTML>
```

Now take a look at `Main.wod` to see how these conditionals are bound:

```
GetNameEntry :WOConditional{
   condition=isNameEntered;
   negate=true;
}

GreetByName: WOConditional {
   condition=isNameEntered;
}

SubmitName: WOConditional{
   condition=isNameEntered;
   negate=true;
}

NameEntryForm: WOForm {
}

UserNameString: WOString {
   value=userName;
}

NameSubmitButton: WOSubmitButton {
   action=submitName;
}

UserNameTextField: WOTextField {
   value=userName;
}
```

For each conditional the condition is set to `isNameEntered`. The first and third conditionals also have the property `negate` set to `true`, that means that they are only displayed when the value of the condition is `false true)`. Looking at the bindings shows us something we wouldn't have realized if we only looked a(the negation of t `Main.java`: the same condition is checked three times. Actually, we could easily reduce this to twice by moving the `WOSubmitButton` up into the body of the first conditional, and eliminating the third conditional.

Sending Information To Other Components

When we write a Java application we construct a bunch of objects that communicate with each other primarily by invoking each other's methods. In this section we'll take a quick look at how WebObject's web components communicate with each other. We'll take the example from the previous section but modify it a little, so that one component is used to gather information from the user, and a second is used to greet the user by name. In other words, we'll repeat the example from our earlier tour, but we'll examine the code in more detail.

Creating the Project

We can either edit our existing file or create a new one. To start a new project from scratch follow these steps:

1. Create a new Web Application called **WOGreeting2**.

2. Use the WebObjects Builder to create a `WOForm` in `Main.wo`. Inside the form place the text **Please enter your name** followed by a `WOTextField`. Add a line break. Then add a `WOSubmitButton`.

3. Use **Edit Source** to add a key. The key is called **userName** and is an instance variable of type `String`.

4. Use **Edit Source** to add an action. The action is called **submitName**. For now you can accept the default value of **null** for the **Page returned**.

5. Bind **userName** by value to the `WOTextField` and bind **submitName** by action to the `WOSubmitButton`. Save the file.

6. Create a new Web Component. On a Windows machine choose **New in Project** from the File menu of ProjectBuilder. Name this component **PersonalizedGreeting**, select **Web Component** and click on the **OK** button, and then choose to create an empty component from the **Component Wizard** dialog box. On Mac OS X, in the **Groups and Files** window, click on **Web Components** to highlight it. Then choose **New File** from the **File** menu, and select **Component** from the **WebObjects** selection. Name this component **PersonalizedGreeting** and choose **Application Server** as the target, and then click on the **Finish** button.

7. Use the WebObjects Builder to set up `PersonalizedGreeting.wo`. Begin with the text **Hello** followed by a `WOString`.

8. Use **Edit Source** to add a key. The key is called **userName** and is an instance variable of type `String` with a set method.

9. Bind **userName** to the `WOString`. Save the file.

Linking To the New Component

We don't have to touch any of the source code in `PersonalizedGreeting.java`. The following is fine the way it is:

```
import com.webobjects.foundation.*;
import com.webobjects.appserver.*;
import com.webobjects.eocontrol.*;
import com.webobjects.eoaccess.*;

public class PersonalizedGreeting extends WOComponent {
  protected String userName;
  public PersonalizedGreeting(WOContext context) {
    super(context);
  }
```

```java
    public void setUserName(String newUserName) {
      userName = newUserName;
    }
  }
```

We do, however, have to make changes to the `submitName()` method in `Main.java` so that it calls the new page and passes along the `userName`. Let's have a look at these changes.

```java
    import com.webobjects.foundation.*;
    import com.webobjects.appserver.*;
    import com.webobjects.eocontrol.*;
    import com.webobjects.eoaccess.*;

    public class Main extends WOComponent {
      protected String userName;

      public Main(WOContext context) {
        super(context);
      }

      public WOComponent submitName() {
```

In the `submitName()` method we'll create an object of type `PersonalizedGreeting` named `greetingPage`. Ordinarily, we would just call a constructor and get back an instance of the class `PersonalizedGreeting`. In this case, however, we use the `pageWithName()` method to create an object of the type whose classname is passed in as a `String`. Here we pass the name `PersonalizedGreeting` to the method, so that an instance of this class is created and returned as a `WOComponent`:

```java
        PersonalizedGreeting greetingPage =
          (PersonalizedGreeting)pageWithName("PersonalizedGreeting");
```

You should note that if the string we pass is `null` we get the `Main` page back again, and if the method cannot create a valid page instance, it throws an exception. We must also cast the returned instance to type `PersonalizedGreeting`.

Now we call the `setUserName()` method on this object:

```java
        greetingPage.setUserName(userName);
```

Finally we must change the object being returned by `submitName()`. The method was originally set up to return `null`, which called the same page. We want to forward to the component we've just constructed, so return `greetingPage` instead:

```java
        return greetingPage;
      }
    } // end of Main.java
```

When we build and run the application, it behaves almost like the version we built before that didn't call a separate component. To make it behave exactly the same we would have to test for acceptable values for the `userName`. If the `userName` isn't acceptable, we return to the input page, otherwise we go to the greeting page. We could code this by adding a few extra lines to `submitName()`:

```
public WOComponent submitName() {
  if (userName==null || userName=="") {
    return null;
  } else {
    PersonalizedGreeting greetingPage =
      (PersonalizedGreeting)pageWithName("PersonalizedGreeting");
    greetingPage.setUserName(userName);
    return greetingPage;
  }
}
```

However, we're going to make a change to the UI in the next section where we won't mind whether the name entered was valid or not, so we won't worry about checking the user input anymore. You now know two very different ways of accomplishing what appears to the user as the same task. Using conditionals you were only changing the presentation logic. In this section, you learned how to communicate between components.

Adding Hyperlinks

We saw earlier how to look at the template and binding files to learn more about the objects we've created. We have also seen that WebObjects Builder provides visual tools to inspect the properties and bindings of the components of your page: the Inspector. The Inspector also allows us to configure **hyperlinks**. Let's add one of these to the `PersonalizedGreeting` component to navigate back to `Main` if the user wants to enter a new name.

Open up `PersonalizedGreeting.wo` with WebObjects Builder. Add the text **If this is not your name you can enter a new name** on the line below the `WOString`. Highlight the words **enter a new name** and click on the hyperlink button in the toolbar (or choose **WOHyperlink** from the **WebObjects** menu). You'll see a hyperlink around the text we highlighted and the text appears in blue. So far it doesn't link anywhere.

Double-click on the link or use the toolbar button and this dynamic inspector window will appear:

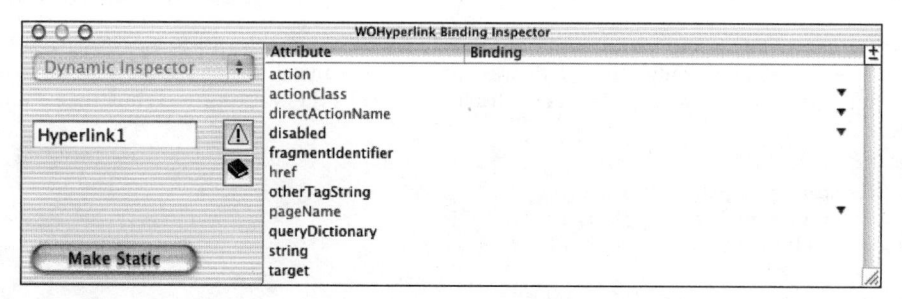

You can see that we can set an action for this link, or choose to link to another page. Click on the arrow to the right of **pageName** and you will see a list of items you could link to. Find **Main** in the dropdown list and select it – you've just created your hyperlink.

Build and run our application with the hyperlink we created. This time when we return to `Main` the `TextField` should be empty – we haven't passed any information back to the page.

Chapter 3

Working with Lists

In this last example, we'll create a list of the usernames entered in the current session, and display it in a table in the browser.

We'll create an `NSMutableArray` to hold the values of past `userNames`. This array will be stored in the `WOSession` object that handles a user session (we'll look at this object in more detail in chapter 4). For the most part working with an `NSMutableArray` feels like working with the WebObjects equivalent of the Java `Vector` or `ArrayList` classes. Adding and accessing elements, as well as determining the length of the `NSMutableArray`, will feel very familiar.

Adding Variables and Methods To the Session

In the Mac OS X version of WebObjects Builder you can open `Main.wo`, highlight **session**, and *Control-click* in the **Sessions** list in the right hand pane of the object browser to add a key or an action to **Session**, or simply to view `Session.java`. On a Windows machine, highlight **session** and right-click in the **Sessions** list to perform these actions. In either case, create a new key in **Session** named `pastUserNames`. Choose to make it a mutable array of type `String` and only create an instance variable.

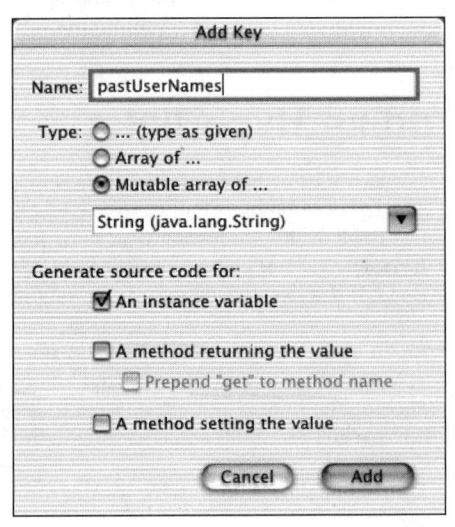

In earlier projects that we built we didn't need to add a new constructor to `Session.java` because it didn't do anything. The default constructor was sufficient because it called the `WOSession` constructor. Now we need to provide a no-argument constructor that calls the `WOSession` constructor and initializes the `NSMutableArray()`:

```
import com.webobjects.foundation.*;
import com.webobjects.appserver.*;
import com.webobjects.eocontrol.*;

public class Session extends WOSession {

    /** @TypeInfo java.lang.String */
    protected NSMutableArray pastUserNames;

    public Session(){
      super();
      pastUserNames = new NSMutableArray();
    }
```

Any time a new `userName` is entered, we want to make sure it is added to the `pastUserNames` array. Therefore we must also add a method to `Session.java` that can add a `userName` to `pastUserNames`. In this case our only choice is to make use of the `addObject()` method. For more information about this, check out the JavaDocs or use the WOInfoCenter for `com.webobjects.foundation.NSMutableArray`.

```java
    public void addUserName(String newUser){
        pastUserNames.addObject(newUser);
    }
```

```
} //end of Session class
```

At this point our `Session` object can initialize and add to a list of former usernames. Now we can call this method from `Main` when the user submits a name. First we invoke the `session()` method. This returns the current session if there is one, or creates a session and returns it if not. The session gets returned as a `WOSession` but we need to call `addUserName()` to add the newly-entered `userName`. This means that we have to cast the result of calling `session()` to be a `Session` object before invoking `addUserName()`. Here's the addition to the `submitName()` method in `Main.java`:

```java
    public WOComponent submitName() {
      PersonalizedGreeting greetingPage =
        (PersonalizedGreeting)pageWithName("PersonalizedGreeting");
      greetingPage.setUserName(userName);
      ((Session)session()).addUserName(userName);
      return greetingPage;
    }
```

We can use output to the console to verify that at this point we are creating an `NSMutableArray` and successfully adding to it every time a `userName` is added. The next step is to output this list using repetitions.

Displaying Lists

Now that all of the information is in the `NSMutableArray`, it is time to display it. We can do this by iterating through `pastUserNames` and displaying the names in turn. Create a new key called **tempUserName** in `PersonalizedGreeting.wo` that is of type `String` and just consists of an instance variable. We'll use this to hold names as you pull them out of `pastUserNames`.

Below the line that contains the hyperlink, enter the text:

So far you have used the following names on this site:

Follow this by a line break. Now, we would like the usernames that are displayed in the browser to be formatted in a table. To do this we will add a table cell. Therefore we create a single table cell below the text we have just typed, by clicking on the **Add table** button and then specifying a table of one column and one row. Let's also make the table cells visible and fixed width. To do this, select the cell, open up the Inspector, give **Border** a value of 1, and **Width** a value of 250 pixels, and close the Inspector.

Now, select the cell again, and either use the circular arrow button on the toolbar or the item in the **WebObjects** menu to create a `WORepetition` around the table. A `WORepetition` is a container element that repeats its contents once for each item in an `NSArray`. We can use a `WORepetition` to create dynamically-generated ordered and unordered lists that may include a column of check boxes, radio buttons or other HTML elements.

Chapter 3

Next, highlight session so that we can see the session variable **pastUserNames**. Click on **pastUserNames** and drag the cursor to the first box following the circular arrow. Then click on **tempUserName** and drag the cursor inside the box following the straight arrow.

Double-clicking on the WORepetition shows that we have a binding between the `list` attribute and `session.pastUserNames` and another binding between the `item` attribute and `tempUserName`.

Finally, add a WOString inside the table cell. This string should be bound by `value` to `tempUserName`; it will display the value of `tempUserName`. The WebObjects Builder window should now look like this:

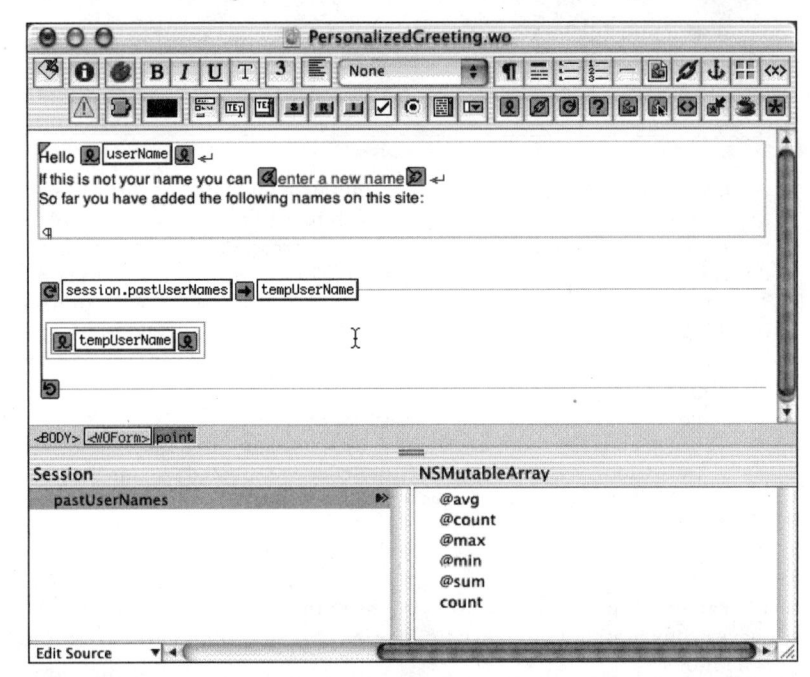

One last time, save the work and build and run the project. Add a couple of usernames by navigating back and forth between the two pages using the **Submit** button and the hyperlink. The output should be a list looking something like this:

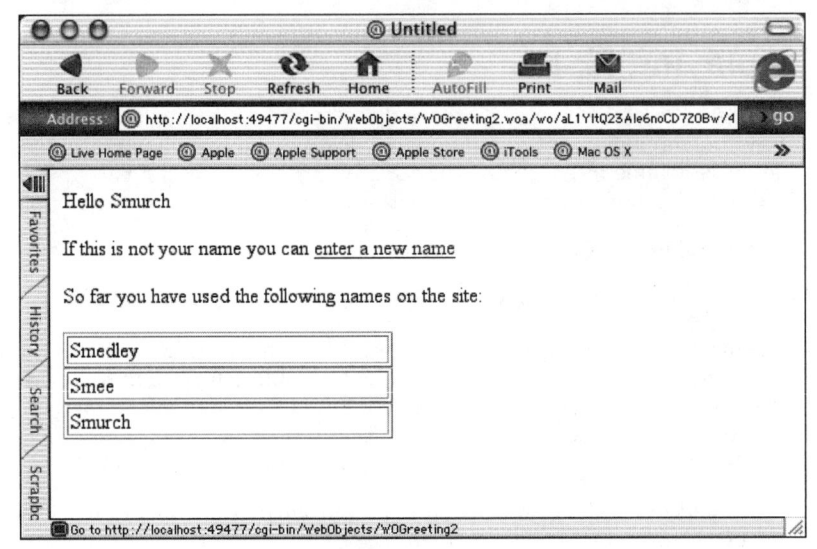

74

Summary

In this chapter we've familiarized ourselves with the WebObjects Builder UI, and written Java code to add functionality to our WebObjects applications. WebObjects provides a lot of presentation functionality allowing you to focus on the business logic in your Java objects. The data contained in our Java objects are synchronized with the values from the UI during the request-response cycle. The code we write to respond to the values input by the user is then reflected in changes to the UI.

We've created variables and methods and tied them to `WOTextFields`, `WOStrings`, and `WOSubmitButtons`. We've also been able to take information from a `WOForm` and used it in our Java code after receiving the request from the client. Then we've sent information on as part of a response.

We've tailored the look of our application in several ways. `WOConditionals` were used to display different parts of a page depending on whether or not a condition is `true`. We also found and communicated with different components using methods from `WOComponent`, and maintained information in a `WOSession` object that we accessed and displayed on a page. At the end of the chapter we created lists using an `NSMutableArray` and displayed the contents of the list using `WORepetitions`. We know that this went by pretty quickly, but we'll return to this concept of repetition later in the book.

In many cases, what we were doing was fairly familiar, we just had to get used to the WebObjects APIs and the tools for generating applications. At this point, we understand the separation of presentation, logic, and data. For the last three chapters we've concentrated on presentation and logic. In the next chapter we will move on and look more closely at the request-response cycle and the classes associated with it, including `WOSession` that we used in this chapter.

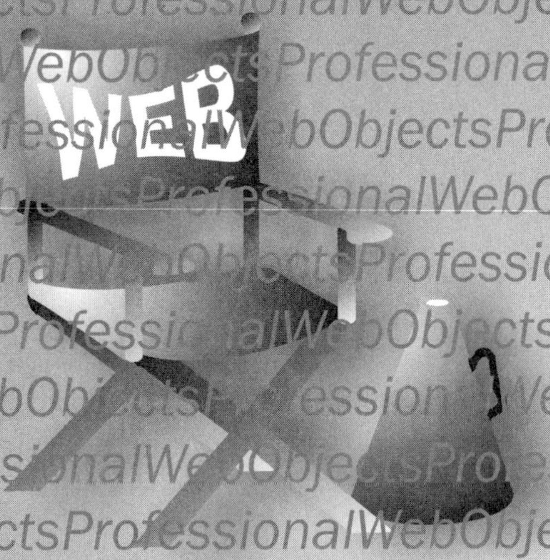
WEB

4

WebObjects Framework Classes

So far we have dabbled in the world of creating WebObjects applications. We've constructed, built, and run some simple applications that make use of dynamic elements and components. However, you are probably curious about what is happening behind the scenes when we run a WebObjects application, since we have largely skimmed over the details. In this chapter we will attempt to satisfy this curiosity by diving under the hood of WebObjects; in particular we will discuss some of the most important objects that are associated with all WebObjects applications, including:

- Request-level objects, including `WORequest`, `WOResponse`, and `WOContext`)
- Server and Application-level objects (`WOAdaptor` and `WOApplication`)
- Session-level objects such as `WOSession`
- Page-level objects, such as `WOComponent`, `WOElement`, `WODynamicElement`
- Database integration-level classes like `WODisplayGroup`

We've already used and modified several of these classes – `WOApplication`, `WOSession`, and `WOComponent` – in order to build our applications in previous chapters, without having a good understanding of them. It's now time to get better acquainted.

The tour of these classes will be followed by an examination of how they and their methods fit into the request-response cycle that we introduced in Chapter 1. At the end of the chapter we will construct an example application that demonstrates the use of these classes and methods in the request-response cycle. By the end of the chapter you will have gained a much deeper understanding of the fundamental WebObjects classes.

Chapter 4

Introducing The WebObjects Framework

In Chapter 1 we introduced the Enterprise Objects Framework (EOF), a collection of classes that allow object-relational mapping to databases in WebObjects applications. However, there are several other frameworks that are associated with WebObjects.

The **Foundation Framework** contains core classes that are used throughout other Apple frameworks. Some of these classes duplicate functionality found in standard Java packages. For instance, the class `NSMutableArray` contains very similar functionality to the utility class `ArrayList`. Although it may seem simpler to use the standard Java packages in Apple's frameworks, replacing the core Foundation classes would involve quite a bit of work. However, the Foundation classes are just as easy to use as the standard Java packages.

The **WebObjects Framework** contains many of the most important classes needed to use WebObjects applications. This framework contains some classes from the foundation Framework, as well as a few from EOF too. In this section we will examine the most important classes of the WebObjects Framework.

As you probably noted from the introduction to this chapter, the fundamental WebObjects classes collected together in the WebObjects Framework can be separated into groups based upon their roles:

- Request
- Server and Application
- Session
- Page
- Database Integration

In addition to creating components for your application, much of your time will be spent overriding the default behavior of the methods contained in the three most important objects of the WebObjects Framework: `WOApplication`, `WOSession`, and `WOComponent`. For example, in the previous chapter we used the `WOComponent` method `pageWithName()` to get a new page instance of the page identified by a `String` argument, and we used the `Session` object towards the end of that chapter too. These objects are particularly useful to us largely because we can use application, session and component objects to persist variables across request-response cycles. Indeed, you'll probably remember that in WebObjects Builder, when you added **userName** as a key, there were already keys available for **application** and **session** too.

All of these classes belong to the `com.webobjects.appserver` package. Let's now study each of the important members of each group of classes.

Request Level Classes

As you've probably guessed, the request level classes store HTTP request and response data. The objects that represent the request and response data, `WORequest` and `WOResponse` respectively, are both subclasses of the parent class `WOMessage`.

Although you will not need to modify these classes as much as others like `WOComponent`, it's certainly worthwhile scanning through the documentation to find out more about them. It is important that you understand their capabilities and how they fit into the overall WebObjects scheme. Eventually you will come across the need to perform some kind of custom manipulation of the browser request (such as pulling out a customer form key-value pair) or need to customize your response (such as adding a cookie). Familiarity with the capabilities of `WOMessage`, `WORequest`, and `WOResponse` will let you solve these kinds of problems quickly and elegantly.

WOMessage

The `WOMessage` class supports HTTP messaging, including support for HTTP headers, cookies, data encoding, HTTP status and of course the HTML (or XML) content itself. `WOMessage` also can do useful things like returning a string based on an HTML string by escaping HTML or an HTML attribute value.

WORequest

`WORequest` objects encapsulate the data sent to an HTTP web server in a request. The objects are created by the WebObjects Adaptor when it is passed request data by the web server. This class extends `WOMessage` quite a bit; some of these extensions are to store application metadata like the application name, instance number and adaptor prefix. Other extensions such as the methods `cookieValueForKey()` and `formValueForKey()` support the manipulation of data sent to the server by the browser.

WOResponse

`WOResponse` represents the HTTP response that is returned to the web server after a WebObjects application has processed the request. This class provides only minimal extensions to `WOMessage`, with cover methods for commonly used items, such as setting the HTTP response status, and disabling caching. There are two main parts to the response: the HTML content, and data used when handling the response (such as headers and status codes).

The `WebObjects` application creates a `WOResponse` object and then passes this object to the session object (`WOSession`), which in turns passes it down to the components associated with the session. The method `appendToResponse()` is called on each component, so that each has the opportunity to add content to the response. We will look at this method in more depth in the example later.

Server and Application Level Classes

Two of the most important classes for WebObjects applications are `WOAdaptor`, and `WOApplication`. In this section we will examine the first two of these.

WOAdaptor

You should recall from Chapter 1 that the WebObjects Adaptor is the interface between the web server and a WebObjects application (or to be precise, a `WOApplication` instance). The functionality performed by the Adaptor is implemented by the `WOAdaptor` class.

The `WOAdaptor` class must first register itself with the `WOApplication` instance, to indicate that it can begin to receive request events. Then, when it is passed a request by the web server, it packages the request up as a `WORequest` object, and forwards it to the `WOApplication` instance. Finally, the `WOAdaptor` will be handed a `WORequest` object from the application, and it then sends this to the client.

WOApplication

As you may have guessed there is exactly one application object WOApplication for each WebObjects application. The purpose of this object is to receive the request from the WOAdaptor, manage the subsequent processing of the request by the WebObjects application, and then pass the generated WOResponse back to the WOAdaptor. The WOApplication listens on a TCP/IP socket and waits for requests indefinitely. Which port the WOApplication will listen on for requests, as well as numerous other parameters, can be specified either as command-line or Monitor arguments, or done programmatically through methods in the WOApplication class.

There is additional important functionality that the WOApplication class provides, including thread coordination, caching of .wod files, caching of actual pages, returning components by name and managing other application resources such as bundles and EOModels.

In the previous chapter we saw that when we create a new WebObjects application, by default we typically get a subclass of WOApplication simply called Application:

```
import com.webobjects.foundation.*;
import com.webobjects.appserver.*;
import com.webobjects.eocontrol.*;

public class Application extends WOApplication {

  public static void main(String argv[]) {
        WOApplication.main(argv, Application.class);
  }

  public Application() {
     super();
     System.out.println("Welcome to " + this.name() + " !");
     /* ** put your initialization code in here ** */
  }
}
```

This class is a shell, with the main() method for the application, and the constructor waiting for you to override methods and provide functionality. We can place any data and functionality we wish to have available through the entire application in here.

Session Level Classes

In the previous chapter we added functionality to the Session class in our sample application. But just what is a session?

A *session* is a period during which a particular client is granted access to an application and its resources. Each session can have associated data. A typical use of the sessions is for e-commerce: each client accesses an on-line shopping application and obtains a session, and then the names of items bought by a particular client are associated with their session. In WebObjects applications, the data and functionality associated are with a session stored in a WOSession object.

WOSession

A `WOSession` object is instantiated for each user session in your application. As well as storing data associated with a particular session, the `WOSession` class includes handling for localization (language), a default editing context for database access, and the session time-out. The session time-out can be set as a command-line parameter and is important since it determines how long a period of inactivity will cause the session to expire and memory to be reclaimed. Long session time-outs can create an application with a large memory footprint, while a time-out that is too short can cause the session to terminate when a user is simply taking a long time between requests, such as typing a long message into a web based e-mail client.

Although state management is handled primarily through the `WOSession` class, the `WOApplication` class has functionality to handle the initial setup of the state – determining which `WOSession` the request is intended for.

In a similar way to `Application.java`, in the last chapter we saw that a new application contains a `Session.java` file that is just a shell that enables you to interact with your `WOSession` object:

```java
import com.webobjects.foundation.*;
import com.webobjects.appserver.*;
import com.webobjects.eocontrol.*;

public class Session extends WOSession {

  public Session() {
    super();
  }

}
```

A WebObjects application uses a *session ID* to identify a session object; this ID is assigned by the `WOApplication` upon receiving the first request of the session. Later we will see how this ID is passed between components of an application using the page URL.

At the end of each request-response cycle, the `WOApplication` must store the `WOSession`. To do this the application passes the `WOSession` object to the `WOSessionStore` object, which determines the storage strategy adopted. Customizing `WOSessionStore` gives us the option to store the session data in the way we want.

In the figure below, we illustrate the relationship between clients, `WOSession` objects, and a `WOApplication` object, as well as a database.

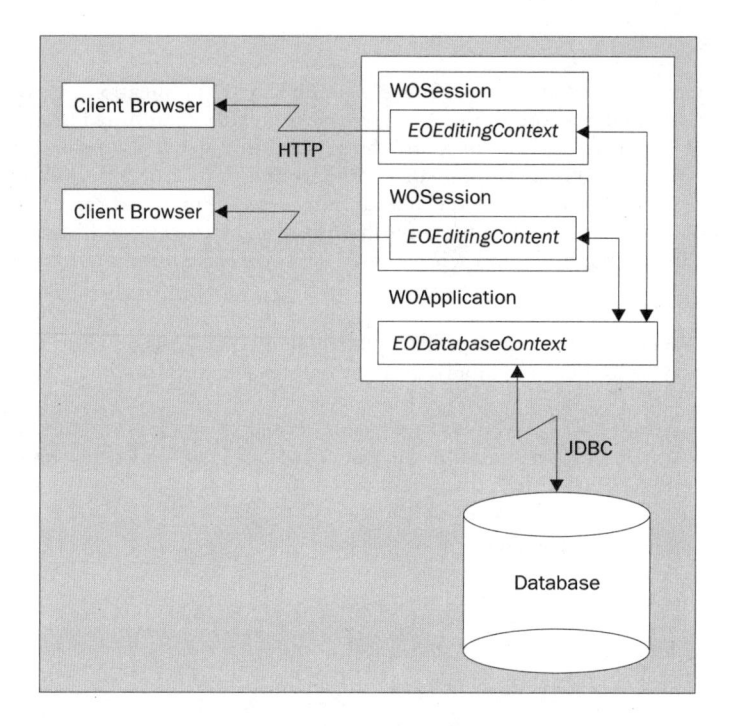

Page Level Classes

In this section we will discuss the WebObjects classes that represent static and dynamic elements on a web page.

WOElement

The `WOElement` class is the parent of all objects that represent page elements in WebObjects. It's an abstract class, so we can't directly instantiate `WOElement` objects; we must create a subclass and generate objects from that instead.

`WOElement` (as well as `WOApplication` and `WOSession`) has three important methods associated with it, that correspond to particular actions that occur in the request-response loop:

- `takeValuesFromRequest()`
- `invokeAction()`
- `appendToResponse()`

All of these methods take a `WOContext` object as argument (we'll discuss this object in a moment), and either the `WORequest` or `WOResponse` object. We'll cover these methods in more depth in a later section.

WOComponent

The `WOComponent` class is the class you typically work with the most in a WebObjects application. A typical WebObjects application may have dozens or even hundreds of `WOComponents`. Typically a given `WOComponent` will represent a single dynamic web page, or a reusable portion of a dynamic web page, and provide a framework for organizing static and dynamic elements within the page.

`WOComponents` can also contain `WOComponents`, giving the developer a high level of reusability for common items. A `WOComponent` reused in another `WOComponent` is known as a subcomponent; each subcomponent keeps track of its own subcomponents and its parent component, so that when it receives a request-response handling message it can forward the message onto its subcomponents too.

The `WOComponent` class has many of the same methods as the `WOApplication` class, but the scope of the methods is limited to the component rather than the application.

WODynamicElement

The `WODynamicElement` class is an abstract superclass from which WebObjects classes representing dynamic elements are derived. Each dynamic element has a name and at least one *property* that is used to store data. As we have seen from chapter 3, this data stored in a property is **bound** to the `WOComponent` that contains the `WODynamicElement`.

When a user submits values into a dynamic element, the data is passed across the bindings to its parent component. When the data has been processed, the component passes data back to dynamic elements that may display that data in the next page representation. We also saw in the previous chapter that dynamic elements can be bound to **actions**, so that when the element is manipulated by the user, it triggers an action method in the `WOComponent`.

WebObjects includes a collection of ready-made dynamic elements that we can include in our components. We've met many of them already; some of the most commonly-used dynamic elements are:

- `WOString`, which renders out a string
- `WOForm`, which renders open/closing tags for a `<FORM>` element
- `WOTextField`, for `<INPUT type="Text"...` elements

There are roughly 40 dynamic elements for a wide variety of primitive HTML elements. These are all well documented with examples, and it's a good idea to review the Apple documentation for all the elements so you understand what elements are available for you to use. WebObjects also ships with a framework called `WOExtensions` that has reusable `WOComponents`. You use these components like a dynamic element or any of your own custom-made reusable components. It is well worthwhile familiarizing yourself with the more sophisticated reusable components available from this framework, as they solve many commonly needed items such as arrays of radio buttons, sort ordering, and so on.

All dynamic elements must implement the `appendToResponse()` method, although those elements that accept values, or respond to user actions (for example buttons), should also obviously implement `takeValuesFromRequest()` or `invokeAction()` respectively.

Database Integration Level Objects

Database integration level objects handle database manipulation – events such as fetches and queries. The most common class of this type is `WODisplayGroup`.

WODisplayGroup

A `WODisplayGroup` object collects objects from an `EODataSource` and then filters and sorts them, ready to be displayed via dynamic elements on a webpage. It manipulates the datasource using a large number of database query-related methods, and registers itself with the `EOEditingContext` for the datasource as an editor and message handler of the datasource (so that the editing context can check with the `WODisplayGroup` for changes to objects).

Chapter 4

Using Context

In addition to those we have already mentioned, one other request-level class, `WOContext`, places a crucial but more behind the scenes role in mapping particular events to particular components in the application.

In a typical WebObjects request-response transaction, there are several important objects: the `WOApplication`, the `WOSession`, the `WOComponents`, and the `WODynamicElements`. Now, it is obviously going to be very useful to have an object that stores the **context** of the transaction: in other words, which important objects are being used in the transaction (the application, session, and so on). A typical transaction can be identified by a *context ID*, which appears in the URL of the web page (along with the session ID).

WOContext

The `WOContext` object is the object used to store a context; it keeps track of the current component (via the `component()` method), and provides information and services related to the current transaction. It can be used to get the full web page URL (or portions of it) if needed. Since the `WOContext` object is passed as argument in calls to the important `takeValuesFromRequest()`, `invokeAction()`, and `appendToResponse()` methods, it allows dynamic elements to know what the current component is, and exchange values with it.

The `WOContext` object also has an `elementID()` method, that returns the *element ID* of the current `WOElement`. We will see how this method is used next, when we take a closer look at the request-response cycle.

A Closer Look At the Request-Response Cycle

In Chapter 1 we gave you an overview of the request-response cycle as applied to a WebObjects application. We saw that when the web server receives an HTTP request, it forwards it to the WebObjects Adaptor, which then determines which WebObjects application the request is intended for, and sends it on. The application receives the request, processes it, and generates a response that it sends to the Adaptor. Finally the Adaptor sends the response back to the client via the web server.

Let's now use our expanded knowledge of the WebObjects Framework classes to gain a deeper understanding of the WebObjects request-response cycle. To do this we must first study some of the most important methods associated with the WebObjects Framework classes and the request-response cycle.

Methods Important To the Request-Response Cycle

Earlier we mentioned that there are three basic fundamental methods implemented by `WOApplication`, `WOSession`, and `WOElement` (and therefore `WOComponent` and `WODynamicElement` too). These methods are:

- ❏   `public void takeValuesFromRequest(WORequest, WOContext)`
- ❏   `public WOActionResults invokeAction(WORequest, WOContext)`
- ❏   `public void appendToResponse(WOResponse, WOContext)`

The methods are declared in all four classes, although they may not actually have an effect in all of the `WODynamicElement` subclasses.

When a request first comes in, it is processed by the `WOApplication` class and then passed off to the appropriate `WOSession` class. This class then passes it to the object at the 'root' of the graph of `WOElements` that comprise the current object graph. This graph will have a root element that typically corresponds to the current page.

Since `WOComponents` can be nested within each other, and are themselves often composed of other `WOComponents` and `WODynamicElements`, a graph similar to an *n*-order tree may result.

The three methods above are sent through this object graph in the order given above. The execution of these three methods corresponds to how the application processes the request-response loop.

As one of the three methods is propagated throughout the graph, each element compares its own `elementID` to that returned by the `elementID()` method in `WOContext`, which is the element ID of the current component. If they are identical then the `WOElement` knows that the method is destined for this component and behaves accordingly. Otherwise it simply passes the method on through the graph.

Let's now take a closer look at these three methods.

takeValuesFromRequest()

As the request arrives, the first thing that is necessary for the application to do is to extract the data the user has submitted to `WOElement` objects. This data is stored in attributes, and then it is passed to the parent component via the bindings.

For instance, a client may be submitting a form with various `WOTextField` elements such as `lastName`, `firstName`. In our application from chapter 3, we had two `WOTextField` elements that were each bound to a Java `String` instance variable in a web page. When the `takeValuesForRequest()` method arrived at each of those elements, they looked at the `WOContext`'s `elementID`, and if it matched they updated the appropriate Java `String` instance variable.

The overall effect of the `takeValuesFromRequest()` method is therefore to synchronize all form values submitted from the browser with their corresponding Java instance variables in the server application.

invokeAction()

The `invokeAction()` method is used to execute actions on the server-side. An action can be invoked through a number of `WODynamicElements` including `WOHyperlink` and `WOSubmitButton`.

The method returns an object of the abstract class `WOActionResults`. This interface has only one method, `WOResponse generateResponse()` and usually in practice the result of the `invokeAction()` method is another `WOComponent` object, the page you wish to return. Of course it could be any object that implements the `WOActionResults` interface. If the method returns `null` then the same `WOComponent` (web page) that handled the `takeValuesFromRequest()` and `invokeAction()` methods will be the ones to create the response. It is very common however for the `invokeAction()` method to return another page or other object. In this case, then the new component is the one to generate the response.

appendToResponse()

The `appendToResponse()` method is responsible for generating the response to the client. For this method, a `WOResponse` object rather than a `WORequest` is passed as a parameter along with the `WOContext`.

Each object that receives this method call may add something to the response to be sent to the client, typically with the `appendContentString(String)` method. It also passes the method on, to any children it may have in the element/component graph.

Eventually at the end of the process the entire `WOResponse` is sent back up to the `WOSession` and `WOApplication` classes (that may also modify it) and then sent back to the client.

Phases of the Request-Response Cycle

We can think of the request-response cycle as consisting of the following five phases:

Awake

When the user presses the **Submit** button, a request is generated that contains all of the information needed to process that request. This includes the values of the form elements, and the fact that the **Submit** button was clicked. The request makes its way to the web server running your application. It arrives at your WebObjects applications and wakes up the relevant processes using methods named `awake()`. The WO adapter handles this interface between the web server and the application. First the `Application` object comes to life, then the `Session` object, and finally the various required components. These awakenings are unsurprisingly known as the **Awake** phase of the request-response cycle. We can initialize instance variables or perform setup operations by overriding the default implementation of these methods.

Sync

The next phase is known as the **Sync** phase. Here the data from the forms is read into the instance variables based on the bindings. In our example, this is when the variable `userName` will be set to the value contained in the `WOTextField` (in other words, the string typed by the user). The actual method that is responsible for syncing is `takeValuesFromRequest()`. In a similar way to the `awake()` method, first the `Application`'s `takeValuesFromRequest()` method is invoked, then the session's, and finally the method belonging to the component(s).

Action

Now that all of the form data has been recorded, it is time for the **Action** phase. In general, this is the phase where the action the user initiated is performed; the `invokeAction()` method is used to call the action bound to the element the user activated. The `invokeAction()` methods are called in the same order as the `awake()` and `takeValuesFromRequest()` methods. In our case, the `WOSubmitButton` is bound to the action `submitName()` and so that method is now called. The default implementation of `WOComponent`'s `invokeAction()` method is to forward the message to the root `WOElement` object of the component template. In this case that would be the `WOForm`.

Now you can see why `submitName()` doesn't have to do very much. The variable `userName` has already been set to the new value. All `submitName()` really has to do is to refresh the screen and display this up-to-date information. It could, however, do much more. We could add code that changes the state of the objects, which in turn would influence what is displayed in the browser.

Response

The **Response** phase is next. This is where the form elements are set to the value of the variables to which they are bound. This is accomplished by the invocation of the method `appendToResponse()`. In our case the `WOTextField` and the `WOString` will both be set to the value of the variable `userName`.

The component walks through its HTML code creating the page's content. When it finds a `<WEBOBJECT>` tag, it invokes the corresponding element's `appendToResponse()` method to get the values of its binding and add the resulting content to the page. This process continues recursively until the entire response page has been created.

Sleep

Once the response is generated and sent back to the client, the component(s), the session, and application are sent the message `sleep()`: this is the **Sleep** phase. Once all of the objects involved in the request-response process are put to sleep, the new page is sent to the WebObjects adaptor. They rest peacefully until the `awake()` method is again invoked.

Demonstrating the Request-Response Cycle

So now we have a basic understanding of the request-response cycle and how the fundamental WebObjects classes and their methods fit into it. Let's reinforce this understanding by demonstrating the use of these objects and methods in a WebObjects application.

The simplest way to do this is to build an application with lots of logging at various key points so that we can see what is happening. We don't need a particularly complex application, so let's use the `WOGreeting2` project we built in chapter 3.

Open up this project using Project Builder. We will need to make some modifications to the Java files of the project so that we can get the application to display which methods are being invoked at which points in the request-response cycle. To do this we are going to override the `takeValuesFromRequest()`, `appendToResponse()`, and `invokeAction()` methods as follows:

```
public void takeValuesFromRequest(WORequest aRequest, WOContext aContext) {
    System.out.println("\r\n=== "
                    + this.getClass().getName()
                    + " takeValuesFromRequest");
    super.takeValuesFromRequest(aRequest, aContext);
}

public void appendToResponse(WOResponse aResponse, WOContext aContext) {
    System.out.println("\r\n=== "
                    + this.getClass().getName()
                    + " appendToResponse");
    super.appendToResponse(aResponse, aContext);
}

public WOActionResults invokeAction(WORequest aRequest, WOContext aContext) {
    System.out.println("\r\n=== "
                    + this.getClass().getName()
                    + " invokeAction");
    return super.invokeAction(aRequest, aContext);
}
```

As you can see, the code we have added to these methods is really simple: we are simply getting the console to display the name of the method as it is called, and the class containing the method too. Add these three methods to the following Java files in your project:

Chapter 4

- `Application.java`
- `Session.java`
- `Main.java`
- `PersonalizedGreeting.java`

When you have added the methods to the Java files, save the files. Then build the project by clicking on the hammer icon, and run it by clicking on the terminal window icon. Your web browser should then open up and after a moment should take you to the first page of the `WOGreeting2` application:

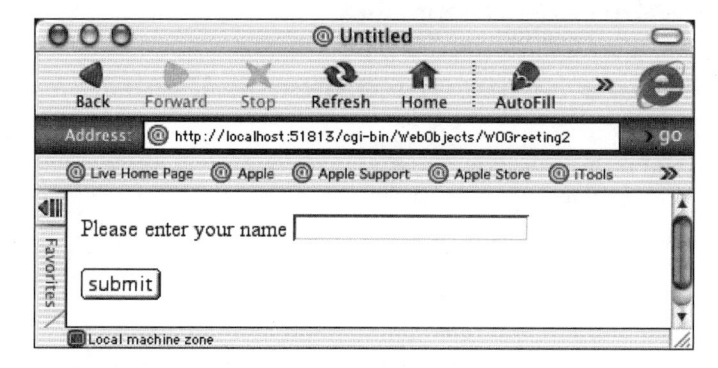

Now take a look at the runtime console (the pane in the top right) of Project Builder. The final text you should see is this:

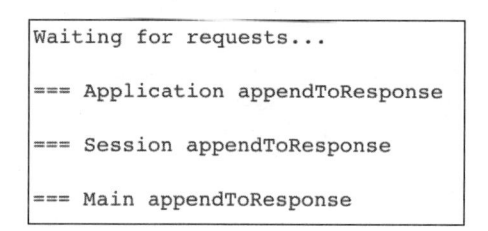

```
Waiting for requests...

=== Application appendToResponse

=== Session appendToResponse

=== Main appendToResponse
```

The **Waiting for requests...** line is where the WebObjects application first starts up and simply waits for a client request. The subsequent lines are from the `println()` statements we put in the code. We can see the request-response loop in action here. Note that there is no request, only a response, since this was the first time the application was accessed by your browser. This is a unique situation and occurs only for the first request. The important thing to note is how the `appendToResponse()` method is called through the application – first from the application object, then the session and then the (Main) component.

Next, enter your name into the text field of the browser and click **Submit**. We see the familiar greeting and table of usernames:

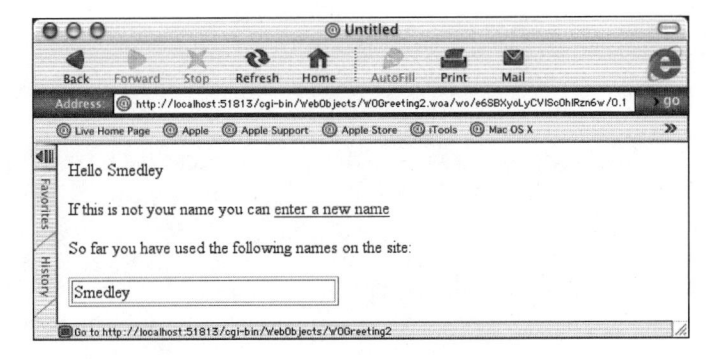

![Browser window screenshot showing a page with "Hello Smedley", "If this is not your name you can enter a new name", "So far you have used the following names on the site:", and a text field containing "Smedley".]

If we jump back to the runtime console, we now see the following lines in the ProjectBuilder console:

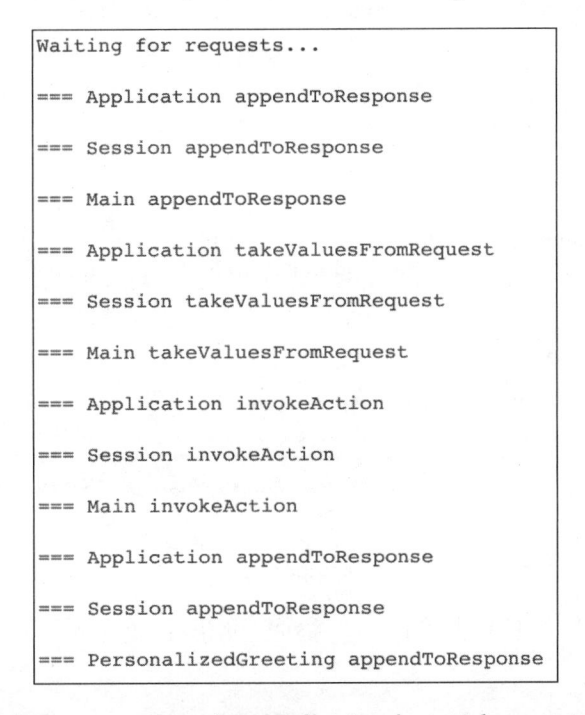

```
Waiting for requests...

=== Application appendToResponse

=== Session appendToResponse

=== Main appendToResponse

=== Application takeValuesFromRequest

=== Session takeValuesFromRequest

=== Main takeValuesFromRequest

=== Application invokeAction

=== Session invokeAction

=== Main invokeAction

=== Application appendToResponse

=== Session appendToResponse

=== PersonalizedGreeting appendToResponse
```

Here we can see the full request-response loop. Following the initial `appendToResponse()` calls that we have already seen, all values submitted by the browser are passed to the application object, the session object and then the component object via the `takeValuesFromRequest()` method. This gives each class a chance to update any instance variables from the form, so that they contain values submitted from the browser.

The second step follows the same chain of events for `invokeAction()`, giving each class a chance to respond to the action request from the browser.

Finally `appendToResponse()` is passed through to the Application and Session but note now that the `Hello` component is the component at the end of the chain, rather than the `Main` component. This is because the `invokeAction()` method in the `Main` class returned the `Hello` component as the `WOActionResults`.

89

You can look in the `Main.java` file to see the method `submitName()` that returns the `PersonalizedGreeting` component:

```
public WOComponent submitName() {
  PersonalizedGreeting greetingPage =
    (PersonalizedGreeting)pageWithName("PersonalizedGreeting");
  greetingPage.setUserName(userName);
  return greetingPage;
}
```

Note how the `pageWithName()` method is used to create a `PersonalizedGreeting` component called `greetingPage`. Then the value of the `userName` property for this component is set.

The `submitName()` method is called from the `invokeAction()` method, which is from the `WOSubmitButton` element in the `Main.wo` component. If you look in ProjectBuilder at the `Main.wod` file you can see:

```
NameSubmitButton: WOSubmitButton {
  action = submitName;
}
```

This entry in the file binds the `submitName()` method to the `action` attribute for this particular `WOSubmitButton` element in the page. When `invokeAction()` is fired, the `WOSubmitButton` looks at its action binding and then calls that method in its parent component, hence the firing of the `submitName()` method.

What's in the URL for a WebObjects Page?

Look at the URL in the web browser after you submitted the name. You will seen something similar to the following:

http://localhost:51813/cgi-bin/WebObjects/WOGreeting2.woa/wo/e6SBXyoLyCVIScOhIRzn6w/0.1

This is the URL to trigger the appropriate action in the application when you clicked the Submit button. We can break this URL down into its constituent parts.

First, we have our standard HTTP URI portion specifying the protocol (HTTP), the host machine (localhost), the port (51813):

http://localhost:51813

Next we specify that the CGI WebObjects Adaptor should be executed:

cgi-bin/WebObjects

Then we define the WebObjects application to send the request to:

WOGreeting2.woa

Now we have a *request handler key*:

wo

This specifies that this action should be processed by a component. Another request handler key, wa, is used for Direct Actions, which we will discuss in Chapter 7.

Then we have the session ID for our session, which in our case is:

e6SBXyoLyCVIScOhIRzn6w

The first digit after this is the context ID:

0

In other words, all of the state information associated with this action is encoded in the URL. The application name tells the WebObjects adaptor which application to forward the request to. The session ID lets the `WOApplication` class know which Session this request is intended for. The context ID and component ID map the request to the `submitName()` method of the `Main WOComponent`.

Summary

When we create applications using WebObjects Builder, it is difficult to appreciate the amount of work that WebObjects is doing for you. So, in this chapter we have looked behind the scenes of WebObjects. applications. In particular, we studied the important classes associated with the WebObjects Framework, such as:

- `WOApplication`
- `WOSession`
- `WOComponent`

Then we discussed how these objects were used in the request-response cycle, and how their important methods were used in it too:

- `takeValuesFromRequest()`
- `appendToResponse()`
- `invokeAction()`

We reinforced our new-found understanding of this cycle by modifying the example application from the previous chapter to demonstrate these objects and methods in action, and looked at how the URL of a WebObjects application is used to store valuable information about the transaction.

Your new-found knowledge of the fundamental WebObjects classes should aid your progress as you construct more and more complex WebObjects applications.

In the next chapter we are going to take you on a tour of the EOModeler tool, showing you how to construct an EOModel.

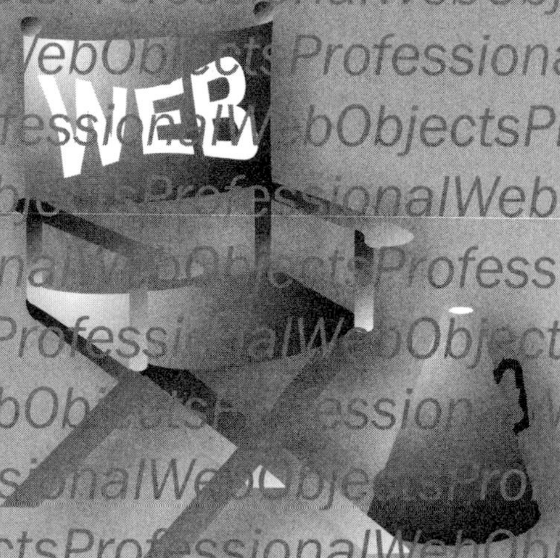
WEB

5

Introducing EOModeler

Data integrity, persistence, and scalability are fundamental requirements in projects that take the challenge to implement business processes on the web. These services are provided by databases and have become almost indispensable for the majority of today's applications. More than before, web applications face the requirement of reusing legacy information residing in existing repositories and shared by other applications.

WebObjects enables developers to leverage the services of the database without getting lost in low-level tasks, so common in the days of CGI. During those days, the web applications often had to include code to manage the database connections, create the SQL used in the various operations, implement caching, and handle user concurrency, among other tasks. More often than not, SQL code was hard coded into the source and was vendor-specific, compromising scalability and increasing maintenance costs.

EOModeler is the tool that allows us to define mappings between the tables in a relational database and Java objects. EOModeler generates Java classes, so that you can programmatically use objects and abstract the database. More than a class modeling tool, more than a code generator, EOModeler is the tool used to design a model that EOF will consult at runtime to get information regarding what needs to be read or updated, and how to talk to the database.

While this modeling process means a performance cost when compared with tightly integrated database-aware code, most WebObjects developers find this cost acceptable when weighed against greatly improved maintainability and greatly abstracted database access.

In this chapter we'll:

- Briefly review database concepts
- Analyze the requirements of an application
- Look at the process of setting up a database connection
- Familiarize ourselves with EOModeler and its layout

Chapter 5

❑ Use entities, attributes, and relationships to model the requirements

Basic Concepts

The services provided by databases to applications are very important, and have become essential to the majority of projects. By briefly reviewing some key database concepts, we'll be able to leverage its services and benefits in our applications. The subject is vast, however we'll limit the scope to the basic concepts that will help us understand the EOModeler tool and our application's interaction with the database.

Database Concepts Reviewed

A database is a collection of entities, or objects. These objects control how the data is stored and how it is managed. A database is self-describing because it maintains not only data but its description as well, what is called the database schema. The schema is, therefore, the definition of the data structure. A database is also an integrated collection of data because it stores the data in the same way, usually, but not always, on one physical computer, called a database server. The data is related, as it represents aspects and relationships between things in the real world. A Database Management System (DBMS) is a collection of software that enables the storage, definition, retrieval, and secure manipulation of data in a database. Common DBMS vendors include Oracle, OpenBase, Sybase, DB2, FrontBase, MySQL, and Microsoft SQL Server (all support JDBC 2.0, the required standard to work with WebObjects – more on this later). We'll be using the more informal term *database* in this chapter to refer to the data collection and the services that a DBMS provides.

Before databases, applications often used the file system to store data. However, the file system presented a number of limitations that compromised the scalability and maintainability of applications. For instance, it was difficult to coordinate concurrent access and changes to files. It was difficult for different applications to share the file access. Each application stored data in a different way, and data was often duplicated, wasting storage and leading to inconsistency problems. Databases store data in a consistent manner, independent of applications. They control the access and enforce data integrity rules, still allowing concurrent access. Databases also provide backup and recovery services, and security.

The schema of the database is important information to be considered when creating a model in EOModeler. This model is the bridge between the database and Java objects. The database schema includes tables, columns, stored procedures, and relationships, among other things. We can have a table to store customer-related information, such as e-mail address and name. The table could then have a row for John, another for Mary, another for Peter, and so on. In the process of mapping the database schema to Java classes using EOModeler, we'll map tables to *entities*, and columns to *attributes*. Each table has a primary key, which is made of one or more columns that uniquely identify one row. A row needs to be uniquely identified because, in order to be referenced and used by the application, it has to be differentiated from other rows. A primary key can be an artificial column, set aside for this purpose (usually a number, for performance), or can be a column that carries user data, like software license key. A primary key is said to be *simple* if it is made of one column, or *compound* otherwise. A foreign key in one table is made of one or more columns that reference the primary key of a second table. A row in an item table may contain a category identifier, which references the category this item belongs to. In other words, a row of one table will reference another row of a second table. This graph of references between rows builds relationships. So, a relationship is an association between two rows of any tables, based in a condition. The condition, usually an equality condition, binds the primary key of one table with the foreign keys of another table. While relationships are often viewed as an association between two rows without direction, in our models we'll consider the direction. Therefore, in EOModeler, we may have a relationship from the category entity to the item entity, and another from the item entity to category.

To retrieve and manipulate the data, the applications interact with the database using SQL. SQL statements manipulate the data and the schema. In our case, WebObjects will translate references and changes we make to Java objects into SQL statements. The following code is the output of an application logging the SQL statements. The EOF sends a SELECT statement to the database, on behalf of the application, because of a FETCH spec (we will encounter these in Chapter 10):

```
=== Begin Internal Transaction
  evaluateExpression: <com.webobjects.jdbcadaptor.OraclePlugIn$OracleExpression:

"SELECT t0.lastName, t0.email, t0.firstName, t0.alternateTelephone, t0.customerID,
t0.loginName, t0.title, t0.password, t0.telephone
 FROM tCustomer t0">

3 row(s) processed
=== Commit Internal Transaction
```

The statement, in the code above, is selecting all the columns from the tCustomer table. A statement can also select from more than one table comparing their attributes. In that case, we say we have a join. When the SQL reaches the database, it analyses it and builds an internal execution plan to perform the query the optimal way. Another way to retrieve data and manipulate it is by using stored procedures. Stored procedures are groups of SQL statements that form a logical unit and perform a specific task in the database. They are often precompiled for performance reasons. The model may also contain these stored procedures. Arguments can be sent to or received from stored procedures. Functions are considered special cases of stored procedures that return one result. You may want to create a stored procedure to allow an external application to access your data, still maintaining the control over how and what is changed. However, in many cases stored procedures are discouraged as they encourage mixing of application-specific rules with the data stored in the database.

During the analysis phase, normalization is the technique commonly used to create a simple and maintainable model. The term is sometimes used informally to denote the division of a table in two, using keys, but it is formally defined in the literature as a multi-step process that goes on refining the schema. Its benefits include easier maintenance, simpler user interface, and reduction of data anomalies, like duplicate data and loss of information. It provides a process for creating the tables, columns and choosing keys. At the end of each refinement, the schema reaches a Normal Form (NF). A model is in the first NF if each attribute has a single, well-defined atomic value, and not several values. In this form no two rows can be identical. A schema is in the second NF if it is in the first NF and all the non-primary key columns are dependent on the whole primary key (tables with simple primary keys are automatically in this form). There are no columns that depend on part of the primary key. A schema is in the third NF if it is in the second NF and it contains no transitive dependencies among the columns. There are no attributes that depend on a non-primary key column that in turn depends on the primary key. There are still other more restrictive NFs, but these ones are the most used ones. Although a normalized schema produces many benefits for maintenance and storage, we may choose to de-normalize some tables for performance. For example, having state, addressID, and country columns in an Address table violates the third NF, because state depends on country, and country depends on addressID. The solution would be to break Address into two tables. But we may still choose to have only one table to avoid SELECT statements with many joins, which degrades performance. So, you may want to normalize as much as possible, granting a few exceptions to tables frequently accessed for performance.

Another basic and important concept is transactions. A transaction is a series of actions performed by one user, which accesses or changes the database, taking the data from one state to another. A transaction has only two outcomes: it either succeeds (COMMIT), or it rolls back (ROLLBACK) to the original state. A database must guarantee the four so-called **ACID** properties:

Chapter 5

- Atomicity
- Consistency
- Isolation
- Durability

Atomicity guarantees that transactions must either complete or the state of the data must remain as it was before the transaction started. In other words, transactions that roll-back should not produce any side effect. Consistency guarantees that, while transactions operate on the data, the database moves from one consistent state to another. Isolation guarantees that each transaction has access to consistent data, even operating concurrently. Finally, durability guarantees that the changes on data made by a transaction persist in the database indefinitely, and in the event of a system crash or media failure, the database is recovered into a consistent state.

An application opens a connection to the database to use the services available from it. While database vendors historically made available libraries for this connection, as time went by, applications sought the best between performance and portability. The JDBC standard is the most common way for Java applications to interact databases is the JDBC standard.

The EOModeler Tool

The main purpose of the EOModeler tool is to map the database schema to Enterprise Objects, and vice-versa. The Enterprise Objects will hold business logic useful for the WebObjects applications. When modeling, we make use of EOModeler's structures: entities, their attributes, and their relationships.

Entities represent a real-world logical structure, and are similar to database tables in functionality. Attributes are the basic unit of data storage, and are similar to columns in functionality. The mapping between objects and tables in the database happens in the following way. Each table or view is mapped to an entity, and each entity is then mapped to a Java class. An entity comprises of attributes that usually correspond to columns in the table. The entity also carries other relevant information for the runtime such as if only a subset of the rows should be used and other configurations, which are related to performance. Attributes contain information such as the Java class that will be used to hold the data and the data type of the column in the database.

Relationships are logical associations between the entities, based on their keys. The model will also contain these relationships. An example of a relationship is that each item is classified into categories. In our example, this is modeled as a relationship between the item and category entities, as we'll see. The relationships contain some basic rules that will be enforced by the EOF. When deleting categories from the database, EOF should also delete its items. Relationships are classified, according to their cardinality, in one-to-one and one-to-many relationships. These terms take the source entity as reference. A one-to-one relationship indicates that one object of the source entity relates to one object of the destination entity at most. A one-to-many relationship indicates that one object of the source entity relates to zero or more objects of the destination entity. We could also classify the relationships taking into account both entities at the same time. From this point of view, we can say that there are three types of relationship: one-to-many, one-to-one, and many-to-many. But usually we are only concerned with whether relationships are to-one-one or one-to-many.

The model creation process consists nothing more than creating the entities, their attributes and relationships, and configuring their properties. At the end of the modeling process, we'll have a set of entities, attributes, and relationships (and stored procedures), stored in the file system, ready to be used by our WebObjects applications. The files, in Windows, are all under the directory (or directories, if you have more than one model) whose name ends in `.eomodeld`. You will see one file on the Mac OSX, wrapper representing the model. When an application starts, EOF parses the model files on demand and maintains the model definition in memory. This definition in memory is accessible from EOF through classes contained in the `com.webobjects.eoaccess` package. The `EOModel` class represents one model, `EOEntity` entities, `EOStoredProcedure` stored procedures, and so on. For simplicity, we'll be using the term **model** in the chapter to denote both the definition of entities, attributes, relationships, fetch specifications, and stored procedures in EOModeler, set at design time, and an `EOModel` object that represents this same information at runtime.

The Requirements of Our Sample Application

The more the requirements specify what is required and the less it defines how it is implemented the better. Specifying the model in a generic way makes it more durable, adaptable, and reusable since tying the model into any specific application model restricts it. We should begin by defining the requirements of the application itself, leaving the discussion of the model for later.

In our example we want an online e-commerce store accessible through the Internet that:

- Allows customers to browse a priced product catalog
- Stores important customer information, such as address and contact information, so that items can be shipped
- Securely authenticates registered customers
- Allows customers to order products
- Processes credit card payments
- Stores relevant statistical information for internal use, such as the volume of orders in a certain period of time

Other requirements might be more detailed in terms of definitions, but having these requirements at hand, we can already begin planning and building our model.

Modeling Requirements

One of the main stresses placed on the developer is the moving goalposts that changing requirements represent. Requirements change as clients understand their needs better and as they react to development throughout the development process. It is therefore very likely that you'll have to change both database structure and the model to fulfill these new requirements. One of our challenges is to minimize the effort needed to implement the requirements. In practice, a model and a database structure are still reviewed and modified throughout the lifecycle of an application.

In this analysis effort, to create a model from requirements, we'll identify the things specified by the requirements in an organized model. In this exercise, we'll create a UML class diagram, and then import it into EOModeler. This facilitates the optimization of the model, and helps the visualization of our system.

Chapter 5

The Application Database Schema

The requirements say that there are customers that will browse and order items. So, we'll create the `Customer`, `Order`, and `Item` classes (UML classes, not Java classes). These classes we will use later in the chapter to create our model in EOModeler. `Item` will represent what is being bought, and `Order` represents the actual order. In order to organize the items in the catalog, we'll classify them in categories using a `Category` class. If items are being shipped, we should store the customer's `Address`. We have a collection of `Items`, but we somehow need to know what the user is buying in a specific `Order`. So we create a class called `LineItem` for that, including the price paid at the time and the quantity ordered. Since the application needs to know when the orders are created for statistics, we'll include that information in the `Order` class. The customer is paying with a credit card. We'll then store `Payment` information in a separate class. It will include information on when the order was paid, how much was it, and the credit card which was used.

Including other class attributes, we'll arrive at a UML class diagram that represents the system. Here is an optimized UML class diagram:

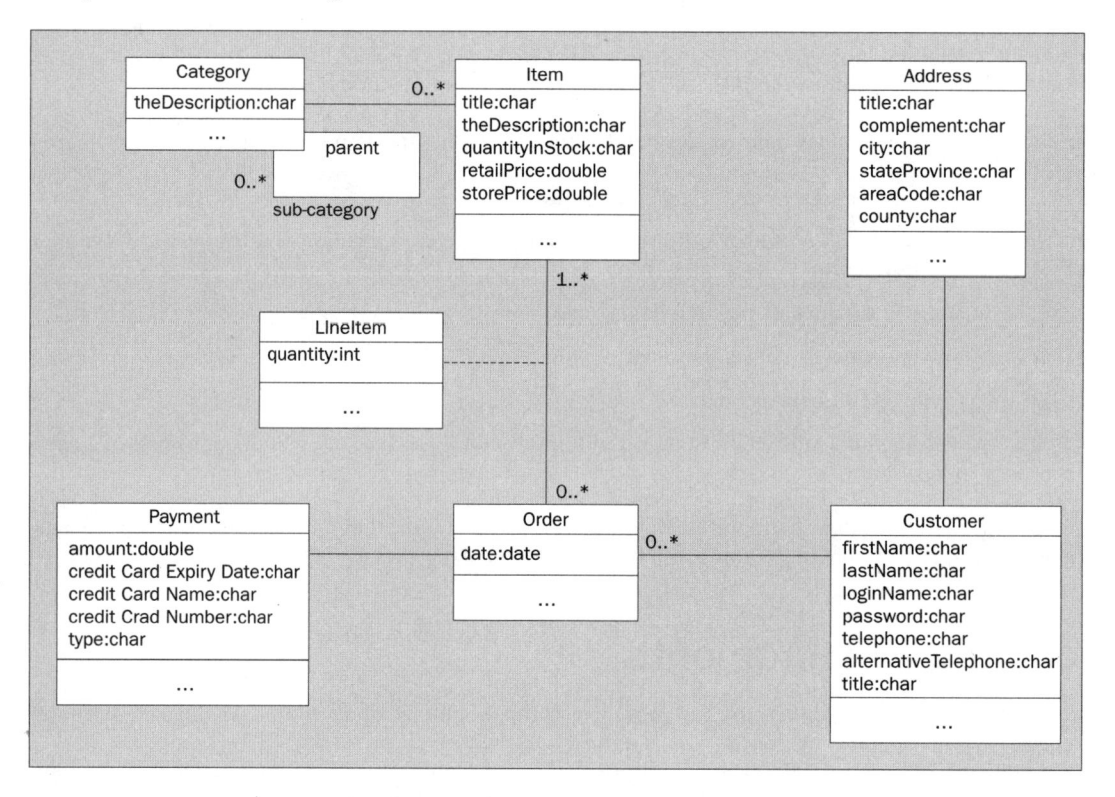

```
┌─────────────────────────┐                    ┌─────────────────────────┐       ┌─────────────────────────┐
│       Category          │         0..*       │          Item           │       │        Address          │
│ theDescription:char     │──────────────      │ title:char              │       │ title:char              │
│          ...            │                    │ theDescription:char     │       │ complement:char         │
└─────────────────────────┘    parent          │ quantityInStock:char    │       │ city:char               │
         0..*                                  │ retailPrice:double      │       │ stateProvince:char      │
                            sub-category       │ storePrice:double       │       │ areaCode:char           │
                                               │          ...            │       │ county:char             │
                                               └─────────────────────────┘       │          ...            │
                                                          1..*                   └─────────────────────────┘
         ┌─────────────────────────┐
         │        LineItem         │
         │ quantity:int            │--------
         │          ...            │
         └─────────────────────────┘

                                                          0..*
┌─────────────────────────┐                    ┌─────────────────────────┐       ┌─────────────────────────┐
│        Payment          │                    │         Order           │       │        Customer         │
│ amount:double           │                    │ date:date               │ 0..*  │ firstName:char          │
│ credit Card Expiry Date:char │                │          ...            │──────│ lastName:char           │
│ credit Card Name:char   │                    │          ...            │       │ loginName:char          │
│ credit Crad Number:char │                    └─────────────────────────┘       │ password:char           │
│ type:char               │                                                      │ telephone:char          │
│          ...            │                                                      │ alternativeTelephone:char│
└─────────────────────────┘                                                      │ title:char              │
                                                                                 │          ...            │
                                                                                 └─────────────────────────┘
```

The diagram contains a good level of normalization, allowing some de-normalization foreseeing performance gains. The `LineItem` association class is a good normalization pattern. The `Payment` class, in turn, has an `amount` property that could be derived by adding of the `prices` in `LineItem`. But that could mean a serious performance hit. Every time we needed to calculate the price of an `Order`, we would need to loop through the prices of each `LineItem`. So, we leave the `amount` attribute in `Payment`, still running the risk of having discrepancies between the values.

Introducing EOModeler

To translate the class diagram to a model in EOModeler, we'll follow some simple steps, (the details on how to do this will be in the section on *Creating Entities*):

1. We transform each class into an entity, including the `LineItem` association class. An association class is an association with properties. However, it is treated as one single element in UML.

2. Next, each class attribute becomes one entity attribute.

3. We then create a new primary key attribute in each entity. The exception here is the `Category` entity, where we'll use the existing `categoryID` attribute as the primary key and `LineItem`, which deserves a different treatment for being an association class. For example, the `Item` entity will have a primary key attribute called `itemID`, and `Customer` will have a primary key attribute called `customerID`.

4. When we have associations with a one-to-many cardinality, we include a foreign key attribute in the entity correspondent to the one-to-many side of the association. As an example, a category contains zero or more items. The one-to-many side of the association is the `Item` class. We then include a `categoryID` foreign key attribute in the `Item` entity.

5. We include in the entity for the association class, `LineItem`, the primary keys of the associated classes. That corresponds to the primary keys of `Order` and `Item`. We include also `LineItem`'s own attributes, `price`, and `quantity`.

Following these steps, we are able to compile a list of entities with their respective attributes.

The model and the database schema are created at the same time in our example. So we must make some decisions regarding the database schema based on the requirements of the application. An example of this is that when creating attributes, we need to create the respective table column names the attributes will be bound to. We'll also need to decide the column width for `String` columns. Since the requirements above don't impose any restriction of this level of granularity, we'll define by ourselves this and other details for this example arbitrarily. There are, nevertheless, some guidelines that we want to keep in mind while building the model and the database schema. We aim at a model that has as little data redundancy as possible; preferably, we want no data redundancy. Yet, the model must contribute, along with all other parts, to a good performance of the deployed application.

Here are the seven entities with their attributes, which are the result of the application of the steps above:

Name of Entity	Attribute	Description
Category	`categoryID`	The identifier for this category
	`theDescription`	This category's description
	`parentID`	The identifier of a less specialized category
Item	`itemID`	Primary key
	`theDescription`	This item's description
	`title`	The name of this item

Table continued on following page

99

Name of Entity	Attribute	Description
	quantityInStock	The quantity in stock for this item
	retailPrice	The retail price
	storePrice	The store price
	categoryID	The identifier of the category this item belongs to
Customer	customerID	Primary key
	title	Customer's title (Mr, Mrs, Dr, and so on)
	firstName	Customer's first name
	lastName	Customer's last name
	loginName	The login name used to access the applications
	password	The password used to grant access to the application
	telephone	The customer's telephone
	alternateTelephone	A second telephone
	email	This customer's email address
	addressID	The key of the customer's address
Address	addressID	Primary key
	address	The actual address
	areaCode	The area code
	city	The city
	country	The country name
	stateProvince	The state or province name
Order	orderID	Primary key
	customerID	The key of the customer who placed this order
	theDate	Date when this order was placed
	paymentID	The key of the payment instance with the payment details
Payment	paymentID	Primary Key
	amount	The total amount of the order
	creditCardExpiryDate	The credit card expiry date
	creditCardName	The name of the customer in the credit card

Name of Entity	Attribute	Description
LineItem	`creditCardNumber`	The credit card number
	`type`	The credit card type (Visa, MasterCard)
	`itemID`	The key of the item purchased
	`quantity`	How many of this item were purchased
	`price`	The unit price paid for the item
	`orderID`	The key of the order

In this section, we have created a UML class diagram and followed five steps to generate a basic list of entities and attributes. We'll now set up the database, in order to use it with EOModeler and the application. After the setup, we'll go through the process of including the entities and attributes in the model.

Setting Up the Database

There are two possible scenarios when it comes to developing an application that makes use of a database.

In the first scenario, the database already exists and the developer starts the project with a target repository whose structure is already defined. In many cases, the database is used by multiple applications. EOModeler, as we will see later in *Modeling an Existing Database*, has a Wizard that can reverse engineer an existing database structure and create a basic model which reflects this structure. This frees the developer from the more mundane tasks of specifying entities, tables, attributes, columns, data types, and relationships, and allows him to concentrate on the finer points of the model.

In the second scenario, the developer or Database Administrator (DBA) designs the database structure from scratch. In our example, we'll assume the second scenario as it will allow a much more detailed examination of the various aspects of EOModeler.

When you launch EOModeler, from **Developer/Applications/EOModeler** on the MacOSX server (**Programs | WebObjects | EOModeler** from the **Start** menu in Windows), you should see the following window:

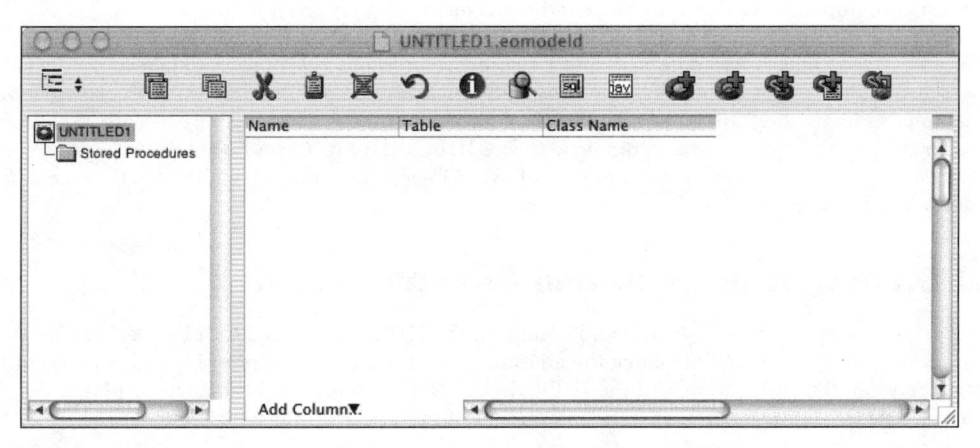

EOModeler starts with an empty model. We'll now set the database connection information.

JDBC

WebObjects uses the JDBC standard for database connectivity. JDBC is an API that provides cross-database connectivity in the Java platform. It is also the *de facto* standard for working with databases in Java. To access databases using this standard, Java applications need a piece of software called a JDBC driver. A JDBC driver is a piece of software that allows Java applications to connect and interact with a database, while maintaining the portability of the application. That is because all JDBC drivers conform to the JDBC API, which defines a set of open interfaces. The Java application, then, is able to use the same API, connecting to different databases without having to change the code. JDBC drivers are installed where the Java application resides, and interacts with the database server which serves the driver requests and manages resources. The JDBC driver from this perspective plays the role of the client in the connection to the database server.

JDBC interacts with the database translating JDBC (Java) calls into calls that the database server can understand. JDBC drivers are categorized into four *types*:

- Type 1 – these are drivers that use a JDBC-ODBC bridge to access the database. The driver calls the ODBC API, which actually does all the work. This type requires ODBC software to be installed on the client machine, which is, in our case, the server where your application runs, and not the end user's computer.

- Type 2 – these drivers directly call the native APIs of the database vendor. This type also requires vendor-specific software, in other words the native drivers, to be present in the database client's system. The driver contains Java code that calls the native protocol used by the database vendor.

- Type 3 – drivers of this type use Java sockets and a generic protocol to communicate to middleware software residing on the database server. The middleware software, in its turn, translates the calls into ODBC or database-specific calls. They don't require vendor-specific software in the client side.

- Type 4 – drivers of this type, also known as "thin" drivers, talk directly to the database using Java sockets. Most of the time, the database vendor is the only supplier of this type of driver. There's no other software required in the client side either.

The most common form of distribution of JDBC drivers is as a jar or zip file.

Historically, WebObjects had database-specific software to interact with each database product. These software was called adaptors, which were provided by each database vendor. WebObjects now has only one adaptor, namely the JDBC adaptor. JDBC adaptors are pieces of code shipped with WebObjects that sit between the application and the driver. The JDBC adaptor uses a JDBC driver, and is part of the EOF. The JDBC adaptor is an important part of WebObjects, as it manages all database access, through the use of the JDBC driver.

JDBC Drivers, Adaptors, and Plugins

In this section, we'll see how to install and configure the JDBC drivers for EOModeler's and application's use. Then, we'll introduce the adaptor, which is a piece of code shipped with WebObjects that sits between the application and the JDBC driver. JDBC drivers and the adaptor play a very important role in the connection and the interaction of our applications with the database.

Introducing EOModeler

WebObjects leaves with you the responsibility of choosing which JDBC driver to use and then installing it. The only exception to this is that WebObjects ships with the JDBC driver for OpenBase. EOModeler will require database access at development time, while manipulating the database schema, browsing data, reverse-engineering the schema, and so on. Our WebObjects applications will also require database access, at development time and when deployed. Depending on the platform used, the fact that both EOModeler and application require database access can decide which JDBC driver(s) to install, as we'll see soon.

When downloading and installing the driver, there are four things to consider: the target development and deployment platforms, the JDK(s) of the driver(s), the database used, and the type of the driver(s).

For deployment, on all platforms, one JDBC driver is required, a JDBC driver for JDK 1.2.X. There is one complication related to Microsoft Windows 2000 and development, though: EOModeler, used at development time, was written in Objective-C and in order to make it available to Java, Apple have written the Java bridge for Windows 2000 in such a way that EOModeler supports only JDK 1.1. The fact that both EOModel and WebObjects applications require database access should be taken into account. EOModeler requires its own JDBC driver for JDK 1.1, and the WebObjects runtime, used by our applications, requires a JDK 1.2.X compatible JDBC driver. So, in Windows 2000, just for the development platform, two JDBC drivers are needed.

The database that you choose for your application will probably depend on a number of criteria, such as licensing costs, familiarity or experience with the database, performance, corporate standards, reliability, and scalability. You must be capable of connecting to this database using a JDBC 2.0 compliant driver, either using a type 1 driver, like a JDBC-ODBC bridge, or a type 2, 3, or 4 driver.

The major database vendors make their JDBC drivers available for download on the Internet. Here are some examples of databases and URLs from where you can download the JDBC drivers:

Database	Download URL
Oracle	http://otn.oracle.com/software/content.html
Sybase	http://www.sybase.com/products/eaimiddleware/jconnectforjdbc
OpenBase	http://store.openbase.com
MySQL	http://mmmysql.sourceforge.net

> Check out Sun's list of JDBC drivers at
> http://industry.java.sun.com/products/jdbc/drivers.

Regarding the driver type, for Mac OSX and Solaris only a type 4 (thin) driver can be used. You can chose between the type 4 or the OCI driver, which is a type 2 driver when using Oracle on Windows. The OCI driver is usually faster than its thin counterpart. OpenBase provides type 4 drivers. You can pick any driver type for any other database, provided it complies with the JDBC 2.0 standard.

While database vendors usually provide JDBC drivers for you to use with their database (mainly drivers of types 2 and 3), that doesn't mean that you can only use the driver provided by that vendor. Always check the driver's documentation.

103

The points made above are summarized in the diagram below. Note the dependencies between driver types, JDKs, and platforms:

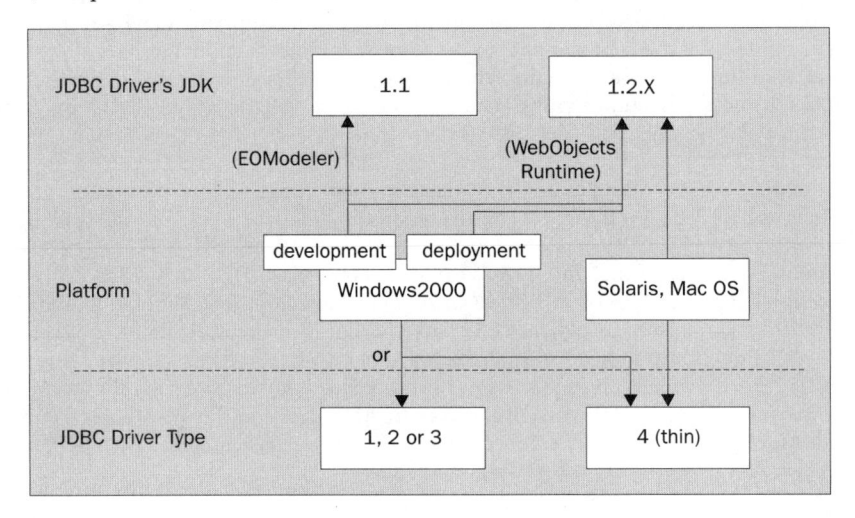

```
JDBC Driver's JDK       1.1              1.2.X
                    (EOModeler)      (WebObjects
                                      Runtime)
                    development  deployment
Platform            Windows2000      Solaris, Mac OS
                         or
JDBC Driver Type     1, 2 or 3         4 (thin)
```

You can put your JDK 1.2.X compatible JDBC driver in your classpath or in the JVM extensions directory, as the following table shows:

Platform	Directory
Windows 2000	`<JRE_directory>\lib\ext\`
Mac OS X	`/Library/Java/Home/lib/ext`
Solaris	`/urs/java/jre/lib/ext`

`<JRE_directory>` is the directory where your Java Runtime Environment (JRE) is installed, usually `<JAVA_HOME>\jre`.

When developing under Windows, follow these steps to install your JDK 1.1 JDBC driver:

1. Login as the administrator user

2. Copy the driver file to `\Apple\Library\Java`

3. Open the file `\Apple\Library\Java\JavaConfig.plist` with a text editor

4. Locate the entry named `DefaultClasspath` and append `<NEXT_ROOT>\Library\Java\<driver_file>` to it, where `<driver_file>` is the driver file. Use the variable `<NEXT_ROOT>` literally, following the pattern of the other values

5. Save `\Apple\Library\Java\JavaConfig.plist`

In Windows 2000, if you have the JDBC driver set for EOModeler but not for the WebObjects runtime, EOModeler works fine at design time, but when the application launches, an exception saying **Driver not found in Java Runtime** is thrown by WebObjects. If that happens, make sure that the JDK 1.2.X driver is located in the proper directory, or in the `CLASSPATH` variable.

Introducing EOModeler

We can create a database for our example after having put the JDBC driver(s) in the proper directories. I'll demonstrate the process using the OpenBase database. OpenBase is a database server that ships with WebObjects, with a limited license for development. You can follow the equivalent procedures of database creation, if using a different database product. At the end of this step of database creation, we should have a new database with an empty schema.

To create the database, we begin by launching OpenBaseManager, OpenBase's database administration tool, that resides in `%NEXT_ROOT%\OpenBase\Apps\OpenBaseManager.app\`. Click in the plus icon, or choose **Database | New** from the menu to create a new database. In the next dialog, choose a name for the new database, and, if you want it to start up at boot time, indicate so checking the first checkbox. The name of the database will soon be used in EOModeler. The window will look like the following:

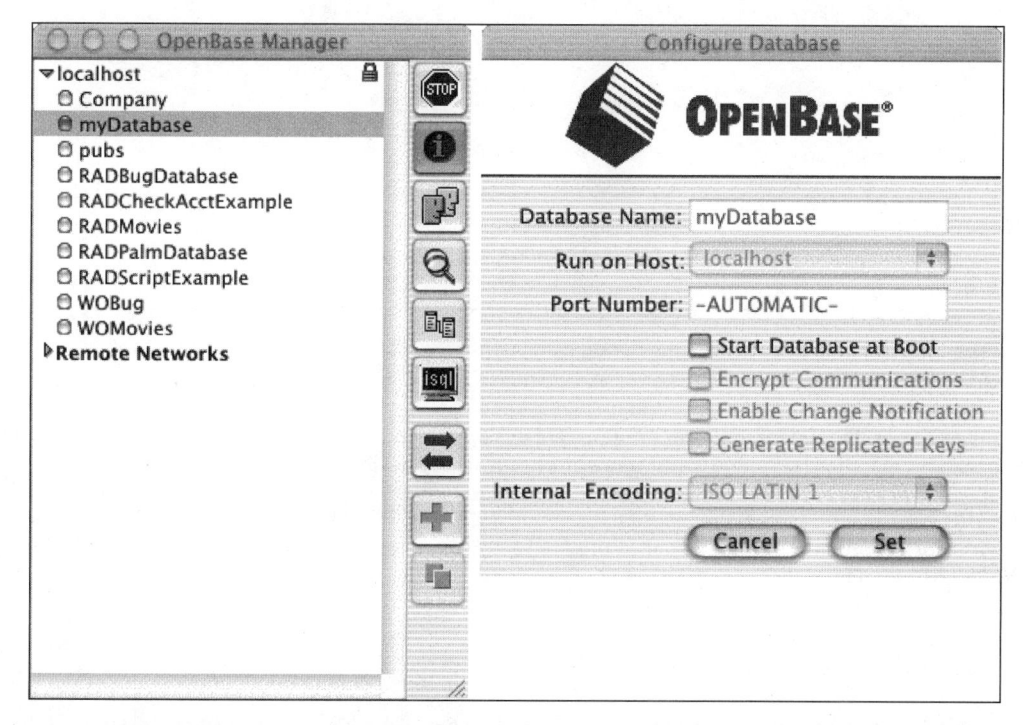

Now click on the **Set** button to create the new database in the local computer. The new database is then listed under the **localhost** section. Click in the button labeled **START** to start it. The database now should be up and running.

Let's go on to create the model that will be used throughout this book for application development. We will create the model from scratch rather than assuming that we have a legacy database to work from.

The premise for the application in this book is that we are developing a new e-commerce application, something that WebObjects is particularly suited for. We will begin by creating a new model. As we create the model, the chosen database will duplicate the work we do to create the table structure that the model implies.

Choose **Switch Adaptor** from the **Model** menu in EOModeler. When prompted about which adaptor to use, select JDBC, in which case you should see a **JDBC Connection** dialog box with blank fields:

Chapter 5

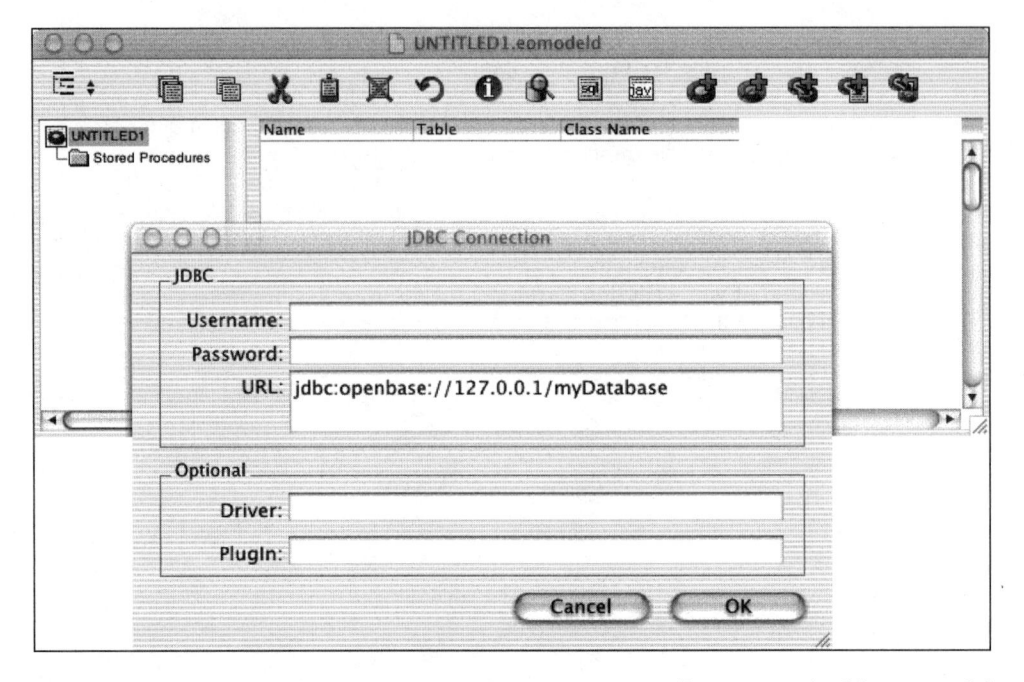

The None option, the only other alternative to the JDBC option, allows you to build your model and defer the connection setup.

In our example, the database doesn't require a username or password. Should a database require this information, use the **Username** and **Password** fields in the **JDBC** section of the dialog.

The URL you enter depends on your database and JDBC driver. The supplier of the driver should provide documentation on the format of the URL, however we will show the use of the URLs for Oracle and OpenBase. The JDBC specification recommends the following URL structure to the database vendors, which has been widely adopted:

```
jdbc:<subprotocol>:<subname>
```

For our example that connects to OpenBase in the local computer, enter the following URL in the dialog's **URL** field:

```
jdbc:openbase://127.0.0.1/myDatabase
```

where myDatabase is the name of the database previously created with OpenBaseManager. Substitute myDatabase with the name of the database that you have previously created.

If you are using Oracle, the URL has this structure:

```
jdbc:oracle:<drivertype>:@<servername>:1521:<database>
```

The last part of the URL, for Oracle's type 4 (thin) driver, following the @ does *not* depend on the entries on your `TNSNAMES.ORA` file, as some Apple documentation states. The number `1521` refers to the port that Oracle typically listens at. If this is different on your setup then it needs to be changed. In Oracle, `TNSNAMES.ORA` is a configuration file that contains the connection information used by the Oracle Client software. A thin JDBC driver doesn't depend on anything on the client side, besides the (pure Java) driver itself. If the database was created on Oracle rather than OpenBase then `myDatabase` would not be an entry in the client's `TNSNAMES.ORA` file, but the `SID` (or the `service name`) of the database (or instance, in oracle terms) on the server, usually assigned during the database creation.

If you are using OpenBase or Oracle, click on the **OK** button to finish the setup of the JDBC connection. If you are using other databases then you may need to include extra information there before finishing with the dialog box later; at the end of this section there is information on the **Optional** fields on this dialog. When the **OK** button is clicked, EOModeler will validate the information entered by trying to connect to the database. If a dialog appears saying java.sql.SQLException: No suitable driver, double-check the directory where the JDBC driver is located.

JDBC is the standard that provides cross-database connectivity using Java. However, even complying with the JDBC standard, many databases still differ in certain aspects, such as SQL statements used for schema creation, stored procedure call syntax, and primary key generation method. The JDBC standard handles these differences by allowing any SQL string to be passed to the databases, leaving the responsibility of how the SQL should be to the client code that in this case is the JDBC adaptor. To address the differences and to allow the use of some database-specific features, the JDBC adaptor allows the use of customizable classes, called plugins. Plugins are helper classes that can be used at development time and at runtime by the JDBC adaptor to enable database-specific features. At runtime, plugins can be used by the EOF to override the default generation of SQL statements. At development time, when using EOModeler, plugins provide a number of customizations; among them, the generation of database-specific SQL statements related to schema creation, the primary key generation method to be used, and the data types available. WebObjects ships with three plugins: the default plugin, the Oracle plugin, and the OpenBase plugin. So, you don't need to worry about plugins if you are using one of these two databases. Other databases can use the default plugin, which should suffice for most of the cases. The default plugin, implemented by the `com.webobjects.jdbcadaptor.JDBCPlugIn` class, provides a generic implementation for features like primary key generation and data types. For example, the default plugin uses SQL statements like `SELECT ... FOR UPDATE` for primary key generation. The MS SQL Server plugin (see later on where to obtain this plugin), however, doesn't support that, and uses its own SQL statements for row locking. The default plugin provides JDBC data types in EOModeler like `INTEGER` and `CHAR`, while the Oracle plugin provides Oracle-specific data types like `NUMBER` and `VARCHAR2`. These are just a couple of the various differences between the databases where the plugins become useful.

While Apple's datasheet states that Oracle is the only officially supported data source, it is clear that it should work with other databases. In fact, WebObjects ships with the OpenBase database embedded. The fact that WebObjects uses JDBC 2.0 means that it should have near universal database connectivity. Indeed, databases like Sybase, MySQL, DB2, FrontBase, and Microsoft SQL Server are commonly used in the WebObjects development community. However, as of this writing, Oracle is the only database extensively tested and supported by Apple. While the default plugin provides generic implementations for most of the databases other than Oracle and OpenBase, some may require a custom plugin. Apple doesn't determine which databases require and which don't require custom plugins. Experience tells us that you may require a custom plugin for overriding certain default operations, like primary key generation. Unfortunately, there isn't a central place from where plugins can be downloaded. At the time of writing, some plugins have been published in different places on the Internet. FrontBase has released a plugin in its web site, http://www.frontbase.com, and volunteer developers made available early versions of plugins for MySQL and Microsoft SQL Server in the Omnigroup discussion list, the URL for this is http://www.omnigroup.com/developer/mailinglists.

You only need to use the Optional section of the dialog if using a database other than Oracle and OpenBase. In the Plugin field, you can enter the name of the plugin class, should you use one. In the Driver field, you can override the JDBC driver class to be used by informing the fully-qualified class name of the JDBC driver. When the OK button is clicked, EOModeler tries to load a plugin class considering the subprotocol part of the URL. Consult the documentation for the plugin which you will use for any specific instructions on the fields for this dialog, as you may not need to inform the class name of the plugin.

Using the EOModeler Tool

Now, let's familiarize ourselves with EOModeler's user interface. EOModeler offers three view modes:

- Diagram view
- Browser mode
- Table mode

The three view modes present the same information in different ways. We'll repeatedly see entities, attributes, and relationships in them. For now, we are only looking at EOModeler's user interface – soon we'll analyze in detail entities, attributes and relationships. You can switch between them by choosing Tools from the menu, or by using the first icon of the toolbar.

The diagram view is perhaps the least used of these. It is the preferred view, though, for documentation because of its graphical layout. Here's a screenshot of the finished model, which we will create in this chapter, using the diagram view:

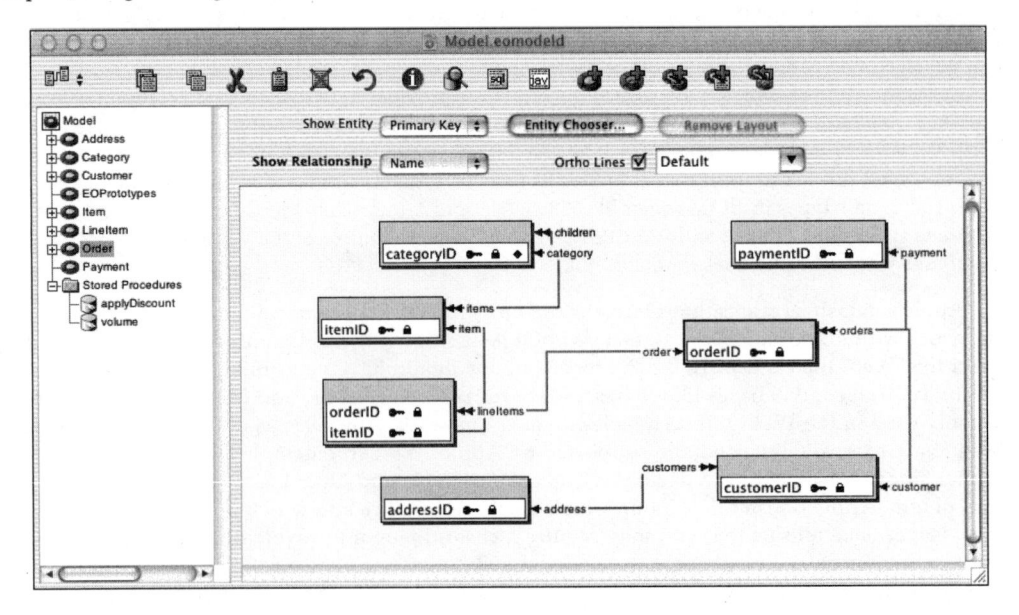

This view contains two panes. The left pane contains a list of entities and stored procedures. Clicking in the plus sign, next to the entity, shows the relationships contained in that entity. Beneath the entities, we have the stored procedures. The right pane shows each entity as a rectangle with routed lines representing relationships. In this view, we can see the relationship between the various entities. The upper part in the pane allows us to set what details to show. Here, we are seeing all the entity's primary key attributes. The `entity chooser` allows us to tailor the diagram for the relevant entities. Unfortunately, this view does not have zooming functionality for greater or lesser detail and cannot be exported to any modeling tools. (As a matter of fact, the only format in which the model is saved is in EOModeler's internal format, comprised of the `.eomodeld` directory.) The view also always shows only *three* properties of the attributes, while it holds many others. These limitations are the reasons that this view is not often used.

The browser mode allows you to easily traverse through the relationships. Here's the same model as before shown in this mode:

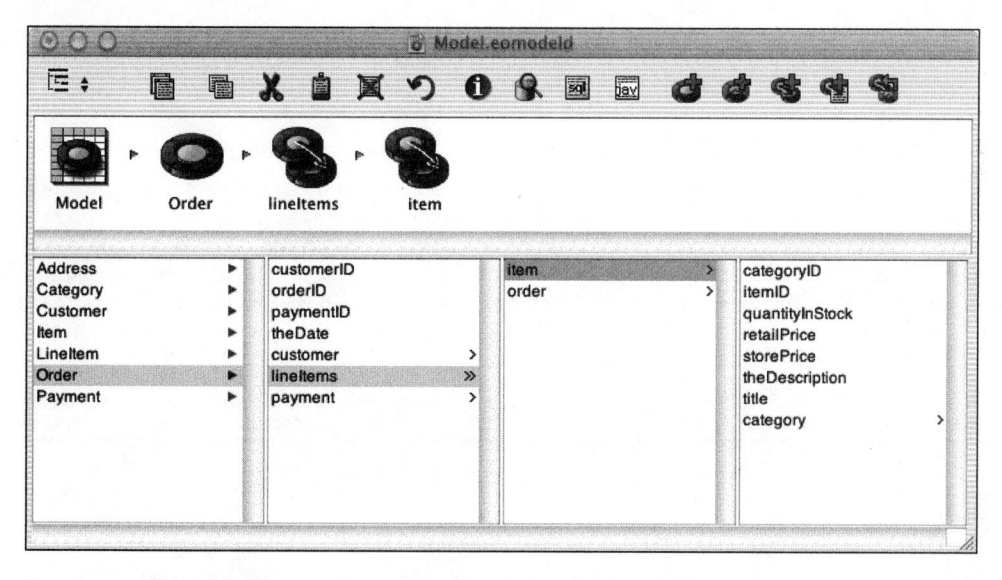

The browse mode divides the window in two horizontal panes. The upper pane highlights an entity and can list relationships and attributes according to the selection in the lower pane. The lower pane contains columns that list the entity's attributes and relationships. The first column contains all entities. When you select a relationship in a column, the attributes and relationships of the destination entity are shown in the next column (again, we'll soon cover relationships in detail later in the section on *Relationships*, when terms like destination entity will be clearer).

Probably the most used of the three views, the table mode is the one that provides the most details. It is divided into three panes. The first pane, to the left, is the list of entities and stored procedures. The top-right pane shows the list of attributes for the entity selected, whereas the lower pane has the list of relationships. The figure overleaf is in the table mode:

109

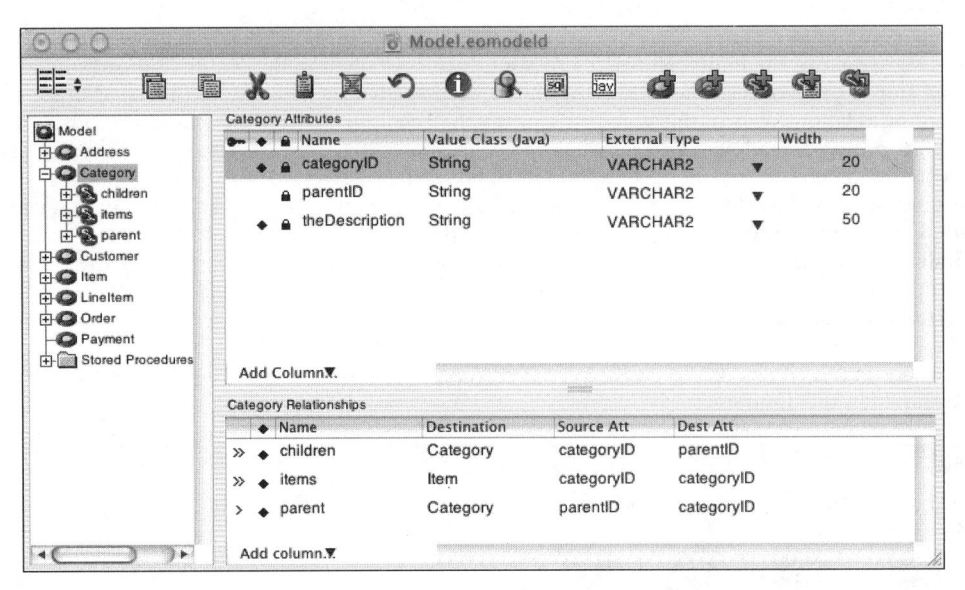

The toolbar provides some helpful actions, some of which apply to the selected item. For example, the eighth icon in the toolbar (from left to right) with the letter *i*, invokes the **inspector** tool. The inspector tool shows detailed information about what is selected. The second group of icons contains the copy, cut, paste, delete, and undo features, even allowing you to copy and paste across different models. A useful tool is the Data Browser, invoked by clicking on the icon with the database and lens images (the ninth icon), or by navigating to **Tools | Data Browser**. This allows us to browse an entity's data.

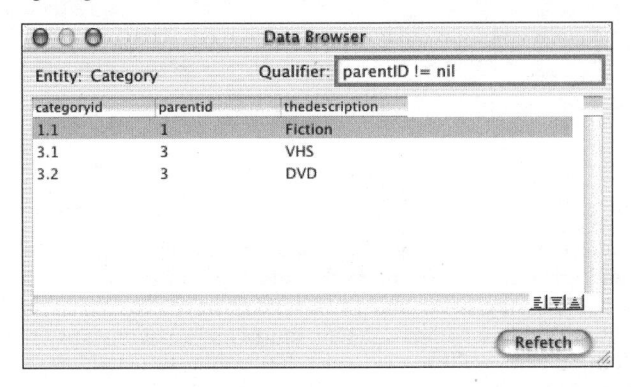

The window lists the entries for the selected entity. In the window above, those entries of the `Category` entity that satisfy the qualifier entered are selected. The data and columns seen on the window will resemble those residing in the database. You can drag and drop the columns to change their order. The icons above the **Refetch** button allow you to sort the entries by the first column. You can also use a nice tool called DBEdit to browse and change the data using an existing model. You can download this from http://www.rubicode.com.

You can save a model at any time by choosing **Model | Save** or **Model | Save As** from the menu. EOModeler will automatically check the consistency of the model just before saving the model. In this verification, EOModeler will warn you if, for example, an entity doesn't have primary keys defined, or if a stored procedure doesn't define the name of the stored procedure in the database. When EOModeler saves the model, all files under the `.eomodeld` directory are touched.

Introducing EOModeler

> The above means that your version control software may assume that some files changed when they actually didn't, depending on how the software verifies changes. If you are using CVS, this behavior shouldn't cause any problems.

If you are using Mac OSX, you will just see the model as one wrapped file. In Windows and Solaris, we can actually see EOModeler's internal representation in the text files inside the .eomodeld directory. It contains:

- One file named index.eomodeld, which lists the contents of the model and the database connection definition
- One .plist file for each entity, containing, among other things, a list of attributes and relationships
- One .storedProcedure file for each stored procedure
- One .fspec file for each fetch specification. A fetch specification allows you to define a set of criteria to fetch data from the database

Now that we are more familiar with EOModeler's user interface, we can begin creating our model. We'll begin with two fundamental things: entities and attributes.

Creating Entities

In the process of modeling our example, we'll take the list of entities and attributes that have been previously compiled. However, since we have seven entities, it would be very repetitive to show how to model all here. So, we'll concentrate on one entity, Category, and we'll see some relevant details related to the other entities afterward.

To store our product catalog, let's begin by creating the first entity, Category. To create a new entity choose **Property | Add Entity** from the menu, or click in the first icon with the green plus sign in it. Name the entity and table by editing the Name and Table fields in the right pane, as shown below:

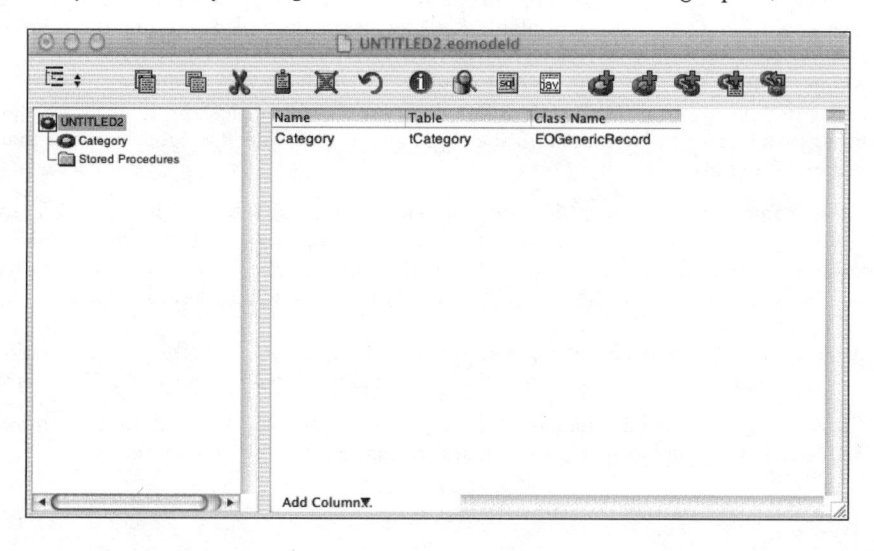

When you inspect the entity selecting **Tools | Inspector**, you see the entity inspector. The **Entity Inspector** is one of the five entity-related inspectors accessible from the **Inspector** panel. Each inspector allows us to edit a different set of related characteristics of the entity. For example, the **Stored Procedure Inspector**, as we'll see in *Advanced Modeling Concepts*, allows us to assign stored procedures to perform a number of database operations related to the entity, like inserting and deleting rows. We'll also analyze in that section the options available in the **Advanced Entity Inspector**. The **Entity Inspector** is similar in functionality to the window in the previous figure, as it allows you to edit the details of the entity:

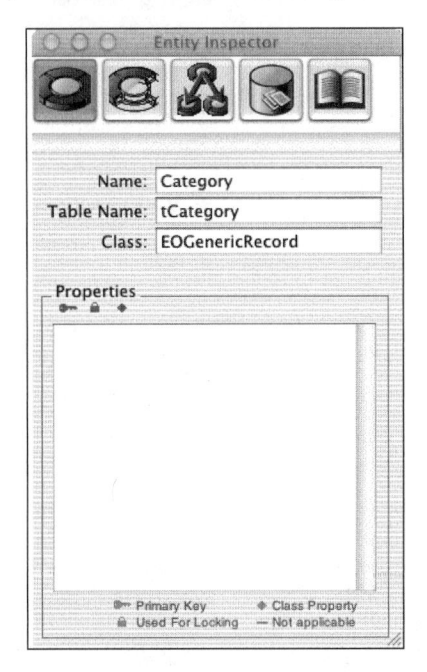

The **Entity Inspector** has a **Properties** section, which will list all this entity's attributes and relationships. Attributes and relationships are considered properties of an entity in EOModeler, at this stage our entity doesn't have any, so that's why it is still blank. Let's take a closer look at the first three fields:

- ❑ **Name** – This is the logical name of the entity. You will use this name when referencing the entity in your application. It is common convention for entities and their classes (as well as other Java classes) to be named in the singular (for example "Category") rather than in the plural ("Categories").

- ❑ **Table Name** – As we saw earlier, entities map to database tables. When you reference the entity's name in your code, say, fetching data, EOF knows that it should fetch data from this table. Be careful not to use reserved words (for your database) here. EOModeler will not warn you if that happens, and the problem will only manifest itself when the application is running.

  As an example, Oracle's list of reserved words includes ORDER, GROUP, and USER. For our example tables, we have chosen to prefix each table name with a t to avoid this potential problem.

- ❑ **Class** – Here you specify the name of the Java class that will be used to programmatically manipulate the data: to insert, delete, and change rows in the database.

Attributes

Columns are the basic unit of storage in the database, and, for that reason, their definition is very important. Attributes play the same role in models and are, therefore, equally important. In this section, we'll create attributes in the model and configure their properties.

We'll begin by including attributes in the `Category` entity, still taking the list of entities and attributes as reference. We'll hold the description of our categories in an attribute named `theDescription`, and not `description`, because `description` is a reserved word for EOF. `categoryID` will uniquely represent one category. `parentID` will reference the category to which this one belongs, or in other words, a less specialized category.

To add a new attribute to the `Category` entity, select it from the left pane in table mode, and add a new attribute by choosing **Property | Add Attribute** from the menu, or by clicking on the second icon with a green plus sign (left to right) in the toolbar. If you select the attribute and select **Tools | Inspector**, or the correspondent toolbar icon, the **Attribute Inspector** window appears. The window shows some properties of the attribute. Let's analyze the fields, using this window as reference:

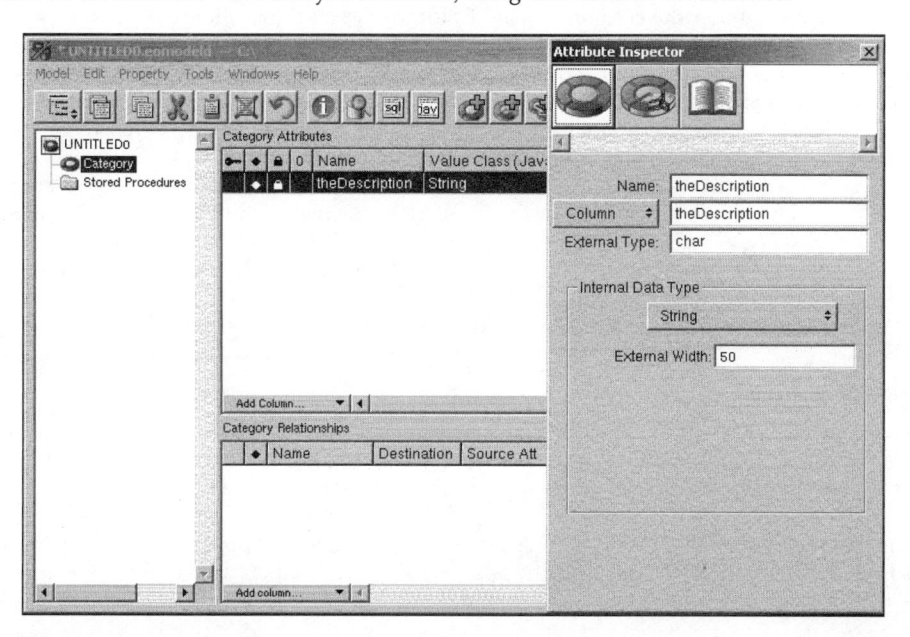

Attribute Inspector

We shall go through all the different properties of the window in this section.

Name

This will be how the attribute will be referenced in your code and in WebObjects Builder. I recommend following the common standard for naming variables in Java, beginning the word with lower-case and capitalizing the first letter in each subsequent word in the variable name. In our example, we're naming our attribute `theDescription`.

113

Column and Derived Options

Attributes usually correspond to columns in a database table on a one-to-one relationship, but may also be derived using a formula. The Column option is the default. The Derived option defines this attribute as being an expression interpreted by the database and is, therefore, database dependent. It is also read-only.

You can have one attribute named name that is derived and defined as a concatenation of three strings, firstName, whitespace, and lastName. In Oracle that would be firstname||' '||lastname and on OpenBase it would be the following, firstName + ' ' + lastName. A similar result can be achieved later by writing methods in your Java code, as we'll see in Chapter 3. Most of the time, you'll just choose the Column option and type the field name. In our case, our attribute is based on the theDescription column.

External Type

This is the data type of the field or expression in the database. Here you can enter the name of the attribute data type. You can, however, more easily select the data type from the drop-down list provided in the main window, under the column labeled External Type (if this column is not visible on the top-right pane in table mode, choose to add it using the drop-down list labeled Add Column that is located between the upper and lower panes. You can also remove a column by selecting it and pressing backspace on the keyboard). The list consists of JDBC data types, but a plugin can override its contents. When using Oracle or OpenBase, the list consists of database-specific types, provided by the plugin. Oracle calls these data types. Some common Oracle data types are VARCHAR2 for variable-length strings, DATE for date and time, and NUMBER for numbers. OpenBase offers two date-related types, date and datetime. The first specifies a day, and the second specifies a point in time, with day and time. Oracle's DATE data type is also a point in time. There is another thing to be aware of regarding date types: if the application computer has a different time zone than the database server, EOF will convert the time when reading from and writing to the database. Consult your database documentation for the various options. Our database is OpenBase, and we want our attribute type to be char.

Internal Data Type

Internal here refers to our Java code. The data type available in the database is mapped to the nearest equivalent in Java. (In Java all the data "types" are classes and not primitive data types. This notation is a throw back to Objective C which allowed primitive data types such as char, and so on.)

The type specified here will determine the class in our code that will hold the data. Depending on your choice here, you'll see other fields. Our theDescription attribute is a string of characters, so we'll choose the String option here. Other internal data types available to you include:

String	The values of this attribute will be represented as objects of class java.lang.String. In External Width enter the maximum length of the field, as defined in the database.
Decimal Number	The values of this attribute will be represented as objects of class java.math.BigDecimal. External Precision refers to the total number of digits and External Scale refers to the number of digits to the right of the decimal point. Check your database documentation for details on range and to confirm the semantics.

`Integer`	The values of this attribute will be represented as objects of class `java.lang.Integer`. If your key is just a numeric sequence of integers, you can choose this option. In our example, we are representing all integers with this class.
`Double`	The values of this attribute will be represented as objects of class `java.lang.Double`.
`Date`	The values of this attribute will be points in time. They will be represented as objects of class `com.webobjects.foundation.NSTimestamp`.
`Data`	Use this type if you want to store a sequence of bytes, like an image, file contents, a serialized Java class, and so on. It is commonly used with large strings of bytes, like Oracle `LOB`s and `RAW`. They will be represented as objects of class `com.webobjects.foundation.NSData`. There are many utility classes in the `com.webobjects.foundation` package; all beginning with `NS`.
`Custom`	With this option, you can define your own class to hold the values from the database. We'll use this option later in the chapter, when we create our own `Password` class.

Many of these options will help EOModeler to generate SQL statements, or more specifically Data Definition Language (DDL) statements, including those that create the tables.

Other Settings

There are other settings that can be specified for an attribute that we should mention.

- **Primary Key Property** – Attributes that have the little key symbol beside it constitute the primary key. The key symbol here denotes *only* attributes pertaining to the primary key and not to foreign key attributes. The attributes that make the primary key should be the same in the database and in the model. Each entity must have a primary key, whose value will uniquely define an instance of this entity. Since the `theDescription` attribute isn't part of the primary key, it shouldn't have the key symbol beside it.

- **Class Property** – The diamond symbol besides an attribute marks it for inclusion in the Java class generated by EOModeler. You probably want to have access to most of the attributes of an entity. However, I advise you not to mark attributes that you don't have to manipulate.

Primary keys uniquely identify a row in a database table. There are also a few cases when primary keys are relevant inside the application code. This is when they also describe meaningful data in some way, like license plate numbers, employee numbers, and so on. The `categoryID` is one of these cases. It is relevant to the user, and we will include it in the user interface.

On the other hand, there are strong reasons for you to never set primary key attributes as being class attributes when they don't represent user data. Firstly, you still can access attributes programmatically using `EOUtilities'` `objectWithPrimaryKeyValue()` method, or some other lower-level EOF methods (accessing row snapshots), even if an attribute isn't marked as a class property. Secondly, if you need to uniquely identify entity instances, you can use EOF's own internal identifiers. Represented by the `EOGlobalID` class, these identifiers are unique across all instances of this entity. For existing database rows, these identifiers equate to the primary keys. You can retrieve them using the `EOEntity`'s `globalIDForRow()` method (EOF also has a mechanism that assigns temporary identifiers to unsaved Enterprise Objects). Lastly, by marking primary keys as class properties you allow the developers to programmatically change them, making the code more susceptible to errors and the data more susceptible to inconsistency. Not marking primary keys as attributes will make it one less thing for you to worry about.

This also applies to foreign keys. It is good practice not to set them as class attributes either. You'll reduce the probability of errors and increase maintainability using the EOF methods that handle relationships. Our `theDescription` attribute is a class property.

- **Used For Locking Property** – The little lock symbol sets the attribute to participate or not in the detection of conflicts when using the "optimistic locking strategy" for this entity. Locking approaches are ways to prevent users from tainting each other's data.

The first time EOF fetches values from the database for a user, it caches them and stores them as snapshots, so that it can supply the cached values to subsequent requests without extra trips to the database. What if another application updates the values without EOF's knowledge? EOF would have stale values. It could also overwrite the first change if it wasn't aware of it.

Optimistic locking is the default strategy to solve this problem. In optimistic locking, EOF serves fetch requests using the cached data, without accessing the database. This allows EOF to respond quicker than actually fetching data from the database every time. When the application updates or deletes the entity instance, EOF will check if the attributes in the database haven't changed since they were cached. If the attributes haven't changed, the database transaction commits. If they have changed, it means that something other than EOF changed them. The database transaction then rolls back and EOF reports the fact to the application by throwing an exception.

There are other alternatives available to solve the same problem, each one with its advantages and disadvantages. The cached snapshots contain all attributes, but just the ones with this option set are used to detect conflicts. This subject is discussed in more detail in Chapter 9. We'll leave the lock in the `theDescription` attribute, but because the whole entity is read-only, this option won't be taken into account. As the comparison between the cached attributes and the current database data changes consume time, we want to include as few attributes as possible. The database overhead in the comparison can be considerable, specially considering web applications, which tend to create a high volume of database operations. As a rule of thumb, do the following:

- Determine the minimal set of attributes in an entity that are guaranteed to change in every update. Attributes that can be changed by external applications should be included in this set.
- Remove from the set binary columns such as Oracle LOBs and LONG RAWs.
- The resulting set is the set of attributes that must be used for locking.

This way, you will guarantee that EOF will check for all the attributes that can change, without including unnecessary ones. Some tables might have a timestamp column that is automatically updated by triggers in every update. In this case, the minimal set of attributes guaranteed to change contains just the attribute bound to this column. Yet, when using a trigger for this, some care must be taken to make EOF discard the data cache immediately after the update. Otherwise, the cached data would become stale, as the changes performed by the trigger would not be reflected in EOF's cache. That would make the cache different from the data in the database, so that the next update operation with optimistic locking would fail. Again, locking strategies are discussed in more detail in Chapter 9. At this point, it is sufficient to say that attributes marked for locking are used in optimistic locking to detect changes made by other users or external applications.

- **Value Type** – it represents the subclass of `java.lang.Number` that will represent this attribute in our Java code. EOModeler should automatically set this value for us when we choose the **Internal Data Type** in the **Attribute Inspector**. It uses the following mapping:

Internal Data Type	Value Type
Integer	i
Long	l
Decimal Number	B
Byte	b
Float	F
Double	D
Short	S

The internal data type of the `theDescription` attribute is `String`. Therefore no value type is defined for it.

Add the other two attributes of the `Category` entity, `categoryID`, and `parentID` as the following window shows:

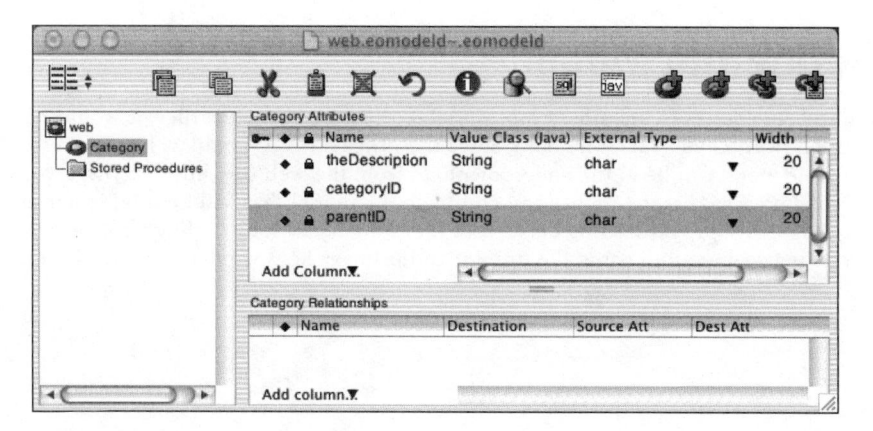

Prototype

EOModeler offers a nice feature called prototype attributes, or simply, prototypes. Prototypes allow us to define standards for attributes, and to apply their settings to another attribute. This allows us to standardize some definitions in a team of developers, and reduce errors avoiding discrepancies between attributes of the same kind. First, you create a prototype attribute with the settings you want for that prototype. Then, when you create a new attribute, you apply the prototype settings to it. The setting of the newly created attribute are initialized from those defined in the prototype. Prototypes also speed up the process of creating a model from scratch, since we don't have to enter each definition for each attribute. You can create a prototype and call it `telephone`, specifying that it is of external type `char`, Value Class `String`, and width `20`. After that, you can create an attribute, say `pager`, and apply the `telephone` prototype to it. EOModeler will set the definition of `pager` to be like `telephone`'s. You can change later `pager`'s settings, if you want.

To create a prototype in the model, simply create an entity called `EOPrototypes`. Include attributes in the entity, with the settings you want for each different prototype. These will be the prototype attributes. Add three prototype attributes to the model, `artificialKey`, `currency`, and `telephone`. We'll apply the `artificialKey` prototype, which defines a `Number`, to the primary keys of all other entities.

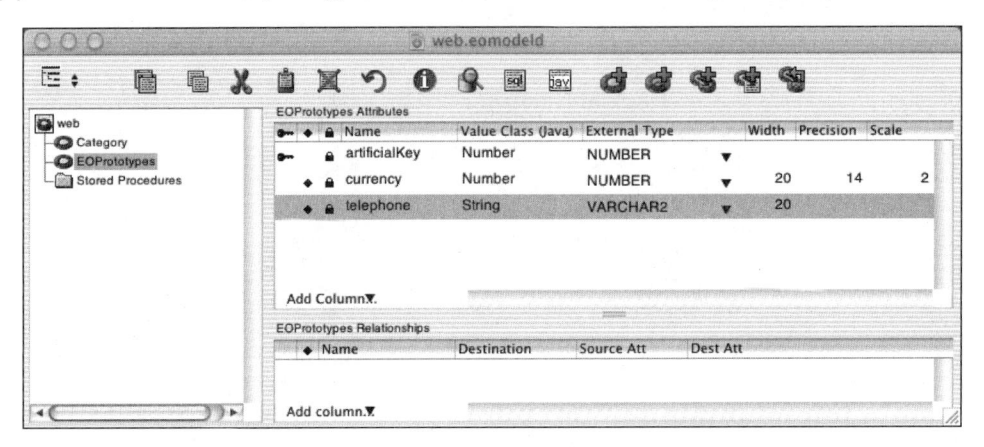

Completing the Model

There are still six entities to include in our model, but, as mentioned earlier, it would be repetitive to demonstrate how to model each one here, since the process is very similar. Figures containing the entities in table mode will be in the code download from the web site, http://www.wrox.com, along with the list of attributes, so that the reader can complete the model that will be used in subsequent examples. Any entity properties that are 'out of the ordinary' will be highlighted. Later, we'll create relationships between entities using the foreign and primary keys we define as attributes.

Introducing EOModeler

Add an `Item` entity to the model, as shown:

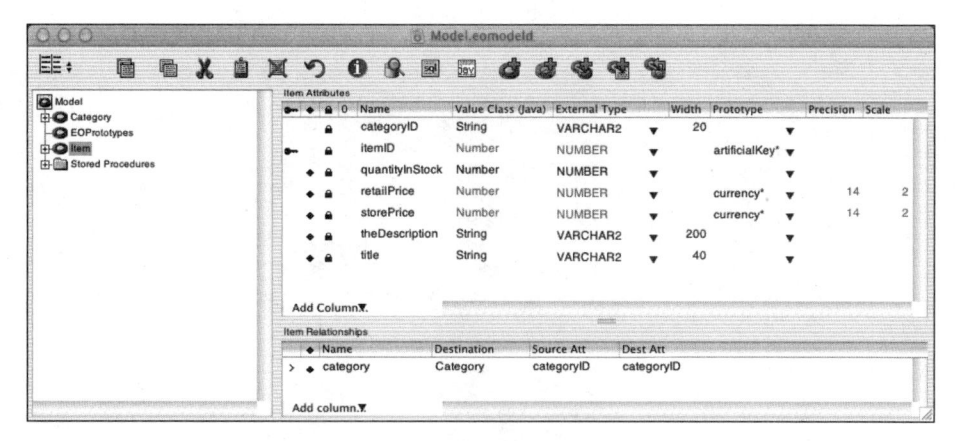

![Model.eomodeld Item Attributes screenshot]

`Item` has attributes of type `double`, that allow us to set the precision and scale. The precision and scale properties can be defined for real numbers, or `BigDecimals`. Precision defines the total number of digits of the number. Scale defines the number of digits to the right of the decimal point. The ranges of each property and restrictions vary from database to database. Oracle, for example, guarantees portability between different servers only with precision ranging from 1 to 38 and scale ranging from 84 to 127. Our application should be safe with 14 digits for precision.

Note that the primary key of the `Item` entity, `itemID`, is not marked as a class property, but `categoryID` in `Category` was marked as such. Previously, `categoryID` was relevant for the application, but `itemID` is an artificial primary key in the entity.

Here's the `Customer` entity:

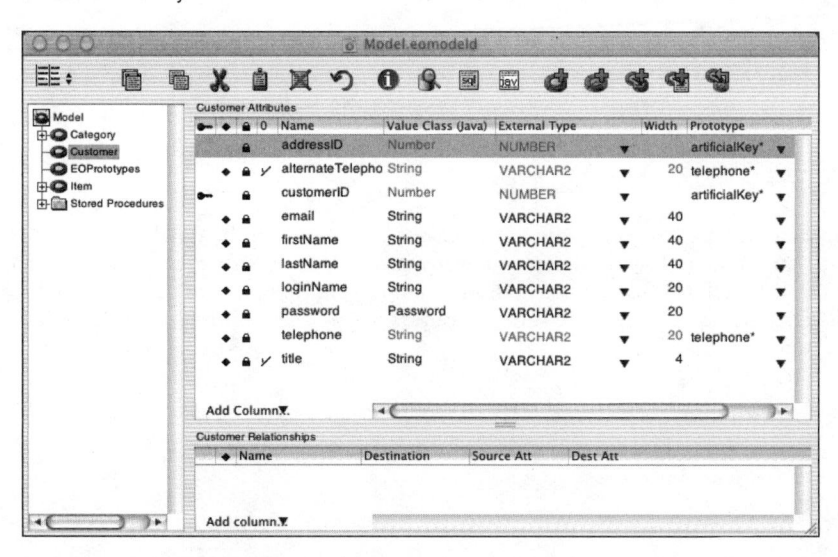

![Model.eomodeld Customer Attributes screenshot]

Note the use of a custom Java class, `Password`, to represent the `password` attribute. EOModeler allows the creation of your own classes to hold attributes, when you choose `Custom` from the internal data type option. In the Chapter 6, we'll go through this process.

119

Add the `Address` entity, as shown in the following figure:

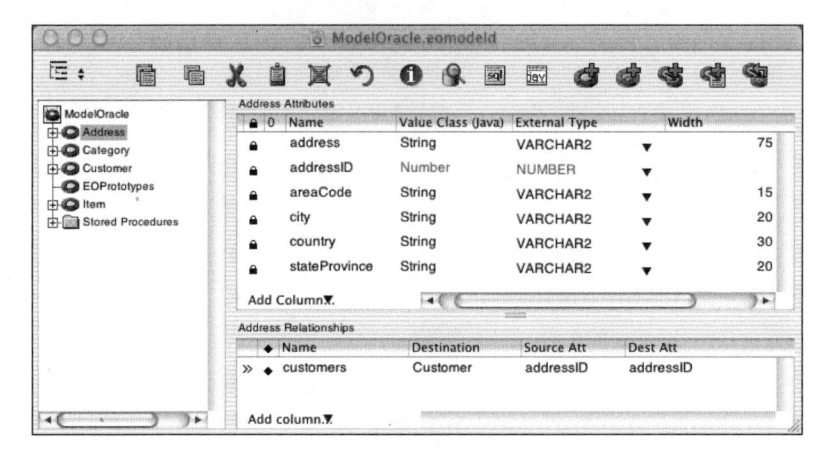

Address Attributes				
Name	Value Class (Java)	External Type		Width
address	String	VARCHAR2	▼	75
addressID	Number	NUMBER	▼	
areaCode	String	VARCHAR2	▼	15
city	String	VARCHAR2	▼	20
country	String	VARCHAR2	▼	30
stateProvince	String	VARCHAR2	▼	20

Address Relationships			
Name	Destination	Source Att	Dest Att
customers	Customer	addressID	addressID

Then we add the `Order` entity:

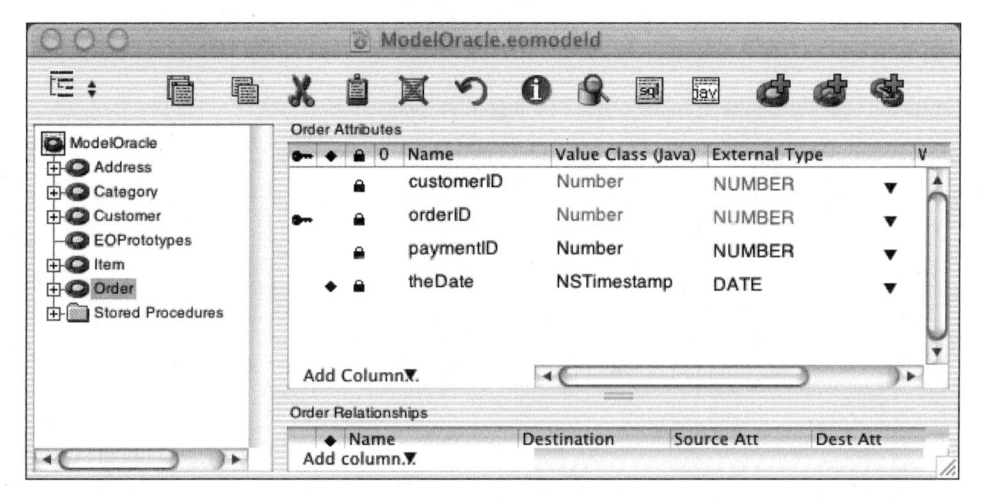

Order Attributes			
Name	Value Class (Java)	External Type	
customerID	Number	NUMBER	▼
orderID	Number	NUMBER	▼
paymentID	Number	NUMBER	▼
theDate	NSTimestamp	DATE	▼

Order Relationships			
Name	Destination	Source Att	Dest Att

We are mapping the `theDate` attribute to the `theDate` column in the database, as the **Column** column shows in the figure above. We are doing so because `DATE` is an ANSI reserved word and can cause problems in some databases like Oracle. Another interesting thing is that `theDate` is the only class property. Its class will be `com.webobjects.foundation.NSTimestamp`, which inherits from `java.sql.Timestamp`.

Introducing EOModeler

Now let's add the `LineItem` entity:

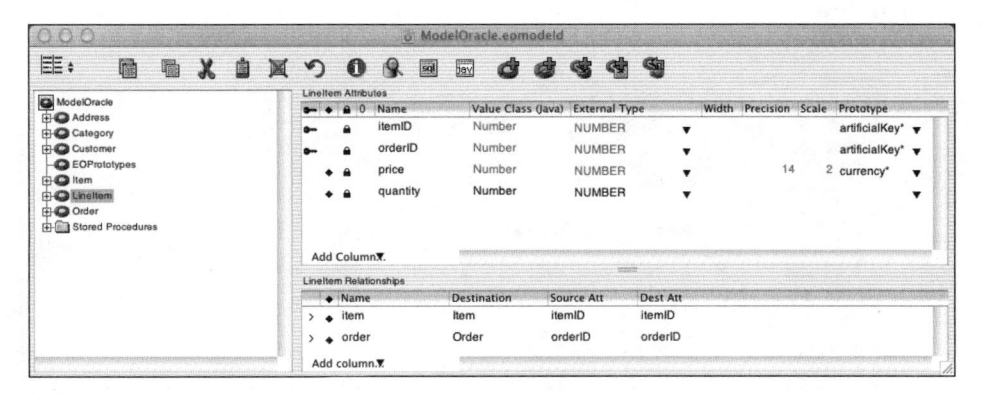

[Screenshot of ModelOracle.eomodeld showing LineItem entity with attributes: itemID (Number/NUMBER/artificialKey*), orderID (Number/NUMBER/artificialKey*), price (Number/NUMBER, Precision 14, Scale 2, currency*), quantity (Number/NUMBER). LineItem Relationships: item → Item (itemID → itemID), order → Order (orderID → orderID).]

The last entity is `Payment`. Add it to the model as shown:

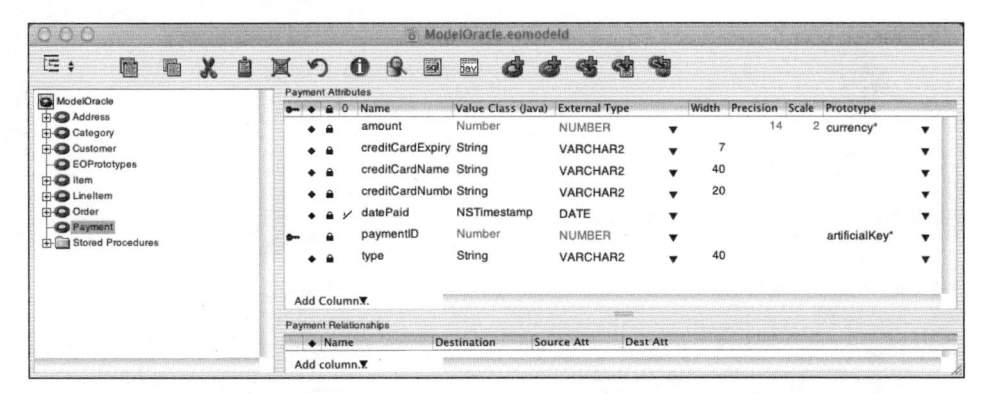

[Screenshot of ModelOracle.eomodeld showing Payment entity with attributes: amount (Number/NUMBER, Precision 14, Scale 2, currency*), creditCardExpiry (String/VARCHAR2, Width 7), creditCardName (String/VARCHAR2, Width 40), creditCardNumber (String/VARCHAR2, Width 20), datePaid (NSTimestamp/DATE), paymentID (Number/NUMBER, artificialKey*), type (String/VARCHAR2, Width 40).]

Now we have a model with entities and attributes. Next, we can add the third fundamental structure of a model: relationships.

Relationships

A relationship defines how two entities relate mutually. We consider pairs of entities, taking one as the source and the other as the destination. For instance, the `Category` and `Item` entities are related. One `category` contains zero or more `items`. One `item` must belong to exactly one `category`.

In EOModeler, there are two types of relationship, generically speaking:

- One-to-one
- One-to-many

To create the one-to-one relationship in the `Item` entity, select it and choose **Property | Add Relationship** from the menu, or click in the corresponding icon in the toolbar. A relationship with a default name will be shown in the lower-right pane.

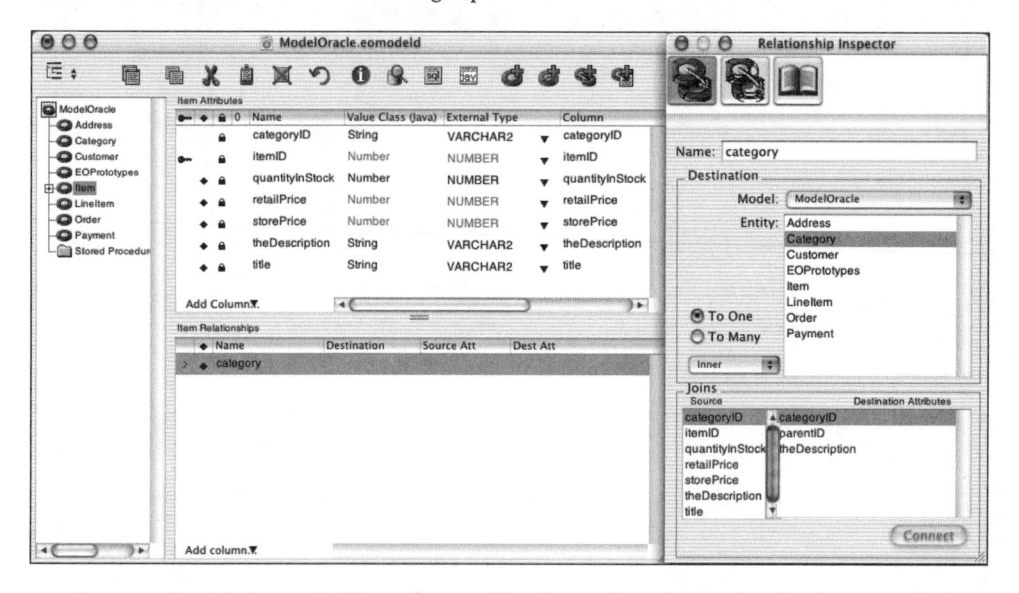

- **Name** – Straightforward. This is how we'll refer to the relationship. In the example above we call it `category` because this is the entity we will relate to `Item`.

- **Destination** – In the `Entity` list, choose the name of the destination entity, `Category`. You should indicate using the radio buttons whether this is a **To One** or a **To Many** relationship. An item must have exactly one category, so we choose **To One**. You should note that we can have more than one model in our project, forming a group of models. Each model can have its own settings, possibly connecting to heterogeneous databases (there are some restrictions on this though, as we will see later). If there are several models available, we must select the appropriate model containing the entity we wish to relate to.

- **Joins** – Here, you indicate which attributes bind the two entities. This will be used later in the SQL joins that EOF will send to the database. The button in the bottom toggles between `Connect` and `Disconnect`. You can bind more than one key in the source entity with the corresponding keys in the destination entity, if you have compound keys. In our example, we'll bind `Items`'s foreign key, `categoryID`, with `Category`'s primary key, `categoryID`.

There are other more advanced options available in the **Advanced Relationship Inspector**. We'll analyze those in the *Advanced Relationship Properties* section in Chapter 6.

To include the remaining relationships of the model of our sample application, use the figure shown in the earlier section on *Using the EOModeler Tool*. It lists all relationships of the model, with their names. Each directed arrow goes from the source to the destination entity. Arrows with a single ending denote a to-one relationship and those with a double ending denote a one-to-many relationship.

With all the entities, attributes and relationships, we have built a complete model. In Chapter 6, in the *Stored Procedures* section, we'll also include stored procedures. But at this point, the first version of the model is complete. You can also download the completed model along with other resources from http://www.wrox.com.

Relationships in the model express the normal association that exists between the existing objects in the real world. At runtime, the Enterprise Objects and their relationships will form a web, or a graph of interconnected Java objects. In the example above, the relationship represents the fact that an Item belongs to one Category. Similarly, in our Java code, we'll be able to access a Category object from an Item object.

Modeling an Existing Database

WebObjects projects ususally have to use existing databases. EOModeler allows us to reverse engineer a database schema, and generates a basic model for us to start with. Having the basic model generated, we are then able to refine it. This saves time and is particularly useful in the beginning of a project. The set of dialogs with this functionality is called the New Model Wizard. In this section, we'll see how to reverse engineer a schema generated by our own model in Oracle, so that we can compare the original model we created with the one the wizard generates.

To start the wizard, choose **Model | New** from the menu. Choose the JDBC adaptor, and enter the JDBC connection details. We'll leave all options checked in the next wizard to see their functionality. The next dialog shows a list of tables that are about to be imported to the model. At the end of the process, the wizard will create one entity per table selected.

The wizard beautifies the names for entities and attributes, based on those in the database. The next set of dialogs may or may not appear, depending on the database used and on the table structures. At this stage, the wizard finds the primary keys for each entity, looking at the definition of the tables. In our case, the wizard passes directly to the next set of dialogs, as it automatically finds keys for all entities. But if an entity didn't have primary keys defined in the database, it would prompt us to assign a primary key, listing the attributes. Next, the wizard defines the relationships between the entities. It will probe the database, looking for integrity constraints and keys. It will then ask for more details on one-to-many relationships. The next dialog shows a series of screens asking details about Tcategory's titems array and so on. You should select the **Cascade** option, this is where when a category is deleted, EOF also deletes all the items that belong to it. Finally, the wizard will probe the database, retrieving the stored procedure names. It will ask which stored procedures to include in the model.

The wizard then builds the model for us, based on the options chosen. Here is the generated model, with its `Titem` entity selected:

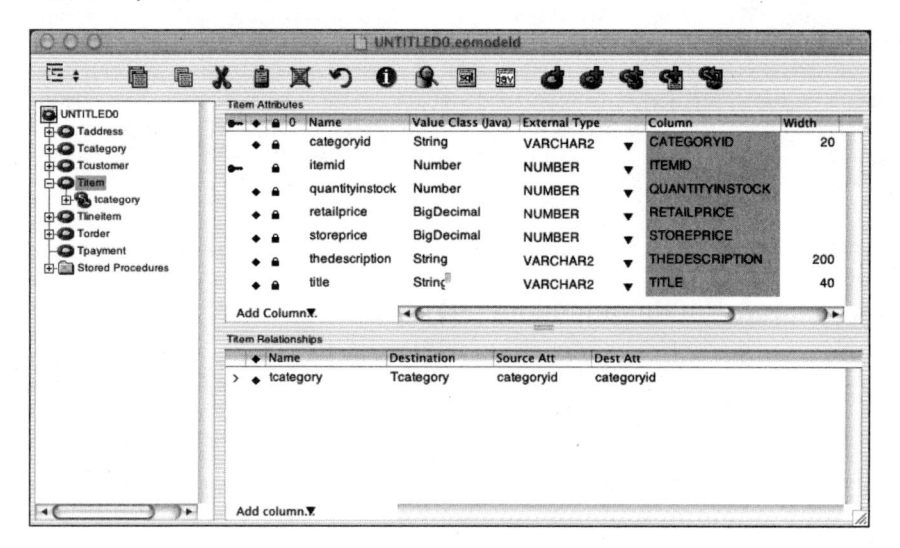

We can see that EOModeler was able to create a model very similar to the one created before. Some relationships are missing, like the ones we had between `Customer` and `Address`, and you may want to include such relationships afterward, according to the needs of the application. The stored procedures are also included, and deserve little or no modifications.

The New Model Wizard allows us to quickly create a model based on an existing database schema. This way we can start working on a model that has most of the information already in it, saving us time especially in the beginning of projects.

Summary

EOModeler is the visual tool that creates and defines the mapping between the database and the WebObjects applications. Using entities, attributes, and relationships, we can create a model that allows us to abstract the details of the database, including connection and other implementation details related to data modifications, while still leveraging the indispensable services offered by databases. EOModeler is capable of generating Java classes, or more specifically, Enterprise Object classes, to represent and manipulate this data. Throughout this chapter, we presented and analyzed the requirements of an online e-commerce store and created a model that is capable of supporting its implementation.

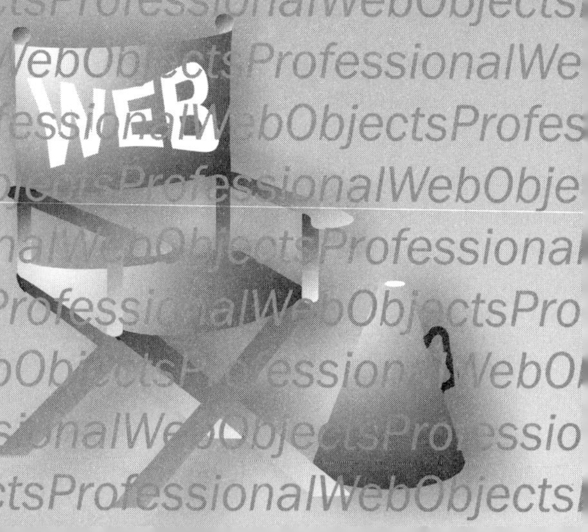
WEB

6

Advanced EOModeler

In the last chapter we created a model from scratch using EOModeler. In this chapter, we will use this model to illustrate some of the more advanced concepts of EOModeler. Also, we will build on some of the things learned in earlier chapters and create a simple project at the end of the chapter using WOBuilder and Project Builder to illustrate how to use Display Groups.

- ❑ We will generate Java files from the entities in the model
- ❑ We will create a database using our model
- ❑ Learn how to synchronize the model with the database
- ❑ We will mention how the model is used with multiple databases
- ❑ How to change the JDBC connection dynamically
- ❑ We will get Advanced Inspectors for entities, attributes, and relationships
- ❑ Then we will go through a tour how to use Display Groups
- ❑ Finally we will see a how stored procedures and functions are handled in EOModeler

Transforming the Model into Java Code

Now that we have a model that maps database structures to objects, we can utilize it in our Java code. Each entity, as we have seen, maps to one Java class. This Java class will represent the data from the database. It gives us the power to manipulate objects without worrying about the underlying details of the database, such as SQL statements or transactions. To the objects of this class, which represents an entity, we give the special name of Enterprise Objects, also referred to in the literature as EOs. Enterprise Objects are important objects, as they hold data and may incorporate other custom business methods, created by us.

Chapter 6

Generating EO Classes

The default Enterprise Object class in EOModeler is `EOGenericRecord`. `EOGenericRecord` is a simple and useful class that allows us to read and manipulate data from the database. But to incorporate our own business rules, like validation, constraints, and initialization, we may want to use our own Java classes. EOModeler allows us to generate customizable Java classes to hold Enterprise Objects. The generated class contains support for accessing attributes and relationships. In Chapter 9, we'll discuss the benefits of using this Java class, and when to use an `EOGenericRecord` or a custom class.

To generate a Java class for an entity, select the entity and choose **Property | Generate Java Files** from the menu, or click on the icon labeled jav. If the default class, `EOGenericRecord`, was previously assigned, EOModeler will suggest a class name.

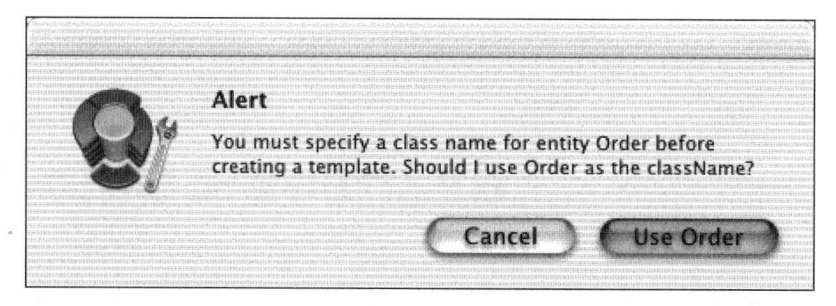

Alert

You must specify a class name for entity Order before creating a template. Should I use Order as the className?

[Cancel] [Use Order]

If the model is in an application, EOModeler will ask you if you want to insert the Java file in the project. If the class already exists, EOModeler will ask you if you want to overwrite it or merge its content with the new one. The contents of the class will be derived from the entity's definition in your model and a template file., probably `EOJavaClass` template, (although this depends upon the project type). This file should be located in `Supporting Files` on `Windows` in your project. Here's the `Order.java` file, generated from the `Order` entity:

```java
// Order.java
// Created on Thu Aug 23 05:52:38  2001 by Apple EOModeler Version 5.0

import java.math.*;
import java.util.*;
import com.webobjects.foundation.*;
import com.webobjects.eocontrol.*;

public class Order extends EOGenericRecord {

  public Order() {
    super();
  }

  /*
  // If you implement the following constructor EOF will use it to
  // create your objects, otherwise it will use the default
  // constructor. For maximum performance, you should only
  // implement this constructor if you depend on the arguments.

  public Order(EOEditingContext context,
               EOClassDescription classDesc,
               EOGlobalID gid) {
```

Advanced EOModeler

```
      super(context, classDesc, gid);
  }

  // If you add instance variables to store property values you
  // should add empty implementations of the Serialization methods
  // to avoid unnecessary overhead (the properties will be
  // serialized for you in the superclass).
  private void writeObject(java.io.ObjectOutputStream out)
              throws java.io.IOException {
  }

  private void readObject(java.io.ObjectInputStream in)
              throws java.io.IOException,
                     java.lang.ClassNotFoundException {
  }
  */

  public NSTimestamp theDate() {
    return (NSTimestamp)storedValueForKey("theDate");
  }

  public void setTheDate(NSTimestamp value) {
    takeStoredValueForKey(value, "theDate");
  }
}
```

The class declaration shows that it extends `EOGenericRecord`. This implements the `EOEnterpriseObject` interface, and allows our Java code to access the attributes and relationships of an entity. It can be used with any entity. Besides the constructor, the `Order` entity has two accessor methods for the `theDate` attribute.

You can customize the template if you want to change the format of the Java classes for all entities that are generated. You can include the following snippet of code in the template to generate a `toString()` method in your Enterprise Objects. The `toString()` method is called by the Java runtime in implicit conversions of objects into a `String`. It can be very handy for debugging. Include it just before the final brackets of the file, and after the `##end` line.

```
  public String toString() {
    return "$entity.classNameWithoutPackage$ [" +
        ##loop $entity.classAttributes$
        " $property.name$:" + $property.name$() +
        ##end
        "]";
  }
```

This portion of the template is instructing EOModeler to loop through the class attributes and substituting their names inside the string. This is the method generated for the `Order` class, in `Order.java`:

```
  public String toString() {
    return "Order [" + " theDate:" + theDate() + "]";
  }
```

You don't need to change the default class, `EOGenericRecord`, until you need to add extra business logic to the entity. Common cases of entities that use `EOGenericRecord` are join tables, which shouldn't have any class properties. However, in many cases we do generate custom classes for entities. It allows us to easily use objects to manipulate our data, abstracting the database layer. Creating and using custom classes is a powerful and commonly used feature of WebObjects.

Some Database Topics

On the other side of the bridge, there's the database. In the next sections, we'll look at some topics related to the database. It will help us know the capabilities that EOModeler has for manipulating the database schema at design time. It will also help us understand how EOF uses the model at runtime to interact to the database, and why should we care about that when building the model.

We begin by looking at EOModeler's process of SQL generation for creating the database and tables. After that, we look at synchronization, when EOModeler applies model changes to the database and imports database changes with the model.

The Generated SQL Script

EOModeler was not designed as a tool to maintain the database schema. However, EOModeler is able to generate scripts to manipulate the database schema, taking the model definition. EOModeler can create the database, tables, integrity constraints, and primary key support. The SQL is generated with the help of the JDBC adaptor and plugin. To generate SQL scripts for an entity, select it and select **Property | Generate SQL** from the menu, or click in the icon with the label **sql**. To generate a SQL script for all entities, select in any view mode the root of the model. It is labeled after the name of the model. A new window will appear, similar to the following:

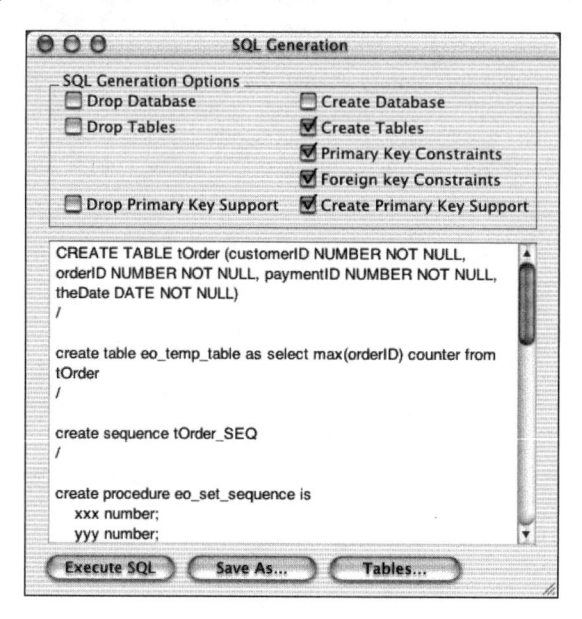

Advanced EOModeler

Not all options are available for all databases, and the SQL generated varies from database to database. In this case, the Order entity was selected, using Oracle as the database.

The first part of the window contains selectable options for the SQL generation. The read-only text area shows the SQL generated and the **Execute SQL** button performs the SQL statements shown against the database. Using the Model that we have created we can select the whole model, generate the SQL for it and then execute it to create the tables and relationships in the database. To populate the database there will be scripts available in the code download or you can create your own sample data in the database.

Be careful with the **Drop Database** and **Drop Tables** options; they drop the table structures and the data. If any error occurs, dialog boxes will report it, including the database error code. There are no dialogs after a successful execution of the SQL script. The **Save As...** button exports the SQL script shown to a file, which can be used later to execute the statements using another tool. The **Tables...** button allows you to select the tables to be used.

Do not choose to *generate* SQL for entities that map to views or aliases. In this case, EOModeler won't know that it isn't a table, and will generate SQL statements to create a table with the same name provided for the entity. Unfortunately, for views we have to have SQL scripts which create them separately. But this is a problem just related to SQL which is generated. There is no problem *mapping* an entity to a view, or a table alias.

The statement:

```
CREATE SEQUENCE tOrder_SEQ
/
```

creates a sequence that is used in the primary key generation mechanism in Oracle. This is one of the customizations of the Oracle plugin. The default plugin uses a table called `EO_PK_TABLE` for the same functionality.

Here is an example of an Oracle referential integrity constraint, generated with the **Foreign Key Constraints** option checked:

```
ALTER TABLE tLineItem ADD CONSTRAINT tLineItem_order_FK FOREIGN KEY (orderID)
REFERENCES tOrder (orderID)
/
```

The SQL statement indicates that for all rows in the `tLineItem` table, at any time, the value of the `orderID` column must match an existing `orderID` value in the `tOrder` table. According to the statement's syntax, the rule will be enforced for each statement within a transaction. Referential integrity constraints are only generated when there is a to-one relationship from one entity to another, and a to-many relationship in the other direction. You may want to include other integrity constraints in the database not generated by EOModeler using another tool. Be advised that you may have to *defer* the time when the database checks the constraints because of EOF. When EOF has two new rows to insert, or a new row and an UPDATE to perform, it will try to order the operations based on the relationship, so that rows with no dependencies are inserted first. However, this is not always possible. The following syntax:

```
ALTER TABLE x ADD CONSTRAINT x_y_fk FOREIGN KEY (ID) REFERENCES y (ID) DEFERRABLE
INITIALLY DEFERRED
/
```

will instruct Oracle to postpone the referential integrity check until a transaction commits. This way, the data will be consistent, regardless of the order EOF uses to insert new rows.

The developers can save the script generated, and run it together with other scripts that set extra database detail. These other scripts commonly include extra referential integrity constraints, indexes for performance, create views, and populate tables with initial values or testing values. If the definitions wanted and the SQL generated are so different then we may want to just ignore the latter. The decision will depend on the complexity of the database schema and how similar the SQL generated is to the SQL needed to create the schema.

Synchronization

EOModeler allows you to synchronize your model with the contents in the database. Synchronization allows us to import new database tables or columns into the model, and create new tables or columns in the database that exist only in the model. It can be useful when changes are introduced to the model or the database, and there's the need to merge the structures.

The model created by EOModeler is not only used to create Java Enterprise Objects, but is also referenced at runtime by the EOF in the various database operations. It is important, for this reason, to keep both database structure and model synchronized. If your model has attributes or tables that don't exist in the database, you'll have problems. The contrary is fine, if the database has other tables or attributes not present in the model, there should be no problem.

When it comes to attribute definitions different from column definitions, behaviors change from case to case. The adaptor will try to convert different types, and you may get either an exception or the value converted to the right type. In Oracle, if your column is a NUMBER, and your attribute in EOModeler lists VARCHAR2 as the External Type and Number as the Value Class, the adaptor will do the conversion for you. However, if EOModeler has an attribute of External Type NUMBER and the database column is defined as VARCHAR2, containing non-numerical values, you will get an exception from the adaptor. This is the reason to try and have the attribute and column definitions synchronized.

Suppose that you delete, intentionally or accidentally, the `Order` and `Payment` entities from the model, and that a new table, `tUndesired`, is created directly in the database. We would then have three unreferenced tables in the database. You can also have a new entity bound to a table that doesn't exist yet in the database. The figure on the right shows this scenario; you can compare your model with the database tables using **Model | Schema Synchronization**. The database has three tables, `TORDER`, `TPAYMENT`, and `TUNDESIRED` that aren't in the model, and the model has a new entity, `newTable`, bound to `tNewTable`.

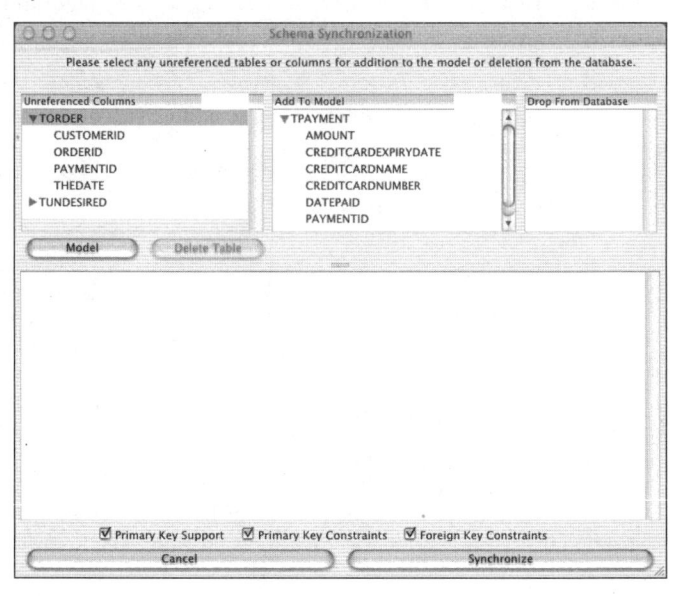

All the columns of the `TPAYMENT` table, from the selections in the figure, are to be added to the model. The new table, `newTable`, is about to be created in the database, the text area shows. You can select the tables to be included in the model from the **Unreferenced Columns** pane. These tables will then be listed in the second pane, **Add To Model**. The lower pane lists SQL statements for the creation and support of new entities that don't exist in the database yet. The **Synchronize** button triggers the synchronization process.

Multiple Databases

In a project, you may want to implement database load balancing to enhance the performance of an application. By distributing the tasks among different databases, you achieve real parallelism and enhance the overall throughput in database operations. Other times, you may want to reuse existing databases that already have a schema defined and hold production data. Whatever is the reason, our applications may need to access different and perhaps heterogeneous databases. How do we model that? We include more than one model in the application, each of which connect to a different database:

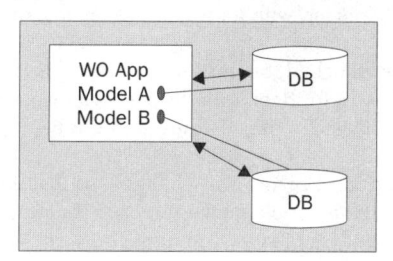

```
WO App
Model A ●────► DB
Model B ●
         ────► DB
```

`com.webobjects.eoaccess.EOModelGroup` is the class that aggregates the models an application references. You can even have relationships between entities in separate models, as we have seen in the **Relationship Inspector** tool.

You do have one limitation in this organization: EOF isn't designed to support distributed transactions. It ensures the atomicity of the transactions for one database. It transparently manages `BEGIN TRANSACTION`s, `COMMIT`s, and `ROLLBACK`s on your behalf for one database. It even uses the JDBC 2.0 API, which supports distributed transactions in its embedded JDBC 2.0 Optional Package API. However, it is not designed to coordinate distributed transactions among different databases. An `EOEditingContext` object, whose class is part of EOF, doesn't even know from which database each Enterprise Object in its object graph comes from. The options are:

- ❑ Not to involve Enterprise Objects from different databases in the same transaction.
- ❑ To integrate EOF with a TP Monitor.
- ❑ To use only one model instead of two, connecting to one database that has database links. You can then delegate the management of the distributed transactions to the database server, which must implement the feature.
- ❑ To code your own transaction management. Depending on the characteristics of the application, like concurrency level, performance requirements, and undo requirements, this option varies from a simple to a very complex task.
- ❑ To live with the risk of inconsistent data, and implement some compensatory process for recovery.

The option that you choose will depend on the characteristics of your application and the database server capabilities. If you are defining the architecture of the databases during the development process, you may want to partition the tables between the servers, having tables that participate in the same transactions residing in the same database. That way, you'll avoid the overhead of distributed transactions, while improving the performance with load balance. However, if you have to use existing databases, you may want to consider the option where you can create database links and delegate the management of distributed transactions to the database server.

Chapter 6

Runtime Connections To the Database

When an application starts, EOF parses the model files and maintains all the model definitions in memory. This gives us the capability of accessing and changing the model programmatically at runtime. One such example is if you want to override the JDBC URL defined in EOModeler at runtime (this is shown in the following code), and thereby switching between development, test, and production databases based on the name of the computer where the application is deployed, or a configuration file. The information available is not limited to just the database connection. We have access to all the model definitions programmatically. This allows us to combine the model definition, built with EOModeler, with information available only at runtime.

When a WebObjects application is launched, the instance is loaded into the JVM, but a database connection is established *only* when the first request for data is made. This way we can change the connection definition, so that when the connection is established, it uses the new definition.

In the following example, `Application.java` was changed, so that it dynamically changes the JDBC URL of the database connection. To test the example, make sure that the model is included in the **resources** folder of the project, and change `Application.java`. You may also want to change the `newURL` variable.

```
import com.webobjects.eoaccess.*;
import com.webobjects.eocontrol.*;
import com.webobjects.foundation.*;
import com.webobjects.appserver.*;

public class Application extends WOApplication {
  String newURL = "jdbc:openbase://127.0.0.1/anotherDatabase";

  public static void main(String argv[]) {
    WOApplication.main(argv, Application.class);
  }

  public Application() {
    super();

    // enable SQL debugging
    NSLog.allowDebugLoggingForGroups(NSLog.DebugGroupSQLGeneration);
    NSLog.allowDebugLoggingForGroups(NSLog.DebugGroupDatabaseAccess);

    // change database connection
    changeDatabaseConnectionInfo();

    // fetch items
    NSArray items =
      EOUtilities.objectsForEntityNamed(new EOEditingContext(), "Item");

    // do something with items
  }

  private void changeDatabaseConnectionInfo() {
    // Our model
    EOModel model;
```

Advanced EOModeler

```
        // The connection definition
        NSMutableDictionary dictionary;

        // retrieve the model group
        EOModelGroup group = EOUtilities.modelGroup(new EOEditingContext());

        // retrieve the current model
        model = group.modelNamed("ModelOB");
        dictionary = new NSMutableDictionary(model.connectionDictionary());

        // assuming newURL already exist
        dictionary.setObjectForKey(newURL, "URL");

        // set new connection information
        model.setConnectionDictionary(dictionary);
    }
}
```

The `changeDatabaseConnectionInfo()` method begins accessing the model group using `EOUtilities'` `modelGroup()` method:

```
EOModelGroup group = EOUtilities.modelGroup(new EOEditingContext());
```

Next, it retrieves the EOModel object, referencing the model by name:

```
model = group.modelNamed("ModelOB");
```

The connection dictionary, containing the username, password, and URL, is retrieved next:

```
dictionary = new NSMutableDictionary(model.connectionDictionary());
```

After changing the URL information in `dictionary`, the new connection information is changed in the model:

```
model.setConnectionDictionary(dictionary);
```

When `EOUtilities'` `objectsForEntityNamed()` method is called here, it retrieves all the categories using the new JDBC URL.

The EOF maintains one connection to the database per application by default. The connection information, (database) user, password, and database definitions are stored in a dictionary objects that resides in the model. All user sessions share that same database connection and consequently the same connection dictionary.

That is relevant from the database perspective, as, by default, the privileges granted and restrictions applied to this user will also apply to the operations requested by all sessions. The fact that all users share a single connection means that there is the possibility of a bottleneck.

Creating multiple users and having multiple connections can avoid this problem. This must be achieved programmatically, though, creating connections within the application.

Chapter 6

Advanced Modeling Concepts

In the next sections we'll be looking into some advanced modeling concepts of EOModeler. We will look at the options made available to use through EOModelers Inspectors. The options related to entities, attributes, and relationships are mainly related to the behavior of EOF. Some concepts are not actually very complex. One example is that the advanced options of an attribute allow us set `null` values. Some other subjects, like faulting and inheritance, are expanded later in the book. The intent is for us to get familiar with the advanced options available in EOModeler, and to know how they influence EOF's behavior.

Advanced Entity Properties

Let's look at some of the advanced configuration settings available to us in the entity inspector. Select the `Category` entity and click in the second icon in the Entity Inspector toolbar. It takes you to the Advanced Entity Inspector:

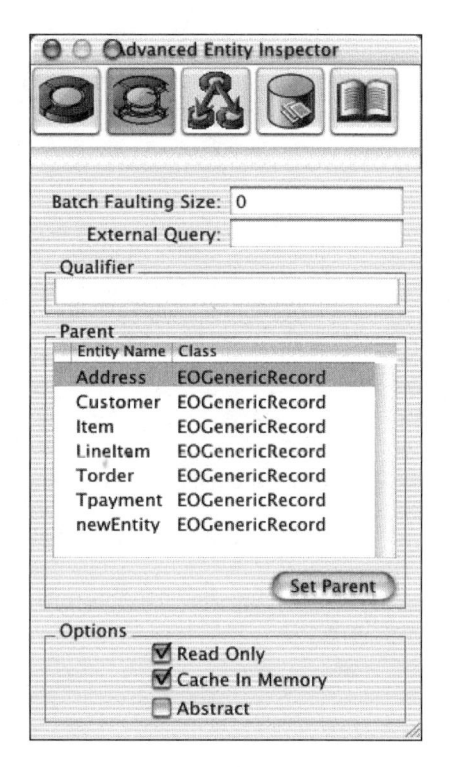

We will now go through all the options to see how we can configure them.

External Query

You can override EOF's SQL statement which is used to select rows for this entity. The EOAccess layer in EOF, by default, generates all expressions sent to the database, considering the set of attributes. This field allows you to set your own SQL, and have the database evaluate the `SELECT` statement. The number of columns selected must match the number of attributes in the entity. The types returned from each expression in the `SELECT` statement defined here must match the external types of the attributes. The order of the attributes in the entity (sorted by name) must match the order of the expressions in the `SELECT` statement. You can also use this feature to filter the entities, including a `SELECT` statement with a `WHERE` clause. We could include a `level` attribute of type `integer` in the `Category` entity to represent the level of the category in the hierarchy. Then in OpenBase, we would set this option to:

Advanced EOModeler

```
SELECT t0.categoryID, (length(t0.categoryID)+1)/2, t0.theDescription, t0.parentID
FROM tCategory t0
```

where `level` corresponds to the second expression, evaluating to an `int`. `level`'s expression which, in this case, is based on `categoryID`'s format. Level one categories have `categoryID`s like 1 and 2, and level two have 1.1, 1.2, and so forth. When browsing data, we can see the values of the new `level` attribute.

This feature may be useful if you want to represent an attribute using expressions, or database-specific features, such as functions. However, it is better to use qualifiers (see below) when database-specific features are not needed. We'll leave this field blank for the `Category` entity.

Qualifier

A qualifier allows you to restrict the set of rows returned from the database using a simple and database-independent language. If you wanted the `Category` entity to not contain root nodes from the tree of categories, you could set the qualifier like this:

```
categoryID != parentID
```

You can easily test your qualifiers before compiling and running your application using the Data Browser tool, previously shown in the *Using the EOModeler Tool* section. This is particularly useful if you are not yet familiar with the expressions and operators used in qualifiers. We'll leave the default value for the qualifier in `Category`: blank.

Options

The **Read-only** option disables any changes to Enterprise Objects associated with this entity. If you try to save an object of a read-only entity, EOF will throw an exception. **Cache in Memory** will make EOF fetch *all* rows from the database upon the first access to an instance of this entity. EOF will then store all these instances in memory, in an attempt to improve performance and avoid other fetches. This option is not creating a new layer of cached objects; it's just informing EOF that it should fetch all rows upon the first access. Since all rows are kept in memory until garbage collection, this option is only recommended for tables with few records in the database and that are referenced a lot in the application. This is the case with the `Category` entity, so we check this option.

Batch Faulting Size

At runtime, when you fetch data from the database for this entity, EOF populates some Java objects with data, but not the objects in the relationships. Instead, EOF substitutes the real data with special objects called faults. Faults are objects that don't carry data, but rather point to some data in the database. Using faults, EOF knows how to fetch data for the relationships too; it's just a matter of sending another SELECT statement with a join to the database. However, EOF will only fetch the data from the database for the relationships when the application requests it. This option controls the number of substitution of faults for real data, for faults that reference this entity. The **Cache in Memory** option overrides this setting, like in the case of `Category`. We'll leave the default value zero (no batch faulting). It has no effect in this case.

Chapter 6

Parent area

The **Parent** area allows you to set a parent entity for this entity, building inheritance. EOF supports entity inheritance, where the attributes of a parent entity are available to the sub-entity. Our `Item` entity could be the parent of two other sub-entities, `OEM` and `Merchandise`. `OEM` and `Merchandise` would, then, mark `Item` as the parent entity. `Item` would then be marked as an abstract entity by checking the **Abstract** checkbox. Using the mapping definition of relational structures to object-oriented structures (Java classes), EOF allows one entity to *inherit* from another entity, allowing us to profit from this fundamental and powerful object-oriented concept. EOF inheritance allows many different setups, each with its advantages and disadvantages. In three different approaches, each entity maps to a different table in a normalized schema, or all entities map to one single table, or all the sub-entities map to one table, with the parent entity not mapping to any table. `Category` won't have any parent entity set.

Advanced Attribute Properties

Clicking on the second icon in the toolbar of the **Attribute Inspector** takes us to the **Advanced Attribute Inspector** window. Here we can set three options, related to changes to the attributes values, optionality, and custom formatting. The options are not very complex, and are often used. Here is the window for the `parentID` attribute in the `Category` entity:

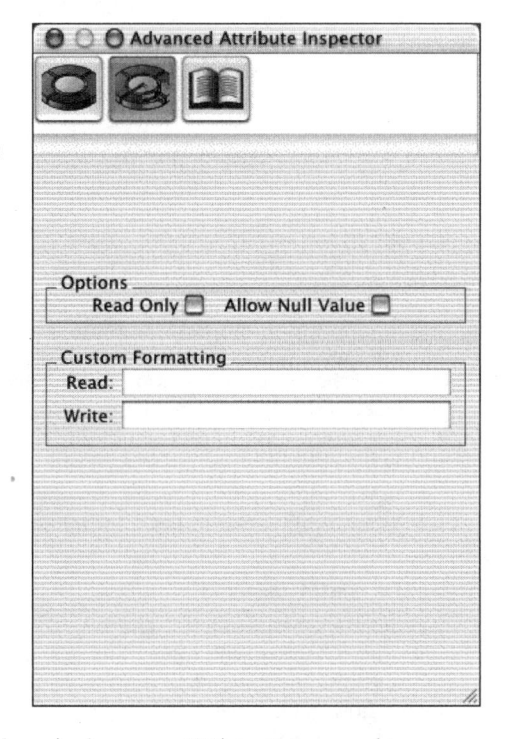

- ❑ **Read Only** – Check this option if your attribute doesn't change or if it's not supposed to change. This option will later on allow the EOF to validate the data in Enterprise Objects, preventing this attribute changing its value. If the application tries to save changes and some attributes marked as read-only changed in memory, EOF won't save the changes to the database, and will report the fact to the application by throwing an exception. We'll leave this option unchecked, as the whole entity is already marked as read-only, and it isn't necessary to mark its attributes individually again.

- **Allow Null Value** – Check this option if this attribute is optional; in other words it can take a `null` value. Otherwise, leave it unchecked. Set this option to carry the same definition of the column in the database. Primary keys should never allow `null` values, because they uniquely identify rows. There would be no way to differentiate two rows with `null`s in their primary keys. If this option is checked and the particular field or expression in the database evaluates to `null`, EOF will provide a `null` value to whatever is accessing this attribute, whether your Java code or the user interface. The column labeled '0', shown in the table view mode, represents the option. This option also will be used by EOF in blocks of code like the following:

```
try {
  session().defaultEditingContext().saveChanges();
  setUserMessage("Changes saved");
} catch (Exception exception) {
```

  This code is saving any changes performed on Enterprise Objects, bound to entities. At runtime, just before saving changes to the database, EOF will validate the state of all Enterprise Objects that have changed, including checking for `null`s when `null`s are not allowed, and signal any problems by throwing exceptions. In the code snippet, if no exception occurs during the save, a method is called to inform the User Interface that the changes were performed. The `catch` block will be able to report to the user any problems that may have occurred during the save attempt. The `parentID` attribute will have `null` values for "root" categories, that is, the least specialized categories. So we'll check the option in the window.

- **Custom Formatting** – You can define two expressions here, one for reading from and another one for writing the attribute value to the database. They allow you to manipulate and modify the attribute value being written to and being read from the database. It can be applied to some transformations that can be expressed by simple expressions, like transforming units of measurement. The expressions can include any type, provided they evaluate to the attribute types. But in practice, these two fields are rarely used. The evaluation of the expressions is performed by the database, and not EOF. In other words, it consumes CPU time in the database, not in WebObject's server. Let's suppose that you want to store weather temperatures in Fahrenheit in the database, but you want your Java class and User Interface to handle the values as Celsius. You could set the following:

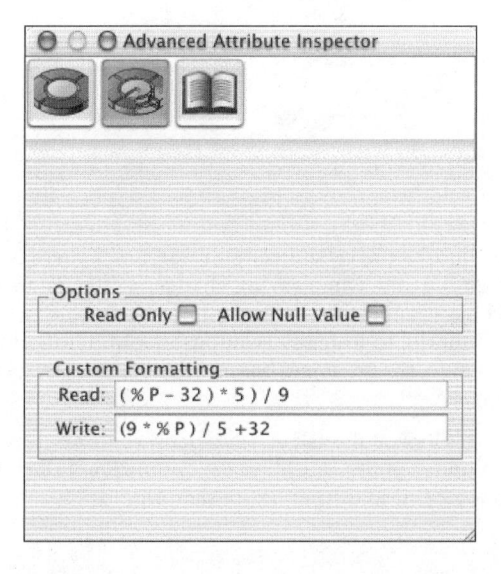

```
Advanced Attribute Inspector

Options
  Read Only []   Allow Null Value []

Custom Formatting
  Read:  ( % P - 32 ) * 5 ) / 9
  Write: (9 * % P ) / 5 +32
```

Note how you represent the attribute within the expression as `%P`. In terms of transparency and maintainability, though, it is better to include such transformations in the Java code generated by EOModeler. The `parentID` attribute won't use any custom formatting.

Clicking in the first icon of the dialog will take us back to the **Attribute Inspector**. There we inform the Java Class that will represent this attribute in our Java code. EOModeler allows us to use our own classes to represent the attributes. This is an alternative to changing the Enterprise Objects classes, when we have simple types of attributes that can be treated as a unit. Using our own custom classes allows us to write and use our own convenience methods. However, be careful not to abuse this option by storing complex structures just in one attribute.

Advanced Relationship Properties

To analyze other options available for relationships, we'll inspect the one-to-one relationship between `Item` and `Category`. Select the `category` relationship from the `Item` entity, and click on the **Inspector** icon in the toolbar. Next, select the second icon on the top part of the inspector window, which will take us to the **Advanced Relationship Inspector**:

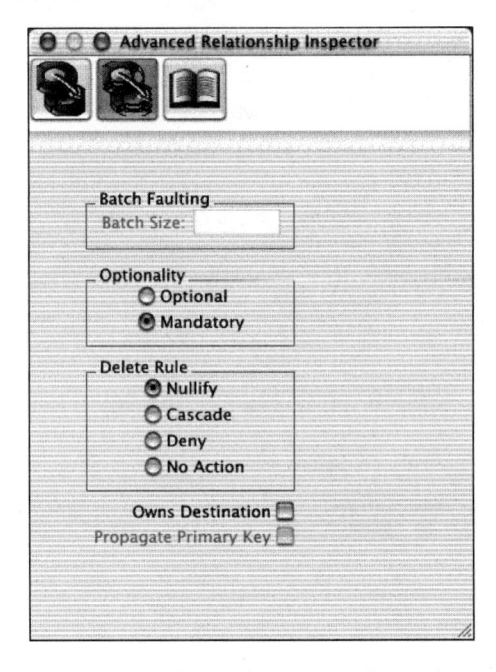

- **Optional** – You can enforce the relationship or not. Since there is a mandatory relationship between `Item` and `Category`, when saving changes to the database at runtime, the EOF will check if each object based on the `Item` entity references exactly one other object based on the `Category` entity. Similarly, in to-many relationships EOF will check if each object based on the source entity has at least one object based on the destination entity.

To analyze the other options, let's look at the relationship between `Category` and `Item`, this is a to-many relationship. `Category` is the source entity and `Item` the destination. Select the relationship and select the **Advanced Relationship Inspector**, as in the previous example.

Advanced EOModeler

- **Batch Faulting** – The batch size specifies the number of to-many relationship faults to resolve, that is, to convert to real data, when one relationship fault is resolved. Like the case of faulting for entities, the option can improve performance by converting faults into objects, hoping that the application will use references to these objects in the future. Again, more on faults will be covered soon.

- **Delete Rule** – When you delete an object of the source entity, what should happen to the objects of the destination entity? Putting the question in our context: when you delete a category, what should happen to its items? The answer depends on the requirements of the application. Let's look at each rule:

    Nullify – With this option, you just disassociate the objects of the destination entity from the object of the source entity being deleted. When deleting a category that has items, leave them all alone in the database, nullifying any foreign keys that reference the category. When selecting this option, the foreign keys must allow `nulls`.

    Cascade – When deleting a `category`, also delete its `items`. We'll choose this option.

    Deny – You are telling the EOF not to allow a category to be deleted if it has any associated item. If the application code tries to delete a category with items, notify it and refuse to delete the category.

    No Action – You are telling the EOF not to do any action with regard to the objects in this to-many relationship. You may choose this option for performance reasons; if you know that there are no objects in the relationship, there is no need to fire the faults. Or you may programmatically nullify back references to the source object being deleted. With this option, the application assumes the responsibility of satisfying integrity constraints.

The JDBC adaptor will issue DELETE FROM statements for each Enterprise Object being deleted when you save changes. Another common alternative to physical deletion of records is "logical deletion". One way to implement logical deletion is to have a "deleted" flag in the database table, and change it to `true` when deleting records. Then, you can build qualifiers in your code or even the model to exclude the logically deleted records. The logically deleted records will then still be available for reporting, or data mining.

- **Owns Destination** and **Propagate Primary Key** – When you flag a relationship saying that the source entity owns the destination, the removal of a destination object from the relationship implies the deletion of the source entity as well. Similarly, including an object in this relationship implies its insertion into the database. In other words, the destination object depends on the source object. If the destination objects don't exist independently from a source object in the database then check **Owns Destination** only. You can check the **Propagate Primary Key** option in a to-one relationship for an object of the source entity to propagate its primary key to the associated destination object. Usually when to-one relationships propagate primary keys, the source entity also owns the destination entity, and the relationship binds the primary key of the source entity to those of the destination entity. You may have an `Employee` entity that stores employee information, and an `EmployeePhoto` entity that stores employee photographs in binary form. Both would have the same primary key definition, `employeeID`, and the to-one relationship between `Employee` and `EmployeePhoto` would be checked to propagate the primary key. However, this not a very common scenario. The advantage of allowing the propagation of the primary key is that we don't need to provide new primary keys for the destination entity. When inserting new records, EOF takes care of the propagation of key from the source entity to the destination entity. We'll leave both options unchecked in our case.

In some cases, the entity can relate to itself. We say, then, that the relationship is a *reflexive* relationship. In our example, a category can contain other categories, and, for a given category, `parentID` references its parent category. Other examples could be an employee that has a manager, who also happens to be an employee. Here are the details of a reflexive to-many relationship named `children` in `Category`:

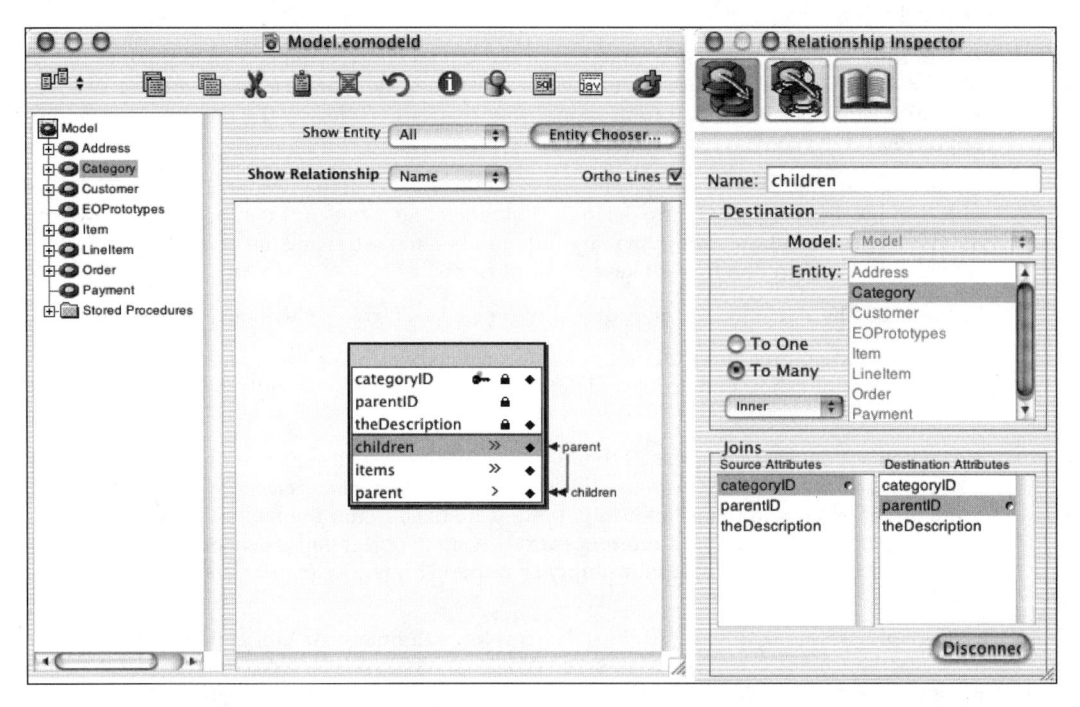

Note that the destination and source entities are the same, `Category`. There is another reflexive relationship in the other direction: the current category has a parent category. This relationship is a one-to-one reflexive relationship.

Flattening Many-to-Many Relationships

The `LineItem` entity in our example is binding one order to items, and one item to many orders. If it wasn't for the `quantity` attribute, it would be what is called a join table in a many-to-many relationship. Let's have an example of a join table. Suppose that in your application you have students and courses. A student can be enrolled in many courses and a course contains many students. Consider the following UML diagram:

The approach to model this in a database is to create a join table, say, STUDENTCOURSE, whose primary keys are also foreign keys to each table. This allows our tables to stay normalized. If we stored foreign keys directly in either table, that wouldn't be the case. Flattening consists of hiding the existence of the join table in our model. Flattening one-to-many relationships allows us to virtually ignore the join table in our code and User Interface, by creating direct to-many relationships on both sides. This will lead to a cleaner, more maintainable code, and a more elegant solution. In EOModeler, it would look like the following:

Advanced EOModeler

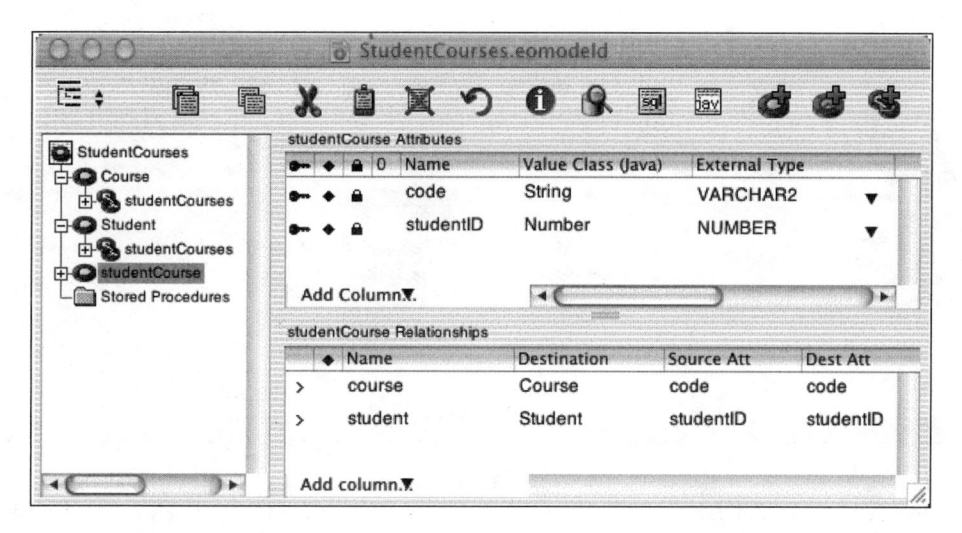

Course and Student have a one-to-many relationship with StudentCourse. StudentCourse has a one-to-one relationship with Student and another with Course. But the join table, StudentCourse, is more an implementation detail than an entity relevant to the application. It has no attributes of its own. We can flatten the relationships between Course and Student, and vice-versa, so that the Java code and the user interface will be able to virtually ignore the join entity. To make the list of courses directly accessible in the Student entity, we expand the StudentCourse relationship and highlight the Course relationship, as the figure below shows.

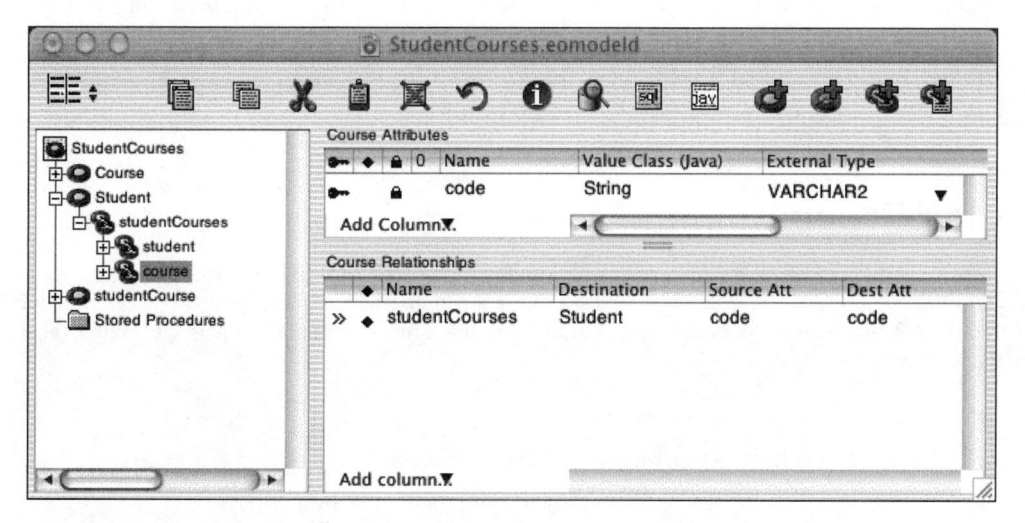

Then, choose Flatten Selected Property from the toolbar, or Property | Flatten Property from the menu. A new one-to-many relationship is created in the Student entity.

143

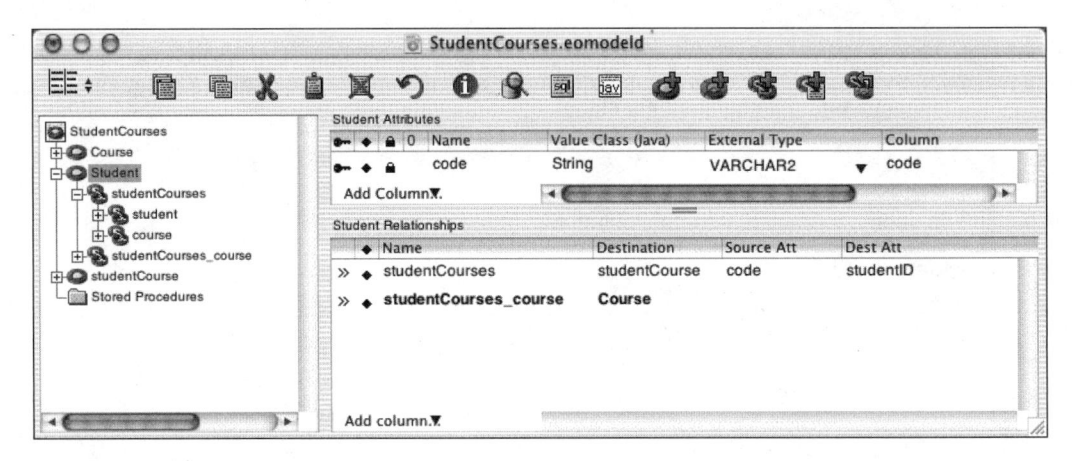

EOF will be able to seamlessly handle this flattened relationship as if it was a direct to-many relationship. It should handle changes, deletions and insertions, primary and foreign keys for you. However, it is highly advisable that you flatten relationships that serve just as join tables and don't carry any other attribute. That is why we can't flatten the relationships between `Order`, `LineItem`, and `Item` in our model.

EOModeler also allows the flattening of attributes of one entity into another. Instead of accessing an attribute of an entity that is accessible through a relationship, the attribute is flattened and made accessible in the current entity. Taking the `Item` entity for example, if we flattened the category's `theDescription` attribute into `Item`, the category's description information would be accessible directly in the `Item` entity. However, this feature is **discouraged**, because at runtime we end up with two Java objects representing the same attribute, and that can lead to data integrity problems. While you update one reference, the other remains unchanged. An alternative to flattening attributes is to customize the Java class generated by EOModeler, so that the accessor methods make use of the relationship. You are then able to access the attribute as if it belonged to the source entity.

Display Groups

There are certain functionalities that are very common across web applications, such as presenting a list of records, browsing through it, ordering it and searching through it with predetermined criteria. A Display Group is an object that can be easily used to implement these functionalities in a page. Its high-level set of methods allow you to:

- Fetch data from the database;
- Render the list in the User Interface, dividing it in batches;
- Build a page with Dynamic Elements and bind them to search criteria;

For pages that require these patterns, Display Groups are a good choice that can save you time and reduce the probability of bugs. A Display Group is an object of the class `com.webobjects.eointerface.EODisplayGroup`.

We will create a page where, on the right side of the page, the user can browse through a list of items using the **Previous** and **Next** hyperlinks. A button allows the user to order the item. To display the list of items we can use a Display Group. The list itself is supplied by the Display Group and is batched item per item. In the left side of the page, we have a list of categories, which doesn't use a Display Group, and is fetched in the page constructor.

Advanced EOModeler

The easiest way to create a Display Group is to drag an entity from EOModeler into your Component in WebObjects Builder, as the next figure shows:

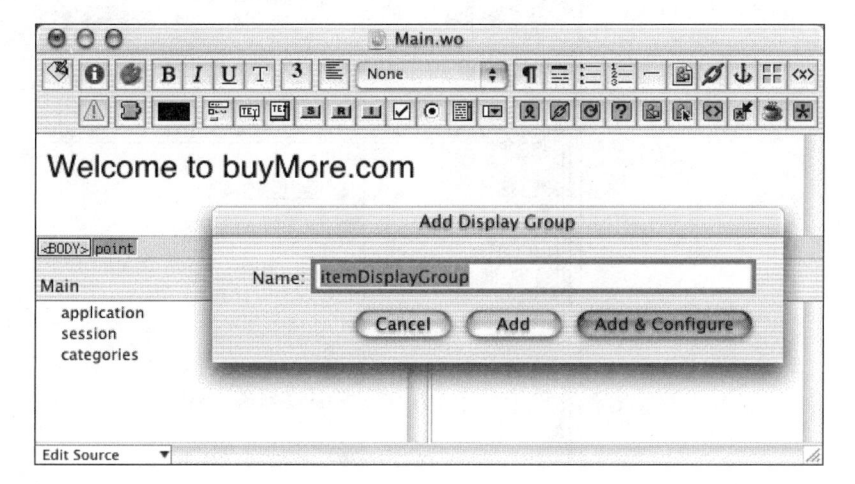

The entity that you drop into the Component is the base entity of the Display Group. In the configuration dialog, you can set the Display Group to use a master-detail setting. In our case, the `Item` entity is detailed, and its master entity is `Category`.

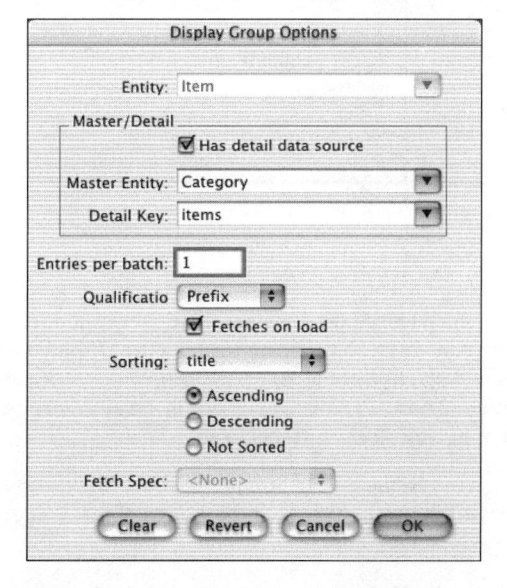

In **Entries per batch** you can specify how many `Items` will be displayed in the page at a time. The **Fetches on load** option makes the display group to automatically fetch data from its source when the page is loaded (checked), or to fetch data programmatically upon a call to the `fetch()` method (unchecked).

145

This figure shows the Main `WOComponent` in Layout View mode in the WebObjects Builder.

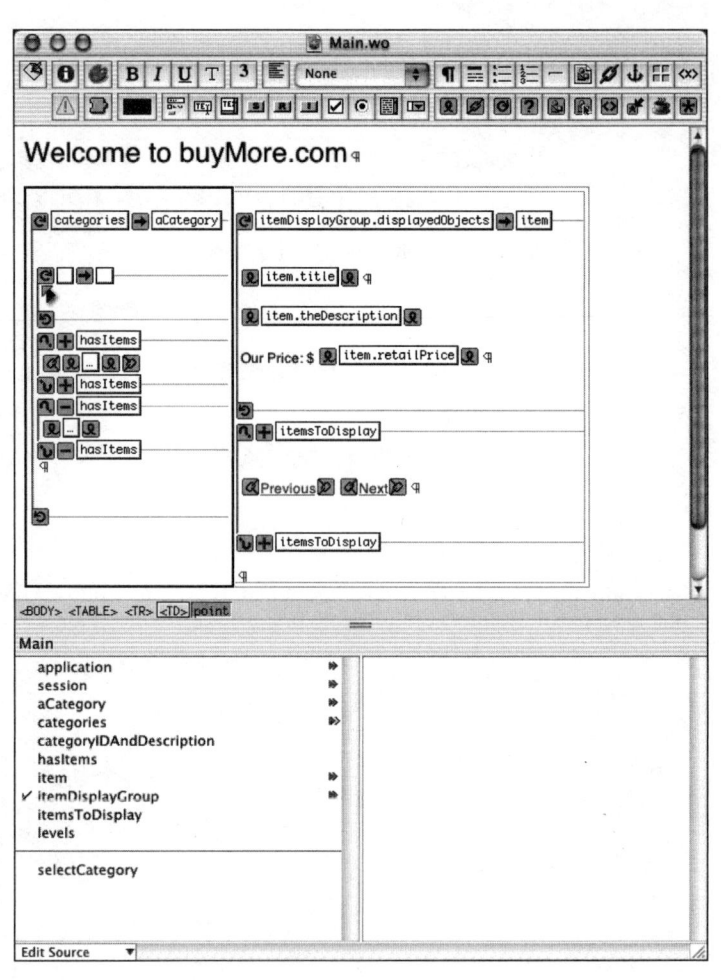

The second cell of the table in the page shows some common Dynamic Elements used in conjunction with Display Groups. We have a `WORepetition` looping through the Display Group's array of Enterprise Objects to be displayed, `itemDisplayGroup.displayedObjects`. It also has two hyperlinks, **Previous** and **Next**, with actions bound to `itemDisplayGroup.displayPreviousBatch` and `itemDisplayGroup.displayNextBatch` respectively.

When the user clicks on a category in the first cell of the table, set that `category` as the Master object of the Display Group. The Display Group will in turn fetch the `items` of that `category`. Here is the method bound to the `category` hyperlink:

```
/** The user selected a category */
WOComponent selectCategory() {

    // the master object is now the selected category
    itemDisplayGroup.setMasterObject(aCategory);

    // display the first item
    itemDisplayGroup.setCurrentBatchIndex(1);
    return null;
}
```

Stored Procedures and Functions

Stored procedures, as we have seen, are callable blocks of SQL statements that reside in the database, often precompiled for performance. While they encapsulate a group of queries and changes as a logical unit, they tend to mix application rules with the actual data. However, for a number of reasons, more than once we can have a situation where our WebObjects applications need to reuse legacy stored procedures.

Let's see, now, how we can use stored procedures in our model and code. Suppose that our client asks us to reuse a stored procedure that was used by the application being replaced by our WebObjects application. This existing stored procedure applies a discount to items that were not sold in the past thirty days.

Here is the script that creates the stored procedure in Oracle. If your database supports stored procedures, then create the procedure `apply_discount`. The syntax may need to be changed, depending on the database you are using, so refer to the documentation for more information on how stored procedures are treated:

```
CREATE OR REPLACE PROCEDURE apply_discount (
  discount     IN NUMBER
) AS
BEGIN
  update tItem set retailPrice = retailPrice / (1 + discount) ,
                  storePrice = storePrice / (1 + discount)
  where itemID in
    (select distinct itemID from tLineItem, tOrder
     where tOrder.orderID = tLineItem.orderID and theDate < sysdate-30);
END ;
```

One easy way to include an existing stored procedure in the model is to let EOModeler's wizard find it in the database and import its definition for us. However, in this example, we'll define the stored procedure ourselves. Select the **Stored Procedures** folder in EOModeler, and choose **Property | Add Stored Procedure** from the menu. A stored procedure called `StoredProcedure` will be created. Change its name to `applyDiscount`, and set the external name to `APPLY_DISCOUNT`.

You can now add arguments by choosing **Property | Add Argument** from the menu. Here is our stored procedure, taking a `Number` as an argument:

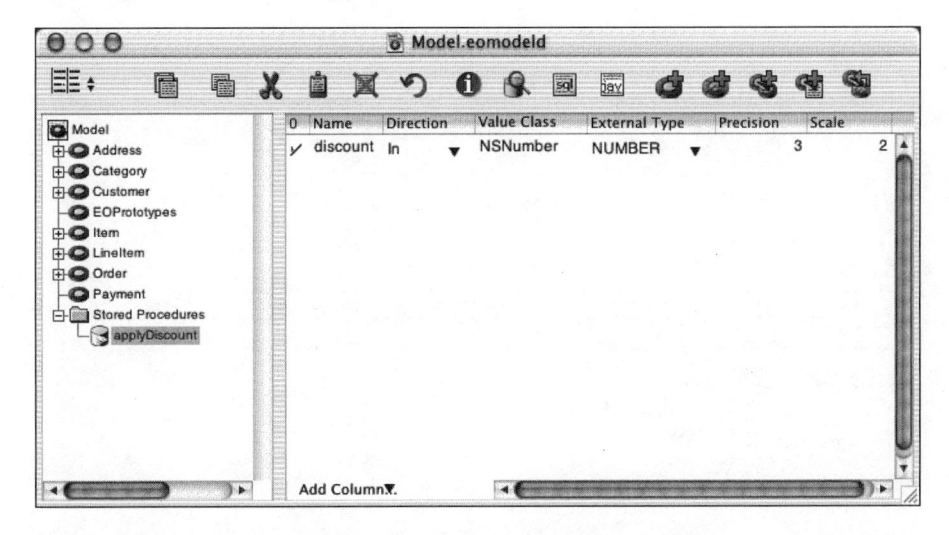

Chapter 6

The **Direction** column is from the database's point of view, `In` arguments are taken as input and `Out` arguments are returned by the stored procedure. `InOut` arguments are `In` and `Out` at the same time. It means that the stored procedure in the database expects the argument to provide input value, and the stored procedure also passes the value back to WebObjects using the same argument. The application passes values to the database, and reads the response using the same (one) attribute. In this example we have only one `In` argument, but we could have as many `In`, `Out`, and `InOut` arguments as we wanted.

You can select the argument and select the Inspector to view its details. You can have either names or numbers in the **Column** field. If you specify names, the order of the arguments is relevant. When the stored procedure is called, the arguments will be bound in the same order, which you specify in the model, regardless of the order that their names are declared in the stored procedure. As EOModeler sorts the arguments by name, you may want to rename them, or use numbers in the **Column** field. If you assign numbers instead, the arguments will be bound in the order of the numbers assigned. The `Out` argument with value zero in **Column** is reserved for the return value of a function, and argument numbers start at one for other arguments.

The stored procedure can then be invoked in your code using EOUtilities' `executeStoredProcedureNamed()` method. To test that, we'll enhance our project.

In Windows, create a new Web Component called `ListOfItems`. When asked about the type of assistance, choose the **Component Wizard**, and click on **Next**. Select the **Item** entity in the next dialog. For the layout, choose **Table** and **Display all Records**. In the next dialog, choose to display all **Item**'s attributes, but don't include any **Category** attribute, and click in the **Finish** button. A new Web Component that browses items will be created for us.

On the Apple OSX, highlight the Web components folder, then go to **File | New File**, then from the window that pops up choose a **Component** from the **Web Object** list and press the **Finish** button. Now, as you may have noticed, this is slightly different than Windows. To create the web page we have to use a display group.

Double-click on this newly created component to open it in WebObjects Builder. On OSX we have to drag the `Item` entity from our model into the web component, as shown in the section on *Display Groups*. Beneath the table, include a `WOForm` with two `WOSubmitButtons`. Soon, we'll associate methods that call the stored procedures with these buttons. Set the value of the buttons to **Apply Discount**, and **Show Sales**, respectively. Still in WebObjects Builder, include a new key named **sales** of type **Number**. Add a `WOString` to show the value of **sales**, and add **Total Volume of sales** to the left of the `WOString`. The component will look like this:

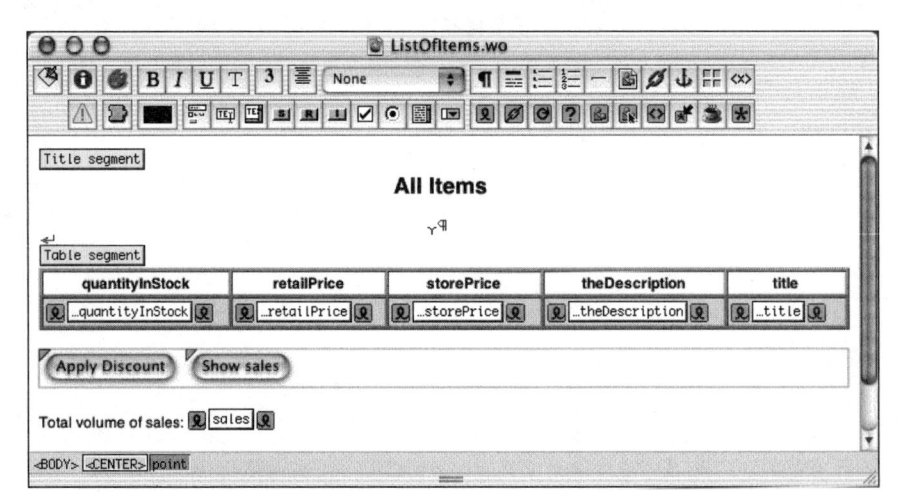

Advanced EOModeler

Include the method below in the `ListOfItems.java` which has been formed:

```java
/** Applies a discount */
public WOComponent applyDiscount() {

  // 15% discount
  NSDictionary arguments = new NSDictionary(new Double(0.15), "discount");

  // invokes the stored procedure
  EOUtilities.executeStoredProcedureNamed(
    session().defaultEditingContext(), "applyDiscount", arguments);
  return null;
}
```

The method is calling the stored procedure named `applyDiscount`. We'll now look at an example of a function. Here's the function called `volume`. Include it in EOModeler, in the same way as a stored procedure; the details can be seen in the following figure:

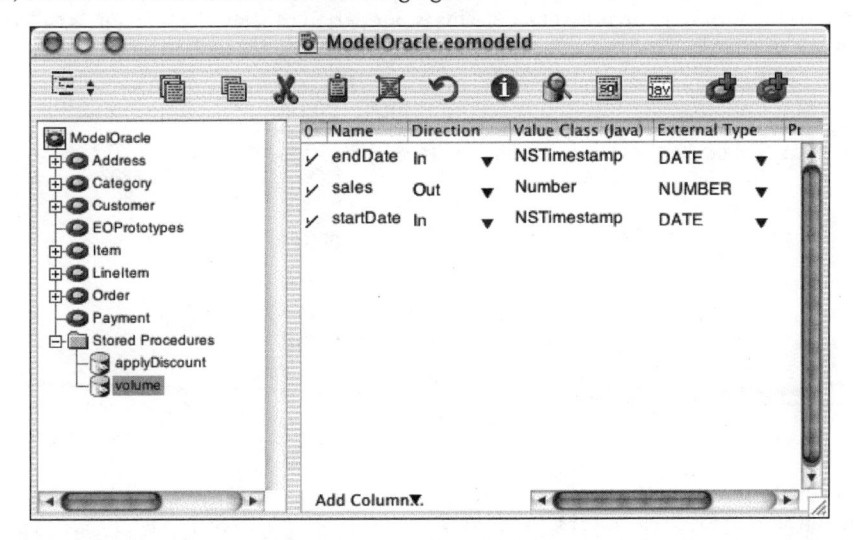

The function returns the amount sold between two dates, and is associated with a function of the same name in the database. We're using numbers in the **Column** fields here, and the zero value is assigned to **sales'** **Column** field. Here's the code for the function as used in Oracle, (as with the stored procedure, the syntax can vary between different databases and you may need to refer to your database documentation):

```sql
CREATE OR REPLACE FUNCTION volume(startDate in DATE, enddate in DATE)
                    return NUMBER AS sales number;
BEGIN
  SELECT sum(amount) INTO sales FROM tpayment, torder WHERE
        torder.thedate > startdate AND torder.thedate < enddate AND
        tpayment.paymentyID = tOrder.paymentID;
  RETURN sales;
END;
```

We can, then, use the function in our Java code. Also include the following method in `ListOfItems.java`:

```java
public WOComponent volumeOfSales() {

  // a dictionary to hold results
  NSDictionary result;
```

After declaring references to hold the result, the method constructs a dictionary with argument values to pass to the function:

```
NSTimestamp now = new NSTimestamp();

// arguments to function
NSDictionary arguments = new NSDictionary(new NSTimestamp [] {

    // starting one month ago
    now.timestampByAddingGregorianUnits(0, -1, 0, 0, 0, 0),

    // two months from now
    now.timestampByAddingGregorianUnits(0, +2, 0, 0, 0, 0) },
    new String [] {"startDate"  , "endDate"} );
```

The dictionary holds two `NSTimestamps`, one referring to one month from the present date, and another referring to two months from the present date. This is our period of sales; the function is called, passing an editing context, the name of the function, and the arguments:

```
// invoke the function
result = EOUtilities.executeStoredProcedureNamed(
            session().defaultEditingContext(), "volume", arguments);
```

After that, we can retrieve the results from the resulting dictionary:

```
// value returned by the function
sales = (Number)result.objectForKey("sales");

// use volumeOfSales ...
return null;
}
```

In WebObjects Builder, bind the action attribute of the first `WOSubmitButton` to the `applyDiscount` action, and the second `WOSubmitButton` to `volumeOfSales`. Also, create a `WOHyperlink` in the Main component, setting its `pageName` attribute to **ListOfItems**, so that we can navigate from the Main component to **ListOfItems**. When you click in the **Apply Discount** button, the stored procedure is called, applying a discount to the items. The component, then, shows the list of items with the discounted prices. When you click in the **Show Sales** button, the stored procedure is executed in the database, and the volume of sales is shown in the component. When logging the SQL, you'll see the call to the stored procedure in the **Launcher** panel. Here is the output of one session, when the **Show Sales** button is pressed:

```
executeStoredProcedure: volume withValues:{startDate = 2001-07-09 17:12:02
America/New_York; endDate = 2001-10-09 17:12:02 America/New_York; }
 === Begin Internal Transaction
 evaluateExpression: <com.webobjects.jdbcadaptor.OraclePlugIn$OracleExpression: "{ ? =
call VOLUME (?, ?)}" withBindings:
1:<com.webobjects.foundation.NSKeyValueCoding$Null>(sales), 2:2001-07-09
17:12:02(startDate), 3:2001-10-09 17:12:02(endDate)>
 === Commit Internal Transaction
```

Summary

EOModeler defines a number of settings for EOF that are used at runtime in EOF's interaction with the database. Even though the model and EOF introduces another layer of abstraction, the benefits of a more scalable and maintainable project, along with the means to handle the database data at a high level, greatly outweigh any overhead or learning curve.

In this chapter, we have learned:

- How to create Java files from our model
- How to generate our database from the model we created in the last chapter and to synchronize our model with the database
- How to modify our code to change the database we need to use at runtime
- Walked through the different Advanced Inspectors in EOModeler and their different options
- How to create a Display Group
- How to use stored procedures and functions with EOModeler

In the next chapter, we will take a closer look at the component architecture of WebObjects, and we will use the model we created in this chapter in component-based applications.

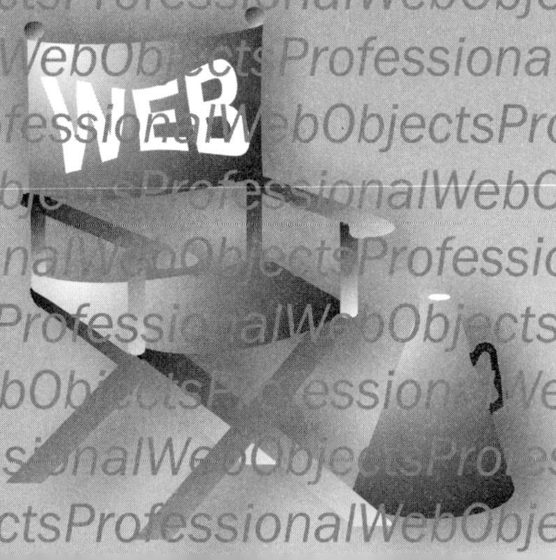
WEB

7
Components

One of the core reasons that WebObjects is so powerful and yet straightforward to use is its component architecture. Components are the building blocks of applications. Mastering WebObjects means mastering components, allowing the developer to build web sites quickly and flexibly. In addition, well-designed components are reusable in a large number of contexts, not to mention highly maintainable. This means that the benefits quoted above are incremental, making your job easier with each project.

WebObjects' component architecture is elegant, simple, and separates code from HTML. Since reading code and reading HTML are very different tasks, separating them can only make both the code and HTML easier to read. Separating code and HTML is obviously also invaluable when working with specialist HTML and JavaScript designers, making their work easier and largely preventing corruption of application code.

In this chapter, we will:

- Define the component
- Design a component for password-protecting portions of web pages
- Develop a navigation menu – in this section we will show the value of developing a super class for our regular and page-level components
- Use two of the more powerful but underused portions of WebObjects, stateless components and direct actions.
- See how the component architecture allows us to develop new pages very quickly and with minimal Java code.

What Is a Component?

In the context of WebObjects, a component is nothing more than a part of an application or web site. A typical component is a navigation menu, a data element, or even a section of HTML that is used by multiple pages.

Web pages are also components. For those of us who are used to object-oriented jargon, a component is either an object, or a number of objects, which exposes methods and properties that describe a given functionality.

For those not so used to object-oriented techniques, it may helpful to think of a component as a subroutine. A subroutine implements a behavior or action. It defines a given set of input parameters, and there is a result to this action. This may be a returned value (or values) and will often have other effects, such as the creation of a new file, updating a data source, and so on.

Just like we use subroutines to structure procedural programs, we use components to structure our application. In the long term, structuring applications as components eases the process of creating applications, as it allows applications to be split into logically partitioned parts.

What makes components powerful is that they can be assembled out of other components. For example, we may begin by building a component for displaying tables, build another for displaying an image hyperlink or button with a JavaScript rollover, and combine the two to create a navigation bar – or to put it another way a table of image buttons with rollover scripting.

Creating Components

Anyone used to developing dynamic web pages will know how easy it is to write scripted code that is very procedural. As each page is designed, the various parts of the page are scripted in sections. In this model, reuse of code translates to copying previously written code between the various pages that require it.

Unfortunately updating that code, or adding functionality, requires changes to be made to each of the pages that contain the code. Certainly not an efficient use of time and is untenable in the long term.

Placing common functionality in components to reduce duplicating code is the first step to using components. For instance, rollover buttons are a very common user interface item on web sites, so creating a component that handles the details of this is very useful.

The next step is creating wrapper components to reduce the duplication of template-type behavior to a component. To illustrate this we should look at web pages. Most web pages have the following structure:

- Head
- Title
- Declarations
- JavaScript
- Body
- Navigation
- Content

All of these, apart from the Content, will often be very similar for any given site regardless of what page the user is looking at in the site. The look and feel of a site will tend to be uniform. It seems natural to group each section into a component, and to represent the site itself, with all of the components in it, as a component. This simplifies the creation of new pages so that it is easier to concentrate on the content.

Why and When To Use Components?

The rules for designing and developing components are the same as those for writing software. This means factoring out code into discrete functionality that is packaged as methods or dependent objects.

Any code that is not strongly related to the current task is placed in a method. Other sections of code that can be described as a set of behaviors, "this code saves data to a file", "this code checks the given parameters against the known username and password", are encapsulated in objects. This is all standard object-oriented code design.

With a web application, "code" includes both Java code and HTML code, so that means that we use a component in the same situations where we would use a method or a new object in a standard application.

The strongest indicator that you need a component is finding that you are cutting and pasting a section of HTML or code. That suggests that that section could be a component to be reused in multiple situations. Grouping sections into components can also be a useful way of reducing an overly complex HTML page to pieces that can be understood more easily.

Separating sections of code out into components also allows multiple developers to work on the various sections in concert. Quite importantly too, any parts of the site that might be customizable should be broken up into components to allow simpler customization by customers.

The Components

In this chapter we will develop several sample components in addition to developing a number of classes that will make future component development easier. These components are:

- ❑ `LoginCheck` and `LoginForm`.
  These two components allow us to password-protect web pages or portions of web pages from view.

- ❑ `MenuElement` and `MenuBar`.
  These components create a site navigation menu, and demonstrate creating components for use by other components.

- ❑ `WROXComponent` and `WROXPage`.
  These components are design as superclasses, defining functionality that components inherit. By creating these superclasses we can build components and pages more quickly.

The first set of components is intended to show how we can use components as building blocks for creating other components. They also show how components can be used most effectively within applications. From this foundation, we will then apply these techniques to see how components will work in action. This will produce the following new components:

- ❑ `CategoryNavigation`, `CategoryMenuBar`, `CategoryMenuElement`.
  These three components will implement a navigation bar that can build itself from our database, specifically the `Category` table. It will allow the user to jump to any location in the store, and will be used throughout the site.

❑ `CatalogPage, ItemList`.
   The heart of any e-commerce site is displaying a list of items for purchase. `CatalogPage` displays those items, linking to another page to display the details for any item. `ItemList` contains the content for the `CatalogPage`, but can also be used on other pages that need to display a list of items. `CatalogPage` uses our `CategoryNavigation` component to display the navigation bar, which in turn uses `CategoryMenubar` and `CategoryMenuElement`.

❑ `ItemPage, ItemDisplay`.
   Once the user has chosen an item, they can view the details about an item, or purchase the item from this page.

Along the way, we will discuss the Model-Façade-View-Controller design pattern.

It should be noted that while WebObjects Builder is certainly useful, it is usual for developers who are becoming comfortable with using WebObjects to favor hand coding the HTML, wod, and Java files, whether in Project Builder or in another editor. If you find that you wish to do this, feel free to copy the code-as-is from the text directly into the source view of Project Builder. We will begin by providing detailed instructions on how to create the files using WebObjects Builder; however, as we progress the instructions will begin to depend on your increased familiarity with WebObject Builder.

LoginCheck

The first component we will develop is one that is extremely reusable but simple to understand, the standard login panel. In addition, this will nicely illustrate the main function of the user session: monitoring user login.

Here's our sample login panel:

Before we begin coding, we should consider the user interface for a moment. In order to protect a section of content, each page with protected content must check if the user is logged in before displaying its content and, if not, redirect them to the login panel.

We can do this in one of two ways; the first is to redirect the user to a login panel, passing the login panel component a reference to the user's requested content. Once the user is logged in, the component redirects the user back to the original page. The second is to hide the restricted content until login. The restricted content is only shown if the user is logged in. For this example we will implement the latter of these two techniques.

The form component is simple enough; it presents the user with the form above. When the form is submitted the component will check the username and password against the details held in the database. On successful login, it initializes a property in the session object called `user`. We'll call this component "LoginForm".

We also need a component that will check the session for a valid user, indicating a successful login, and display the login form if it cannot find one. This component, `LoginCheck`, must be included in each page that contains restricted content. This will allow it to redirect the user to a new page that contains the login form component or hide the content of the page the user is trying to view until they have successfully logged in.

Components

The `LoginForm` component is straightforward. Begin by creating a new project called `Login` and associate the EOModel developed in Chapters 5 and 6 with it. In OS X, we can simply drag and drop the `eomodeld` file to the resources folder of the `Login` project. On windows, we can do this by double clicking the resources folder and adding the `eomodeld` file to the project resources using the dialog window that opens.

On Mac OS X we create a new web component, choosing File | New File, select Components from the WebObjects sub menu, and enter LoginForm as the component name.

On Windows, choose File | New In Project, select Web Component and enter LoginForm as the component name. The following file is the HTML file for our component.

LoginForm.html

```
<WEBOBJECT name=form>
  Username:<WEBOBJECT name=username></WEBOBJECT><BR>
  Password:<WEBOBJECT name=password></WEBOBJECT><BR>
  <WEBOBJECT NAME=login></WEBOBJECT>
</WEBOBJECT>
```

We will begin by deleting the HTML created by default by Project Builder. This component will always be used from another component that will provide the required HTML page structure, so we don't need the usual <HTML>, <HEAD>, <BODY>, structure that WebObjects provides by default. Select the Source View from the Edit menu. The top window is the HTML: delete all of the text in that window.

Selecting the file in Project Builder will bring up the source code in the bottom window of Project Builder. This source code can be directly edited to avoid using WebObject Builder. Alternatively, double-click `LoginForm.wo` in Project Builder. This will bring WebObjects Builder up in Layout View.

Select Forms | WOForm to insert a form into `LoginForm`. Bring up the inspector and change the name of the form to "form". Next, delete any text automatically inserted by WebObjects Builder and type "Username:". Now, insert a text field selecting WOTextField from the Forms menu.

We will now insert an entry for the password. Type "Password:" on a new line and insert a `WOPasswordField`, again from the Forms menu. Finally insert a `WOSubmitButton`. `LoginForm` will now look as in the screenshot below in WebObjects Builder:

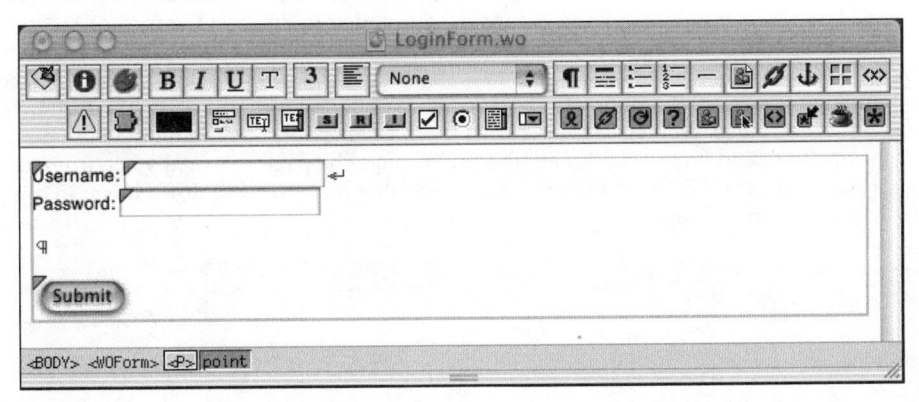

157

Creating the bindings for this file is quite simple. Select the first text field for the username and bring up the inspector. It is better to change the name of the text field to something meaningful, such as username. The value attribute should be bound to username.

We can do this by double-clicking in the Binding column of the Binding Inspector that corresponds to the value Attribute so that the cursor appears in it and typing "**username**". This effectively means that when the user enters a value for the user name, WebObjects will map this value to an instance variable in LoginForm.java called username. Click **Enter**.

At this point, WebObjects Builder will recognize that LoginForm.java does not have an instance variable called "username" and will offer to add it to the Java file. Choose to add this variable. The next window gives us a chance to amend the variable name, and offers to automatically generate an accessor/mutator pair. Select these options and select Add:

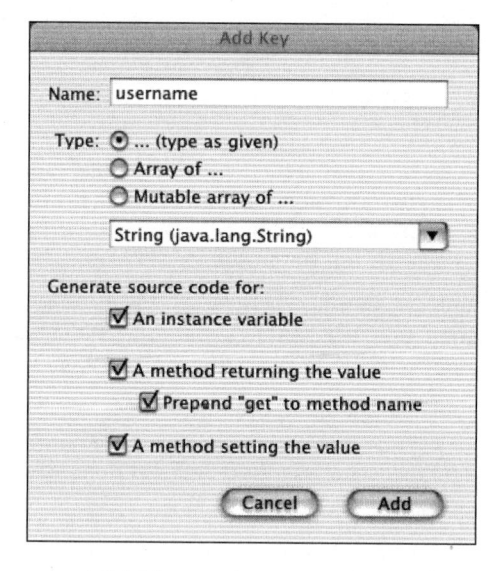

Now do the same for the password field (remembering to rename the form text field) to create the binding and have the variable and its accessor methods added to the Java file for LoginForm.

Finally, we must bind the **submit** button to an action method that we will call login(). Select the submit button and bring up the inspector, rename it to **login**, and bind the action attribute to the value login. Again, WebObjects Builder will detect that there is no action method defined in LoginForm and will ask if we wish to add an action. Accept this and change the page returned value from null to WOComponent. Note that "**WOComponent**" is not available from the pull down menu in this dialog window, just type it in by hand.

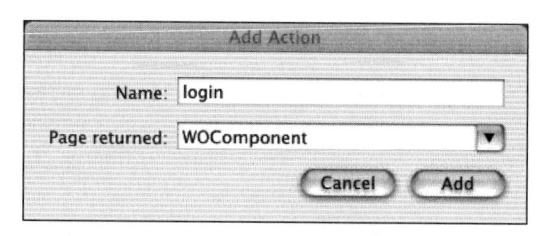

Components

Now change the value attribute to **Login**. This time, however, do not add the key to the class. This will change the label of the submit button to **Login**:

The resultant wod file will look like this:

LoginForm.wod

```
form : WOForm {
}
login:WOSubmitButton {
  action = login;
  value = Login;
}
password : WOPasswordField {
  value = password;
}
username : WOTextField {
  value = username;
}
```

LoginForm.java

The Java file now has two protected properties, the username and password.

```
public class LoginForm extends WOComponent {
  protected String username;
  protected String password;
```

The accessors and mutators for these properties have public access:

```
public String getUsername() {
  return username;
}
public void setUsername(String newUsername) {
  username = newUsername;
}
public String getPassword() {
  return password;
}
public void setPassword(String newPassword) {
  password = newPassword;
}
```

Delete the code that WebObjects has created for the `login()` action method. We will rewrite this method.

Selecting the **Login** button on the HTML page will invoke the action defined below to check the input values against the database. The login query code is better placed in the session object, since it is the session's responsibility to login the user rather than the components. In this example, however, it is provided in the `LoginForm` component for simplicity. We begin by defining an `NSMutableDictionary` named `lookup`.

As a reminder, a dictionary object stores key-value properties. We use the `setObjectForKey()` method to add the username and password provided by the user with key names "**loginname**" and "**password**". If you recall, these are property names of the `Customer` entity defined in the previously created model, `wrox.eomodel`.

```
public WOComponent login() {
  NSMutableDictionary lookup = new NSMutableDictionary();

  lookup.setObjectForKey(username, "loginname");
  lookup.setObjectForKey(password, "password");
```

We place the data into a dictionary, which we will submit to the `objectsMatchingValues()` method of the `EOUtilities` class. This static method checks the provided entity in the `EOEditingContext` object for an object whose properties match those provided in the dictionary object.

The entity we are concerned with in this case is the `Customer` entity (populated from the database we created earlier in this book). Practically, this translates to searching through the customers for a loginname and password matching those given by the user. This trims several lines of EOF code to just one call.

We retrieve the default editing context and call the `objectsMatchingValues()` method with it, the entity name as "`Customer`", and the values given by the user. If a match is found, the appropriate `Customer` object will be returned. Remember that in this case more than one match should not happen.

```
Session sess = (Session)session();

EOEditingContext ec = sess.defaultEditingContext();
NSArray result = EOUtilities.objectsMatchingValues(ec, "Customer", lookup);
```

Finally, as long as at least one resulting match (ideally the maximum number of matches too) is found, we retrieve the current session for this user and add the retrieved customer object to the current session:

```
    if (result.count() >= 1) {
      sess.setUser( (Customer) result.objectAtIndex(0));
    }

    return null;
  }
}
```

We return `null` regardless of the result; if the login is successful, we set the `session.user` property (we will create this property in just a moment) and return the same page we were on. Recall that returning `null` will send the user back to the originating page.

Here is the completed code for the `Session.java`. We have added a `user` variable of type `Customer`, and provided a method called `userIsLoggedIn()` that returns a Boolean indicating if the user has logged in.

Session.java

```
public class Session extends WOSession {
  Customer user;
  // accessor and mutator omitted for clarity
```

```
    public boolean userIsLoggedIn() {
      if(user == null) {
        return false;
      } else {
        return true;
      }
    }
  }
```

When the user has been returned to the page they originally requested, the `session` object's user variable should be set with a valid customer object, so the `LoginCheck` component will allow the page to be drawn with the previously hidden content rather than the `LoginForm` component.

If the login is not successful, we still return the same page, and `LoginCheck` will hide the content and display the login form again. The main benefit of this is that users can bookmark pages deep in the site and login directly from that page without needing to navigate from the home page to it after login.

The technique above is a nice simple design as the user can continue from where they were. If we returned some other page here, such as the Main page, the user may have to navigate through the site to get back to this location.

This is what `LoginCheck` looks like in code:

LoginCheck.html

```
<WEBOBJECT name=isLoggedIn>
  <WEBOBJECT name=parentContent></WEBOBJECT>
</WEBOBJECT>

<WEBOBJECT name=NOTisLoggedIn>
  <WEBOBJECT name=LoginForm></WEBOBJECT>
</WEBOBJECT>
```

Understanding this file should not present too many difficulties; if the user is logged in, something that is checked by the first `WEBOBJECT` tag, we show the content of the page. If the user is not logged in, indicated by entering the `NOTisLoggedIn` tag, we show the `LoginForm` component.

We can create this file in WebObjects Builder in the following way. Create a new Component in Project Builder and call it **LoginCheck**. Double-click the resulting .wo file and WebObjects Builder should open. Begin by deleting the HTML automatically created in the source view, as we did above.

In **Layout View**, add a `WOConditional` from the **WebObjects** menu and bind the condition to the session's `isUserLoggedIn()` method by selecting the session object in the object browser and dragging **isUserLogged** to either of the two boxes belonging to the `WOConditional` object:

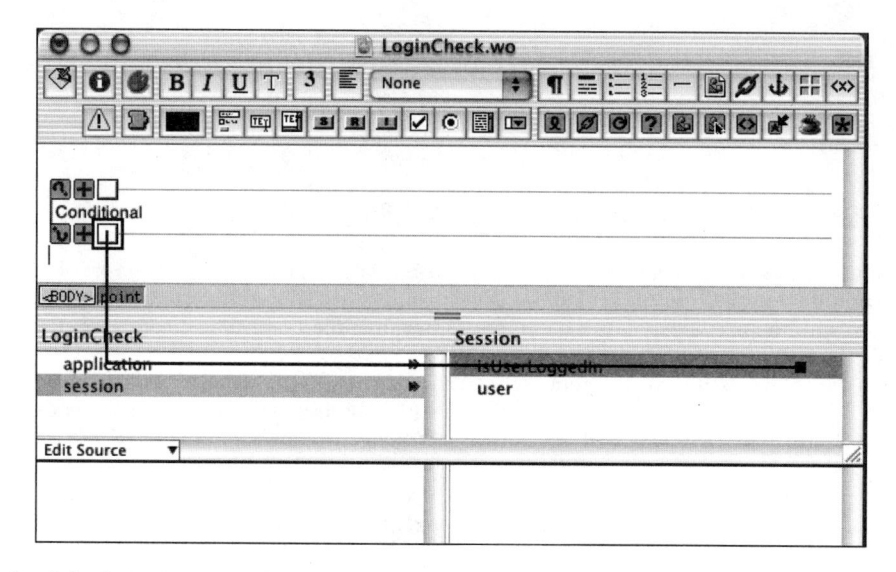

Delete the default text given and replace it with a **WOComponentContent** from the **WebObjects** menu. Rename this component **parentContent**.

In order to understand this, recall that `LoginCheck` is used to restrict access to content. The content to be restricted is defined by the page that uses `LoginCheck` however, also known as its parent. `WOComponentContent` is a special WebObjects tag that includes the content of its parent component: the page or component using our `LoginCheck` component.

A component that uses `LoginCheck` will therefore have the following code somewhere in its HTML page:

```
<WEBOBJECT name=loginCheck>This content needs to be protected</WEBOBJECT>
```

This is very powerful, because it allows us to create "wrapper" components that depend on their parent component for their final outcome. This is what allows us to hide the content of the parent component or page until the user has successfully logged in.

Add a second `WOConditional`, bind it to the same method, however this time, click on the conditional's plus sign to negate the condition. This means that the second conditional will only show its contents if the `isUserLoggedIn()` method returns `false`.

If the user is not logged in, we must present the login form. In order to do this, select and delete the default content of the second conditional, select **Custom WebObject** from the **WebObjects** menu, and type in **LoginForm** and **loginForm** as the object and object name respectively. Now select OK.

The resulting wod file for this component should resemble the following listing:

LoginCheck.wod

```
isLoggedIn: WOConditional {
   condition=session.userIsLoggedIn;
```

```
    }

    NOTisLoggedIn: WOConditional {
      condition=session.userIsLoggedIn;
      negate=true;
    }

    parentContent: WOComponentContent {
    }

    loginForm: LoginForm {
    }
```

isLoggedIn simply calls the isUserLoggedIn() method of the session object and returns the relevant value. NOTisLoggedIn returns the inverse of this value by using the negate binding. If there is no user stored in the session, the first conditional above will return false and the second true and vice versa for a successful log in.

We can see that the current file does not require any code in LoginCheck.java, the real work is being done in the session object. This results in the following Java file for LoginCheck:

LoginCheck.java

```
public class LoginCheck extends WOComponent {
  public LoginCheck(WOContext context) {
    super(context);
  }
}
```

With LoginCheck completed, we need to wrap up the LoginForm component.

LoginCheck and LoginForm in Action

We can now show our components in action using a test page. Open Main.wo in WebObjects Builder and insert the text "Try using brett/ichtus to login" at the top of the page as a hint to yourself of a valid username and password (these values are provided with the example database in the code download available for this book on www.wrox.com).

Now insert a custom Web Object from the WebObjects menu, entering **LoginCheck** as the class name, and **loginCheck** as the object name. Finally, enter some text to be protected in the area wrapped by login check. While we have entered a single line of text, anything could go in here, from other components, to complex tables, or some other HTML.

The following are the resulting html and wod files for the Main component:

Main.html

```
<!DOCTYPE HTML PUBLIC "-//W3C//DTD HTML 3.2//EN">
<HTML>
  <HEAD>
    <META NAME="generator" CONTENT="WebObjects 5">
    <TITLE>Testing Login Check</TITLE>
  </HEAD>
```

```
<BODY>
    Try using brett/ichtus to login.<P>
    <WEBOBJECT name=LoginCheck>
      This text is protected.
    </WEBOBJECT>
  </BODY>
</HTML>
```

Main.wod

```
loginCheck : LoginCheck {
}
```

The Java file for this component does not need to be amended. Compiling and running this application will result in the following page:

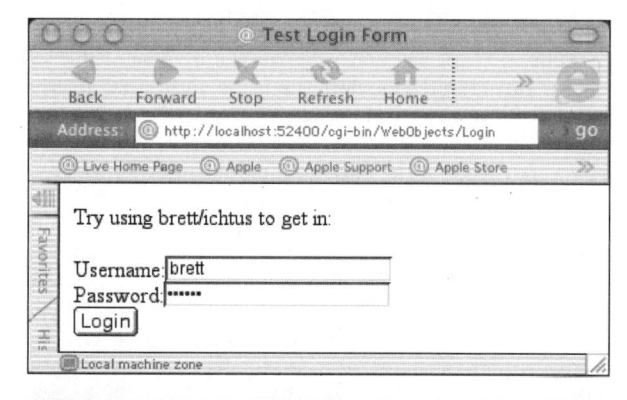

Signing in with a username and password from the database (`LoginTestPage` suggests one if you are not sure) will result in the following output:

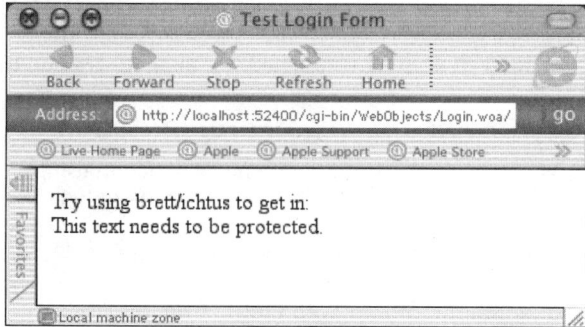

An Aside

Notice that much of the Java code in `LoginForm` consists of accessor and mutator methods for password and username. Since they're very obvious code and are getting in the way, we will omit the accessor and mutator methods in the code listings in the text from now on as follows:

```
public String username;
public String password;
//accessors for username and password omitted for clarity
```

The code in the download this book from the Wrox web site contains these methods.

Building Components with Components

`LoginCheck` is a useful component, but it doesn't display any data or use any data to determine what to display. 99% of WebObjects components, however, do draw themselves based on data held in objects. So while it is very useful, it is not a typical WebObjects component.

Let's look at a more typical component, a navigation bar. In order to do this, we will develop a couple of superclasses that contain functionality shared by all page level components. We will also develop a superclass for our Java classes.

We'll develop these superclasses, which we'll call `WROXComponent` and `WROXPage` as we develop our navigation menu. In order to create this application, begin by creating a new project named "Menu".

Navigation Menus

For our e-commerce site, we will need a menu that lists each type of merchandize. At the end of the menu, there will be a "checkout" menu item that will allow the customer to complete their purchase.

The menu item that corresponds to the users position in the site will be highlighted to show the user where they are in the site.

For our menu, we will use a set of hyperlinks in a table. For the purpose of this example we will indicate the user's current position in the site by changing the background color of the relevant table cell.

The navigation menu is a good example of a component that uses contextual information because it needs to know where in the site the user is in order to highlight the correct menu item.

WebObjects applications have 4 types of information:

- ❑ Application level information
- ❑ Session level information
- ❑ Page information
- ❑ Component information

Application information includes global variables and caches of commonly used EOF objects. Session information is information relating to the current user and what they're doing on the site. The most used session variable is a pointer to the user object. We saw an example of this in `LoginCheck` above.

Examples of page level information are what images need to be preloaded (for rollover scripting), or the URL of the current page. Component level information is generally a single object or collection of objects that the component needs in order to draw itself.

In our site, each page will also need to know what section of the site the user is in so that it can render the menu appropriately. We will define two classes, `WROXComponent` that defines generic component behavior that we will develop later in the chapter, and `WROXPage`, which extends `WROXComponent` to define behavior specific to components that have associated output.

We will begin by defining a methods for `WROXComponent`, `getArea()` that returns the name of area in the site where the current component or page belongs. For example, a book details page that lists the price, description, and ISBN of the book belongs in the bookstore part of the application. This component would return a value representing the bookstore area. The menu items also have output and so will be instances of `WROXPage`, to determine the menu item to highlight, we will compare the value returned by the menu item's `getArea()` method and the area value for the page that contains the menu item.

We don't need anything fancy for the result of `getArea()`, a string such as **Books** is good enough.

Let's have a look at the code:

WROXComponent.java

```
public abstract class WROXComponent extends WOComponent {
  public WROXComponent(WOContext context) {
    super(context);
  }

  abstract public String getArea();
}
```

To create this Java class, select **New File** (**New in Project** in Windows) and name it `WROXComponent.java`. The file must be made to inherit from `WOComponent` and should provide a constructor and method as shown in the code above. Any classes that extend `WROXComponent` must implement the `getArea()` to return a value representing the area of the site they belong in.

WROXPage.java

```
public abstract class WROXPage extends WROXComponent {

  public WROXPage getPage() {
    return (WROXPage)context().page();
  }
}
```

We define the `getPage()` method that returns the top-level page in the current response. The top-level page is the one that was originally requested by the user. The method casts the return value to `WROXPage`. `WROXPage` is declared as abstract as it does not implement `getArea()`.

We will now create a component representing each menu choice. We will call this component `MenuElement`. `MenuElement` will manage its background color according to whether the web page that contains the menu is in the area that is described by the menu element. So, in the books area, the books menu choice will be colored differently to the other menu choices. This will show the user that they are in the books area of the site.

Begin by creating a new component, `MenuElement`, and insert a `WOGenericContainer` into it using WebObjects Builder. Name the WOGenericContainer "menuItem". Next insert a `WOComponentContent` in place of the text inserted by WebObjects Builder by default and name it `parentContent`. The resulting file is shown below:

MenuElement.html

```
<WEBOBJECT name=menuItem>
  <WEBOBJECT name=parentContent></WEBOBJECT>
</WEBOBJECT>
```

Components

The `WOGenericContainer` creates tags in the output document. Its `elementName` attribute creates WebObjects tags for generating HTML tags. In this context, a container element is a tag that has both an opening and a closing tag, and usually has content between those tags.

The alternative to this is the `WOGenericElement`, which represents an element that has no content. As a result, this type of tag often has no end tag. Examples of content-less HTML elements are `<hr/>` and `<br/>`.

In the inspector for this object, add the following values against the relevant attributes:

```
elementName="TD";
bgcolor=getColor;
align=^align
valign=^valign;
width=^width;
height=^height;
```

Make sure that the value for **elementName** is surrounded by quotation marks as otherwise you will get a compilation error.

Here is where we start to see areas where it is much faster to directly edit the source files. Creating these attributes in WebObjects Builder means creating new bindings. We can do this by selecting the button in the top right hand corner of inspector and selecting **add new binding**:

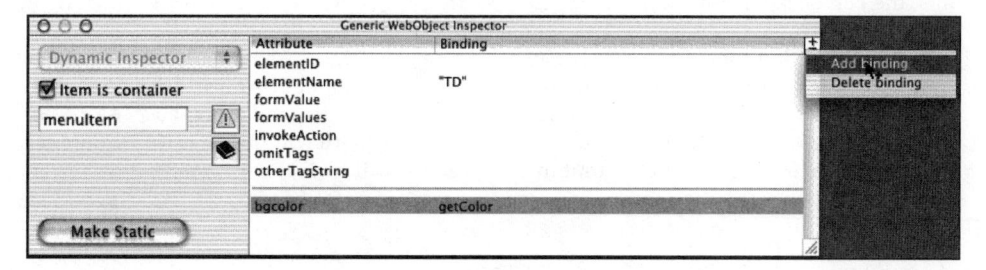

In each case, the value will be passed from this parent component in to the child, `MenuElement`.

Now insert a `WOComponentContent` and name it `parentContent` as in the example above for `LoginCheck`. Table cells are container HTML tags, so we need a `WOGenericContainer`. The resulting code will generate one of the following outputs:

`<TD bgcolor="#CCCCCC" align="center" width="72">content</TD>`

or

`<TD bgcolor="#FFFFFF" align="center" width="72">content</TD>`

Which of the two will be output will depend on whether the content (the menu item) describes the position of the current page in the site. We will use the `MenuElement` component to do this. It has an align property that describes the alignment of the text within the table cell and a width property that sets the table cell's width.

167

Chapter 7

MenuElement.wod

```
buttonCell : WOGenericContainer {
  elementName = "TD";
  bgcolor = getColor;
}

parentContent: WOComponentContent {
}
```

Make sure that the **elementName** value is **"TD"** (double quotes must be present) or it will look for a key called **TD** in the `MenuElement` class file.

When you add the `getColor` binding, WebObjects Builder will ask if it should add an action for it. Accept this request. The logic to determine the background color of the table cell will be provided by the `getColor()` action method as shown in the wod declaration above.

Change `MenuElement.java` so that it extends `WROXPage`. We add two keys, `highlight` and `background`, that describe the colors of the table cell in highlighted and normal mode. Create two more keys, `align` and `width` that will determine the horizontal alignment of content within a table cell, and the width of a table cell respectively. Allow WebObjects Builder to create accessors and mutators for both. We also define a key called `area` that will be compared against the containing page's area to determine the cell background color.

Finally, we add an action method `getColor()` with a return type of `String`. Be sure to amend the code created by WebObjects Builder as follows: `align`'s value should be set to `"center"`, `width`'s to `"72"`. Quite importantly, `background` and `highlight` must be assigned the values `"#FFFF00"` and `"CE0031"` or at least two dissimilar colors. If we don't do this there will be no visible difference in coloring between menu items and the point of this exercise will be lost.

MenuElement.java

```
public class MenuElement extends WROXPage {
  String align="center";
  String width="72";

  protected static String background = "#CE0031";
  protected static String highlight = "#FFFF00";

  String area;
  // accessors and mutators omitted for brevity's sake

  public String getColor() {
```

The `getColor()` method begins by checking if the current page area is the same as the menu item's area in the site. If so, it returns its color value as the highlighted background color. Otherwise it returns the normal background color.

```
    if (getPage().getArea().equals(area)) {
      return highlight;
    } else {
      return background;
    }
  }
}
```

The sections representing the changes to be made to the source code generated by WebObjects Builder are highlighted in the text above. Now we have the table cell, but we don't have the table. We need a menu bar component:

We can create this component as follows: Insert a table into `MenuBar.html` using the **Table...** menu item from the **Elements** menu or alternatively click the **insert table** button. In the dialog box that comes up select 1 row of 5 cells, a width of 360 pixels and some arbitrary height, say 40 pixels.

Now highlight the whole table and select the inspector. Choose to make this table dynamic. The table will then become an instance of `WOGenericContainer` with its value set to "TABLE" and named `menuTable`. The next part we will need to do in **Source View**, as it is not possible to do in Layout view: we will insert 5 `menuElement` components.

In the first three `MenuElement` components and the last in the page insert a `WOHyperlink`. The `MenuElement` components are named "Books", "Music", "Electronics", and "Checkout" respectively, while the links are named after their parent `MenuElement` with the word "Link" appended.

The resulting HTML is shown below:

MenuBar.html

```
<WEBOBJECT NAME=menuTable>
  <TR>
    <WEBOBJECT NAME=books>
      <WEBOBJECT name="booksLink">Books</WEBOBJECT>
    </WEBOBJECT>

    <WEBOBJECT NAME=music>
      <WEBOBJECT name="musicLink">Music</WEBOBJECT>
    </WEBOBJECT>

    <WEBOBJECT NAME=electronics>
      <WEBOBJECT name="electronicsLink">Electronics</WEBOBJECT>
    </WEBOBJECT>

    <WEBOBJECT NAME=emptyCell> </WEBOBJECT>

    <WEBOBJECT NAME=checkout>
      <WEBOBJECT name="checkoutLink">Checkout</WEBOBJECT>
    </WEBOBJECT>
  </TR>
</WEBOBJECT>
```

The fourth component is called `emptyCell` and is appropriately empty. The reason for this is as follows: In our menu we want to have a space between shopping areas of the site and the checkout link as shown in the diagram below.

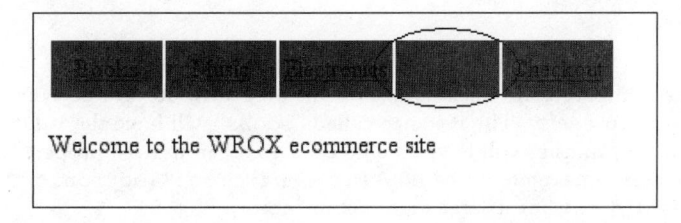

Chapter 7

If, however, we had inserted a standard <TD> element with its background color set to "#CE0031" to match the values currently in `MenuElement.java` we would lose a vital flexibility in the site.

Imagine that we change our corporate colors overnight, from red and yellow to green and blue. The site now needs changing. We can change the menu items colors quite simply, by amending the wod bindings to set the background and highlight keys. However, if we also got TD elements with the site colors hard coded in we would have multiple places to update. By creating an empty menu item element, we are focusing the number of places where changes need to be made to a single wod file, `MenuBar.wod`.

The related bindings are:

MenuBar.wod

```
emptyCell : MenuElement {
  area = "none";
}
books : MenuElement {
  area = "Books";
}

booksLink : WOHyperlink {
  pageName = "BooksTop";
}

music : MenuElement {
  area = "Music";
}

musicLink : WOHyperlink {
  pageName = "MusicTop";
}

electronics : MenuElement {
  area = "Music";
}

electronicsLink : WOHyperlink {
  pageName = "ElectronicsTop";
}

checkout : MenuElement {
  area = "Cart";
}

checkoutLink : WOHyperlink {
  pageName = "Checkout";
}

menuTable : WOGenericContainer {
  elementName = "TABLE";
  width = 360;
  height = 40;
}
```

Each binding of the `MenuElement` declarations for the area attribute will be synchronized with `MenuElement`'s area property. The instance called "books" will have the value `Books` assigned to it when it is instantiated, "music" will have a value of `Music` in its area property, etc. Clicking on the links will cause the user to navigate to the `BooksTop`, `MusicTop`, `ElectronicsTop`, and Checkout pages in our site. `emptyCell` has its area value set to "none".

Both `MenuBar` and `MenuElement` can be very simple, because the `MenuBar` component is using the `MenuElement` component to generate almost the same HTML for each menu item but with different data.

The Java file does not need to do anything at this time, however remember to change its inheritance to `WROXPage`.

MenuBar.java

```java
public class MenuBar extends WROXPage {
  public MenuBar(WOContext context) {
    super(context);
  }
}
```

Testing MenuBar So Far

In order to test `MenuBar`, we will need to create the top level pages for each department in the site; Music, Electronics, and Books, plus a page that represents the Checkout entry page. Create a new component named "`MusicTop`". Add a menu bar using the **Custom Object** menu choice from the **WebObjects** menu. Now add some text to represent typical content for the top level page of a site area. The content in the download reads: "The music department fulfills all your music needs".

Next add a key `area`, request that access methods be provided and amend the source code so that `area` is defined as "`Music`" matching the value defined in **MenuBar.wod** for the `Music` menu item.

```java
import com.webobjects.foundation.*;
import com.webobjects.appserver.*;
import com.webobjects.eocontrol.*;
import com.webobjects.eoaccess.*;

public class MusicTop extends WOComponent {
  protected String area = "Music";

    public MusicTop(WOContext context) {
        super(context);
    }


  public String getArea() {
    return area;
  }
  public void setArea(String newArea) {
    area = newArea;
  }

}
```

Now create three more components: `BooksTop`, `ElectronicsTop`, and `Checkout`, and follow the instructions as above for `MusicTop`. One last step remains, in order to be able to use `MenuBar` from the Main class, we will need to amend the Java file for it to extend our `WROXPage` class, rather than the default class. Add a MenuBar and some text saying "Welcome to the WROX ecommerce store."

Chapter 7

Compile and run this application. Now select a link, you should get output similar to that we saw earlier:

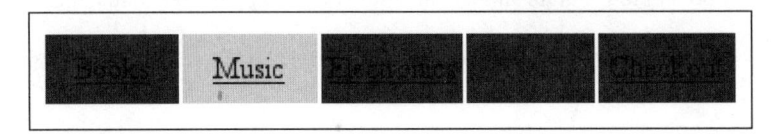

Let's also test the flexibility of this application. Change the wod bindings as follows to amend the color values of this menu:

MenuBar.wod

```
emptyCell : MenuElement {
  area = "none";
  background = "#1005A5";
  highlight = "#069817"
}

books : MenuElement {
  area = "Books";
  background = "#1005A5";
  highlight = "#069817"
}

booksLink : WOHyperlink {
  pageName = "BooksTop";
}

checkout : MenuElement {
  area = "Checkout";
  background = "#1005A5";
  highlight = "#069817"
}

checkoutLink : WOHyperlink {
  pageName = "Checkout";
}

electronics : MenuElement {
  area = "Electronics";
  background = "#1005A5";
  highlight = "#069817"
}

electronicsLink : WOHyperlink {
  pageName = "ElectronicsTop";
}

music : MenuElement {
  area = "Music";
  background = "#1005A5";
  highlight = "#069817"
}

musicLink : WOHyperlink {
  pageName = "MusicTop";
```

```
    }
    menuTable : WOGenericContainer {
      elementName = "TABLE";
      width = 360;
      height = 40
    }
```

Now recompile and run the application. You should have the following output:

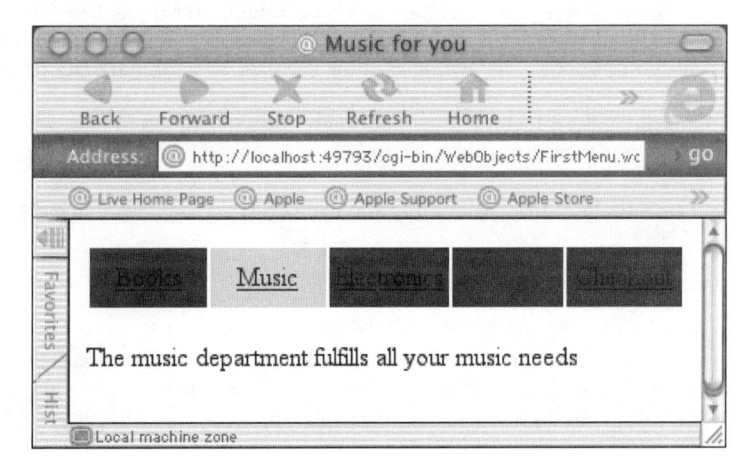

Hmm, maybe not.

Adding Direct Actions

Now, let's look at what could be improved about this component. Each `WOHyperlink` is an action-less hyperlink that takes the user to the page for the selected area. However, because we're using a component action style link, the link it generates is going to be different on each page. If you recall, component actions, also simply known as actions, are links that return a HTML page, a file to download, or a redirection. Direct actions allow us to create links that are not dependent on the location of the user in the application.

In order to understand this we will look at an example. For the purpose of illustration, the link to the MusicTop page is going to be:

http://localhost:52912/cgi-bin/WebObjects/FirstMenu.woa/wo/qz5PhbJRqYfJFHQQ95RK1g/1.1.3.0.1

```
/cgi-bin/WebObjects/FirstMenu.woa/wo/JaPhwpak8tNeZbna7fWq8w/0.1.3.0.1
```

on the first page but:

```
/cgi-bin/WebObjects/FirstMenu.woa/wo/qz5PhbJRqYfJFHQQ95RK1g/1.1.3.0.1
```

on the second page, despite the fact that they are going to the same place. Why is this? WebObjects maintains state information including history in the hyperlink in order to know which component to direct an action to which it does by counting the components.

Why is this a problem? Imagine that the user opens many windows in order to explore the store. The default cache size for history in WebObjects is 64. The user can easily go through more than 64 steps inside a reasonably large store. If the user were now to go back to their initial window and select a link the WebObjects server will not be able to serve the link because the history cache will no longer hold the relevant information.

More seriously, the user cannot come back to this page using a bookmark once they have left the site. The links above are very specific to the current session and cannot be saved for later return.

While the default history cache size can be changed, it would be better if we were able to set a value such that we were not dependent on local conditions for the correct functioning of our pages. We can do this by changing our component. This will also allow the user to bookmark the page for later.

Hyperlinks that contain navigation history information are only useful for the current session. That means users can't share hyperlinks for interesting products or return to their shopping after time out.

What we'd really like is static-like links. Well, one way we could do that is replace the WOHyperlinks with static hyperlinks:

```
<A href="/cgi-bin/WebObjects/MyStore.woa/wo/MusicTop">Music</A>
```

That link is a WebObjects trick using the component action request handler that will take us directly to MusicTop. The /wo/ part of the URL directs WebObjects to load the MusicTop page. Of course, we are hard coding values that WebObjects normally dynamically generates and therefore adding to the maintenance costs associated with this application.

Let's see if there isn't some way to generate links that look static, but that contain dynamic information. We can do this with direct actions. Direct actions generate the types of links usually associated with cgi programs. An example of a direct action link is shown below:

```
/cgi-bin/WebObjects/FirstMenu.woa/wa/MusicTop?parameter=value
```

The link above will 'break' in the future should we change the name of `MyStore.woa` or the number of parameter or values required. The main problem, however, of the short to medium-term reliability of the hyperlinks generated will be avoided. So if we use direct actions, our links can be dynamically generated, but they will act like static links for as long as the application is not changed.

Before we look at this we should review how direct actions are implemented. For each application WebObjects create a subclass of the `WODirectAction` class, called `DirectAction` by default.

There are a number of ways to implement direct actions. The first is to add methods to the `DirectAction` class that are specified in the wod file as follows:

```
myLink : WOHyperLink {
   actionClass = "DirectAction";
   directActionName = "myActionMethod";
}
```

Alternatively, and this is the preferred technique, we can subclass the `DirectAction` class and add the relevant action methods in it. In this way, the site direct action methods can be implemented in either one or as many classes as is deemed necessary.

As an example, say we develop a method in a page named `MyPage`. We create a class called `MyPageAction` of type `DirectAction` (or some other subclass of `WODirectAction`). A typical method will look something like this:

```
public WOComponent myPageAction() {
  WOComponent mypage = pageWithName("MyPage");
  takeFormValue("data");
  mypage.setData(data);
  return mypage;
}
```

`myPageAction()` pulls some data from the URL, calls `pageWithName("MyPage")` to build the page, shoves each URL query string parameter into the page, and then returns the page.

Notice, however, that when we put the `WOHyperlink` into the `MenuBar`, we knew what page we were linking to, and it was even in the wod file:

```
pageName="MusicTop"
```

Once it goes to the user and back again, that information is lost, and WebObjects has to map the direct action name back to the method that then maps it back to the desired page.

`WODirectAction` begins by calling a method called `performActionNamed()` with the `directActionName` from the URL that we specified in the wod file. The default behavior of this method is to append `Action` to the end of the name, and look for methods with that name. What we're going to do instead, is change it to use the `directActionName` to the page name:

MyDirectAction.java

```
public class MyDirectAction extends DirectAction {

  public MyDirectAction(WORequest aRequest) {
    super(aRequest);
  }

  public WOActionResults performActionNamed(String name) {

    WROXPage nextPage=(WROXPage) pageWithName(name);
    nextPage.takeFormValues (request().formValues());

    return nextPage;
  }
}
```

Add this file to the `DirectActions` project as a new Java class file.

If we need special handling for other direct action types, we can place that handling in a different subclass of `WODirectAction`, and access it through the `className` binding on `WOHyperlink`.

Processing Parameters in Direct Actions

The first part of the code uses `pageWithName()` to retrieve the name passed in from the wod file. The second simply passes the URL query parameters to the forwarded page. Appending URL query parameters can be done in wod files using code such as that below:

```
DisplayLink : WOHyperlink {
  directActionName="BookDisplay";
  ?ISBN= book.getISBN();
}
```

`directActionName="BookDisplay"` we've seen before. This will bring up the `BookDisplay` page. The following line:

```
?ISBN = book.getISBN();
```

will cause a link to be generated with the book's ISBN number in the URL as follows:

/cgi-bin/WebObjects/MyStore.woa/wa/BookDisplay?ISBN=1-861004-33-1

In fact, any number of query parameters can be appended to the direct action URL using separate lines in the wod file.

In the example above, the `BookDisplay` will extract this information from the URL in order to identify the book whose details should be displayed.

In order to understand the code above, we will need to look more closely at the following line of code:

```
nextPage.takeFormValues(request().formValues());
```

This code extracts a dictionary object from the request and submits it to the `takeFormValues()` method of the destination page.

The Apple documentation talks about using `takeFormValuesForKey()` to push those form values into the `DirectAction` object, from where they can be pushed into the page object's properties.

This, however, turns out to be very cumbersome, because we then need an instance variable for every query string parameter name in the direct action class. In addition, we also have to push the value into the direct action and back out into the page.

What we will do instead is to pass the parsed URL as a dictionary to the page object, which will programmatically extract the values it requires. Create a new project, `DirectionActions`, and import the work we have done so far into it. We will be amending and adding to the code we have done so far.

Since we now need this method to be defined in every page in our site, the method belongs in our `WROXPage` object and looks like this:

WROXPage.java

```
// class as before

public void takeFormValues(NSDictionary value) {
  java.util.Enumeration enum = getValueList().objectEnumerator();
```

The `getValueList()` method returns an `NSArray` object containing the list of values that should be extracted from the URL. We retrieve an enumeration of those values, iterating through the values stored in the enumeration, and extracting them. Notice the check at the end that makes sure that the value retrieved is not `null`:

```
    while(enum.hasMoreElements()) {
      String key=(String) enum.nextElement();

      Object obj = context().request().formValueForKey(key);
      if (obj != null) {
        takeValueForKey(obj,key);
      }
    }

    public NSArray getValueList() {
      return NSArray.EmptyArray;
    }
  }
```

With this method available in all subclasses of `WROXPage`, our `BookDisplay` page rather than overriding `takeFormValues()`, will override `getValueList()` to provide the list of query parameters to extract as follows:

```
public NSArray getValueList(){
  return new NSArray("ISBN");
}
```

Another advantage of this technique is that we can easily see what items a component will pull from a URL. With the above code, we can rewrite our menu links as:

MenuBar.wod

```
// menuElement bindings as before

booksLink: WOHyperlink {
  directActionName="BooksTop";
}

musicLink: WOHyperlink {
  directActionName="MusicTop";
}

electronicsLink: WOHyperlink {
  directActionName="ElectronicsTop";
}

checkoutLink: WOHyperlink {
  directActionName="Checkout";
}
```

Replace `pageName` with `directActionName` in the wod file. This makes the site work better and takes up less code. The resulting output is identical to that as before, however this time we can bookmark the pages, and even restart the server, and the links will still work.

So now, any book page link can be a direct action, which means it can be bookmarked; people can e-mail it to their friends, authors can put it on their web pages, and so on. This architecture will work for any page in our site, so almost any link can be a direct action. This type of linking also provides benefits in UI, giving a unified look to the site. In addition, it allows the browser to cache resulting pages thus giving (perceived) improvements in performance.

When Not To Use Direct Actions

The link architecture above can be used in pages where the content to display is completely determined by the URL and does not depend on state information (except perhaps on whether the user is logged in).

Like any rule, however, there are exceptions. Direct actions are perfect for "view only" pages or forms that are actually navigational tools, like search boxes. What they are not useful for, are pages that have state, of which the most common example is a form. In an e-commerce site, the best example of this is the checkout procedure.

The pages that the user goes through during the checkout stage are usually done in sequence: Firstly, the customer is given a chance to review and confirm their order. They are then prompted to enter credit card details, shipping address, and billing address (for sending the receipt to). When finished, there is a last chance to review the total, and the order is then submitted.

This is not a part of the site where it is necessary or even particularly useful to allow the user to jump to any position in the process. Using direct actions to link between participating pages becomes cumbersome, as the results of the previous page must be passed to the next. Moreover, the user entries are usually validated before continuing with the process. If entries do not pass validation (incorrect credit card number, zip code, or address) the user is returned to the originating page.

While it is possible to use direct actions in this case to convey the data between pages, perhaps by using hidden fields, it is not recommended and it is usually better to use action methods. As a basic rule of thumb, a link can be encoded as a direct action, while a form submission should be encoded as an action method. Perhaps a more complex version of this rule is that only form submissions that are not part of a sequence, and therefore do not have to keep prior state information, should be encoded as action methods.

A stock quote page might use a direct action coupled to a form. It doesn't need to keep track of any state before or after the form submission. By using a direct action, the quote page can then be bookmarked by symbol. Rather than use an action method, the stock quote form would generate a direct action hyperlink:

```
/cgi-bin/WebObjects/MyStocks.woa/wa/Quote?symbol=AAPL
```

which will take the user to the `Quote` page directly.

Stateless Components

There's one step left to finish our menu components, and that's to make them stateless. Looking at the `MenuBar` and `MenuElement` components, we can see that `MenuBar` doesn't have any instance variables. `MenuElement` has one; `myarea`, and in that case constant values are being passed into and out of the component. So we could make this a stateless component pretty easily.

Why should we make it stateless? There are two benefits to stateless components: memory and speed. When WebObjects detects that a component is stateless (by checking the value of its `isStateless()` method), it knows that it doesn't have to create an instance of the component for each web page. This also means that WebObjects does not have to keep that copy in memory for each web page in the backtracking queue of each session.

That means savings in both memory and time. The process of WebObjects pulling a page out of storage, reanimating it, and putting it back again takes some time. WebObjects doesn't have to do that for stateless components, and it can reuse the same stateless component for multiple users and sessions, something it can't do for stateful components.

WebObjects only needs one instance of each stateless component for the entire application. Since we use the navigation menu on every page that means that a single copy of the menu for the entire application represents a significant saving.

That sounds wonderful but there are three things to be aware of. First, a stateless component cannot contain a component that is not stateless. That can create a significant amount of work to ensure that all contained components are also stateless. This means that, in practice, there will be some components that are themselves stateless but that won't declare themselves stateless in order to operate with stateful components like forms.

The second issue is that stateless components need to reinitialize themselves after each use. That is, if the component is stateless, it will need to reset any temporary instance variables when WebObjects is done with it. This is actually easily done, as WebObjects calls the `reset()` method of stateless components between requests.

For `MenuBar`, this is simple, because it doesn't have any variables to reinitialize. For `MenuElement`, we have one, so the resulting code would be:

MenuElement.java

```
...
public void reset() {
  area = null;
}
...
```

However, don't amend the source code for `MenuElement` at this time, this functionality will be useful in other components, so we should make it available in `WROXComponent`. We will look at this later in the chapter.

The final and most complex issue is that stateless components don't get their bindings automatically pushed in and pulled out again. Synchronizing components, (the default for components) pull in the values for the variables from the parent before each phase, and push those values back to the parent at the end of each phase.

Stateless components are also considered non-synchronizing components, which means that WebObjects won't try to synchronize any variables with their bindings. It is the responsibility of the developer to synchronize the values with their bindings if required.

This is another speed optimization because, by default, (with synchronizing components), the pushing and pulling of values goes on before and after each of the three phases of the request/response loop (`takeValuesFromRequest()`, `invokeAction()`, `appendToResponse()`). It does this even if the values haven't been changed by the components.

That means that any parameters to our components won't be set, we have to pull them in manually using `valueForBinding()`, and push them out manually using `setValueForBinding()`.

For `MenuBar`, that doesn't matter because it doesn't take any parameters, and doesn't set any. For `MenuElement`, we have several choices. The first is that we could use `valueForBinding("myArea")` before each use of `myArea`. That would look like this:

Chapter 7

```
public String getColor() {

    String area = (String)valueForBinding("area");
    if (getPage().getArea().equals(area) {
      return background;
    } else {
      return highlight;
    }
}
```

Which is a pretty small change. If we did that, strictly speaking we wouldn't need the `area` instance variable at all, which means we wouldn't need the reset method above either.

Automatic Bindings

An alternative would be to pull the bindings automatically via a list, using the same technique we used above in direct actions. This may seem like a contradiction, because we previously said that there are performance benefits to avoiding pushing and pulling bindings for stateless components; however, this is a special case.

WebObjects pushes and pulls these bindings three times per request. By comparison, we pull the bindings in once only. This works well for components that are only reading their parameters, as most components do. This will still be faster than using the default (not to mention the other benefits of reduced memory and improved performance associated with stateless components.

We will pull the bindings just before the component gets used, by inserting a method call to pull all of the bindings and store them in our instance variables. As we briefly mentioned earlier, there are three methods that WebObjects calls during a request:

- ❑ `appendToResponse()` generates response content
- ❑ `takeValuesFromRequest()` parses form values and places them in objects stored in or accessible to the component
- ❑ `invokeAction()` invokes component actions

These methods define the request/response cycle, so overriding them to do initialization or post processing is quite common.

We provide a `getBindingList()` method that returns the list of bindings. This can then be used by both `pullBindings()` and the `reset()` method to pull the binding values, and set the instance variables back to `null`, respectively. The `pullBindings()` method iterates through the enumeration binding the values of all the listed items.

WROXComponent.java

```
public class WROXComponent extends WOComponent {
  public WROXComponent(WOContext context) {
    super(context);
  }

  public abstract String getArea();

  void pullBindings() {
```

```
      java.util.Enumeration enum = getBindingList().objectEnumerator();

      while(enum.hasMoreElements()) {
        String key = (String) enum.nextElement();
        takeValueForKey(valueForBinding(key), key);
      }
    }

    public NSArray getBindingList() {
      return NSArray.EmptyArray;
    }
```

What we'll do is override each of these methods to call `pullBindings()` before calling the original method call through to the superclass. When `pullBindings()` is called it will simply call `valueForBinding()` for each binding.

```
    public void appendToResponse (WOResponse response, WOContext context) {
      if (isStateless()) {
        pullBindings();
      }
      super.appendToResponse(response, context);
    }

    public void takeValuesFromRequest( WORequest request, WOContext context) {
      if (isStateless()) {
        pullBindings();
      }
      super.takeValuesFromRequest(request, context);
    }

    public WOActionResults invokeAction(WORequest request,
                                        WOContext context) {
      if (isStateless()) {
        pullBindings();
      }
      return super.invokeAction(request, context);
    }
```

We also add a `reset()` method to the `WROXComponent` class, to make this available to every class. The `reset()` method follows the same pattern as above to set the variables to `null`.

```
    public void reset() {
      java.util.Enumeration enum = getBindingList().objectEnumerator();
      while(enum.hasMoreElements()) {
        String key = (String) enum.nextElement();
        takeValueForKey(null, key);
      }
    }
```

Any component that extends `WROXComponent` can now take advantage of this method, although that class will need to override `getBindingList()` to provide the list of keys to set to `null`. Remember that we don't need to do anything else: WebObjects will call the reset method at the end of each request and so simply providing a list of keys in the `getBindingList()` method will be all that is required.

The effect on `MenuElement` is as follows:

MenuElement.java

```
public class MenuElement extends WROXComponent {
..// menu element as before

  public NSArray bindingList() {
    return new NSArray("area");
  }
}
```

MenuElement now inherits the reset() method from WROXComponent, which calls the method above to return a annul the area key or property for this class.

Now that the one instance variable in MenuElement is taken care of, there's nothing keeping MenuBar and MenuElement from being stateless. In order to make them stateless, all we need to do is to override isStateless() in both:

MenuBar.java

```
public class MenuBar extends WROXComponent {
  public boolean isStateless() {
    return true;
  }
}
```

MenuElement.java

```
public class MenuElement extends WROXComponent {
..// rest of class as before

  public boolean isStateless() {
    return true;
  }
}
```

As a note, should any of our components change the value of a bound variable in a stateless component, we will need to call setValueForBinding() in order to update the bound value. In this case, we have no reason to do so, as MenuBar and MenuItem don't change the values of any bound variables.

In most cases, there shouldn't be any need to push values out of a stateless component as they rarely calculate values for use elsewhere in the page. An exception is the index variable in a WORepetition which can be used to alternate the colors of rows, to name one example.

Pass Through Bindings in Stateless Components

Now that all the components are stateless, there are further advantages. Since WebObjects is no longer pushing and pulling values in and out of our component, we can have bindings that aren't tied to variables; bindings that are only referenced in the wod file. These bindings are called "pass-through" bindings, because they aren't backed by instance variables. The values are passed through from the component above the current component, and may be passed on to components below.

We will use this to allow anyone using MenuBar and MenuElement to specify the background and highlight color, or any extra formatting information needed.

First, let's do the background and highlight color in MenuElement as regular variables with optional bindings. The changed code looks like this:

MenuElement.java

```
public class MenuElement extends WROXPage {
  protected String area;
  protected String highlight = "FFFF00";
  protected String background = "CE0031";
  // rest of menu element class as before
```

```
  public NSArray bindingList() {
    return new NSArray(
          new Object[] {"area","highlight","background"});
  }
}
```

So we can now use `MenuElement` with modifiable background and highlight colors.

We can now add some parameters to the `<TD>` tag as well without adding code or instance variables.

MenuElement.wod

```
buttonCell : WOGenericContainer {
  elementName="TD";
  bgcolor=getColor;
  align=^align
  valign=^valign;
  width=^width;
  height=^height;
}
```

The `^` notation tells WebObjects to call `valueForBinding(name)` to get the value of name. So when `WOGenericContainer` is building the `<TD>` tag it will add `align="left"` if the value of `MenuElement`'s `align` binding is specified as `"left"`, and similarly for the other values.

Each of the last four values above is passed through from `MenuItem` to `WOGenericContainer`, untouched by our code. We didn't have to declare instance variables for these parameters, or manually retrieve the values for the bindings in the Java code.

We can use pass-through bindings to make components more flexible by making sure that we pass through bindings for child components even if we are not currently using them. This will allow us to use them in the future should we wish to. For example, whenever we use a `WOGenericContainer` tag in a stateless component, we may want to think about adding a set of optional bindings for each possible tag attribute, especially for table tags such as `<TABLE>`, `<TD>`, `<TR>`, and `<TH>`.

Now our four pass-through bindings from `MenuElement` (`align`, `valign`, `width`, `height`) and our two new variable bindings (`background` and `highlight`) must be provided in `MenuBar` or its parent. We can do this in the wod file like this:

MenuBar.wod

```
books: MenuElement {
  source = area;
  align = ^itemalign;
  valign = ^itemvalign;
  width = ^itemwidth;
```

```
    height = ^itemheight;
    background = ^background;
    highlight = ^highlight;
}
```

`MenuBar` now takes six new parameters: `background`, `highlight`, `itemalign`, `itemvalign`, `itemheight`, and `itemwidth`. All are passed straight through to `MenuElement`, which passes the four table tag attributes through to the `WOGenericContainer` tag. Even though these are pulled directly from bindings via the caret, they work just like regular bindings.

Also, on the way through `MenuBar`, `height` and `width` change name to `itemheight` and `itemwidth`. That's to differentiate between the width of the table, which `MenuBar` sets and the width of individual cells, and similarly for the table height. So we use a different name, but uses a `^` binding to avoid declaring any variables. This allows us to make the following declaration in `MenuBar`:

MenuBar.wod

```
menuTable : WOGenericContainer {
    elementName="TABLE";
    bgcolor=^bgcolor;
    width=^width;
    height=^height;
    cellpadding=^cellpadding;
    cellspacing=^cellspacing;
    align=^align;
}
```

The end result is that our `MenuBar` component is now very flexible. We can specify the `height`, `width`, `background` color, `cellpadding`, `cellspacing`, `align`, `itemalign`, `itemvalign`, `background`, `highlight`, `itemheight`, and `itemwidth` attributes, where before they were hard coded in the code.

Non-Synchronizing Components

In order to use pass-through variables in stateful components, we must make our component non-synchronizing. In fact, stateless components are actually a special type of non-synchronizing component.

All we need to do is tell WebObjects not to push and pull values out of the component, as is the default for a synchronizing component. This can be done as shown in the code excerpt below:

```
boolean synchronizesVariablesWithBindings() {
    return false;
}
```

When WebObjects sees this, it will not automatically push or pull the bindings to and from the component. This means that the code above that overrides `appendToResponse()`, `takeValuesFromRequestInContext()`, and `invokeActionForRequest()` has a small problem because we're checking to see if a component is stateless rather than if it synchronizes.

We could change the code to check both values, however, it makes more sense to put the logic in the `synchronizesVariablesWithBindings()` method. Callling `isStateless()` implies that the component does not synchronize, but that's implied, not explicit, and it's not even documented.

Because of this we will override the default definition of `synchronizesVariablesWithBindings()` so that the relationship is explicit, and then check for that instead. In our Java code this looks like this:

WROXComponent.java

```java
// WROXComponent as before

public boolean synchronizesVariablesWithBindings() {
   if (isStateless()) {
     return false;
   }
   return true;
}

public void appendToResponse(WOResponse response, WOContext context) {
   if (synchronizesVariablesWithBindings ()) {
     pullBindings();
   }
   super.appendToResponse(response, context);
}

public void takeValuesFromRequest( WORequest request, WOContext context) {
   if (synchronizesVariablesWithBindings ()) {
     pullBindings();
   }
   super.takeValuesFromRequest(request, context);
}

public WOActionResults invokeAction(WORequest request, WOContext context) {
   if (synchronizesVariablesWithBindings ()) {
     pullBindings();
   }
   return super.invokeAction(request, context);
}

// rest of class as before
```

Now, whether a component is non-synchronizing only, or also stateless, our components will pull in their bindings automatically.

Stateless vs. Non-synchronizing

As mentioned above, stateless components are preferred because they're faster and more efficient. This is most useful for navigation components like the `MenuBar` component. Components that wrap other components are much harder to make stateless because they can only contain other stateless components. In that case, make them non-synchronizing only, especially if they need to use pass-through bindings.

The Finished Components

Well, here is the completed application:

MenuBar.wod

```
emptyCell : MenuElement {
   area = "none";
   align = ^itemalign;
   valign = ^itemvalign;
```

```
    width = ^itemwidth;
    height = ^itemheight;
    background = ^background;
    highlight = ^highlight;
}

books: MenuElement {
    area = "Books";
    align = ^itemalign;
    valign = ^itemvalign;
    width = ^itemwidth;
    height = ^itemheight;
    background = ^background;
    highlight = ^highlight;
}

music: MenuElement {
    area ="Music";
    align=^itemalign;
    valign=^itemvalign;
    width=^itemwidth;
    height=^itemheight;
    background=^background;
    highlight=^highlight;
}

electronics: MenuElement {
    area ="Electronics";
    align=^itemalign;
    valign=^itemvalign;
    width=^itemwidth;
    height=^itemheight;
    background=^background;
    highlight=^highlight;
}

checkout: MenuElement {
    area ="Checkout";
    align=^itemalign;
    valign=^itemvalign;
    width=^itemwidth;
    height=^itemheight;
    background=^background;
    highlight=^highlight;
}

booksLink: WOHyperlink {
    directActionName="BooksTop";
}

musicLink: WOHyperlink {
    directActionName="MusicTop";
}

electronicsLink: WOHyperlink {
    directActionName="ElectronicsTop";
}

checkoutLink: WOHyperlink {
    directActionName="Checkout";
}
```

```
menuTable : WOGenericContainer {
    elementName = "TABLE";
    bgcolor = ^bgcolor;
    width = ^width;
    height = ^height;
    cellpadding = ^cellpadding;
    cellspacing = ^cellspacing;
    align = ^align;
}
```

Compiling and running this application should give you much the same output as before. This time, however, we can make changes to the look of the menu in far more ways than before. We have control over a large number of the table attributes through the wod bindings of the `MenuBar` component. We don't have to use them, but if they are there we do. This makes the component useful in other settings – and not only on this site.

`WROXComponent` is finished, though we have a bit more work to do on `WROXPage` to make it work better with direct actions.

Summary

Now it seems like we talked about a lot of code, where did it all go? The application works much in the same way that it did before, and the only visible difference is the type of links that are generated. What happened is that as we went along, we found some general functionality that we put into our `WROXComponent` and `WROXPage` superclasses. So a lot of the code ended up there.

Well, there are still some improvements to be made: we are not yet done. However, we have learned some valuable lessons in this chapter. We have shown how to implement direct actions in order to allow bookmarking of pages on our site. We have also implemented several superclasses that give us some valuable functionality and simplify the code greatly. Finding where code really belongs cuts the length of code to implement a given functionality significantly and simplifies the application.

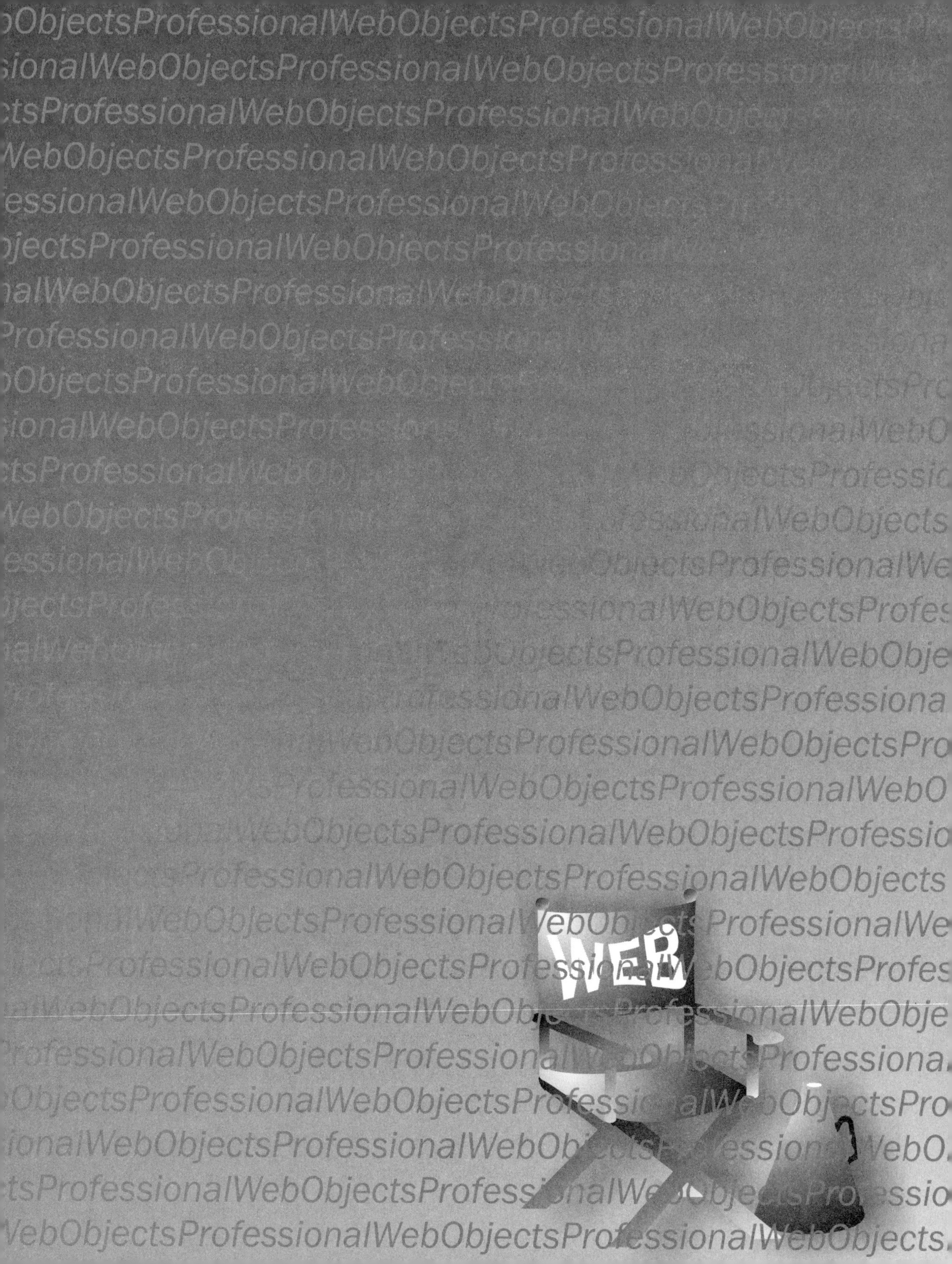
WebObjectsProfessional
WEB

Writing Fetch Specifications

As we have learned, WebObjects provides a scalable, robust server-side architecture using compiled Java code to build solutions where business logic is separated from the presentation layer. Of course, that is only half the story – a WebObjects application also connects to persistent data stores such as a database.

Searching for data and presenting it to the user is a primary goal of many WebObjects applications. Allowing one or more users to edit records and write them to the database is also important. In this chapter we will define fetch specifications, explain the relevance of the editing context, and cover the following:

- Using EOModeler to create advanced queries called fetch specifications
- Sorting the resultant data
- Enabling data modification through the editing context
- Presenting data for use by our application

We will create a fetch specification using our example application, then discuss several advanced concepts and their usefulness. In a simple example, we will build a fetch specification in our model, and make use of it in a search component in our application. In a more complex example, we will build a fetch specification entirely in code, and introduce the use of an editing context.

EOF – an Intermediate Lens On Our Database

The model created in EOModeler can be considered an intermediate lens that our application uses, via the Enterprise Objects Framework, to access data in our database. EOF uses entity relationship modeling to describe a persistent data store's structure in a way that allows it to be mapped to enterprise objects. The EOModeler application is used to specify the mapping between the database contents and our enterprise objects, creating our model. If the model presents an object-oriented picture of the database to our application, a fetch specification is the template for querying that database.

EOF manages the subtleties of data persistence, and presents data in an object-oriented manner so you can make use of it in our application – relational database concepts such as tables and rows are transformed by EOF into classes and instances so you have a uniform means of accessing and manipulating database data from your WebObjects application.

An EOModel file maps how the schema of our database is represented in an object model. Much like a set of class definitions in Java, the model file determines the names of entities, their attributes, their relationships to other parts of the database, and what Java classes will represent them. But how do you extract data from the database to present it in the user's browser? You *fetch* enterprise objects!

To complete a query of the database, we will fetch data from a persistent data store, and make it available in a WebObjects application that is using EOF. We will then present the fetched information in the user's browser using typical form elements. In the examples following, we will use EOModeler to build a fetch specification, and construct a code-based one ourselves.

The Editing Context: Keeping Track of Changes

In Chapter 6 we learned about Display Groups, but limitations to their functionality become clear as our applications grow more sophisticated. Luckily, WebObjects offers a variety of means to retrieve objects from a database. The Enterprise Objects Framework can be accessed directly when we have more sophisticated requirements such as creating a variety of queries, or when the `WODisplayGroup` cannot be used, such as when incorporating Direct Actions. An editing context manages a selection of enterprise objects and keeps track of changes that need to be transmitted to the database, in the event the application (or the user, as the case may be) decides to save those changes.

- ❏ Fetches data from the database
- ❏ Keeps track of changes to all objects formed from the data
- ❏ Tracks inserts and deletes made to the set of objects
- ❏ Stores these changes until the object is saved back to the database, or the changes are abandoned

The `EOEditingContext` class is found in the `EOControl` layer, and is used to keep track of all the changes made to enterprise objects that we have retrieved from the database. The editing context provides methods for retrieving, inserting, and deleting objects, and provides methods for saving and canceling changes made to objects. Edits can be made without affecting other users of the same data, until the data is written back to the database. An `EOEditingContext` object represents a single object space or document in an application. Its primary responsibility is managing a graph of enterprise objects. This object graph is a group of related business objects that represent an internally consistent view of one or more external stores, usually a database.

Methods for undoing and redoing modifications to objects are also provided; EOF is designed to work with desktop applications as well as WebObjects applications, and so provides methods that follow standard application conventions such as undo and redo. In a web application with multiple users potentially accessing records simultaneously, we do not want the possibility of confusing which operations from which users may be undone. The editing context offers a solution in dealing with this potential problem. In many cases, users are dealing with objects managed by their own private editing contexts, and each editing context has its own undo stack. Changes made by a user to enterprise objects in an editing context remain local to those objects in that editing context. Similarly, any undo actions performed by the user are applied only to those same objects in that same editing context. For WebObjects applications, we recommend setting the undo manager for the editing context to `null` to reduce overhead.

The `EOEditingContext` can be used to retrieve enterprise objects from the persistent data store. The exact objects to be collected are determined by the `EOQualifier` object used. `EOQualifier` is an abstract class that holds information used to restrict selections on objects or database rows according to specified criteria. The same qualifier can be used both to perform in-memory searches and to fetch from the database. We can set the order in which such objects are retrieved with an `NSArray` of `EOQualifier` objects.

To retrieve enterprise objects with our `EOEditingContext`, we need an `EOQualifier` that specifies objects to be retrieved. We then need an `NSArray` of `EOSortOrdering` that specifies the order of retrieval of our objects; an `EOFetchSpecification` that uses the qualifiers and sort orderings; and, of course, we need an `EOEditingContext`.

Note that raw SQL can be used with similar results, but we would lose the operability of EOF: the ability to abstract and customize database operations from the specific back-end database.

What is a Fetch Specification?

A fetch specification is the set of parameters defining a query (or *fetch*) we can use in our application. The basic approach to performing a query is to create a fetch specification, of the type `EOFetchSpecification`. Then the class named `EOEditingContext` is used to retrieve objects from the database via the model, and detect changes made to those objects while used by a session. For our purposes, the editing context will accept the fetch specification and return an array contains all the objects that match the requirements of the query.

The `EOFetchSpecification` object is used to select which objects will be retrieved from the database, and, optionally, in what order. By creating a fetch specification with EOModeler (or programmatically), we can create one or more such fetch specifications and reuse them every time we need to return the content of records from the database.

Much like a SQL query, the fetch specification defines certain attributes of our EOF-based query. The first attribute is the entity from which data will be drawn. The entity name is a string. The next attribute is the qualifier or qualifiers, a specification of which data objects are sought. The qualifier is given as an object of class `EOQualifier`. Finally, the last attribute is the sort ordering, which defines the order of the data objects as they are presented in the array. This order is an array of the `EOSortOrdering` objects.

Qualified vs. Unqualified Fetching

By merely calling `EOFetchSpecification` and providing it with the name of the table to be fetched, with `null` for the other two arguments, we get an unqualified fetch. All the data in the table will be retrieved, and in whatever order it is stored in the database. The other two arguments that we will examine in detail later are the qualifier(s), which define the parameters of the actual query, and sort orderings, which define the keys to sort on.

When we want to pull subsets of data and retrieve only certain records, we apply an `EOQualifier` to the fetch. Such a fetch can be a selection of objects having an attribute that matches a key field or a column name in the table with a value (specified as an `EOKeyValueQualifier`). Making a qualified fetch does not mean building a hierarchy of objects ourselves, such as in SQL. `EOQualifier` accepts a string and builds the appropriate object combinations for us. A hierarchy of `EOQualifiers` makes the restrictions that select objects from the database. Compare this with a `WHERE` clause in SQL, but with the hierarchy of qualifiers you do not have to create such a search by hand; you can use a string, that will be parsed to construct the qualifiers.

Advanced Fetching Concepts

The most typical advanced form of a fetch is qualifying, but there are other factors we can consider when retrieving data. Foremost, we will want to present data to the user in some order; we can also reorder data as needed. For example, we may provide the user with a button to change the presentation of records in an ascending or descending sequence. We can also enhance our application's performance by applying several techniques, such as prefetch and caching data.

Ordering During the Initial Fetch

Unless we want the database to define the order in which objects are retrieved and presented, we will need to define a sort ordering at the time of the fetch. Many databases present the rows in the same order they were inserted; rows do not have an intrinsic order in the database. Do not rely on the database order – it is a good practice to set the order in the fetch specification.

To do so, we have to supply an attribute to sort by, then whether to sort in ascending or descending order. For identical value items, we may specify a second or third attribute to sort on. Create an `EOSortOrdering` object with the `sortOrderingWithKey()` static method, and provide the key to order on, and an ascending or descending value. Note that `EOSortOrderings` are used both to generate SQL when fetching rows from a database server, and to sort objects in memory. The advanced example following contains details on these procedures.

EOModeler gives us a means to specify the sort ordering using the graphical user interface, demonstrated in the example later.

In-Memory Ordering

Once data has been retrieved we may want to reorder the information, perhaps for presentation reasons, or because data has been added or deleted. Rather than subjecting our application to the overhead of posting another query to the database, we can apply an in-memory sort using the method `EOSortOrdering.SortedArrayUsingKeyOrderArray()`. The first parameter required is the array of objects to be ordered; the second is an `NSArray` of `EOSortOrderings`. This method returns an ordered `NSArray` containing the exact same objects as the `NSArray` given to it, as specified by the `NSArray` of `EOSortOrderings`.

To order an array in place, use `EOSortOrdering.SortArrayUsingKeyOrderArray()`. The first parameter is an `NSMutableArray` of enterprise objects that will be ordered after the method finishes; the second is an `NSArray` of `EOSortOrderings` that determines how the mutable array is to be ordered. The advanced example following contains details on these procedures.

Fetching Raw Rows

A raw row fetch specification is used to identify which attributes of an entity are to be returned without creating an enterprise object for them. A raw row fetch returns an `NSArray` of `NSDictionary`, where each entry in the `NSArray` represents the rows from the selected table. These can be used as read-only objects only, or you can use the adaptor to update the database with raw rows. Take the `EOAdaptorChannel.updateValuesInRowDescribedByQualifier()` method, for instance. Using a raw row fetch reduces our application's memory overhead by not creating enterprise objects. Raw rows can be easily converted to enterprise objects at any time, if you keep track of primary key attributes.

Let's shift gears and discuss raw SQL. You can use raw SQL in a fetch specification to retrieve enterprise objects. Or you could use a regular fetch specification without any custom SQL to retrieve raw rows. A raw row fetch specification enables us to specify SQL directly, subject to the requirements of the database being used. Be aware that supplying SQL directly to the database means code may have to be modified if the database is changed later. Common SQL statements such as `GROUP BY` can be used. You can `setUsesDistinct(true)` on a fetch spec that returns full enterprise objects – you don't have to use raw row fetches in order to use `distinct`. In addition, since standard fetch specification operators are limited, we can use a raw row fetch specification to construct database aggregations such as a sum or average. Note that when using raw row fetching, we lose some important features: the `NSDictionary` objects are not unique; the `NSDictionary` objects are not tracked by an editing context; and: we cannot access `to-many` relationship information.

EOModeler gives us a means to create fetch specifications for fetching raw rows using the graphical user interface, demonstrated in the following example.

Improving Performance

We have three options that can be utilized to improve application performance, prefetching, caching and sharing.

Prefetching

Prefetching searches out the objects across relationships in our database, using the fetch specifications. Keys are the mechanism used to add prefetching relationships to a fetch spec. In a model-based fetch specification, keys are defined in the graphical user interface. In a code-based fetch specification, the method `EOFetchSpecification()` can be used to set the keys to be prefetched. Performance can be significantly enhanced, but watch out: pulling too much data into memory when it is not needed can overload your server. Although prefetching can increase the initial hit to our database, it can improve overall performance by reducing return hits to the database.

For instance, when EOF fetches an enterprise object, it creates `EOFault` objects for the enterprise object's relationships. Each time we access one of these `EOFaults`, EOF fetches the data from the database. This procedure works well and minimizes the amount of unnecessary data fetching from the database. However, each time an `EOFault` is accessed, a separate database query is performed. Using a technique called "batch faulting" can reduce the number of database queries. If we know that we will be faulting all instances of a particular relationship, you can use prefetching to skip the `EOFault` creating stage and produce a single database query to load all related objects.

Caching

Caching moves all the objects for an entity to be loaded into memory the first time an object is requested. After that, every time an object is sought, it is returned from memory. In addition, cached objects are available to all sessions and to all components, saving time since data does not have to be retrieved multiple times for each session. Note that caching should be used sparingly since loading significant amounts of data into memory may have the adverse effect on our database server.

The problem, in this situation, can be exacerbated for the application server, as the memory consumed can greatly increase the Java heap size. This can put a heavy load on the CPU for the database server, but is not a memory problem; the reverse is true for the application server, creating a memory problem, not a CPU problem.

Cached objects can only be used in qualifiers that are resolved in-memory, and changes made would not be resolved in objects retrieved from the persistent data source. Cached objects are most useful when reserved for lookup entities that rarely change; a small number of non-transient records that are read-only would be the ideal situation to use caching.

Objects are cached in `EODataBaseContext`, which shares the same `EOObjectsStoreCoordinator` with the `EOEditingContext` objects used on our application code. Using the same connection information for each user ensures getting the most benefit from caching.

Sharing

Reusing, the mantra of object-oriented development, can be extended even further with objects by enabling sharing. Objects in a shared editing context do not have the same restrictions as cached versions; shared objects can be accessed by users with different `EOEditingContexts`. Shared objects do not have to include all records for a particular entity, unlike cached objects. Each application has one shared editing context, accessed using the `WOApplication's sharedEditingContext()` method.

EOModeler gives us a means to prefetch, cache, and share data using the graphical user interface, and several techniques are demonstrated in the following example.

Two Ways To Create and Use a Fetch Specification

Fetching from our database for our application requires several items: an EOModel that maps the related tables and rows to an object model; a fetch specification that details the exact objects needed from the database; an editing context to initiate the fetch (query); and a variable to hold the array of fetched objects. To demonstrate assembling of components used with the editing context, we will walk through a sample application that searches for records in the `Customer` table. Our sample application will use the same database and EOModel as previously described.

Manually Creating a Fetch Specification

Let's walk through the longhand version of creating a fetch specification. Understanding how these operations work behind the scene will open doors to possibilities tinkering with code can bring. Sometimes an application may require built-on-the-fly fetch specifications. With the plethora of techniques available to fetch data, keep in mind that all use the same underlying steps:

Writing Fetch Specifications

- ❑ Build a fetch specification
- ❑ Direct the editing context to query the database using the fetch specification
- ❑ Present an array of objects

Step One: Gathering What We Need

To demonstrate building a code-based fetch, accessing our Enterprise Objects, editing them, and returning the results to the back-end database, let's add a component to our sample application. The component we build in this example will enable a user to search for a customer, and, if successful, display a list of results. If the customer search is not successful, a message will be displayed saying that the search was not successful.

We will build a sample application that lets us view records in the Customer entity, using the sample database and model used in Chapter 5. Don't forget to add the Java classes representing the database entities being used.

To get started, create a new project called Sample in Project Builder. Add the EOModel file by selecting **Add Files** from the **Project** menu. In Project Builder, double-click on the EOModel file, which will launch EOModeler and open the selected file. Select the database, and then choose **Generate Java Source Code for Selected Entities**. EOModeler will then ask for class names for each entity. Choose the default names to keep this simple. In ProjectBuilder, under the **Project** menu, choose **Add Files** and select your newly created Java class files to add to your project for the Application Server target. Exit EOModeler.

Step Two: Creating the Interface in WebObjects Builder

In Project Builder, select **New** from the **File** menu, and choose a WebObjects component from the **Assistant** dialog. For **Component Name**, type **CustomerLookup**. For **Location**, set the location where WebObjects projects are stored on your local drive, and click **Finish**. Open the Main.wo component with WebObjects Builder, and add a WOHyperlink to the CustomerLookup component with the text **Go to Customer Lookup Page**.

Double-click the CustomerLookup.wo icon to launch WebObjects Builder and edit the CustomerLookup Web Component to contain the field for names to be searched. The values the user enters in these fields will be used to create the EOQualifier. A String instance variable will be needed: customerName2Find. Add as a key in the component and bind to the value attribute of the WOTextField in the search form. Bind an action named lookUpCustomer to the WOSubmit button. Place a WOForm around this section.

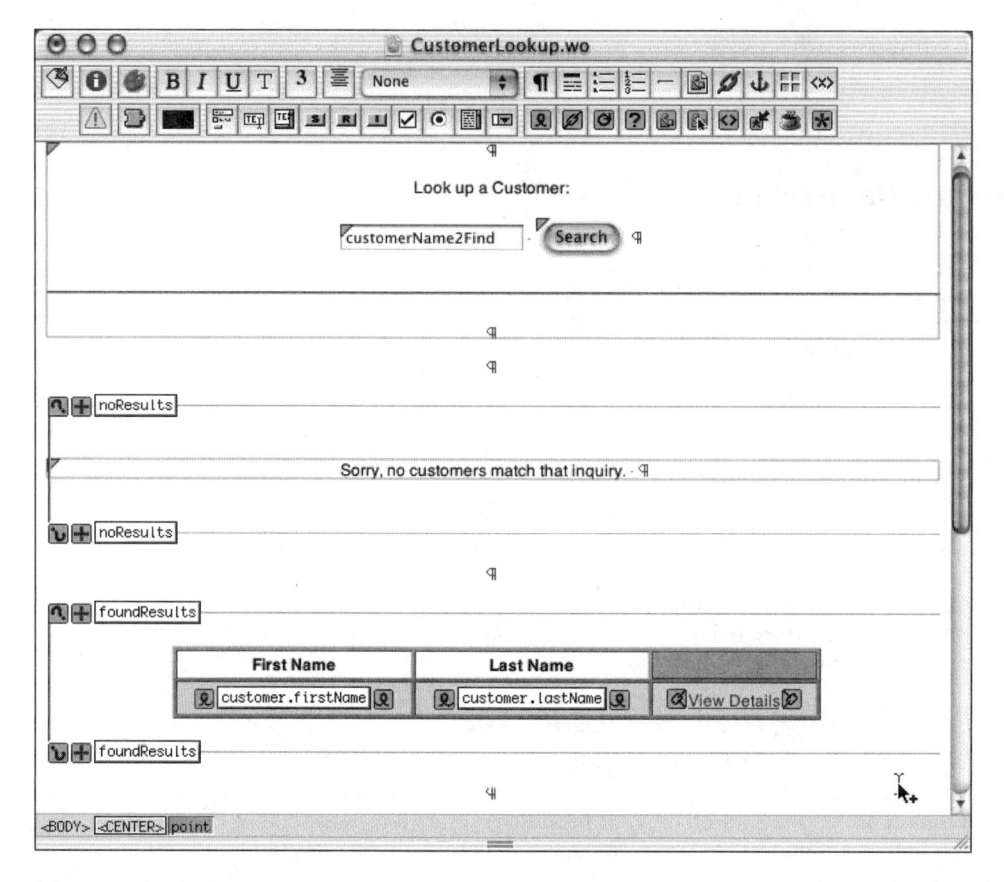

By adding conditionals, we can make the interface look clean, and control the amount of information a user is exposed to – supplying the right amount of detail when needed so as not to overwhelm. The conditionals we will use are `foundResults` and `showDetails`. Add keys specified as `booleans`, and bind to the appropriate `WOConditional` elements.

We need to add other elements to this user interface; a message to display when the results are returned `null` is added first. In an evolved version of this application, we could also include a `WOHyperlink` to an `Add Record` component. We also need a table with `WORepetition` to display the successful results of a search. Add `WOStrings` for the column (or field) names, and a `WOHyperlink` that gets bound to an action named `viewDetails`.

Writing Fetch Specifications

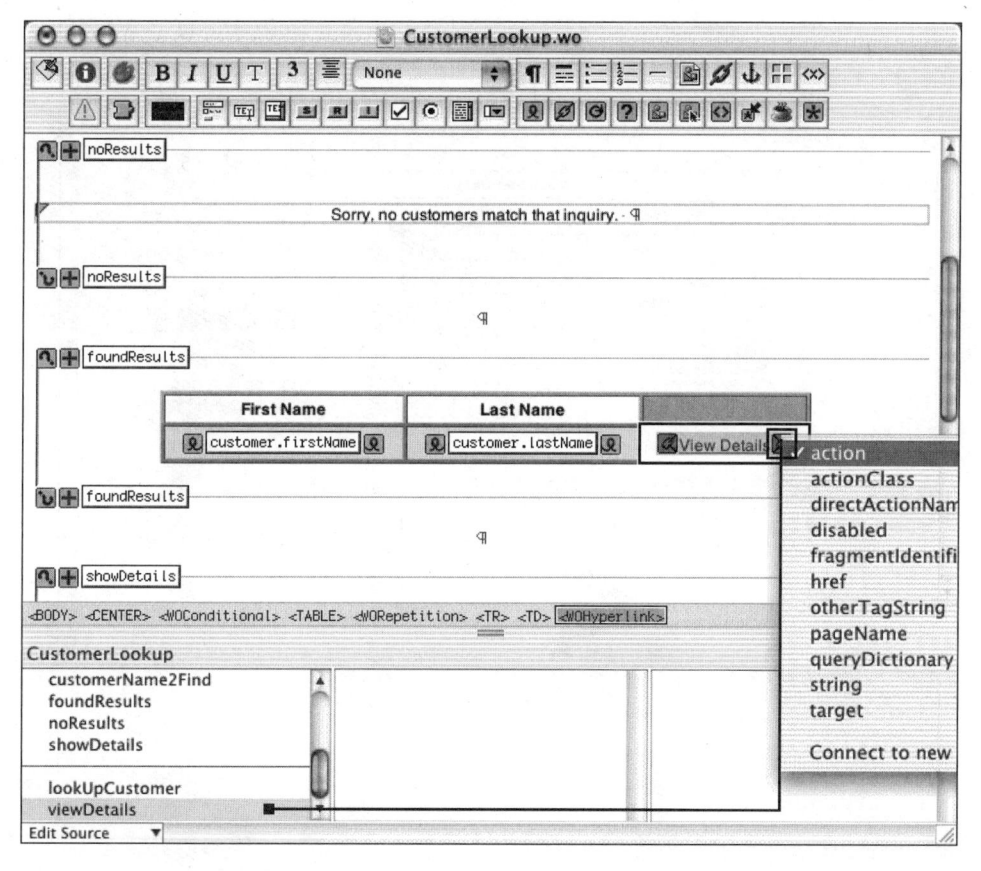

[Screenshot of CustomerLookup.wo in WebObjects Builder]

Finally, in the `WOConditional showDetails`, we will add a table to display the individual information from a selected record. This conditional will remain hidden unless the user clicks the **View Details** link. We now need to add these keys: `customer`, of class `Customer`; and `customerList`, an `NSArray`. Set the `WORepetition` list to `customers` and the item to `customer`. The customer data in this table is presented in `WOStrings` bound to various columns from our database.

197

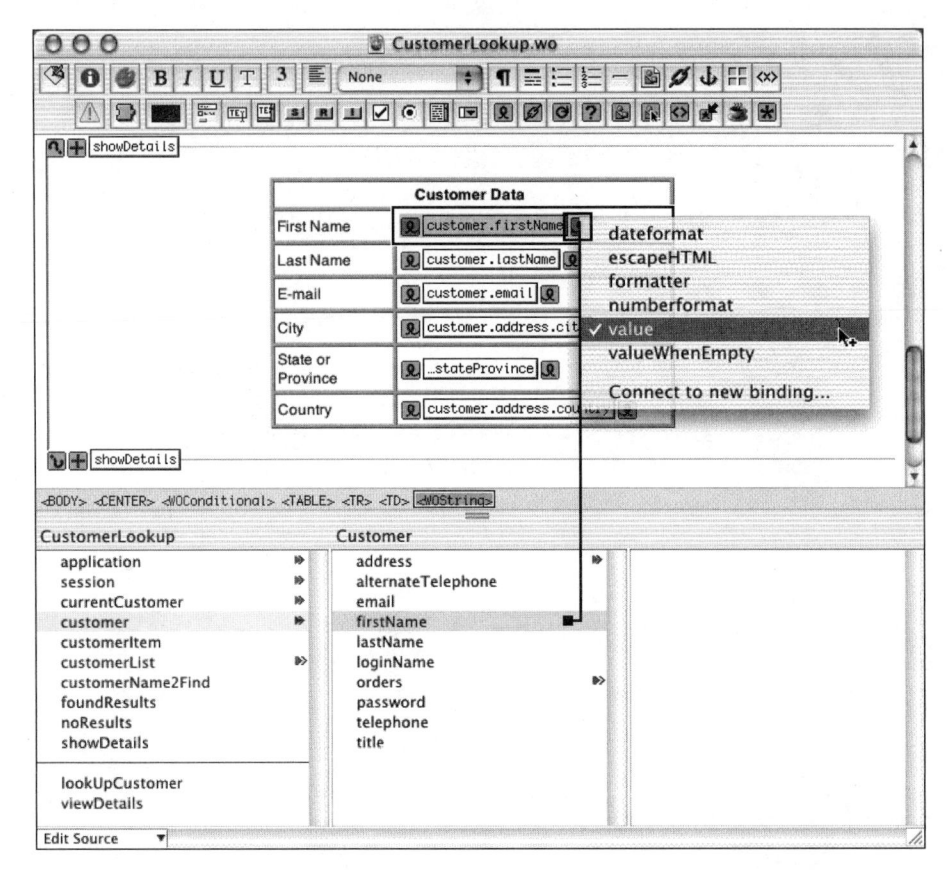

[Screenshot of CustomerLookup.wo component in WebObjects Builder]

The **Customer Data** is a good candidate for using a subcomponent. While our example does not use a subcomponent, this is a good habit that stimulates reusability. The `lookUpCustomer` action method will initiate the search using a fetch specification that we will build in the `CustomerLookup.java` file. The `viewDetails` action will enable display of the table in the `showDetails WOConditional`.

Step Three: Adding Custom Code in Project Builder

At this point we can view the Java class file for our `WOComponent` in Project Builder. We will now build the qualifiers for the first and last names, and then add a `WORepetition` to the component in WebObjects Builder.

While sometimes it is convenient to just retrieve all rows from a particular table in our database, this search form is used to locate a specific customer. Performing an unqualified fetch requires creating a new `EOFetchSpecification` (using the 3 argument constructor) and providing the name of the table to be fetched. Specify `null` for the remaining two arguments, and we get an unqualified and unsorted fetch.

The `EOQualifier` is used to specify which objects will be retrieved from the database, that is, it's used to "qualify" the otherwise unqualified set of objects to be retrieved. There are a number of useful subclasses as well: `EOAndQualifier`, `EOKeyComparisonQualifier`, and so on. A basic qualifier is the `EOKeyValueQualifier`, which compares a property of the object to some value using one of the `NSSelector` constants that specify the comparison operator. Using `EOAndQualifier` or `EOOrQualifier`, we can build complex queries.

Writing Fetch Specifications

To make it easy for the user, we will create a means so that either first or last name can be entered into the search text field:

```
String name2FindString = "*";
if (customerName2Find != null) {
  name2FindString = customerName2Find+"*";
}
NSArray bindings = new String( new Object[] {name2FindString, name2FindString});
```

This creates the string `customerName2Find` that is then used to build the qualifier. This is a case where building our own fetch specification gives us more flexibility: we can append the asterisk to the end of the search string, so that, used with the SQL `like` operator, the user can type part of a search query and get a list of matching results.

```
EOQualifier qualifier = EOQualifier.qualifierWithQualifierFormat(
                            "firstName like %@ or lastName like %@",
                            bindings);
```

Let's take a look at the syntax of qualifiers, which are database independent. `QualifierWithBindings` returns a new qualifier created by substituting all `EOQualifierVariables` with the values contained in the provided argument. The object passed to this method contains the values to which the `EOQualifierVariables` are bound, such as those entered by the user. If the second argument is `true`, then the new qualifier requires all its variables. If a value is not found for a variable in the provided object, an `EOQualifierVariableSubstitutionException` is raised. If the second argument is `false`, then the new qualifier does not require all its variables; and if the user has left that field for the qualifier blank, the element of the query is discarded or ignored.

Another element, `bindingKeys`, returns an array of strings representing the binding keys for the `EOQualifierVariables` contained in the qualifier. For example, if you have a qualifier such as `customerSince = $date`, this method returns an array of the string `date`. Multiple occurrences would only appear once in the returned array. When you use a qualified binding, another element, `keyPathForBindingKey`, returns the method needed for the key, `customer` in `customer.customerSince= $date`.

Of course, we want to sort the returned data. Because there are two fields (first and last name), we want to sort by last name as the primary, and first name as the secondary keys. The orderings are then stored in an array.

```
EOSortOrdering lastNameSortOrdering = EOSortOrdering.sortOrderingWithKey(
                            "lastName", EOSortOrdering.CompareAscending);
EOSortOrdering firstNameSortOrdering = EOSortOrdering.sortOrderingWithKey(
                            "firstName", EOSortOrdering.CompareAscending);
NSArray sortOrderings = new NSArray(new Object[]{ lastNameSortOrdering,
                            firstNameSortOrdering });
```

Now we can create the fetch specification, which we'll name `fetchSpec`. Remember that we need to specify the entity to search (`Customer` table), the qualifier (in our case, either the `firstName` or `lastName`), and finally the `sortOrderings` (an array of the keys to sort on, `lastName` and `firstName`).

```
EOFetchSpecification fetchSpec = new EOFetchSpecification("Customer",
                                                          qualifier,
                                                          sortOrderings);
```

To use the data fetched from the database, we will use an editing context. For example, rather than just viewing a customer's detailed information, we could permit the user to edit the data and re-post it to the database. We will use the editing context to populate the `customerList` that is returned when a successful search is made.

```
EOEditingContext myEditingContext = this.session().defaultEditingContext();
customerList = myEditingContext.objectsWithFetchSpecification(fetchSpec);
```

`EOEditingContexts` can be viewed as working areas into which objects are fetched and modified. By default, every session is given its own `defaultEditingContext` as a means of separating different user's objects.

A bit of housekeeping comes next. We want to display a message when no records match the query; if successful, we want to display a table of returned records summarized for the user.

```
    if (customerList.count() == 0) {
      noResults = true;
      foundResults = false;

    } else {
      noResults = false;
      foundResults = true;

    }
    showDetails = false;
    return null;
}
```

Here is the complete code for `CustomerLookup.java`:

```java
import com.webobjects.foundation.*;
import com.webobjects.appserver.*;
import com.webobjects.eocontrol.*;
import com.webobjects.eoaccess.*;

public class CustomerLookup extends WOComponent {
  protected String customerName2Find;

  /** @TypeInfo com.webobjects.eocontrol.Customer */
  protected NSArray customerList;
  protected Customer customer;
  protected boolean foundResults;
  protected boolean showDetails;
  protected boolean noResults = false;

  public CustomerLookup(WOContext context) {
    super(context);
  }
```

```java
// This is where we do our intitial search
public WOComponent lookUpCustomer() {

  String name2FindString = "*";
  if (customerName2Find != null) {
    name2FindString = customerName2Find + "*";
  }

  NSArray bindings = new NSArray(new Object[] {
    name2FindString, name2FindString
  });

  EOQualifier qualifier =
    EOQualifier
      .qualifierWithQualifierFormat("firstName like %@ or lastName like %@",
                                    bindings);

  EOSortOrdering lastNameSortOrdering =
    EOSortOrdering.sortOrderingWithKey("lastName",
                                       EOSortOrdering.CompareAscending);

  EOSortOrdering firstNameSortOrdering =
    EOSortOrdering.sortOrderingWithKey("firstName",
                                       EOSortOrdering.CompareAscending);

  NSArray sortOrderings = new NSArray(new Object[] {
    lastNameSortOrdering, firstNameSortOrdering
  });

  EOFetchSpecification fetchSpec = new EOFetchSpecification("Customer",
        qualifier, sortOrderings);

  EOEditingContext myEditingContext =
    this.session().defaultEditingContext();

  customerList =
    myEditingContext.objectsWithFetchSpecification(fetchSpec);

  if (customerList.count() == 0) {
    noResults = true;
    foundResults = false;

  } else {
    noResults = false;
    foundResults = true;

  }
  showDetails = false;
  return null;
}

// The View Customer conditional component
public WOComponent viewDetails() {
  showDetails = true;
  foundResults = false;
```

Chapter 8

```
        noResults = false;
        return null;
    }
}
```

Doing a fetch by hand can be cumbersome, but provides flexibility. When building a fetch specification, think of what is needed from the database, starting with the entity name, or table. Next, which items do we want to look for? The qualifier or qualifiers (think of the `where` statement in SQL) that determine which fields to search in – this is an object-oriented way to describe criteria for picking the items sought. Finally, we present an array of sort orderings, so we don't rely on the lack of order of items as they appear in the database. The finished application looks like this:

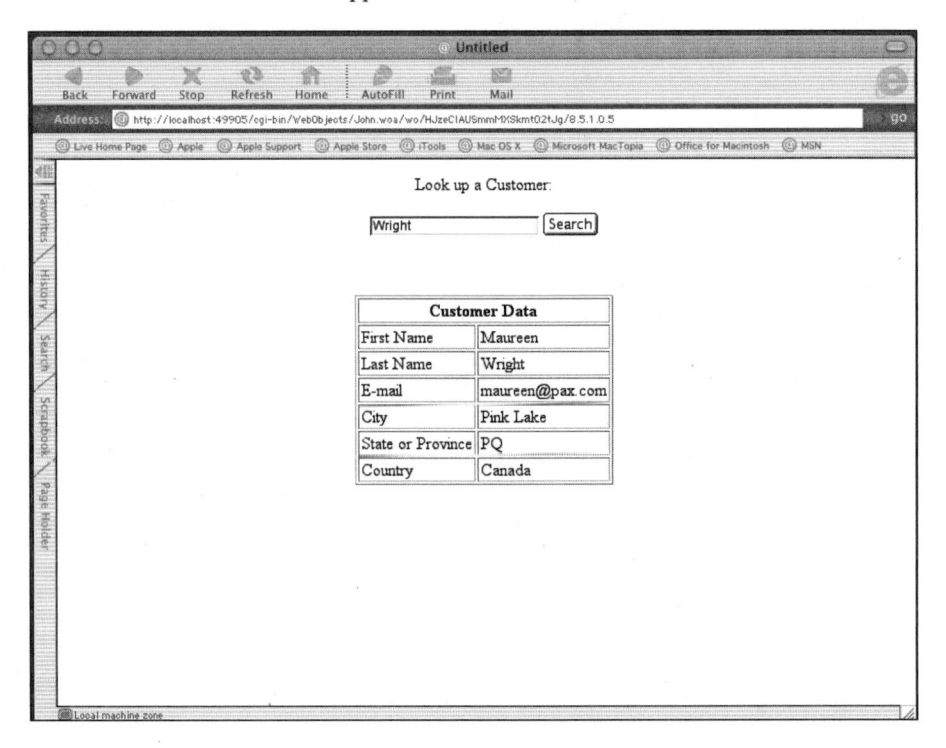

Creating a Fetch Specification Using EOModeler

The integrated development environment Apple has provided also gives us an easy way to build fetch specifications in EOModeler. Stored in our model file, we can then refer to these fetch specifications by name anywhere in our application. The functionality available programmatically is also present in EOModeler. If we need to modify a given query, we can do it once in the model file and not worry where occurrences are in our application – the hallmark of object-oriented design.

Step One: Starting with EOModeler

WebObjects provides the tools needed to create robust fetches. A fetch is associated with a specific entity, so the first step is to open our model in EOModeler. Once open, select the **Customer** entity.

Writing Fetch Specifications

Then choose the New Fetch Specification in Selected Entity button to create Fetch Spec1; rename to lastNameFetchSpec.

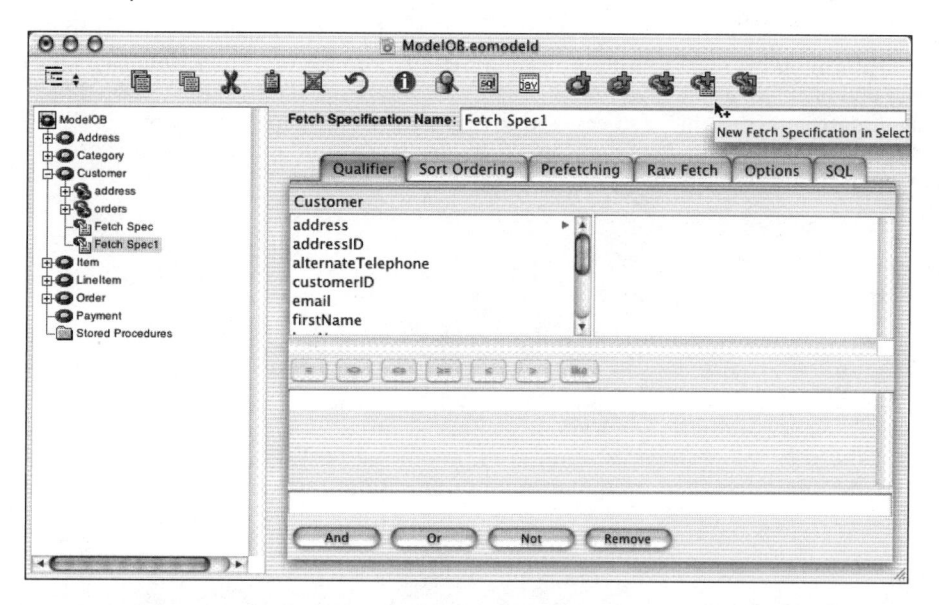

To modify the qualifier, we associate attributes with operators and values. Buttons at the bottom of EOModeler's Qualifier tab let us build complex qualifiers using And, Or, and Not. Click on the lastName field specified in the list of columns under the Customer table. Don't forget to click on the top input field to enable selecting the column names. The column name lastName now appears in the input area. Choose the like button, which, along with the other operators, will be active.

Because we want to have the user input the values to be searched for, we will add a placeholder to capture the data input from the application, and to be stored in an NSDictionary. We will add $lastNameValue to the input field so that, at runtime, an NSDictionary containing a key equal to our string lastNameValue will be substituted. It is the value represented by this qualifier that will be associated with the key.

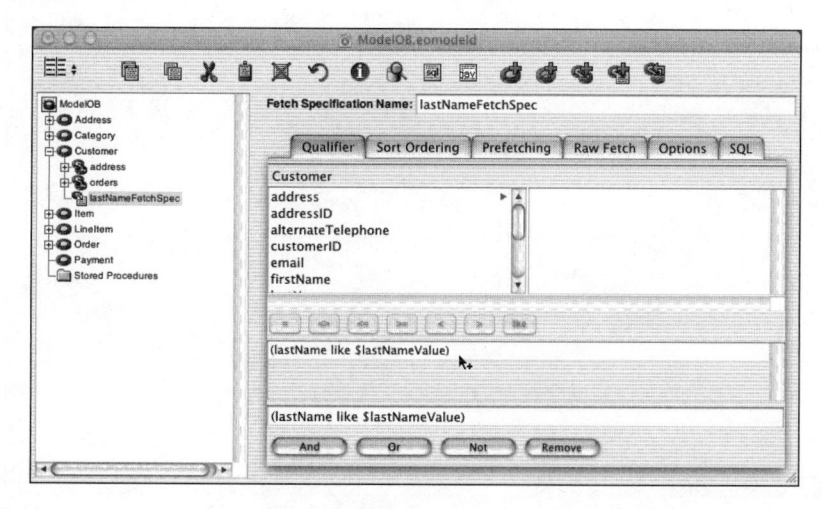

Chapter 8

Adding statements with the And, Or, and Not buttons means we can build complex searches in EOModeler with minimal effort – the parentheses will be added automatically. For this example, we will use just one statement.

The next step is to set the sort ordering: click on the **Sort Ordering** tab, choose the field **lastName** from the column and click the now-active **Add** button. The two icons at the right of the added field indicate ascending or descending sorting, and case sensitivity. Turn on case insensitivity by clicking the **s** icon to turn it into an **i**, then select the field **firstName** from the list and add it to the sort ordering. Turn on case insensitivity for this ordering as well.

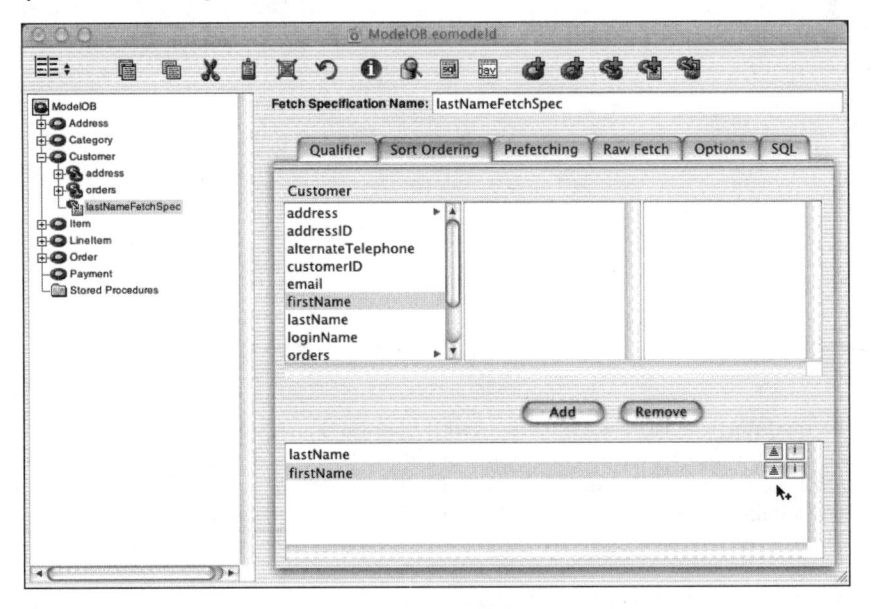

Have the EOModeler generate the Java source code files for the tables (entities) in the sample to use in our application, using their names as the default class names.

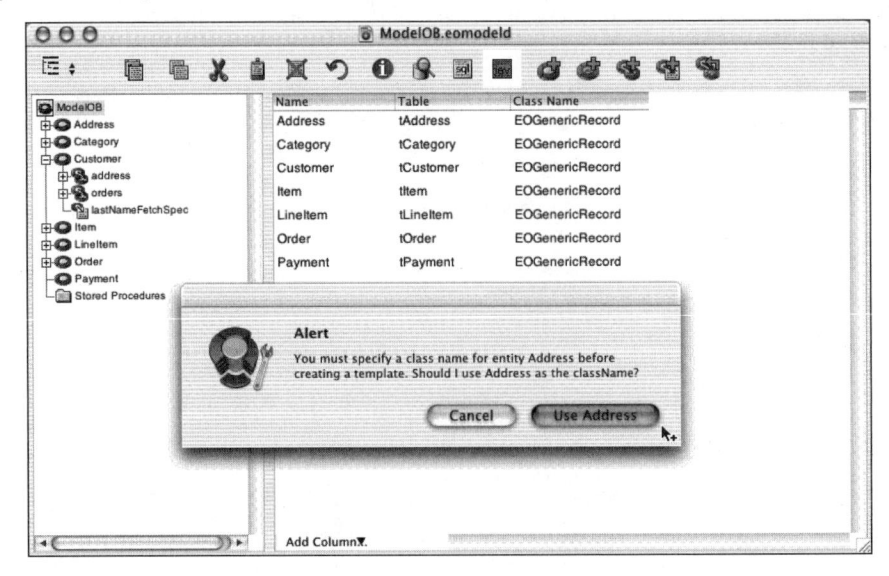

There are four other tabs in the Fetch Specification editing pane, offering advanced features that can be used for a particular fetch specification: setting the sort ordering of rows retrieved; defining prefetching rules; setting the type of objects returned, either as enterprise objects or as raw rows; setting fetch limits setting various options (fetch limits, locking, whether to fetch distinct rows, whether to refresh existing EOs from prefetched objects, and whether the fetch spec requires all variable bindings); and finally a SQL tab that lets you write your own SQL if you need to, rather than using a qualifier specified under the GUI's **Qualifier** tab. Also, the SQL tab enables you to enter in raw SQL to use for the fetch. Remember that raw SQL must conform to the constraints of the back-end database. If you change databases, raw SQL specific to one database might not work. The EOModeler application can be used to define all the details of a fetch specification instead of having to do so programmatically, and is especially useful for building frequently used fetches.

What's Going On Here?

Now we want to retrieve the fetch specification in our application. Getting at this object means we must delve into the `EOEntity` object that is associated with the entity containing our fetch specification – the `Customer` entity in this example. An `EOEntity` describes a table in a database and associates a name internal to the Framework with an external name by which the table is known to the database. We will use a static method called `fetchSpecificationNamed()`, using the name of the entity and name of the fetch specification.

There is a variety of means to retrieve a fetch specification, and if we have many associated with any given entity, we may want to choose a more code-intensive means of accessing the fetch specifications. A model-based fetch specification can be retrieved using the model group and entity classes. In addition, while it is possible to just get the `EOEntity` object from the `EOModel` object, we may likely want to include fetch specifications from more than one model for use in our application. So we could retrieve the object via the `EOModelGroup`, which contains all models for the application.

To bind the substitution values in our code using an `NSDictionary`, we want to create an `NSMutableDictionary` containing the keys named in the fetch specification – `lastName` in our example. In the `EOFetchSpecification` class we use the `fetchSpecificationWithQualifierBindings()` method. In a query with multiple keys, we may want part of the qualifier to go unused if not supplied. EOModeler also provides the option of requiring all variables, depending on the application demands. EOModeler lets you set this, but it is an `EOFetchSpecification` configuration and can also be specified programmatically.

We need to initialize the dictionary, not necessarily in the constructor. We can also bind in WebObjects builder, as long as the dictionary is an instance variable and is created as part of a component's constructor. Remember to always create a `NSMutableDictionary` before calling `setObjectForKey()` on it.

Substitution values are entered in WebObjects Builder; we would use an `NSMutableDictionary` and enter the key `lastNameValue`. Since `NSDictionary` implements `NSKeyValueCoding`, you can specify a key path which specifies a key name that will be used to set and access an object in the dictionary. Naming the dictionary `bindingsDictionary`, the `WOTextField` value binding is then designated `bindingsDictionary.lastNameValue`. This makes sense to reduce code overhead, but we lose some functionality because the asterisk we appended in our code-based approach is not present. When a query uses the `like` operator, this means the user must add the asterisk along with the characters entered. Other operators do not have this drawback – one reason using this approach has limitations.

To demonstrate using a model-based fetch specification, let's add a component to our Sample application. The component we will build for this sample will allow users to search for customers by last name, returning a list of found customers. Our user interface will consist of a field to input the customer's last name, a button to initiate the search, and a table to display the results. The process behind this will consist of holding the name to be searched for in a string variable; accessing the fetch specification from the model; delivering the name to be searched for; and returning the results (if any) to the user.

Step Two: Creating the Interface in WebObjects Builder

Let's put the pieces together by adding a new WebObjects Component to our Sample application in Project Builder.

We want to build the web interface and create our code. Add a Web Component named **Search**. Double-click the Main.wo file found in the Web Component named Main to open it in WebObjects Builder. Add a WOHyperLink, and select the Search page as the target.

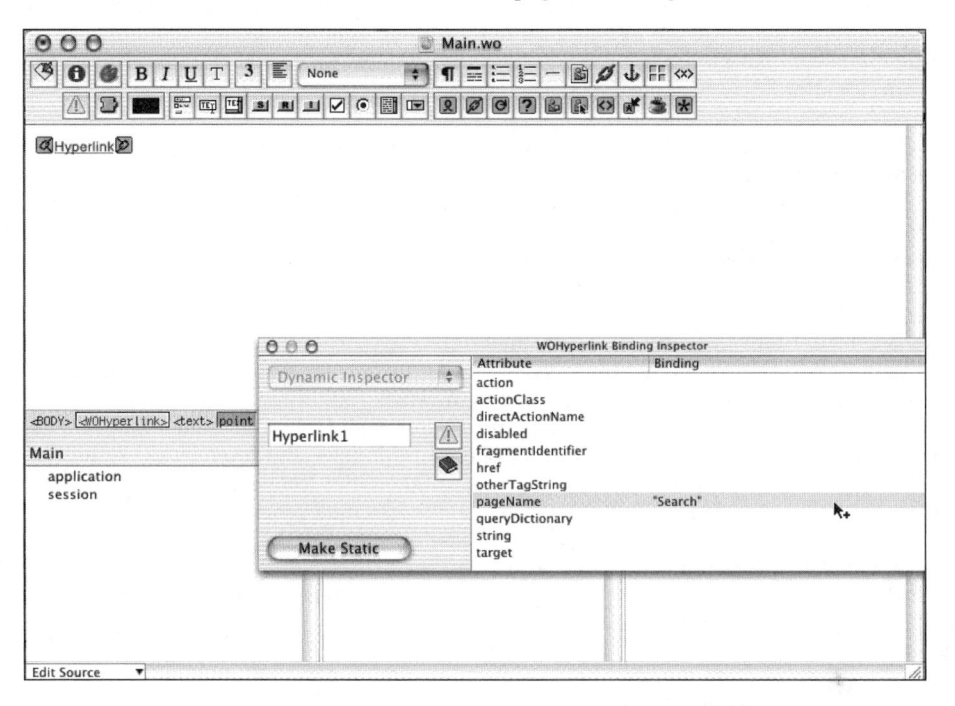

Now we'll design the Search page. Open Search.wo in WebObjects builder, add text to describe the user action desired, and add a WOTextField. Add a WOSubmit button as well, then select the WOTextField and WOSubmit button, and wrap in a WOForm. To display the results of our search, add a table to contain the WORepetition. Set up your page to resemble the figure following, with a **WOTextField** where the user will enter the lastName value. Name the WOSubmit button **Search**. Add a message **Sorry, no customers with that last name found** in a WOConditional named **noResults**.

Writing Fetch Specifications

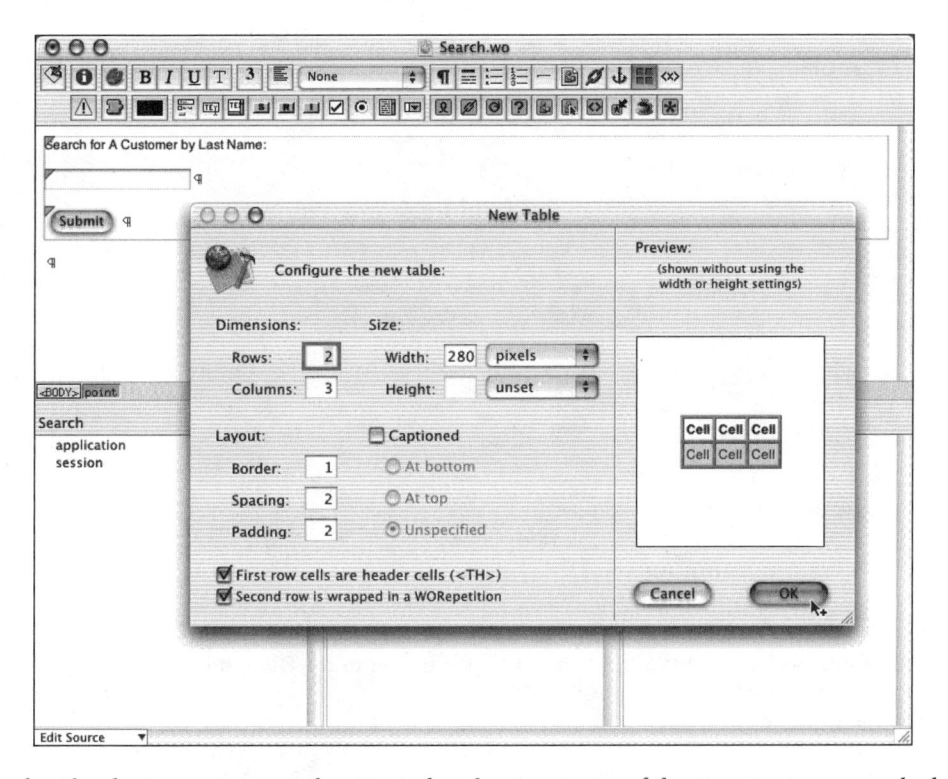

Add a key for the `lastname` search string, a key for `customer` of the type `Customer`, and a key named `customers` that is an `NSArray` of `Customer`.

Now create a key named `queryBindings` that is defined as an `NSMutableDictionary`. Bind the key `queryBindings` to the `WOTextField`, and set the value to the `keyPath` that specifies the key to access the dictionary (`queryBindings.lastNameValue`) we created with EOModeler in our model file. You don't need the $ symbol.

Set the `WORepetition` list to `customers` and the item to `customer`. Add `WOStrings` for first and last names, and e-mail. This repetition will display the results of our search; we want to display additional information associated with the customer record retrieved: the customer's first name and e-mail address.

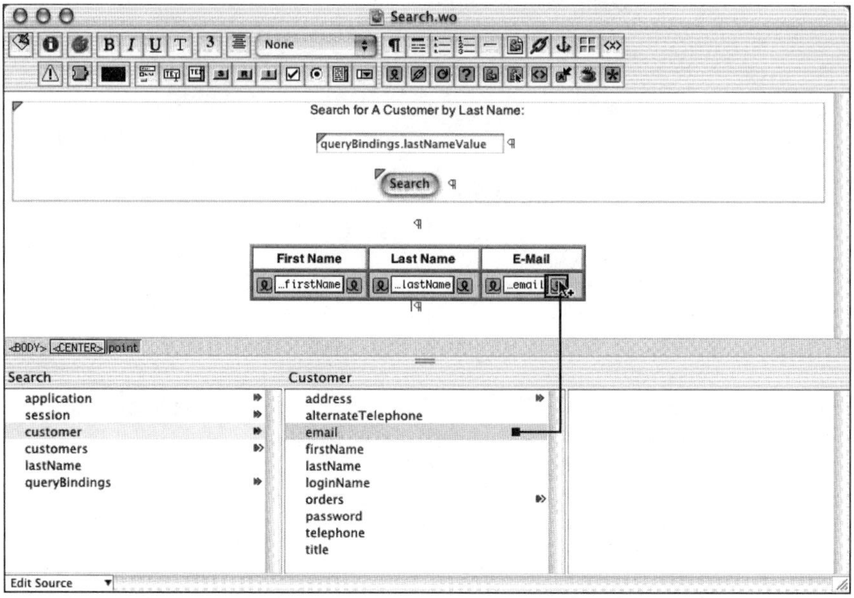
Search.wo
None
Search for A Customer by Last Name:
queryBindings.lastNameValue
Search
First Name
Last Name
E-Mail
...firstName
...lastName
...email
<BODY> <CENTER> point
Search
Customer
application
session
customer
customers
lastName
queryBindings
address
alternateTelephone
email
firstName
lastName
loginName
orders
password
telephone
title
Edit Source

Add an action named `searchForCustomers` that is linked to the **Search** button in the `WOForm`.

To neaten things up, we will put a `WOConditional` around the results table; add a `boolean` key named `showResults` and bind it to the `WOConditional`. Now that we've completed our interface, we will return to Project Builder to add the remaining code needed.

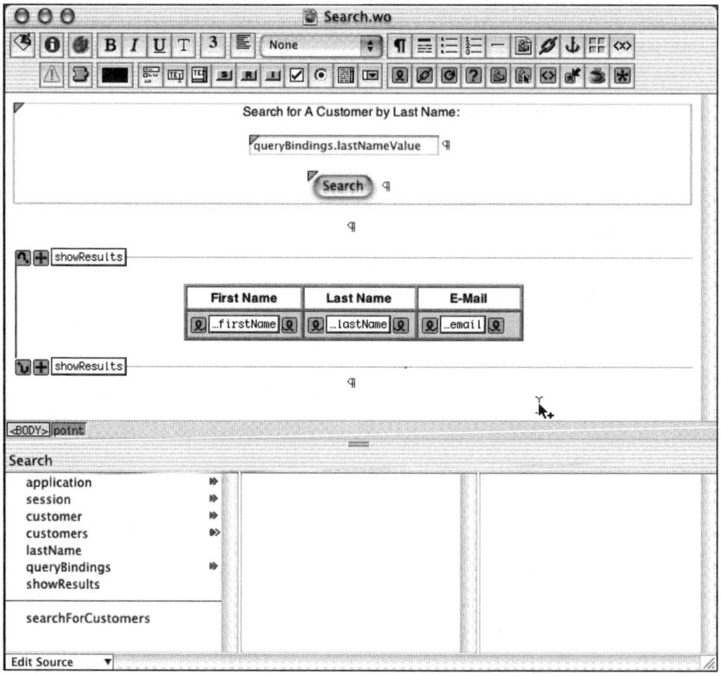
Search.wo
None
Search for A Customer by Last Name:
queryBindings.lastNameValue
Search
showResults
First Name
Last Name
E-Mail
...firstName
...lastName
...email
showResults
<BODY> point
Search
application
session
customer
customers
lastName
queryBindings
showResults
searchForCustomers
Edit Source

Writing Fetch Specifications

Step Three: Adding Custom Code in Project Builder

When we added the user interface components in WebObjects Builder, the basic structure of the code we will need was inserted into the `Search.java` file in Project Builder. But there are several bits of code we'll still need to add the old fashioned way: by typing it in. First, we need to create the dictionary that will hold the string (or strings) that will be searched for:

```
queryBindings = new NSMutableDictionary();
```

Now we need to get the fetch specification we created in our model. The arguments supplied will be the name of the fetch specification, and the entity in the database it is associated with:

```
EOFetchSpecification fetchSpec = EOFetchSpecification.fetchSpecificationNamed(
                                     "lastNameFetchSpec","Customer");
```

Because we are building a string to search for (the value supplied to the fetch specification), we will obtain the string from the user, and put it in a dictionary under the key that we specified in the named fetch specification in the model. Now we need to hand over that dictionary to the fetch specification:

```
fetchSpec = fetchSpec.fetchSpecificationWithQualifierBindings(queryBindings);
```

Let's copy a reference to the Editing Context to a local variable, for convenience named `myEditingContext`:

```
EOEditingContext myEditingContext = this.session().defaultEditingContext();
```

The list of results of the fetch, which we'll display in the `WORepetition`, is returned by our editing context associated with the objects retrieved:

```
customers = myEditingContext.objectsWithFetchSpecification(fetchSpec);
```

Finally, we show the results in the conditional, or show a message if the results are empty:

```
    if (customers.count() != 1) {
      showResults = false;
      noResults = true;
      return null;
    } else {
      showResults = true;
      noResults = false;
      return null;
    }
```

This is the final content of the `Search.java` file:

```
import com.webobjects.foundation.*;
import com.webobjects.appserver.*;
import com.webobjects.eocontrol.*;
import com.webobjects.eoaccess.*;
```

```
public class Search extends WOComponent {
  protected String lastName;
  protected Customer customer;

  /** @TypeInfo Customer */
  protected NSArray customers;
  protected NSMutableDictionary queryBindings;
  protected boolean showResults;
  protected boolean noResults;

  public Search(WOContext context) {
    super(context);

    queryBindings = new NSMutableDictionary();

  }

  public WOComponent searchForCustomers() {

    EOFetchSpecification fetchSpec =
      EOFetchSpecification.fetchSpecificationNamed("lastNameFetchSpec",
          "Customer");

    fetchSpec =
      fetchSpec.fetchSpecificationWithQualifierBindings(queryBindings);

    EOEditingContext myEditingContext = this.session().defaultEditingContext();

    customers = myEditingContext.objectsWithFetchSpecification(fetchSpec);

    if (customers.count() != 1) {
      showResults = false;
      noResults = true;
      return null;
    } else {
      showResults = true;
      noResults = false;
      return null;
    }
  }
}
```

To complete the application we need to add another `WOHyperlink` to the Main page linking to the Search page we have just created.

The compiled application is clean but has some limitations. The user must know the whole last name of the customer to search for. We could construct a string that would allow partial searches, appending an asterisk to the search string. But the fetch specification resides in the model file; it can be accessed from anywhere within our application. Also, changes made to the fetch specification in the model are accommodated easily – no code needs to change in the application. Here's the compiled application:

Writing Fetch Specifications

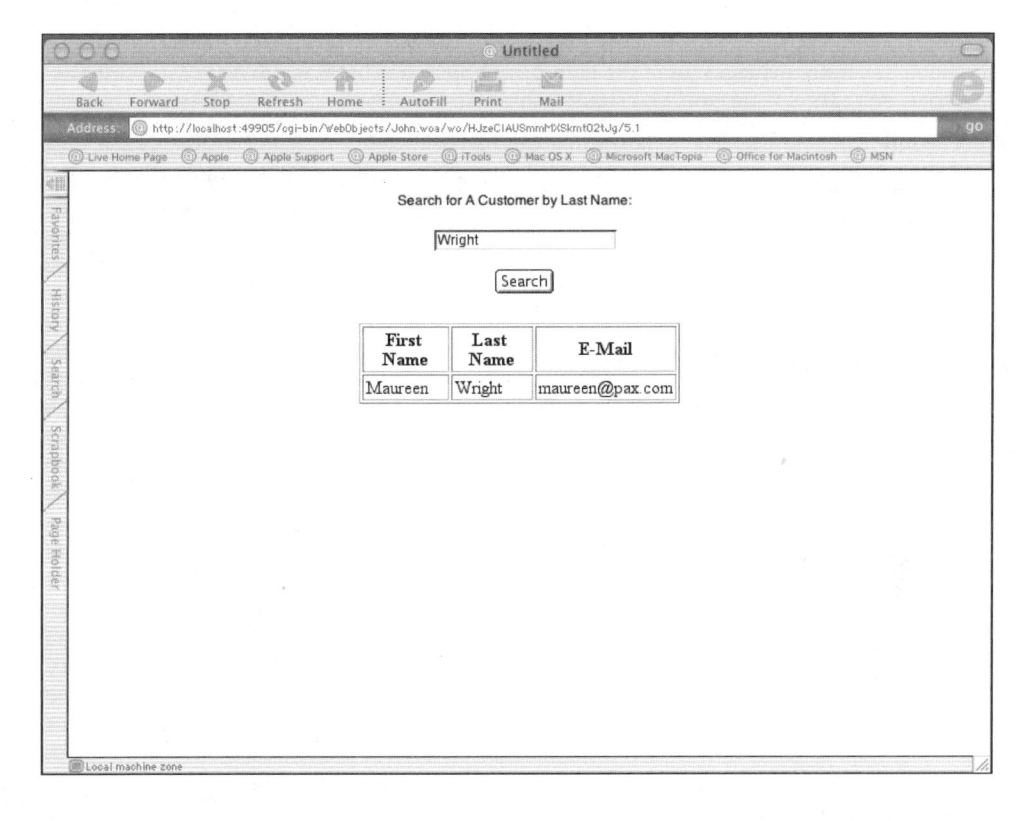

Summary

Performing a query of our database is as simple as asking the `EOEditingContext` for the records matching our fetch specification. Keep in mind that each session we invoke has a default editing context, and that we can use the enterprise objects fetched from a database just like any other object in our application. We can build our own fetch specifications programmatically or use EOModeler's graphical user interface. After reviewing this section, you should understand the following concepts relating to fetch specifications and the editing context:

- ❑ The process of fetching from the database requires these elements used by an `EOFetchSpecification`: the name of the entity to fetch from; an `EOQualifier` to qualify the data; and an array of `EOSortOrderings` to determine order. Of course, a model is needed as well as an `EOEditingContext`. Just follow the same elements – `qualifier`, `sortOrder`, `fetchSpec`, `fetch`.

- ❑ After we have defined a fetch specification, it can be used to fetch data from the object store. WebObjects translates the fetch specification into SQL statements that your database system can understand. The database returns a list of rows that WebObjects translates into enterprise objects (instances of `EOGenericRecord`) before returning them in an `NSArray`.

- ❑ An Editing Context is needed to perform the fetches, and is responsible for maintaining the object graph for the fetched objects. You keep your own collection of these objects, through which you access them. This includes persistent objects (such as data that already exists in some external store such as a database) as well as transient objects such as objects in memory, – even if they have never been represented in the back-end database.

- You access a session's default editing context by calling the session's default editing context, which generally manages all of the enterprise objects in that session: `editingContext = this.session().defaultEditingContext()`.
- The following are important classes that can be reviewed: `EOKeyValueQualifier`, `EOFetchSpecification`, `EOSortOrdering`, `EOQualifier`, `EOAndQualifier`, `EOOrQualifier`

Writing Fetch Specifications

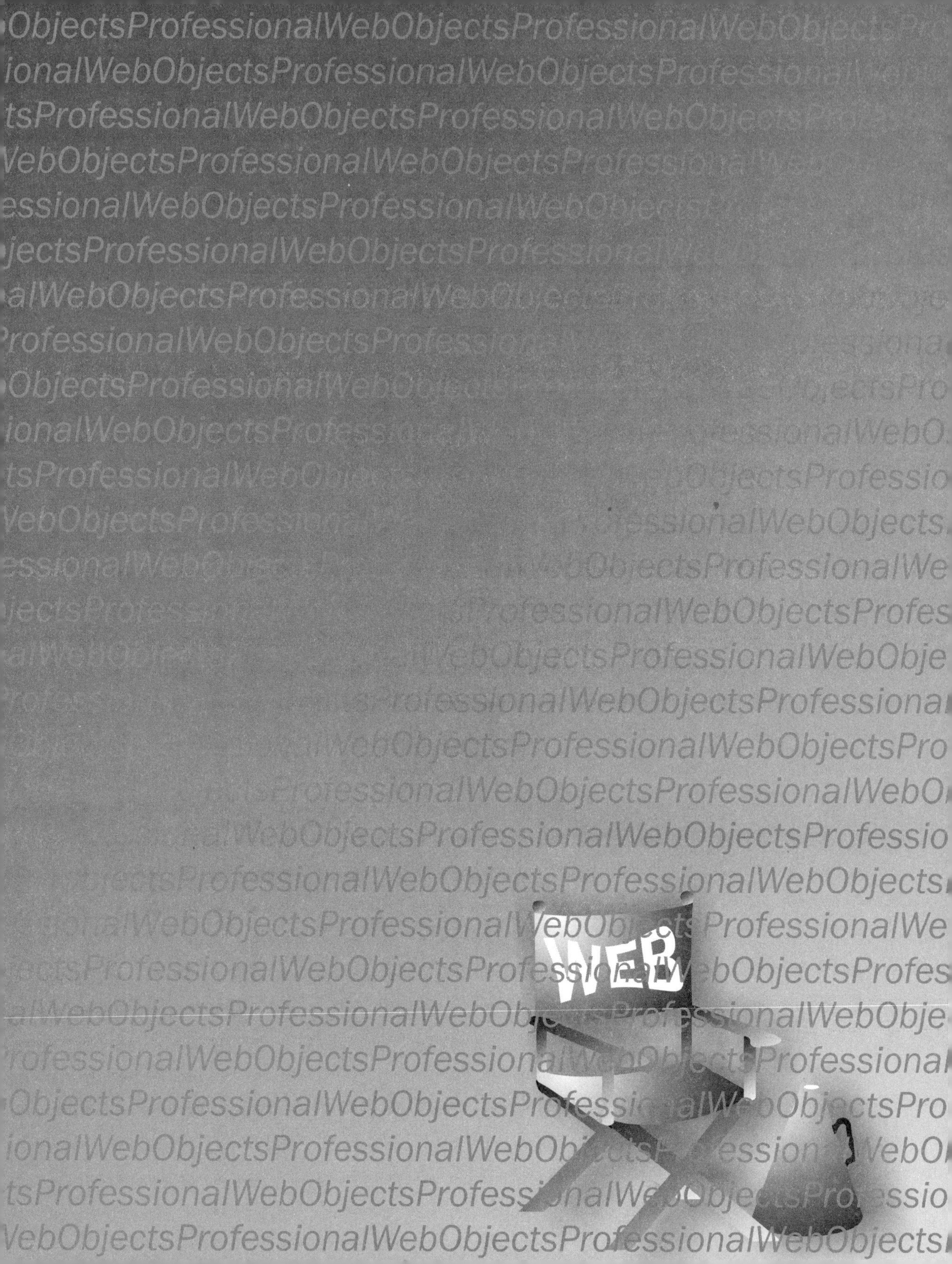
WebObjectsProfessional
WEB

9

Advanced EOF

This chapter discusses three main topics in relation to EOF: key-value coding, validation and locking. We will first explore how key-value coding works, where it is used and the advantages of using it, before discussing validation strategies and locking techniques. We will see how EOF utilizes these mechanisms and how they are all interrelated.

We will begin by exploring how key-value coding works, where it is used and the advantages of using it. We will see how EOF utilizes key-value coding, and what special circumstances have to be taken into account when incorporating it into our custom classes. We will then discuss how we can validate data and what techniques we should use to carry out validation. Finally we will look at how to protect our data from accidental changes and how we can implement data locking. We will be presenting relevant code templates and snippets throughout this chapter, where italicised code should be replaced with specific custom code words.

Key-Value Coding

Key-value coding (KVC) is a mechanism used for accessing object properties through a defined interface. It enables access to these properties by a key name, which means that we do not have to access an instance variable directly or use a pre-learned custom accessor method.

A **key** in WebObjects is a string that is the name of an object attribute. This attribute can be derived or directly related to an instance variable. Key-value coding enables you to retrieve or set the values of these attributes by referring to the key, rather than by calling a specific object method. When key-value coding is used in conjunction with EOF, the attributes of objects are called properties.

Keys are heavily used in WebObjects; for example, we bind an instance variable by using its name as the key to a dynamic element. An instance variable named `foo` can be bound to a dynamic element by the key `foo`. However, we could also use `bar` as the key to access the property `foo` of our Enterprise Object (you can think of `bar` as a derived attribute here), so long as we conform to the WebObjects key-value coding convention.

This convention is defined by the interface `NSKeyValueCoding` in the Foundation Framework of WebObjects. In conjunction with the Enterprise Objects Framework (which we use for doing any data storage operations) there is a second convention defined by `EOKeyValueCoding`, to address the special needs of the EOF.

The benefit of key-value coding is that it gives us a consistent way of accessing attributes of objects and it does not rely on other data transportation mechanisms. By using key-value coding, we place a further abstraction wrapper around our Enterprise Objects. Key-value coding gives us a standardized easy-to-use interface to every Enterprise Object. We can think of keys as a language-independent way of accessing object properties. We can even resolve values across multiple object references by using key paths.

Keys are used by WebObjects primarily in WebObjects Builder. We bind a key or key path to dynamic elements or custom components. The WebObjects Framework uses these keys to access the properties of our components or Enterprise Objects, to store or retrieve data. We can even bind properties of custom classes to these components or dynamic elements, if they implement the key-value coding interface.

The objects specified by the keys are not typed and this means that we can use a key path to access a property of referenced objects without knowing what kind of objects we are dealing with.

WebObjects offers two different flavors of key-value coding. One general approach, which is usable with any kind of object, and one supplemental approach used for handling Enterprise Objects. The next section will cover both ways.

General Key-Value Coding: NSKeyValueCoding

Key-value coding is defined by the abstract interface `NSKeyValueCoding`. There is also a default implementation `NSKeyValueCoding.DefaultImplementation` that is used by most WebObjects classes notably `WOComponent` and `EOGenericRecord` (as a subclass of `EOCustomObject`, which implements the interface).

Key-value coding is defined in the Foundation Framework (see Appendix A) and is made up of several interfaces and classes, as the table below illustrates:

Interface/Class	Description
`NSKeyValueCoding`	Interface that defines the basic access methods
`NSKeyValueCoding.DefaultImplementation`	Class that provides a default implementation of the `NSKeyValueCoding` and `NSKeyValueCoding.ErrorHandling` interfaces
`NSKeyValueCoding.ErrorHandling`	Interface that defines the interface used in case of errors
`NSKeyValueCoding.Utility`	Class that uses key-value coding on non-enhanced classes

Advanced EOF

Interface/Class	Description
`NSKeyValueCodingAdditions`	Interface that enhances the standard interface to handle key paths
`NSKeyValueCodingAdditions.DefaultImplementation`	Class that is equivalent to `NSKeyValueCoding.DefaultImplementation` but is used for handling key paths
`NSKeyValueCodingAdditions.Utility`	Class that is equivalent to `NSKeyValueCoding.DefaultImplementation` but which is used when handling key paths

There is also a special constant: `NSKeyValueCoding.Null` that is used to handle `null` values.

If we are going to prepare a class to use key-value coding, we would simply implement the two methods defined by the interface of `NSKeyValueCoding`.

To set a value we use the following method:

```
void takeValueForKey(Object object, String key)
```

To retrieve a value, we use:

```
Object valueForKey(String key)
```

In our custom code, the implementation of these methods would call the default implementation.

> Because keys are just names, they do not need to correspond to variable names. Although a certain key's name will be the same as the variable name, it does not have to be! In fact, WebObjects Builder will scan the source code and provide keys which it recognizes. Only as a last resort does it present accessible instance variable names as keys!

A third method can be implemented to return `true` if direct access to instance variables is allowed and `false` if no direct access is allowed:

```
Boolean canAccessFieldsDirectly(){
```

This method is useful if we use the default implementation in our code or if we want to add additional protection to our class to ensure that access to properties by keys or key paths is performed using a corresponding accessor method rather than by accessing the instance variable directly. Ultimately this would help in writing better code although this would only be cosmetic if we don't make the instance variables private.

If we wanted to implement key-value coding and utilize the default implementation that is provided by Apple – which is highly recommended due to its performance optimizations – we would implement the following code (which in this case is used in a custom class called `Car`):

```
// import the NSKeyValueCoding interface
// located in the foundation framework of WebObjects

import com.webobjects.foundation.*;

public class Car extends ... implements NSKeyValueCoding, ... {
  //instance variables
  protected String color;
    ...

  //implementation of the key-value coding interface
  public Object valueForKey(String aKey) {
    return NSKeyValueCoding.DefaultImplementation.valueForKey(this, aKey);
  }

  public void takeValueForKey(Object aValue, String aKey) {
    NSKeyValueCoding.DefaultImplementation.
                     takeValueForKey(this, aValue, aKey);
  }
  // end of key-value coding interface
  // accessor methods
  public void setColor(String aColorName) {
    // some checks on the color name can go in here
    ...
    color = aColorName;
  }

  // other methods follow
  ...
}
```

In this code example, whenever a color property is set by using key-value coding (for example when bound in WebObjectsBuilder) the default key-value coding implementation will first call the `setColor()` method. If a color name is found, then the default implementation will not look for a `getColor()` or `color()` method and it would therefore access the instance variable `color` directly.

> We don't have to implement the key-value coding interface methods, if we are subclassing any classes of the WebObjects Frameworks which already implement the **NSKeyValueCoding** protocol, for example **WOComponent**. If not stated otherwise, these classes will utilize the default implementation and we get fully featured key-value coding for free.

All our key-value accessed property values are just store and retrieve values. This is useful when we want to get values from the user input and use retrieved values with other objects. The first step of handling this input might be to use a dictionary to hold all these values in the class accepting the user input. In this case, the key-value coding logic is simply:

```
// import the NSKeyValueCoding interface
import com.webobjects.foundation.*;

public class Car extends ... implements NSKeyValueCoding,{
  NSMutableDictionary keysDict = new NSMutableDictionary();
```

```
    // implementation of the key-value coding interface
    public Object valueForKey(String aKey){
      return keysDict.objectForKey(aKey);
    }

    public void takeValueForKey(Object aValue, String aKey){
      keysDict.setObjectForKey(aValue, aKey);
    }

    // end of key-value coding interface
    // other methods follow
}
```

The above example moves every key into the class' dictionary, enabling us to handle as many values as we want. Additionally we might want to enlarge this class by adding further instance variables with set and get accessor methods. These instance variables would be accessible by key-value coding because we already implemented the `NSKeyValueCoding` interface.

To enhance an existing business class unrelated to WebObjects, we would check the key first and call our own set and get accessor according to the given key in our implementation of the `valueForKey()` and `takeValueForKey()` methods.

The Default Implementation

To take full advantage of key-value coding, we need to know how the default implementation provided by `NSKeyValueCoding.DefaultImplementation` really works.

The default implementation uses three different ways to access the property with the following logic (replace *key* with the specific name of the key that should be accessed):

1. It looks for public accessor methods named `getKey()` or `key()` or `setKey()` for setting the value.

2. If this fails, it looks for private methods beginning with an underscore (`_getKey()` or `_key()` and `_setKey()` respectively).

3. If that fails again and the `canAccessFieldsDirectly()` returns `true`, the instance variables are accessed directly.

4. Otherwise the `handleQueryWithUnboundKey()` method or `handleTakeValueForUnboundKey()` if setting a value is invoked. This method implements the `NSKeyValueCoding.ErrorHandling` interface.

5. Finally if `handleQueryWithUnboundKey()` fails, an exception is raised (`NSKeyValueCoding.UnknownKeyException`). The exception provides information about the object throwing the exception (`TargetObjectUserInfoKey`) and the unknown key (`UnknownUserInfoKey`) in the exceptions info dictionary.

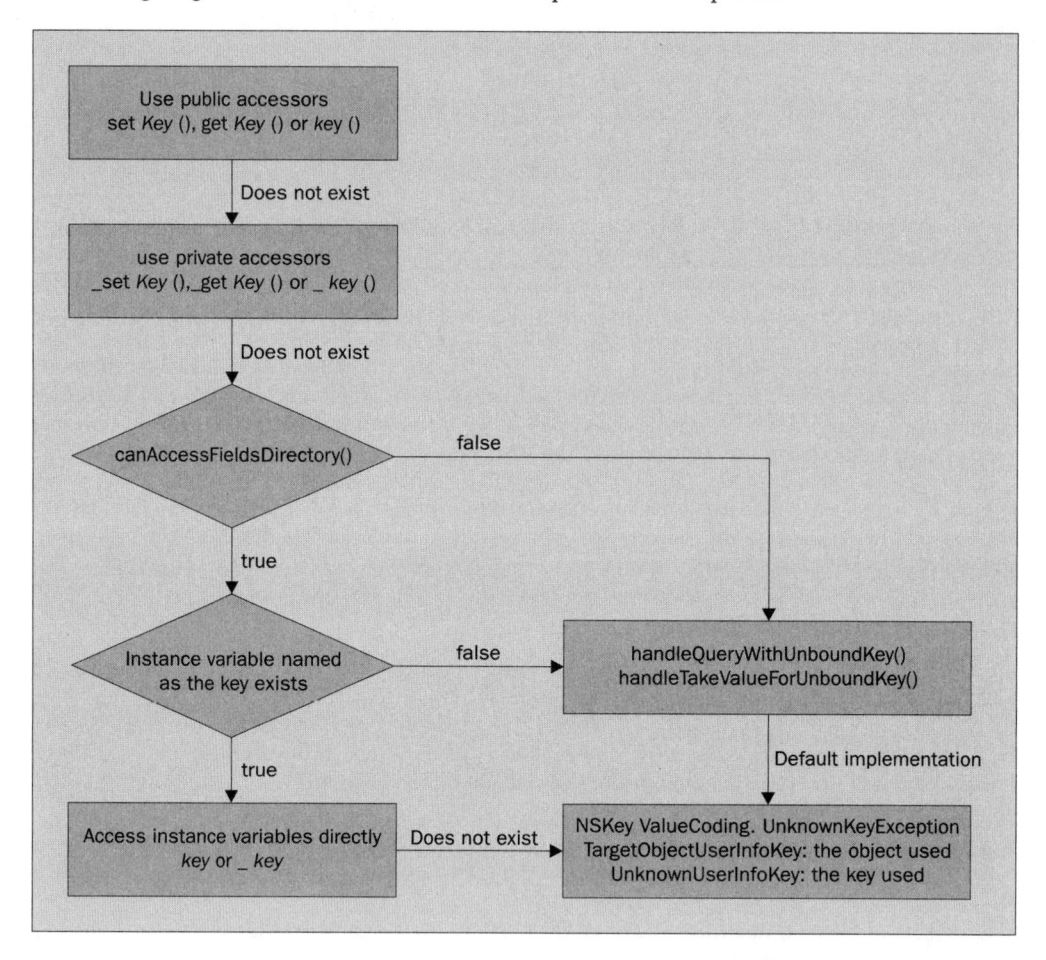

The following diagram illustrates how the default implementation operates:

```
┌─────────────────────────────────────────────────────────────────────┐
│                    ┌──────────────────────────┐                     │
│                    │    Use public accessors  │                     │
│                    │ set Key (), get Key () or key ()│              │
│                    └──────────┬───────────────┘                     │
│                               │ Does not exist                      │
│                    ┌──────────▼───────────────┐                     │
│                    │    use private accessors │                     │
│                    │ _set Key (),_get Key () or _ key ()│           │
│                    └──────────┬───────────────┘                     │
│                               │ Does not exist                      │
│                          ◇────┴────◇                                │
│                         ╱           ╲    false                      │
│                    canAccessFieldsDirectory()─────────────┐         │
│                         ╲           ╱                     │         │
│                          ◇────┬────◇                      │         │
│                               │ true                      │         │
│                          ◇────┴────◇    false    ┌────────▼──────┐  │
│                         ╱ Instance    ╲──────────▶│handleQueryWithUnboundKey()│
│                    variable named as              │handleTakeValueForUnboundKey()│
│                         ╲ the key exists╱         └────────┬──────┘  │
│                          ◇────┬────◇                       │ Default implementation
│                               │ true                       │         │
│                    ┌──────────▼───────────────┐  Does not exist ┌────▼────────────────────┐
│                    │Access instance variables │──────────▶│NSKeyValueCoding.UnknownKeyException│
│                    │   directly key or _ key  │           │TargetObjectUserInfoKey: the object used│
│                    └──────────────────────────┘           │UnknownUserInfoKey: the key used│
│                                                           └─────────────────────────┘
└─────────────────────────────────────────────────────────────────────┘
```

To handle key paths, key-value coding uses an additional interface NSKeyValueCodingAdditions, with the corresponding classes NSKeyValueCodingAdditions.DefaultImplementation and NSKeyValueCodingAdditions.Utility. This interface defines the standard key path separator (KeyPathSeparator) as a single dot. The default implementation uses the standard NSKeyValueCoding methods for resolving each part of the key path before accessing the final key.

Generalizing the Usage of Key-Value Coding

If we are going to write our own reusable WebObjects components, we might want to write our own key-value coding. In this case we would ask another object of unknown type to set or get values by key, but as we would not know what kind of object we are dealing with we would also not know whether this object implements NSKeyValueCoding.

How can we solve this situation? One way can be to ask the object whether it implements the NSKeyValueCoding interface and call the appropriate accessor methods. If the object does not implement the interface we could use a private accessor or access the instance variable directly.

Advanced EOF

Our custom code for setting a color would not know whether it deals with cars, bikes, iMacs, or anything else for that matter. It only knows that the object has a property, which can be set through the usage of the key `color`. As a result we would need to implement the following code:

```
if (anObject instanceof NSKeyValueCoding){
    ((NSKeyValueCoding)anObject).takeValueForKey("tangerine", "color");
} else {
    NSKeyValueCoding.DefaultImplementation.takeValueForKey(anObject,
                                                           "tangerine",
                                                           "color");
}
```

However, this would be quite annoying and time-consuming if we needed to do it quite often, and this is exactly where the `NSKeyValueCoding.Utility` class comes in.

`NSKeyValueCoding.Utility` is a small class which uses `NSKeyValueCoding` on an object. The methods are the same as defined by `NSKeyValueCoding`, but with an additional first argument, which is the object the key-value coding is going to be used on. Therefore, the preceding code example can be replaced with a call to the `NSKeyValueCoding.Utility` method:

```
NSKeyValueCoding.Utility.takeValueForKey(anObject, "tangerine", "color")
```

This method will then try to use key-value coding on the object `anObject` to set the `color` key to the string `tangerine`.

The Value of Dictionaries

Dictionaries are very useful in WebObjects. They allow you to store any key-value pairs you need and provide a single point of storage for data you do not need to add custom logic for.

In addition, dictionaries in WebObjects implement the `NSKeyValueCoding` interface. This can cause problems if, for example, we want to show the number of key-value pairs of a dictionary with a `WOString` element. We would probably bind `myDictionary.count` to the desired `WOString` dynamic element. However, this would probably result in an empty string. As `NSDictionary` implements `NSKeyValueCoding`, the binding for `count` would be interpreted as the name of a key and looked up in the dictionary itself. In most cases, we would probably not store a `count` key with value in our dictionary. To solve this problem, we need to write our own accessor method for count and bind it to the desired string.

Nevertheless, how could you take advantage of this feature? Dictionaries are most commonly used for fetch specifications. As you will see, fetch specifications can use variables. The variable names are of course keys, and a dictionary serves as an argument container for setting up a whole host of variables for a fetch specification, by supplying the needed key-value pairs.

This makes it easy to write a generic fetch specification and use a single dictionary in our search page's component, to store the user input. You do not need to have a separate instance variable for every possible user input.

The following example will illustrate the usage of a dictionary with WOBuilder in conjunction with a new fetch specification in our EOModel.

Chapter 9

1. First, let's specify a new fetch specification in EOModeler. To do so, open the example model file that we have been working with in EOModeler. Select the **Customer** entity and add a new fetch specification. Name it "**genericFetchSpec**" and provide the qualifier as shown in the screenshot:

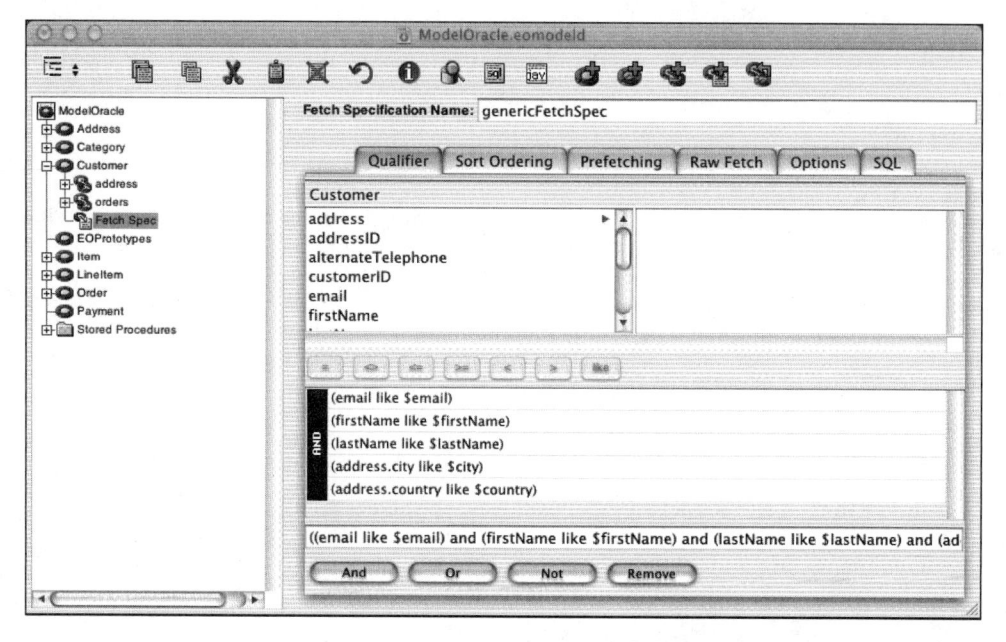

    [Screenshot of EOModeler showing ModelOracle.eomodeld with Fetch Specification Name: genericFetchSpec. The Qualifier tab shows the following expressions joined by AND:
    - (email like $email)
    - (firstName like $firstName)
    - (lastName like $lastName)
    - (address.city like $city)
    - (address.country like $country)

    Full qualifier: ((email like $email) and (firstName like $firstName) and (lastName like $lastName) and (ad...]

    This fetch specification uses more than one variable all connected by an **AND** clause. If any variable is not set, this evaluation of the expression using this variable will be ignored. Therefore, the more variables we set later, the more precise the fetch will be when it is finally used in our code.

2. Next we need to modify the fetch request page in WOBuilder to produce a table with five input fields asking users to enter their **Last name**, **First name**, **City**, **Country** and **E-mail**. In this example, the fetch is very simple and uses the **Main** page to set the search values and to supply the result. We need the variable `queryBindings` of type `NSMutableDictionary` that was created in the last chapter. As before, the values will be the user's input in the corresponding text fields and we should end up with a table that looks like this:

222

Advanced EOF

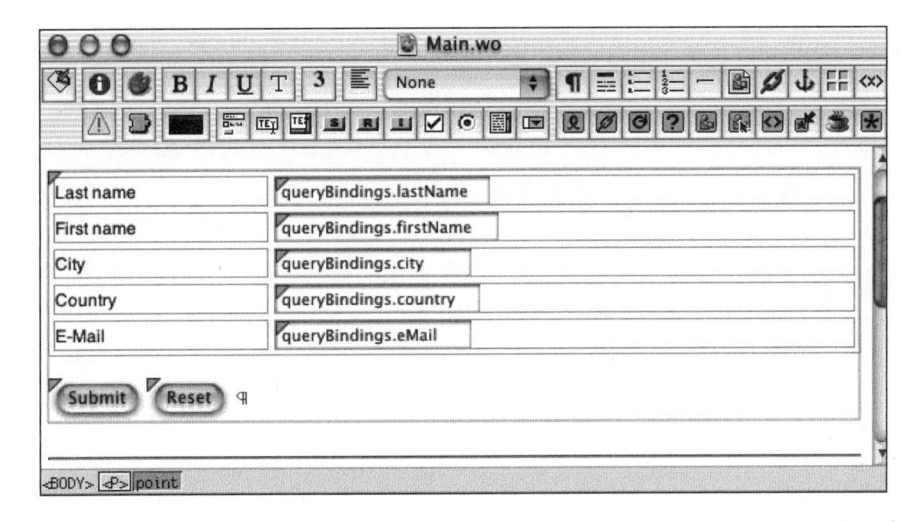

3. To create the above page, the `queryBindings` dictionary should be bound using drag and drop to the text fields and edited with the Inspector tool. You need to add the variable names to the value key by hand. This way, the dictionary `queryBindings` is asked for the keys (`lastName`, `firstName`, and so on) when displaying this page and the keys are used for setting the values, when you press Submit. Using this method, you avoid having to use extra local variables in the `Main.java` class for each search criteria and you make use of the key-value coding support of the dictionary class.

Special Key-Value Coding with EOF: EOKeyValueCoding

EOF takes key-value coding one step further. In addition to the standard mechanism of the key-value coding interface, EOF uses a different default implementation to store and retrieve data. This is because EOF needs to update values independently from business logic.

In most cases, you are using the default key-value coding mechanism as implemented by `NSKeyValueCoding.DefaultImplementation`. This implementation will call your custom set and get accessor method. It is likely that business logic was implemented into accessor methods, but this implies that different properties are interdependent. Therefore if you set the value of property A this will also change property B and maybe affect property C and D.

How It Works

The key-value coding methodology is inappropriate for data that is fetched from a database or restored from a snapshot. This is because we only need to store the values directly and no business logic is involved. The same applies when the current state of an Enterprise Object needs to be written to the database or a snapshot. In that case, the get accessor methods must not use business logic, which can influence already read values for storing.

This problem can be solved. When the EOF needs to access the Enterprise Object directly (due to private framework logic), the "stored" key-value coding accessor methods are called. The `EOKeyValueCoding` interface defines the main data access mechanism within EOF, where the application logic uses the standard key-value coding interface.

223

This is achieved by `EOCustomObject` and `EOGenericRecord`, which implements `EOKeyValueCoding` as an informal interface. This informal interface includes `NSKeyValueCoding` so you also get the standard interface for all subclasses of `EOCustomObject` and `EOGenericRecord`.

Similar to the standard key-value coding, EOF's key-value coding for **stored** values is made up of the following interfaces and classes:

- `EOKeyValueCoding` (interface)
- `EOKeyValueCoding.DefaultImplementation` (class)
- `EOKeyValueCoding.Utility` (class)
- `EOKeyValueCodingAdditions` (interface)
- `EOKeyValueCodingAdditions.DefaultImplementation` (class)
- `EOKeyValueCodingAdditions.Utility` (class)

EOF's key-value coding is similar to the standard key-value coding, and we will be highlighting the differences between the two approaches later on in the chapter.

When the `EOKeyValueCoding` interface addresses the problem to get and set stored property values, the method names are changed. `EOFKeyValueCoding` defines `takeStoredValueForKey()` and `storedValueForKey()`.

The default implementation of these two methods is different to that of `NSKeyValueCoding` because it addresses the issue of accessing data more directly and takes the following course:

1. It looks for a private accessor method (a method preceded by an underscore) for the desired key (`_getKey()`, `_key()` or `_setKey()`).

2. If no private accessor method is found, it tries to access the private/public instance variable directly by accessing `_key` or `key`.

3. If there is no instance variable (neither private or public) it tries to access the public accessor method (`getKey()`, `key()` or `setKey()` respectively).

4. If either fails, it will call `handleQueryForUnboundKey()` and `handleTakeValueForUnboundKey()`, respectively if the class implements the supplemental `NSKeyValueCoding.ErrorHandling` interface.

5. Analogous to `NSKeyValueCoding`, if the last step fails, an exception is raised. (Note that `EOKeyValueCoding` uses the implementation of `NSKeyValueCoding.ErrorHandling` and does not define its own error handling.)

Advanced EOF

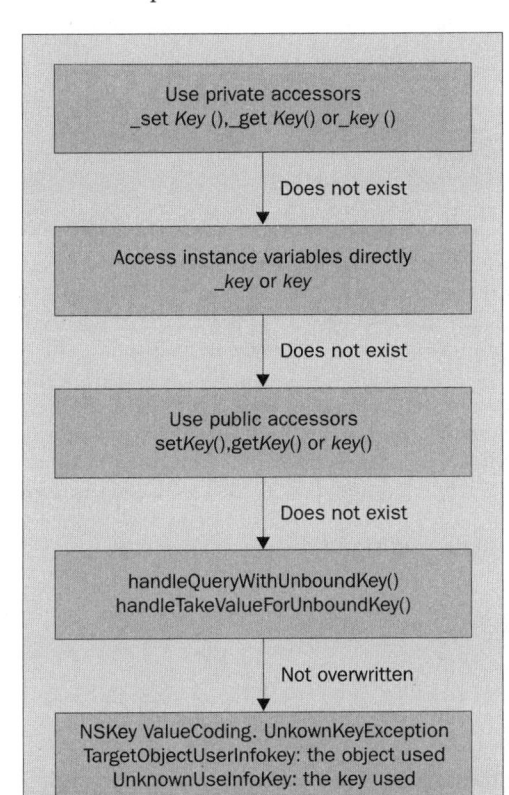

The following diagram illustrates this operation:

```
┌─────────────────────────────────────┐
│  Use private accessors              │
│  _set Key (),_get Key() or _key ()  │
└─────────────────────────────────────┘
                │ Does not exist
                ▼
┌─────────────────────────────────────┐
│  Access instance variables directly │
│  _key or key                        │
└─────────────────────────────────────┘
                │ Does not exist
                ▼
┌─────────────────────────────────────┐
│  Use public accessors               │
│  setKey(),getKey() or key()         │
└─────────────────────────────────────┘
                │ Does not exist
                ▼
┌─────────────────────────────────────┐
│  handleQueryWithUnboundKey()        │
│  handleTakeValueForUnboundKey()     │
└─────────────────────────────────────┘
                │ Not overwritten
                ▼
┌─────────────────────────────────────────────┐
│  NSKey ValueCoding. UnkownKeyException      │
│  TargetObjectUserInfokey: the object used   │
│  UnknownUseInfoKey: the key used            │
└─────────────────────────────────────────────┘
```

> `EOKeyValueCoding` is supplemental to `NSKeyValueCoding`. `EOKeyValueCoding` should throw the same exceptions as `NSKeyValueCoding`.

Implementing EOF's Key-Value Coding

By default, key-value coding should be implemented using the following guidelines:

- If our class is not already a subclass of any WebObjects class that implements the `NSKeyValueCoding` or `EOKeyValueCoding` interfaces, implement the methods as previously stated. Use the suitable default implementation.

- Implement set and get accessor methods. Avoid using the default implementation feature to access the instance variables directly, because this goes against the Object Oriented programming concept of handling a class as a black box.

- If our class is being used as an Enterprise Object, implement the set and get accessor to take advantage of the `EOKeyValueCoding` by calling the stored property key-value coding methods. This is the default if the class code is generated by EOModeler.

225

The default implementation for Enterprise Objects uses the following code template for set and get accessors:

```
public ObjectType key(){
  return (ObjectType)storedValueForKey("key");
}

public void setKey(ObjectType value){
  takeStoredValueForKey(value, "key");
}
```

This code template works with the dictionaries of subclasses of `EOGenericRecord`, or with explicitly declared instance variables named as the key. If you use a subclass of `EOGenericRecord` (the default code, generated by EOModeler) and you use instance variables too, the instance variables are accessed first, before the dictionary of the `EOGenericRecord` is accessed.

Alternatively, if we need type coercion, we could consider using another form of set and get methods for Enterprise Objects. Because the EOF normally handles objects, these methods are suitable if we need type coercion to primitive types (especially for numbers and booleans). The EOF will take care of the necessary type conversions needed between its internal object representation and our primitives.

Our Enterprise Object should have the following accessor methods:

```
public int getAmount();
public void setAmount(int value);
```

The key-value coding implemented by Enterprise Objects will automatically convert the `int` value to a Number.

If we needed to implement our own accessor methods, they might look like this:

```
//explicit instance variable
  Type key;
public Type key(){
  willRead();
  return key;
}

public void setKey(Type value) {
  willChange();
  key = value;
}
```

In this case, there are additional calls `willRead()` and `willChange()` which are necessary for the EOF to track changes and faulting. In the previous example, this functionality was handled implicitly by using the stored property accessor methods.

> When using this with primitives, we need to remember that EOF is only able to convert **Number** objects. Therefore, if you want to set a value and the source object is of type **String**, this has to be converted to a **Number** first. In WebObjects this can be easily achieved by supplying a formatter to the **numberformat** attribute of input fields.

Advanced EOF

Handling relationships is like handling properties. This is especially true for to-one relationships, where, on the function call, you cannot distinguish whether you set an object property or an object relationship. However, the set and get methods have to look different. You need to set the returned and set value types to `EOEnterpriseObject`.

To-many relationships are handled differently. The property of a to-many relationship is an `NSArray`. This array holds all the related/referenced objects. Therefore, we need to add or remove an object from this array. If we use set and get on the to-many relationship property, we would accidentally set and get the relationship array. Therefore the naming convention for adding or removing an object to a to-many relationship follows the naming schema for set and get, by naming the corresponding methods `addTo`*Key*`()` and `removeFrom`*Key*`()`. Although these methods look like key-value coding methods, they are not. They are used by other methods like `addToBothSidesOfRelationshipWithKey()`.

The default implementation (as produced by EOModeler as well) is as shown:

```
public NSArray key(){
   return storedValueForKey("key");
}

public void setKey(NSMutableArray value){
   take storedValueForKey(value,"key");
}

public void addToKey(ObjectType object){
   NSMutableArray array = (NSMutableArray)storedValueForKey("key");
   willChange();
   array.addObject(object);
}

public void removeFromKey(ObjectType object){
   NSMutableArray array = (NSMutableArray)storedValueForKey("key");
   willChange();
   array.removeObject(object);
}
```

Again, replace `key` with the name of the entity attribute name and `ObjectType` by its type. You should consider naming the key/attribute in plural form for a better reading of the code. EOModeler will name to-many relationship keys in plural for you by default.

Type Checking, Type Conversion and Null Values

By using keys, instead of variables, the compiler has no chance to check for types. Therefore it is possible to send a string value to an object by using `takeValueForKey()` where the receiver expects a value of type `NSData`. Because of this, the sender is responsible for checking the type. This could be achieved by calling `validateValueForKey()` and is discussed in more detail later on in the chapter.

There is one exception to this rule. The default implementation of the key-value coding methods supports the `int`, `float` and `double` scalar data types. Therefore it is possible to automatically convert from a `Number` object to one of these scalar types. This is achieved by using the corresponding `intValue()`, `floatValue()` methods on the object, but you will encounter an error if you are using objects which don't support these methods.

Of course, these methods cannot set a `null` value for a scalar type, even if the database can allow a `null` value. If a `null` value is encountered by setting a scalar type, the methods will invoke `unableToSetNullForKey()`, which by default throws a runtime exception. We can consider overwriting this method and reinvoking `takeValueForKey()` with the desired value for example to set -1 as a value where otherwise only positive values are allowed.

To represent a `null` value when data is retrieved from the database, `NSKeyValueCoding` defines a final class `NSKeyValueCoding.NullValue`. You can safely check for `null` for any value in a snapshot of objects, fetched from the database, by using the following code snippet:

```
if (value == NSKeyValueCoding.NullValue){
  //your code
}
```

Luckily, you will rarely use this, because EOF is able to translate these null values for you to `null`. You only need to be aware of this, if you are dealing with the snapshot directly.

How To Use Package Access Instance Variables

By default, the default implementation of `NSKeyValueCoding` cannot access the package access instance variables. This means, if you want the default mechanism of `NSKeyValueCoding`, you have two options:

- **Make all instance variables where you want to use key-value coding public.**
  This is the easiest method, however it breaks the black-box concept. Nevertheless, this is the fastest method and acceptable for prototyping.

- **Implement the default set and get accessor methods to obtain object properties.**
  This is the preferred method, because it preserves the object-oriented approach of viewing objects as a black box.

If you need access to package access instance variables, you might also consider another third option:

- **Add a subclass of `NSKeyValueCoding.ValueAccessor` named `NSKeyValueCodingProtectedAccessor` to your package.**
  This method gives you access to protected variables by using Java introspection. Because it breaks the way things should work, this should be only considered as a short-term solution.

If you wish to know more about creating an `NSKeyValueCodingProtectedAccessor` class, you should note that there is an implementation of this class shown in the Apple documentation at:

http://developer.apple.com/techpubs/webobjects/FoundationRef/Java/Classes/NSKVCValAcc.html

The class should obviously extend `NSKeyValuecoding.ValueAccessor`, and should contain your implementations of the following classes:

- `fieldValue()` – returns the value of the field of the object
- `setFieldValue()` – sets the value of the object's field
- `methodValue()` – uses a method (supplied as argument) to return the value of the object's field
- `setMethodValue()` – uses a method (supplied as argument) to set the value of the object's field

We will now look at validation and exception handling and discuss their significance in relation to WebObjects and the EOF.

Validation and Exception Handling

Validation is central to most applications. It is even more important in client-server applications like WebObjects, where roundtrips back and forth from the user due to invalid values are expensive and time consuming. Validation in WebObjects includes single attributes that map directly to database columns, and derived attributes.

Now that we have seen which mechanisms are used in WebObjects to store and retrieve values from objects, you are probably wondering how to validate these values. How can we tell whether the value the user just stored is suitable for the object? How do we handle error conditions if a certain value is not suitable? If all values are valid independently, will they still remain valid all together when the object will be saved?

As validation can occur over many different key-values, we must handle validation exceptions efficiently. If we have stored a whole host of new values, we would likewise want to handle a host of exceptions altogether. To do this, exception handling in WebObjects is based on Java exceptions.

We can use several mechanisms to implement our validation logic. To assist this process, WebObjects uses a validation mechanism, defined by the NSValidation interface, to validate object properties. In conjunction with business objects, represented by Enterprise Objects in WebObjects applications, an additional validation technique exists to validate an object during operations as a whole. This is defined by EOValidation. We will first have a look at the NSValidation interface.

Property Validation: NSValidation

The NSValidation interface and the default implementation provided by the NSValidation.DefaultImplementation inner class defines a mechanism for generic validation. Several interfaces and classes in the Foundation Framework of WebObjects define the way basic validation works:

- NSValidation (interface) – defines the basic access methods.
- NSValidation.DefaultImplementation (class) – implements a default way of handling validation.
- NSValidation.Utility (class) – uses validation on non-enhanced classes.

The NSValidation interface defines the way validation works. It has two methods, validateValueForKey() and validateTakeValueForKeyPath() that set up the whole mechanism. By implementing these methods, object properties can be validated by key rather than by calling some object-specific validation methods. As with any other interface, objects implementing the NSValidation interface can be validated in a consistent manner.

WebObjects Framework classes are supposed to call these two validation methods whenever validation is required. Generally, we would not need to implement our own logic to determine at which time to call these methods, as the Framework's classes handle this for us.

Values are validated in one simple way: any value which should be validated is accepted by a validation method as a generic object. The validation method itself can carry out tasks such as checking whether the type of the object matches, eventually converting or changing it, and finally returning some value or throwing an exception of type NSValidation.ValidationException. If no exception is thrown, the value is accepted, so every validation is successful if the validation methods return any value including null.

validateValueForKey() is a basic method. It either returns a value for a given key-value pair (the value is accepted) or throws a NSValidation.ValidationException (the value is rejected). The second method, validateTakeValueForKeyPath() is a superset. It is capable of working with a key-path, and if the validation method accepts the value, it is stored in the property specified by the key.

> Always remember that a validation is successful, if it returns **null**. Because validation is usually called before values are stored in object properties, your set accessor methods should be prepared to handle **null** values too before sending any further messages to the validated value.

To enhance our custom class Car with the validation mechanism by using the default implementation provided by Apple, we would need to implement the following code:

```
//import the NSValidation interface
//located in the foundation framework of WebObjects
import com.webobjects.foundation.*;

public class Car extends ... implements NSValidation,NSKeyValueCoding,{
  //implementation of the validation interface
  public Object validateValueForKey (Object aValue, String aKey)
                          throws NSValidation.ValidationException {
    return NSValidation.DefaultImplementation.validateValueForKey(this,
                                                                  aValue,
                                                                  aKey);
  }

  public Object validateTakeValueForKeyPath(Object aValue, String aKeyPath)
                          throws NSValidation.ValidationException {
    return NSValidation.DefaultImplementation.validateTakeValueForKeyPath(
                                                                  this,
                                                                  aValue,
                                                                  aKeyPath);
  }
  //end of validation interface
  //other methods follow
}
```

Although it is not implemented in the above code example, it is also a good idea to implement the NSKeyValueCoding interface (for example by using NSKeyValueCoding.DefaultImplementation), because this can be used by NSValidation.

Note that you don't have to implement these methods if you are subclassing any classes of the WebObjects frameworks which implement the NSValidation interface, like WOComponent. These classes utilize the default implementation.

The Default Implementation

Generally you would not want to implement your own NSValidation interface but utilize the default implementation by NSValidation.DefaultImplementation that is highly optimized.

The default implementation works hand in hand with the key-value coding mechanism. validateValueForKey() takes the key argument and looks for a method named validateKey() and invokes it, if it exists. These methods will either raise an exception NSValidation.ValidationException (value rejected), or return the value returned by validateKey() (value accepted).

Advanced EOF

The default implementation of `validateTakeValueForKeyPath()` is a superset of the functionality of `validateValueForKey()` and works by using `valueForKey()` for the path elements and by calling `validateValueForKey()` on the final receiver. If the value is accepted and is different from the current property's value, the value is stored using key-value coding's mechanism for storing values.

> It is important to note that the object's set accessor methods are not called if the value taken for validation is not different from the current stored value. Therefore, if you depend on having the set accessor methods called in any way, you probably want to override `validateTakeValueForKey()` and implement your own strategy.

Generalizing the Usage of Property Validation

In general, we would not need to call the validation methods ourselves, they are called by other classes such as `EOEditingContext` when values are going to be saved, or `WOComponent` when values are going to be stored after a user input, which would implement the validation logic for you.

If we wanted to access the object with the `NSValidation` API we would have to amend our code. The code would check whether the object we want to operate on implements the `NSValidation` interface. If it does, our code will call the corresponding `NSValidation` method, otherwise it can fall back on the standard validation way implemented by `NSValidation.DefaultImplementation`.

The following code snippet illustrates this:

```
if (object instanceof NSValidation) {
  myValue = ((NSValidation)object).validateValueForKey(key);
} else {
  myValue = NSValidation.DefaultImplementation.validateValueForKey(object,
                                                                   value,
                                                                   key);
}
```

To avoid numerous `if` statements, we can use the `NSValidation.Utility` inner class. `NSValidation.Utility` implements both validation methods (`validateValueForKey()` and `validateTakeValueForKey()`) using a third argument for the object to operate on. Therefore we could replace the above code snippet with the following line of code:

```
myalue = NSValidation.Utility.validateValueForKey(object, value, key);
```

Writing Property Validation Methods

Implementing validation methods in our custom code is very simple. As we have seen, the Foundation Framework uses a key to access a certain attribute of an object for validation. Therefore, if we wanted to implement validation for an attribute, we would need to implement a `validateKey()` method for each property we wanted to validate. We would have to implement the following validation methods:

```
public Object validateKey(Object aValue) throws
                            NSValidation.ValidationException
```

We would need to replace *Key* with the specific key's name.

As shown, the `aValue` argument is of type `Object`. This is not always the case, but it is most suitable, because a validation method should perform the following tasks:

- Check whether `aValue` is of legal object type.
- Convert `aValue` to the proper type if needed.
- Check whether `aValue` is of legal value.
- Throw a `NSValidation.ValidationException` exception if `aValue` is not legal.
- Return the validated value if `aValue` is legal.

The return type of a validation method does not necessarily have to be of type `Object`. In fact, we would probably want to set it to the type of the validated attribute. This is also true for the validated value `aValue`, but you should avoid this providing a type for the `aValue` in `validateKey()` whenever possible, as it is not wise to overload the validation methods to handle different argument types. Always write one method for a certain key and handle the type checking within the validation method. There is only one exception to this rule: attributes of Enterprise Objects, which have a to-one relationship with other Enterprise Objects, should accept `aValue` of type `EOEnterpriseObject`.

Using `Object` as the only argument type for a validation method allows more flexibility. For example a property for a numeric value may be set by a string value. In this case, the validation method does have the chance to convert the type as needed. Note that the return type is also allowed to be `null` as a legal value and we might want to use this if we are trying to validate and set an empty string for a property.

The following two validation methods show a sample implementation of the `LineItem` class of our sample EOModel, as one possible implementation:

```java
public Number validateQuantity(Object aValue) throws
                                NSValidation.ValidationException{
  Integer numberValue;
  int quantity;

  if (aValue instanceof String){
    //Convert the String to an Integer.
    try {
      numberValue = new Integer((String)aValue);
    } catch (NumberFormatException numberFormatException) {
      throw new NSValidation.ValidationException
          ("Validation exception: Unable to convert the String " + aValue
          + " to an Integer");
    }
  } else if (aValue instanceof Number) {
    numberValue = new Integer(((Number)aValue).intValue());
  } else {
    throw new NSValidation.ValidationException
          ("Validation exception: Unable to convert the Object " + aValue
                                              + "to an Integer");
  }

  quantity = numberValue.intValue();
  if (quantity < 1) {
    throw new NSValidation.ValidationException
          ("Quantity is negative or zero!", this, "quantity");
  }
  return numberValue;
}
```

Advanced EOF

This `validateQuantity()` method two main tasks. Firstly, it accepts any object and tries to convert it to be able to present an integer (`Integer` or `Number` class). If conversion fails, an exception is thrown. The final exception will carry the key which was checked, and the object which threw the exception, as additional arguments. This will enable further exception handling and debugging. Secondly, this method does a business logic check. In this case, the quantity can not be zero or negative.

While validating these values, we must take care if we are depending on other attributes, as we cannot be sure of the order validation takes places for the different keys! Therefore this should be avoided and placed in operational validation methods.

Special Validation with EOF: EOValidation

Enterprise Objects have special requirements for validation. Firstly, Enterprise Objects are based on a corresponding EOModel. The model itself specifies certain attributes, which need to be checked. This includes the checking for database `null` (if allowed or not), field lengths, and precision. Secondly, by using the EOF you get additional control points for validation. EOF is designed to handle persistent data stores, so objects have to be checked when they are about to be inserted, deleted, updated or saved to the database. This means that the generic `NSValidation`, which is used for **property** validation, is supplemented by the `EOValidation` interface, which specifies whether an Enterprise Object is ready for a certain **operation**.

How It Works

The `EOValidation` methods trigger the `NSValidation` methods. The validation rules are called when you trigger them yourself, or when another object like `EOEditingContext` triggers validation.

To help you with the implementation, the EOF basic classes already provide most of the needed functionality. These basic classes are `EOCustomObject` and `EOGenericRecord`. Both implementations make use of a default `NSValidation` and `EOValidation` interface implementation. These interfaces are implemented by `EOCustomObject` and `EOGenericRecord`, as a subclass of `EOCustomObjects`, inherits this functionality.

`EOValidation` defines four additional validation methods, which are called by the Framework. You implement these methods only if you wish to have additional control over the validation process. The table lists these four methods:

Method	Description
`void validateForInsert()`	This method is called whenever an Enterprise Object is about to be added to existing data.
`void validateForDelete()`	This method will be called when an Enterprise Object is about to be removed from an existing data store.
`void validateForUpdate()`	This method will be called whenever an Enterprise Object is about to be updated. You will override this method to check whether the object's current state is valid for any object's unspecific update.
`void validateForSave()`	This is probably the most used validation method. It is called whenever an Enterprise Object is about to be stored permanently in the data store.

When implementing custom operational validation logic, it's a good idea to remember that a save operation (which will probably be applied after a successful `validateForSave()` call) can affect other applications using this instance in completely different contexts. In contrast an update, insert or delete validation might occur without touching the database, although this is unlikely and the default implementation for `validateForInsert()` and `validateForUpdate()`, as we will see, will call `validateForSave()` anyway. Therefore if we are validating anything which is not absolutely specific to an update or insert, this should go into the `validateForSave()` implementation.

These descriptions become more concrete, if we look at the Framework when it calls these operations. Enterprise Objects are managed by instances of `EOEditingContext`. The editing context will therefore trigger all these validation calls for us. Whenever we tell the editing context to insert, delete or save, the corresponding validation methods will be called. Updating is done implicitly by simply setting a value for a certain property.

As with the general validation methods, defined by `NSValidation`, the `EOValidation` methods are required to throw exceptions, whenever an validation error is encountered. The procedure to throw an exception is the same as the procedure for validation methods of the `NSValidation` interface when a `NSValidation.ValidationException` is thrown.

The Default Implementation for Operation Validation

The basic classes `EOCustomObject` and `EOGenericRecord`, (as a subclass of `EOCustomObject`) implement the `EOValidation` interface, and so also inherit the `EOValidation.DefaultImplementation` inner class too. Therefore, there is no need for us to implement a validation class with the same functionality as the default implementation (and we don't require a `EOValidation.Utility` class either).

Since all objects based on `EOCustomObject` inherit the default implementation of the `EOValidation` interface, what can the default implementations of `EOCustomObject` do for us in terms of validation? `EOCustomObject` implements basic operation validation based on information stored in the EOModel. However the information in the model for operational checks are currently only used for validation checks on delete operations. This means that the `validateForDelete()` implementation will honor the delete rules we specified in our EOModel. This does not look too complicated, but if we remember that deletes can be cascaded, this can lead to more complication.

The default implementation will call `validateForSave()` in the `validateForInsert()` and `validateForUpdate()` method implementations. The `validateForDelete()` will only be triggered if the data is about to be saved back to the database. So you need to take special care of the `validateForSave()` method.

The `validateForSave()` implementation of `EOCustomObject` will first call its inherited validation method, named `validateObjectForSave()`. This implementation will check values based on the information provided in the EOModel. After this call, the implementation iterates through all properties and will again call its inherited validation method of the superclass version first (named `validateValueForKey()`), before calling your own implementation of `validateKey()`, which utilizes the `NSValidation` interface.

> **validateForDelete()** and **validateForSave()** are currently the only concrete implementations. **validateForUpdate()** and **validateForInsert()** just calls **validateForSave()**. When overwriting these methods, you are required to make a call to **super()**.

Handling Validation Errors

Now that we implemented all the validation methods and strategies, we need to know when validation will be performed. Within WebObject applications validation methods are called in the following situations:

- ❑ When form values are pushed into attributes of an object and this object implements the `NSValidation` interface.
- ❑ When you trigger save changes on an editing context, by calling `saveChanges()`.

Obviously, this implies that if we need validation at different points in time, we need to call the different validation methods ourselves.

Because each validation method potentially throws an exception to indicate failure, we need to catch these exceptions when calling validation methods, as shown on the next page:

```
//custom call to validation methods
try{
  myEnterpriseObject.validateValueForKey(aValue, "aKey");
  myEnterpriseObject.validateForUpdate();
}catch (NSValidation.ValidationException){
  //handle errors
}
```

We will also need to deal with validation errors of user input, for example when the user submits a form. These form values are checked one by one, by using an attached formatter first and then by calling the appropriate validation method (attaching formatters is discussed in greater detail later on). If any step fails, an exception will be thrown and your component will be notified with a call:

```
void validationFailedWithException(Throwable anException,
                                   Object value,
                                   String key);
```

We can intercept the exception handling at this point and process the exception. The default implementation of `WOComponent` simply ignores any exception, so no error page will be generated by property validation.

Whenever you call `saveChanges()` or any other method on the editing context, this action will cease after the first exception is encountered. However, a `validateForSave()` of a single Enterprise Object within the bundle of objects one editing context controls, will stop any further validation of the other objects if it fails.

By default, the operational validation methods of `EOValidation.DefaultImplementation` do aggregate exceptions. An operational validation method of a single object, which is supposed to do property validation on every property, like `validateForSave()`, will aggregate all property validations. This means, that the editing context will stop validation after the first Enterprise Object will throw an exception.

To override this behavior and force the validation of every object, we need to configure the editing context by adding the following code:

```
//enables continuous validation checking
myEditingContext.setStopsValidationAfterFirstError (false);
```

If we enabled continuous validation checking, we would expect to receive many individual exceptions. It would be convenient to get all occurred exceptions at one single point, and that is exactly what happens. If you disable the stopping of further validation this way, the editing context will aggregate all exceptions and present us with one single exception after processing.

By default, the operational validation methods of `EOValidation.DefaultImplementation` also produce aggregate exceptions. An operational validation method of a single object, which is supposed to do property validation on every property, like `validateForSave()`, will already aggregate all property validations.

We may also aggregate exceptions ourselves by using the following code, in a custom implementation of the `validateForOperation()` method:

```
public void validateForOperation() throws NSValidation.ValidationException {
  NSValidation.ValidationException superException = null;
  NSValidation.ValidationException myException = null;

  try{
    super.validateForOperation()
  }catch (NSValidation.ValidationException s){
    superException = s;
  }

  if (operationWillFailClause){
    myException = new NSValidation.ValidationException(
                   "Something terrible went wrong");
  }

  if (superException && myException){
    NSMutableArray exceptions = new NSMutableArray();

    exceptions.addObject(superException);
    exceptions.addObject(myException);

    throw NSValidation.ValidationException.aggregateExceptionWithExceptions(
                                           exceptions);
  } else if (superException){
    throw(superException);
  } else if (myException){
    throw(myException);
  }
}
```

Whenever you receive validation exceptions, you can "ask" the exception, whether it holds information about further exceptions by accessing an array of further exceptions by calling `additionalExceptions()` on the `userInfo()` dictionary. The returned array will contain all the other aggregated exceptions. You can ask any exception for the key which caused the validation exception by sending it the `key()` method, and you can ask for the object on which the key was used by sending it the `object()` method. This dictionary will also contain an array of further exceptions, when the exception was aggregated.

Alternative Validation Strategies

We are not limited to the proposed concepts explained here. Most database programmers utilize database constraints, to ensure that correct data values are stored in the database. Many HTML programmers also like to use JavaScript, to utilize client-side value checking. This means that values transferred from the client are prechecked already by a simple JavaScript. We also have the formatters feature of WebObjects which can be very helpful.

To take advantage of most validation strategies we should combine the following strategies with the validation methods to achieve the best results:

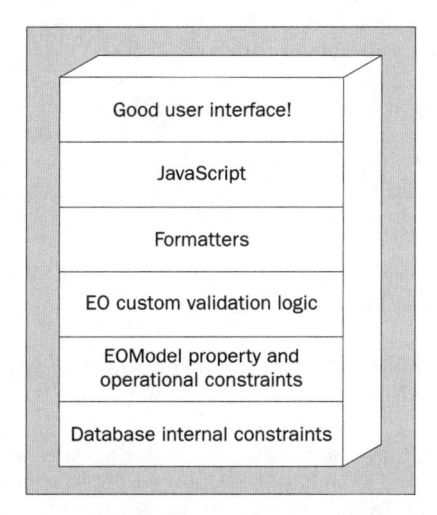

```
┌─────────────────────────────────┐
│   Good user interface!          │
├─────────────────────────────────┤
│   JavaScript                    │
├─────────────────────────────────┤
│   Formatters                    │
├─────────────────────────────────┤
│   EO custom validation logic    │
├─────────────────────────────────┤
│   EOModel property and          │
│   operational constraints       │
├─────────────────────────────────┤
│   Database internal constraints │
└─────────────────────────────────┘
```

Working with Database Constraints

If we are going to work with an existing database, we must analyze the constraints of the database. We will encounter constraints that we cannot model (such as dependencies between tables and content). Although we cannot discuss these constraints in detail here, we should be aware of the more generic constraints, like the number of characters allowed for a string or the precision of a number because we need to set the attributes in our EOModel to be in compliance with the database. However we must not always obey the rules of the database! Here are a few examples of when we might defy these rules:

- ❑ The database defines a user's password field to be of fixed length of 255 characters. Your technical specification however, limits passwords to a minimum length of 8 characters and maximum length of 30 characters. We could then reduce the model's length attribute to 30 and include an additional check in your `validatePassword()` for minimum length method.

- ❑ The database allows anonymous user attributes. Users generally do not need to specify their gender, give their age or postal address. These database fields are allowed to be `null`. If the application you are writing specifies that at least the gender (`string`) has to be given for a valid user before it will be stored in the database, your model will therefore overwrite the `allow null` attribute for gender and age (forcing the internal checks to fail if no values are set). Your `validateGender()` method will have to check, whether the given value can be used as a string value and can be set to one of the constants for gender used in the database.

As you can see, we cannot overcome the constraints defined in the database, but we can limit them so that they conform to our more specific technical specifications.

Working with JavaScript

The advantage of JavaScript is that it runs on the client, reducing the roundtrip overhead for value checking. If values are already checked on the client, this reduces the possibility that wrong values are sent to your application thus forcing the application to generate an error page, requiring the user to correct his/her values.

In short, JavaScript validation works within the browser and is typically triggered by some GUI events within the browser (an input field is changed, a submit button is pressed and so on). The browser's JavaScript engine will then perform the JavaScript validation method and check whether the input is valid. These JavaScript methods can be very powerful for example if an error is encountered, the user will often get an error message immediately, with an explanation as to why the input value was wrong. In this case, the applications logic will not get triggered, and no values will be sent to the application.

However, this also introduces more code to maintain. We should not just maintain client-side checking because users can disable JavaScript. Therefore, we still need to maintain our own validation methods. The overhead arises if we change the validation logic. In this case, we need to take care of the validation methods within our application and our client-side code. Even worse, we need to maintain three languages: JavaScript on the client, which is embedded in HTML, and Java on the server side.

In the following example will use some simple JavaScript on the client side, to validate a text input field to be a number, in JavaScript. This involves two steps:

1. Select the desired text field and open the Inspector. Add another attribute, by clicking the + button in the right corner and selecting **Add binding**.

2. Enter the binding name to read `onBlur` and enter a value to read `"checkNotNegative(this.value)"` (do not forget to include the quotation marks). This step will trigger a JavaScript call to `checkNumbercheckNotNegative()`:

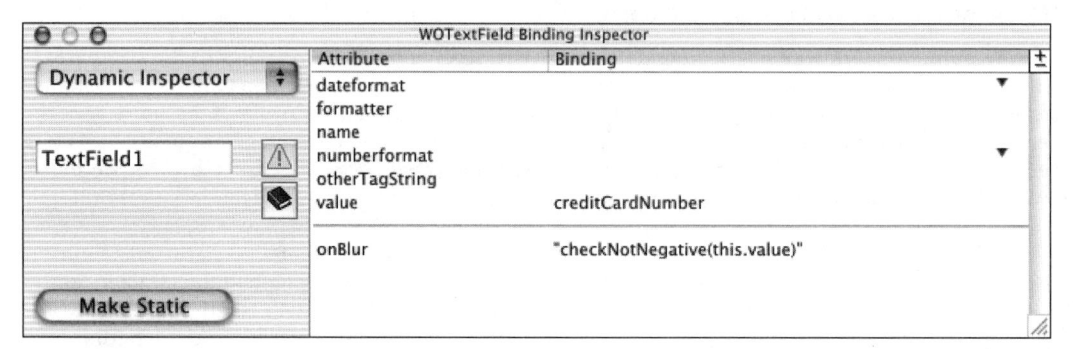

Attribute	Binding
dateformat	
formatter	
name	
numberformat	
otherTagString	
value	creditCardNumber
onBlur	"checkNotNegative(this.value)"

3. At the top of your page, add a `WOCustomObject` by clicking on the asterisk button from the tools menu. In the selection panel that appears set the **WebObject class to use** to `WOJavaScript`. In the Dynamic Inspector bind the **scriptString** attribute of the newly inserted `WOJavaScript` element to read: `"function checkNotNegative(number) {if (number < 0) alert ('Please enter a non-negative number');}"` – do not forget to include the quotation marks.

Advanced EOF

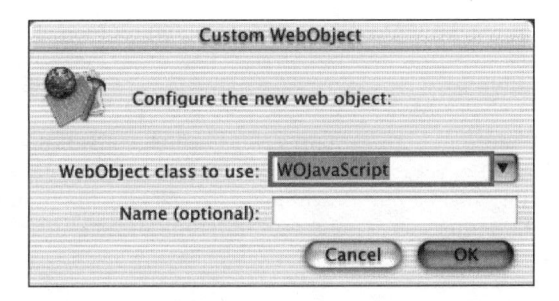

The JavaScript will then be directly connected to the text field and when a user enters a negative number, a dialog box will appear telling them to **Please enter a non-negative number**.

We can also embed larger JavaScripts, by putting the code into a separate file, adding the file to your projects resources and reference this file in the script file attribute of the `WOJavaScript` element. The `WOJavaScript` also accepts a string value to provide the needed JavaScript code, so we can even produce the JavaScript code dynamically during the page generation phase.

To further simplify the process, Apple have added the sample component `JSValidatedField`, which combines the two steps mentioned above in a single reusable component where you specify the error text, the validation function and the name of form when this script is used.

Working with Formatters

Formatters are general conversion objects. They work bi-directionally, which means they can format an object for output and convert the output back into an object. Usually the output is just a string. Remember that for this reason you need a number-formatter in your text fields, if you require a primitive like `int` in the receiver.

Formatters do not really carry out validation for you, but they aid in providing good values to your code. This is because if a formatter is unable to convert a value, it simply throws an exception.

> **Values that are not different from the current property values, will not be stored again, even if they passed the formatter successfully!**

If we want to use formatters in WebObjects, we need to connect an instance of a formatter to the appropriate attribute in the bindings inspector, as exemplified in the screenshot:

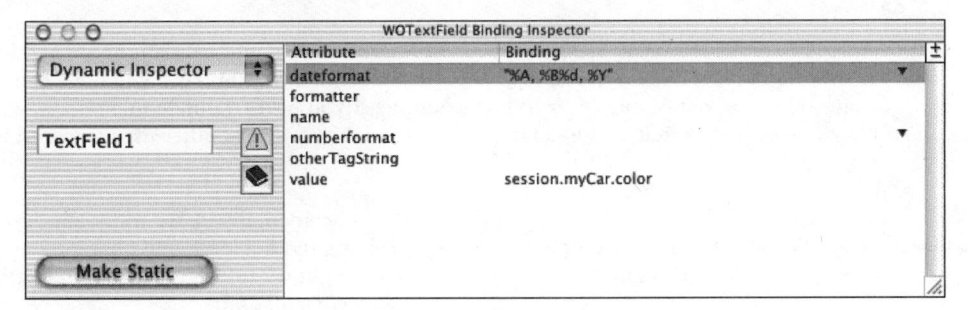

We would need to bind a format string to **dateformat** or **numberformat**. Rather than binding a string, we could instead bind an instance of `NSNumberFormatter` or `NSTimestampFormatter` or any other formatter instance to **formatter**.

The **dateformat** and **numberformat** both contain strings, which convert numbers or dates according to the specification of `NSNumberFormatter` or `NSTimestampFormatter`. We could choose the most commonly used format strings from a pull-down menu, by clicking the triangle on the right of the desired format. A custom formatter can even accept different formats and output accordingly. This will improve user experience.

Handling the GUI

Designing a good graphical GUI is always a difficult task. The HTML-based GUIs of today differ significantly from the interactivity and clarity of traditional native applications. We will not discuss GUI graphical design issues here, but instead we will focus on a way to improve functionality.

Generally, the workflow for user input in web-based applications is the same: present input page, parse input as form values, return input page with error notifications and retry or continue when no errors occurred.

The focus should be on reducing the overhead of re-entering values. However, web applications are not interactive by design, and therefore the application cannot check user input instantly. If the application can only check all values at once in a single action method, it is not possible, as in traditional applications, to connect each input element with a corresponding controller method. Such a controller method would normally check the value and instantly deliver a response to the user.

Such interactivity cannot be integrated with web application logic. There are some workarounds provided by using JavaScript, Applets and other interactive browser plug-in functionalities like QuickTime, Flash or others. All these alternatives work on the client side and help to reduce roundtrips and produce better user feedback.

These add-ons try to bring back some of the functionality that we are used to from native applications of our operating system. However due to the design of web applications, which are designed for client server stateless communication, they will never give us the convenience that a native application could offer. In addition, the programmer cannot rely on them, because s/he has no control over the client's hardware and software configuration. Even a Java applet today will often not work on all platforms, due to different implementations of the JVM.

Locking

Now that we have discussed the basic mechanisms of key-value coding and validation, we will focus on techniques for locking objects. This is useful if we encounter validation problems which we cannot overcome, because they are out of our control. For example, if you try to validate one object, which relies on another object, and save it to the database, before realizing that another user changed the other object you have used!

Locking is a mechanism used for protecting objects from being accidentally changed by another user, task, thread or application. Imagine that one user is just accessing the database and changing value X. The same value would be also available to a second user who might try to change this value at the same time. Locking the value for concurrent access will help avoid such situations.

There is more than one way to perform locking. Each approach has its pro and cons, so you would probably mix the different techniques to solve any problems. We will discuss two basic approaches named optimistic and pessimistic locking, and two additional locking strategies: locking on a column and application based-locking.

Optimistic Locking

Optimistic locking is the default strategy used by EOF. You will always automatically use optimistic locking, if you do not implement another locking strategy. Optimistic locking actually does not lock anything actively on the database, so this approach is supported by any database.

Optimistic locking works in a simple way. In our EOModel for each entity we specify the attributes that we want to be locked, by adding the lock symbol to the attribute. This is set by default for each attribute, so we would probably remove the lock, rather than set it.

After a fetch, EOF will remember the values fetched from the database in a so-called "snapshot" of the data. When we save the data back to the database, the EOF will compare the snapshot data with the data in the database. If the data is still the same, the save or update operation will complete, otherwise it fails and throws an exception. We would need to catch these exceptions on updates. The following code shows how this can be done:

```
//try to save changes
try{
  myObject.editingContext().saveChanges();
}catch (Exception exception){
  //handle the error, by either presenting an error page
  //or rolling back the last transaction
  //until a save state is established again
}
```

This method is easy to use; it does not require any additional database calls and is supported by all data stores. However, we will not get notified about changes until we actually try to save the data back to the database, and because of the additional requirement of comparing snapshot data with the database, this method is a little slower than a direct update operation.

This procedure is called optimistic locking. It is unlikely that conflicts will arise and we would not want other users being blocked while our data access and update operation is completed. Everybody is free to access the values. We are only concerned if data is actually being changed on the database.

When we consider using optimistic locking, we need to look at whether we should lock all or just some of the attributes (column). To answer this question we need to remember how optimistic locking works. As already stated, the EOF supplies an additional qualifier to the update operation and this qualifier includes every attribute value we specified for locking.

The more attributes we lock, the more values will be included in the qualifier and this can slow down the database operation. Therefore, if we know that some attributes will never be changed by our application code, there would be no need to lock it. This will reduce the amount of locked attributes and the complexity of the update qualifier.

In addition, there are attributes, which map to certain database types like float, double or binary large objects (BLOB). These types are not suitable for this kind of database qualifier. This is either because the internal representation of such types differs from the database or due to the amount of data involved (comparing your snapshot data with the BLOB data in the database will make the application much slower).

You can choose to lock one single attribute. If you do this, you have to choose an attribute which will always change if an object gets updated, for example an update counter. The advantage of this is that it leaves a small footprint on the checking qualifier and therefore results in virtually no overhead on the database side.

We would also be able to tune our database more efficiently by creating a compound index containing only the primary key(s) and our locking attribute. This is because the EOF will always include the primary key in SQL clauses to the database (whether it is marked for optimistic locking or not). Our problem will be to identify this attribute and to change it every time we update our object, for example by overwriting the `willChange()` method or by catching a notification for message changes from EOF (`EOObjectsChangedInEditingContextNotification`).

Another idea would be to use this method, but move the modification of the lock attribute to the database side. Most databases support such triggers. By using this method, we would be subject to all the benefits and disadvantages as before, with the difference that we would have to write some database-specific code (the triggers), too. The advantage is that the value will only be updated when the object is saved back to the database and not every time a single update occurs. The disadvantage is of course, that we would need to maintain database code along with our application code.

Pessimistic Locking

Pessimistic locking works on the database level by actively preventing other access calls from retrieving or updating the data that is currently locked.

Pessimistic locking can easily be combined with optimistic locking by enabling it for certain objects, or setting it to be the default strategy. However, if you set up pessimistic locking as the default strategy, you cannot use optimistic locking on other objects.

Once an object is locked, the lock will only be removed if we save the data back to the database or tell EOF to undo the change transaction on the data. The EOF will also refault objects when such a transaction is over, so we are guaranteed to always work with up-to-date data.

There are some general caveats with pessimistic locking. If you accidentally forget to save back the data or refault the locked object, the lock will remain. This does mean that we would need to code much more accurately when compared to using optimistic locking. Additionally we would need to be prepared for errors as if a lock operation fails, EOF will throw an exception.

Pessimistic locking is often unsuitable in WebObjects applications because data is usually held in a user's session. You don't have full control of the session: because the user's connection might fail or s/he might accidentally close the browser resulting in our session – including the data it might have locked pessimistically – stalling.

Pessimistic locking can be very powerful but also very tricky to handle because different databases use different pessimistic locking mechanisms. One database might lock a single row, another will lock a group of data and others might not support pessimistic locking at all. There are also differences in the way databases react when locked data is being accessed. One database adaptor might just block access, the other will raise an exception. As you can see, it is crucial to check your database documentation before using this feature.

To make matters more complex, there are three different pessimistic locking strategies, which are all supported by the EOF. The first strategy "Lock on Select" comes in two flavors. These strategies are now discussed in more detail.

Lock on Select

This strategy works globally. If we fetch any data from the database it will automatically become locked. This strategy changes the default locking strategy.

A lock for an object will automatically be released when we save the data using `saveChanges()` or when we roll back the transaction by using any method which undoes our change (`revert()`, `invalidatAllObjects()`, ...). After calling one of those methods, the data will be available to others again. If we fetch the data again, a new lock will be established.

To establish this strategy, we tell the database context we are using for the fetch of the data, to use a pessimistic locking strategy. The `EODatabaseContext` is an object used by the EOF framework internally, which controls access to the database like `EOEditingContext` objects track access to your Enterprise Objects:

```
//previously set up fetch specification
EOFetchSpecification myFetchSpecification;

EOObjectStoreCoordinator myOSC =
                    EOObjectStoreCoordinator.defaultCoordinator();
EODatabaseContext myDBC =
         myOSC.objectStoreForFetchSpecification( myFetchSpecification );

myDBC.setUpdateStrategy( EODatabaseContext.UpdateWithPessimisticLocking );
```

The above code sets the update strategy for pessimistic locking. As you can see, we need to inform the database context of a database connection to carry out this strategy. This way, the update strategy works globally on any fetch done using the specified database context only. If you were using multiple database channels to different databases, you probably would want to set the update strategy on every connection to be the same to really have an application-wide global unique strategy. You should use the object store coordinator to iterate over the different database contexts.

This is easy to set up. It works directly when fetching data, so the number of roundtrips to the database is low. However, we are setting a default strategy and this could result in exceptions if we get into deadlock situations during a fetch operation. Additionally, if we perform more read operations than write operations, we would probably lock more data than we actually need to.

If we want EOF to only lock certain objects for a specific fetch, we can tell the fetch specification that we are using, to lock the objects which are about to be fetched from the database.

The following code snippet shows how to do this:

```
//previously set up fetch specification
EOFetchSpecification myFetchSpecification;

//activate the method to lock objects
myFetchSpecification.setLocksObjects(true);

//safety measure to always get fresh data
myFetchSpecification.setRefreshesRefetchedObjects(true);
```

If we are using this technique then we should use the `setRefreshesRefetchedObjects()` call to enable refreshing of objects on every fetch. This will ensure that the internal cache of fetched objects will not get used and that we always get fresh data from the database. If we were using the EOModeler to define a fetch specification, we can activate both features (locking and refreshing) directly in the EOModel. Just open the fetch specification you already defined, click on the **Options** tab and select **Lock all fetched objects** and **Refresh refetched objects**:

Chapter 9

[screenshot of ModelOracle.eomodeld showing Fetch Specification with Options tab selected, including Fetch Limit (Max Rows: 0, Prompt on limit) and checkboxes: Perform deep inheritance fetch, Fetch distinct rows, Lock all fetched objects, Refresh refetched objects, Require all variable bindings]

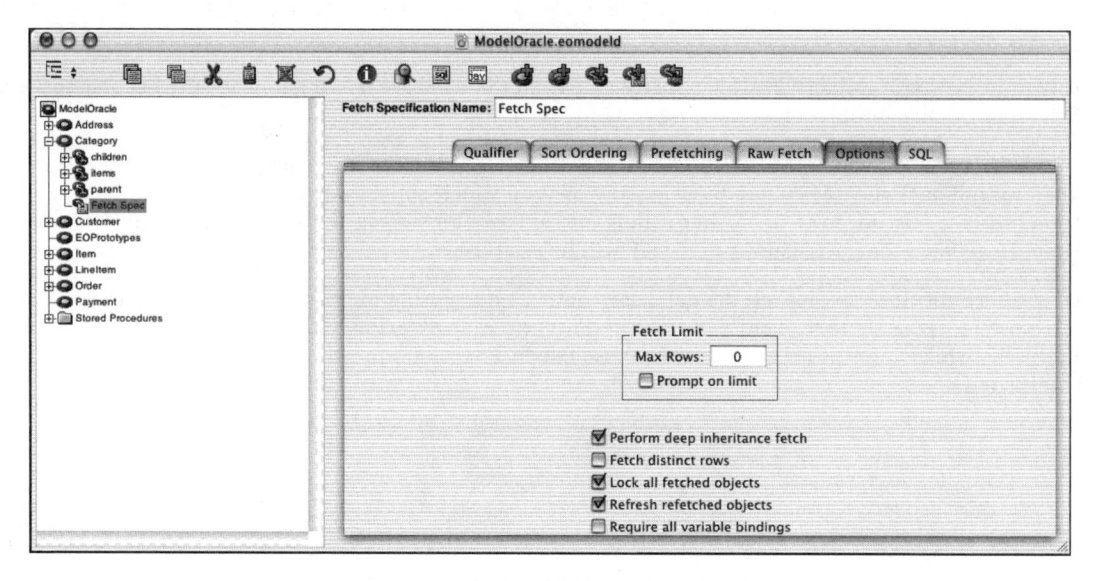

This strategy is probably the most convenient way to lock the data of a certain fetch for data that will change, especially when using the EOModeler. Do not forget to release the lock again by either refaulting, reverting or saving the locked objects back to the database!

Lock on Update

If we wanted to reduce the amount of locked objects as well as lock the objects we are about to modify, then the lock on update method is the most suitable. By using the lock on update method, objects become locked when the EOF encounters changes on a previously fetched object. In this case, the EOF will refetch the object from the database and put a lock on it.

The following code snippet will activate this mechanism by telling the currently used editing context to explicitly lock objects when they are about to become modified:

```
//this is the data object we just fetched
EOGenericRecord myData;

//tell the editing context to use lock on demands
myData.editingContext().setLocksObjectsBeforeFirstModification(true);
```

Establishing this locking strategy is quite easy. It reduces the locking overhead that the locking on select strategy has, but it will throw an exception if the database is in a deadlock situation. Another 'disadvantage' is the way this strategy works: an additional roundtrip to the database is required each time an object is about to be modified.

Lock on Demand

This last strategy reduces the number of locks required even further. The lock on select strategy was globally set up on a certain fetch specification and therefore is always used if this fetch specification is used. Lock on demand will disable automatic pessimistic locking. When using this strategy, you are completely on your own and decide which objects to lock as needed.

To set the lock, we invoke the `lockObject()` method on the editing context our object belongs to. This gives us greater control over possible exceptions, so we would catch exceptions directly when locking the object, as shown:

```
//locking with exception catching
try {
  myObjects.editingContext().lockObject(myObject);
} catch (Exception exception){
  //doesn't require lock
  //provide a wait or error page or try again after a certain time
}
```

This strategy requires an extra fetch on the object, so the overhead is slightly higher than when locking it directly when fetched.

Locking a Column

Optimistic and pessimistic locking both have one disadvantage: your lock will be removed whenever the locked data is reverted or saved back to the database. So if we wanted to keep the lock over several save operations or over a longer period of time, and do not want to establish the lock over and over again, we need a different approach.

We can use an additional column in our table to keep the locking information. This is somewhat similar to the concept of using a semaphore or operating system lock to prevent access to shared data, but this time the semaphore resides together with the data it protects, in the database itself. It also implies that the logic for the lock needs to be implemented on the application side, because the database will know nothing about the real usage of the extra column.

Because we are using an extra column in the database, we will also allocate more space for the table. This could be used to store more information than just the lock. A simple lock would probably be represented by a column containing `Boolean` values, storing `true` for a lock, and `false` if the column is free.

It would be a good idea to store the `sessionID` or `userID` to keep track of who locked the column. This can be a good starting point for sharing access by the same user or session over different application instances. To indicate that a row is not locked, the stored value does not contain a concrete value but `null`.

What information to store in the extra column, depends on what kind of extra data we want to keep. Of course we can use multiple columns to store combined information, for example if we wanted to store both the mentioned timestamp and user information.

Although this approach seems very powerful and useful, especially if we are using the lock to store extra information to implement further features, the implementation can be tricky.

Of course we still need to combine this mechanism with optimistic or pessimistic locking to prevent others from changing our lock, so the pros and cons of optimistic and pessimistic locking mechanisms also apply to this technique. For example, if you are using optimistic locking, you will only mark the extra column for optimistic locking with the lock symbol.

There is another disadvantage. If we need to set the lock, we need to save the object which should be locked to the database. To do this, the object usually resides within an editing context, and the `saveChanges()` operation of the editing context will not only save our special object, but every object currently controlled by the editing context. Therefore it is a good idea to set up a new editing context for this task, which should only contain the object which needs to be locked.

The following code snippet from the WebObjects documentation may be used to enable this locking strategy. How you handle access to the object while it is locked, depends on your specific needs. You can check for the lock on every modification (by overwriting `willChange()`) or just on operations like `validateForSave()` for the save operation, as we can see:

```
//set a lock
public void lock(){
  EOEditingContext tempContext = new EOEditingContext();
  EOEnterpriseObject myEO;
  myEO = tempContext.faultForGlobalID(
        this.editingContext().globalIDForObject(this), tempContext);
  myEO.setLock(true);
  myContext.saveChanges ();
}

//release the lock
public void unlock(){
  EOEditingContext tempContext = new EOEditingContext;
  EOEnterpriseObject myEO;
  myEO = tempContext.faultForGlobalID(
        this.editingContext().globalIDForObject(this), tempContext);
  myEO.setLock(false);
  myContext.saveChanges();
}
```

The above code uses a tricky method to set itself into the editing context. Instead of inserting itself into the new allocated editing store by using `tempContext.insertObject(this)`, it uses the `globalId` to generate a fault for itself in the new editing context. This way it avoids the `awakeFromInsertion()` message and others which would normally be triggered. We might want to overwrite the `setLock()` and other methods of `EOEditingContext`, to utilize this approach.

Locking By Application Logic

The final technique to lock objects is to use the traditional approach: locking at the application level. This is probably the most flexible way, but also the most complicated way. This strategy requires the application to keep track of all locked objects by itself. This means extra work is needed to implement the tracking logic, but this does provide greater flexibility than the other methods.

Of course, locking at the application level requires no database logic to be triggered; neither does it allocate extra space on the database. This leads to more code complexity, if for example, you want to notify other applications about the lock status changes. In this case we would need to implement further communication code and use appropriate data transportation mechanisms between applications.

One thing that prevents the usage of such a technique is the shared use of the database. If we are integrating our WebObjects application into an established environment, our application will probably not be the only one accessing the data. Application-based locking is based on the commitment of all applications to the same strategy and this will be hindered if just one application is not aware of a lock outside the scope of the database.

Summary

This chapter discussed key-value coding, validation and locking strategies within typical WebObjects applications. Key-value coding is a generic way of accessing properties of objects. Through the use of key words we can access object properties and avoid using a custom accessor method. Every value we store and retrieve in the WebObjects Framework relies on keys.

Whenever we store data to objects, we require data validation too. Many of the validation mechanisms presented here are generic but there are also special EOF validation mechanisms. Validation in WebObjects relies on the implementation of interfaces and classes that enable validation to occur on relevant data.

Finally we explored different locking strategies such as optimistic and pessimistic locking, which help us protect our data from accidental changes caused by other users or programs. Optimistic locking requires us to mark the attributes we want to lock. Pessimistic locking prevents other users from accessing locked data. We could also lock data by column, which would protect our data over several save operations or use application logic to lock objects.

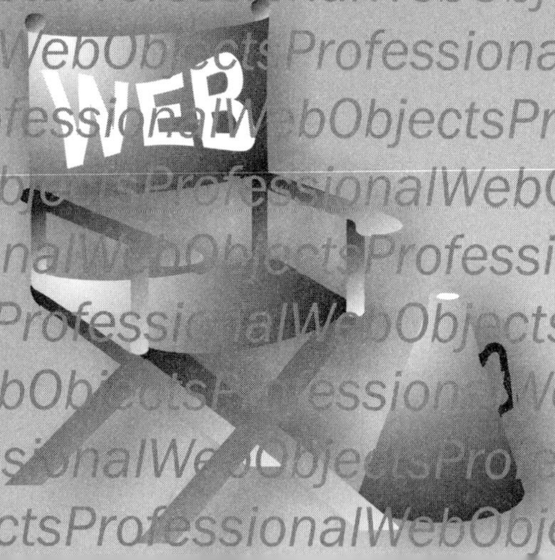
WEB

10
Direct To Web and Templating

Forget everything you think you know about Direct To Web (D2W). Direct To Web is a remarkably powerful, remarkably misunderstood technology. The material available to date about Direct To Web focuses on how Direct To Web applications are different from non-Direct To Web applications. This has lead to some confusion regarding Direct To Web. We will show how D2W applications are simply WebObjects applications with an extra brain helping out – the Direct To Web Rule System.

Direct To Web is such a large topic within WebObjects that we have split the discussion into two chapters. This chapter deals with templating techniques and Chapter 12 covers the Rule System in detail.

What is Direct To Web?

Direct To Web is a template-oriented environment for database-driven web applications. It leverages all of the information you provide about your data in your business logic blueprint, the EOModel, and all of the robust capabilities that WebObjects provides developers and users.

It complements these technologies with an innovative "Rule System" that configures your application with rules you supply. These rules shape your application; tell it what to do, when to do it, and how it should look when it does it.

A simple application can be created without writing any Java code, but, in addition to the Rule System, Direct To Web provides many Java hooks you can take advantage of to create a powerful, yet still very adaptable application. It's comforting to know that Direct To Web is very scalable. It is effective in the simplest Create, Read, Update and Delete applications, and in huge, highly dynamic, user-centric systems with hundreds of tables and very complex requirements.

Most importantly, Direct To Web is not a code-generation system. It is designed from the ground up to be a code **reuse** system. Ultimately, Direct To Web will save you time, money, and keep you ahead of your competition.

Why Use Direct To Web?

Direct to Web applications enjoy all the benefits of code-reuse – decreased development time, decreased debugging and testing time, and increased stability through the use of highly-exercised code. Also, because of the rules you write using Rule Editor, Direct To Web applications are easy to maintain and adapt to changing requirements.

For example, changing the word "Lorry" to "Truck" throughout your application is usually as easy as editing a single rule in Rule Editor. Your entire application will react to the change and use the new terminology. When you add a new entity to your application, Direct To Web pages generated at run time to manage that entity automatically adopt the look and feel mandated by the rules you applied to the rest of your application. Your users benefit greatly from the consistent user-interface that results. This adaptability minimizes the amount of simple but time-consuming work required to improve your application, and gives you the time to focus on business logic and valuable features.

Direct to Web applications take full advantage of the information provided by your EOModel, to ensure applications will not violate database integrity. You can achieve this without Direct To Web, but you have to write code to avoid such situations and write code to handle errors generated by bad data.

Direct To Web also fully leverages the validation services provided by WebObjects and EnterpriseObjects, which are very powerful, but can be time consuming to integrate into a non-Direct to Web application.

When Should You Use Direct To Web?

Once you have designed your database and created an EOModel file you can quickly get a web application up and running with Direct To Web. At first you can use the application to seed your database with data and test your EOModel. You can mix Direct To Web and non- Direct To Web pages in your application as desired. Prototyping is made easy with D2W reusable components, which are covered later in this chapter. The early stages of the application life-cycle is when the requirements change most often and most drastically – the agility of Direct To Web lets you respond to change requests quickly, letting you focus on implementing important features instead of struggling to keep up with shifts in business-terminology and color schemes.

Your application doesn't have to be 100% Direct To Web or 0% Direct To Web – it can be any mixture you want. Even if your application does not end up using Direct To Web in pages shown to your users, it can still be useful for prototyping new features, and testing new EnterpriseObjects entities and business logic while you're developing.

If you anticipate a lot of changing requirements, sticking to Direct To Web will maximize your engineering team's agility and minimize head counts.

Where Is Direct To Web?

Direct To Web is comprised of three frameworks that are added to your project by default when you create a Direct To Web WebObjects application.

Direct To Web and Templating

```
▼ 📁 Frameworks
    ▶ [F] JavaFoundation.framework
    ▶ [F] JavaEOControl.framework
    ▶ [F] JavaEOAccess.framework
    ▶ [F] JavaWebObjects.framework
    ▶ [F] JavaJDBCAdaptor.framework
    ▶ [F] JavaWOExtensions.framework
    ▶ [F] JavaXML.framework
    ▶ [F] JavaDTWGeneration.framework
    ▶ [F] JavaDirectToWeb.framework
    ▶ [F] JavaEOProject.framework
```

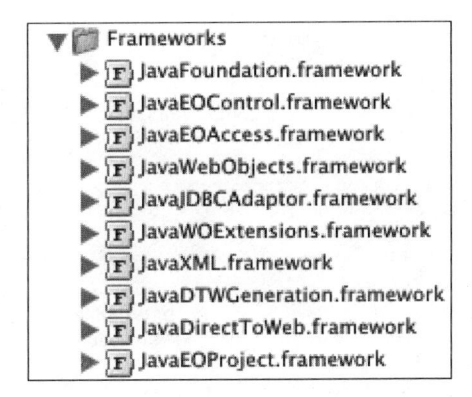

The `JavaDirectToWeb` framework implements all the features of Direct To Web except the "page freezing" functionality, which is implemented by the `JavaDTWGeneration` framework.

In addition to these frameworks and the usual WebObjects and EnterpriseObjects-related frameworks, a new Direct To Web application also includes the `JavaEOProject` framework, which implements functionality related to `JavaClient` and `DirectToJavaClient` applications.

Rule files (files ending with `.d2wmodel`) are edited using `RuleEditor`, which is found in your developer's application folder.

Direct To Web Documentation

Documentation for Direct To Web can be found in the following locations on your hard drive:

Developing WebObjects Applications With Direct To Web:
/Developer/Documentation/WebObjects/DirectToWeb/ (Mac OS X)
C:\Apple\Documentation\Developer\WebObjects\DirectToWeb (Windows)

WebObjects Overview: Direct To Web Applications:
/Developer/Documentation/WebObjects/WebObjectsOverview/D2W/ (Mac OS X)
C:\Apple\Documentation\Developer\WebObjects\WebObjectsOverview\D2W (Windows)

JavaDirectToWeb.framework Reference:
/System/Library/Frameworks/JavaDirectToWeb.framework/Resources/English.lproj/Documentation/Reference/Java/ (Mac OS X)
C:\Apple\Library\Frameworks\DirectToWeb.framework\Resources\English.lproj\Documentation\Reference\Java (Windows)

The Architecture of Direct To Web Applications

As you see from the diagram below, Direct To Web adds only a few extra pieces to the architecture of a WebObjects application.

Chapter 10

```
         D2W.          Your WebObjects Components and         Your
       factory()         D2W's WebObjects Components        EOModels
                                                           and Business
                                                              Logic

                              Keymaster
                              D2WConext
                              Gatekeeper

     Legend
     creates        Your      DirectToWeb      D2W's
     uses          Rules      Rule System       Base
                                               Rules
```

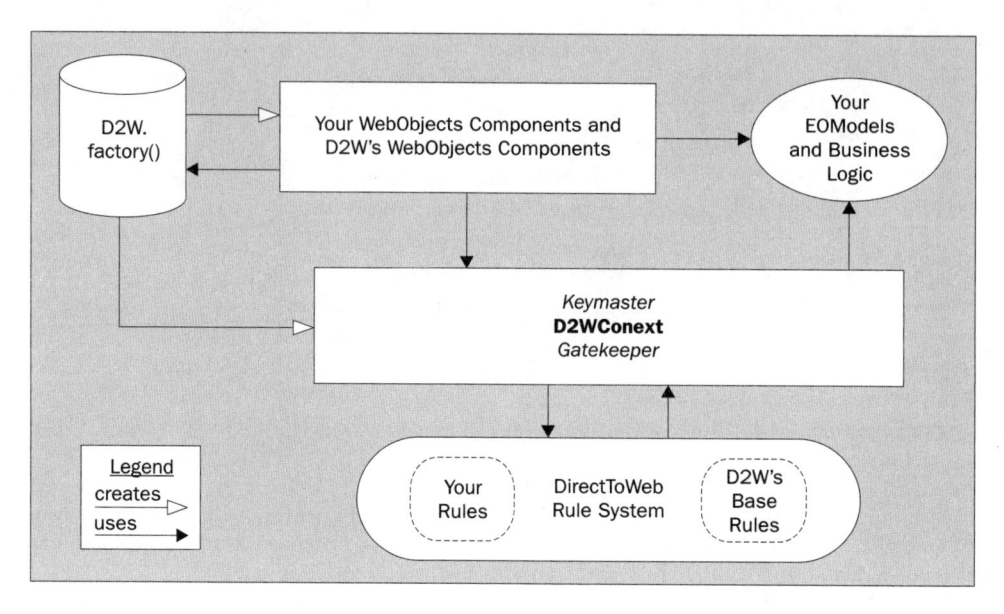

Fundamentally, Direct To Web adds two things – **templates** and **rules**. Templates are WebObjects Components that implement Direct To Web's different page types, which are called **tasks**. Rules dictate what templates to use, and what they should display.

The **Direct To Web Context**, implemented by the D2WContext class, ties the two together. The D2WContext is what allows Direct To Web templates to be completely reusable, to work with every WebObjects application and any EOModel. We'll be covering D2WContext in detail in Chapter 12.

The catalyst in this equation is the **D2W Factory** (implemented by the D2W class). It creates Direct To Web pages and provides the D2WContext with information to serve the templates and rules effectively.

D2W Factory

The **D2W Factory** is the Direct To Web page manufacturing facility. Its customers are you, and the pages it creates. Direct To Web pages create other Direct To Web pages when a link or button is clicked in the browser – meaning less work for you.

The D2W class, as you might expect from its name, uses the **Factory design pattern** to create and return instances of different classes of WOComponents. As is normal with a Factory class, you do not need to know the exact class of the page it returns. However, it helps to know which interface(s) the created page implements. Direct To Web's task specific Page Interfaces will be covered thoroughly in this chapter.

Direct To Web Apps Are WebObjects Apps

Direct To Web pages are WOComponents too. Like all components, they have bindings to keys that determine what content to include in generated pages. The home page of a Direct To Web application is Main.wo as usual, and can be edited to your heart's content.

Direct To Web and Templating

Two ready-made reusable subcomponents are included with new Direct To Web projects. They can be used as-is, modified in WebObjects Builder to suit your requirements, or simply ignored or removed altogether.

- `MenuHeader.wo` is a navigation bar for basic Direct To Web functionality
- `PageWrapper.wo` is your site's template (not to be confused with a Direct To Web task template – covered later), which you'll undoubtedly want to edit to incorporate your organization's standard colors/logos/branding. This component wraps around Direct To Web pages (hence the name PageWrapper) using the powerful `WOComponentContent` dynamic element.

In a new Direct To Web Application project, `Main.wo` implements a simple login page. The Login button is bound to the `defaultAction` method in `Main.java`. Clicking Login in a web browser configures the WebAssistant and returns a Direct To Web page. Your `Main.wo` component doesn't have to be a login page, and doesn't have to configure the WebAssistant. It can be, and do, anything you want it to.

Direct To Web projects include `EOModel` files and EnterpriseObject business logic classes, just like any other WebObjects project. Your `Application`, `Session` and `DirectAction` classes work as they always have. There is nothing D2W-specific in any of these classes in a new Direct To Web project.

Also included in Direct To Web projects is a "rule file" called **user.d2wmodel**. This file contains rules for the Direct To Web Rule System. The only rule you'll find in a brand new `user.d2wmodel` file is the one that configures the "look" you choose when creating. Your rules configure your application and you will find out more about them in Chapter 12.

What Are Templates?

At some point you're going to have to think more about how your users will interface with your database. One of the nice things about WebObjects is that you can easily maintain a separation of presentation, business logic, and data. In fact, the pieces that go into producing the look of your site are contained in many different elements. In Chapter 3 you learned about the template and binding files. For a Web Component named `Foo`, these would be the files `Foo.html` and `Foo.wod`.

There are other notions of templates that we'll look at in this chapter. You may want to have a common look and feel across your site by including some sort of navigation bar on each page – this is done for you automatically by Direct To Web and you'll see how to do this yourself in other applications. Much of the Direct To Web pages are generated on the fly from pre-built templates. There are several advantages to working with D2W templates:

- Templates allow you to modify the properties and page appearance using the visual tool WebAssistant
- Templates can be used for any entity
- A template is a WebObjects component so you can modify its visual appearance using familiar tools such as WebObjects Builder
- Because a template is a WebObjects component you can add functionality by editing the component's Java code as well as by editing the bindings of the component's dynamic elements

253

Chapter 10

Creating a Direct To Web Application

Let's start by automatically generating an application from the database developed in Chapter 5. Getting started is slightly different on Windows and on Mac OS X.

Instructions for Mac OS X

On the Mac, start up Project Builder and follow these steps.

- ❏ Select **New Project** from the File Menu. Scroll down to the **WebObjects** offerings, choose to create a **Direct To Web Application** and then click the **Next** button.

- ❏ The Direct To Web Project Assistant pops up and prompts you to enter a project name. Call this project `WOWroxExample` and tab so that the location is automatically assigned to `~/WOWroxExample/`. This will place the folder containing the project inside of the `Mac OS X/Users/<your user short name>/` directory. Again click the **Next** button.

- ❏ The assistant then asks you to choose to add in any needed frameworks. We don't need any so just hit the **Next** button again.

- ❏ The assistant then asks you to choose an **EOModel**. In other words, navigate to the database on which you are basing this application. Click the **Add** button and navigate to the `.eomodeld` file you created in Chapter 5. Click the **Choose** button. You should now see the path to the file you just selected listed under the heading **EOModels**. Click the **Next** button.

- ❏ You are now asked to pick a look for your project. The three choices are **Basic Look**, **Neutral Look**, and **WebObjects Look**. Throughout this chapter you'll see screenshots from these different looks and will be able to better decide the look you want. For now, choose **Basic Look** by clicking on it and then click the **Next** button.

> You need to think carefully about the look you want for your site before making your selection, as it isn't easy to change your mind after you get started. Check out the screenshots in the section *Comparing the Default Looks* for a quick idea of the differences.

- ❏ You can then choose whether or not to build and launch the project right away. It doesn't really matter. If you'd like to play around with the application a bit, go ahead and check the box labeled **Build and launch project now**. In either case click on the **Finish** button and you're done.

Instructions for Windows

On a Windows box you begin by starting up Project Builder.

- ❏ Select **New** from the **Project Menu**. From the dropdown list choose **Java WebObjects Application**.

- ❏ Next complete the Project Path. This will also name your project. The Direct To Web Project Assistant pops up and prompts you to enter a project name. For example, if you enter `C:\WOWroxExample`, then you are naming your project `WOWroxExample`. Click the **OK** button.

254

- The WebObjects Application Wizard appears and asks you to Choose type of assistance in your Java project. This is Wizard for "what kind of project are you building?" Your choices are Direct to Java Client, Direct To Web, Wizard, Java Client, and None. Select the radio button in front of Direct To Web and click the Next button.

- The assistant then asks you to Specify a model that defines your database-to-objects mapping. Select the radio button labeled Open existing model file. Click the Browse button and navigate to the .eomodeld directory from Chapter 5. Click the Open button. You should now see the path to the file you just selected listed to the right of the heading Model File. Click the Next button.

- You are now asked to pick a look for your project. The three choices are Basic Look, Neutral Look, and WebObjects Look. Choose Basic Look by clicking on it and then click on the Next button.

- You can then choose whether or not to build and launch the project right away. Click on the Finish button and you're done.

The Elements of a Web Component

Now that you've built your sample project, take a look at the Web Components. One of them is Main.wo. On the Windows platform this contains the files Main.html and Main.wod.

Comparing the Default Looks

There are three looks you can generate for Direct To Web. The easiest way for you to get a quick feel for each of these looks is to generate three Direct To Web projects that all use the same EOModel and differ only in the look being selected.

Follow the steps for setting up a Direct To Web application and choose to build and launch the project at the last step. All three versions will display log in screens. They are slightly different, but you really get a feel for the differences at the next screen. Select the checkbox that is labeled either Assistant or Enable Assistant and then click the Login button. This takes you to a page from which you can search by address, customer, line item, order, or payment.

Notice that you didn't do anything to build these views. You'll later be able to fine-tune this look and only include the properties you want to expose to the user. So far the point is that you get a functional, easy to understand UI that users can use to search your database.

The Basic Look

In the basic look the control header runs across the top of the screen. You have what appear to be navigation buttons. This is a familiar metaphor for browser users who are used to having a navigation button bar at the top of their browser. The dropdown list at the left side allows users to select the property from which a query will be constructed. If they select Address and then click on Build Query they will be taken to an Address Query screen that allows them to construct a more sophisticated query based on the Address field.

As the user navigates around the site, the control header stays in place and the rest of the screen changes. The bottom part of the screen is made up of tables. This look is very boxy. In this screenshot you can see that each row corresponds to a different entity and that dropdown lists and text fields are used to define fairly broad searches.

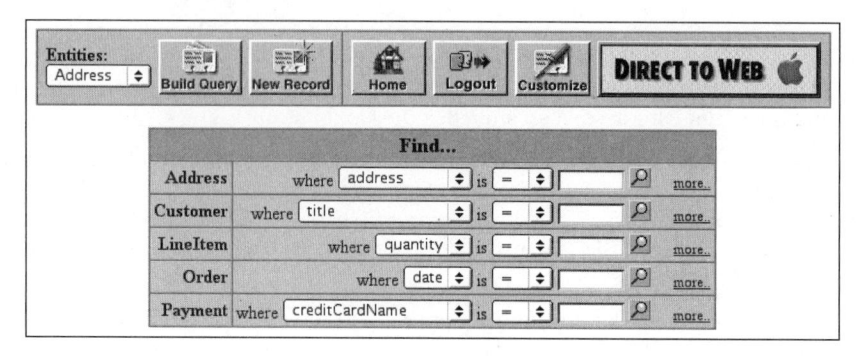

The Neutral Look

With the Neutral look the navigation element moves to the left column and runs vertically as text based choices instead of buttons. When you press Search... or New... the word Find changes to Search and Edit respectively and the word Entities changes to the entity being searched on or edited. The buttons added to this look on the search page and others have a brushed metal look to them. The query screen looks like this:

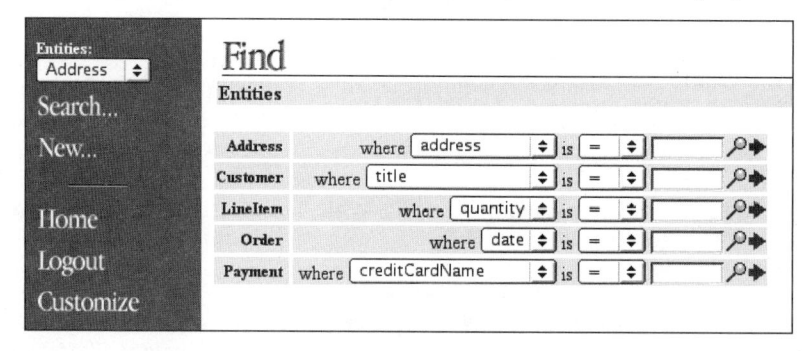

The WebObjects Look

The WebObjects look is very similar to the Neutral look. The navigation appears on the left and the organization is the same. The difference is that this site is branded as a WebObjects site. In addition to the badge saying Powered by WebObjects, the Apple logo sits at the top of the navigation frame and the WebObjects image appears on various fields and buttons. Here's a look at the WebObjects version of this page:

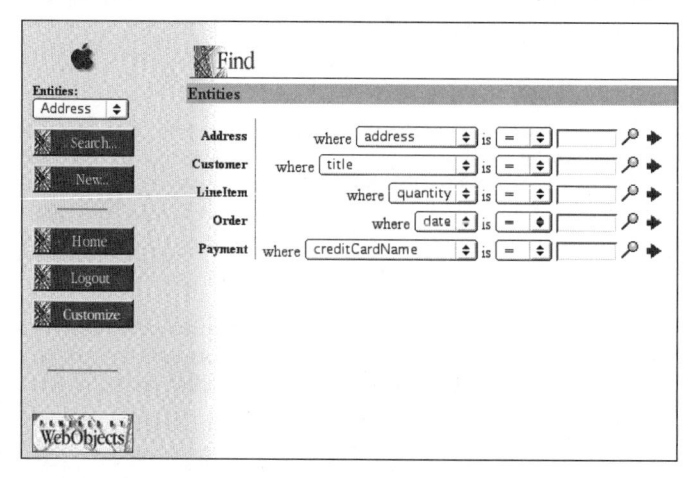

Changing the Look

If you look at the .html and .wod files for the three components you'll see no mention of the look they're using. If you look for clues in the .java files, again you'll see no mention of the look. The file where the value of the look is set is user.d2wmodel, which can be found under **Resources**. It should look like this:

```
{
  rules = (
    {
      class = com.webobjects.directtoweb.Rule;
      author = 100;
      rhs = {
        class = com.webobjects.directtoweb.Assignment;
        keyPath = look;
        value = "BasicLook";
      };
    }
  );
}
```

Replace the string BasicLook with the string NeutralLook. Save user.d2wmodel and build and run the application again. The result tells you a lot about what is going on and when. The top of the page is the same as the Basic look while the bottom of the page is now in the Neutral look. This is easy to see as the toolbar in the Neutral look runs along the left side of the browser window and doesn't have the Apple logo on it. Next, change the value from the string NeutralLook to WebObjectsLook, save, build and run the application. Again the top of the page is the same as the Basic look but the bottom of the page is now rendered in the WebObjects look.

You can see how easy it is to change the look of the elements that are rendered on the fly. In the section *Creating and Using a Custom Template* you'll see how to create your own template to modify the look of various elements.

Inside Main.java

Now that you are familiar with what a Direct To Web page looks like we'll take a more detailed look at some of the components. This section will look at improving the standard login page and introduce the different page types and interfaces.

Open up a new Direct To Web Application using Project Builder as before and open the Main.wo component by double-clicking the Main.wo folder. It is a simple login page for your application. When a visitor clicks on the **Login** button, they will invoke the defaultPage action method.

Here is the code created by Direct To Web's Project Builder Wizard for Main.java:

```
import com.webobjects.appserver.*;
import com.webobjects.directtoweb.*;

public class Main extends WOComponent {

  public String username;
```

```
    public String password;
    public boolean wantsWebAssistant = false;

    public Main(WOContext aContext) {
      super(aContext);
    }

    public WOComponent defaultPage() {
      D2W.factory().setWebAssistantEnabled(wantsWebAssistant);
      return D2W.factory().defaultPage(session());
    }

}
```

The first statement in the `defaultPage()` method tells Direct To Web whether or not your user wants to be able to use the WebAssistant during their session. The `wantsWebAssistant` boolean instance variable is bound to the `Assistant` checkbox on the page. The second line returns the default Direct To Web page for the application. This is usually a page that lets the visitor perform a Query against all the entities in your EOModels (called a QueryAll page).

The username and password variables bound to the page's text fields aren't authenticated, so the stock login page is not very useful. It's easy to check the username and password against your database of user accounts – you use familiar WebObjects and EnterpriseObjects techniques to do this.

This enhanced `defaultPage()` action method will only return the next page if the login name and password matches a `Customer` record in the database. Assume you have a `Customer` entity in your EOModel with `loginName` and `password` attributes and have generated a `Customer` class for this entity.

```
import com.webobjects.appserver.*;
import com.webobjects.directtoweb.*;
import com.webobjects.foundation.*;
import com.webobjects.eoaccess.*;
import com.webobjects.eocontrol.*;

public class Main extends WOComponent {
  public String username;
  public String password;
  public boolean wantsWebAssistant = false;

  public Main(WOContext aContext) {
    super(context);
  }

  // bind this new instance variable to a WOString in Main.wo
  public String errorMessage = null;    // display any error message

  private static final String LOGIN_ERR_MSG =
    "The username or password is incorrect. Try again...";

  public WOComponent defaultPage() {
    D2W.factory().setWebAssistantEnabled(wantsWebAssistant);
    WOComponent result = null;
    try {                                 // fetch customer object for this session
      NSArray customers =
```

```
                EOUtilities.objectsMatchingValues(session().defaultEditingContext(),
                                                                      "Customer",
                                                new NSDictionary(new Object[] {
            username, password
        }, new Object[] {
            "loginName", "password"
        })));
        if (customers.count() == 1) {     // AUTHENTICATION PASSED!
            Session s = (Session) session();

            // add a customer property to Session
            s.setCustomer((Customer) customers.objectAtIndex(0));

            // create the next page - can be anything you want!
            result = D2W.factory().defaultPage(s);
        } else {                          // AUTHENTICATION FAILED!
            throw new IllegalArgumentException(LOGIN_ERR_MSG);
        }
    } catch (Exception e) {

        // reset the password field for security purposes
        password = null;
        errorMessage = e.getMessage();
        result = null;                    // show the login page again
    }
    return result;
}
```

If `EOUtilities.objectsMatchingValues(…)` returns an array with one `Customer` object, the `Customer` object is handed to the `Session` so it remembers who logged in, and then `D2W.factory().defaultPage()` is returned as usual. If zero or more than one `Customer` objects are in the array, an `IllegalArgumentException` is thrown with the `LOGIN_ERR_MSG`. An exception is thrown because it simplifies the handling of errors – all exceptions are caught in the `catch` block where the `errorMessage` can be set to the message of an `Exception`.

Don't forget to put a `WOString` on `Main.wo`, and bind its `value` to `errorMessage`.

Direct To Web Tasks

What makes templates a bit confusing in WebObjects is that the word is used to mean different things. The `HTML` files such as `Main.html` that you learned about in Chapter 3 are often referred to as template files. Components such as `PageWrapper.wo` are used to set the look for all of the pages except, in the first case, the login page – and can be thought of as a template for the site. To avoid confusion, we referred to it as a common element so that we wouldn't be applying the word template to yet another concept. In this section we're going to begin to look at templates used in a more technical WebObjects specific way.

In D2W, the part of the web page that is not the `MenuHeader` is, by default, generated on the fly from the rules specified in the `d2wmodel` and the previous user actions, filled in with the relevant data stored in the database. These parts get rendered into HTML the way you see them because they use predefined templates provided as part of WebObjects. Direct To Web generates these task web pages using instances of the `D2WPage` class called Direct To Web templates. Direct To Web includes templates for the Basic look, the Neutral look, and for the WebObjects look.

There are nine templates corresponding to each default look. On a Windows Machine you can find them in this directory:

`Apple\Library\Frameworks\JavaDirectToWeb.framework\Resources`

and on Mac OS X you can find them at:

`System/Library/Frameworks/JavaDirectToWeb.framework/Resources`.

The nine templates, or **tasks** for the Basic look are the `BASConfirmPage`, `BASEditRelationshipPage`, `BASErrorPage`, `BASInspectPage`, `BASListPage`, `BASMasterDetailPage`, `BASPlainListPage`, `BASQueryAllEntitiesPage`, and the `BASQueryPage`. The naming conventions for the Neutral look is the same except the letters `BAS` are replaced by the letters `NEU`. Similarly, to get the templates for the WebObjects look, replace the letters `BAS` with the letters `WOL`. Later on you'll see how to modify these templates to create your own.

The D2W Factory provides methods you use to create Direct To Web pages corresponding to each task. Action methods in task template components also use the D2W Factory to create new pages for these tasks. Tasks are a central concept in Direct To Web, so let's review what each does and how to create them:

- **Query** pages display a search form to the user and a Query button. When the user clicks the button, a List page is shown that displays the result of the search. You create a Query page using this method on `D2W.factory()`:

    `QueryPageInterface queryPageForEntityNamed(String entityName, WOSession session)`

- **List** pages display a list of objects in a tabular format. The user can sort the objects by any column in ascending or descending fashion. The page also batches the objects and lets the user page through them to keep each page a manageable size. Clicking on the icon to the left of each row will display an Inspect page if the object's entity is read-only, or an Edit page if it isn't. If the object's entity is not read-only, a "Delete" button or trashcan icon will display a Confirm page, asking the user to confirm the deletion of the object. You create a List page using this method on `D2W.factory()`:

    `ListPageInterface listPageForEntityNamed(String entityName, WOSession session)`

- **Inspect** pages display a single object to the user. Each attribute or relationship of the object is shown on a separate line. If the Entity for the object is configured to be editable, an "Edit" button will appear at the bottom of the page. When clicked, an Edit page will be displayed. If the object's entity is not read-only, a "Delete" button will delete the object when clicked. Note that the deletion isn't confirmed! You create an Inspect page using this method on `D2W.factory()`:

    `InspectPageInterface inspectPageForEntityNamed(String entityName, WOSession session)`

- **Edit** pages allow the user to edit a single object using an HTML form. Attributes are typically displayed in text fields or with checkboxes. Relationships are shown in various ways depending on the type of relationship it is. If the object's entity is not read-only, a "Delete" button will delete the object when clicked. Note that the deletion isn't confirmed! You create an Edit page using one of these methods on `D2W.factory()`:

```
EditPageInterface editPageForEntityNamed(String entityName, WOSession session)

EditPageInterface editPageForNewObjectWithConfigurationNamed(String
                                      pageConfigurationName, WOSession session)

EditPageInterface editPageForNewObjectWithEntityNamed(String entityName,
                                                      WOSession session)
```

Use the first method when you want the user to edit an existing object. The second and third methods let the user edit a new object, which it instantiates for you. Use the second method when you want to use a specific page configuration. (Page configurations are covered in Chapter 12.)

The second and third methods insert the new object in a peer editing context. This way, an "empty" row won't appear in the database later if the edit page is never saved or canceled and a different page saves the session's `defaultEditingContext`.

❑ **Select** pages show a list of objects like the list task, but allows the user to choose one of them by clicking on a "Select" button that's shown next to each row. Select pages are used by EditRelationship pages and MasterDetail pages (a special aggregate page that has a `D2WSelect` reusable component at the top and a `D2WEdit` reusable component at the bottom). D2W reusable components are covered later in the chapter. You create a Select page using this method on `D2W.factory()`:

```
SelectPageInterface selectPageForEntityNamed(String entityName, WOSession session)
```

❑ **EditRelationship** pages are the most complex of all Direct To Web pages. They are created by Edit pages when the user wants to change a relationship property of an object. EditRelationship pages handle to-one and to-many relationships, and can perform sub-queries to allow the user to find object(s) to use in the relationship. If the entity for the relationship's entity are not marked read-only, the EditRelationship also allows the user to create a brand new object to use for the relationship. You create an EditRelationship page using this method on `D2W.factory()`:

```
EditRelationshipPageInterface editRelationshipPageForEntityNamed(String
                                                 entityName, WOSession session)
```

❑ **QueryAll** pages show a vertical list of small search forms – one for each visible entity in your application. Clicking the search button on a row brings up a List page with the result of the search for that row's entity. Each row also has a link to the full Query page for the corresponding entity. You create a QueryAll page using this method on `D2W.factory()`:

```
QueryAllPageInterface queryAllPage(WOSession session)
```

❑ **Confirm** pages display a message, and **Yes** and **No** buttons. The message should be in the form of a Yes/No question to make sense to the user. Clicking **Yes** confirms the action, and clicking **No** cancels the action. You create a Confirm page using this method on `D2W.factory()`:

```
ConfirmPageInterface confirmPageForEntityNamed(String entityName,
                                               WOSession session)
```

❏ **Error** pages display a message to the user, which should inform them that some kind of error has occurred. A "Return" button will take them to the next page. If there is no next page to go to, a "Login" button will be displayed which takes the user to the start of the application. You create an Error page using this method on `D2W.factory()`:

```
ErrorPageInterface errorPage(WOSession session)
ErrorPageInterface errorPage(WOContext context)
```

The D2W Factory can also create a Direct To Web page for a **Page Configuration**. Page Configurations are covered in Chapter 12, but for the sake of showing you all the ways to create pages with the D2W Factory, here is the corresponding method on `D2W.factory()`:

```
WOComponent pageForConfigurationNamed(String configurationName, WOSession session)
```

Direct To Web Page Interfaces

All of the pages (`WOComponents`) returned by the D2W Factory implement a Java interface defined in the Direct To Web framework, such as `ListPageInterface` or `QueryPageInterface`. These interfaces make it possible to have multiple template components to choose from for each task.

WebObjects comes with three sets of templates – one set for each of the three standard "looks": Basic Look, Neutral Look, and WebObjects look. Each set has a template for each task (although the Edit and Inspect tasks share the Inspect template, and the List and Select tasks share the List template). Each look's Inspect template is a different class, but all Inspect templates implement the `InspectPageInterface` interface, so you can use that interface to interact with any Inspect page you get from the D2W Factory.

Single Object pages

Edit, EditRelationship and Inspect pages display a single object, and need to be told which object to operate on. When one of these pages is created by another Direct To Web page, the originating page provides the information it needs to continue, so you don't have to do this yourself. When you create one of these pages, you need to configure the page using the methods in their respective interfaces.

InspectPageInterface and EditPageInterface

```
void setObject(EOEnterpriseObject eo);
void setNextPage(WOComponent component);
void setNextPageDelegate(NextPageDelegate delegate);
```

Call `setObject`, and one of `setNextPage` or `setNextPageDelegate` to configure an Inspect page or Edit page.

EditRelationshipPageInterface

```
void setMasterObjectAndRelationshipKey(EOEnterpriseObject eo, String key);
void setNextPage(WOComponent component);
void setNextPageDelegate(NextPageDelegate delegate);
```

Call `setMasterObjectAndRelationshipKey`, and one of `setNextPage` or `setNextPageDelegate` to configure an EditRelationship page.

Direct To Web and Templating

Here's an example of creating an Edit page for the `Customer` object stored in the Session using the D2W factory. This code builds on the previous code example from `Main.java`:

```java
import com.webobjects.appserver.*;
import com.webobjects.directtoweb.*;
import com.webobjects.foundation.*;
import com.webobjects.eoaccess.*;
import com.webobjects.eocontrol.*;

public class Main extends WOComponent {
  public String username;
  public String password;
  public boolean wantsWebAssistant = false;

  public Main(WOContext aContext) {
    super(context);
  }

  // bind this new instance variable to a WOString in Main.wo
  public String errorMessage = null;    // display any error message

  private static final String LOGIN_ERR_MSG =
    "The username or password is incorrect. Try again...";

  public WOComponent defaultPage() {
    D2W.factory().setWebAssistantEnabled(wantsWebAssistant);
    WOComponent result = null;
    try {                          // fetch customer object for this session
      NSArray customers =
        EOUtilities.objectsMatchingValues(session().defaultEditingContext(),
                                          "Customer",
                                          new NSDictionary(new Object[] {
          username, password
        }, new Object[] {
          "loginName", "password"
        }));
      if (users.count() == 1) {    // AUTHENTICATION PASSED!
        Session s = (Session) session();

        // add a customer property to Session
        s.setCustomer((Customer) customers.objectAtIndex(0));

        // Create a new Edit page using the D2W factory
        EditPageInterface epi =
          D2W.factory().editPageForEntityNamed("Customer", s);

        // tell the Edit page which Customer to display
        epi.setObject(s.customer());

        // tell the Edit page to go to the QueryAll page
        // when the user clicks "Save" or "Cancel"
        epi.setNextPage(D2W.factory().defaultPage(s));
        result = (WOComponent) epi;
      } else {                     // AUTHENTICATION FAILED!
        throw new IllegalArgumentException(LOGIN_ERR_MSG);
      }
```

```
        } catch (Exception e) {
            // reset the password field for security purposes
            password = null;
            errorMessage = e.getMessage();
            result = null;           // show the login page again
        }
        return result;
    }
}
```

With the modification above, visitors arrive at a page where they can edit their Customer profile after authenticating. When the user clicks on **Cancel** or **Save** on the Edit page, they arrive at the default D2W page. Clicking the **Save** button will save the `Customer` object before returning the QueryAll page.

Multiple Object Pages

List and Select pages operate on a list of objects, and need to be given an `EODataSource` of objects to operate on. When a List or Select page is created by another Direct To Web page, the page that creates it gives it the list of objects it needs, so you don't have to do this yourself.

ListPageInterface

```
void setDataSource(EODataSource dataSource);
void setNextPage(WOComponent component);
void setNextPageDelegate(NextPageDelegate delegate);
```

Call `setDataSource`, and `setNextPage` or `setNextPageDelegate` to configure a List page.

SelectPageInterface

```
void setDataSource(EODataSource dataSource);
void setNextPageDelegate(NextPageDelegate delegate);
void setSelectedObject(EOEnterpriseObject eo);
EOEnterpriseObject selectedObject();
NextPageDelegate nextPageDelegate();
```

Call `setDataSource` and `setNextPageDelegate` to configure a select page. Your `NextPageDelegate` can find out which object was selected by calling `selectedObject` on the `WOComponent` passed in as the sender to its `nextPage` method. `NextPageDelegates` are covered later in the chapter.

Here's an example of creating a List page using the D2W Factory to display the current Customer's past orders. This code builds on the previous code examples which have a `customer()` accessor method in the Session class. The action method below is put in the `Session.java` file; your components can bind their `WOHyperlink` and `WOSumbitButton` actions to `session.listMyOrders` to use this method.

```
import com.webobjects.directtoweb.*;

    public WOComponent listMyOrders() {
        // remember the current page
        WOComponent currentPage = this.context().page();
        // create the List page
```

```
            ListPageInterface result = D2W.factory().
                listPageForEntityNamed("Order", this);
            // create a data source for the Customer entity
            EOEditingContext ec = this.customer().editingContext();
            EODataSource ds = new EODatabaseDataSource(ec, "Customer");
            // this next line creates the master-detail data source
            ds = ds.dataSourceQualifiedByKey("orders");
            // this line specifies which customer's orders to use
            ds.qualifyWithRelationshipKey("orders", this.customer());
            // tell the List page to list the customer's orders
            result.setDataSource(ds);
            // clicking "Return" goes back to the current page
            result.setNextPage(currentPage);
            return (WOComponent)result;
        }
```

When a button or hyperlink bound to `session.listMyOrders` is clicked, the originating page, accessible from `this.context().page()` (where `this` is the `Session` object) is remembered. Then a List page is created for the `Order` entity.

The next few lines of code creates a master-detail `EODetailDataSource` whose master object is the session's `customer()` object, and the detail relationship is `orders`.

The List page is given the `EODetailDataSource`, and told to return to the originating page when the "Return" button is pressed on the List page. The List page is then returned from the action method so the response can be generated and returned to the user's browser.

Query pages operate on all the objects of the `EOEntity` provided by the `entityName` parameter to the `queryPageForEntityNamed` method. When the user clicks on the "Query" button on a Query page, a List page is generated, and the Query page provides the List page with an `EODataSource` containing the objects matching the query parameters.

QueryPageInterface and QueryAllPageInterface

```
    void setNextPageDelegate(NextPageDelegate delegate);
    EODataSource queryDataSource();
```

A `Query` page is ready once you create it. If you want something other than a List page with the search results to appear when the user clicks the **Query** button, provide the `Query` page with a `NextPageDelegate` by calling `setNextPageDelegate` on the `Query` page. `NextPageDelegate`s are covered later in the chapter.

`QueryAll` pages offer miniature query forms for all entities visible in the application. The interface works the same, except you have to ask the `queryDataSource()` for its `classDescriptionForObjects()` to find out which entity was searched.

Here is an example of creating a `Query` page that displays a custom `WOComponent` to display its results instead of a Direct To Web list page. This demonstrates mixing Direct To Web and non-Direct To Web components in your application. Put this method in your `Session.java` file.

The example assumes you have a `WOComponent` called `CoolProducts` with methods `void setItems(NSArray objects)` and `void setSearchPage(WOComponent page)`. Presumably this page will display the search results in some incredibly appealing manner.

Chapter 10

```
    import com.webobjects.directtoweb.*;

  public WOComponent searchProducts() {
    // create the query Items page
    QueryPageInterface result =
            D2W.factory().queryPageForEntityNamed("Item", this);
    // a SearchResultsDelegate will set up the search results
    result.setNextPageDelegate(new SearchResultsDelegate(result));
    return (WOComponent)result;
  }

  public static class SearchResultsDelegate implements NextPageDelegate {
    private QueryPageInterface qpi;
    // this constructor remembers the originating query page
    public SearchResultsDelegate(QueryPageInterface searchPage) {
      qpi = searchPage;
    }

    // called when the Query button was pressed
    // return the page you want the customer to see next
    public WOComponent nextPage(WOComponent sender) {
      // create the product listing page
      CoolProducts result =
              (CoolProducts)sender.pageWithName("CoolProducts");
      // send the query results to the page
      result.setItems(qpi.queryDataSource().fetchObjects());
      // give it the query page too, so the user can modify
      // their search criteria by returning to the query page
      result.setSearchPage((WOComponent)qpi);
      return result;
    }
  }
```

Bind a `WOHyperlink`'s action to `session.searchProducts`. When the hyperlink is clicked, a Query page will be displayed that allows the user to search the product database. When the Query page's "Query" button is clicked, the query page creates the `EOQualifier` to be used when fetching the results using `queryDataSource().fetchObjects()`.

Since the Query page has a `nextPageDelegate` set (an instance of `SearchResultsDelegate`), the NextPage method of the `nextPageDelegate` is called. The component it returns is the one that the user will see next.

The `nextPage()` method simply creates an instance of the fictitious `CoolProducts` component, and then provides it with the search results from the Query page, and the Query page instance itself. The CoolProducts page can provide a link back to the originating Query page. This is handy because the Query page will still have the user's criteria filled in, and the CoolProducts page can be used from different types of search pages, not just Direct To Web Query pages.

Message Pages

Message pages display a message (a String containing useful information) to the user and allow them to continue past them. They are very simple to set up, and not terribly robust.

ConfirmPageInterface

```
    void setConfirmDelegate(NextPageDelegate confirmDelegate);
    void setCancelDelegate(NextPageDelegate cancelDelegate);
    void setMessage(String message);
```

Direct To Web and Templating

Call all three methods to configure a Confirm page. When the user clicks Yes on the page, the NextPage method of the `confirmDelegate` is called, and the component it returns is displayed to the user. If the user clicks No, the NextPage method of the `cancelDelegate` is called, and the component returned is displayed to the user. `NextPageDelegates` are covered in greater detail later in Chapter 12.

ErrorPageInterface

```
void setMessage(String message);
void setNextPage(WOComponent component);
```

Call `setMesssage` and `setNextPage` to configure an Error page. When the user clicks the "Return" button on the Error page, the `component` passed to `setNextPage` will be displayed.

To demonstrate using an Error page, the `defaultPage()` action method in `Main.java` will once again be modified.

```
// the errorMessage instance variable is not needed anymore
// public String errorMessage = null; // display any error message

    private static final String LOGIN_ERR_MSG =
        "The username or password is incorrect. Try again...";

    public WOComponent defaultPage() {
...
...
...
    }
    } catch (Exception e) {
        // reset the password field for security purposes
        password = null;
        // create an error page, and give it the errorMessage
        ErrorPageInterface epi = D2W.factory().errorPage(session());
        epi.setMessage(e.getMessage());
        // tell the error page where to return to
        epi.setNextPage(this.context().page());
        result = (WOComponent)epi;
    }
    return result;
}
```

Instead of setting the `errorMessage` to the exception's message, and returning `null`, an Error page is created that displays the exception's message and a "Return" button that takes the user back to originating page.

The Generated Web Components

To reinforce your understanding and to learn how to quickly generate a consistent look for your web site, we'll take a look at what has been generated by the Wizard you used to build your application in the Creating a Direct To Web Application section. To help you completely understand the structure of Web Components and therefore to better design your own, we'll take a look at the graphical side of these components.

Start by opening up the `WOWroxExample` project you created in Project Builder. On a Windows box you'll open the file `PB.project` inside the `WOWroxExample` folder. On Mac OS X open the file `WOWroxExample.pbproj` inside the `WOWroxExample` directory. The Project Builder main window contains a browser that allows you to look through the various parts of the project. On the Mac this is on the left side and on Windows it's across the top. Under **Web Components** you'll see **Main**, **MenuHeader**, and **PageWrapper**. These are arranged and packaged differently on the Mac and in Windows, but in both cases you can take a look inside by double clicking on files with the suffix wo. Let's take a look at these three components starting with **Main**.

The Main Component

Double click on **Main.wo** and the WebObjects Builder application will open. You should see a window like this on your screen.

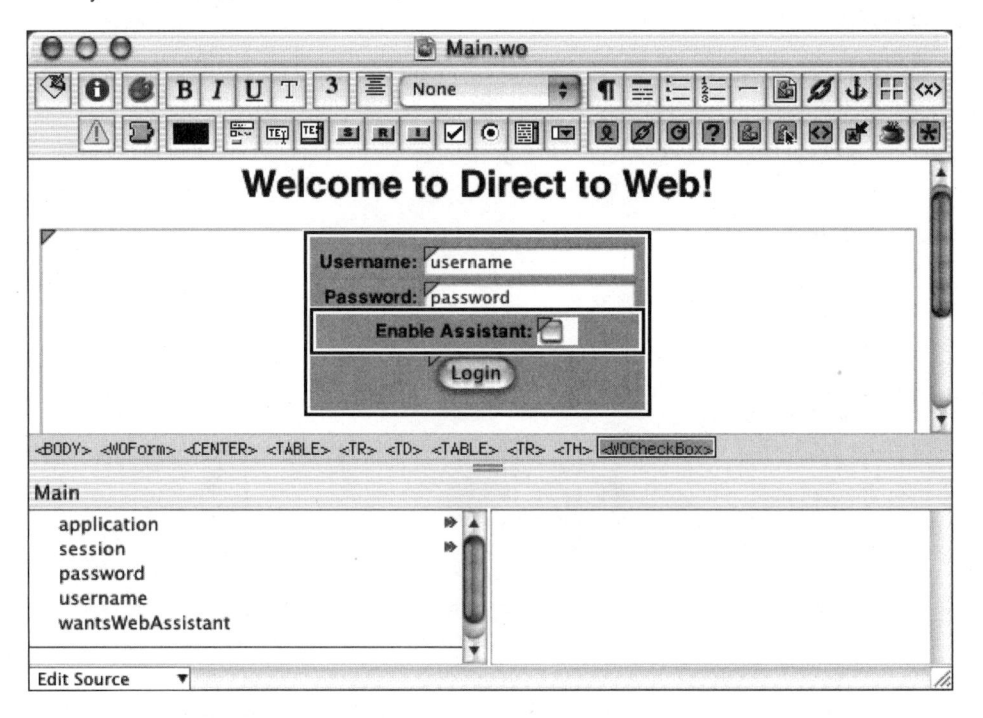

You can see the Basic look login screen made up of various components you should recognize – `WOTextField`, a `WOPasswordField`, a `WOCheckBox`, and a `WOSubmitButton`. In the image, the `WOCheckBox` has been clicked on. You can see in the line below the image that the `WOCheckBox` element is inside of one `TABLE` that is inside of another `TABLE`. The outer table has been `CENTER`ed inside of a `WOForm` contained in the `BODY` of the document. In fact, when we look at the `Main.html` file you'll see that it describes this page with familiar HTML except for the WebObjects specific tags.

To find information about the `WOCheckBox`'s binding, double click on the `WOCheckBox` and a Binding Inspector window opens up that tells you the `checked` attribute is bound to the variable `wantsWebAssistant`. This information is found in the `Main.wod` file.

Direct To Web and Templating

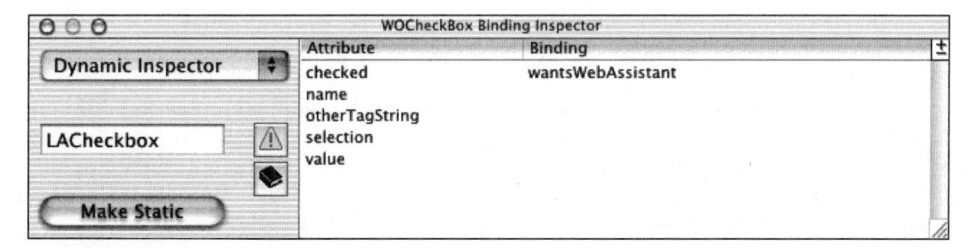

It's interesting to note that there is no particular information that lets you know this page has been constructed using the Basic look. Let's move on and look at the other two Web components in this application.

The MenuHeader Component

The MenuHeader is what gives this site its common look and feel. We said before that in the Basic look, it looks as if we have a collection of navigation buttons on the top bar. If you had run your mouse over the buttons you would have seen that the left two are buttons and the four elements to the right of the divider are just hyperlinked images. Once you view MenuHeader.wo in the WebObjects Builder you can confirm that the header consists of a WOPopUpButton, two WOImageButtons and four WOImages inside of WOHyperlinks. The final component, D2WRemoteControl, is a custom WebObject.

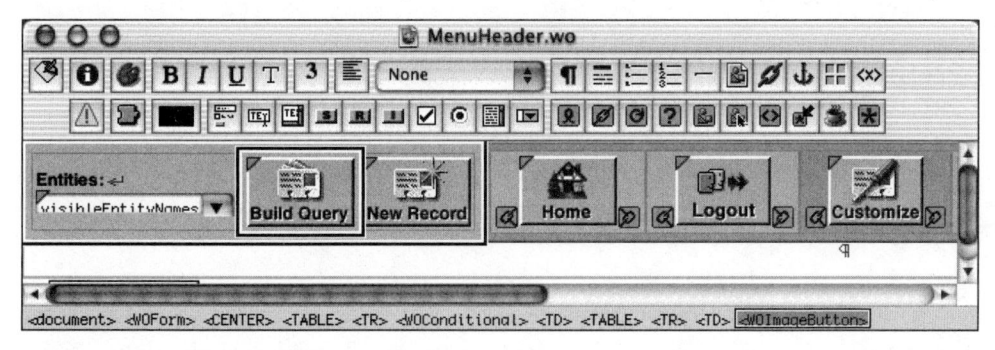

A quick look at the inspector shows that this MenuHeader component is a WOConditional that is tied to the field isWebAssistantEnabled boolean property that was set during the login. It is interesting to look at this same Web Component in the Neutral look. This time the WebObjects builder looks like this.

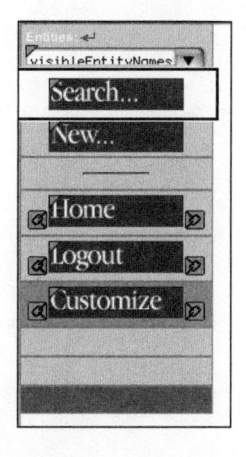

You can see that the components are still the same types and that the only differences are the image files used and the layout of the components on the screen.

Take a minute to inspect the bindings for each component. Each button and hyperlink is bound to a method of the class `MenuHeader`: **BuildQuery** (or **Search**) is bound to the action `findEntityAction`; **NewRecord** (or **New**) is bound to the action `newObjectAction`; the hyperlink containing the **Home** button has the action `homeAction`; the hyperlink containing the **Logout** button has the action `logout`; and the hyperlink containing the **Customize** button has the action `showWebAssistant`.

Notice in the file `MenuHeader.java` that each method that generates a new page uses the `D2W.factory()` method.

```java
import com.webobjects.directtoweb.*;
import com.webobjects.appserver.*;
import com.webobjects.eocontrol.*;
import com.webobjects.eoaccess.*;
import com.webobjects.foundation.*;

public class MenuHeader extends WOComponent {

  public String entityNameInList;

  public MenuHeader(WOContext aContext) {
    super(aContext);
  }

  private String _manipulatedEntityName;
  public String manipulatedEntityName() {
    if (_manipulatedEntityName == null) {
      WOComponent currentPage = context().page();
      _manipulatedEntityName =D2W.factory().entityNameFromPage(currentPage);
    }
    return _manipulatedEntityName;
  }

  public void setManipulatedEntityName(String newValue) {
    _manipulatedEntityName = newValue;
  }

  public NSArray visibleEntityNames() {
    return D2W.factory().visibleEntityNames(session());
  }

  // generates Query Page when user selects "Build Query"
  public WOComponent findEntityAction() {
    QueryPageInterface newQueryPage =
      D2W.factory().queryPageForEntityNamed(_manipulatedEntityName,
         session());
    return (WOComponent) newQueryPage;
  }    // generates record entry page when user selects "New Record"
   public WOComponent newObjectAction() {
    WOComponent nextPage = null;
    try {
      EditPageInterface epi =
        D2W.factory()
          .editPageForNewObjectWithEntityNamed(_manipulatedEntityName,
             session());
      epi.setNextPage(context().page());
      nextPage = (WOComponent) epi;
    } catch (IllegalArgumentException e) {
```

```
      ErrorPageInterface epf = D2W.factory().errorPage(session());
      epf.setMessage(e.toString());
      epf.setNextPage(context().page());
      nextPage = (WOComponent) epf;
    }
    return nextPage;
  }

  // generates logout page when user selects "LogOut"
  public WOComponent logout() {
    WOComponent redirectPage = pageWithName("WORedirect");
    ((WORedirect)redirectPage).setURL(D2W.factory().homeHrefInContext(context()));
    session().terminate();
    return redirectPage;
  }

  // generates home page when user selects "Home"
  public WOComponent homeAction() {
    return D2W.factory().defaultPage(session());
  }

  // brings up WebAssistant applet when user selects "Customize"
  public WOComponent showWebAssistant() {
    return D2W.factory().webAssistantInContext(context());
  }
  public boolean isWebAssistantEnabled() {
    return D2W.factory().isWebAssistantEnabled();
  }
}
```

The static method call `D2W.factory()` returns an instance of class `D2W` that is used to create all of the Direct To Web pages in your application. Once you hold a reference to an instance of `D2W`, you call its methods to perform tasks such as creating pages, obtaining page information, managing the WebAssistant, and managing the Direct To Web factory. For example, the method `findEntityAction()` created and returned a new query page and the method `queryPageForEntityNamed()` was called by the instance of `D2W` returned by the `factory()`. The name of the entity for which the query page is to be built is passed in as the first parameter and a handle to the current Session object is handed in as the other parameter. The way the new page looks is based on the evaluation of the rules that are set up in the file `user.d2wmodel`.

You can override any of the methods in `D2W.java` by extending `D2W`. You'll find the documentation for D2W in `.../Documentation/WebObjects/DirectToWebRef/Java/Classes` (Mac OS X) or `C:\Apple\Library\Frameworks\JavaDirectToWeb.framework\Resources\English.lproj\Documentation\Reference\Java\Classes` (Windows). The class `com.webobjects.directtoweb.D2W` is responsible for creating the Direct To Web pages. The way you change what is produced by the Direct To Web factory is to extend D2W and place your custom code in the subclass.

For example, call your subclass, `MyD2W`, override or add methods, and save it where it will be visible to your application. Now you have to ensure that your application will use `MyD2W` and not `D2W`. To do this you will have to add a line to the constructor in the file `Application.java` where we are instructed to place our initialization code.

Chapter 10

```
public Application(){
  super();
  NSLog.out.appendln("Welcome to " + this.name() + " !");
  /* ** put your initialization code in here ** */
  D2W.setFactory(new MyD2W());
}
```

The PageWrapper Component

When you have designed a menu component that you like, you just need to provide the framework that displays this menu in the proper position for your look. That is the job of the `PageWrapper` component. Every page on your site other than the login page described by `Main.wo` will be displayed with the help of `PageWrapper`. Bring up this component in the WebObjects Builder and you'll see this screen:

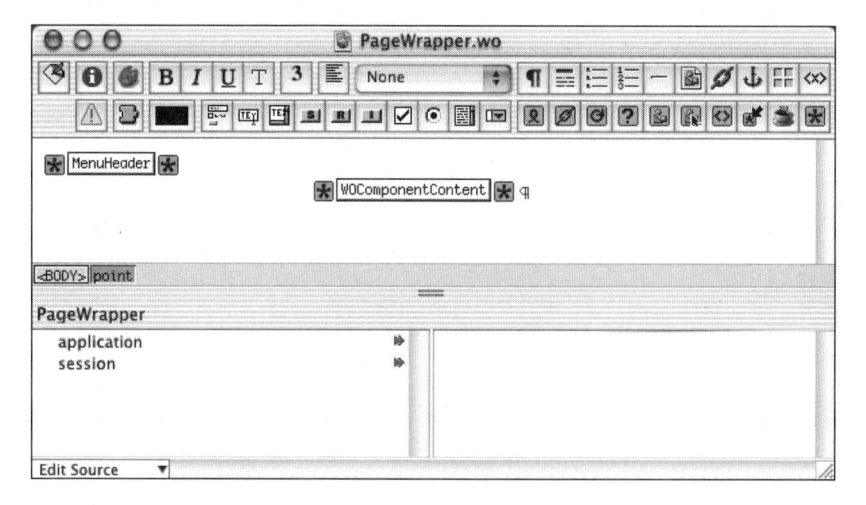

It doesn't look like there's a lot here – and that's the point. The `PageWrapper` just places the `MenuHeader` on top and the relevant page on the bottom. In the other views the placement is different but the behavior is exactly the same. All of the components generated from the database will appear in place of the custom component `WOComponentContent`. You've already seen what a list looks like. If you click the button labeled **New Record**, you'll see a screen with a lower half that looks like this.

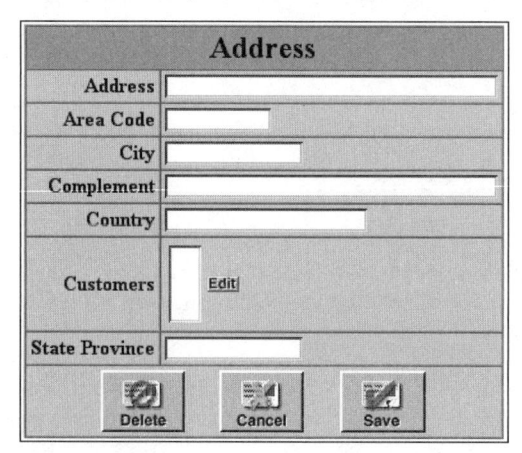

Direct To Web and Templating

This is quite a different look from the previous query page – there are navigation buttons at the bottom of the panel. This is possible because `PageWrapper.wo` is not the top level WebObjects component involved in the layout of the page. In the Basic look, the Direct To Web template `BASInspectPage.wo` contains `PageWrapper.wo`. `BASInspectPage.wo` includes a place to display errors and displays the buttons appropriate to the page being displayed based on the value of `booleans` using `WOConditionals`. This is how the buttons are displayed when you are adding a new record but not when you are viewing a list. There are corresponding versions for the Neutral and WebObjects looks. Here's a portion of `BASInspectPage.wo` from the JavaDirectToWeb framework. This can be found in `System/Library/Frameworks/JavaDirectToWeb.framework/Resources/` (Mac OS X) or `C:\Apple\Library\Frameworks\JavaDirectToWeb.framework\Resources` (Windows).

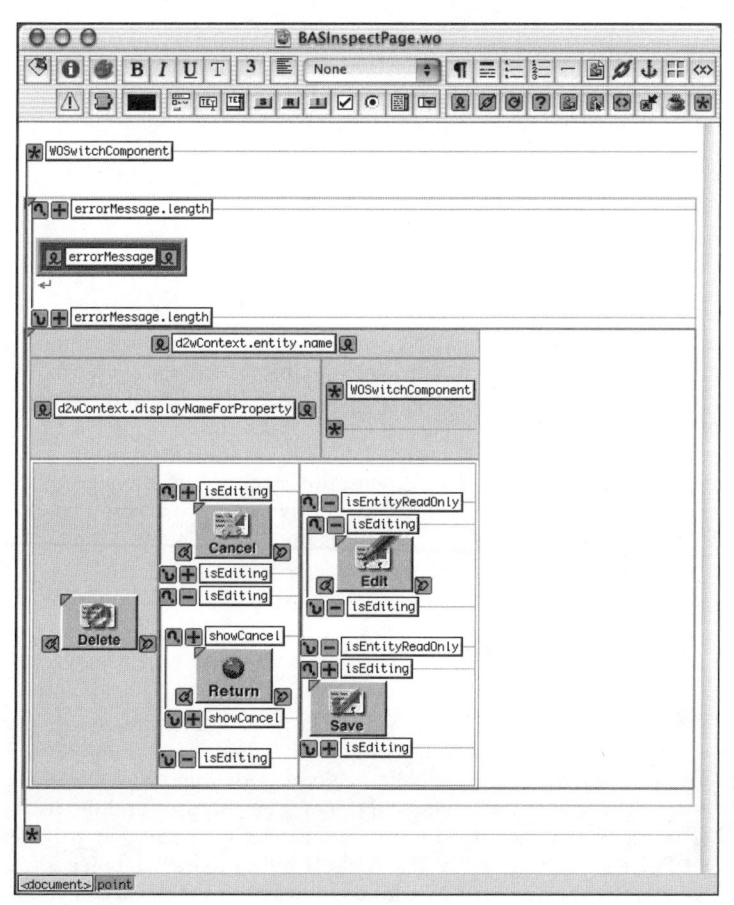

Common Elements in a Web Application

The technique of including the `MenuHeader` on each page creates a nice uniformity for your site. The good news is that this technique is not just limited to Direct To Web applications. Let's pause in our exploration of Direct To Web to see how to apply these same techniques to applications that you write from the ground up. In general, Direct To Web is a quick way to get a working application up and running. For full control, however, you will design your own applications. You can and should employ some of the same design principles incorporated automatically into the Direct To Web process.

273

In this section you'll adapt an example from Chapter 3 to show how you can build common elements into an ordinary web application. In the example, you asked the users to enter their name. After they did, they were taken to a second page that displayed a greeting and listed all of the names under which they had accessed the site in this session. They could then navigate back to the login page and enter a different name. Let's modify the example so that the list of names appears on both pages. Before you create your own version in a non Direct To Web application, take a quick look at what is created for you using Direct To Web. The Direct To Web context returns `PageWrapper` for the `WOComponentName` binding. `WOSwitchComponent` displays the application's `PageWrapper.wo` component. Direct To Web's `PageWrapper` shows you how to include the common element in all pages, but there are some other differences. Open up the file `PageWrapper.html`:

```
<!DOCTYPE HTML PUBLIC "-//W3C//DTD HTML 3.2//EN">
<HTML>
    <WEBOBJECT NAME=Head></WEBOBJECT>
  <BODY>
     <WEBOBJECT NAME=Header></WEBOBJECT>
     <CENTER>
        <WEBOBJECT NAME=Body></WEBOBJECT>
     </CENTER>
  </BODY>
</HTML>
```

This HTML code that is generated by default by the WebObjects Builder includes `<HTML>` and `<BODY>` tags and the `MenuHeader` that was also built with WebObjects Builder. You can't have nested `<HTML>` and `<BODY>` tags. Either the application would have to parse them out of the inner file or the inner file would have to not include them to begin with.

With these common components, WebObjects takes the second, easier approach. The `MenuHeader.html` file doesn't include `<HTML>` or `<BODY>` tags. To accomplish this, you need to indicate to WebObjects Builder that this component is not a complete document. You then need to tie the two elements together.

Creating the PageWrapper

You may have to consult Chapter 3 for instructions on how to perform some of these steps on your platform, but we'll repeat some of them here. Start up ProjectBuilder and choose to create a Web Application called **WOGreeting4**. Add a new Component called `PageWrapper` to the **Web Components** group that has the target **Application Server**. Open up `PageWrapper.wo` in WebObjects Builder. The `PageWrapper` will include the component it is wrapping and the list of all past names the user has entered. This list will be generated from an `NSMutableArray` that grows every time the user enters a new name. The `NSMutableArray` is a variable in the `Session` object. You'll also need an instance variable in `PageWrapper.java` that holds the values of the array as you access them.

The Code in Session.java

From your view of `PageWrapper.wo` in WebObjects Builder add a `Session` variable by selecting **session** and then either right-clicking or Control-clicking in the `Session` pane and selecting **Add Key to Session**. Your key should be named `pastUserNames` and be a Mutable array of type `String`. You should choose to only generate source code for an instance variable.

Now open `Session.java` and add a line to the constructor to initialize the array and the method `addUserName()` so that you can add `userNames` to the `NSMutableArray`.

```java
import com.webobjects.foundation.*;
import com.webobjects.appserver.*;
import com.webobjects.eocontrol.*;

public class Session extends WOSession {
  /** @TypeInfo java.lang.String */
  protected NSMutableArray pastUserNames;

  public Session(){
    super();
    pastUserNames = new NSMutableArray();
  }
  public void addUserName(String newUser){
    pastUserNames.addObject(newUser);
  }
}
```

Finishing the PageWrapper

`PageWrapper.java` needs a `String` to keep the value of the user names being retrieved from the `NSMutableArray pastUserNames`. Add a key to the component `PageWrapper.wo` from WebObjects Builder called `tempUserName`. Next you'll add components to your page so it looks like this.

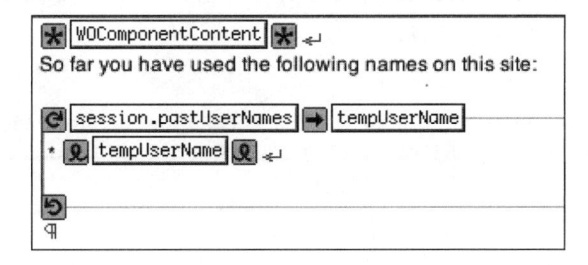

```
[*] WOComponentContent [*] ↵
So far you have used the following names on this site:

[G] session.pastUserNames [→] tempUserName
* [Q] tempUserName [Q] ↵

[⟲]
¶
```

Follow these steps:

❑   Add a custom WebObject by clicking on the asterisk button in the toolbar or by selecting **Custom WebObject** from the **WebObjects** menu. Either type in or scroll down to the WebObject class **WOComponentContent** and click the **OK** button. Hold the *Shift* key while you press the *Return* key.

❑   Type in the text **So far you have used the following names on this site:** and again *Shift-Return*

❑   Add a repetition by clicking on the circular arrow from the toolbar or by selecting **WORepetition** from the **WebObjects** menu. Bind `pastUserNames` to the first box following the circular arrow by clicking on `session.pastUserNames` and dragging into the box. Also bind `tempUserName` to the second box (the one following the horizontal arrow).

❑   Inside the body of the repetition type a * and add a **WOString** using the loop button on the toolbar or using the **WOString** item in the **WebObjects** menu. Bind `tempUserName` to the value of the **WOString**. Press *Return* so that the names will appear on different lines and won't all run together. Save your work.

You don't need to make any changes or additions to the `PageWrapper.java` file.

Redesigning Main

Open `Main.wo` in WebObjects builder. Add a key called `userName` that is a `String`. You won't need accessor methods for it, as its value will be set during the Sync phase of the request-response cycle, when the instance variables are given the value of the WebObjects elements to which they are bound. Add an action called `submitName`; for now you can leave the value of `PageReturned` as `null`. Next you'll add components to your page so it looks like this:

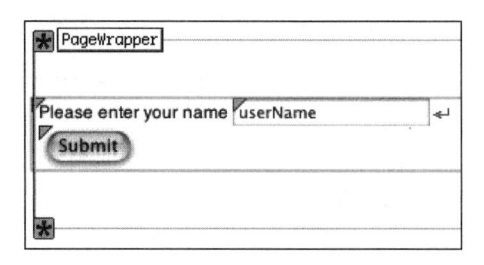

Follow these steps:

- Create a `WOForm` using the toolbar or the item from the **Forms** menu. Inside of it add the text **Please enter your name.**

- Add a textfield using the toolbar or the `WOTextField` item from the **Forms** menu. Bind `userName` to the `value` attribute of the `WOTextField`. *Shift-Return* and then save your work.

- Add a submit button using the toolbar or the `WOSubmitButton` item in the **Forms** menu. Bind `submitName` to the `action` attribute of the `WOSubmitButton`.

If you click on the submit button at this point you'll see, from the section of the window below where you're working, that the current structure is `<BODY>` `<WOForm>` `<WOSubmitButton>`. You can't have the `WOForm` inside of a `<BODY>` element if you want to include it as part of the `PageWrapper` page since the `PageWrapper` page has its own `<BODY>` element. The point is, that if this page is going to be included in other pages, it can't have its own `<BODY>` or `<HTML>` tags. This next step will remove the `<BODY>` and `<HTML>` tags that might be enclosing your visible work.

- Double click on any element on the page to bring up the Inspector window. Click on the `<BODY>` tag or somewhere else in the `Main.wo` window that will turn this into the Page Inspector. In the Page Inspector window you will see a drop down list that currently **says Full document**. Click on it and select **Partial Document** instead. You will get a warning that this action will remove the `<BODY>` tag. In this case, that is exactly what you want to do. Choose **Continue**.

- Your final step is to wrap this Main up so that it sits inside of `PageWrapper`. From the **Edit** menu choose **Select All**. Now click the asterisk button on the toolbar or **choose Custom WebObject** from the **WebObjects** menu. Scroll down in the list to find `PageWrapper` and click the **OK** button.

To get the page to work correctly, you have to edit the `submitName()` method in `Main.java` so that it looks like this:

```
import com.webobjects.foundation.*;
import com.webobjects.appserver.*;
import com.webobjects.eocontrol.*;
import com.webobjects.eoaccess.*;
```

Direct To Web and Templating

```
public class Main extends WOComponent {
  protected String userName;

  public Main(WOContext context) {
    super(context);
  }

  public WOComponent submitName() {
    PersonalizedGreeting greetingPage =
                  (PersonalizedGreeting)pageWithName( "PersonalizedGreeting");
    greetingPage.setUserName(userName);
    ((Session)session()).addUserName(userName);
    return greetingPage;
  }
}
```

This won't compile correctly until you complete the next section because your code says that you are forwarding to the page that has the name `PersonalizedGreeting` and you haven't created it yet.

PersonalizedGreeting

Now that you understand what you're doing, you can take a more direct approach. Create a new component called `PersonalizedGreeting` in the `WebComponents` directory with the `Application Server` as its target. Open `PersonalizedGreeting.wo` in WebObjects Builder. Do the following:

- Add a key named **userName** that has type `String`. This time you want to generate code for both an instance variable and for a set method.

- Add a **Custom WebObject** and select **PageWrapper** from the drop down menu

- Insert the word **Hello** followed by a `WOString` that is bound by value to `userName`

- Add the text **If this is not your name you can enter a new name.**

- Highlight **enter a new name** and add a `WOHyperlink`. Use the Inspector to set the value of page to `Main` using the drop down list. Save your work.

The structure of the element looks like this.

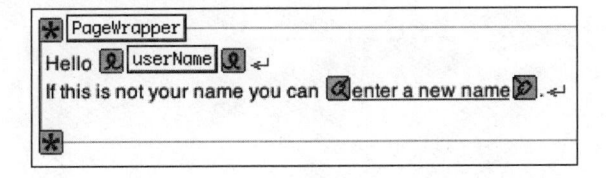

```
┌─ PageWrapper ────────────────────────────────────┐
│ Hello [ ][userName][ ] ↵                         │
│ If this is not your name you can [ ]enter a new name[ ]. ↵ │
│                                                  │
└──────────────────────────────────────────────────┘
```

277

The file `PersonalizedGreeting.java` doesn't need to be changed in any way. Build and run your application and you'll see that the pages all have the running list of names at the bottom. In this screen shot composite, the page built from `Main` is on the left and from `PersonalizedGreeting` is on the right.

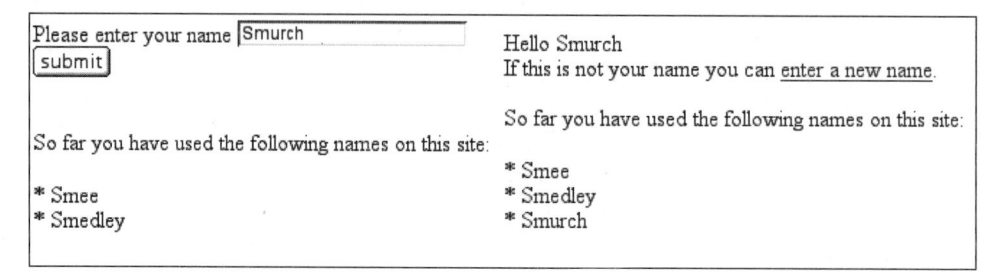

```
Please enter your name [Smurch        ]        Hello Smurch
[submit]                                        If this is not your name you can enter a new name.

                                                So far you have used the following names on this site:
So far you have used the following names on this site:
                                                * Smee
* Smee                                          * Smedley
* Smedley                                       * Smurch
```

Modifying Templates Using WebAssistant

In the section *Changing the Look*, you changed the look of your generated web pages by changing the value of `look` in the `user.d2wmodel` file. You can also use the WebAssistant to change the look of the generated web pages by creating new templates and modifying the existing ones. To start up WebAssistant, run the `WOWroxExample`. When you get to the login page make sure you check the box labeled **Enable Assistant**. On the next screen, click on the **Customize** button.

> Consider whether you want to allow your users to be able to continue to customize the look of the website after you've deployed your application. If not, then add the Launch Argument `-D2WLiveAssistantEnabled NO` before you deploy.

When the WebAssistant opens, select the **Expert Mode**. Note that your experience with the WebAssistant may be different on different platforms and using different browsers. If you find the WebAssistant is not responsive, you may want to try a different browser. Once you select the Expert Mode, your choices are **Properties, Page, Generation,** and **Entities**. Here's a look at **Page**:

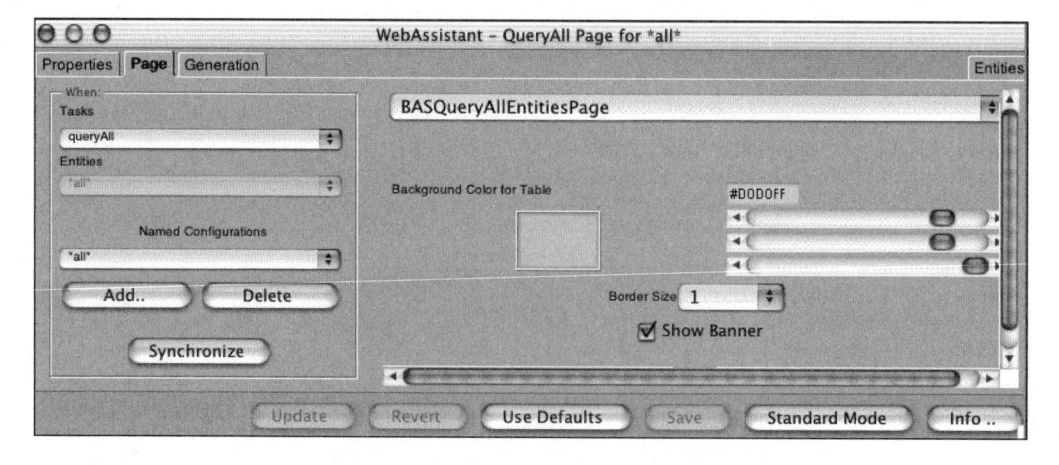

You can tell that this shot is from the Expert Mode because you are able to change pages other than the one you are currently viewing. Play around with it a bit and change the background color for the table and choose the query task instead of queryAll. To see your changes reflected in the running application click on the Update button. If, for example, you choose to turn the background color to blue, move the top two sliders all the way to the left, your table should change from a light purple to deep blue. If you want to check that this change is local to your application, generate another Direct to Web application from the same database. Once you get past the login page you'll see the familiar light purple color for the background of the table.

Once you're satisfied and want to save your changes press the Save button. These changes to the template are only reflected in the current application. Even though you may have changed the background color for the queryAll task, this won't be reflected in other applications. The reason is that you aren't really making changes to the underlying template, you are adding rules to your `user.d2wmodel` file.

> It is considered bad programming style to change the standard Direct to Web basic components. Although you can do it, these changes have global effects. You are changing the style for every other application that depends on the same component. If you need to modify a basic component, copy it into a private framework and modify it there.

Open up `user.d2wmodel`. At the end you can see the rule you saw a few sections ago in *Changing the look*. The last rule is the one that assigned BasicLook as the look. We didn't pay a lot of attention to the other components of the rule. The rule assigning the look only has a right hand side denoted rhs. The author value of 100 tells us which rules this one has priority over. Now look at the newly added rule.

```
{
  "rules" = (
    {
      "class" = "com.webobjects.directtoweb.Rule";
      "author" = "100";
      "rhs" = {
        "class" = "com.webobjects.directtoweb.Assignment";
        "value" = "#0000f5";
        "keyPath" = "backgroundColorForTable";
      };
      "lhs" = {
        "class" = "com.webobjects.eocontrol.EOKeyValueQualifier";
        "value" = "queryAll";
        "selectorName" = "isEqualTo";
        "key" = "task";
      };
    },
    {
      "class" = "com.webobjects.directtoweb.Rule";
      "author" = "100";
      "rhs" = {
        "class" = "com.webobjects.directtoweb.Assignment";
        "value" = "BasicLook";
        "keyPath" = "look";
      };
    }
  );
}
```

The new rule has a left hand side and a right hand side. This rule is only fired when the left hand side is true. In this case, if the task has the value `queryAll` then the rule will be fired. That is exactly how you set up the rule using the WebAssistant. The result of the rule is that the `backgroundColorForTable` will be assigned the value of `0000f5`. This is the deep blue you saw on the screen. There is no reason for you to directly set the value of `backgroundColorForTable`. This example just showed you the result of making a simple adjustment in WebAssistant. Modifying a template using WebAssistant results in adding rules to `user.d2wmodel`. As you know from the section *Changing the Look*, the rules are consulted as part of the process of generating any new page. This means that changes to `user.d2wmodel` will be apparent very quickly.

If you want to add or edit rules by hand you can either work with the source code or you can also bring up the `RuleEditor` by double clicking on `user.d2wmodel`. In particular, you can undo changes by removing the rule from `user.d2wmodel`. You will find out a lot more about D2W rules Chapter 12.

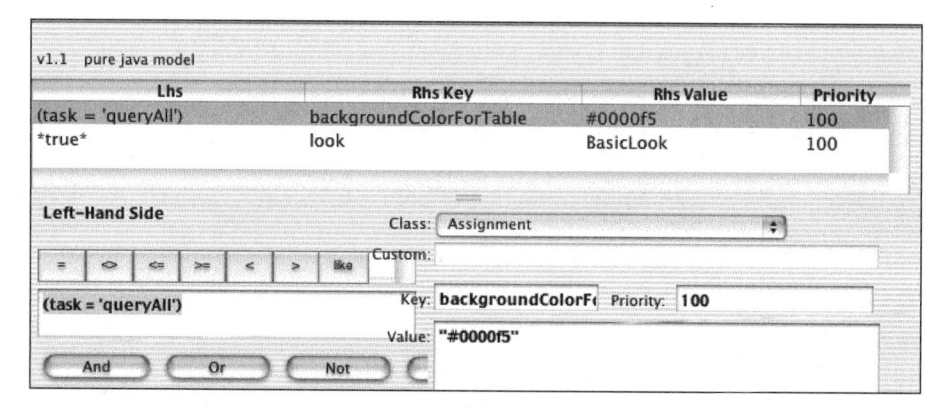

Lhs	Rhs Key	Rhs Value	Priority
(task = 'queryAll')	backgroundColorForTable	#0000f5	100
true	look	BasicLook	100

Left-Hand Side — Class: Assignment

(task = 'queryAll') Key: backgroundColorFc Priority: 100
Value: "#0000f5"

Creating and Using a Custom Template

You can go further than just modifying the basic look of a page; you can create your own template. Remember that each pre-built template corresponds to a given task. This means that you create a custom template by specifying which task you are addressing. In this example you'll create a custom template for the task `queryAll`.

Open up WebAssistant, select **Expert Mode** and click on the **Generation** tab. Click on the button labeled **Generate Template** and a pop-up window will appear prompting you to **Pick a name for your template**. Call it NewQueryAll and click the Ok button. Before closing the WebAssistant make sure that the **QueryAll** tasks will be using your **NewQueryAll** template. If not, use the drop down list with the **BASQueryAllEntitiesPage** showing to select **NewQueryAll**.

Go back to the ProjectBuilder window and you will see that **NewQueryAll** has been added to your **Web Components** folder. Stop the project from running. Open up `NewQueryAll.wo` in WebObjects Builder. You can now customize this template by adding elements, hyperlinks, and action buttons. To demonstrate the changes, just change the text **Find...** to something like **What would you like to find...**. Save your changes, build and run the project. After you login you'll see your changes reflected.

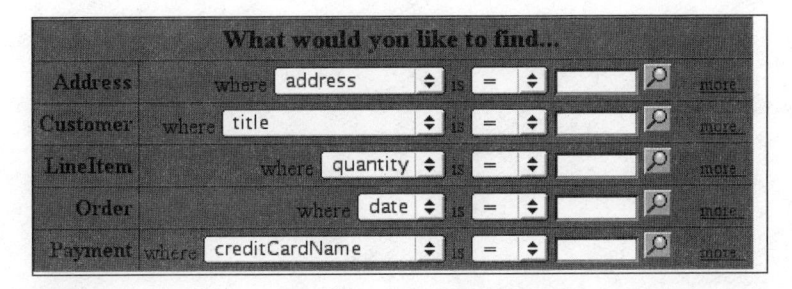

So, where are the changes? Under **Resources** you'll see a property list called d2wclientConfiguration.plist. Open it up and you will see that NewQueryAll has been added as one of your components. Also if you open up user.d2wmodel you'll see two new rules. One specifies that when the task is queryAll and the look is BasicLook that the pageAvailable should be assigned the value NewQueryAll. The second rule specifies that when the task is queryAll that the pageName should be assigned to NewQueryAll. This time your changes were saved in the new template and the rules act as a mapping to the template when the conditions are met.

Summary

You've seen how to quickly create a web site from a database using Direct To Web. Templates allow you to customize this look by changing small items such as the background color and which elements are displayed in which order. You can also take an existing template and modify it using WebObjects Builder and then have it used by the pages generated by Direct To Web.

Even if you are building an application from the ground up, you can benefit from looking at the architecture of web sites built with Direct To Web. Including common elements by using a page wrapper is a great way to add uniformity to your site. You saw how to modify a previous project with changes in WebObjects Builder and modest refactoring to the associated Java code.

This chapter has also shown how you can make adjustments to the look of your site by adding rules to the user.d2wmodel file – this will be expanded in greater detail in Chapter 11.

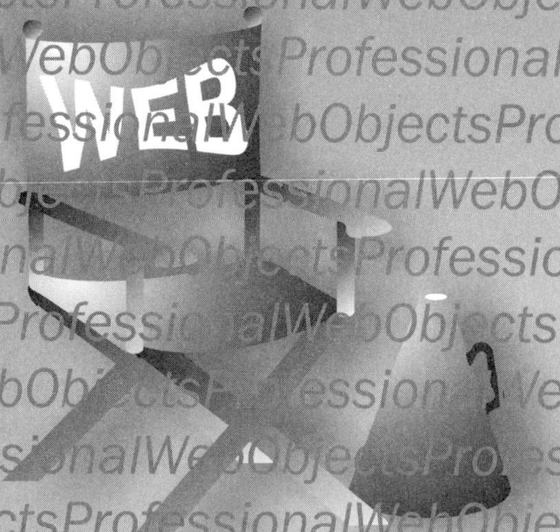
WEB

11

Direct To Web and Rules

As we mentioned in the previous chapter, Direct To Web uses templates and rules. Templates are WebObjects Components that implement Direct To Web's different page types and rules dictate what templates to use, and what they should display.

The Rule System is the brains behind the D2WContext. The D2W Factory that we looked at in Chapter 10 doesn't give the D2WContext nearly enough information to serve the templates' needs. The Rule System fills in the gaps.

The Rule System needs knowledge to fill in those gaps correctly. The Rule System is pre-configured with knowledge about web applications in general, but needs your rules to make your application behave exactly as you want.

D2WContext: Bridging Two Worlds

It is worth stressing that the Direct To Web Context ties templates and rules together – allowing Direct To Web templates to be completely reusable, to work with every WebObjects application and any EOModel. D2WContext is like a Keymaster, and a Gatekeeper:

- ❑ To **templates**, it is the Keymaster – it holds all of the keys that WOComponents and dynamic elements need to display the right information
- ❑ To **rules**, it is the Gatekeeper – the gateway to all of the things specific to your application they need to know when to be applied

Let's look at how D2WContext is used before going into the details. Open the Inspect page template for the Basic look in WebObjects Builder. The name of this component is BASInspectPage.wo, and can be found in the Resources folder of the JavaDirectToWeb.framework. The full path is:

```
/System/Library/Frameworks/JavaDirectToWeb.framework/Resources/BASInspectPage.
wo (Mac OS X)
C:\Apple\Library\Frameworks\JavaDirectToWeb.framework\Resources\BASInspectPage
.wo (Windows)
```

This template is used when inspecting (viewing) or editing an enterprise object. It works by repeating over the attributes and relationships configured for display for that entity or `pageConfiguration` using a `WORepetition`, an element you should be familiar with.

Look at the `WORepetition`'s bindings in the `.wod` file. Here they are:

```
AttributeRepetition: WORepetition {
    _unroll = true;
    item = d2wContext.propertyKey;
    list = d2wContext.displayPropertyKeys;
}
```

(The `_unroll` binding is used by the JavaDTWGeneration framework when freezing Direct To Web pages, and is not important right now.)

The `D2WContext` is used by dynamic elements in D2W templates. When the D2W Factory creates a page, it also creates a `D2WContext`, provides it with the **task** and **entity**, or `pageConfiguration` for the page. After configuring the new `D2WContext`, the page receives it from the D2W Factory by the setter method defined in `D2WComponent` called `setLocalContext(D2WContext d2wContext)`.

The `WORepetition` in the template binds its `list` key to `d2wContext.displayPropertyKeys`. Like all things correctly bound to the `list` key, `d2wContext.displayPropertyKeys` returns an `NSArray`.

Here's a theoretical `displayPropertyKeys` array for the Item entity:

```
("title", "theDescription", "retailPrice", "quantityInStock")
```

> Each time the **WORepetition** begins an iteration, the **propertyKey** of the **d2wContext** is set to the next value in the list, as you'd expect to happen with a **WORepetition**.

The only thing curious about this is...where does `d2wContext` actually get the `NSArray` for `displayPropertyKeys`? The answer is: The Rules System.

Now that you know the `WORepetition` is going to repeat over an array of Strings, let's look inside that `WORepetition`.

The table row inside the `WORepetition` contains two cells: one for the current `propertyKey`'s label, displayed by a `WOString`, and one with a `WOSwitchComponent`. The `WOSwitchComponent` replaces itself with the correct **property-level component** (covered later in the chapter), which in turn displays the value for the key the `propertyKey` refers to.

Direct To Web and Rules

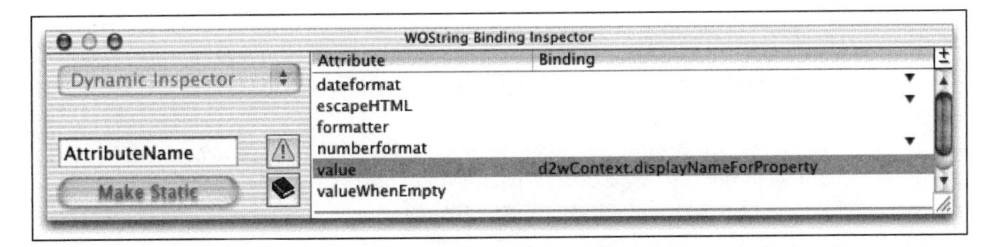

	WOString Binding Inspector	
	Attribute	Binding
Dynamic Inspector	dateformat	
	escapeHTML	
	formatter	
AttributeName	numberformat	
	value	d2wContext.displayNameForProperty
Make Static	valueWhenEmpty	

The `WOString` is bound to `d2wContext.displayNameForProperty`. `D2WContext` will return a beautified version of the `propertyKey` for `displayNameForProperty`. For example, when the repetition's item is `"quantityInStock"`, the `displayNameForProperty` is `"Quantity In Stock"`.

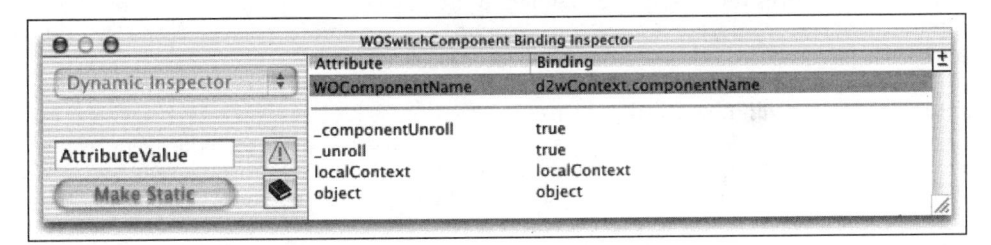

	WOSwitchComponent Binding Inspector	
	Attribute	Binding
Dynamic Inspector	WOComponentName	d2wContext.componentName
	_componentUnroll	true
	_unroll	true
AttributeValue	localContext	localContext
Make Static	object	object

The `WOSwitchComponent` is the placeholder for the actual property-level component that is best suited to display the value of the current `propertyKey`. Its `WOComponentName` key is bound to `d2wContext`'s `componentName` key, which returns the name of the best suited property-level component.

For example, when `d2wContext.propertyKey` is `"quantityInStock"`, `d2wContext.componentName` will return `"D2WDisplayNumber"`, so that is the property-level component that will display the value of the `Item`'s `quantityInStock` attribute. For Edit pages, `d2wContext.componentName` returns `"D2WEditNumber"` instead.

> You can find Direct To Web's property-level components in the same folder you found Direct To Web's template components:
>
> `/System/Library/Frameworks/JavaDirectToWeb.framework/Resources/`

The other bindings for the `WOSwitchComponent` are forwarded to the property-level component.

The Direct To Web Context provides the information to the templates that makes them work. There are many more keys available to templates from the D2WContext.

Basic and Derived D2WContext Keys

The D2W Factory provides the `D2WContext` with the `task` and `entity` keys, or the `pageConfiguration` key. Using that information, and with help from the template setting `D2WContext`'s `propertyKey` as it iterates over the list of `displayPropertyKeys`, the `D2WContext` is able to derive these keys:

- **propertyKeyIsKeyPath**: if `propertyKey` is of the form `key.subKey`, `propertyKeyIsKeyPath` is `true`. Otherwise it is `false`.

- **propertyType**: if `propertyKey` is a key path, `propertyType` returns "k". If it refers to an attribute in the entity, `propertyType` returns "a". If it refers to a relationship in the entity, `propertyType` returns "r". Otherwise, the `propertyKey` is considered a "custom property" and `propertyType` returns "c".
- **attribute**: if `propertyKey` resolves to an attribute, attribute returns the `EOAttribute` object (defined in the `JavaEOAccess` framework) corresponding to the current `propertyKey`. Otherwise attribute returns `null`.
- **relationship**: if `propertyKey` resolves to a relationship, `relationship` returns the `EORelationship` object (defined in the `JavaEOAccess` framework) corresponding to the current `propertyKey`. Otherwise relationship returns `null`.

The `entity` key returns the `EOEntity` (defined in the `JavaEOAccess` framework) for the current page. If the page is created from a `pageConfiguration` instead of a `task` and `entity`, the value of the `entity` key is resolved using the Rule System.

If the page is created with `D2W.factory().pageForConfigurationNamed(String configurationName, WOSession session)`, the `pageConfiguration` key returns the value of `configurationName` the page was created with. Otherwise, the `pageConfiguration` key returns `null`. Page Configurations are covered in more detail later in this chapter.

The `D2WContext` also makes the current `Session` object available under the `session` key. Everything in your `Session` class, and anything accessible from it, is available to templates and rules.

You might be thinking, "those few keys aren't much information to go by to generate a page, and, what about the other keys I found in the `BASInspectPage.wod` file, like `d2wContext.backgroundColorForTable`, and `d2wContext.border`... how does `D2WContext` get the values of those keys?"

The Direct To Web Rule System determines the value of any key not listed above. The `displayPropertyKeys` key, as mentioned previously, also comes from the Rule System. It is important to understand there is no finite list of keys available from the `D2WContext`. Any key, even ones you invent yourself, can yield a value from the `D2WContext`, if a rule exists for it in the Rule System. The Direct To Web Context gets most of its information from the Rule System. As stated above, the `D2WContext` is not only the Keymaster for the templates, but it is also the Gatekeeper for the Rules.

To complete your understanding of the `D2WContext`, you will benefit greatly from knowing how all this information comes to exist. Therefore, the time has come to discover the wonder that is the Direct To Web Rule System!

The Rule System's brain works a lot like the human brain. This is best explained with an example.

The Rule System

When you teach a new employee at an ice cream parlor how to scoop ice cream, you do not have to teach the same technique for each flavor in the store – they recognize that all flavors are scooped the same way. The new employee will scoop all flavors the way you taught them how to scoop the first flavor.

Imagine your store receives a new flavor (Fooberry) that must be scooped with a plastic scoop instead of the regular metal scoop. Failure to use a plastic scoop will sour the ice cream and make your customers sick!

Direct To Web and Rules

How do you avoid sick customers? You give your employees a new rule: "When you are scooping Fooberry ice cream, *use the plastic scoop*". Since your employees are smart, they know that all the other flavors can still be scooped with the regular metal scoops. Once they've learned the "Fooberry scoop rule", you will be able to ask them to scoop any flavor of ice cream in your store, and they will use the right scoop every time.

These rules "configure" your employees to do their job as you want them to. An employee that knows the "Fooberry scoop rule" is more specialized than one that doesn't.

Direct To Web's Rule System works the same way as the employees in the ice cream parlor. It will work the way it has been taught to work. When you give it new rules, it learns them and becomes more specialized at its job.

When Does the Rule System Come Into Play?

If you like the way Direct To Web works... great, you won't need to give it any specialized rules! Direct To Web's Rule System brain has already been taught a base level of knowledge that will make it an effective brain for the D2WContext for all applications.

Chances are, though, that you want your Direct To Web applications to work differently than they did when you first created them. To do this you add rules to a "rule file". Rule file filenames end with .d2wmodel and are edited with the RuleEditor application. Each Direct To Web application has a rule file called user.d2wmodel, and each framework can have a rule file called d2w.d2wmodel. When a Direct To Web application starts, it teaches itself the rules in user.d2wmodel and all d2w.d2wmodel files from the frameworks it uses.

Since every Direct To Web application uses the `JavaDirectToWeb` framework, they always find the d2w.d2wmodel file in the `JavaDirectToWeb` framework – this is the rule file that gives Direct To Web's Rule System brain the base knowledge it needs to be a good brain for the `D2WContext`.

A Real Direct To Web Example

Your Item entity, which represents a product your company sells, has an attribute called quantityInStock. Direct To Web will put "Quantity In Stock" in the web pages that use the Item entity, but you need to make sure it puts "Qty. in Stock" in the pages instead, everywhere in your application.

This is very easy to do, first, let's write this rule in plain English. If asked for the user-friendly name for quantityInStock, you should answer "Qty. in Stock".

If you mix in Direct To Web terminology with the English, the rule reads like this:

If asked for the `displayNameForProperty` when the value of `propertyKey` is "quantityInStock", you should answer "Qty. in Stock".

This is how you describe the rule in pure Direct To Web pseudocode:

```
(propertyKey = 'quantityInStock') => displayNameForProperty =
                                              "Qty. in Stock"
```

Yes, it worked! You decide to put this rule in the d2w.d2wmodel file in your "BusinessLogic" framework, so all of your WebObjects applications will learn this rule. Then, out of nowhere, the Marketing VP comes to your door and says:

"I noticed the site says 'Qty. in Stock' now. Great job! But it's still too wide on the pages that list our products. Make it say '# left' in all the product listing pages."

Oh no! You have 50 different pages on your site that list products! As soon as you remember your WebObjects application has a brain, you feel much better.

Here is the rule in English:

"If asked for the `displayNameForProperty` for list pages when the value of `propertyKey` is "quantityInStock", you should answer "# left"."

And now in Direct To Web pseudocode:

```
((propertyKey = 'quantityInStock') and (task = 'list')) =>
                               displayNameForProperty = "# left"
```

With that one piece of information added to the Rule System's consciousness, all 50 Direct To Web pages that list your products will put '`# left`' in the `quantityInStock` column header! And better still, when you or someone else adds the 51st product listing page Direct To Web will already know you want it to put '`# left`' in that column, and you won't have to tell it again!

Of course, if this 51st page is yet another special case from Marketing, you can write another rule to teach the Rule System brain how to handle whatever minor detail needs tweaking, but you'll save time because all of the previous rules you have written will take part in shaping the page to look exactly how you want.

Rules: Cause and Effect

In the previous section, you saw how rules have cause and effect on your Direct To Web application. The Rule System is asked for the value of a key by the D2WContext. The syntax of a rule looks something like this:

```
Left Hand Side => Right Hand Side
```

The left-hand side (the cause, also known as the LHS) is made up of one or more expressions called the condition. The right-hand side (the effect, also known as the RHS) is an assignment that holds a key and value. Assignments are instances of the `Assignment` class (or a subclass, which is covered in the next section).

```
condition => key = value
```

Rules also have a **priority** level. The higher the priority level, the more "important" it is. Priority levels are not usually included when expressing a rule in writing, but they are a part of the rule.

```
expressions => key = value [priority #]
```

When the Rule System is asked about a key, it finds all of the rules with that RHS key whose condition evaluates to `true` at that time. Those rules are called the **candidates**. The candidate with the highest priority level is the rule chosen. The Rule System answers the question about the key by "firing" the assignment of the chosen rule. Firing an `Assignment` object returns the RHS value of the rule.

If multiple candidates have the highest priority level, rules with lower priority levels are removed from the candidate list, and the Rule System chooses the candidate with the most expressions in its condition. If this does not result in a single candidate, the Rule System chooses one of the remaining candidates arbitrarily. You should give your rules varying priority levels so this situation does not occur!

If there are *no* candidates, the Rule System will throw an exception. Thankfully, the `JavaDirectToWeb` framework's `d2w.d2wmodel` rule file has rules for all of the common keys (with very low priority levels), so an exception will only be thrown when you mistype something, such as the right-hand side key in a rule, or a key in the bindings of a template component.

Assignments: The Effect

Let's open the `JavaDirectToWeb` framework's `d2w.d2wmodel` rule file, and look at the rules that define the basic behavior of Direct To Web applications. Open that `d2w.d2wmodel` file by double-clicking its icon from the Finder, or dragging its icon from Project Builder onto the RuleEditor application icon. (Unfortunately, double-clicking on the file in Project Builder will open the rule file in a Project Builder text editor window.)

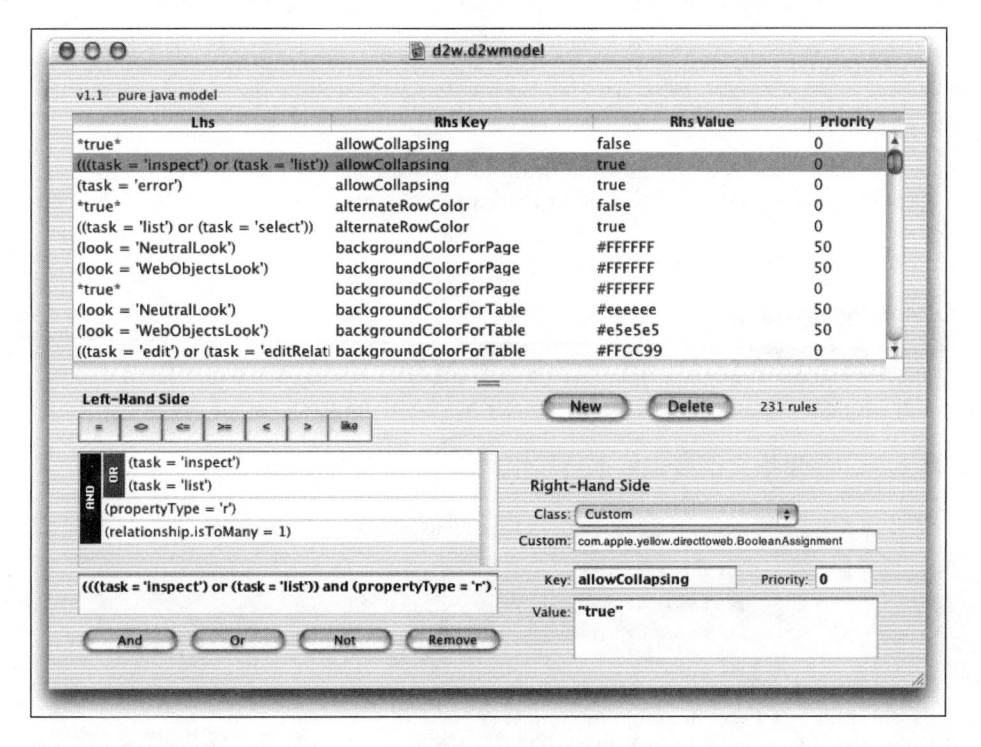

The full path to the file is:

`/System/Library/Frameworks/JavaDirectToWeb.framework/Resources/d2w.d2wmodel`

Select the first rule in the list. You should be looking at this rule:

```
*true* => allowCollapsing = false, priority 0 (BooleanAssignment)
```

The bottom half of the RuleEditor shows the left and right-hand sides of the rule, and lets you edit them.

Notice that RuleEditor also has a popup menu labeled **Class:**, and a text field beneath the popup menu labeled **Custom:**. The **Class:** popup is set to **Custom**, and the **Custom:** field is set to com.apple.yellow.directtoweb.BooleanAssignment.

> *This is actually a bug in RuleEditor. The* `com.apple.yellow` *package was used in WebObjects 4.5 and earlier. Starting with WebObjects 5, the package is* `com.webobjects`*. If you open the rule file in a text editor you'll see the* `Assignment` *class is specified correctly as* `com.webobjects.directtoweb.BooleanAssignment`*, but RuleEditor is doing some funky translation of the class packages. See the section "Custom Assignment Class Packages" later in the chapter for more details.*

When the rule candidate is chosen to fire, its `Assignment` object (which might be a subclass of `Assignment`, like `BooleanAssignment` as shown above) returns the value of the rule. The `Assignment` class's fire method will return the object in the RHS value of the rule. In the case of this `allowCollapsing` rule, the RHS value is `false` – so why is there a Custom `Assignment` class involved?

The `Assignment` class can only return a `String`, `Number`, `NSArray`, or `NSDictionary`. The `allowCollapsing` key wants to return a `Boolean` object, not a `String`, so it uses a specialized `Assignment` class called `BooleanAssignment` that can return Boolean objects.

There are two main reasons why you would want to use a subclass of `Assignment`. The first is the reason just explained, to return a value other than that which the `Assignment` class can return. The second reason is to be able to execute some special logic to return a value, which might or might not be based on the RHS value.

The DefaultAssignment class

With `JavaDirectToWeb.framework`'s d2w.d2wmodel rule file still open in RuleEditor, choose **Filter Rules...** from the **File** menu. If you've already filtered the rules, click the **Reset** button, and then choose **Filter Rules...** again. Pick displayPropertyKeys from the RHS key popup menu. Click **Filter**.

Only two rules should be displayed at this point:

```
*true* => displayPropertyKeys = "defaultPropertyKeysFromEntity" [priority 0]
                                                     (DefaultAssignment)

((task = 'list') or (task = 'select')) => displayPropertyKeys =
           "defaultPropertyKeysFromEntityWithoutRelationships" [priority 0]
                                                     (DefaultAssignment)
```

Notice that both have a Custom assignment class specified: com.apple.yellow.directtoweb.DefaultAssignment. *(which should read* com.webobjects.directtoweb.DefaultAssignment, *but RuleEditor has a bug, see above)*

As the name implies, the `DefaultAssignment` class provides default values for RHS keys. When a `DefaultAssignment` rule fires, it in turn calls the method on the `DefaultAssignment` class named in the RHS value of the rule, such as `defaultPropertyKeysFromEntity` in the first example above. The `fire` method gets the `D2WContext` as a parameter, so it has access to all the keys in the `D2WContext`, such as `task`, `entity`, `propertyKey`, and so on. It uses this information to derive the result for the RHS key.

Direct To Web and Rules

If you look at the `DefaultAssignment` class in the `JavaBrowser` application, you'll see it has these instance methods (and more):

```
// the "fire" method itself. Called on the winning candidate
Object fire(D2WContext d2wContext)

// some of the methods you can specify in the RHS value
// these are called by the fire method
NSArray defaultPropertyKeysFromEntity()
NSArray defaultPropertyKeysFromEntityWithoutRelationships()
String defaultDisplayNameForProperty()
```

The two rules above give the `D2WContext` the array of `propertyKeys` to iterate over in templates. If you don't provide a specific rule for the `displayPropertyKeys` RHS key for a particular condition, those `DefaultAssignment` rules will apply. As the condition of the second rule implies, it only takes effect for list and select pages, and the array of properties from the entity it returns does not include keys for the entity's relationships.

There is another interesting `DefaultAssignment` rule in the `d2w.d2wmodel` rule file in the `JavaDirectToWeb` framework:

```
*true* => displayNameForProperty = "defaultDisplayNameForProperty"
                                   [priority 0] (DefaultAssignment)
```

Recall that `displayNameForProperty` is used to display the user-friendly name for each property in a template. In List and Select pages they are the column headers, and in Query, QueryAll, Inspect, Edit, and EditRelationship pages, they are the labels in front of the value of the current property.

The way `defaultDisplayNameForProperty` works is by capitalizing the first letter in the `propertyKey`, and then putting a space in front of each subsequent capital letter. For example, the `displayNameForProperty` for the "quantityInStock" `propertyKey` is "Quantity In Stock". Similarly, "thisIsASuperLongPropertyKey" becomes "This Is A Super Long Property Key".

Now you know how Direct To Web chooses which attributes to show on Direct To Web pages, and how it manages to give each attribute and relationship a more user-friendly name! There's no magic to it, just a brain that has learned some rules – the `DefaultAssignment` class.

Now that we have covered the RHS of rules, let's focus on the LHS: the `condition`.

Conditions: The Cause

If you have experience with SQL, you'll notice how a rule's `condition` resembles the WHERE clause of a SQL statement.

```
((task = 'list') and (propertyKey = 'quantityInStock')) =>
                                    displayNameForProperty = "# left"
```

You could imagine this rule looking something like the following if it was written in SQL:

```
UPDATE D2W_CONTEXT
SET display_name_for_property = '# left'
WHERE (task = 'list') AND (property_key = 'quantityInStock')
```

291

Chapter 11

However, think of the condition as a **WHEN** statement, not a WHERE statement.

Conditions are made up of expressions called **qualifiers**. Qualifiers should be familiar to you from the `EnterpriseObjects` framework – in fact, Direct To Web uses `EOQualifiers` internally to represent and evaluate the qualifiers in the LHS of the rule.

Each expression has a "qualifier operator" – you can use all of the normal qualifier operators from the `EOQualifier` class:

=	Equals
<>	Not equals
<=	Less than or equal to
>=	Greater than or equal to
<	Less than
>	Greater than
like	Like, used with the * wildcard character

When the Rule System is finding rules for a RHS key, it has to evaluate the condition of **all** the rules with that RHS key to find out which ones are candidates. Let's look at a rule with a couple of qualifiers:

```
((task = 'list') and (look = 'WebObjectsLook')) => pageName = "WOLListPage"
```

The pageName key is used by the D2W Factory to choose which template to use for a page being created. This rule's condition translates into an `EOAndQualifier` with two `EOKeyValueQualifiers`:

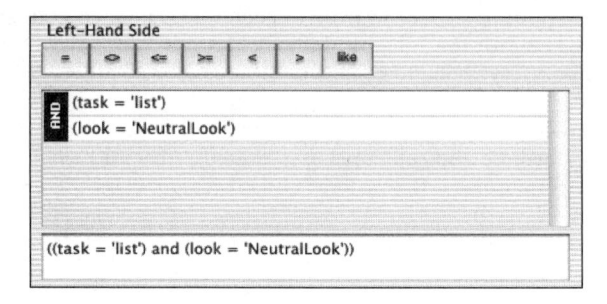

Left-Hand Side

| = | <> | <= | >= | < | > | like |

AND
- (task = 'list')
- (look = 'NeutralLook')

`((task = 'list') and (look = 'NeutralLook'))`

The Rule System evaluates the rule's condition by traversing the qualifiers and testing each expression. If it is evaluating the rule above it means the D2WContext has asked the Rule System to resolve the pageName key.

Let's run through this example to see how it works:

The Rule System asks the D2WContext for the value of task. If the page is created using `D2W.factory().listPageForEntityNamed("Item", session())`, the D2WContext already knows the value of the task key, so it can simply return it. However, if the page was created using `D2W.factory().pageForConfigurationName("MyItemListPage", session())`, the D2WContext doesn't know what the task is, so it has to ask the Rule System to resolve the task key.

Direct To Web and Rules

When you create a page from a `pageConfiguration`, you have to provide rules for the `task`, `entity`, and `displayPropertyKeys` keys. For example:

```
(pageConfiguration = 'MyItemListPage') => task = "list"

(pageConfiguration = 'MyItemListPage') => entity = "Customer"
                                                    (EntityAssignment)

(pageConfiguration = 'MyItemListPage') => displayPropertyKeys = (title,
                                                    retailPrice, quantityInStock)
```

The Rule System will fire the rule with the `task` RHS key to resolve the `task` for the original rule.

The `task` rule returns `"list"`, so the first qualifier, (`task` = `"list"`), an `EOKeyValueQualifier`, evaluates to `true`.

Next, the Rule System asks the `D2WContext` for the value of `look`. The `D2WContext` won't know the value of `look` so it will have to ask the Rule System. When you create a Direct To Web application, the Project Builder Direct To Web wizard will ask you if you want to use Basic Look, Neutral Look, or WebObjects Look. Assume you choose WebObjects Look. In this case, the following rule will appear in the `user.d2wmodel` file in your application's project:

```
*true* => look = "WebObjectsLook"
```

This rule will always be a candidate for the `look`, because its `condition` is `*true*`. Usually, this is the only `look` rule in your application, unless you want different sections of your application to use different looks (which is perfectly acceptable if that's what you want).

The `look` rule returns `"WebObjectsLook"`, so the second qualifier, (`look` = `'WebObjectsLook'`), an `EOKeyValueQualifier`, also evaluates to `true`.

The entire `condition` evaluates to `true`, so this `pageName` rule is a candidate. It's safe to say this rule will be chosen to fire because you wouldn't want to add a rule to change the List page template for the `WebObjectsLook` specifically.

Notice that the Rule System actually asks the `D2WContext` for the value of all of its keys. This is why the `D2WContext` is said to be the *Gatekeeper* for the Rule System. And as you saw from this example, rule firing can be recursive – every qualifier in the LHS could potentially cause another rule to be fired.

Another reason the `D2WContext` is said to be the Rule System's Gatekeeper is because it is the gateway between the Direct To Web world and the `EnterpriseObjects` world. Consider this rule:

```
((entity.name = 'Customer') and (propertyKey = 'loginName')) =>
                                    displayNameForProperty = "User ID"
```

The `entity` key returns an instance of `EOEntity`, defined in the `JavaEOAccess` framework. Using Key-Value Coding, you have access to all of the members of the `EOEntity` class, which you configure using the EOModeler application! In the rule above, the LHS key `entity.name` returns the name of the `EOEntity` for the page being generated. Similarly, you have full access to the information for all of the attributes and relationships in your EOModel using the `attribute` and `relationship` keys in the `D2WContext`. If you read through the `d2w.d2wmodel` rule file you'll see how Direct To Web takes advantage of these objects to pick the right property-level components, formatters, and other options.

One rarely used feature of `EnterpriseObjects` and `EOModeler` is the `userInfo Dictionary` available for each attribute, relationship, entity and fetch specification in your `EOModel`. You can access the `userInfo Dictionary` and access from the Rule System. For example, you might want to show certain date attributes in long format. You can add a key to those date attributes' `userInfo Dictionary` and then act on that information in a new rule for the Rule System.

Add a key called `dateFormat` to the `userInfo dictionary` of the `date` attribute of the `Order` entity in the `EOModel`. Set the value of this key to `Long`.

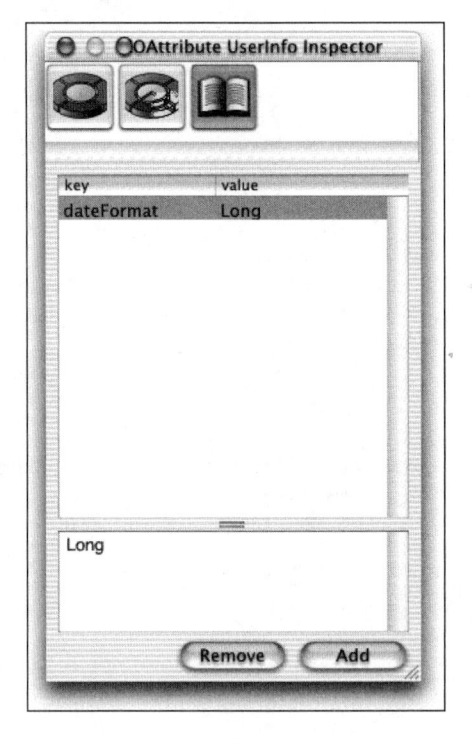

Then add this rule to your `user.d2wmodel` rule file:

```
(((not (attribute = null)) and (attribute.className =
   'com.webobjects.foundation.NSTimestamp') and
   (attribute.userInfo.dateFormat = 'Long')) => formatter = "%A, %d %B, %Y"
```

Now, whenever Direct To Web shows the value of a date attribute, and that date attribute was configured in `EOModeler` to have a `dateFormat` key with the value `Long`, the date will be displayed like "Thursday, August 23, 2001", instead of the default format, "Aug 23, 2001". Adding that `userInfo` key and one rule is much easier than changing all the pages in your application to use a different `dateformat` binding for all the `WOStrings` that bind to date values you want changed to the long format.

There are many other potential uses for the `userInfo` dictionary. It's there for you to add information to, and Direct To Web makes it very easy to take advantage of it.

Another useful thing about the D2WContext is it can access the `Session` object. That means you can use anything in the session in the Rule System. Consider these rules:

```
((pageConfiguration = 'ListItems') and (session.user.isAdmin = 1)) =>
  displayPropertyKeys = (title, theDescription, retailPrice, storePrice,
    quantityInStock)

((pageConfiguration = 'ListItems') and (session.user.isAdmin = 0)) =>
  displayPropertyKeys = (title, theDescription, retailPrice )
```

With this rule, administrators will see the wholesale price and inventory levels of the products offered for sale, but customers only see the retail price.

Unfortunately, as you'll learn in the next section, there is a caveat to accessing the session from the Rule System. Thankfully, there is a simple workaround, but you need to be aware of it.

For a complete list of the keys you can use in the LHS of a rule, refer to the *Basic and Derived D2WContext Keys Section* earlier in this chapter.

Rule Firing Is Cached

The previous section said, "When the Rule System is finding rules for a RHS `key`, it has to evaluate the `condition` of **all** the rules with that RHS `key` to find out which ones are candidates." If you're thinking that could become a very time and CPU intensive operation, you're absolutely right!

To optimize this as much as possible, the Rule System actually caches the result of rules that fire so that it doesn't have to go through the whole process described in the previous section each time the Rule System is invoked. As a result of this cache, resolving RHS keys is actually much faster than you might think!

This caching isn't without its problems, however. Caching is based on a list of **significant keys**. Only the LHS keys marked significant by Direct To Web are considered when looking up a RHS value from the cache. The standard significant keys are:

- task
- entity
- pageConfiguration
- propertyKey

When a rule fires, a cache entry is created which records the values of the significant keys, the RHS key, and the value returned. If the Rule System is asked for the same key later, and the cache contains an entry with the same values for the significant keys, all rules are ignored, and the value from the cache is returned.

As a result, you can get into a situation where the Rule System returns the *wrong RHS value* because one of the rule's LHS keys wasn't "significant" enough and the cached value for a similar, but still different, LHS is returned. For example, consider the rules from the previous section whose LHS accessed `session.user.isAdmin`.

```
((pageConfiguration = 'ListItems') and (session.user.isAdmin = 1)) =>
  displayPropertyKeys = (title, theDescription, retailPrice, storePrice,
    quantityInStock)

((pageConfiguration = 'ListItems') and (session.user.isAdmin = 0)) =>
  displayPropertyKeys = (title, theDescription, retailPrice )
```

If an administrator logs into the application before any customers do and goes to the `ListItems` page, the Rule System creates a rule cache entry for `displayPropertyKeys` and the significant keys. In this case, the only significant key from this rule is `pageConfiguration`. The task is `list` and entity is the `Item` entity, found from the other rules for the `pageConfiguration`:

```
(pageConfiguration = 'ListItems') => task = "list"

(pageConfiguration = 'ListItems') => entity = "Item" (EntityAssignment)
```

(You should enter the fully qualified assignment class name in RuleEditor; in this case, `com.webobjects.directtoweb.EntityAssignment`)

Afterwards, a customer logs in and visits the ListItem page. The D2WContext asks the Rule System for the `displayPropertyKeys`. Before the rules are considered, the cache is checked. It finds a cache entry containing:

```
task = "list"
entity = Item
pageConfiguration = "ListItems"
propertyKey = null
RHS key = displayPropertyKeys
value = (title, theDescription, retailPrice, storePrice, quantityInStock)
```

The current D2WContext has those *exact values* for the significant keys, so the cache entry wins! The second rule whose RHS `value` prevents customers from seeing sensitive business information is not consulted! Thankfully, there is a way to avoid this.

You can add a new significant key to the Rule System that will be recorded with the default significant keys for all cache entries. It's simple to do. Add this statement to your Application class' constructor:

```
D2W.factory().newSignificantKey("session.user.isAdmin");
```

Now the value of `session.user.isAdmin` will be stored in the cache along with the other significant keys, and both the first and second rule will be guaranteed to fire and create *separate* cache entries.

Customizing D2W Factory Using Rules

In Chapter 10 you saw how to customize the behavior of the Direct To Web Factory's `defaultPage` method by registering an instance of a subclass of the `D2W` class as the `D2W.factory()`.

The easiest way is to add rules for `startupTask` and `startupEntityName` to your `user.d2wmodel` rule file. This customization will be covered later in the chapter.

```
*true* => startupTask = "list", priority = 100
*true* => startupEntityName = "Customer", priority = 100
```

Those rules will override the rule in `JavaDirectToWeb.framework`'s `d2w.d2wmodel` rule file that says:

```
*true* => startupTask = "queryAll", priority = 0
```

Any RHS key in `JavaDirectToWeb.framework`'s `d2w.d2wmodel` file can be overriden by creating a rule for that key in another rule file with a **higher priority** and a different RHS value. This isn't usually necessary, but when it is, it's an easy way to subtly or radically alter Direct To Web's behavior.

NetStruxr's ERDirectToWeb Framework

NetStruxr (http://www.netstruxr.com/), which you will find out more about in Chapter 15, use Direct To Web extensively in their mission-critical customer-facing WebObjects applications. They developed numerous extensions for Direct To Web and collected them in a framework called **ERDirectToWeb**. This framework is generously made available, with full source code, under an open source license.

One significant improvement in `ERDirectToWeb` is that the caching scheme has been replaced with a smarter cache that does not require significant keys to be added! Also included are much more advanced templates that you can use to create more robust Direct To Web applications.

As of this writing, `ERDirectToWeb` is only available for WebObjects 4.5, but the WebObjects 5 porting effort is well underway. Hopefully the WebObjects 5-compatible version will be available by the time you read this, or shortly thereafter.

You can try `ERDirectToWeb` by downloading it from the following URL: http://www.netstruxr.com/developer/

RuleEditor Traits

RuleEditor is a simple, elegant application. You can easily enter new rules, find existing rules, and modify them. Like all software, however, it is not without its quirks.

Custom Assignment Packages

As mentioned previously, RuleEditor has some problems with entering custom assignment class names, confusing the old YellowBox-based class packages with the new pure-Java class packages for WebObjects 5. Enter custom assignments using the YellowBox package specifier for Direct To Web's assignment classes.

For example, instead of typing com.webobjects.directtoweb.BooleanAssignment into RuleEditor's Custom field, type com.apple.yellow.directtoweb.BooleanAssignment. RuleEditor does the proper translation when saving and opening the rule file.

This bug has been filed with Apple, so hopefully this bug will be fixed soon.

RuleEditor and CVS

If you are working on a Direct To Web project with a team of developers, you need to be aware of some challenges regarding CVS and merging changes. The rule file format is the old-style PLIST text format. Each rule takes up a number of lines in the file, intended to be human readable. CVS' diff routines do not handle conflicts well with this kind of file. Resolving conflicts in rule files can be a mind-numbing experience!

To combat this, it is necessary for your development team come up with some kind of **exclusive-locking mechanism** so that only one person is editing any particular rule file at a time. CVS does not support file locking so you need to devise your own way to distribute access to rule files.

Until recently, NetStruxr had a hat-tree loaded with labeled baseball caps, one for each framework and application containing a rule file. When someone wanted to edit a rule file, they first had to get possession of the corresponding hat. If someone else had it, they had to wait until the hat-holder was done with the rule file and had committed their changes to CVS. Once a person got possession of a hat, they would do a `cvs update` of the file, and **then** open it in RuleEditor.

> Make sure you `update` the file before you open it in RuleEditor.

RuleEditor does not warn you that the file has changed on disk since it was opened, so if you are not careful, you can easily save your changes over the updated file.

Recently, a Direct To Web-based "online hat system" was added on to NetStruxr's bug-tracking application, so the hat-tree is now retired. Use whatever mechanism, electronic or otherwise that is comfortable with your development team to ensure that multiple people don't try to edit the same rule file concurrently.

One potential solution, which to our knowledge has not been experimented with, is a CVS filter to translate the rule file before committing to the repository, putting each rule on its own line. RuleEditor is happy to open any valid PLIST-formatted file, and line spacing is not significant with the PLIST format. Theoretically, CVS' diff routines would be better able to handle conflicts in rule files if each rule was restricted to a single line in the file.

A Note About Data Entry in Rule Editor

After editing any field in RuleEditor, make sure you press the *Enter* or *Tab* key when you are finished to commit your changes to the field. If you do not press one of those keys, RuleEditor will not save your changes to that rule and your changes will not be saved to disk next time you save your rule file.

Hopefully Apple will update RuleEditor to address these issues and upgrade its functionality, which is adequate, but not stellar.

Page Configurations

We've touched on **pageConfigurations** a few times so far, but now that the Rule System is your friend, it's time to learn about them in more depth.

Page Configurations exist for a few reasons. First, it's familiar and comfortable to refer to a page by name. Secondly, it's actually easier to configure pages using `pageConfigurations` than without them. And thirdly, without them, you'd only have one style of List page for Customers, one for Items and so on. For each `task` and `entity`, you'd be limited to one style of page, unless you wrote a lot of overly complex rules with exotic LHS conditions. Of course, you want to be able to list Items, Customers, Orders in various different ways, and you want to be able to show very different Inspect and Edit pages, for example, to different kinds of users. Using Page Configurations, this is easy.

Recall that a page is created using a `pageConfiguration` with this method on the `D2W` Factory:

```
D2W.factory().pageForConfigurationNamed(String configurationName,
                                        WOSession session)
```

For example:

```
EditPageInterface epi =
  (EditPageInterface)D2W.factory().
    pageForConfigurationNamed("EditCustomer", session());
```

Direct To Web and Rules

You set up the `pageConfiguration` entirely in RuleEditor. As a minimum, you need to provide rules for `task` and `entity` so the D2W Factory can determine what kind of page `"EditCustomer"` is, and create the right template component for the page.

```
(pageConfiguration = 'EditCustomer') => task = "edit"

(pageConfiguration = 'EditCustomer') => entity = "Customer"
                                                 (EntityAssignment)
```

You'll probably also want to add a rule for `displayPropertyKeys`, which lets you choose the attributes and relationships to be shown on the page.

```
(pageConfiguration = 'EditCustomer') => displayPropertyKeys = (firstName,
                                        lastName, title, email, telephone)
```

You can configure the page any way you want to – just refer to the `pageConfiguration` in the LHS condition. You can choose different labels for the attributes:

```
((pageConfiguration = 'EditCustomer') and (propertyKey = 'lastName') =>
                                displaynameForProperty = "Surname"

((pageConfiguration = 'EditCustomer') and (propertyKey = 'email') =>
                        displaynameForProperty = "Internet e-mail Address"

((pageConfiguration = 'EditCustomer') and (propertyKey = 'telephone') =>
                                displaynameForProperty = "Home Ph. #"
```

and different field lengths:

```
(pageConfiguration = 'EditCustomer') => length = "25"

((pageConfiguration = 'EditCustomer') and (propertyKey = 'email')) =>
                                                        length = "35"

((pageConfiguration = 'EditCustomer') and (propertyKey = 'telephone')) =>
                                                        length = "15"

((pageConfiguration = 'EditCustomer') and (propertyKey = 'title')) =>
                                                        length = "35"
```

The length RHS key is bound to the "size" binding of the WOTextField used by the D2WEditString property-level component. The first length rule above sets the "default length" for all the fields to 25 characters wide. The next three rules mandate different lengths for e-mail, telephone, and title.

PageConfigurations and the like Qualifier Operator

Remember that you can use the `like` operator in a LHS qualifier. When you use `like`, you can put the * wildcard character in the value of the qualifier:

```
((pageConfiguration = 'EditCustomer') and (propertyKey like '*Name')) =>
                                                        length = "20"
```

Chapter 11

The rule above makes the EditCustomer page size the `WOTextField` to 20 characters for all `propertyKeys` that end with `Name`. That is somewhat interesting, but there is a really great use for the `like` operator with `pageConfigurations` – in the `pageConfiguration` qualifier itself.

If you rewrote all the rules above to use a wildcard as the `pageConfiguration` qualifier, you could create other `pageConfigurations` that were similar to the original, and not have to write rules for all of the pages if you wanted to change something on all of them. Here's a scenario:

```
(pageConfiguration like 'InspectItem*') => task = "inspect"

(pageConfiguration like 'InspectItem*') => entity = "Item"
                                                        (EntityAssignment)

(pageConfiguration like 'InspectItem*') => displayPropertyKeys =
                                   (title, theDescription, retailPrice)

((pageConfiguration like 'InspectItem*') and (propertyKey =
       'theDescription') => displayNameForProperty = "About this Product:"

((pageConfiguration like 'InspectItem*') and (propertyKey =
          'theDescription') => componentName = "D2WDisplayStyledString"

((pageConfiguration like 'InspectItem*') and (propertyKey =
          'theDescription') => componentName = "D2WDisplayStyledString"

((pageConfiguration like 'InspectItem*') and (propertyKey = 'retailPrice' =>
                 displayNameForProperty = "Our Everyday Low Price:"
```

These rules configure all pages whose `pageConfiguration` begins with "`InspectItem`". If you want to create a special internal-only page for inspecting Items, you can customize the page without having to duplicate all of the existing rules. Here's the sensitive internal-only version:

```
(pageConfiguration = 'InspectItemINTERNAL') => displayPropertyKeys =
         (title, theDescription, storePrice, retailPrice, quantityInStock)

((pageConfiguration = 'InspectItemINTERNAL') and
 (propertyKey = 'retailPrice') => displayNameForProperty = "Customer Price:"

((pageConfiguration = 'InspectItemINTERNAL') and
    (propertyKey = 'retailPrice') => componentName = "D2WDisplayStyledString"

((pageConfiguration = 'InspectItemINTERNAL') and
                            (propertyKey = 'retailPrice') => bold = 1

((pageConfiguration = 'InspectItemINTERNAL') and
                          (propertyKey = 'retailPrice') => color = "red"

((pageConfiguration = 'InspectItemINTERNAL') and (propertyKey =
              'storePrice') => displayNameForProperty = "Wholesale Cost:"
```

The important concept here is that the internal version's rules specify `pageConfiguration = 'InspectItemINTERNAL'` instead of `pageConfiguration like 'InspectItem*'`. All the rules for `'InspectItem*'` apply to the internal version, unless a rule for the same RHS key exists for `InspectItemINTERNAL`.

Give `InspectItemINTERNAL` rules a higher priority value than the `InspectItem*` rules – most of the rules above have the same number of qualifiers, so if the priorities are equal as well, the Rule System won't know which one to pick, and will pick one arbitrarily!

The internal version's page differs from the standard version in a few ways. First and foremost, it displays the `storePrice` and `quantityInStock` fields, which are not shown on the standard (for Customer eyes) version.

The `retailPrice` field will be displayed in a bold, red typeface so it stands out on the screen. You wouldn't want one of your telephone operators accidentally quoting a customer the wholesale Cost! It does this by telling Direct To Web to use the `D2WDisplayStyledString` property-level component to display the `retailPrice` field. The `D2WDisplayStyledString` component can make the value it displays **bold**, *italic*, and have a particular color. The rules above illustrate how to make that happen.

Make Your Life Easier: Use Page Configurations

If you stick to a consistent naming convention, you can greatly reduce the number of rules you have to write to set up new `pageConfigurations`.

Add a rule for each `task` in your rule file with a low priority (75 should do):

```
(pageConfiguration like 'Inspect*') => task = 'inspect'

(pageConfiguration like 'Edit*') => task = 'edit'

(pageConfiguration like 'List*') => task = 'list'

(pageConfiguration like 'Select*') => task = 'select'

(pageConfiguration like 'EditRelationship*') => task = 'editRelationship'

(pageConfiguration like 'Query*') => task = 'query'

(pageConfiguration like 'QueryAll*') => task = 'queryAll'

(pageConfiguration like 'Confirm*') => task = 'confirm'

(pageConfiguration like 'Error*') => task = 'error'
```

Now you don't have to add a `task` rule for each `pageConfiguration`. Just make sure to start Edit page names with `Edit`, List pages with `List`, and so forth.

Similarly, you can add rules that save you from having to write the `entity` rules:

```
(pageConfiguration like '*Customer*') => entity = "Customer"
                                              (EntityAssignment

(pageConfiguration like '*Item*') => entity = "Item" (EntityAssignment

(pageConfiguration like '*Order*') => entity = "Order" (EntityAssignment
```

And so on...

Now the only rule you have to specify is for `displayPropertyKeys`, and that's only if the default value isn't what you want.

Go wild... create pages using `D2W.factory().pageForConfigurationNamed(String configurationName, WOSession session)` with different names – "ListOrders", "QueryItems", "InspectCustomer"... The D2W Factory will create the right page every time, with the help of the D2WContext, the Rule System, and your rules!

Property Level Components

Property-Level components have been mentioned throughout this chapter. By now, you may have figured out that these little components are responsible for actually displaying your data on the web page.

Back in the section *D2WContext: Bridging two worlds*, we opened up the `BASInspectPage.wo` template component and peeked inside. You might want to go back and re-read the part about the `WOSwitchComponent` inside the `WORepetition` before you continue.

Direct To Web chooses the property-level component that matches the task and the type of data the attribute displays. There are three types of property-level components:

- `D2WEdit____`: used when editing attributes and relationships. For example, D2WEditString, `D2WEditLargeString, D2WEditBoolean, D2WEditToManyRelationship`.

- `D2WQuery____`: used when querying attributes and relationships. For example, `D2WQueryStringComponent, D2WQueryNumerRange`.

- `D2WDisplay____`: used when displaying attributes, relationships, and custom `propertyKeys`. For example, `D2WDisplayString, D2WDisplayImage, D2WDisplayHyperlink, D2WDisplayMailTo, D2WDisplayToOne`.

The `d2w.d2wmodel` rule file in the `JavaDirectToWeb` framework's Resource folder contains some fallback rules that tell Direct To Web which property-level components to use. If you open that rule file in RuleEditor, and filter the rules by the `componentName` RHS key, you'll see how Direct To Web chooses which property-level component to use in each situation.

Custom Property-Level Components

One of the best things about Direct To Web is you can easily create custom property-level components (and templates) and use them in your Direct To Web pages!

It is recommended that property-level components be stateless, unless there is a good reason for requiring state in the component. This keeps the pages fast, and lowers the memory footprint of your application, since WebObjects caches a single instance of stateless components.

If you're using `pageConfigurations` in your application, a very common need is to link to a particular `pageConfiguration` from another Direct To Web page. This is easily done with a custom property-level component.

Direct To Web and Rules

Let's expand on the `InspectItemINTERNAL` example from the previous section. You want your employees to have a link to an order history page from the product detail page. It should list the orders for the product.

First, create a new `WOComponent` for your Project. Call it `LinkToViewOrderHistory`. All this component has to do is display a `WOHyperlink` that says "View Order History", and go to the `ListOrderHistory pageConfiguration` when the `WOHyperlink` is clicked.

Here is the Java source code:

```java
import com.webobjects.foundation.*;
import com.webobjects.appserver.*;
import com.webobjects.eocontrol.*;
import com.webobjects.eoaccess.*;
import com.webobjects.directtoweb.*;

public class LinkToViewOrderHistory extends WOComponent {

  public LinkToViewOrderHistory(WOContext context) {
      super(context);
  }

  // make this a stateless component, improving performance
  public boolean isStateless() { return true; }
  public boolean synchronizesVariablesWithBindings() { return false; }

  // action method - return the ListOrderHistory pageConfiguration page
  public WOComponent viewOrderHistory() {
      WOComponent result = null;
      if (item() == null) {
          // WHOA, you've misconfigured something!
          ErrorPageInterface epi = (ErrorPageInterface)
              D2W.factory().errorPage(session());
          epi.setMessage("ERROR!  I don't know what the item is!");
          // tell the error page to return to the current page
          epi.setNextPage(context().page());
          result = (WOComponent)epi;
      } else {
          // create a data source for the Order entity
          // To run this you must create a fetch specification
          // in the EOModel called "OrderHistoryByItem"
          // with the qualifier: (lineItems.item = $item)
          // It should sort by date in descending order
          EODatabaseDataSource ds = new EODatabaseDataSource(ec,
                                              "Order",
                                         "OrderHistoryByItem")
          // qualify the fetch specification with the Item we want
          // the order history for.  "item" corresponds to $item above
          ds.setQualifierBindings(new NSDictionary(item(), "item"));
          // create the list page
          ListPageInterface lpi = (ListPageInterface)
              D2W.factory().pageForConfigurationNamed(
                  "ListOrderHistory",
                  session()
              );
```

303

```
            // set the dataSource for the list page
            lpi.setDataSource(ds);
            // clicking "Return" on this list page goes to current page
            lpi.setNextPage(context().page());
            result = (WOComponent)lpi;
        }
        return result;
    }

    public EOEnterpriseObject item() {
        // get the Item object from the object binding
        EOEnterpriseObject eo = (EOEnterpriseObject)
            valueForBinding("object");
        if (eo.entityName().equals("Item"))
            return eo;
        else {
            // the object isn't an Item, maybe the object.key is?
            Object obj = eo.valueForKeyPath(
                (String)valueForBinding("key")
            );
            // the key binding is the current propertyKey
            if (obj instanceof EOEnterpriseObject) {
                eo = (EOEnterpriseObject)obj;
                if  (eo.entityName().equals("Item"))
                    return eo;
            }
        }
        // if we're here, there's no Item here. :-(
        return null;
    }
}
```

The HTML code is very simple – it's just a single WEBOBJECT tag for a WOHyperlink:

```
<WEBOBJECT NAME=Link>View Order History</WEBOBJECT>
```

The .wod file contains the bindings for the link:

```
Link: WOHyperlink {
    action = viewOrderHistory;
}
```

To use this component, add a fake propertyKey to the displayPropertyKeys for the InspectItemINTERNAL pageConfiguration, and configure it to use the new property-level component:

```
(pageConfiguration = 'InspectItemINTERNAL') => displayPropertyKeys =
        (title, theDescription, storePrice, retailPrice, quantityInStock,
            orderHistory)

((pageConfiguration = 'InspectItemINTERNAL') and
     (propertyKey = 'orderHistory')) => componentName = "D2WCustomComponent"

((pageConfiguration = 'InspectItemINTERNAL') and (propertyKey =
        'orderHistory')) => customComponentName = "LinkToViewObjectHistory"
```

You'll also want to set the `displayNameForProperty` for the fake `orderHistory` key to an empty String, since the link speaks for itself and having a label in front of it wouldn't help.

```
((pageConfiguration = 'InspectItemINTERNAL') and (propertyKey =
                    'orderHistory')) => displayNameForProperty = ""
```

If you've added the fallback rules for `task` and `entity` suggested in the *Page Configurations* section, you won't have to add *any* rules for the `ListOrderHistory` page, assuming you're happy with the `displayPropertyKeys` DirectToWeb's `DefaultAssignment` class chose for you!

NextPageDelegates

One of the keys to developing a user-friendly application is doing smart things when a user clicks on a link or button. A basic Direct To Web application will do the simplest, but not necessarily best/smartest thing, because it doesn't know anything about your application's real needs – it only knows about your database!

Many of the Page Interfaces can accept a `NextPageDelegate` by calling the `setNextPageDelegate(NextPageDelegate nextPageDelegate)` method on the page. `NextPageDelegate` is a very simple Java interface – it contains one method:

```
WOComponent nextPage(WOComponent sender)
```

The component that calls the `nextPage(WOComponent sender)` method will pass itself in as the sender. Having access to the current page gives you access to a lot of useful things from inside the `nextPage()` method: the current `WOContext` (`sender.context()`), Session (`sender.session()`), the current page (`sender.context().page()`), the current `WORequest` (`sender.context().request()`), and perhaps most importantly, things available from Direct To Web Page Interfaces, such as the `object()` or `dataSource()` being displayed.

You can do whatever you want inside the `nextPage()` method. You are expected to return a `WOComponent` at the end, but what you do before that is up to you. The component returned doesn't have to be a Direct To Web page; it can be any `WOComponent` you want!

To create a `NextPageDelegate`, you create a class (it is often convenient to make it a **static inner class** of another class) that implements `NextPageDelegate`.

You might create a Select page that lists some objects. The object selected by the user should be deleted immediately. You can create a `NextPageDelegate` to delete the object and attach it to a Select page. Here's a code example. First, the action method that creates the Select page:

```
public WOComponent deleteACustomer() {
  // create a select page for Customers
  SelectPageInterface spi = (SelectPageInterface)
     D2W.factory().selectPageForEntityNamed(
        "Customer", session()
     );
  // tell the select page to list ALL Customer records
  EOEditingContext ec = session().defaultEditingContext();
  spi.setDataSource(new EODatabaseDataSource(ec, "Customer"));
  // tell the select page what to do when a customer is chosen
```

Chapter 11

```
        spi.setNextPageDelegate(
            new DeleteSelectedObjectDelegate(
                // return to the current page after deleting the customer.
                context().page()
            )
        );
        // return the page
        return (WOComponent)spi;
    }
```

Now, here's the `DeleteSelectedObjectDelegate` class. Note that this class is *completely reusable* – it can delete any single object and then return any page afterwards.

```
public class DeleteSelectedObjectDelegate implements NextPageDelegate {

    public DeleteSelectedObjectDelete(WOComponent afterDeleting) {
        // remember where to go after deleting the object!
        theRealNextPage = afterDeleting;
    }
    private WOComponent theRealNextPage;

    // when the user clicks "Select", this
    // method will be called!
    public WOComponent nextPage(WOComponent sender) {
        // get a reference to the current select page
        SelectPageInterface spi =
            (SelectPageInterface)sender.context().page();
        // get the selected object, and its editing context
        EOEnterpriseObject eo = spi.selectedObject();
        EOEditingContext ec = eo.editingContext();
        // delete the object, and save the editing context
        ec.deleteObject(eo);
        ec.saveChanges();
        // go to the REAL next page
        return theRealNextPage;
    }
}
```

And there you have it, custom workflow in a Direct To Web application. It's that easy!

D2W Embedded Components

Tucked away in the third of six palettes that come with WebObjects Builder are five true gems:

- ❑ D2WList
- ❑ D2WEdit
- ❑ D2WInspect
- ❑ D2WQuery
- ❑ D2WSelect

To find them, choose **Palette...** from the **Window** menu in WebObjects Builder (or type *Cmd-2*), and click on the D2W icon.

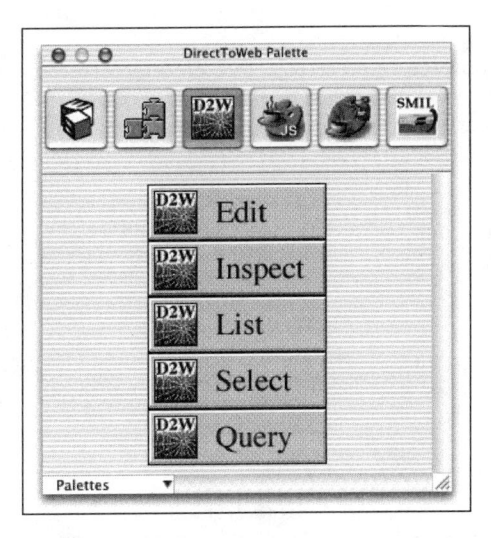

Each is a Direct To Web Reusable Component you can drag-and-drop onto a WOComponent to add DirectToWeb functionality to it. They are also known as **Direct To Web Embedded Components** because each inherits from `D2WEmbeddedComponent`.

> **Using D2W embedded components is a great way to ease into using Direct To Web development, and a great way to integrate Direct To Web technology with existing WebObjects applications.**

For example, putting a `D2WList` on a `WOComponent` puts a D2W-style list of objects on your page. Bind an `EODataSource` to the embedded component's `dataSource` binding, and the name of the `entity` it lists to its `entityName` binding, and it's ready to go!

Drag-and-dropping an Entity or Fetch Specification from EOModeler onto a WebObjects Builder window creates a `WODisplayGroup` for you. WODisplayGroups have a `dataSource` key you can bind to D2WList or D2WSelect's `dataSource` binding.

If you don't want to use a `WODisplayGroup`, you can create your own `EODataSource` programmatically *(see `EODatabaseDataSource`, `EODetailDataSource`, and `EOArrayDataSource` in the `EOAccess` and `EOControl` references, respectively, for more information)*, or simply bind an `NSArray` of objects to the `D2WList`'s (or `D2WSelect`'s) `list` binding. If you are trying to list the contents of a to-many relationship, the `list` binding is probably the easiest route. Here's the .wod source for a `D2WList` that should display the items for a particular category of a store:

```
ListPastOrders: D2WList {
    entityName = "Item";
    list = someCategory.items;
}
```

Chapter 11

D2W embedded components fully support the Rule System like any other Direct To Web template. You can bind a `pageConfiguration` name to the `pageConfiguration` binding of an embedded component to use that configuration.

Embedded components also provide a `displayKeys` binding for providing a custom `displayPropertyKeys` array to the Direct To Web template, in the absence of a `pageConfiguration`, overriding any default `displayPropertyKeys` you might have configured in your rule files.

The `displayKeys` binding expects a `String` representing an `NSArray` in property-list format, or an `NSArray` itself. Here's an example of a `displayKeys` binding (the double quotes are significant):

```
"(firstName, lastName, telephone)"
```

`D2WEdit` and `D2WInspect` operate on a single object you provide through the required `object` binding. The simple example below allows a logged-in customer to edit his or her first and last name. D2W embedded components include their own `WOForm` and form submit buttons, so they're self-contained and don't require extra setup.

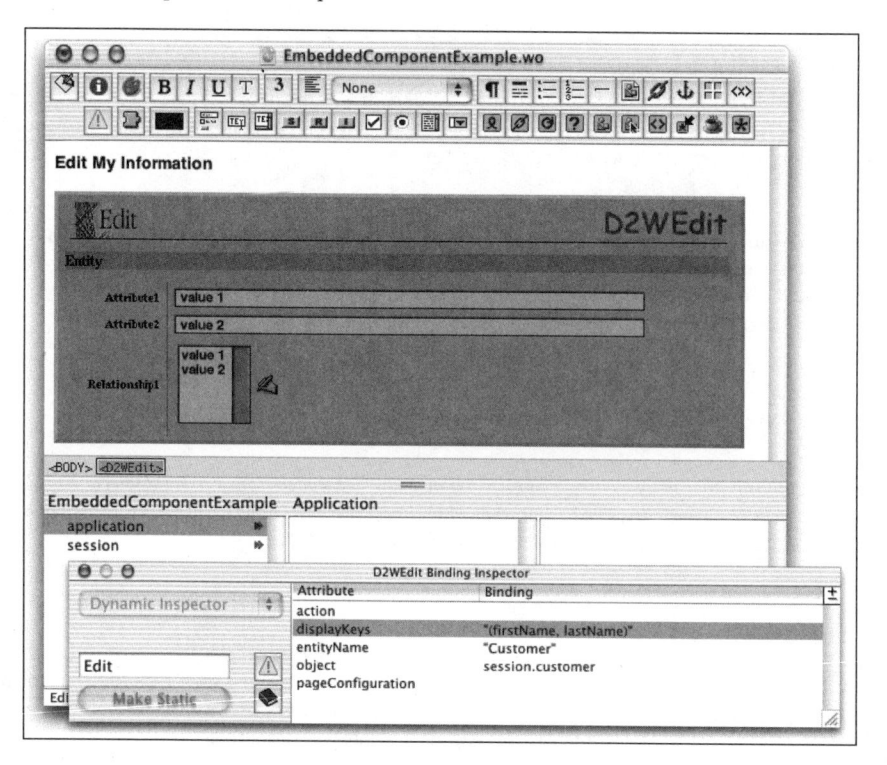

`D2WQuery` has a `queryDataSource` binding. Bind an `EODataSource` variable to this binding and `D2WQuery` will set that variable to an `EODataSource` containing the objects that match the query! You could bind that same `EODataSource` to the `dataSource` binding of a `D2WList` or `D2WSelect` on the same or next page to provide the results of the query – or get an `NSArray` containing the query matches by calling `fetchObjects()` on the `EODataSource` object.

Finally, each D2W embedded component also has an `action` binding. Bind an action method (that is, a public, no-argument instance method that returns a `WOComponent`) to the `action` binding to impose your own workflow for an embedded component.

- For `D2WEdit`, the `action` is invoked when the user clicks the **Save** or **Cancel** button. The object's `EOEditingContext` is saved before the `action` method is called (if the **Save** button was clicked), so you only need to worry about which page should appear next.
- For `D2WInspect` **and** `D2WList`, the `action` is invoked when the user clicks the **Return** button.
- For `D2WSelect`, the `action` is invoked when the user clicks **Select** or **Return**. If the user clicked the **Select** button, the variable you bound to its `selectedObject` binding will contain the object corresponding to the **Select** button clicked.
- For `D2WQuery`, the `action` is invoked when the user clicks the **Query** button, after the objects matching the query bindings have been fetched. The `EODataSource` variable bound to the `queryDataSource` binding contains the matching objects.

Embedded components are yet another way you can benefit from the reusability of the Direct To Web frameworks and the Rule System.

Direct To Web Techniques

Once you have some experience with Direct To Web you'll see useful patterns emerge, and ways to optimize your work patterns.

One excellent technique, if you have multiple Direct To Web applications to maintain, or multiple developers working on one or more applications, is to segment your rules across multiple rule files across frameworks. Of course, each application has its own rule file called `user.d2wmodel`.

It is recommended you try to keep these rule files as small as possible. Try to develop reusable property-level components, and put them in a framework that is shared by your applications. Your component framework should contain a `d2w.d2wmodel` file that has rules that are common to any application that uses that framework and/or component. Put `pageConfigurations` that use those components and are shared across applications in this `d2w.d2wmodel` file. Your applications should link to this framework.

Create a framework for your custom template components. Put a `d2w.d2wmodel` rule file in that framework as well – it should contain the base rules that provide default values for those templates (the rules in the `JavaDirectToWeb` framework's `d2w.d2wmodel` file still apply to all your frameworks, so you don't have to duplicate those rules in your `d2w.d2wmodel` files – just add the rules you want to override or augment the base rules). Your reusable components framework and applications should link to this framework.

Put your enterprise object business logic classes in a separate framework with your `EOModel` file and a `d2w.d2wmodel` file. Put base rules in that rule file that are specific to your data – for example, custom `displayNameForProperty` rules, base `EntityAssignment` rules as described in the *Make Your life Easier: Use Page Configurations* section, `keyWhenRelationship` rules, special `formatter` rules, and so on. Chances are your reusable components frameworks are going to need your business logic classes, so that framework should link in your business logic framework, as should your applications, of course.

You should endeavor to make your template/look framework free of dependencies on any specific business logic so it can be used by any application, regardless of which set of business logic classes or frameworks it uses. It's quite common to have business-logic specific classes in the `PageWrapper.wo` and/or `MenuHeader.wo` component in each application – this is expected and encouraged.

You might create separate frameworks for different "modules" of your application, so that you can swap features in and out of applications essentially by linking and de-linking those frameworks from your application. By introducing the rules in a module's rule file to an application by linking its framework to your application, and configuring the module in the static initializer or a static method of a class in its framework, you can do some pretty amazing things.

Try to adopt a strict naming convention for the names of your attributes, relationships, entities, and page configurations. If you stick to a convention, you can take advantage of that in your rules, enabling you to write very powerful rules that can apply across a number of scenarios, by virtue of the similarity in the names of those aspects of your design. The "`like`" `EOQualifierOperator` and the wildcard character (`*`) will become two of your biggest assets when your naming strategy is consistent! You can put multiple wildcard characters in the value of an `EOKeyValueQualifier`, even in the middle. For example: (`pageConfiguration = 'List*Customers*'`) is a very flexible qualifier that can apply to many `pageConfigurations`, such as `ListNewCustomers`, `ListCustomersAdmin`, and so on.

For many more specific techniques and technologies you can incorporate into your WebObjects and Direct To Web applications, it is recommended that you read the NetStruxr case study in Chapter 15.

Summary

In this chapter we have covered the major features of the DirectToWeb frameworks and seen a few ways that Direct To Web can be integrated into your WebObjects applications, and vice versa.

The chapter focused on how to get D2W pages to look and do what you want them to, using the Rule System and `NextPageDelegates` respectively.

We saw how Direct To Web pages (which are actually `task` and `look` specific WOComponent templates) can be configured on many levels, be it by `task`, `entity`, `pageConfiguration`, or a combination of these and other aspects.

We created a reusable property-level component and showed how to configure the Rule System to use it in a custom `pageConfiguration`. We also used Reusable Embedded D2W components such as `D2WEdit` to incorporate D2W functionality into a regular WOComponent.

Techniques for reducing the number of rules that have to be written were shown, as were ways to keep development teams from corrupting each other's rules in a team environment that relies on CVS for source control.

Direct To Web is a large topic that could easily span an entire book on its own. With this guide and resources that come with WebObjects and on the Internet, you should be able to turbo-charge your WebObjects development by taking advantage of this remarkable system.

Direct To Web and Rules

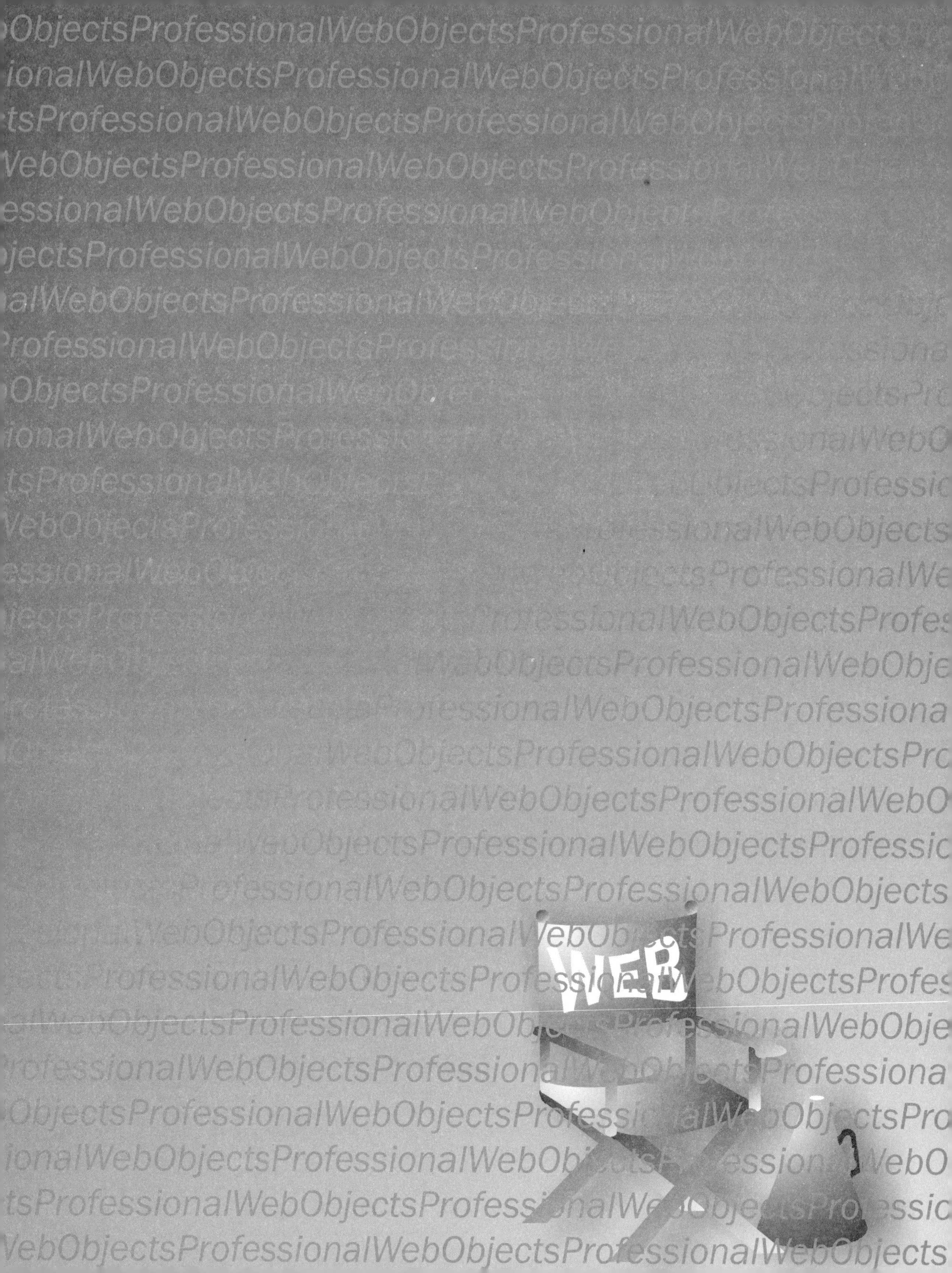
WEB

12

JavaClient/DirectToJavaClient

WebObjects' JavaClient and DirectToJavaClient frameworks can be used to create pure Java desktop applications. These user interfaces look and feel more like typical applications, and allow you to overcome some of the weaknesses inherent in HTML applications, such as statelessness.

JavaClient is a framework for creating three-tier applications – there is a database layer, an application server layer, and a client layer. The database and application server layer (EOF, and WebObjects) have already been discussed in Chapters 4 and 5. Every JavaClient application is at its core a WebObjects application. There is always a server component, which queries a database in response to HTTP request; the response is not HTML, but serialized EnterpriseObjects.

Explaining JavaClient, or DirectToJavaClient could fill an entire book, and in many ways it already has. The JavaClient APIs are based on the NextStep/OpenStep APIs, and so are very mature, and have had several books written to describe their workings. DirectToJavaClient is built on top of JavaClient – it uses all of the JavaClient APIs, and also uses the rule system of DirectToWeb.

This chapter will describe three scenarios where you are required to use either JavaClient, or DirectToJavaClient to solve a problem. We'll walk you through creating example applications, and then explain the concepts used to build them. The first example will be quite low-level (at least for the JavaClient framework, people familiar with normal Swing applications may be astonished at how little work they need to do), each subsequent example will involve less custom code, and will use more of JavaClient/DirectToJavaClient's built-in functionality.

This chapter aims to provide you with a good explanation of how to actually use the JavaClient frameworks, discuss underlying ideas, and give you a better understanding of how they work.

The One Week Scenario

You work for an e-commerce company of thirty people. They've just hired a customer support representative, Mike, but have no administrative tools. The CEO asks if you can put something together by the end of the week, that will allow Mike to quickly, and easily, view a customer's orders.

Creating the Application On Mac OS X

Start by creating a new Java Client Application project called OneWeek. At the Choose Frameworks panel, simply press Next. Now you have to Choose EOModels; press the Add button, and add the EOModel that you created in Chapter 5. Press Next. On this panel you'll fill in the class name, and the package name. For the class name enter OrderLookupController, and for the package name enter com.wrox.client. On the next panel, press Finish.

You've just created a very basic JavaClient application. Before launching the client you need to add some startup arguments to the server application. Go to the Executables tab of the OneWeek target and add the line -WOAutoOpenInBrowser NO -WOPort 8088. WOAutoOpenInBrowser, which defaults to yes, will automatically open up your default browser, and attempt to run the OneWeek client as an applet. It is easier to run the client as a command line application every time, especially if you specify the default port. Once you've added the launch arguments, build and run the server application.

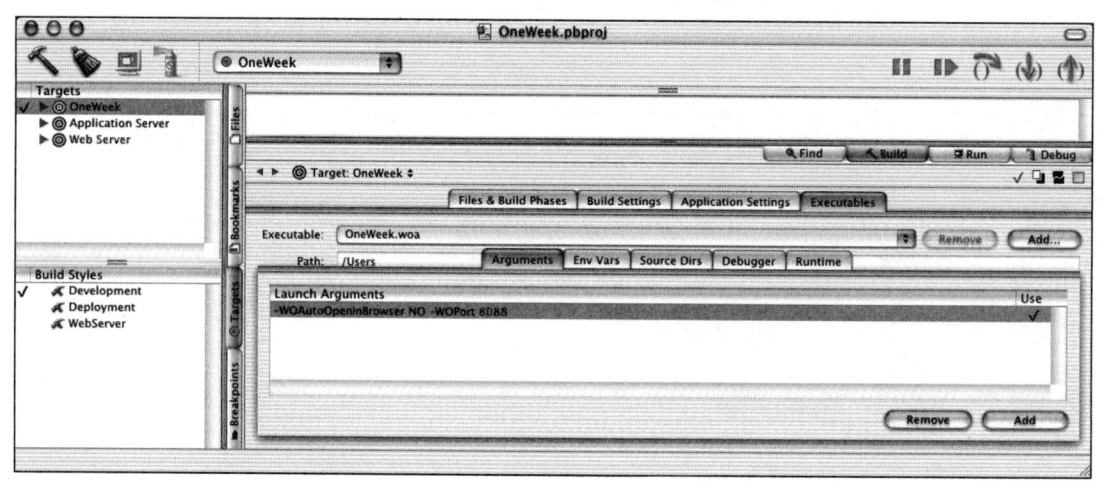

To launch the client, go to a Terminal window, and enter:

<path-to-OneWeek.woa>**/Contents/MacOS/OneWeek_Client http://127.0.0.1:8088/cgi-bin/WebObjects/OneWeek.woa**

You should see your running application – an empty window labeled Window. Select Quit from the Java menu in the menu bar to exit the application.

Creating the Application On Windows

Start a new Java WebObjects Application called OneWeek and select JavaClient from the WebObjects Application Wizard. Next, browse to the EOModel that you created in Chapter 5. At the next page, press Finish. The Windows version does not give you the option of changing the class name or package name. The default class name is the same as the filename and the default package is <filename>.client.

You've just created a very basic JavaClient application. Before launching the client you need to add some startup arguments to the server application. Select the Launch Options icon (the 'Blue Tick') from the Launch panel. Go to the **Arguments** tab of the `OneWeek` target and add the line `-WOAutoOpenInBrowser NO -WOPort 8088`. WOAutoOpenInBrowser, which defaults to `yes`, will automatically open up your default browser, and attempt to run the `OneWeek` client as an applet. It is easier to run the client as a command line application every time, especially if you specify the default port. Once you've added the launch arguments, build and run the server application.

To launch the client, go to a command window, and enter:

C:\<path-to-OneWeek.woa>\Contents\Windows>**oneweek http://127.0.0.1:8088/cgi-bin/WebObjects/OneWeek.woa**

You should now see an empty window.

Inside the Project

Now let's look at the project itself. In the **Classes** group you'll find the typical `Application.java`, `Session.java`, and `DirectAction.java` files. In the **Interfaces** folder you'll find two files, `OrderLookupController.nib`, and `OrderLookupController.java`. For Window users, the files are called `OneWeek.nib` which can be found under `SUBPROJECTS>ClientSideJava.subproject>Interfaces>English` and `OneWeek.java` which is at `SUBPROJECTS>ClientSideJava.subproject>Classes`.

The `.nib` file contains information about your application's UI. The `.java` file is a controller, from the classic Model-View-Controller paradigm, at runtime it will read information from the `.nib` file, and create the actual UI elements that the application uses. Finally, in the **WebComponents** group, you'll find the `Main` component. Open up the `Main` component, in WebObjects Builder. The `Main` component contains a single `WOComponent` a `WOJavaClientApplet`. Using the inspector to view the components bindings, you'll see that only one key is bound, `interfaceControllerClassName`. The `interfaceControllerClassName` binding is used to specify which `.nib` file should be loaded by default when running the application.

Now go back to the **Interfaces** folder, and double-click on the `OrderLookupController.nib` file. Choose **Hide Others** from the Interface Builder menu, and your desktop should look something like the figure shown overleaf:

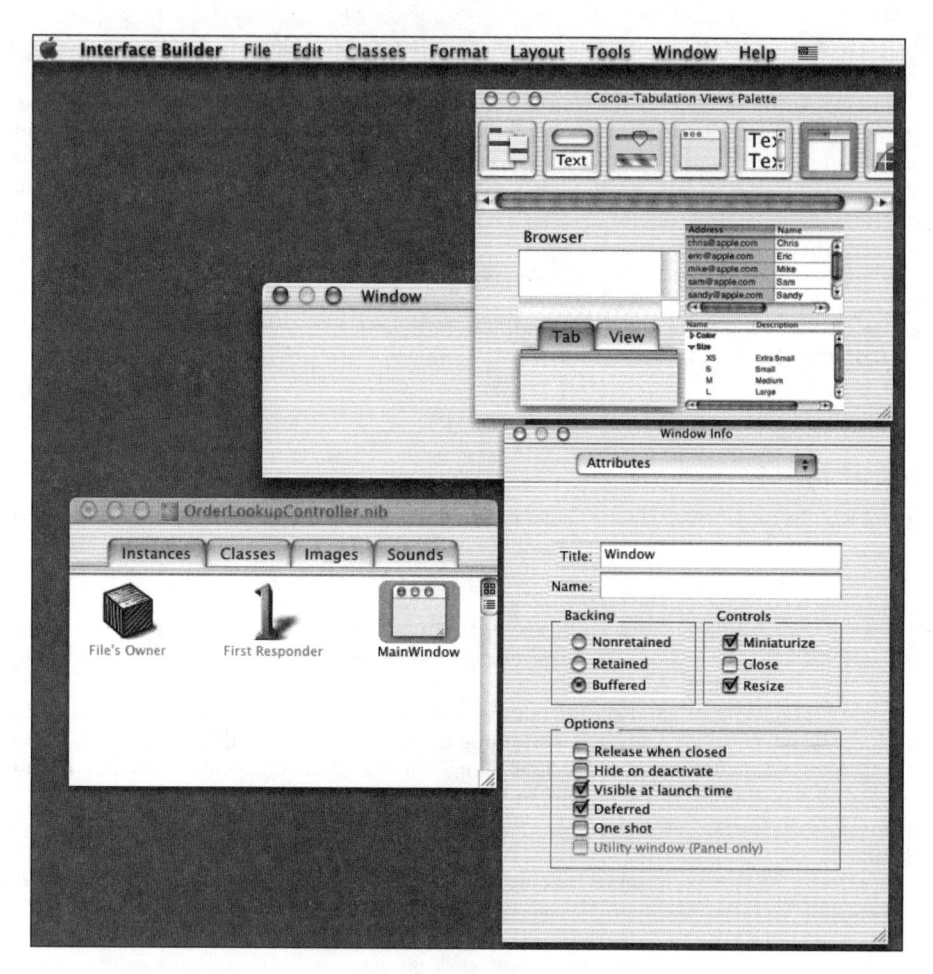

In the middle of your screen you'll see a blank window labeled **Window**; this is the window that will be displayed whenever you load, and display the `OrderLookupController`. On the bottom left you'll see a window labeled **OrderLookupController.nib**, this window contains information about all of the different non-UI objects available for you to work with. The window labeled **Window Info** at bottom right is an inspector panel, which will allow you to modify many different values for the currently selected object. If this window is not displayed, you can view it by selecting **Window Inspector** from the **Window** menu in Windows or **Show Info** from the **Tools** menu in Mac OS X. Last is the **Palette** window, which holds generic elements, mostly UI widgets that can be added to the interface.

Let's start by giving our main window a descriptive name. Click on the title bar of the main window, and then make sure that **Attributes** is selected from the combo box at the top of the inspector. Change the value of the **Title** text field to **Customer Lookup**. Tab from the text field, and you'll notice that the title of the window has changed to **Customer Lookup**.

Now let's start adding the UI widget, such as buttons, textfields, and labels. Start by pressing the **Views** palette button at the top of the **Palette** panel (we'll reference these buttons by their tool tip text).

Now, drag the **Message Text** label to the main window. As you move the label around the window, you may notice that dashed blue lines appear – these are known as guide lines, and they help you to line up widgets, both next to and within each other (Note, this is only a Mac OS X feature and lines will not show up on Windows so Windows users will have to line up by eye). Drop the label in the upper left-hand corner of the window, so that there is a guide line to the left of, and on top of the label, as below.

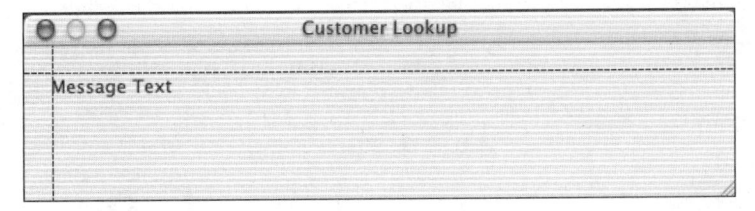

Double-click on the **Message Text** label, and it becomes editable; replace **Message Text** with **Customer Login Name:**. It is possible that, you'll only be able to see the word **Customer** until you resize the label. To resize a widget, click once on it, and you will see 9 dots (or handles) around the edges of it. Grab any of the dots, and drag to resize.

Now add a text field next to the **Customer Login Name:** label, and resize it until it stretches to the guide line that appears on the far right of the window. Below the text field, but still against the far right of the window, add a button. Change the button title to **Lookup** by double-clicking on the button widget.

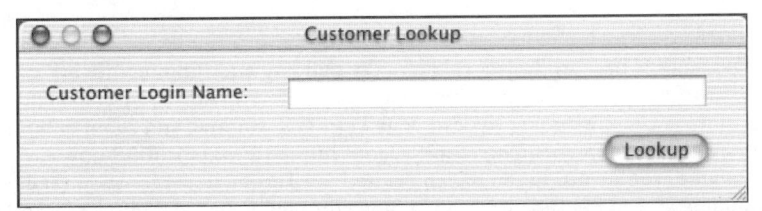

Finally, add a table, which will be used to display a customer's order. Press the **Tabulation Views palette** button, and drag the table widget, pointed to by the mouse in the image below, to the window.

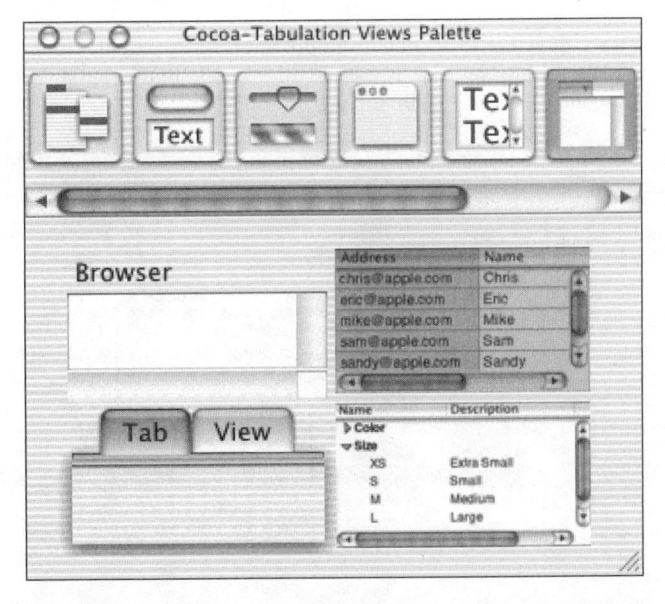

Resize the table to take up the remaining space at the bottom of the window. Double-click in the table region, the table should turn gray. Now you can set the title for the two columns by double-clicking in the header section. Edit the header on the left to read **Date**, and the one on the right to be **Amount**. Resize the date column by dragging the line that separates the two columns to the right.

Your window should now look something like this:

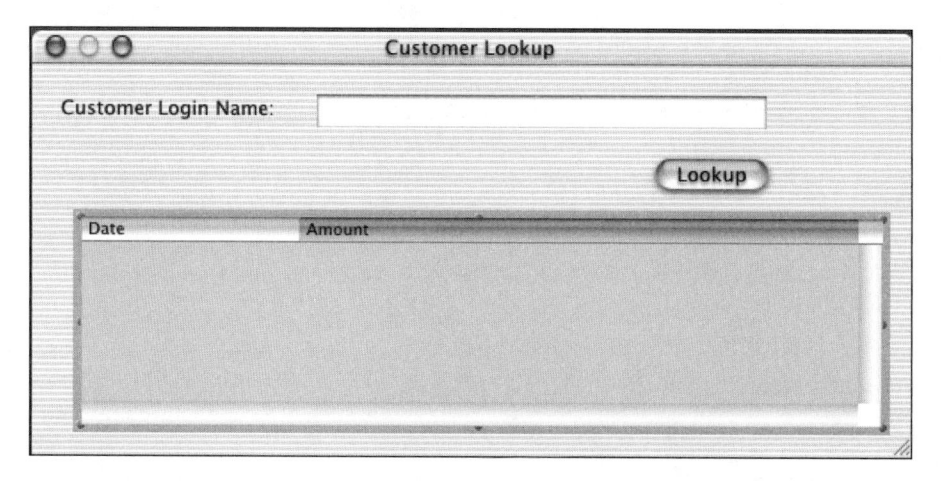

Save your changes, and go back to Project Builder. Try building and running the server application again, but make sure that you've stopped the last running application before building, by clicking the **Quit** button. Once the server is up, run the client by going back to your Terminal window, and again entering <path-to-OneWeek.woa>/Contents/MacOS/OneWeek_Client http://127.0.0.1:8088/cgi-bin/WebObjects/OneWeek.woa. If you haven't closed the Terminal window you used to launch the client before, you should be able to use the up arrow to move through your old commands, and reuse the last one. You should get a window very similar to the one created with Interface Builder.

Outlets and Actions

OK, so now you have a window that looks like it should, but doesn't actually do anything useful – it's time to add some functionality. What we want to do is use the information in the text field to find a customer, and display their orders in the table, whenever the lookup button is pressed.

To start, double-click on the icon labeled **File's Owner** in the OrderLookupController.nib window. You'll see a listing like this:

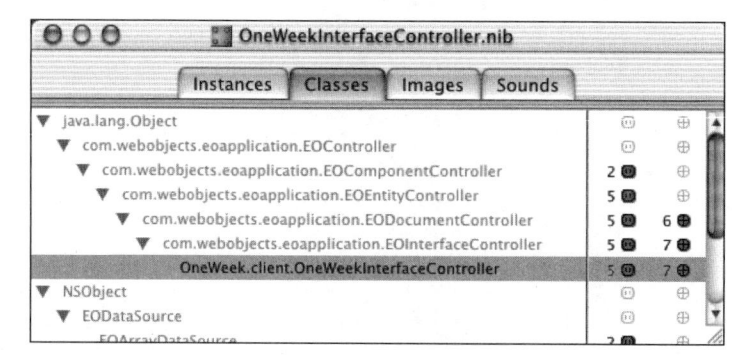

JavaClient/DirectToJavaClient

The tree list on the left represents the class hierarchy of the `File's Owner` object. It is an instance of `com.wrox.client.OrderLookupController`, and a direct descendant of `com.webobject.eoapplication.EOInterfaceController`. `EOInterfaceController` contains the code that reads a `.nib` file, and based on that information, constructs a user interface. On the right are two columns, the outlet column represented by a symbol that looks, faintly, like an electrical outlet. The other column, which is shown as a circle with a cross in the middle, is the action column. Click on the outlet column and you should see:

This is how you add outlets (which correspond to instance variables), and actions (which represent methods). Pressing *enter* now will add a new line to outlets – change the name of this outlet from myOutlet to loginNameTextField. Click the Instances tab. Now *control-click* on the File's Owner icon, and drag to the text field in our lookup window.

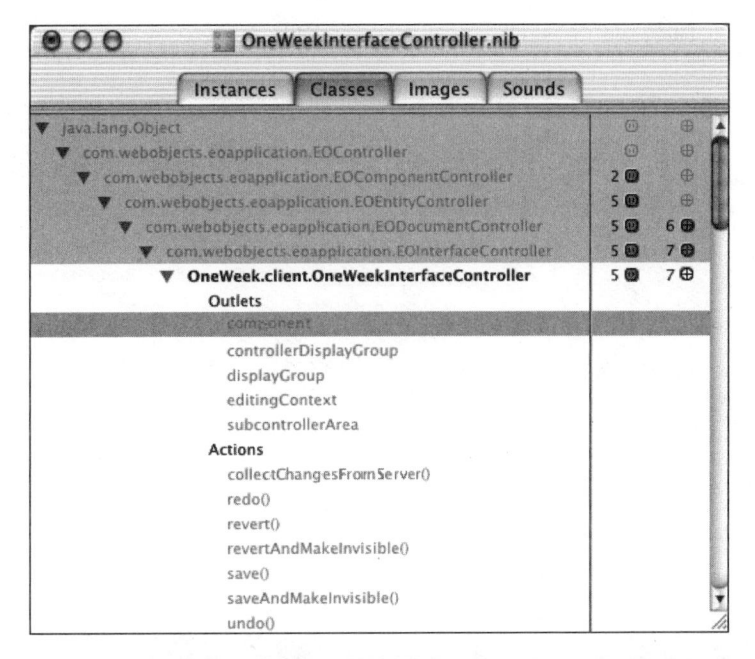

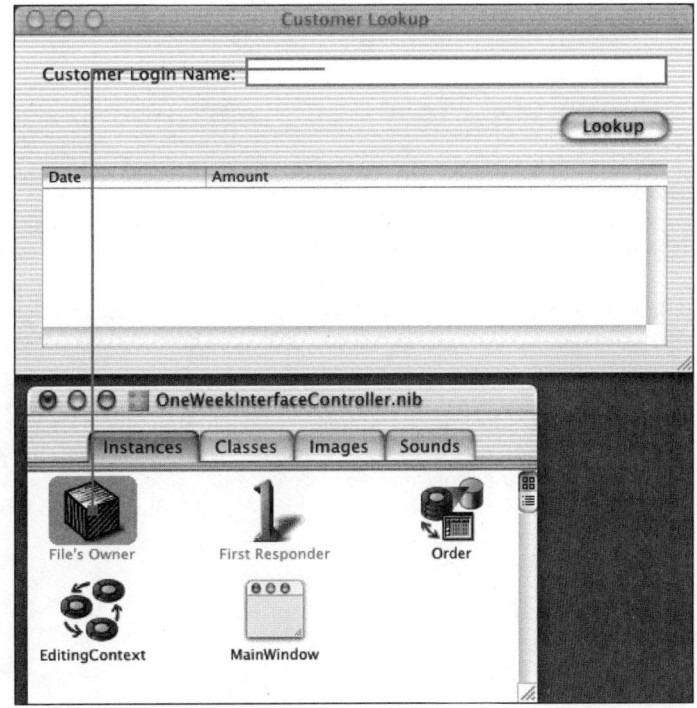

319

The inspector window should now look like this:

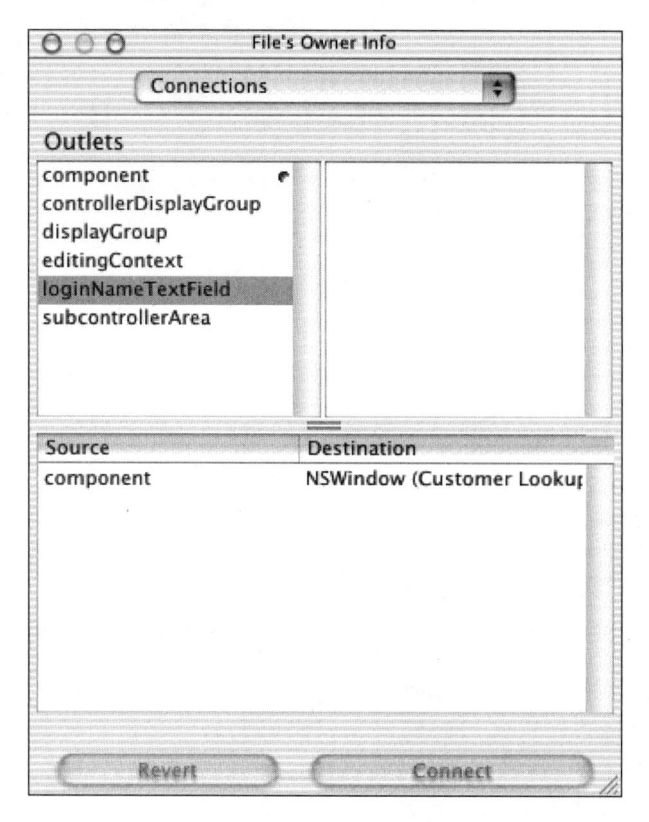

Select **loginNameTextField** in the upper left-hand panel, as is shown above, and then press the **Connect** button on the bottom right. By connecting the text field widget to the loginNameTextField outlet of the `File's Owner` object you have set up the `OrderLookupController`, also known as `File's Owner`, to have its `loginNameTextField` controller bound to the text field widget, that is, in the `OrderLookupController` class you'll be able to retrieve the contents of the text field by using the code fragment `loginNameTextField.getText()`.

Now let's make the **Lookup** button actually do something when pressed. Go back to the Class view of the `File's Owner` object, by double-clicking its icon, this time click on the action icon – the circle with a cross in it. Hit *enter*, and replace `myAction()` with `lookupAction()`. Now *control-drag* from the **Lookup** button to the `File's Owner` object, and change the bindings combo box in the inspector panel to **Outlets**, as shown opposite:

JavaClient/DirectToJavaClient

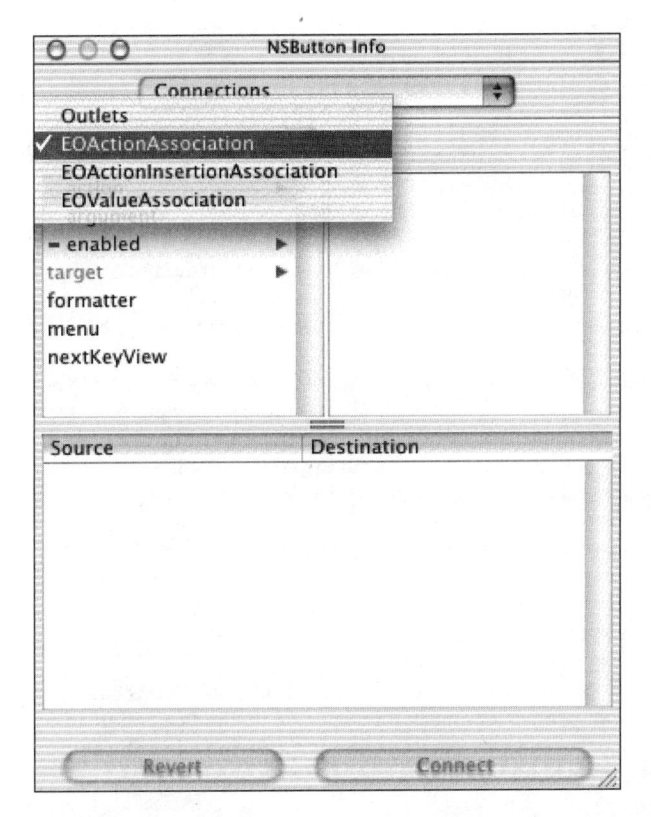

The top left panel should now display a list of possible outlets: **target**, **formatter**, **nextKeyView**, and **menu**. The target outlet should automatically be selected, and the list on the right should be populated with all of the available actions for the `OrderLookupController` class. Select `lookupAction()`, and press the **Connect** button. At runtime, pressing the **Lookup** button will now cause `lookupAction()` to be called on `File's Owner`, which is an instance of `OrderLookupController`. To verify that everything is working as expected save your `.nib` in Interface Builder, go back to Project Builder, and modify the `OrderLookupController.java` file to look like this:

```
// OrderLookupController.java

package com.wrox.client;

import com.webobjects.foundation.*;
import com.webobjects.eocontrol.*;
import com.webobjects.eoapplication.*;

public class OrderLookupController extends EOInterfaceController {

  public Object loginNameTextField;

  public OrderLookupController() {
    super();
  }

  public OrderLookupController(EOEditingContext substitutionEditingContext) {
```

```
        super(substitutionEditingContext);
    }

    public void LookupAction () {
        System.out.println("loginNameTextField class = "
                           + loginNameTextField.getClass());
    }
}
```

Now build and run the application again. When you press the **Lookup** button, the class of the `loginNameTextField` will be printed to the Terminal; it should be `com.webobjects.eointerface.swing.EOTextField`, which is a subclass of the Swing `JTextField`.

But what have we really just done? How do outlets and actions really work? When you *click*, or *control-click*, on a button, the inspector updates to display all of the button's relevant information. In particular, the `Outlets` panel is updated to display all of a button's outlets, or in Java-speak, all of the buttons publicly visible instance variables (it's useful to note that the instance variable itself need not be public, but if it is not, it must have publicly accessible accessor methods). By *control-dragging* from one element to another, you are graphically binding objects, that is by *control-dragging* from the button to the `File's Owner` object, and connecting it to the target outlet, you are telling interface builder to set the button's `target` variable to reference the `File's Owner` object. By *control-dragging* from the `File's Owner` object to the text field, and binding to the `loginNameTextField`, you have ensured that `File's Owner` will hold a reference to that text field with its `loginNameTextField` variable.

Actions are much more obvious – actions represent method calls. In this case, it's the `lookupAction()` method. A button's target isn't just an object, it's a specific method called on an object. You can't simply tell a button to call the method `lookupAction()` without specifying what object to call it on, so you also include the object when creating the binding – in this case `File's Owner`.

EODisplayGroups, and Associations

So now that we know what method will be called when the **Lookup** button is pressed, and we have a reference to the text field that will contain the customer's login name, how do we display the customers' orders?

First off we'll need to add a display group to our `nib`. `EODisplayGroups` are very similar to `WODisplayGroups` – their main purpose is to hold a collection of a specific type of `Entity`, and to store user interface related information, that is, the currently selected object in the collection. To add a `displayGroup` to the nib, simply open the EOModel, and drag the type of entity you need to the `OneWeekInterfaceBuilder.nib` window in Interface Builder – in this case the `Order` entity.

JavaClient/DirectToJavaClient

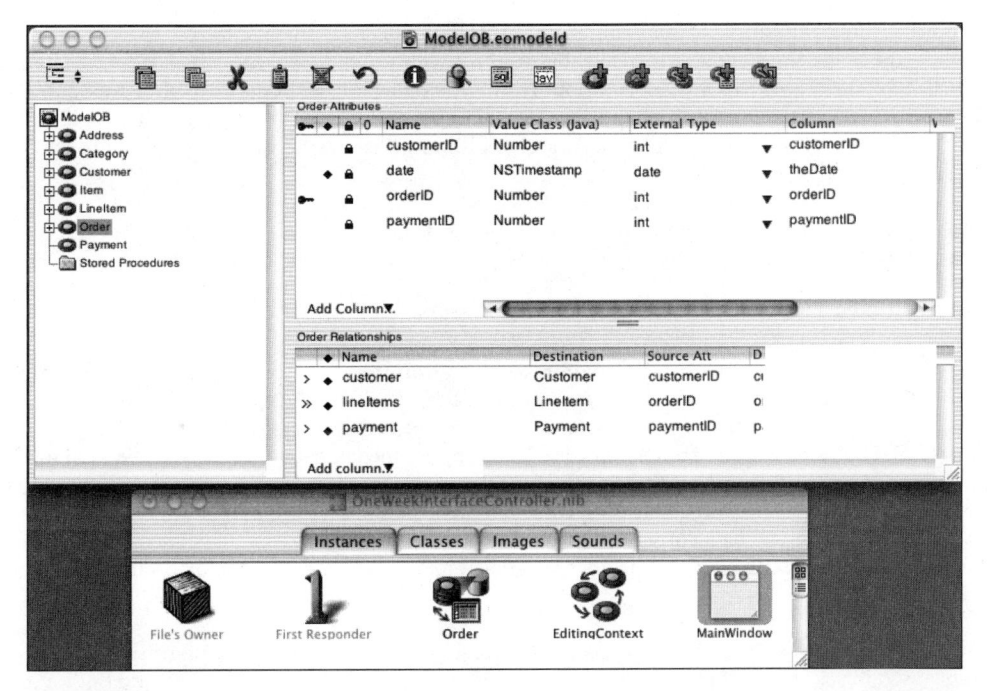

You'll now see two new objects in the window, one labeled **Order**, and the other named **EditingContext**. The `Order` object is a display group that will contain an array of orders; the `Editing Context` object represents the editing context that will be used by the `Orders` display group.

Select the `File's Owner` object, and *control-drag* to the `Orders` object. Connect the `Orders` display group to the `File's Owner displayGroup` outlet by selecting `displayGroup` from the `Outlets` list, and pressing the **Connect** button. Repeat the procedure to bind the `Editing Context` object to the `editingContext` outlet.

Now go to our user interface window, and double-click the table. Once the table becomes gray, click on the column labeled **Date**, and *control-drag* to the Orders object in the `OrderLookupController.nib` window. In the Inspector window make sure that `EOTableColumnAssociation` is visible from the bindings combo box, and choose **value** from the table list on the top left. Choose **date** from the list on the top right, and press the **Connect** button. When you're done the Inspector window should look like this:

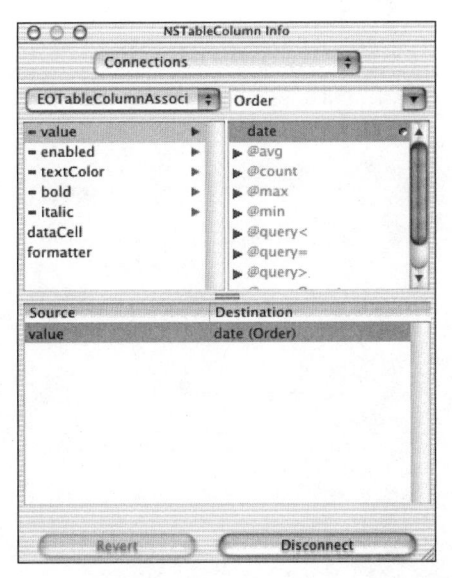

323

Do the same thing with the **Amount** column, only this time select the triangle next to the grayed-out payment row of the top right listing. You should get a new list in the top right, which displays all of the attributes of the `Payment` entity. Select **amount**, and press the **Connect** button. With these bindings, each order in the Order display group will appear as a row in the table. The **Date** column will display an individual order's date attribute, while the **Amount** column will show the value of the amount attribute from an order's payment relationship.

By default the Orders display group will load and display every `Order` object, so build and rerun your application now to see all of the orders in the table.

So, what have we done? What are associations, and how do they work?

In the classic Model-View-Controller pattern, associations are the `Controller` – they make sure that the value of the `Model` objects, those found in the `EODisplayGroup`, are kept in sync with the `View` objects, or user interface widgets. Associations, subclasses of `com.webobjects.eointerface.EOAssociation`, use the concept of aspects to keep the model and view in sync. Above we bound an `EOTableColumnAssociation`'s value aspect to an `Order`'s date attribute and a table column. In essence we created an association that will make sure that for every Order in a display group, there will be a corresponding row in a table displaying the date value of that order, and if the value in that cell is edited by a user, the association will make sure to update the date value of the corresponding row.

One of the most confusing concepts when dealing with aspects is that they can be directional: some aspects are only used to set up the display, some are only used to modify the model, and some do both. For example, the `EOTableColumnAssociation`'s value aspect is bi-directional – it's used by the view to discover what string to display in a given table cell, and if a cell is modified, it's used to update the model object with the new value. On the other hand, the bold aspect is unidirectional; it is only used by the view to decide if a given cell should draw its contents using a bolded font. Keep this in mind if you find yourself getting confused while setting up an association – it can often clear things up.

Putting It Together

So now we've got a single object, the `OrderLookupController`, which contains a reference to the `JTextField` in which users will enter a customer's login name, we have a method that will be called whenever the **Lookup** button is pressed, and we have a reference to the `EODisplayGroup` whose Orders are used to populate a table which displays an order's date, and payment amount. With all of this, here's what the `OrderLookupController.java` file should look like to finish this application.

```
// OrderLookupController.java

package com.wrox.client;

import com.webobjects.foundation.*;
import com.webobjects.eocontrol.*;
import com.webobjects.eoapplication.*;
import com.webobjects.eointerface.*;
import com.webobjects.eointerface.swing.*;

public class OrderLookupController extends EOInterfaceController {

    protected EOTextField loginNameTextField;
```

```
// CONSTRUCTORS
public OrderLookupController() {
  super();
}

public OrderLookupController(EOEditingContext substitutionEditingContext) {
  super(substitutionEditingContext);
}

// ACCESSOR METHODS
public EOTextField loginNameTextField() {
  return (loginNameTextField);
}

public void setLoginNameTextField(EOTextField aTextField) {
  loginNameTextField = aTextField;
}

// PUBLIC API
public void LookupAction() {
  displayGroup().setQualifier(loginNameQualifier());
  displayGroup().updateDisplayedObjects();
}

public void establishConnection() {
  super.establishConnection();
  LookupAction();
}

// PROTECTED API
protected EOQualifier loginNameQualifier() {
  return (new EOKeyValueQualifier("customer.loginName",
                                  EOQualifier.QualifierOperatorEqual,
                                  loginName()));
}

protected String loginName() {
  return (loginNameTextField().getText());
}
}
```

Here are the major changes:

- ❑ We imported `com.webobjects.eointerface.*`, and `com.webobjects.eointerface.swing.*`

- ❑ We made the `loginNameTextField` an instance of `EOTextFieldController`, changed its visibility to `protected`, and added accessor methods for it. This is not strictly necessary, but is a better coding style for object-oriented programs.

- ❑ We added a method that creates a qualifier based on the `loginName`. The qualifier does *not* fetch a customer based on the `loginName` – it simply qualifies the `DisplayGroup` based on an order's `customer.loginName` value. The qualifier will match any order for which `order.valueForKey("customer.loginName")` equals the value in the `loginNameTextField`. Equals comparison is done using the `equals()` method, not the equality comparator `==`.

- After setting the qualifier on the `displayGroup`, we needed to call `displayGroup().updateDisplayedObjects()` to get it to refresh using the new qualifier.
- We override the `establishConnection()` method inherited from `com.webobjects.eoapplication.EOController`, and add a call to `lookupCustomer()`. `establishConnection()` is called before the interface controller becomes visible, but after it's been initialized (although the method name may sound like it's causing a connection to be made with the server, it's not – the method name refers to the DirectToJavaClient controller hierarchy that will be discussed later). Calling `lookupCustomer()` at this point will filter out all of the orders from the table (assuming you don't have a customer whose login name is the empty string).

Build and run the client and server applications – this is the final version of the application. There should be no orders in the order table when the application starts up. Enter a customer's login name, press the **Lookup** button, and all of the orders for that customer should appear in the table.

The One Day Scenario

The company you work for has grown to about 300 people, and has caught the eyes of a larger e-commerce company. The owner of your company comes up to you one morning, looking a little anxious, and says that he's going to be showing off the customer support system to a prospective buyer. He's hoping that maybe you can improve it a little bit, by maybe adding the ability to view the line items for a selected order. And maybe we could also do lookups using the customer's last name, or e-mail address. Oh, and the changes need to be in place by 4 o'clock today!

Creating the Application

Create a new Java Client Application project named `OneDay`, and add the EOModel. Name the main controller `OrderLookupController` again, and put it in the `com.wrox.client` package. This time use the `Master Detail` template, and uncheck the **Fields** checkbox in the `Main DisplayGroup` list and the `Detail DisplayGroup` list. At the next panel, labeled **Choose the Main EOEntity**, select **Order**. The next panel has a browser on the left side, and a list on the right. Choose **customer** from the first browser pane, and then **lastName** from the second. Press the button with the **>>** label, and **customer.lastName** should appear in the list on the right. Do this for **customer.firstName**, **date**, and **payment.amount**. When you're done, the window should look like this:

JavaClient/DirectToJavaClient

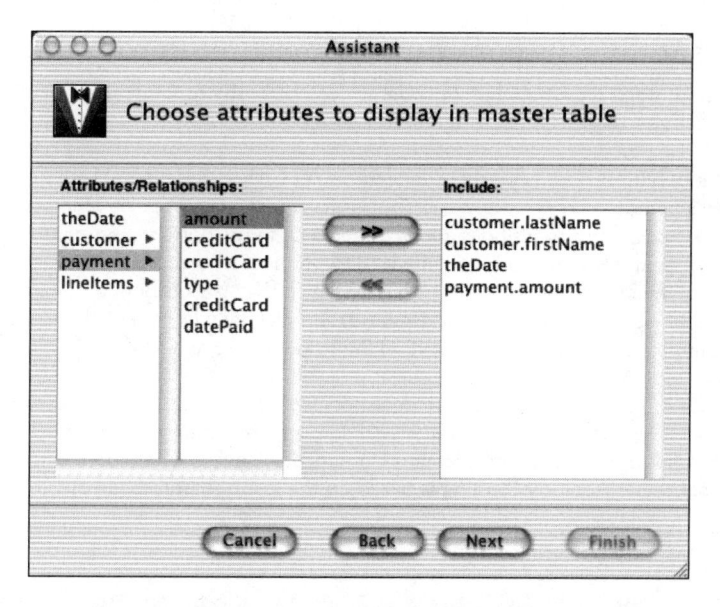

Go to the next panel and choose customer.lastName, customer.loginName, and customer.email. In the next panel you choose what relationship of Order you are going to display – choose lineItems in the first browser panel, and then press the >> button. In the next panel select item.title, quantity, and price – these are the three values to display for each line item in an order. Press Finish, and open `OrderLookupController.nib` from Project Builder. Modify the `nib` so that the user interface looks something like the screenshot below, build and run your application and you're done!

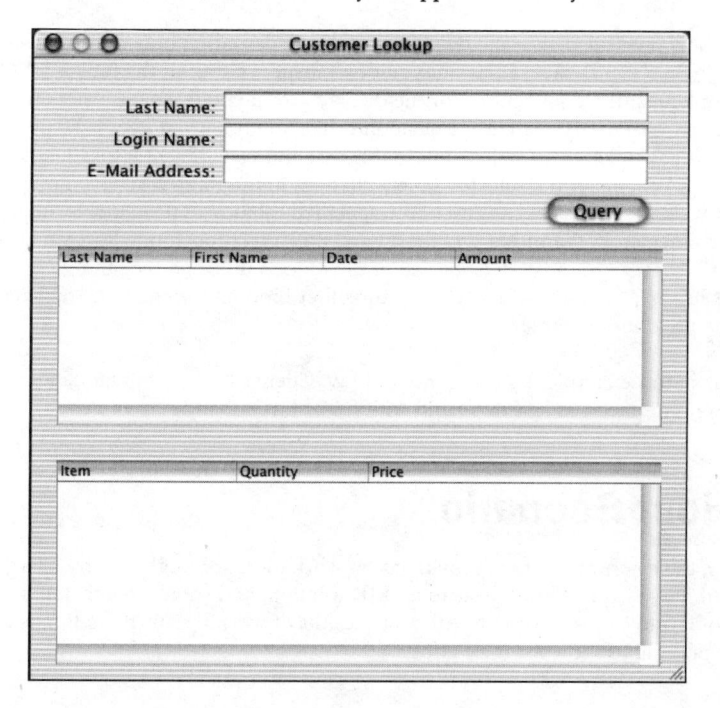

Inside the Project

How is it that without writing a single line of code, we've got a fully functional application? Open the `OrderLookupController.nib` file to see what's going on.

First, select the Query button, and inspect its connections. You'll see that the only connection that's bound is the target outlet, and it's bound to an `EODisplayGroups qualifyDataSource` method. Unfortunately you can't tell *which* `EODisplayGroup` it's bound to. Too see that, in the bottom command *click* on the highlighted target line – the line should become unhighlighted. *Click* on the line again, and Interface Builder will draw a connection line from the button to the display group to which the target is bound; the Order display group. When the Query button is pressed, the Order display group will have its `qualifyDataSource()` method called, which apparently filters the Orders based on the values in the text field.

Now inspect the Login Name text field. Its value aspect is bound to `@query=.customer.loginName`. When `qualifyDataSource()` is called on an `EODisplayGroup`, it creates an `EOQualifier` based on all of the values bound to `@query`, and refetches from its data source using the qualifier. The `EOQualifier` that is used for a particular `@query` binding is based on the symbol after `@query`:

Binding	EOQualifiers
`@query=`	Uses an `EOQualifier.EOQualifierOperatorEqual`
`@query<`	Uses an `EOQualifier.EOQualifierOperatorLessThanOrEqual`
`@query>`	Uses an `EOQualifier.EOQualifierGreaterThanOrEqual`

All of the `@query` bindings are then added to an `EOAndQualifier`.

So now that we know how the orders get displayed in the Order table, how does the Line Item table know which line items to display? To figure this out you don't inspect either of the tables, but the actual `LineItem` display group. Looking at the connections for the display group you'll see it's using an `EOMasterDetailAssociation`. This association is like any other – it keeps the objects in its master display group in sync with its `view` object, but in this case the view object is another `EODisplayGroup`, the detail display group. Whenever the selected object changes in the master display group, the detail display group is updated with the objects at the end of the specified relationship. In our example, where the detail display group is connected to the master via the `lineItems` relationship, whenever the selected order changes, the detail display group is filled with all of the objects returned by calling `order.valueForKey("lineItems")`. All of the other bindings, namely the table columns, are exactly the same as in the previous example.

As you can see from this example, by using more of JavaClient's built-in functionality you can often create more complex user interfaces, in less time, and with fewer lines of code.

The One Hour Scenario

About a year ago, the e-commerce company that you work for was bought out by a larger player. The new regime decided to move from WebObjects to an EJB solution, and spun the development of customer support admin tools into its own division. After 11 months of working on "the ultimate admin app", the 6 developers have nothing to show for their efforts.

JavaClient/DirectToJavaClient

Your team is in a meeting getting ripped apart by the Chief Technical Officer – they want to know why the project is taking so long. You, either being very good (or very bad) at the game of politics, state that their decision to use EJBs instead of WebObjects is the reason things are taking so long and to prove it, you say you can build the same application in an hour using WebObjects.

Creating the Application

Create a new 'Direct To Java Client Application' project, named OneHour. Add your EOmodel. On the next panel uncheck the **Build and launch now** checkbox, and press **Finish**. Add the `-WOAutoOpenInBrowser NO -WOPort 8088` startup arguments to the application, build, and run.

Technically at this point you're done – you can find and edit any relationship or attribute diagrammed in the EOModel. Without any modification the user interface is confusing though, so let's make a few changes. First, instead of having **Address** and **Customer** as the entities in the main query window, let's use **Customer**, and **Item**; next, we should remove any widgets that display a user's password; let's have Category selection as a combo box, instead of free form text field, and lastly, let's use a text area for an Item's description value instead of a text field.

Go to the **Tool** menu of the client, and select **Assistant**. The assistant has six tabs across the top: Entities, Properties, Widgets, Windows, Miscellaneous, and XML:

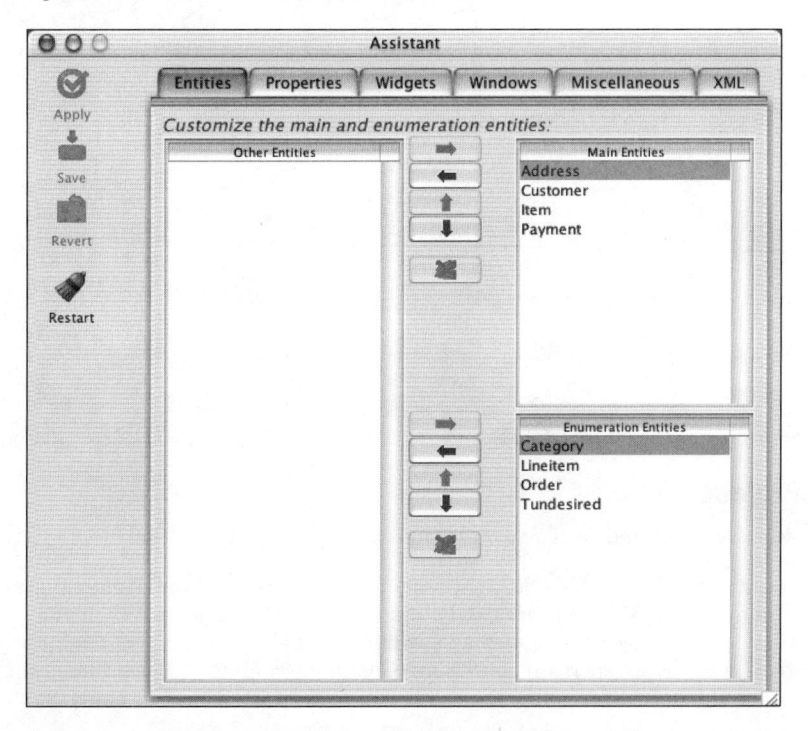

Go to the Entities tab, and remove **Address** from the **Main Entities** list by selecting **Address** from the table, and pressing the left arrow button to the left of the **Main Entities** table. Select Item from the **Other Entities** table, and press the right arrow button. Now add **Category** to the enumeration entities list.

329

To remove the password column from tables which display customer information, you go to the **Properties** tab, and set **Question** to **<All>**, **Task** to **list**, and **Entity** to **Customer**, then remove the line password from the **Property Keys** table on the right. Do the same thing for the **identify**, and **query** tasks.

To use a text area, instead of a text field for editing an item's description attribute: go to the **Widget** tab; set the **task** to **form**; set the entity to **Item**; set the **property key** to **thedescription**; choose **EOTextAreaController** from the **Widget Type** combo box.

These changes are enough for the DirectToJavaClient rules engine to create a very usable interface. Press the **save** button on the left of the assistant, and restart the client (note: the restart button should allow you to restart the client without having to actually shutdown and restart the whole JVM, but as of this writing, there is a bug that keeps this from working). You should now see a query window with two tabs – **Customer**, and **Item**. Fill in a search value, and press the **Find** button at the top; the list at the bottom will become populated with all of the Customer objects that met your search criteria. Double-click on a customer in the results table, and you'll get a form window, where you can edit any of the customers attributes, and also any of the objects that customer has a relationship to. Each relationship appears as a tab in a tab pane. The panel of a to-one relationship simply displays a form panel for the corresponding entity type; the panel of a to-many relationship displays a table listing all of the corresponding objects, and a form panel below the table, which allows you to edit the selected sub-object.

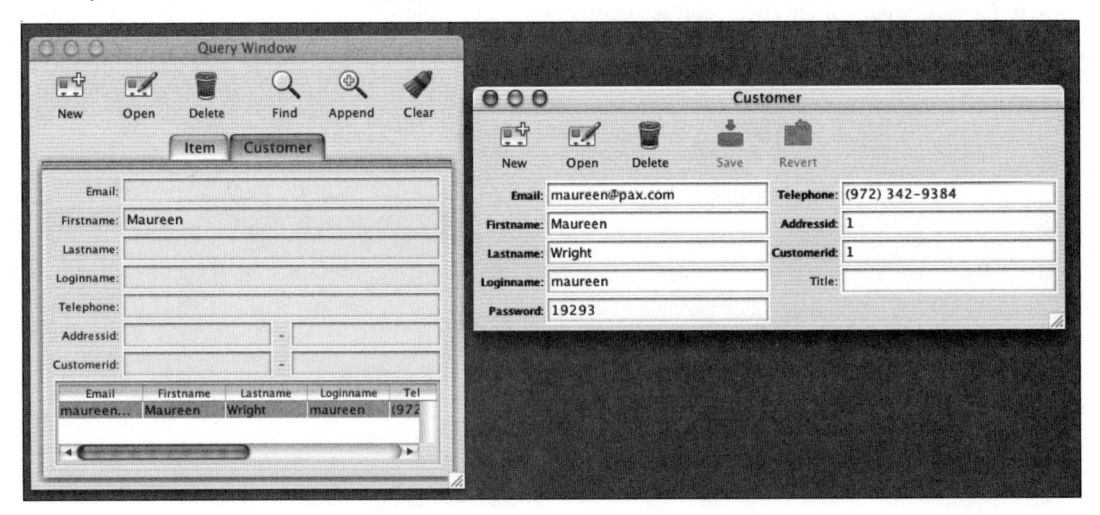

Inside the Project

Bring the Assistant back up, and we'll go over what each tab does in more detail.

- The Entities tab: DirectToJavaClient separates Entities into three distinct types, Main, Other, and Enumeration. Main entities can be thought of as root objects. When you start up a D2JC application it will, by default, display a window that allows you to search for any of the main Entities. In this case our main entities are **Customer**, and **Item**. From these root objects, you should be able to traverse, via relationships, to just about any other entity.

  Enumeration entities usually represent group entities that are frequently selected from a list. For example, a **Country** entity might be considered an **Enumeration** entity – end users would be modifying the object as much as they would be selecting a single country from the list of all countries. In our case we set **Category** as an enumeration entity.

JavaClient/DirectToJavaClient

- The Properties tab: This tab is used to modify what attributes, and relationships should be displayed in different situations. The top combo box, **Question**, allows you to select whether your changes take effect when the window is a dialog box, or a normal window. The second combo box, Task, has four choices: **Form**, **Identify**, **List**, and Query. The Form task relates to what properties will be displayed in the UI when editing an objects values; **Identify** when selecting an object for a to-one relationship; **List** when displaying a group of objects in a table, and **Query** when searching for a specific set of objects. The Entity combo box allows you to select which entity type you're working with.
- The Widgets tab: This tab also has a **task**, and **entity** combo box, but also adds one for **property key**. When you modify the values in this panel, it affects how a specific widget will be drawn in different situations.
- The Window tab: This tab is a cross between the Properties tab, and the Widgets tab. It has the same combo boxes as the Properties tab, but is used to modify the physical properties of the windows that will be created.
- The Miscellaneous tab: This tab allows you to set a couple of default values for all widgets. For example setting the highlight tab to `true` will cause all labels to be drawn in a dark blue.
- The XML tab: Although you can't make any changes to the user interface here, in some ways this is the most important tab. DirectToJavaClient is built on top of the DirectToWeb framework, and uses the same rules engine to generate the user interface.

The client generates specifications, and passes them to the rules engine on the server. Most specifications are based on the entity to display, the task to perform, and the question. The question normally maps to the type of window the interface will be displayed in. On the server the main difference between the DirectToWeb framework and DirectToJavaClient, is that the DirectToJavaClient components generate XML instead of HTML. There's no trick or magic to having WebObjects output XML instead of HTML, simply put XML in your `.wo`'s `.html` file; you can still include `<webobjects>` tags to dynamically generate content.

The XML that gets returned to the client represents a hierarchy of controller objects, all descendants of `com.webobjects.eoapplication.EOController`. The `EOController` class contains the generic code necessary to create and traverse a controller hierarchy.

There are two main subclasses of `EOController` – `EOComponentController`, and `EOEntityController`. `EOEntityControllers` contain a display group, and use the information they find in their XML tag to populate the display group with entities. Subclasses of `EOComponentController` handle creating user interface widgets based on their XML attributes. They also create associations to connect their widgets to display groups found in `EOEntityControllers` found higher up in the controller chain.

In the XML tab you see a list of available specifications, and the XML that the server generates for each of them. A description of all the `EOController` classes and their XML equivalent is beyond the scope of this book, but by looking at the XML generated for different specifications, and using the documentation available from Apple, you should begin to get a feel for how things work.

Summary

In this brief introduction to JavaClient we've walked through three different scenarios showing how you can easily create JavaClient and DirectToJavaClient applications. The first application, `OneWeek`, was relatively low-level and involved manually inserting widgets, connecting outlets and actions and changing Java code. `OneDay` was much easier to create using the `Master Detail` template, but was just as functional and adaptable as the previous application. Finally, you created a DirectToJavaClient application called `OneHour`. This application was even quicker to create and was easily updated on the fly using the `Assistant`.

In the next chapter we will discuss the best ways to manage the data in our applixations.

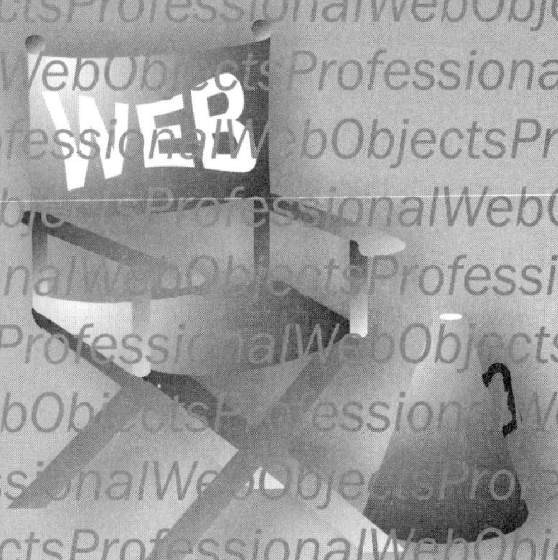
WEB

13
Managing Data

There are many types of data in even a simple program of any software system, and many ways to organize that data. First of all, the physical and logical locations of data are quite varied. Placing data in a particular location brings a set of abilities and restrictions for access to that data. Knowing when to create data *state*, what to put in it, and where to put it, are important skills to possess. Of course, once the state is created, it probably needs to be maintained. Deciding when to update state can also be tricky.

The answers to these questions are very inter-related. For instance, let's say you decide to put a customer's orders in a table in the database. There are many consequences to that decision, common to any data stored in a database:

- ❑ The data values representing the order must conform to the available database storage types. Putting the data for all orders into one table means that this order table must have all the data required for every kind of order.

- ❑ If at some point in the program, the data for a particular customer is loaded into the application, and that customer's orders are needed from the database, then the model should contain a relationship from the customer to the order.

- ❑ If only some users of the application are allowed to view a customer's order, then the application must contain a mechanism to enforce access restrictions.

- ❑ If only certain orders are needed by a particular part of the application, an appropriate mechanism must be selected to retrieve the desired subset of orders.

- ❑ Once certain orders are retrieved by an application, it might need to modify or delete them, and these changes must be consistent with the rest of the data in the database.

- ❑ The same order may need to be accessed by more than one piece of code in the application. If the processing time for making that request is long enough, it might make sense to share the reference to the data.

❏ One of the order data items may distinguish types of orders, such as shipping type. If the application code makes a test on shipping type, then the dependency between code and database content must be handled carefully.

❏ An order may have a shipping address, which may come from a customer record initially. However, an existing order's shipping address should not change when a customer's address changes. This might be accomplished by "breaking" the relationship to the customer's address in the order by inserting a copy of that address in the order.

In this chapter, we are going to cover the issues brought to light by this customer order example. Some of these address database design, but others address how the database design affects the application code. We will examine the consequences of the various database design and code decisions, and offer some examples that illustrate the decision process. We also delve into some basic design principles, to clarify the process and keep it consistent and focused on solving a particular software problem. In short, we cover the management of data from selecting the best data type to selecting the best location for the data. The ideas will be both generally applicable to all such software design endeavors, and specifically applicable to WebObjects applications.

Data Design

Before we attempt to describe the variety of ways to manage data, let's look at some general data design principles. Then, as we discuss different specifics of data locations and data management techniques, we can do so with regard to some generally good ideas that help us make our decisions.

You should note that there are many books written on software design methodologies. We do not go so far as to present a complete design methodology here, only a review of the most important principles.

❏ Use a methodology – a repeatable process for creating software.

❏ Make sure it includes creating a conceptual model with a vocabulary.

❏ Separate things which change from things which do not change.

Repeatable Steps in the Design Process

When you design data, it is important to pick a methodology. WebObjects is such a powerful tool that it is easy to get lost in the details. You can learn all the API's and know how to solve low-level problems, or even how to organize a database and create object-relational maps in model files. However, don't be lulled into thinking that the strength of WebObjects somehow replaces the need for good design practices.

Using a methodology implies that we apply the same methodology for each data design problem that we face. This **repeatability** helps while developing projects, because each new assignment will then benefit from the systematic approach taken in previous projects. The design result of a single developer can be audited by another, checked by a team of developers in a "walk-through" of the design, or even independently recreated and compared.

Of course, independent teams will not produce identical results. Often there are many equally good designs. But, with a repeatable design process, the chances are that each design will afford adequate solutions to the same problem.

With some creative statistics gathering, the repeatable process can produce software metrics – statistical hints that can help predict, among other things, how much work the next project will entail. There is nothing more impressive, short of creating software that does what it is expected to do, than being able to predict how much time and money a software project will take.

A repeatable process is of course a requirement for any standards-based quality control protocol. Part of that process might be to identify the opportunities for creating reusable components and identifying the potential uses for existing reusable components. If true, then repeatability also leads to reusability.

Create a Model Vocabulary

The beginning of good communication is agreeing to a vocabulary. Usually the party who wants the software created is distinct from the party who creates the software. Or, the party who both wants and creates the software may be different from the party who maintains the software. In either case, communication is better when the basic language between both parties is written down and understood.

Now, the same party might specify, create and maintain a software system. But even in this case, they may, in time, forget why they implemented particular parts of the software in the way they did. The solution to this is to create a model vocabulary. Here are the ways that it can help:

- All the people involved in the software development project have a common reference of definitions.
- The descriptions of terms make sense to even the least technical of the participants, often including the client.
- Once the client approves the vocabulary, the designers can move forward with confidence that they have a common understanding of the problem with the client.
- When the client is not satisfied with the functionality of the program, he or she may refer to the vocabulary.
- Designers may analyze requests for change in functionality by comparing design issues against proposed changes in the vocabulary.
- Testers use the vocabulary to validate and inspire the creation of the test cases.

Even if all the "people" involved in the software are just various roles played by one person, the vocabulary is still very helpful. It keeps thoughts organized, allows decisions made early to be remembered after time has passed, and provides continuity to the next developer that takes over the project.

This model vocabulary should contain terms that make sense to the client. Describe both the data and the processes that operate on them. Even describe the users of the system. Save technical terms that only make sense to the software creators to a different document. Don't include references to things like "objects", "classes" or "interfaces" – save these for the design documents.

Pay particular attention to common expressions like name, address, or price. The most common expressions are often the ones that cause the most misunderstanding. Each user assumes that everyone else knows exactly what he or she is saying. You need to pin down the meanings of them at the beginning of the project.

Creating a vague vocabulary is worse than not having one at all. A vague data description will introduce errors in interpretation that will probably not be caught until very late in the development cycle, possibly in production. This is due to the fact that the developers believe that they have a concrete definition, and they will not question its validity. With no vocabulary at all, they're at least forced to go back to the client. It should be possible to determine from the vocabulary any detail required about a particular term. What is often left out, and just as important, is how the terms relate to each other. For data definitions in particular, try to include all of the following information:

Related Data Items

Data items never exist as "islands" of totally independent information. It's the proper association of a variety of data that makes up a substantial part of any software system. Be sure to capture in the vocabulary any term that is directly related to any other. Describe that relationship in terms of any conditions that are required for that relationship to exist.

Data Restriction

To properly select the data representations, various restrictions on the data need to be considered.

- Only certain values need to be used to represent the data.
- Some data items depend on the existence of others.
- Some data items need to be repeated.
- Data items may need be used differently by different users.

Permissible Values

If a rule will suffice to describe the permissible values, use that. At the very *least*, give a list of examples that shows all the important variations in that data item. Remember to stay focused on describing the logical system. Don't confine the definition to a particular implementation data type at this stage. You may discover, for instance, that a particular logical data value may be implemented as several different data types. But you won't know whether that is necessary unless you have the freedom to describe the data as it actually exists in the real world of the problem domain.

Counts and Existence

Describe how many instances of data items might exist. Describe how many of this data item might be required for other related data items. If this vocabulary is describing an existing system that you are trying to automate, include a reference here to how many of this kind of data item already exists. If you are inventing a new system with no historical counts, add some estimates of how many of these you anticipate in a full-scale version of this system. If the number of data items will seriously change over the anticipated life of the application, consider including a more detailed description which allows you to state how many data items may exist at different times in the future.

Access and Modification Rights

Which users can access this data item? If there is enough variety here, it will require some effort designing access privileges to a system. Since we are defining users in this vocabulary, this is where role-based definitions of a user may come in handy. You may only need to specify which user roles have access to this information.

Of course, things could get more complicated. Perhaps, in a particular role, for instance, a user may have permission to create a data item, but not destroy it or update it. Please specify data item access to whatever level is appropriate. Be sure to include every different role of user. This may include a variety of roles, for example:

- Retail customers
- Wholesale vendors
- Accounting auditors
- System administrators

The ways in which the data might be used include:

- Creating new data
- Modifying existing data
- Deleting data
- Fetching data

Use Cases

Use cases provide a mechanism to go beyond the data items and the relationships between data items. They allow a structure for expressing the goals of each individual user role in the system. Taken together, they provide glue that holds the entire software development life cycle together.

Describe the Use Cases

Use Cases get much attention these days, and quite a variety of definitions. The "Extreme Programming" movement makes use of another, more general concept which I will discuss first – the story.

Write a Story

A story is a narrative that describes how the software system is used. It answers the question "Who?" in that it tells the tale of a noble user. It answers "What?" by describing the valiant quest that the user undertakes. It answers "How?" by relaying the actions performed by the user to achieve their quest. It answers "When?" by describing any prerequisite dragon slayings that might be required, or magical data items that might need to be created first.

Use cases in the literature may be defined with much less information than the "story" described above. However, I prefer a good, stout story to a watered-down use case any day. From this point on, we will use the phrase "use case" to a relatively detailed description of one use of the software. The point of the story is to provide the equivalent of a simulation test case for your design. In other words, consider the effects of any design decision with respect to the use case.

One helpful technique to keep use cases simple is to constrain the size of the description. Again, from the Extreme Programming camp, keep the use case contained on one side of a 3" by 5" card. An electronic version might be to describe the use case in 75 words or less.

Whatever process you follow, you will need a use case, a story, or some definition of roles and responsibilities. It doesn't really matter what methodology you use, but you do need some idea of who will have access to the various data records and fields, and what actions they are permitted to perform on that data.

Be Complete

Try to include enough use cases to cover all the possibilities. In the literature, slight variations of a use case (to cover slightly different data inputs, handle error recovery, and so on) are termed scenarios. If you do a thorough job of creating use cases, then the software system design will be complete when all the use cases are satisfied.

In some development workplaces, the use case is actually the unit of work for design, implementation, and testing. Schedules and deliverables are designed around creating use cases, designing use cases, implementing use cases, and creating test plans from the use cases. Users create software change requests based on new or updated vocabulary and use cases. Test designers work from the use cases and the system design to discover problems in the implementation.

In practice, the use cases will never be complete. The client and software developers should work together to keep the use cases up-to-date. As a project progresses, understanding of technology limitations, discovery of new business requirements, or reality of changing availability of money or time can affect what the client wants from the project. The methodology should contain ample opportunities for review of the use cases.

Maintenance

Don't leave out the system maintenance needs from the use cases. Whoever has to keep this system running once it is put into production is just as much a system user as the customer hitting the website over the Internet. But, the maintainer may have very different needs, the ability to change access by roles, the backup and restore of the data, reorganize file system references, and so on. Any action the maintenance user must perform should find its way into a use case. This might include normal backup procedures, emergency procedures, and usage statistics reporting.

Separate the Constant and Variable Data

I apologize for not giving this a proper attribute, but I have read it in several places now and find it to be very valuable advice. When you stop and think about it, this is a very fundamental goal of life and finds expression in much of religion and philosophy. So, why not use it with WebObjects!

Where does it come into play? Almost everywhere. The following are some shining examples.

Constants

What could be more unchanging than a constant? In Java, an instance variable or static variable in a class can be typed `final`. This means that once this value is initialized, neither the code in a method of that class nor any other class that has access to that variable may change it by assignment. One rarely is forced to declare a member variable as `final`. It removes from the variable a perfectly valid operation, which is the assignment of a new value. Why would a programmer give up his right to assign a value to a variable voluntarily?

It is expressing the intent to anyone reading the code or using the code that they should *not* change that value. There may be another value elsewhere that depends on this variable having that value. There may simply be a processing step that behaves unpredictably unless the variable has that value. There may be several pieces of code that need to work together in such a way that they can all depend on that variable having a common value.

The programmer has explicitly separated variable values that are allowed to change from those that are unchanging by affixing a `final` type specifier to a variable declaration. If only all unchanging truths of the universe could be so clearly marked!

Keep in mind, that we are not just discussing Enterprise Objects here. Data representations become implicit or explicit in a software system in a variety of ways. It is not unreasonable to include final values in an Enterprise Object. Say there is a field in an EO that is a `shipping` type. A final array can be created inside that EO that lists specific code values for different `shipping` types. These exist in code so that code that is different per shipping type may distinguish a shipping record by its `shipping` type. This eliminates the need to have the integrity of a piece of code dependent on a `shipping` type display string. One might want to edit the display without having to change the corresponding code that tests for `shipping` type. This can be accomplished by creating final values, encoding the `shipping` type in the EO.

Anything Can Change

Here's another way of looking at data that changes from that which stays the same. There really are no data values that can't be changed. After all, this is all data entered by some human or machine existing in some physical device. Even if it's burned into a circuit, you can burn another circuit representing a different value and replace the old circuit with the new one.

The question becomes, how difficult is it to change the data item? In the case of a constant described above, a programmer may remove the final type specifier, and then make other changes to the code that allow the previous constant variable to take assignments. Mind you, this may have far reaching consequences in many places in data and code. But, it is possible. So, the variable remains constant, until the code is changed.

This is the general principle for isolating and describing things that don't change. What effort does it take to effect the change? For a final variable, we have to recompile code. This probably involves at least stopping the application, changing code, recompiling, redeploying, and starting (assuming you don't want to also test your changes!) In other words, recompiling requires programmer intervention and should be avoided for any routine changes of data item content.

On the other hand, a field in a table of a database that contains a customer's last name is probably changed by the customer. Perhaps the first time the customer enters the name, it is misspelled. This might happen as the customer edits his own profile with a WebObjects application from his browser client. This kind of change should be supported by a use case.

Editor Versus Auditor

Let's say that each order is created in the database, with a relation back to a customer record. Let's also say that there is a report that runs periodically to show each item shipped in a given week, which shows the name of the customer. Let's also say that one of the use cases says an auditor must be able to match the shipping reports back to the orders in the database. Let's say the shipping report did not have a unique customer-identifying number on it, but only the customer information entered in the system at the time the shipping occurred. Now, say the customer has changed his name, but wants an audit performed by the auditor to show him all the orders he has made and all the shipping reports. He won't be able to get his shipping reports unless he remembers the proper original misspelling of his name. In other words, the part of the system responsible for the auditor action unfortunately made a bad assumption. That was, the customer name does not change after a shipping report is created. A thorough exercise of the use cases, comparing the user's ability to change his name, with the auditor's ability to match shipping reports with orders, would have uncovered this bug. The bug was caused, in part, by the assumption that a customer's name doesn't change, when in fact it can easily.

The point of this example is to illustrate how important it is to understand what values should not change with respect to other values. It is incorrect to create a compound primary key for the shipping record based on any component of the user editable user name. An automatically generated primary key for this shipping record is probably the correct choice.

Anything Can Stay the Same

Yet another way of looking at this constancy versus change issue is to look at the periods over which something can remain the same. Of course, measuring a physical timing doesn't make much sense. The important question is: "Between what events in a system can I count on a data item to stay the same?"

This question is especially critical for certain data items. Enterprise Objects that represent database fetch results come to mind. So does any data item that is a common resource between multiple threads. For instance, one does not want to always assume a rapidly accessible "cached" copy of some data item is as fresh as the slowly accessible original data item. Cached data usually becomes stale after a point and needs refreshing from the original. It is essential to know what deciding events determine that point. In between the deciding events, the cached data item is constant.

Class Design

One place that temporary data may reside is in member variables of instances of custom classes that you create. If the data does not need to persist beyond an instance of the application or a user session, then it is not appropriate to use a database for storage via EnterpriseObjects. Otherwise, it is appropriate to use EnterpriseObjects.

If you need to create your own classes to store data, then consider the following questions:

- ❑ "What is the list of attributes that describes everything I ever want to know about this kind of object?" That is, find the non-changing list of attributes for this class. These become the instance variables.

- ❑ "What is the list of all actions I would ever perform on this collection of attributes?" That is, find the non-changing list of actions for this class. These become the instance methods.

- ❑ "Where do I put the data items that I can't predict ahead of time?" That is, find a place to put the attributes that are not unchanging. Java provides a `java.util.Dictionary` object for storing "key-value pairs". WebObjects maintains its own variety of dictionary classes, like `com.webobjects.foundation.NSMutableDictionary`.

- ❑ "What values do I pass in as arguments to a method?" That is, find the data items required by this method that are not in my non-changing list of class attributes. Those become method arguments.

- ❑ "What methods and attributes do I make part of a class and which do I leave to an extension of that class?" That is, find the data items and methods that do not change over the set of all the varieties of this class. These attributes and methods belong in the class. Remember that the method name, return values and argument list are what compose the "signature" which is the design of a method. This can be implemented in different ways in extended classes. Be careful that the extended class always implements the unchanging intention of the method from the base class. Otherwise, this violates the principle of separation of changing from unchanging principle and will make the extended class difficult to manage.

Managing Data

Understand the Available Data Types

Both Java 1.3 and WebObjects via the Foundation classes provide data types to manage a wide variety of data item requirements. The various EO frameworks also contain elements with some consequences for data management. It's beyond the scope of this chapter to provide a complete description of all the available native data types and collection classes. However, we'll discuss some of the basic choices that lead to the use of various data types. Also, watch out for some common mistakes described below.

Java 1.3.1 Types

Remember that Java itself has several native data types for handling logical, text, and numeric data. One of the common things forgotten about a numerical data type is its range. Storing a number that is out of range in a numerical value will usually not produce a runtime error. Instead, a misrepresentation of that data is stored instead. However, accessing that value later will give a different value than the one you intended to store there, leading to much grief. Listed below is a reminder of the native types and their upper and lower limits.

Integer Types

Type	Minimum Value	Maximum Value
byte	-128	127
short	-32768	32767
char	(\u0000) 0	(\uffff) 65535
int	-2147483648	2147483647
long	-9223372036854775808	9223372036854775807

Floating Point Types

Floating types are a little harder to understand. There is a "mantissa" and an "exponent" and a "sign" which combine together to make the entire value. The size of the mantissa determines the number of significant digits. The exponent determines the power of 2 that is used to multiply the mantissa. The sign is simply whether the number is positive or negative. This representation is described most naturally in binary.

Of course, most of us don't deal with base 2 comfortably. So, here is a table that shows the smallest and largest positive numbers that can be stored in either of the two native floating point types, float and double. Note that the values relative to powers of 2 have been converted below into powers of 10.

Type	Significant Digits Binary	Smallest Positive	Largest Positive	Significant Digits Decimal
float	24	$1.17549435 \times 10^{-38}$	$3.40282347 \times 10^{+38}$	6-9
double	53	$2.2250738585072014 \times 10^{-308}$	$1.7976931348623157 \times 10^{+308}$	15-17

The smallest and largest negative integers can be simply found by adding a negative sign to their positive equivalents. Now, there is a concept of "non-normalized" numbers than can squeeze a tiny bit larger than the largest number and a tiny bit smaller than the smallest number. Compilers may vary in when they allow normalized versus non-normalized numbers to be used. The Java Language specification actually allows compilers to support an extended precision data set that may be substituted for the non-extended set. And be careful about the display of formatting routines and formatted to binary conversions for numbers that are "close to the edges" of the representation ranges for the data types. If you would like more information then IEEE 754 is the ultimate reference that defines float and double standards; it can be purchased from http://www.ieee.org/.

The point of all this detail is that any floating point number is likely to not exactly represent the physical quantity that you need for a perfect description of a business state or a business rule. However, if the constraints, as described above, are tolerable, then use the appropriate fixed or floating point data type.

Also note that the purpose of `char` type is to hold a Unicode encoded character. Remember that Java natively represents its strings in a Unicode encoding, which occupies 2-bytes for most characters. This distinction is important when dealing with Java IO framework. `char` and `String` types often hold data which has been encoded to the Unicode encoding, whereas byte data type is used to hold data from arbitrary encodings.

Each of these native data types has an object wrapper class counterpart. For instance, the integer data type has a `java.lang.Integer` class. The wrappers can be very useful when you have a value that might be undefined. A variable of type `Integer` can hold a `null` object reference, which can indicate an undefined value; a variable whose type is native `int` cannot.

Floating for Dollars

A particular common mistake to make with money is to use a floating point value for dollars. Remember that certain values of cents, like 3 cents, when saved as dollars, are saved as 0.03 dollars. The value 0.03 as a float or double value will be represented by a binary value which is slightly less than 0.03. Consequently, comparisons on that value or arithmetic operations on that value may give undesirable results. These are due to round-off errors, which accumulate in the process of, say, adding a list of numbers.

What are the alternatives? If you only need accuracy to cents, then why not use cents in the calculation? Save the values in `int` type variables. There will be no round-off errors. Be sure and check the maximum values you may need to store and use `short`, `int`, or `long` as appropriate. This solution is also very fast when it comes to calculations involving these values.

Another way to deal with the numbers is to use arbitrary precision arithmetic. Note that the programmer does not have to define the precision explicitly. This allows exact representation of cents or any other decimal value without the use of the IEEE 754 standards for floating point. While they do maintain accuracy, they do so at a cost. They can take up many more bytes per number, and also are much slower to use in calculations than the native integer or floating point types. This is because the hardware on any microprocessor running a Java virtual machine supports directly the Java native floating point types (or something very close to them). Arbitrary precision is not supported directly in hardware, so software routines must do more work to handle the extra digits and do it more slowly. Watch out what you get with EOModeler when you start with a database schema and generate the classes. If the Java data type in the EOModel for a floating point value is specified as `BigDecimal`, then you might be in for some performance penalties when you use this value in a calculation. The Java library supplied class for arbitrary precision floating point numbers is `java.math.BigDecimal`. Java supplies `java.math.BigInteger` for arbitrarily large integers.

Java Collections

With Java SDK 1.1.8 and beyond, there is a very useful set of collection classes and interfaces defined in the package `java.util`. The classes `java.util.ArrayList` and `java.util.Hashmap` are especially useful.

`ArrayList` gives you a variable-length array, in which you may store instances of an Object or its extensions. If it makes sense to find the element again by remembering its position in the list, then `ArrayList` is a good choice. `ArrayList` also works if you don't care about an element's position in the list, but simply need to conveniently operate on each element of the list via an iterator.

`HashMap` is more useful when the identifier for accessing the data is naturally a name rather than a number. The object you store is the *value* and a `String` object representing the name of the object is the *key*. When the object is required, use the key to retrieve it. Another useful feature of `HashMap` is that you can have a `null` key, as well as a `null` value.

If you have your own custom object you would like to use for a key in the `HashMap` (instead of `String`), just remember to create a reasonable `equals()` method and `hashcode()` method for the class of the keys.

Neither `ArrayList` nor `HashMap` are automatically synchronized for access by multiple threads. This is only a problem if you design your code with multiple threads that may be making structural modifications (inserting or deleting items) to the same `ArrayList` or `HashMap`. If you want to use these collections from multiple threads, then you can either synchronize calls to them on some common object, or you can use a special constructor to add synchronization to all the methods of the `ArrayList` or `HashMap`. These collections, of course, work faster when not synchronized.

The older `Vector` class is pretty much replaced these days by `ArrayList`, mostly because `ArrayList` is not synchronized, and so outperforms `Vector`.

WebObjects Foundation Collections

WebObjects began life way before there was a Java, much less a Java 1.2 SDK with Collections. So, the Foundation framework, `com.webobjects.foundation`, for historical reasons contains its own collection classes. You must learn to live with them, because many of the other frameworks use them too.

The array functionality is handled by `NSArray` and `NSMutableArray`. If you need to alter the structure of an array after it is created, then you need an instance of `NSMutableArray`. `NSArray` instances, once constructed, do not allow elements to be added or deleted. In the same way, `hashMap` functionality is provided by `NSDictionary` and `NSMutableDictionary`.

As mentioned before, you may want to use an arbitrary key to fetch a particular value from a member variable. If so, then use `NSDictionary` or `NSMutableDictionary`. Use the latter if you need to add or delete data after you have created the instance.

One thing to note about the difference between the Java and WebObjects variety of collections is the way they handle `null`s. In general, Java Collection containers deal with `null` object references in arrays and `HashMap`s comfortably, while in the WebObjects Foundation classes, `null` object references are generally forbidden. This can sometimes be the deciding factor as to which variety of collection objects you choose.

Designing the Methods

If you needed custom classes and have chosen data types for your member variables, then you should add appropriate methods for accessing (`get()` methods) and modifying (`set()` methods) the member variables.

I recommend using the JavaBean style of interface for data items that are gathered together in classes. Use `get()` and `set()` accessors – even when you don't have to. Say you have a member variable:

    String name;

although you can use this value in an expression in any method you create in this class, use the `getName()` method instead. Similarly, you could set the value `name` with the assignment operator:

    name = defaultName;

but you should use the `setName()` method instead:

    setName(defaultName);

One very simple reason for doing this is for debugging purposes. A frequent kind of bug tracking exercise involves determining when a data item changes. If that data item happens to reside in an instance of a class, and its values are always set with a `set()` accessor, then it is easier to find the events at which the data item is modified. Simply set a breakpoint on the `set()` accessor, and you can trace every instance where the data item might change.

You should name methods clearly. A hint can be taken from the old Objective-C naming convention. There, because of the syntax of a function call, the name of the method included an action followed by names for all the arguments in the order they were called. This has the benefit of making it trivial to remember what arguments to pass in a method call. It also motivates you to design simple interfaces to methods that don't require extravagantly long argument lists. A disadvantage of this is that you can't use the same method name to accommodate the feature of "method overloading," where different methods can be implemented with the same name, but different combinations of data types.

Now that WebObjects is Java based, you might take advantage of a useful documentation generator – Javadoc Other automatic documentation tools are available (for example, HeaderDoc). Automatic documentation is wonderful for those who have to use your interfaces, those who have to implement your code, and those that have to read your code to maintain it. The most important part about managing data is communicating what it means to all interested parties. It is particularly useful in method documentation to comment about any assumptions you make about the input data, as well as describing the results and how they depend on the inputs.

Designing the User Interface

In an ideal world, we have a clean separation between user interface (the way data is presented and manipulated) and the data model (the representation and persistence of the data itself). In the "Model View Controller" paradigm, there is another clean separation – controller – which serves as an coordination point between the data model and the views.

With this ideal situation in mind, it sounds as though you should be able to design user interfaces independently of the underlying model. However, have you ever worked on a WebObjects project where a separate graphic design company designs the user interfaces? Unless the efforts of user interface design are carefully coordinated with the data model, it is possible to get into trouble. Sometimes a party in charge of only graphic design may make assumptions about what data can be easily and efficiently displayed together on the same page. When the back-end programmer attempts to implement the display, various problems can occur. For instance:

- Too much information to retrieve in a reasonable time.
- No feedback is available for user data entry validation.
- Complex relationships between user interface elements are difficult to keep synchronized.
- Space is too small to accommodate the size of the maximum size of the data elements on the smallest supported screen sizes.

A particular project comes to mind to illustrate this. A car company wants to display how much their car costs, depending on what options you want selected. Sounds simple, right? However, the interactions between various sets of options have dependencies (one option requires others) and restrictions (you can't have the value of option a if a particular value for option b is selected). The result is that in order to show option selection choices properly on a single page, and not take 30 minutes per query to find the right option choices to display, a lot of work had to be done. Special indexes have to be created to filter the option possibilities periodically, and a special controller layer was added to select options through the special indices.

This is the case where a situation that seemed like a relatively simple user interface ended up requiring extensive work on the data item side.

Other issues can arise regarding the use of a web browser for a client interface. It can be very tricky to design a user interface that behaves the same with a web browser as it would as a desktop application. Attempting to include client code as JavaScript is possible. But anything other than the most trivial examples requires extreme care to work properly across even a few different combinations of browser vendor, browser version, and browser platform.

The lesson here is to keep the interfaces extremely simple, honoring the limitations of the technology. Even if this means envisioning the user interactions in a different way, creating more pages that are each simpler, or sending the web page design back to the drawing board. Be involved in the user interface design process, even as the architect or data model designer.

Direct To Java Client has some promise for being able to make a web-based application more like a desktop-based one. But it requires that the proper Java environment exists on the client machine, which may be easy to guarantee on a corporate intranet. On some platforms, you can count on Java 1.2 to be available if not installed on the platform. Unfortunately, the rather large installed base of Macintoshes with OS 9 and earlier will never have a Java VM greater than Java 1.1.8.

Data Storage Considerations

In this section, we'll examine the different locations data can reside in your system. Then, we'll analyze what makes one place different from another. Last, we'll look at how these differences should affect the way you design your software.

Chapter 13

Where Are the Possibilities?

The data storage can reside in any internal or external memory location, such as:

- Database
- URL
- File System
- Enterprise Object
- Application Member Variable
- Session Member Variable
- Cookie
- Other Locations

What Makes Each Location Different from the Others?

The different places can be distinguished by the following characteristics:

- Some provide persistence of the data across multiple application instances, while some may only be valid inside a single call of a method.
- Some allow data to stand alone, while others may require synchronization with data in a different place.
- Some of them can be in places accessible by only particular kinds of users.
- Some places restrict access to the methods of some classes.
- Some of them are obvious and intentional, while some are subtle and hidden.
- Some of them keep data constant, but only between certain events. To put it a slightly different way, some data can only be updated on certain events.

Look for the above considerations in the descriptions of the different possible storage locations for data in a WebObjects application.

Databases

The first place WebObjects programmers think about when storing data is the database. Since the database is such an important place for data items, the discussion about this will be rather lengthy. So, let's examine the persistence properties of the database in WebObjects.

Object-Relational Mapping

One value of Enterprise Objects is the ability to map Java-oriented data to and from relational database oriented data. Implicit in this is the ability to save values of Java objects to a database and restore the values of Java objects from a database. This happens most easily in WebObjects with a database and data stored in instances of extensions of `EOGenericRecords` or `EOCustomObjects`. It requires creating an EOModel to explicitly define how you want the mapping to work; this was shown in Chapter 5 where an EOModel was created.

It requires, for all practical purposes, two layers of classes for the Enterprise Objects. Any custom code added for a persistence class ought to live in a separate class from the automatically generated classes that EOModeler creates for you. This way when anything changes in the model file that affects the automatically generated code, you don't have to re-enter all your changes into the automatically re-generated code.

Stored Procedures – a Good Thing

Enterprise Objects provides you with a profound layer of database independence. If you write your code in the proper spirit of Enterprise Objects, then you can switch database vendors, and the code that depends on the Enterprise Objects does not have to change. If you write code that takes advantage of features specific to a particular database, like a stored procedure in a database, then you are not so lucky. All stored procedures must be rewritten for the new database. Different database vendors have their own ways of implementing stored procedures and their own flavors of SQL and as such it makes difficult to port code that, for example, was written for Oracle into SQL Server. Also, features may have been used that are peculiar to a certain database vendor.

Stored procedures are not always to be avoided, either, even though they increase the difficulty of porting from one database to another. Databases are generally fast at finding result sets for a particular SQL based query. With Enterprise Objects and no stored procedures, we frequently find ourselves fetching too much data into some `EOEditingContext`, either directly or indirectly, and pulling out what we need with Java code. There is an extra performance penalty on the Java virtual machine, executing code less efficiently than a database engine would. Then there is the extra bandwidth required to pump all that extra information across the database connection into the application, which must then dispose of data it shouldn't have had to request in the first place. Generally, a stored procedure executed on the database might have done the job much faster, and delivered less data to a less burdened Java virtual machine.

Databases Are a Shared Resource

A database has another desirable property – the ability to manage database transactions. For single database operations, Enterprise Objects and the `EOEditingContext` (we discussed this in Chapter 8) do a good job of managing transactions for you. But beware of the oversimplified examples that catch an Exception when asking an editing context to `saveChanges`, then print an error message and continue. You must plan a consistent strategy for dealing with cases where updating the database or fetching from the database fails. This includes choosing a pessimistic or optimistic locking strategy. This includes automatic recovery attempts. It also may include different routes through the pages to handle notification and presentation of recovery options to the user.

The database is likely to be shared by all the editing contexts in a single instance of your WebObject application, and instances of your WebObjects application, but also by other WebObjects and even other application servers or SQL scripts. Pay particular attention to what happens when an administrative user attempts to access parts of the database that another user is using; this may cause problems with data integrity due to the way some databases implement locking.

Independence of Database Content

A database ought to be consistent and self-sufficient. It's great that you have WebObjects to help you write database-enabled applications. But try to keep the information in the database so complete that a completely different application server could use the database too. In other words, try not to design a data item that is dependent on a WebObject and then have other items in the database depend on it.

And, of course, use the database's ability to apply integrity constraints very early on in the development process. You are more likely to introduce inconsistencies into your database when you are first testing your code than when your code is thoroughly tested.

Here is another helpful hint on database integrity constraints. When EOModeler generates database constraints on some database platforms (Oracle comes to mind), the name assigned to the generated constraint is constructed from table and column names. It is easy to end up with a database constraint whose name is so long that the underlying database system can't use the constraint!

Elsewhere in this chapter, I advised you to use long names in methods to make them more self-documenting. Don't take that advice with database column names. Short is sweet! Check with the database vendor documentation to find out what the maximum integrity constraint name is. When you generate SQL from the EOModel, check the display of the SQL generated and look for the longest constraint name you can find, it should correspond to a long column name for some table. Then, after you execute the SQL to set the constraints, use your database tool to check the long constraint to make sure it made it in its entirety into your database.

WebObjects Applications Are Not Independent

Remember that all the Enterprise Object classes normally have their code generated by EOModeler from the database schema itself. So, even though the database can stand alone, the WebObjects application can be totally broken by even the slightest change to the database schema. As long as the WebObjects application uses a database, it is very dependent on the integrity of the database, as well as the parallel structure between the database schema and the Enterprise Object derived classes.

Databases With Dependencies and Synchronization

Sometimes, you don't want an entirely independent database. This usually means that some external reference is required. Perhaps the data item in the database is a URL to a web resource. Perhaps, it is a reference to a file on a local file system. This opens up the possibility that the database content can be out of synchronization with the outside world unless you and your DBA (database administrator) have strategies to keep this information up-to-date.

Where Is That String?

The less obvious case is when code also depends on content of the database. A qualifier for an editing context fetch specification may hard code a search for US in order to determine whether a user had specified his address selection with a country value indicating the United States of America. If, later, someone (with appropriate privileges) decides that the abbreviation in the database for United States should be USA, and changes it, then the search looking for US will never find it. To find this value in the code, you must do a string search for US in any source code file that might have a hard-coded fetch specification in it. Of course, since the fetch specification takes a string expression for the qualifier, you could easily refer indirectly to US from some other data item, in which case it may take even longer to track down.

No Fake IDs

The moral of the story here is this. If you have a list in the database, and your code needs to uniquely identify items in the list, then the table containing that list needs a column for a unique item ID that identifies that item. It should not to be the other unique ID (primary key) associated with the row for that list item. The reason you can't use the primary key is this: dropping the table and adding it again, or deleting the rows in the table and adding them back, may generate another set of primary keys. They will be unique, of course, but they may be different than the first set of primary keys. Since you want your code to continue to work even if you have to restore the database from a backup, you shouldn't use primary key values in your code. (Separate the item ID's which should never change from the primary keys, which might change. Sound familiar?)

Now it is true that primary keys can be designed to be real data, like a social security number. But social security numbers are recycled and hence do not uniquely identify a person for the long term. If you allow user-supplied data to be primary key values, then you must catch the inevitable exception that is thrown when you try to save a record to a database that does not have a unique primary key. This may be more trouble than it is worth.

From the earlier argument about country having the value US, you also want to keep a separate display string for each item in the list. This is what will appear in reports or popup menus, which are related to this list. They can be edited and re-spelled to your hearts content, and your code won't have to change. For lists of items that may ever need to be displayed in something other than increasing alphabetical order, I usually include another column of unique keys that controls the sorting order. This way, the list can be arbitrarily rearranged, and I still don't have to change the code!

Make Them Choose

One more synchronization issue: bend over backwards to use fixed lists whenever you anticipate searching for that value. Never create an opportunity for a user to insert "US", "USA", "United States", "U.S.A.", and "America" in the country code if you ever hope to do a search by country. Either use fixed choice lists, like radio buttons, popup menus, or browsers. If you have to allow free form text, please validate it to an appropriate fixed list item, and let the user review your substitution and confirm that is correct, or re-enter the information. Just make sure it doesn't get into the database in such a way that several different values all are effectively the same search key.

Accessibility To the Database

All databases come with some sort of security scheme, whereby different database users have different levels of access. Some allow a very detailed breakdown of database functionality assigned to a user. That user is assigned some identification information like user id and password to gain access to the database.

In WebObjects, it is more common to toss the concept of individual user access and fine control over user actions out the window. The "application" makes a connection or a pool of connections to the database, and hence has to "login" as a special user. All users of the application hence get the same level of access as far as the database is concerned. That doesn't mean that the WebObjects application itself can't implement its own business rules for user access – and they frequently do. But, that is access to the application, not the database itself.

Typically, an application that needs users with individual permissions implements it own access mechanism. One way is to create an entity of roles. Create another entity of permissions. A user can be assigned to a single role through a one-to-one relationship. A role can be assigned permissions via an association table with a one-to-many relationship pointing in each direction. The administrative code to add a new user can then enter not only the user ID and password, but also assign the user a role. (You could even do multiple roles if it makes sense for your application.) The administrative application can also assign permissions to roles.

User interface code can have `WOConditional` dynamic elements controlling which elements appear on a page according to the permissions allocated to the role of the current user assigned to a page's session.

Bolders, Pebbles, and Sand

To allow different levels of access to the database, with a coarse resolution, make separate WebObjects applications. For instance, create an administrative application to accompany a customer application. The administrative application could access the database with different login information, and hence different privileges, from the customer application. Of course, the default place to store connection information is in the EOModel, which is probably going to be shared between the two applications. So, it is probably best not to use the connection information there if you are going to use database security to enforce restrictions between administrative and customer access.

Chapter 13

For a finer resolution you might try this. It is possible that a WebObjects application could be designed in the following manner. A single session could have its own database connection to the database, which that session's editing context could use. The web application could prompt the user for her actual database user ID and password. This would prevent you from having to use a completely different mechanism for securing access to the application than for securing access to the underlying database. However, it would be more work and require extra database connections, since they wouldn't be shared between users, which could slow things down. But you can't get much finer-grained than that!

In the roles and permissions example above, you are providing "action" level access. Each action is controlled by a permission connected to a role. The database login scenario would only give "data" level access. The former is more flexible and efficient.

The Database is Your Friend

Databases can be edited outside your WebObjects application. Totally different application servers can access the database. They can be backed up and restored independently. They have their own constraint mechanism for catching problems as they occur.

But, someone with sufficient privileges can alter the structure of a database without "notifying" the programmer that a change has occurred. Care must be taken in an application server to respond appropriately to violations of the constraints. The database is a shared resource, so you must address all the problems surrounding access of the same data items by different users.

The URL

The main way to use a URL is to embed the data within the URL itself. When you do this, it is now called a URI (Uniform Resource Identifier). If you look at the URL on a search engine such as Google, when you do a search, the query words are placed in the URL and then sent to the search engine. The problem with this is that the URL on various operating systems is limited in its length, typically to about 256 characters in length. However, with the introduction of web services, all of this may change and URLs may be used as data stores more often.

You can also use a web page as a data store. However, HTML does not have any meta data associated with it, and thus to find the information on the page can quite difficult as various different web servers parse HTML differently. They can be also coded using different versions of the HTML so the information may be in a different place on the web page, so finding the information may become difficult.

Of course, unless the web site is your own, you may have no control over when the content of a web site changes. You may have no control over when the link becomes bad – that is, the server returns a "404 File Not Found" error response, or some such.

However, for URLs that refer to resources for which you do have control, or for "normative" references that are not likely to change, go ahead and use URLs.

The File System

If a data item is complex, it may not make sense to put it in a field of a database. Modern databases do support some variation of the binary large object. These can hold arbitrary data chunks, but with restrictions. For instance, a particular database product may only allow one column in any table to hold such a `blob`. Sometimes, the `blob` cannot be indexed easily. Worst of all, the data cannot be viewed with a simple database viewer.

However, some products exist specifically for holding large objects and indexing them in databases. If you find one of those products suits your needs, then feel free to store proprietary information in `blob`s in the database.

Managing Data

So, a file system is a convenient place to store complex or proprietarily formatted information. The usual need is to provide access to an entire file as a standalone document, and not to some portion of a file's content. Again, this is slippery, because file system locations can change at the whim of the file's owner.

I have found it useful in the past to keep collections of files specified hierarchically in the referencing data item. Let's say I have a set of banner images to display and I want to keep them in the file system. My means of organizing the banners is one directory for the entire set of images, within that directory there is another directory for each advertiser, and then the individual banners for each advertiser are in their respective folders. In the database, I have a field that allows me to specify a string for the overall location of banners. Then for each advertiser, there is a column for banner directory name. Each banner ad image is referred to by its filename. To access a particular banner, I concatenate the appropriate strings together from overall location, advertiser directory followed by image name. If I need to move the whole directory structure to a different file system place, I can do so fairly easily as long as I also set the overall location directory path name in the overall location data item in the database.

Another possible alternative to a file system store is really more of an alternative to the URL example above. A product called WebDAV allows you treat a web server as a file system. It can be administered remotely and provides easy access to common resources for team programming efforts. You reference data via URLs but serve and administer the data through the web server.

Enterprise Objects

Enterprise Objects (EO) are normally only used to conveniently map data to and from table/column structure to a class/member variable structure. But even the simplest EOs also include relationships. The relationships return results from one entity based on matching values of attributes in one entity to values of a corresponding attribute in another entity. The Enterprise Object system does its best to make sure that simple table fetches and some slightly more sophisticated SQL queries are handled as simple references to the Java object graph of Enterprise Objects.

Application Member Variables

WebObjects applications have instances of `WOApplication` to provide high-level access to data items that are accessible by many other WebObjects instances in the system. In particular, instances of `WOSession` always have access to the `WOApplication` that created them. By "Application Member Variable" I mean considering an instance of `WOApplication` as a place to store data items.

It might be best to consider initializing `WOSession` instances. What might a session need that might change from the beginning of one session to the next? Any meta data about sessions might be a likely candidate. Information such as average lengths of sessions, number of sessions in a recent time period, number of recent database timeout errors might be useful to effect the initialization of a new session.

An application starts up only once, and can therefore load information that won't change during the application's life. This might be data items loaded from the file system or some other non-database source. Loading them in the application reduces the amount of time spent accessing that data (compared to loading it separately for each session). It also reduces the amount of memory required. If the data items are the same, they don't need to occupy multiple bytes on the same machine.

I specifically excluded database information above because it needs careful consideration. Remember that Enterprise Objects containing data items fetched from a database each have a home – an editing context. A `WOApplication` instance needs to create its own editing context if it plans on fetching EOs during their lifetime. There is no particular concern here if the application needs the EOs for its own functionality.

The problem arises when other subordinates to the application need the data. It is tempting, for instance, to load an array of commonly used data items that won't change over the run of the application, and store those items as member variables in the application. Then, later, when a session needs access to that list of data, it simply refers to it by means of the session's access to its own application.

Let's say the session is trying to access EOs in an editing context of the application. Let's say further that it tries to create a relationship to one of those EO data items in the application. The session has its own default editing context. Most simple WebObjects examples show a session doing all of its fetching from the default editing context. The session default editing context is not the same as the editing context created in the application. Therefore two EOs representing exactly the same database, where one is in the application editing context and one in the session editing context are *not* the same EO. What's more, one cannot be added to a relationship of the other – an error will result.

You need to pay careful attention to the advice and techniques given in the section *Working With Objects Across Multiple EOEditingContexts* in the Apple-supplied documentation entitled *EOEditingContext Concepts*. This is a tricky issue and must be handled with care. Suffice to say, there are ways of creating a second EO in a second editing context that represents the same data as the first EO from the first editing context. The methods that handle this are in *EOUtilities*.

If you know exactly what extra data items you want to store at the application level at design time, you may add these variables to your own extension of the *WOApplication* object. If you need something more dynamic, *WOApplication* also implements `takeValueForKey` and `valueForKey`. Just add your own data on-the-fly to your application's own implicit dictionary.

Remember that a well-designed WebObjects application is pretty stable these days. Make sure you do not depend on the creation of new instances of an application instance in order to update some not-so-frequently changing data. (In some older version of WebObjects, you had to restart applications on a regular basis, due to some framework memory management issues.) It is better to add a mechanism to the application that will periodically refresh data. Actually there are some methods in EOF that allow you to set expiration dates on data so that it will automatically refresh. This is particularly helpful if you have an administrative application that can alter a few key application-level parameters to fine-tune its operation. If you want things to happen sooner than a predetermined periodic rate would allow, you might consider using an event notification mechanism for your application.

The Session

Here we are speaking of using an instance of your extension of `WOSession` (which we will refer to as "session") as a place for storing data items. This was seen in the `WOGreeting2` example in Chapter 3. There are the same consequences for including these items as member variables as in the application. They can only change structure at design time. For the session, they only last as long as a session lasts. Remember, a session has an automatic timeout value (although you can override the default or turn off the feature). Tuning your application by setting the expiration time for a session is a good idea. Having sessions never expire would normally not be a good idea, unless you had some mechanism of your own to delete sessions that you could detect as expired. Extra sessions just occupy memory resources until they are deleted, so your WebObjects server could run out of memory prematurely if sessions lived forever.

Otherwise, it is hard to know when a session for a particular user is complete. Unless you include in your user interface design an explicit "logout" functionality, there is no way of getting feedback from the browser client side that the user is through with the session. Providing such functionality is a good idea, as it lets the user manually assist your efforts to keep the minimum number of sessions open at any one time. Just remember, the session timeout value or some similar mechanism must also be in place, because you cannot compel the user to log-out of a session.

The other thing with a session is its implicit dictionary to save and retrieve data whose natural identifiers are not known until runtime.

If you want to use Direct To Web, you should probably only use one editing context – that is, the session's default editing context. It is quite a challenge to get D2W to deal with alternative editing contexts.

Another caution about the session involves object references to it. Any class that has reference to a session can hold references to it. A `WOComponent` extension can get to its own session, which might be cached. It is a bad idea to cache an object reference, such as a `WOSession`, in an object, like a `WOComponent`, if the first object normally maintains any references to the second object. Since `WOSession` instances indirectly hold references to `WOComponents` that are used to display that session's information, there is potential for disaster. If Java object A refers to Java object B in one of its member variables (or indirectly through another object reference), and Java object B refers similarly to A, a circular object reference exists. Not all Java virtual machines can detect these properly, so when Java garbage collection time comes, the session and the component may never get deleted, because they each have active references to each other.

This may be a rare occurrence in WebObjects 5 because the latter uses Java 1.3, and because of the way that later JVM's do garbage collection. But, it is still a good idea to set variables containing object references to `null` after the reference is no longer needed. This improves garbage collection performance and prevents the use of a non-`null` reference to an object that is already deleted.

The Cookie

It is possible to save information that would normally be put into a session member variable or the session dictionary, into the client browser instead. This happens using a cookie. Cookies can store information, similar to what you could store in member variables of your session. Actually, it's more like the implicit session dictionary, since you can name cookies whatever you like, and put whatever text content you want. You might not want to use it to serialize an object for a value in a cookie; strings are better.

`com.webobject.appserver.WOCookie`

Create one of these for your session. Either use the constructor or the shortcut static method in that class `cookieWithName(String name, String value)`. Create more than one cookie to store multiple values. At some point in the request/response cycle before the final response is returned (perhaps in the page component's `appendToResponse()` method), call the response's `addCookie()` method as many times as necessary to add all the cookies required to the response. Later when a request comes back (perhaps in the page component's `takeValuesFromRequest()` method, call one of the cookie accessors of the request: `cookieValues()`, `cookieValueForKey()` or `cookieValuesForKey()`. At this point you should probably have a method in the session to call to notify the session of all the cookie values it has retrieved. This way the session can pick up where it left off.

Two points need to be made here. First, if you are really going to use the cookie mechanism to save and restore a session, pretty much all of your custom member variables in your own subclass of `WOSession` are going to be encoded to and decoded from a cookie. This may prove to be a lot of work, especially if some of your session state is composed of EO references. You may have to use the cookie values to imply what EO references need to be restored from the database.

What might be simpler is to only store a session restoration identifier in the cookie, and save all the values keyed by that identifier in the database. This probably speeds the response time to the user, both in posting requests and receiving responses. Of course, then you are not taking advantage of using the browser client to store the session state.

Chapter 13

The grim reality is that many people are paranoid about cookies and so they deactivate them, and some don't go to web-sites that require them. So, if you are using them for a public web-site, you may get reduced traffic. Besides security problems, the cookie list from each browser can be big and thus noticeably consume bandwidth. Also, there are limits to the length of cookies that can be passed, which are browser dependent.

It is more reasonable to try to use cookies in a corporate intranet environment. Here, the policy can be enforced to require the use of cookies to access the corporate software. There is also the ability of WebObjects to direct your session to a different application server in a WebObjects cluster if cookies are being used to save session state.

Other Locations

It is hard to keep data out of the other places, but it will happen. Almost anytime an expression contains a hard coded constant, the programmer should examine whether anyone is going to a) be confused by that constant or b) want to change it. For instance, if an expression needed to convert days to seconds, it could do this:

```
int days = seconds * 86400;
```

Where does the "magic number" 86400 come from? It would be better to declare a constant:

```
final int SECONDS_PER_DAY= 86400; //the number of seconds in a day
```

and compute:

```
int days = seconds * SECONDS_PER_DAY;
```

In either case, the hard-coded constant should be given a proper name, a place, and documentation.

Such expressions can appear in almost any line of code in any method of any class. They can also appear in places such as stored procedures, which is still code, but running on the database server instead. Take it on as an exercise during the code review or code re-writing process to look for hard coded constants and give them the attention they deserve.

Other more subtle things to check are simply assumptions in the code that imply a hard coded constant without the benefit of an explicit expression containing it! Think about creating a fixed size array in one part of your code, then adding lines to initialize each of its members. Just the existence of 4 lines of code to initialize that array implies that the size of that array is 4, no matter what the actual dimension is. Should the array be changed to a size of 5, you will not get a compiler error and perhaps not a warning, and no error when you don't initialize the fifth element. You may not even get an error when you access that fifth element if it is a native data type. Even using it may not cause a problem if it is a numeric type and zero is a reasonable value for that array position most of the time.

Try to keep track of all places in your code that are joined by a common assumption. Add comments on **both** sides of such an assumption. Say what the consequences are of changing a value here to other data or code that exists over there. If possible, design data representations so that this linking of data values to each other or data values in one place and code in another is kept to a minimum. If it is necessary, document these things thoroughly wherever one end of the dependency is exposed.

Better still, write unit tests in both methods that are designed to fail if the assumptions are not met. Then the developer will catch the problem at unit test time and can see the failure occurred on the assumption testing code line.

Summary

There are many places to insert and retrieve data in a WebObjects application. Many of the principles and thinking patterns we have discussed, apply to data modeling in general and implementation patterns applicable to many different languages and frameworks.

- Keep aware of just when data changes and who might change it.
- Isolate the data that changes from that which does not.
- Watch out for common Java problems, like circular object references, and using the wrong data types.
- Watch out for database related intricacies inherent in editing contexts, transaction handling and properly identifying data.
- Be aware of the limits of web browsers, as compared to desktop applications.
- Keep things simple and well documented, especially relationships and assumptions that apply across different places.

Now that we have discussed how to manage data, we shall look at how we can managethe deployment of our WebObjects projects.

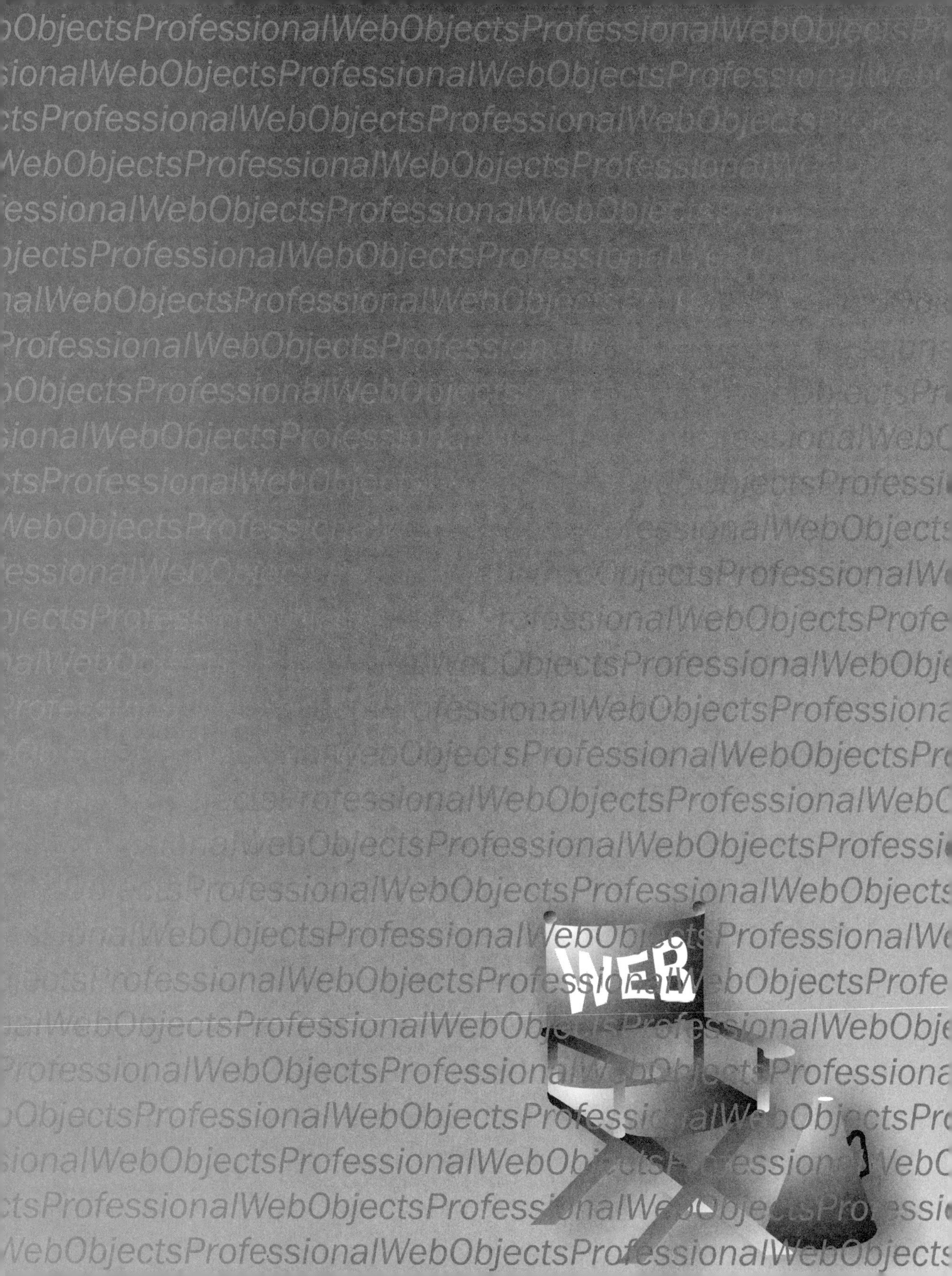
WEB

14

Managing the Deployment Environment

WebObjects comes equipped with graphical tools to assist developers in the deployment process. WebObjects 5.0 has undergone a lot of changes since version 4.0. These changes have made the deployment tools more intuitive, and the deployment environment more reliable.

The deployment environment is very flexible and allows individuals to deploy distributed and non-distributed applications with ease. This chapter will focus on deploying WebObjects 5.0 on the Mac OS X, Windows 2000 Pro, and Sun Solaris operating system. We will also look at deployment on the Oracle database and the Apache web server.

In this chapter we will also:

- Use the `JavaMonitor` tool to set up applications
- Discuss the role of wotaskd in the deployment environment
- View deployment architectures
- See how the web server fits into the deployment environment

From Development To Deployment

WebObjects 5.0 offers developers the choice of developing applications on either the Mac OS X, or the Windows 2000 Professional operating system. Once the application has been developed and tested, it can be deployed on Mac OS X, Windows 2000, or Sun Solaris systems.

Chapter 14

In the install documents, Apple states that the WebObjects 5.0 deployment software can be installed on any platform that has the Java 2 Platform, Standard Edition 1.3. One important fact to keep in mind is that Apple only tested WebObjects 5.0 on three platforms which were:

- Mac OS X Server
- Windows 2000 Professional with Java SDK 1.3
- Sun Solaris v 2.8

Some WebObjects developers have managed to install WebObjects 5.0 on RedHat Linux (v 7.1). Although this is possible, it should be noted that Apple does not officially support this platform and therefore if your application encounters problems in deployment, Apple Iservices may not be able to help you.

It is also important to note the difference in licenses between development and deployment. With a Developer License you will have the following restrictions:

- Applications cannot be multithreaded
- Application requests are limited to only 50 transactions per minute
- Application build tools are installed on the system "make"
- The user can only deploy one instance of an application

A Deployment License will allow you to have:

- More than one instance of an application deployed
- Unlimited amount of application requests per minute
- Multithreaded Applications

When comparing the differences between the two licenses, it is obvious that the deployment license is optimized to run more efficiently in the production environment.

Installing WebObjects for Deployment

The WebObjects 5.0 software package comes with 2 CDs. One CD contains the Developer and Deployment installation for the on Mac OS X. The other contains the Developer and Deployment installation for Unix and Windows 2000.

Before proceeding with the Deployment installation, the Java 1.3 runtime must be installed on the machine. If it is not, the installer will issue a warning stating that the installation cannot proceed until the Java 1.3 JVM is installed. It is also easier to install WebObjects after the web server has been installed. During the installation process, WebObjects files are copied to the script root and document root directory of the web server. Some WebObjects configuration files, which contain the web server information, are also set up at this stage.

The Developer installation loads all of the necessary tools that developers need to create WebObjects applications (such as EOModeler). The deployment installation will only install the software that is required to run the applications. With this type of installation, developers will not be able to build applications on the deployment machine, as the build tools are not installed on the machine.

Managing the Deployment Environment

When it comes to production machines, it should be noted that all production machines should have the deployment version of WebObjects installed. In certain cases, it may be convenient to install the developer tools on the deployment machine. This can be accomplished by simply using the `WebObjects 5 License Upgrader` application to change the license from Developer to Deployment. This is advantageous if you choose to have the development tools handy for quick code fixes in the deployment environment.

Installing Patches

Apple is continuously releasing application patches for WebObjects. At the time of writing, Apple had 1 patch out for WebObjects 5.0. These patches can be located on the WebObjects web site (http://www.webobjects.com) and should be installed as soon as the patch has proven to be stable. When setting up a new deployment system, it is always best to have the latest patch.

At the time of writing, the following builds were the latest for WebObjects 5.0:

- `Monet3P4` – WebObjects 5.0
- `Monet3R2` – WebObjects 5.0 Update 1 for Mac OS X and Solaris
- `Monet3R4` – WebObjects 5.0 Update 1 for Windows 2000

In order to determine which version of the software is installed on your computer use the following rules:

- **Windows**
  Use the **Add Remove** system feature in the **Control Panel** to view the software version that is installed.

- **Sun Solaris**
  View the contents of the `software.ver` file that is located in `$NEXT_ROOT/Library/Receipts/PDO/`.

- **Mac OS X (v.10.0)**
  Go into the `Library/Receipts` directory and open the `WO5MacOSXDepUpdate1.pkg` directory. Inspect the subdirectory `Contents/Resources` within `WO5MacOSXDepUpdate1.pkg`, and a `software_version` file will be present. Open this file and read the version number. Note that this version number will not have the prefix of `Monet`.

Building and Installing the Application

The process of building and installing a WebObjects application is straightforward. During the development cycle of the application, the project is compiled countless times to test modifications to application logic and user interface changes. When the application is compiled in development, the project is stored within the root directory of the project in the format `$project.woa`. Each time the application is compiled, this folder is updated with the latest source and application resources. When the developer runs the application to test the change that has been made, the application is run from this directory.

Chapter 14

Structure of the Build Directory

The following screenshot shows the files that are placed within the $project.woa directory, after the application has been compiled:

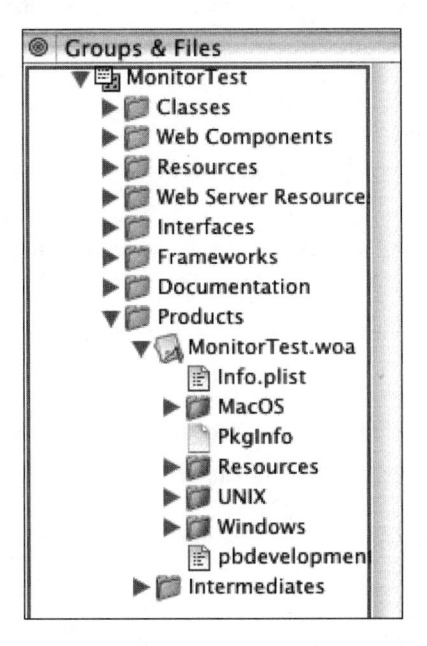

```
Groups & Files
  MonitorTest
    Classes
    Web Components
    Resources
    Web Server Resource
    Interfaces
    Frameworks
    Documentation
    Products
      MonitorTest.woa
        Info.plist
        MacOS
        PkgInfo
        Resources
        UNIX
        Windows
        pbdevelopmen
    Intermediates
```

- **MonitorTest.woa**
  This directory contains two scripts that start the application. One has the name `MonitorTest` and the other has the name `MonitorTest.cmd`. The `MonitorTest` script is used to start WebObjects instances in Sun Solaris and Mac OS X platforms. The `MonitorTest.cmd` script is used to start instances within the Windows environment.

- **Mac OS X, Unix, Windows**
  These three directories contain property files that are used to run applications on each operating system.

- **Resources**
  All of the application logic that was produced by developers is stored within this directory. All of the Java classes are put together into a jar file and placed under this directory. Each `WOComponent` that is created within the application has its own directory. If a `WOComponent` called `LogoutPage` is created within the application, then a folder named `LogoutPage.wo` will be created within the Resources directory when the application is compiled.

There is no executable code in any of the files that are contained within the $project.woa folder to tie the application to a specific platform. This is one of the great features of WebObjects v 5.0.

How to Select the Right Platform

The two main criteria for selecting the deployment platform for any application are customer needs and the developers preferred operating system. There are also many other factors that influence this decision:

- Is the support staff familiar with the platform?
- Which operating system has more robust automated administration features, such as cron jobs?
- Which platform will provide the most reliability?

At the time of writing, there are no metrics from Apple with regards to WebObjects deployment.

Transferring Application To Deployment Environment

Before an application is placed in the deployment environment, a series of steps must take place. The deployment platform does not have any build tools so the building of the application must be carried out on the development platform.

The first step is to clean the application and rebuild it. At times, Project Builder will not flag the correct Java files for recompilation and this can cause problems when the application starts up. A clean-up ensures a fresh rebuild from scratch of all Java classes. Once the application has been cleaned and recompiled, it must be moved to the deployment server.

Monitoring Application Performance

When the WebObjects applications are up and running, system administrators do have tools at their disposal to monitor the performance of the application instances. They are:

- The `Top` command on Unix systems to monitor memory and CPU usage of the "Java" processes that represent WebObjects instances
- `Task Manager` within the Windows 2000 environment to monitor memory and CPU usage of the "Java" processes that represent WebObjects instances
- `PlaybackManager` to stress-test applications before they are released into the production environment

JavaMonitor

`JavaMonitor` is the main piece of software that system administrators use to configure the deployment environment (it itself is a WebObjects application). With the new release, the Java class that starts this application is called `JavaMonitor` but before WebObjects 5.0 it was called `Monitor`. `JavaMonitor`. carries out the following functions:

- Adds and deletes application instances
- Displays a global view of all application instances on all related hosts
- Allows users to set up scheduling of application instances
- Starts and stops application instances

Chapter 14

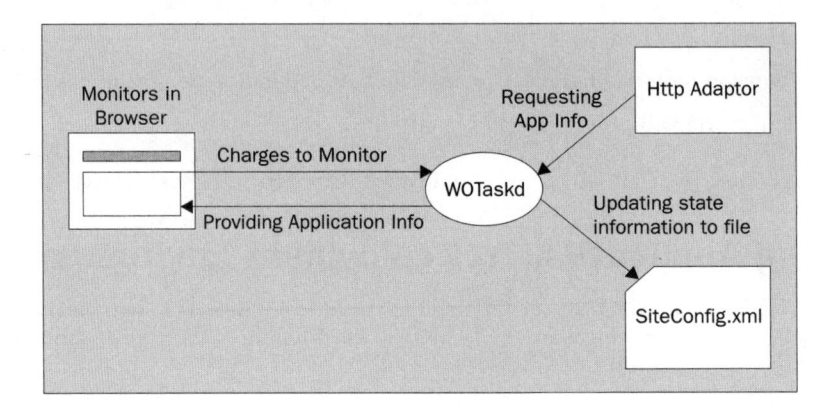

`JavaMonitor` provides a graphical method to manipulate wotaskd. Wotaskd is a daemon and will be explained in more detail later on in the chapter. For now, all we need to know is that we are simply changing the configuration information within wotaskd by using `JavaMonitor`. The information that is changed in the wotaskd is provided to the HTTP adaptor so that it can find application instances. The data is also written to a static file called `SiteConfig.xml` which is located in the `$NEXT_ROOT/Local/Library/WebObjects/Configuration` directory. This file is used to restore state to Monitor if it crashes or if the system is rebooted.

In the deployment environment, there is only one machine that has to have the `JavaMonitor` software running. This would link to all the machines that are running the wotaskd daemon. Monitor gains access to these machines when hosts are added.

Location of JavaMonitor

The executable for `JavaMonitor` is located in the following directory:

`$NEXT_ROOT\Library\WebObjects\JavaApplications\JavaMonitor.woa`

To run `JavaMonitor` on Windows 2000, navigate to the aforementioned directory and enter `JavaMonitor`.

To run `JavaMonitor` on the Mac OS X, you must open the Terminal and enter the following command:

/System/Library/WebObjects/JavaApplications/JavaMonitor.woa/JavaMonitor

Once `JavaMonitor` has been started, the following screen will be presented within the default web browser:

Managing the Deployment Environment

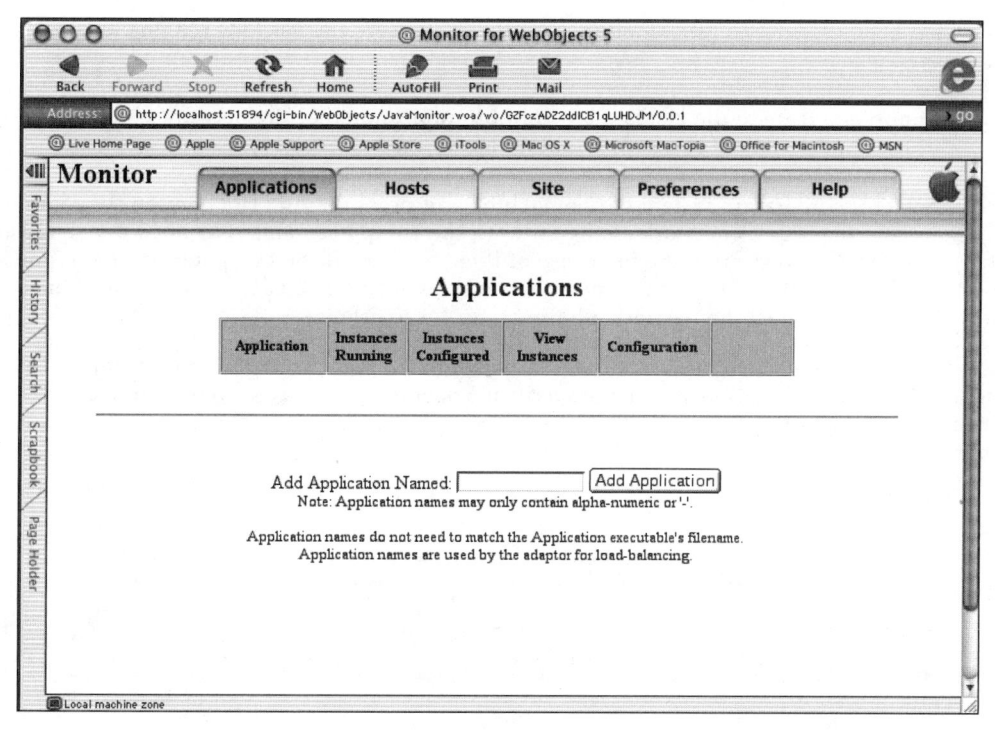

Note that if the browser window does not open automatically with the home page of `JavaMonitor`, simply note the port that it was started on in the command prompt/Terminal window and enter that port number into the browser URL (such as http://host:port).

The `JavaMonitor` application (Monitor) is divided up into 5 sections: **Applications, Hosts, Site, Preferences** and **Help**.

Setting Up a Host within Monitor

Before any work can be done, Monitor must be set up with hosts running wotaskd. Monitor is used to configure *n* number of wotaskd daemons.

Any computer that is running the wotaskd daemon can be added as a host. The only condition is that each computer must have a wotaskd running in order for it to be part of the WebObjects deployment architecture. To set up a new host, simply enter the hostname or IP address of a computer that is running the wotaskd service daemon. In relation to Monitor in the deployment environment, Monitor has a one-to-many relationship to the wotaskd daemons running on all of the machines.

It is possible to have hosts running on different platforms, one on Windows 2000, one on Mac OS X and one on Sun Solaris. This makes no difference to Monitor as the wotaskd daemons use the TCP/IP protocol to communicate.

To set up a host, the first step is to make certain the machine to be added can be seen by the Monitor application on the network. One of the easiest tests to perform is to simply ping the host machine from the machine that is running Monitor. In most cases this is not an issue, as applications are usually deployed on the same machine Monitor is running on.

Once it has been determined that Monitor has network access to the machine running wotaskd, you can add a host:

1. Simply navigate to the **Hosts** tab within Monitor and enter the network name/ IP address of a computer that is currently running the wotaskd daemon.

2. Select the operating system of the machine and press the **Add Host** button. It is important to note that due to network configurations, the computer name may not work. Firewalls and DNS settings might be the cause of this behavior. If the computer name does not work, simply enter the IP address of the machine. If the IP address of the machine does not work, contact the network administrator for assistance.

Once the host has been added, a new entry will appear in the hosts listing. The entry will tell the user if wotaskd on the host machine is running properly, the operating system and version of the host and how many instances are running on the host. There is also a hyperlink to resynchronize the host computer with the `JavaMonitor` information of the host:

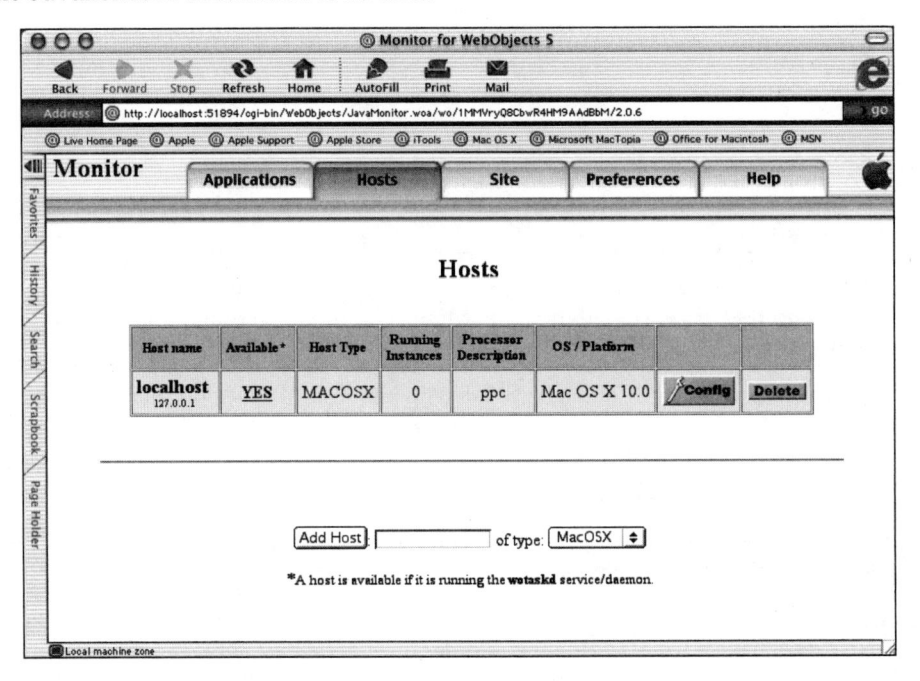

Adding Applications

After hosts have been successfully added to the Monitor application, we can then proceed to add applications.

To add an application, you must follow these instructions:

1. Navigate to the **Applications** tab of Monitor and enter the name of the application into the text field to the left of the **Add Application** button. The application can be given any name. In this example we shall use the name `MonitorTest` as we are testing the Monitor application. Otherwise it is good practice to use the name of the project as the application name.

2. Once the **Add Application** button is pressed, the user will be presented with a screen where they enter application configuration information:

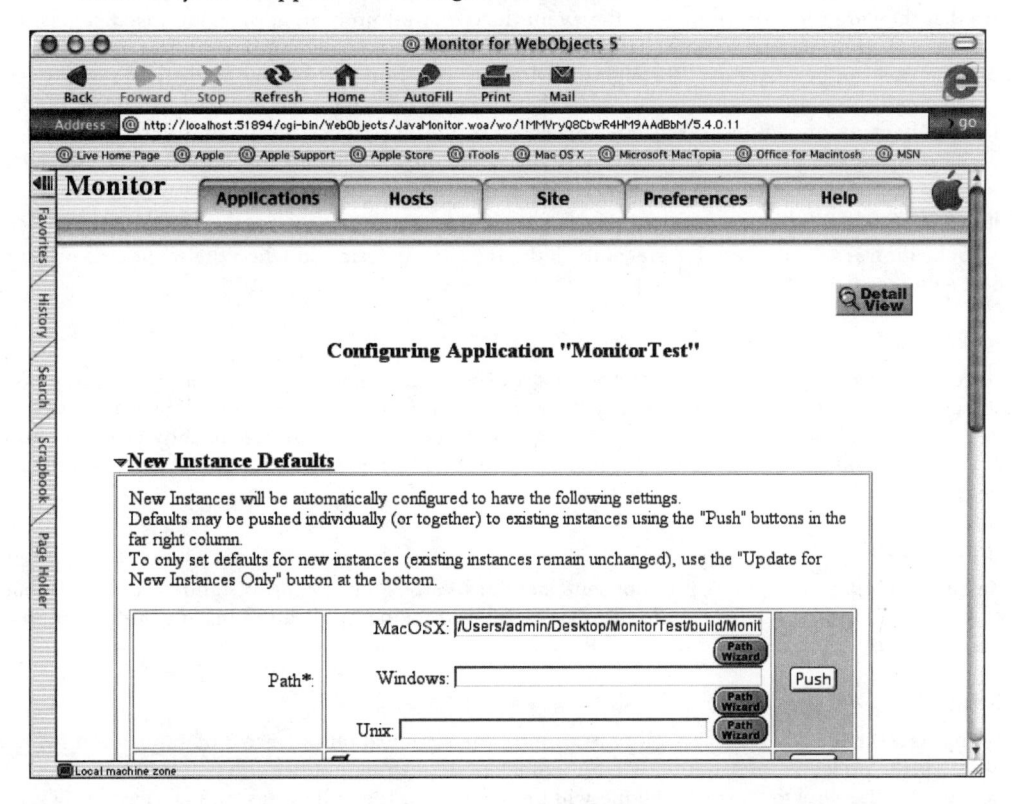

[screenshot: Monitor for WebObjects 5 — Configuring Application "MonitorTest", showing New Instance Defaults with Path fields for MacOSX, Windows, and Unix, each with a Path Wizard button, and a Push button]

Within this page, users can set application instance defaults that will apply to all application instances that are added. This information is entered under the **New Instance Defaults** section it is used to start all instances of that application. Each instance configuration can be modified after it is created but in most cases, each instance of an application has the same settings.

At minimum the user must provide the path of the application on the host machine. Simply select the **Path Wizard** for the operating system of the host machine. The **Path Wizard** is a great tool to make certain that no formatting or spelling mistakes are made when entering the path value.

Configuring Applications

Monitor contains many other options. We will not go through every single option, but the following sections list the most commonly used options when configuring new WebObjects applications.

Path

This setting indicates where the startup script is for the application instance. In the Windows 2000 environment, this will be a `cmd` script. In the Unix and Mac OS X environment, this will be a shell script that bears the name of the project.

Chapter 14

Auto Recover

This checkbox indicates whether or not new application instances should be monitored by wotaskd to ensure that they are up and running. In the event that wotaskd finds an application instance has died, it will restart it. It is important to note that wotaskd will try to restart the application instance even if the application was stopped by a user through the Monitor tool. Some system administrators might use cron jobs to manually stop application instances. If this option is activated, the wotaskd will bring the application back up once it has restarted. This was a common practice in previous versions of WebObjects (for example version 4.0) because the scheduling feature within Monitor was not reliable.

Minimum Active Sessions

If an application is set to schedule "gracefully", the instance is restarted when the session count is less than or equal to this value.

Caching Enabled

If this feature is enabled, component templates (`WOComponent` files in `wo` directories) will only be parsed once, and all subsequent uses of this template will not require re-parsing. This is used to improve the performance of the application. If an application needs the ability to dynamically change templates while the application is running then this feature should be turned off. Generally, it is a good idea to cache templates.

Debugging Enabled

By default, WebObjects instances do not send standard verbose messages to standard out. This feature will turn the debugging on. This could be very useful in tracking application instance information when the standard output is being captured in a log file.

Output Path

WebObjects 5.0 has added the capability to capture the standard output/error of application instances to a file. This is priceless information when it comes to debugging application issues. Users simply select the location of the directory where the file will be saved. The file will be saved in a directory with the following format `<ApplicationName>`-`<ID>` where `<ID>` represents the unique number of the running application instance. Every application instance should have a log file. Sometimes WebObjects instances will die with no apparent reason. When this happens, application instances are good at dumping information to standard error but if this information is not being logged, then it cannot be used to solve the problem.

AutoOpenInBrowser

By default this is set to off. This command does exactly what it implies. In the deployment environment, there is no need for this to be activated.

LifeBeat Interval

All WebObjects instances report into wotaskd at a specified interval to say "Hey I am alive and doing well". By default this value is set to 30 seconds. If your application has certain features that extend beyond the time limit of 30 seconds (such as long reports) then this value should be changed accordingly. It is possible that a user requests something that takes 40 seconds. If the application is multithreaded, then lifebeats are sent from their own thread. In this case, long running requests should not prevent the lifebeat from occurring on time. This in turn causes wotaskd to assume that the application instance is dead. If the **Auto Recover** option is turned on, wotaskd will try to start a new instance of that application because it thinks it is not running. As you can see this can cause a lot of problems in the deployment environment.

Managing the Deployment Environment

Once this information has been entered and saved by clicking the appropriate buttons, the user is returned to the main page of the application where the added application is listed. At this point, we have simply set up the default application settings for all instances that are created. In order for end users to gain access to it, application instances must be set up.

Adding Application Instances

The next step in the deployment process is to add instances. This is accomplished by clicking on the Detail icon on the application row. This will bring up a screen that lists all of the application instances. Because this application has just been added to Monitor, it does not have any application instances by default:

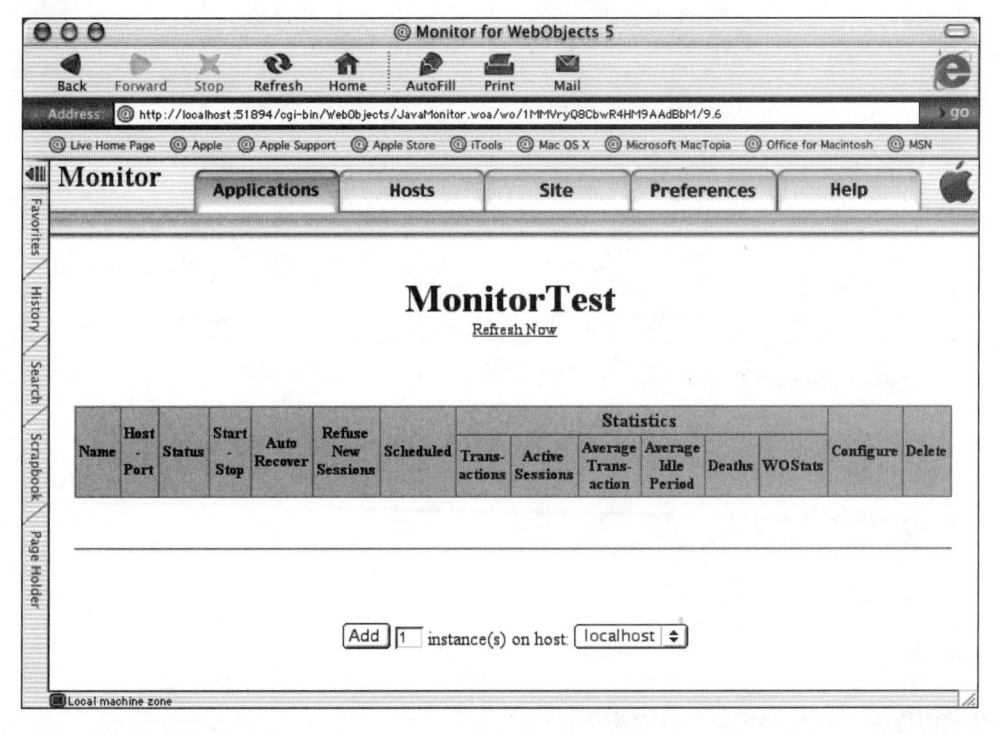

At this point we are ready to add instances of the application to Monitor. This is accomplished by entering the number of application instances into the number text field and selecting the host computer that will be running these instances.

It is important to note that all WebObjects applications should have more than 1 application instance running in the production environment. By having more than 1 instance running, fault tolerance is increased so that if one instance dies, there are n number of instances still running to take new requests.

There is one very important thing to consider when running more than 1 instance of an application in production. WebObjects does not synchronize cached application instance information by default. WebObjects does have methods to deal with this programmatically and it is an issue that has to be dealt with during the development phase of the application.

With WebObjects version 4.0 and 4.5, a framework was available to synchronize cached information across instances. The framework was called `ChangeNotification` and was written by David Neumann. At the time of writing, a port of this framework is available at http://www.wirehose.com/download/.

After adding more instances, Monitor returns to the Detail View page of the application. At this point we see that *n* number of lines have been added to this list as per the number of instances that were added:

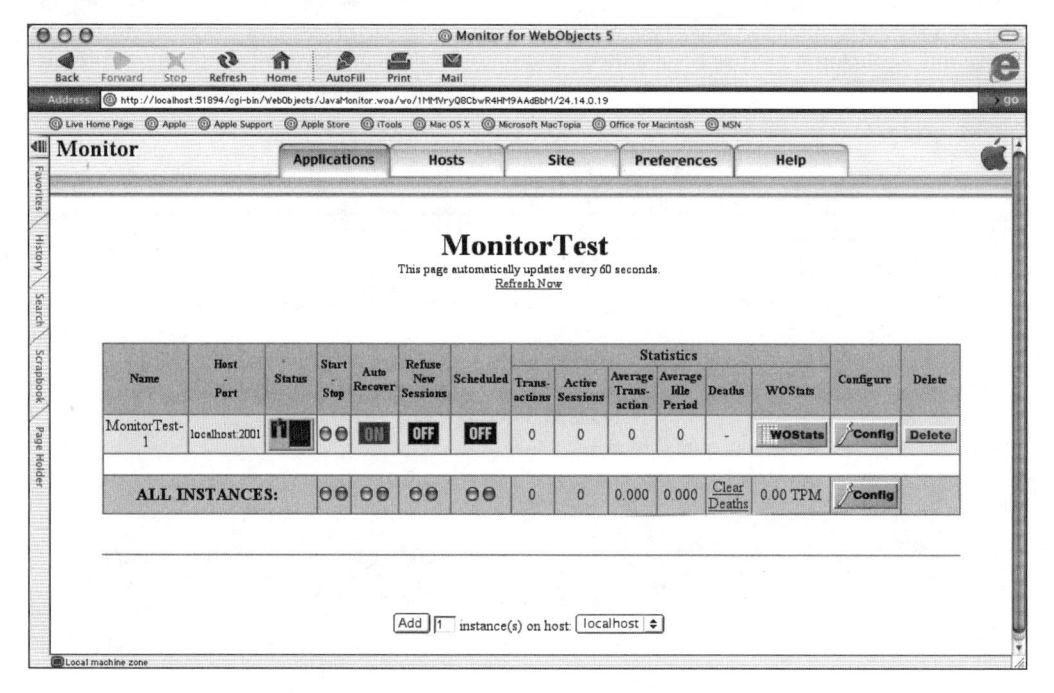

Just as we can configure applications, we also have the ability to configure individual application instances. We can start/stop instances, change configuration information, or monitor the behavior of one application instance.

When Should Monitor Be Running?

Even though the Monitor application is a tool that is used extensively to deploy applications, it does not have to be running in order for application instances to be running. This tool is only needed to set up application instances and remote administration of the instances.

The main thing to remember about Monitor is that it is a tool that gives individuals the ability to modify the `SiteConfig.xml` and `WOConfig.xml` files (which we will explore in greater detail later on in the chapter) via a graphical tool. The required service wotaskd and the HTTP adaptor in the deployment environment use both of these files respectively. It is possible to manually modify these files to achieve the desired results, but the Monitor tool is a much quicker and less error-prone method to modify these files.

Scheduling

Scheduling is a feature within Monitor that automates the recycling of applications. Due to the architecture of the EOF, it is possible that a WebObjects application can end up pulling an entire database into memory in the form of Enterprise Objects (EOs). If a WebObjects application is not designed correctly, the caching mechanism of the EOF will allow this to happen.

All EOs that are used in an application are stored as `NSDictionaries` objects in the `EODatabase` layer of the application instance. This behavior is a result of poor architecture and is not to be blamed on the WebObjects software. Developers do have to access the methods to deal with this cached data but sometimes do not put thought into this issue until the application has been deployed and the symptoms start appearing.

The time at which an application should be rescheduled depends on the usage of the application. If for example an application is being heavily used during the course of a day and it consumes a lot of memory, then it might be a good idea to recycle the instances on a daily basis. If an application receives moderate usage then it could go on for days without being recycled.

Once the frequency of restarts has been determined, the next thing to determine is when the application instances should be restarted. Most applications can be restarted in the early hours of the morning when the least amount of users are present on the system (for example 03:00 am):

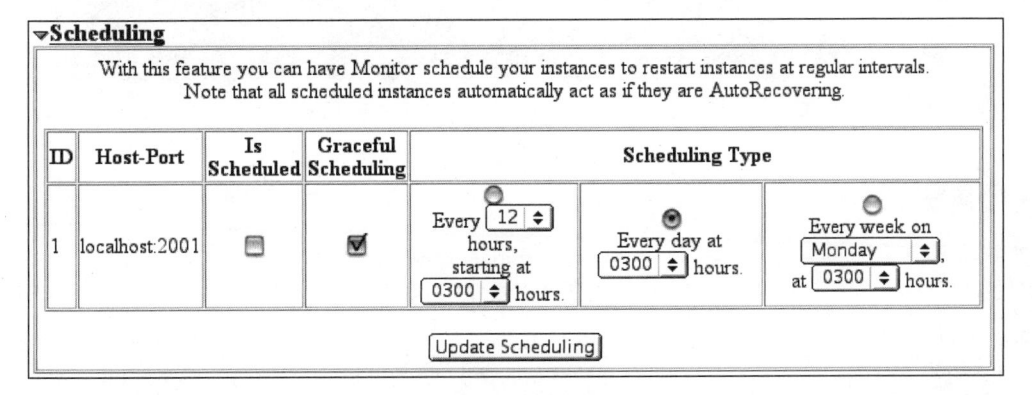

▼**Scheduling**

With this feature you can have Monitor schedule your instances to restart instances at regular intervals. Note that all scheduled instances automatically act as if they are AutoRecovering.

ID	Host-Port	Is Scheduled	Graceful Scheduling	Scheduling Type		
1	localhost:2001	☐	☑	Every 12 ♦ hours, starting at 0300 ♦ hours	Every day at 0300 ♦ hours	Every week on Monday ♦, at 0300 ♦ hours

[Update Scheduling]

All WebObjects applications should have more than 1 instance running. If only 1 application is configured, then users will not be able to log into the application when it is cycling. Having more than 1 instance ensures no end user interruption during cycling as the instances are restarted at staggered times (2:00 am, 2:30 am, and 3:00 am). It is important to note that end users will not be interrupted if the applications are scheduled to recycle gracefully. This means that the application instance will wait for all of the sessions to timeout before exiting. Once the application instance has exited, wotaskd will take care of restarting the instance.

It is important to note that even though scheduling is set up via the Monitor GUI, the job of restarting the application instances is performed by wotaskd. One important bug that exists on Windows 2000 Pro with the WebObjects deployment software is that the wotaskd is killed when the user logs out of their session. In order to get around this bug, a user must stayed logged into the system and lock the screen to prevent unauthorized access.

Debugging Tip

In the Windows 2000 environment, application instances that are started from Monitor, on occasions, will not start. This behavior is usually encountered when setting up a new machine in the deployment environment. When this happens, it is a good idea to try and start the application from the command line and see what comments are redirected to standard out. If there were no problems with the application starting up, then the last line in the command prompt window should read Waiting for requests:

```
MonitorTest.woa
WOUserDirectory=C:\MonitorTest\MonitorTest.woa
WOWorkerThreadCountMax=256
WOMonitorEnabled=false
WODirectConnectEnabled=true
WOAdaptorURL=http://localhost/Scripts/WebObjects.exe
WOPort=-1
WOApplicationBaseURL=/WebObjects
WOAutoOpenInBrowser=true
WOLifebeatInterval=30
WOLocalRootDirectory=C:\Apple\Local
WOIncludeCommentsInResponse=false
------------------------
Created adaptor of class WODefaultAdaptor on port 1087 and address tabh/192.168.
10.142 with WOWorkerThread minimum of 16 and maximum of 256
NSBundle is unable to find "ExtensionsForResources.plist" in the main bundle.  I
gnoring optional configuration file.
Application project found: Will locate resources in 'C:\MonitorTest' rather than
 'C:\MonitorTest\MonitorTest.woa'.
Creating LifebeatThread now with: MonitorTest 1087 tabh/192.168.10.142 1085 3000
0
Welcome to MonitorTest !
Opening application's URL in browser:
http://tabh:1087/Scripts/WebObjects.exe/MonitorTest
Waiting for requests...
```

Had there been a problem with starting the application, the error would have been written to standard out.

WOTASKD

The wotaskd process is a very important part of the deployment environment. This process can be referred to as a daemon. This term originated in the Unix environments and stands for a process that is constantly running in the background, even when users log out of the system. Within WebObjects, the wotaskd daemon is used to carry out functions such as application scheduling and updating adaptor and application configuration files. Wotaskd brings together the Monitor tool with the WebObjects HTTPD adaptor. The following diagram demonstrates the role that wotaskd has in the deployment environment:

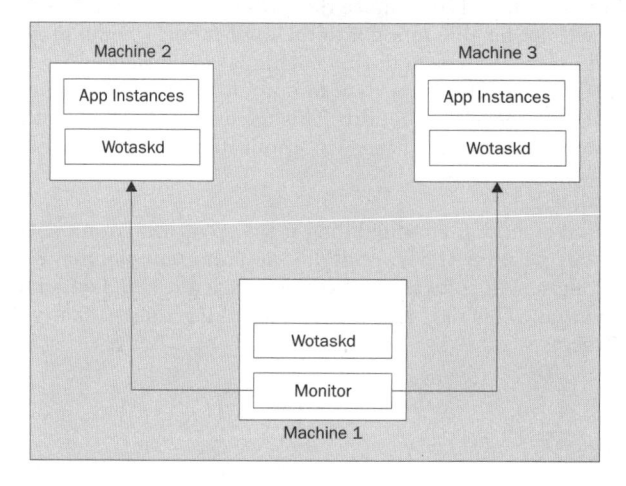

Managing the Deployment Environment

Every machine that is running application instances must be running wotaskd. Monitor is used to administer all of the hosts from one location.

When changes are made in the Monitor Application such as adding an application, Wotaskd writes the application configuration information to the SiteConfig.xml file. In addition to writing the configuration information for the application, the adaptor information is also written to an XML file WOConfig.xml which is used by the WebObjects HTTP adaptor to route application requests to the proper application instance.

Features such as scheduling and auto recover are carried out by wotaskd; it is wotaskd that does the scheduling of the application and not Monitor. The wotaskd daemon is not needed for application instances to run. Keep in mind that wotaskd modifies the deployment XML files and automates tasks such as scheduling and **Auto Recover**.

The wotaskd daemon is located in:

$NEXT_ROOT\Library\WebObjects\JavaApplications\wotaskd.woa

Accessing wotaskd Configuration

By default the wotaskd daemon starts up on port 1085. There are two ways to access the configuration information of a wotaskd process:

- Enter the address http://hostname:1085

- Under the **Hosts** tab in Monitor click on the **YES** hyperlink in the **Available** column,. This will launch a new browser window that will contain the requested information.

The following output is generated when wotaskd is queried:

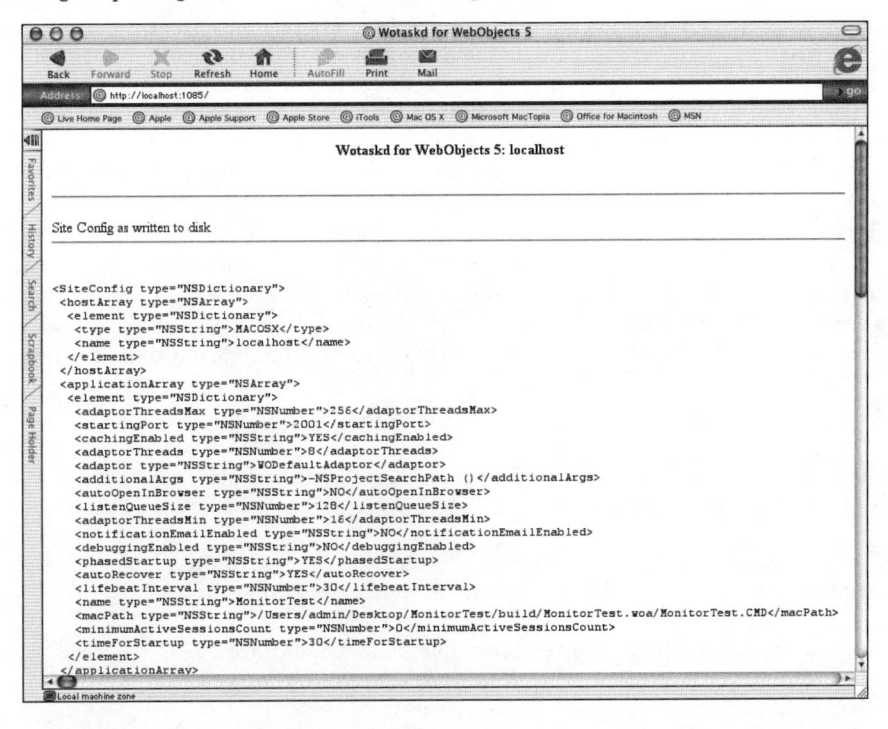

```
Wotaskd for WebObjects 5: localhost

Site Config as written to disk

<SiteConfig type="NSDictionary">
  <hostArray type="NSArray">
    <element type="NSDictionary">
      <type type="NSString">MACOSX</type>
      <name type="NSString">localhost</name>
    </element>
  </hostArray>
  <applicationArray type="NSArray">
    <element type="NSDictionary">
      <adaptorThreadsMax type="NSNumber">256</adaptorThreadsMax>
      <startingPort type="NSNumber">2001</startingPort>
      <cachingEnabled type="NSString">YES</cachingEnabled>
      <adaptorThreads type="NSNumber">8</adaptorThreads>
      <adaptor type="NSString">WODefaultAdaptor</adaptor>
      <additionalArgs type="NSString">-NSProjectSearchPath ()</additionalArgs>
      <autoOpenInBrowser type="NSString">NO</autoOpenInBrowser>
      <listenQueueSize type="NSNumber">128</listenQueueSize>
      <adaptorThreadsMin type="NSNumber">16</adaptorThreadsMin>
      <notificationEmailEnabled type="NSString">NO</notificationEmailEnabled>
      <debuggingEnabled type="NSString">NO</debuggingEnabled>
      <phasedStartup type="NSString">YES</phasedStartup>
      <autoRecover type="NSString">YES</autoRecover>
      <lifebeatInterval type="NSNumber">30</lifebeatInterval>
      <name type="NSString">MonitorTest</name>
      <macPath type="NSString">/Users/admin/Desktop/MonitorTest/build/MonitorTest.woa/MonitorTest.CMD</macPath>
      <minimumActiveSessionsCount type="NSNumber">0</minimumActiveSessionsCount>
      <timeForStartup type="NSNumber">30</timeForStartup>
    </element>
  </applicationArray>
```

The output from querying the wotaskd produces a document that contains 5 entries:

- Site Config as written to disk
  When the Monitor application is used to set up new application instances, all of this information is written to the `SiteConfig.xml` file in the `$NEXT_ROOT/Local/Library/WebObjects/Configuration` directory. Monitor simply reads this file to get the appropriate configuration information. When the computer is rebooted, this file is read by the wotaskd process and is used to start up appropriate applications.

- Adaptor config as sent to Local WOAdaptors — All Running applications and instances
  This information is sent to local `WOAdaptors` and lists all of the running applications that have checked into wotaskd with a lifebeat when they started up.

- Adaptor config sent to Remote WOAdaptors — All Registered and Running Applications and Instances
  This should only contain instances that have been set up within the Monitor tool and are running.

- Adaptor config as written to disk — All registered Applications and Instances
  This represents a stateful copy of the information that is sent to Remote Adaptors. If at any time the remote `WOAdaptor` is not working correctly then this is one of the first places to look for errors.

- Properties of this wotaskd
  This lists important configuration information about the wotaskd instance that is running on the machine. One of the most important settings visible in this section is the location of the `SiteConfig.xml` file that is used to back up instance information.

Password Protection

As wotaskd contains vital information about the setup of the production system and functionality to configure, it is wise to prevent unwanted individuals from viewing the output that is issued by http://hostname:1085. All users will be able to access this configuration information so long as the Monitor password has not been set. Once the Monitor password has been set, the http://hostname:1085 will not return the wotaskd configuration information.

HTTP Adaptors

The http adaptor is the bridge between the web server and the WebObjects instance. WebObjects supports many web servers for different platforms. This piece of software is responsible for features such as load balancing. Every request that comes to a deployed WebObjects goes through the following steps:

1. Request is made from the application through the browser window

2. The request is received by the Web Server where it is then directed to the WebObjects HTTP adaptor in the scripts direct

3. The WebObjects HTTP adaptor then forwards the request to the requested application based on the information located in the `WOConfig.xml` file

4. The application instance receives the request via its `WOAdaptor`

Managing the Deployment Environment

5. The application processes the request and pulls any required data from the database, then returns the request to the web server in HTML form

6. The web server receives the HTML response; if the application is a split installation, then the appropriate application resources are added

7. The request is then returned to the browser that made the original request

The following diagram demonstrates the central role that the HTTP adaptor plays in deployment:

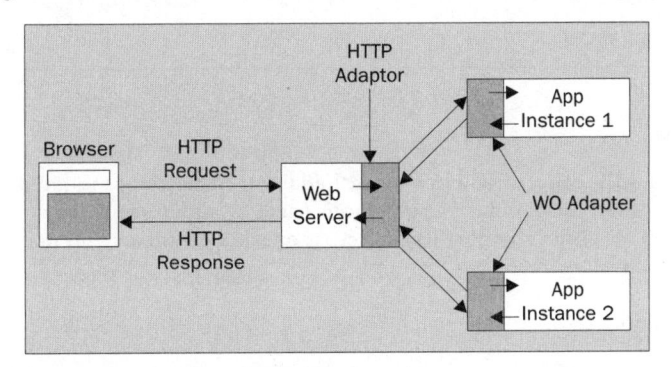

By tracing the process flow from the user's original request, we can see that every application request passes through the HTTP adaptor. The HTTP adaptor connects with the `WOAdaptor` of each application instance. It is the `WOAdaptor` of each application instance that accepts incoming requests and sends out the appropriate responses once the instance has produced them.

When a user requests access to a WebObjects application in the deployment environment for the first time, the request is captured by the WebObjects HTTP adaptor. At this point, the adaptor realizes that no application instance number is stored in the requesting URL, so it uses the configured load-balancing algorithm to forward the request to an available instance. The WOApplication receives the request and realizes that this request does not have a session, so it creates one.

When the response is sent back to the user, the URL contains the instance ID and the session ID. Now that this information is stored in the requesting URL, the WebObjects HTTP adaptor will know which instance to forward the request to. Once the request is forwarded to the correct instance, the application uses the session ID in the URL to retrieve the user's session information. Therefore once a user is assigned to an instance, all subsequent requests are forwarded to that same instance by the adaptor. This makes sense, as WebObjects does not support cross instance synchronization of session objects by default. Each instance is its own island of data.

Types of Adaptors

WebObjects can use two different types of HTTP adaptors: CGI and API-Based. It is important to note that, by default, the CGI HTTP adaptor is installed with WebObjects. The CGI adaptor will work with almost any web server. This generality has a trade-off, in the form of performance. Whenever possible, the CGI HTTP adaptor should be replaced with the native API-based adaptor. Each request that comes into the CGI adaptor requires a fork to process the request. This behavior is resource intensive and does slow down the request-response loop for users.

The API adaptors produce better performance in the deployment environment as they are incorporated directly into memory within the web server and in return are able to process requests more efficiently.

Chapter 14

Supported Platforms

The following is a list of adaptors and what platforms they can be used on:

	CGI	Apache	NSAPI	ISAPI
Windows 2000	X		X	X
Solaris	X	X	X	
Mac OS X	X	X		

Source Code

WebObjects includes the source code for the API adaptors. This comes in handy when special requirements are needed for deployed applications (such as added security features). The source code is in the C language. This ensures compatibility across operating systems and maximum performance on the deployment machine.

The code is located in:

$NEXT_ROOT/Developer/Examples/WebObjects/Source/Adaptors

All of the binaries for the HTTP adaptors along with the installation instructions are located in:

$NEXT_ROOT/Library/WebObjects/Adaptors

Configuring Adaptor Settings

The adaptor can be configured through the Monitor UI. Within Monitor, navigating to the **Site** tab and selecting the **HTTP Adaptor Settings** allows a developer to set global values. It is also possible to configure individual instances by clicking on the **config** button for the application instance.

When the adaptor settings are configured, the one thing that is usually changed is the adaptor timeout values. Once a request is submitted to a WebObjects application instance, a default timeout value of 30 seconds is applied to the request. If the HTTPD adaptor does not receive a response for the original request then it will timeout and present the user with an error message stating **Invalid response received from application**.

If this behavior is encountered within a deployed application it should be viewed as a design flaw, as end users would not want to wait in excess of 30 seconds for an application response. A solution to this problem is to increase the adaptor timeout value to a value higher than 30 seconds. This requires modifications of the application logic, web server or database tuning, in order to come up with a permanent solution.

WebObjects URL Format

A WebObjects application can be accessed through several different URLs. These URLs differ based on whether the application is running in development, production, or testing.

Direct-Connect

When developing an application, this is the URL format that is used when the application is started by Project Builder or through the command line in Direct-Connect mode:

http://machine:port/cgi-bin/WebObjects/AppName

This URL breaks down as follows:

- http://machine:port/cgi-bin/WebObjects
  The http address of the machine hosting the WebObjects HTTP adaptor. Note that depending on the web server that is being used, this executable directory will be different. For Netscape and Apache, the `cgi-bin` directory is used; for IIS, the `scripts` directory is used.

- AppName
  The case-sensitive name of the application that the user is trying to access.

It is also useful to know that the application can be accessed directly by entering the following URL http://machine:port. This will have the same effect as entering the application through the full Direct Connect URL. This entrance to the application instance comes in handy when it is required to quickly test if the application instance is still running.

Deployed URL (Before Logging into Application)

The deployment URL is used once the application has been deployed. In the deployment environment, a request is received by the web server, then it is forwarded to the WebObjects HTTP adaptor. The adaptor is the middleman who accepts incoming requests from the outside world and routes them to the appropriate application instance. Because of this, the port number of the application instance is not embedded within the URL:

http://machine/cgi-bin/WebObjects/AppName

Deployed URL (After Logging into Application – Session Based)

Once a user submits a request to the application and the application is built with session-based components, the URL on subsequent WebObject application generated pages will include all this information. We came across this in Chapter 4, but here is a recap:

http://host[:port]/cgi-in/WebObjects/App[[.woa][/instance]/wo[/componentName]/sessionID/elementID

This would be, for example:

http://machine/cgi-bin/WebObjects/AppName.woa/1/wo/rXH1a7X8aYM0Nm1rmDGW/0.1

By comparing this URL to the one prior to logging into the application, it is clear that the response from the application has appended extra data to the end of the URL. This extra data can be broken down as follows:

- /1

  The instance number for the application that is being accessed. This value tells the reader what instance the session is stored in. This value will stay the same for all subsequent requests.

- /wo

  The request handler type that is being used, wo = component request handler, wa = direct action based request handler. It is possible for the application URL to switch between component and direct actions. If an application has this logic, then the request handler will change states from wo to wa.

- /rXH1a7X8aYM0Nm1rmDGW

  The unique session ID that is used to identify users. This value will stay the same for all subsequent requests.

- /0.1

  The context ID of the component.

Deployed URL (Test Instance)

This is a new URL format that is only found in the WebObjects 5.0 deployment environment. This URL is used within the deployment environment to let the adaptor know that it is accessing an application instance that has not been set up through the Monitor UI. The load-balancing algorithm will not forward application requests to this instance, as it is not meant for production. This allows developers to test an application in the deployment with the web server without having to set it up through Monitor:

http://machine/cgi-bin/WebObjects/AppName.woa/-2054

Direct Action URL

The majority of WebObjects applications use component-based request/responses. This is a result of most WebObjects applications using the EOF as the data persistence layer, which requires a stateful request/response loop. WebObjects does offer the option of using stateless request/response loops; this is accomplished by using direct actions:

http://host[:port]/cgi-bin/WebObjects/App[[.woa] [/instance]/wa/ [actionClass|actionName|actionClass/actionName][?key=value&key=value...]

wich for example is:

http://machine/cgi-bin/WebObjects/AppName.woa/wa/gotoSec?zone=h2&area=j4

Notice that the application URL looks the same up until the wa part of it. The wa signifies that the direct action request handler will handle the request.

Load Balancing

The preferred way to deploy WebObjects applications requires the need for more than one application instance to be running. When more than 1 application instance is running, the problem arises of making certain that users are spread equally across all of the available instances to ensure maximum performance gains. The WebObjects adaptors implement load balancing but depending on the adaptor that is being used, only certain algorithms may be used.

Managing the Deployment Environment

The following load balancing algorithms are available within WebObjects:

- **Round Robin**
  This algorithm works on a looping premise. If several application instances are available, the first request is handed to the first application instance, the second request to the second instance and so on until all instances have received a request. Once the last instance has received a request, the scheduler loops back around and starts at the beginning again. It is important to note that the CGI adaptor cannot use this algorithm, as it requires state in order to keep track of which instances have already received requests.

- **Random**
  This is the default load-balancing algorithm that is used in deployment. This is a basic load-balancing algorithm that picks an instance at random and forwards the request to it. All adaptors can use this type of algorithm.

- **Load Average**
  This algorithm tries to spread the number of sessions evenly throughout all application instances. This is different from Round Robin as not all sessions die at the same time.

Adaptors and Configuration Information

There are two different methods for the WebObjects HTTP adaptor to get configuration information about deployed application instances. The first is by querying all available wotaskd daemons for the information and the second is to use an XML configuration file that is manually configured.

When the HTTP adaptors are first used, they send out a multicast request on the local subnet directed at all running wotaskd daemons. The wotaskd daemon listens for these requests on the IP address 239.128.14.2 and port 1085. Both of these settings can be changed to new values. When a wotaskd daemon receives this request, it responds with its machine address http://machineIP:1085. The adaptor can receive *n* number of responses from running wotaskd processes.

Now that the adaptor has all of the wotaskd responses, it constructs a list of all the available wotaskd processes and their address and places it within a list. The adaptor then uses this list to query for application configuration information.

It is also possible to provide the adaptor with the required configuration information via an XML file. By default, if the adaptor cannot find a valid wotaskd host running, it will then look for an XML file. Instructions on how to build the adaptor file are given in the woadaptor.xml and example.xml files located in:

$NEXT_ROOT/Developer/Examples/WebObjects/Source/Adaptors/

Obtaining Configuration Information

There are three different sources from which the WebObjects HTTP adaptor gets configuration information about deployed application instances:

- Multicast request
- Host List
- Configuration file

Chapter 14

With Multicast, when the HTTP adaptors are first used, they query the hosts, which were added to the deployment environment using `JavaMonitor`, the local subnet directed at all running wotaskd daemons. The wotaskd daemon listens for these requests on the IP address 239.128.14.2 and port 1085. Both of these settings can be changed to new values. When a wotaskd daemon receives this request, it responds with its machine address (http://hostname:1085). The adaptor builds a list of all the wotaskd processes that responded. The adaptor then polls this list for future changes with the wotaskd processes.

Multicast is the method that is used by default for all adaptors when a WebObjects machine is first set up. The Host List method is half way between the Multicast and Configuration file options. With this, the administrator must enter the hostnames of the servers running wotaskd. Once this list is created, the adaptor will then poll it for future changes.

The configuration file is the last method to provide the HTTP adaptor with information. The required information is stored within an XML file. By default, if the adaptor cannot find a valid wotaskd host running, it will then look for an XML file. Instructions on how to build the adaptor file are given in the `woadaptor.xml` and `example.xml` files located in:

- On Mac OS X systems
  `/Developer/Examples/WebObjects/Source/Adaptors`
- On Windows and Sun Solaris
  `$NEXT_ROOT/Developer/Examples/WebObjects/Source/Adaptors/`

Available Applications

The WOAdaptorInfo page will list all the applications that are visible to the HTTP adaptor. If for some reason you are not able to access an application but you know that it is running, check this list to see if your application is listed. If your application does not appear in the list, then the source of information that the adaptor is using for routing is not configured properly. Remember that this is the HTTP adaptor view of available WebObjects applications.

Each entry will have useful statistics about each application instance such as port numbers, unique instance number. This output is useful to cross-reference with the wotaskd output information. The WOAdaptorInfo page represents what applications are accessible by the adaptor whereas the wotaskd output represents all of the applications that are configured under a wotaskd daemon. See the earlier section on *wotaskd* on how to query the configuration information for wotaskd.

Web Servers

Out of the three main deployment components (besides database and app server), the web server is the easiest to configure and administer. In WebObjects applications, the web server is responsible for handling incoming http requests. Once it receives the requests, they are routed to the HTTP adaptor where they are then forwarded on to the appropriate application instance. Application instances then process the request and return the information to the web server where it is then directed back to the requesting user. The job of the web server boils down to accepting and returning http requests for WebObjects application instances.

When the WebObjects software is installed into the deployment machine, one of the questions that the installer asks for is the root directory for the executable directory and the document root directory. With this knowledge, the installer then proceeds to copy the HTTP adaptor to the executable directory and application `WebServerResources` to the document root directory.

By default, the cgi-bin HTTP adaptor is installed into the executable root directory. In order for the adaptor to be changed, the new adaptor must be installed as per the installation instructions provided by Apple Inc.

WebServerResources

This directory is used to store resources that applications use but do not want to serve from the WebObjects instance. Instead, the web server will serve these resources as it is accustomed to this work and will take added stress away from the application instance.

When a WebObjects application is built, a $project.woa file is produced. Within the root directory of the project, the WebServerResources is located within the **Contents** directory. This is the same directory that gets copied to the document root of the web server:

There are two main items installed in the document root directory, the Frameworks and individual web server resources. The web server resources are located within the $project.woa directory by looking at what is installed when the deployment software is installed. The deployment installer installs all of the WebServerResources for the deployment applications (such as JavaMonitor) and application examples that are used in WOInfoCenter (such as VirtualStoreLite). The WebServerResources directory usually contains application images.

Split Installations

When a WebObjects application is installed in the deployment environment that does not have the appropriate build tools, the WebServerResources must be manually transferred over to $WEB_SERVER_HOME/scripts/WebObjects directory. Simply copy over the same project folder that is created when the application is built but only include the $projRoot/Contents/WebServerResources directory.

In Windows 2000, it is also important to modify the Makefile.preamble file to tell the application to perform a split installation. Simply uncomment the INSTALLDIR_WEBSERVER attribute and build the application.

If the deployment machine has the build tools, the make install command will take care of installing the right files into the web server.

WebObjects Deployment Files

Once an application has been deployed, there are several files that can be used to configure the deployment environment. These files control web server properties, Java properties and a host of other deployment-related functions.

WebServerConfig.plist

When installing the WebObjects software into the deployment environment, one of the questions that the installer asks for is the location of the web server's script and documents directory. This information is then taken and stored in two files for use by the WebObjects application server.

It is placed in the $NEXT_ROOT/Library/Frameworks/JavaWebObjects/Resources/ directory and will have the following contents:

```
{
DocumentRoot = "D:/Apache/Apache/htdocs";
WOAdaptorURL = "http://localhost/cgi-bin/WebObjects.exe";
}
```

If in the future the web server is changed or the directory structure of the web server is changed, then both files need to be modified to reflect the change; both should have the same contents at all times. If the web servers document directory changes, then the contents of the previous web server's directory must be copied to the new location.

JavaConfig.plist

This file is responsible for configuring the WebObjects application server to use the Java Virtual Machine installed.

The file is located in $NEXT_ROOT/Library/Java and has the following contents:

```
Vendor = sun;
sun = {
VM = "$NEXT_ROOT/Library/JDK/bin/java.exe";
DefaultClasspath =
"$HOME/Library/Java;$NEXT_ROOT/Local/Library/Java;$NEXT_ROOT/Library/Java;$NEXT_RO
OT/Library/JDK/lib/classes.zip;$NEXT_ROOT/Library/Frameworks/JavaVM.framework/Clas
ses/awt.jar;$NEXT_ROOT/Library/JDK/lib/swingall.jar";
DefaultBeanpath =
"$HOME/Library/JavaBeans;$NEXT_ROOT/Local/Library/JavaBeans;$NEXT_ROOT/Library/Jav
aBeans";
Compiler = "$NEXT_ROOT/Library/JDK/bin/javac.exe";
Headers = "$NEXT_ROOT/Library/JDK/include $NEXT_ROOT/Library/JDK/include/winnt";
Library = "$NEXT_ROOT/Library/JDK/lib/javai.lib";
DebugLibrary = "$NEXT_ROOT/Library/JDK/lib/javai_g.lib";
};
}
```

If your application requires a specific JDBC driver, this file would be used to set this up. Under the DefaultClassPath entry, the location of the JDBC jar package would be entered. In addition, some WebObjects developers have managed to change the JVM that is being used in the deployment environment (that is, Jikes JVM by IBM). In order to do this, this file would have to be modified. Note that Apple will not provide technical assistance to anyone who uses anything but the JVM version that is specified with the installation instructions.

SiteConfig.xml

When applications are set up via the Monitor tool, this information is expected to stay the same even when the machine is rebooted or when the system crashes. The `SiteConfig.xml` file is a way for wotaskd to store state information on application instances. When the machine boots, wotaskd reads this file to see what applications should be started up by default. Monitor also reads this file to see what applications have been set up.

In Windows 2000, this file is located in:

`$NEXT_ROOT\Local\Library\WebObjects\Configuration`

In the Mac OS X, the file is in:

`$NEXT_ROOT/Library/WebObjects/Configuration`

Instance Logfile

All instances should be deployed with logging on. Not all WebObjects application errors will be visible by daily use of the application, as the error might occur during the request/response loop but the response loop never reaches the requesting browser. This logging helps to find the cause of a particular problem at an instance level. This feature is controlled through the Monitor UI in the application/instance detail page.

In addition to capturing all of the normal information that is generated by a WebObjects application instance, developers can create custom messages to send to the log file. One way of doing this is to use the `WOApplication.logString` method to redirect the output to standard error, which in turn is redirected to the application logfile that is specified in the Monitor UI.

The following piece of code can be used within any component to log messages to the log file:

```
application().logString("This is a comment 2");
```

Makefiles

On Windows 2000, each WebObjects application has three `Makefiles` by default, `Makefile.preamble`, `Makefile` and `Makefile.postamble`. These makefiles are configuration files for the "make" utility that is responsible for compiling the application. They can be located within the root directory of the project folder. Each file has differing tasks:

- `Makefile.preamble`
  Used to set custom application attributes that are required to build the application (such as frameworks)
- `Makefile`
  Inherits the properties set in the `Makefile.preamble` file and is not to be modified as it is maintained by Project Builder
- `Makefile.postamble`
  Inherits the properties set in the `Makefile.preamble` and `Makefile` files and can be modified for the purpose of overriding attributes set in previous `Makefiles`

Chapter 14

License.key

When WebObjects is installed onto a machine, it is copied into a file located on the local system.

- This is located in `$NEXT_ROOT /System/Library/Frameworks/JavaWebObjects.framework/Resources` on Mac OS X systems

- This is located in `$NEXT_ROOT/Library/Frameworks/JavaWebObjects.framework/Resources` on Windows 2000 and Sun Solaris machines

If the license on a certain machine must be changed (such as Developer to Deployment), there are two ways to carry out this change. Within Windows and Mac OS X, use the **LicenseUpgrader** tool to perform the license change or simply change the license that is visible in the file. The other option, which can be used with all platforms, is to simply modify the license in the file by hand, resave, and restart all WebObjects related services for the change to take effect.

Frameworks

All WebObjects applications use frameworks during the development and deployment phase. When deploying an application, certain frameworks such as the JavaWebObjects and Foundation frameworks are included in the WebObjects installation. A lot of applications require custom-built or third-party frameworks. In order to do this they must be installed on the deployment machine.

Frameworks are divided into two categories on each developer/deployment machine:

- **Apple Frameworks**
  Located in `$NEXT_ROOT/Library/Frameworks` directory and contains the frameworks that are created by Apple for use with WebObjects.

- **Third Party Frameworks**
  Located in `$NEXT_ROOT/Local/Library/Frameworks` directory and contains the frameworks that are produced for individual projects and third-party frameworks.

On Mac OS X, there is only one directory for frameworks:

- Frameworks directory located in `System/Library/Frameworks`

Installing Frameworks

When setting up the deployment environment, you must install the application-related frameworks before the application itself can be installed. In order to do this, copy the `MyFramework.framework` directory to the appropriate directory.

- On Mac OS X, copy the framework to the `$NEXT_ROOT /System/Library/Frameworks` directory

- In Windows 2000 and Sun Solaris, copy the framework to the `$NEXT_ROOT/Local/Library/Frameworks` directory.

Managing the Deployment Environment

Note that frameworks that are installed on Windows 2000 systems also require a DLL file. When a framework is compiled, this DLL file which bears the name `MyFramework.framework` is placed within the build directory. This DLL must be placed in the Executables directory within the `$NEXT_ROOT/Local/Library/Executables` directory.

Large WebObjects applications tend to have a large number of frameworks. When a lot of frameworks exist, it is possible to end up with one framework referencing another. In this case, care must be taken when compiling the frameworks to ensure that they are compiled and installed in the proper order.

Important WebObjects Services

When the WebObjects deployment software is installed, important services are installed to make sure that the WebObjects application instances start up properly when the machine is rebooted and that the required services are always running (such as wotaskd).

One thing to note is that the Monitor application is not started as a service on one of the platforms. It is started only when an application has to be configured. Here is a list of these important services on each of the three platforms.

On Windows 2000:

- **Apple Mac Daemon** -- is set up as a service in the service control panel
- **Apple Netname Server** – is set up as a service in the service control panel
- **Wotaskd** – started by script in the `Startup` directory of the machine when users log into the machine

Note – At the time of writing, there is a bug within the Windows 2000 deployment environment. Whenever the administrator logs out of their Windows session, wotaskd is killed. The workaround is to lock the server (screensaver) so that wotaskd could be run therefore taking care of scheduling and Auto Recover.

On Solaris:

- `S79WOServices` script installed in the `/etc/rc2.d` directory of the server. This script starts up wotaskd using the `javawoservice.sh` script. The `javawoservice.sh` script constantly polls wotaskd to ensure that it is always running. If wotaskd happens to die for some reason, then the `javawoservice.sh` script will restart it.

On Mac OS X:

- `WebObjects` script located in the `/System/Library/StatupItems/WebObjects` directory. The WebObjects script carries out the same function as the `S79WOServices` script on the Solaris platform.

Note that when wotaskd is started on all platforms, a log file is generated. Simply editing the startup scripts can modify the location and name of this logfile.

Deployment Architecture

WebObjects can be deployed under several different architectures. These range from the easiest where everything is contained on one computer to the most complex where several computers are connected to serve up the application.

The one important thing to keep in mind when deciding on how to configure the deployment environment is that the deployment environment is composed of three main parts: the web server, database and application server.

For purpose of demonstration, assume that there are four common types of deployments. We shall go through these in the following sections.

Simple Web Application

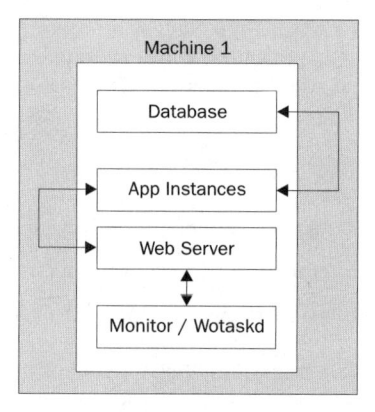

This is the most basic setup of any WebObjects application. In this scenario, the web server, application server, and database are all located on the same machine.

This setup reduces the expense on hardware, increases the simplicity of the deployment and allows easier administration of the machine. The one downside about this setup is that all three components of the deployed application will be competing for system resources, which will slow down the end-user's experience.

The best use for this type of deployment would be a small application that does not get a lot of activity.

Small Database Intensive Applications

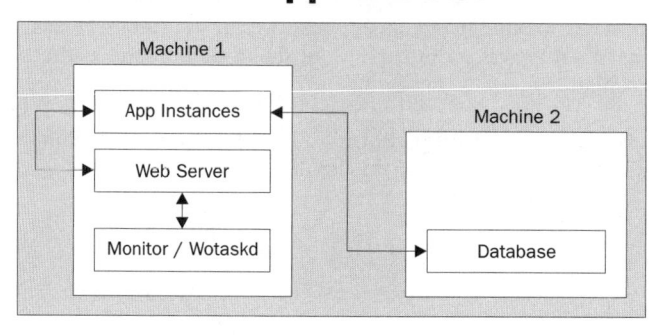

This setup is ideal for small applications that require a lot of database processing and in many cases, companies have machines whose whole purpose for existing is to serve databases.

Medium-Sized Web Applications

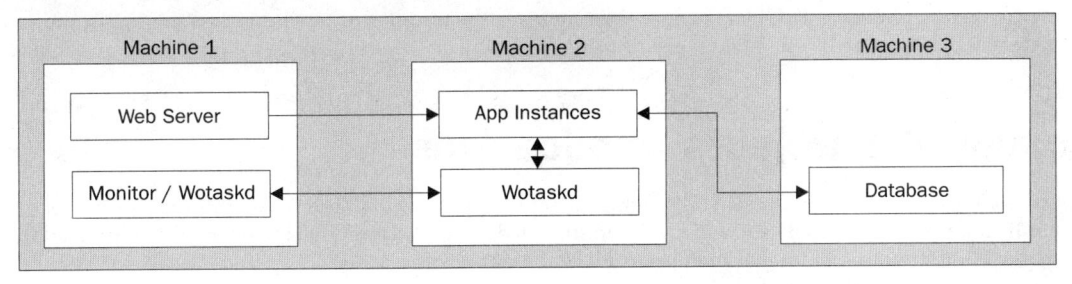

```
Machine 1: Web Server, Monitor / Wotaskd
Machine 2: App Instances, Wotaskd
Machine 3: Database
```

Actually, the title should be "medium sized web applications with mild database access". This setup is meant for large applications that require all three components of the deployment environment to perform at their maximum level.

This does introduce added cost to have a machine for each component. With the option, administration is increased, as there are 3 machines to configure and watch out for.

Large Web Applications

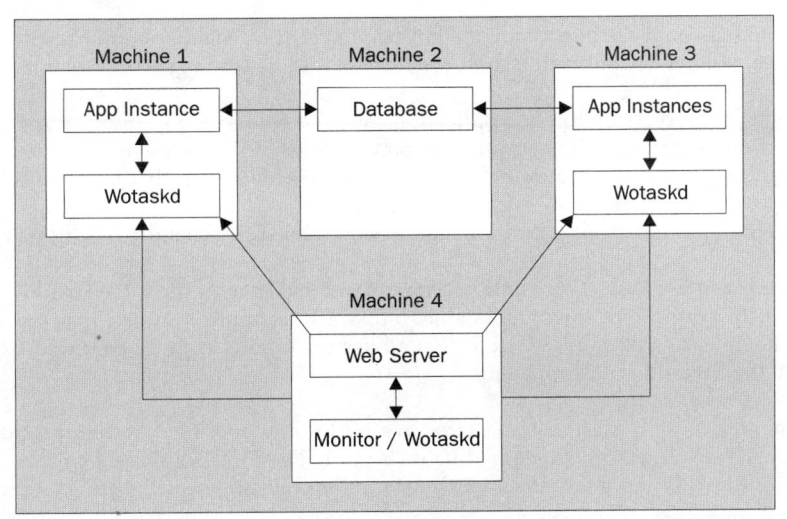

```
Machine 1: App Instance, Wotaskd
Machine 2: Database
Machine 3: App Instances, Wotaskd
Machine 4: Web Server, Monitor / Wotaskd
```

This setup is common when the application requires a lot of processing within user-written code. In addition, this setup provides fault tolerance in the sense that if one of the machines happens to die then the other is available to accept user requests.

Chapter 14

Many Deployment Scenarios

Even though 4 example deployment architectures were described, there are many ways to configure the deployment environment to meet the needs of the application. If for instance the application will be serving a lot of web pages, then increase the number of web servers. If the application requires a lot of processing within the WebObjects code, then increase the number of machines hosting application instances. This is one of the advantages of using WebObjects when it comes to deploying an application.

Scaling WebObjects Applications

One of the nice features about the WebObjects deployment architecture is the ability to improve application performance by focusing only on the needed areas. In many cases, when the application is deployed, the setup is sufficient to support all of the application users.

As time passes, more users are added to the system, the database grows and the application logic has been updated from a simple application to a complex business system. Within the deployment environment, we can add more machines for instances and web servers. This approach to improving application performance is substantially less expensive than having application developers increase the performance through application code.

How Many Instances To Deploy

Along with thinking about the best hardware arrangement for the deployment, planning must go into determining the number of application instances that should be running.

As a rule of thumb, every WebObjects application should have more than 1 application instance running. By default, every WebObjects application processes SQL statements in a queue manner, one after the other. If an application has a long request/response loop, then that instance is keeping other users from accessing the application. By default the WebObjects applications are single threaded. This can be modified programmatically. Extra instances would be able to handle new users requests.

Fault tolerance is another reason for running more than 1 instance. If for some reason instance A crashes unexpectedly, instance B would be able to pick up the application requests that were headed to instance A. The downside of this scenario is that all users on the A instance would lose their data and would have to log back into the application.

Obviously, the more application instances that are started, the more the system resources are consumed. Each WebObjects instance had its own JVM. The JVM requires a large amount of memory and if there are too many instances started, then the system will not have enough memory to perform its normal duties.

A simple rule to follow when calculating the number of instances to deploy is find the amount of memory that one instance uses during the business day. If for instance the system memory is 256 MB and the application instance takes 30 MB during the course of the business day, simply deduct the memory that is used by the system (256 – 50). Then simply divide the rest by the projected usage of the application. (256-50 / 30) = 7 instances.

Database Connections

WebObjects 5.0 changed the way that connections are made to the database. In previous versions, each database had to have its own EOAdaptor in order to make use of the EOF. In v 5.0 this architecture has been replaced with the more open JDBC drivers. The WebObjects runtime will only work with JDBC 2.0 versions. For reference on the driver types and operating system specific information, refer to Chapter 5.

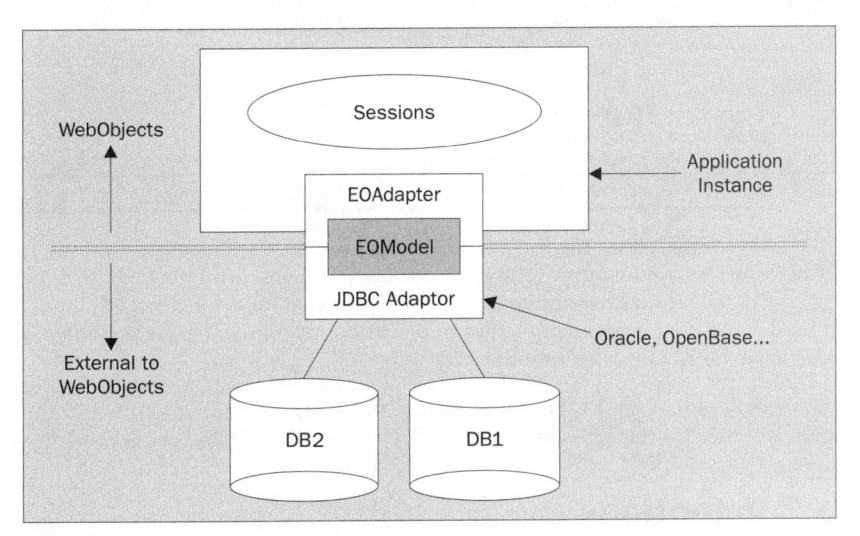

Before running the application, the JDBC driver must be installed. It is the developer's responsibility to locate the proper JDBC-type adaptor for the database they are connecting to. Windows is the only operating system that can use type 2 adaptors, all others use type 4. Once the adaptor classes have been located, the following steps must be carried out to install the adaptor.

Once the adaptor has been located, the compressed jar (or zip) file must be moved into a location where the JVM will be able to see it. This is accomplished by setting the classpath to point to the archive or placing the archive in the extensions directory for the JVM.

- Mac OS X – `/Library/Java/Home/lib/ext/`
- Windows 2000 – `$JAVA_ROOT\jre\lib\ext\`
- Solaris – `$JAVA_ROOT/jre/lib/ext`

Now that the adaptor is installed, it is important to make sure that all of the EOModels are pointing to the correct database. When developing a WebObjects application, the EOModeler is used to set the JDBC connection string for the database. Any changes made to the EOModel are saved to text files.

In Windows 2000, when a WebObjects application connects to a database through the Enterprise Objects Frameworks (EOF), it must have an EOModel for the database schema. When using the EOModeler, all changes that are made graphically are kept within a series of files within a directory with the format `MyModel.eomodeld`. Within this directory, you will find a file called `index` and you can open this file with a text editor:

Chapter 14

```
{
    EOModelVersion = 2.1;
    adaptorName = JDBC;
    connectionDictionary = {
        LC_ALL = iso_1;
        URL = "jdbc:openbase://127.0.0.1/WOMovies";
        databaseEncoding = "ISO Latin-1";
    };
    entities = (
        {className = EOGenericRecord; name = Director; },
        {className = EOGenericRecord; name = Movie; },
```

This file is the base configuration file for the model and also stores the connection information of the database. Often when an application is moved from the testing environment to the deployment environment, the database that the application is connecting to must be changed. One way to do this is to open the model and change the connection information manually. This is the only way to do it on the Solaris platform, as the EOModeler tool does not run on this platform.

To change the database that the EOModel points to, three keys must be modified: the URL, password and username. In order for this change to take effect, the application instances must be restarted.

Instance Connections

When an instance starts up, all of the EOModels within the project are read and kept in memory. The `connectionDictionary` section of the EOModel file will be used to connect to the database.

A WebObjects instance forms the connection to the database the first time the application requires database information. This information is useful in debugging application outages. Once the connection is formed, WebObjects will hold the connection open until the instance dies or it is restarted. If the connection to the database is lost while the application is running (such as bad network traffic), the adaptor will try to reconnect to the database.

Deployment Checklist

The following is a quick WebObjects Deployment checklist that can be used with any WebObjects installation. This checklist assumes that the user has already installed the web server and WebObjects software on the deployment machine and that Monitor and wotaskd and the HTTP adaptor are configured properly.

1. Move the build folder (`$project.woa`) over to the deployment machine. Make certain to watch out for line breaks when moving from one operating system to another (such as Windows to Mac OS X) as they could cause compilation problems.

2. Copy the application's `WebServerResources` directory over to the web server's document root directory. The whole contents of `$project.woa/Contents/WebServerResources/*` must be installed in the `<document root>/WebObjects/` directory.

3. Move all project-related frameworks over to the deployment machine and install them.

4. Modify all the EOModel files within the application to point to the correct databases.

5. Navigate to the root directory of the application and start the application from the command line to ensure that it will run by itself. At times, Monitor will not be able to start the application, but it will start from the command line.

6. Make certain that wotaskd is running by displaying the status page http://hostname:1085. Be mindful of whether the Monitor password has been set or not.

7. Start up Monitor. This does not have be to running all of the time, it should only be running when the deployment environment needs some configuration.

8. Set up one instance of the application in the `JavaMonitor` with the proper default arguments. Make certain to include a log file for the application instance. The common error for Monitor not starting application instances is an incorrect application path. It is also common not to include the executable name after the project directory. This error will result in the application not starting and no error message will be displayed.

9. Start the application through Monitor and try accessing the application through the standard WebObjects URL format (http://machine/cgi-bin/scripts/WebObjects/AppName).

10. Provided the instance starts with no problems, set up the rest of the application instances. If problems are encountered look at the instance log file to see if any errors were captured. It is also worthwhile to look at the wotaskd log file for the system.

11. If scheduling is being used, which it should be, then set up scheduling on all application instances.

12. Make certain that all deployment services are password protected (such as Monitor, wotaskd).

13. Stop Monitor as it is no longer required once the deployment environment has been configured.

Summary

This chapter has demonstrated that the WebObjects deployment environment allows developers to deploy applications with little trouble. It also described the components within the deployment architecture and what administrators should worry about when dealing with them. With the new knowledge, you have the knowledge to:

- Set up WebObjects applications with the Monitor tool
- Deal with WebObjects HTTP adaptors and web servers
- Troubleshoot deployment problems
- Understand the three main deployment components: web server, database, and application server

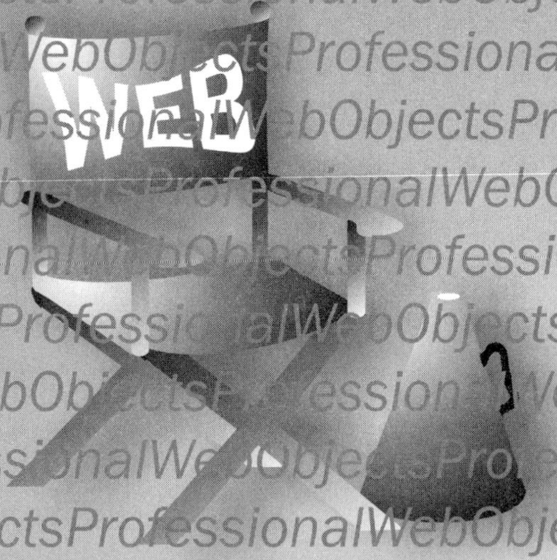
WEB

15

Corporate Real Estate Case Study

Real estate has been one of the worst stories of the web. Venture capitalists have poured more than one billion dollars into corporate real estate Internet start-ups, all of them hoping to cash in on some piece of the five trillion dollar pie that is global corporate real estate. Unfortunately, as most real estate start-ups were quick to learn, building a corporate real estate platform isn't like building an ordinary online store. It turns out that really there are two very difficult problems with online corporate real estate:

- An incredibly fragmented marketplace (the top 100 property owners in the USA make up less than 5% of the market place)
- Transaction lengths of between three and six months

How is it possible then that one little start-up from San Francisco with five engineers (including the CTO) was able to build in one year what nobody else has? You'll discover the answer to that question in this case study.

NetStruxr (http://www.netstruxr.com/), located in San Francisco, California, developed an online corporate real estate transaction platform using WebObjects. NetStruxr was founded in November of 1999. In the summer of 2000, three Fortune 50 companies – Bank of America, IBM, and Prudential Insurance – began beta testing the company's SPACEdirect real estate transaction platform.

In November 2000, these companies agreed to be strategic partners of NetStruxr and committed to using SPACEdirect for their space transactions. A growing number of companies – such as ADP, Chase Mortgage and Duke Energy – are joining the NetStruxr marketplace. To date, we represent 1.3 billion square feet in space acquisition projects on our system.

One of the reasons we succeeded where so many others failed, and therefore the focus of this chapter, is choosing the right tool for the job. In this case WebObjects was, and is without a doubt, the right tool.

Chapter 15

In this case study we'll be covering the following main areas:

- ❏ We'll examine the solution NetStruxr used
- ❏ We'll discuss the framework architecture and some of the considerations that should be applied when building large suites of applications with WebObjects
- ❏ We'll discuss rapid turnaround development and some of the ways to get the most 'bang for the buck' in terms of developer resources
- ❏ We'll cover extending `DirectToWeb` templates and creating custom look frameworks to 'skin' a WebObjects application
- ❏ The final section covers some patterns and techniques that NetStruxr has employed to build a better WebObjects application. Of notable interest are a login-required `WODirectAction` subclass and a user preference system

While theory is helpful, a case study is far more valuable with real examples that can be taken away and used. Consequently, I have tried to choose a collection of highlights from the WebObjects solution that we feel has enabled us to be successful as a software development team, and as a company.

Thanks to our executive team, NetStruxr has open sourced all of our base frameworks (the frameworks plus other resources can be found at http://www.netstruxr.com/developer). So, during many of the topic explanations, I refer to real code we use in production as a means of further illustration. In addition, I have broken out code from our production open source frameworks that is directly relevant to the topics in this case study, and included it in a 'mini-framework', ERMiniExtensions.

> At this time, these frameworks are only developed and tested on WebObjects 4.5. It is our intention to make them available for Mac OS X by the time this book is on the shelves or as soon as possible afterwards.

This framework is used in the NetStruxrCaseStudy WebObjects Application, which provides working examples of all the topics covered in this chapter. It is my hope that having real working code available to go along with each topic, will enable readers to implement any of the solutions presented in this chapter in their own WebObjects applications. Note, this chapter is not intended to somehow sell Netstruxr; we are in no way a consulting company.

The Example Application

An example application, NetstruxrCaseStudy is provided to accompany this case study. This application showcases most of the topics covered in this chapter, including log4j, a login-required direct action, dynamically switching DirectToWeb templates, and a user preference system for remembering the batch size and sort orderings of DirectToWeb list pages.

The application code provided here was designed for WebObjects 4.5, however, a version for 5.0 is available with the download for this book.

This highly contrived application manages a many-to-many relationship between users and groups. Of special interest is the ability to completely change the look of the entire application by simply selecting which of the 'looks' you would like the application to assume. The only looks provided with the application are Default and Ugly, which can be changed by a popup on the User's homepage.

Also of interest is that the list pages will 'remember' the last sort ordering and the number of items to display on a per-user per-page basis. For example try signing up two different users and changing the number of items to be displayed in the "List All Users" page for each logged-in user: restart the application and note that the number of items per batch has been remembered for each user.

The application also demonstrates the use of a login-required direct action. The same link "Super Secret Action" appears on both the login page and on the user's homepage. Note that if clicked from the homepage then the action requires the user to log in before proceeding to the secret page, but when clicked from the User's homepage the action allows the user to proceed directly to the secret page.

The `NetstruxrCaseStudy` application relies on three frameworks: `ERMiniExtensions`, `ERMiniUglyLook` and Log4j. The `ERMiniExtensions` framework contains a small subset of two of NetStruxr's open-source frameworks, `ERExtensions` and `ERDirectToWeb`.

The `ERMiniUglyLook` contains two DirectToWeb templates for the Ugly look that are used to demonstrate dynamically switching the appearance of the application's pages. The third framework, Log4j, is nothing more than a framework wrapper around the `log4j.jar` file. The main advantage to using a framework wrapper is that you don't have to modify your classpath for every jar added.

The case study frameworks and applications can be found from www.wrox.com. Before running the application the database access will need to be configured and the frameworks installed. Inside the NetstruxrCaseStudy application you will find an EOModel named **CaseStudy.eomodeld**. By default the JDBC adaptor of this model is pointing to an OpenBase database named CaseStudy, which is on the local machine.

If you use the default configuration you will need to first create a new database using the OpenBaseManager on the localhost. Next start the database via the start button in the OpenBaseManager application. Open **CaseStudy.eomodeld** in EOModeler. Click the SQL button to generate the SQL needed to create all three of the tables in the database.

To test that the database has been set up properly, try using the data browser in EOModeler. If you can successfully use the data browser, then the NetstruxrCaseStudy application should be able to run after being built. If on the other hand EOModeler is unable to connect to the database, I would refer you to Chapter 5, which covers using EOModeler and configuring the JDBC adaptor in more detail.

The Solution

So what exactly is it that we built? After all this is a case study, so we should spend a bit of time describing the solution before getting to the good stuff (code, WebObjects design patterns and more code). Unfortunately, I must briefly bore you with corporate real estate jargon in order to describe NetStruxr's corporate real estate procurement and transaction platform.

Imagine you are in charge of operations for Acme Corporation. Business is booming, and your company needs to expand in order to keep up with demand. After a long meeting, you and the other top managers decide the most strategic way to grow your business is to open a branch office in another part of the country.

In the past, you would have called various real estate brokers to find out about available office space in your location of interest. Of course, these brokers work on commission, so they only tell you about the space they represent. This process could take weeks just to locate a handful of potentially interesting office spaces. However, using NetStruxr's corporate real estate marketplace, you can find specific descriptions of properties available, prices, pictures, floor plans, and so on, within a matter of hours. All that is needed is to follow a few simple steps.

The first step to finding office space is to create a space requirement. This requirement would contain all of the particulars of your space needs. Possible criteria might include: the date you need the space from, geographic areas you are limited to, and the type of space you wish to obtain (office, industrial, retail, and so on). Once the requirement has been refined to your liking, the next step is to post your requirement to all the potential space providers who meet your criteria.

A space provider will have previously set up market search notification criteria so that they can be automatically notified when possible lessees post requirements that match their criteria. When a space provider reads a space requirement that they might be interested in, they might choose to create a space response. In the space response, they would provide detailed information about the space and terms of the lease.

You, the lessee, would then get a chance to review all of the space responses that your requirement has generated, rejecting those that you don't like and choosing to engage those responses that you would like to know more about.

Once you have engaged one or more space responses, you would proceed to exchange documents and participate in online discussions with your space candidates. Eventually, each space provider will create a lease proposal, which will contain all of the nitty gritty details of the lease.

With the space proposals in hand, you should be able to narrow down the selection even further, eventually deciding on one or two proposals that you think will fit your needs perfectly. At this point, you would create a lease term sheet that outlines all the terms of the lease based on the lease proposal, but of course only after they have been tweaked by you (a lot of negotiation of the finer points of the lease occurs at this phase).

After negotiating the fine points with the candidate, the lease term sheet would be finalized, and NetStruxr takes half a percent of the total cost of the lease (as opposed to the 6% a traditional real estate broker would take).

Right now the NetStruxr suite of applications generates around 1,000 different web pages, inserts, updates and deletes data from around 250 tables in a database, and rolls out a new version of the applications with around 400 – 500 changes and additions every six weeks.

The system also has the ability to have the entire look customized (all 1,000 pages) to a licensee's look – in other words the web application supports different skins.

One of the key decisions that made this possible was to base the entire user interface of the applications on `DirectToWeb`'s template and rule driven approach. About 95% of all the pages (about 950) generated by NetStruxr's applications are `DirectToWeb` pages. What is unique about our applications is that these pages are generated by around 3300 rules and 35 templates as opposed to the usual approach of creating and maintaining one WOComponent for every page (which in this case would be close to 1,000 WOComponents).

Framework Architecture

One aspect of WebObjects development that is rarely covered in any detail is how to organize classes and resources into frameworks that promote reuse and design flexibility. To see what I am getting at, let's mentally walk through a beginning developer's first real WebObjects development effort.

They might begin with an idea: "Wow, what the Internet really needs is interactive hangman!" They then register the domain name www.interactivehangman.com. Next they create the WebObjects application MyHangMan in ProjectBuilder on OS X.

Thinking that this will be a small application they throw in an EOModel, a few custom display components and presto: one little online hangman application. As luck would have it the venture capitalists get hold of our developer and throw lots of money at him to hire more developers and build an entire online hangman-centric community and web portal.

So the MyHangMan application grows into a fully-integrated community site with weekly hangman competitions that are well documented in the HangNews community newsletter.

However, now our developer is facing a bit of a crisis: he realizes the need for an administrative application to keep track of everything that is taking place on the MyHangMan application, but right now the EOModel and all of the custom enterprise objects are all in one application.

Worse yet, because everything was in one spot it was so easy to make the enterprise objects depend on the Session and the Application classes. Now the real problems appear, the MyHangMan application has become so popular that other sites want to license it for use in their site, but only if it can match the look and feel of their site.

With the plurality of dependencies and interconnections between the class files of the project, developing a new front end quickly or a new administrative application that reuses all the effort already put into the business logic will be a tremendous amount of work.

So, what would have been a better approach? Well, for the purposes of this case study, let's compare it with the NetStruxr suite of applications:

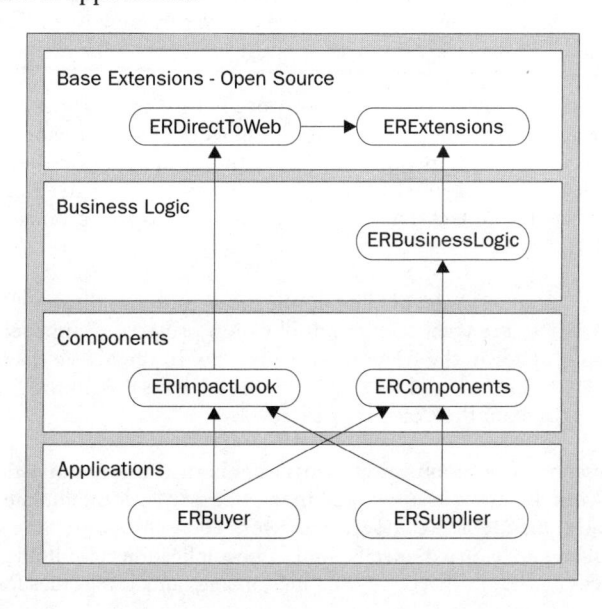

As a side-note, if you are curious as to why all of our frameworks and classes are prefixed with ER, it is because NetStruxr's original name was eResource. When switching to the name NetStruxr we felt it unlucky to start prefixing everything NS so we stayed with ER.

As the previous diagram shows, NetStruxr's frameworks can be organized into four basic levels:

- Base Extensions
- Business Logic
- Components
- Applications

Notice the levels are hierarchical, with Base Extensions at the top. For example, Applications depends on Components, but Components does not depend on Applications. The top level is the Extensions level. Classes at this level do not have anything to do with NetStruxr-specific applications or business logic. This level contains all of our base `WebObjects`, `EOF` and `DirectToWeb` extension frameworks as well as unit testing and integration of Apache's log4j, a popular logging package written in Java.

> **Throughout the rest of this case study, when a file that is public domain is referred to, the framework it is in will also be noted.**

The second level is the Business Logic level. Frameworks at this level are only composed of EOModels and enterprise objects. NetStruxr has focused from day one on stressing that business logic related activities belong in the custom classes the enterprise objects are mapped to, or in controllers of the enterprise objects. We have had great success using this methodology, especially when combined with `DirectToWeb`'s template approach toward building dynamic web interfaces.

The third level of frameworks is the Components level. This is where all of the NetStruxr-specific components reside. These components are shared across multiple applications. This level is also where NetStruxr's DirectToWeb `look` frameworks are located (`look` frameworks will be discussed in further detail in the section titled: "*Skinnable applications*").

If a component is only used for one very specific purpose in one application, that component should be located in the application, not in a component level framework. As a real world example, let's look at a component from one of our applications, `ERSupplier`. In this application there is a special component named `LinkToViewMyResponses`, which takes a landlord user to a page displaying all of his responses to a space requirement. Due to the fact that only landlord users create responses, this component was put into the `ERLandlord` project.

The final level is the `Applications` level. The applications found at this level are the consumers of the underlying frameworks. These are `WebObjects` application projects as opposed to `WebObjects` framework projects found higher in the framework hierarchy. In the above diagram we can see two NetStruxr applications `ERSupplier` and `ERBuyer`, both of which link in the `ERComponents` and `ERImpactLook` frameworks from the `Components` level.

This allows for the abstracting of common components from both of these applications into the `ERComponents` framework. Likewise as is covered in the `DirectToWeb` template section (DirectToWeb Template Based Approach), the `ERImpactLook` framework allows for abstracting style-sheets and custom images in addition to holding a NetStruxr-specific look. The applications also hold application-specific components and resources (like `DirectToWeb` rule files, images and strings files for localization).

The real benefit of this approach becomes apparent as the complexity of the requirements rise. By working mostly at the framework level, not at the application level, NetStruxr has been able to leverage all of the rich and tested business logic in internal administration and bug tracking applications.

Likewise by having a set of buckets defined for where resources belong developers are less likely to strike out on their own, which usually leads to mass chaos about the time the fourth developer 'heads out'. Also by having a strict separation between the business logic level and the application logic level there is less chance of commingling between `WOApplication`, `WOSession` and `EOEnterpriseObject` subclasses. You should always be very wary of having to include the application server import (`com.webobjects.appserver`) in an `EOEnterpriseObject`.

Rapid Turnaround Development

Rapid-turnaround is being able to change, for example, a `WOComponent` or `DirectToWeb` rule file located in a framework or application and then see the changes by just hitting the reload button on a browser. Rapid turnaround is more than just a buzzword; it is vital for the success of a business. When you have more than 1100 shared enterprise objects spread over 70 reference tables and between ten and fifteen frameworks being linked into each application, it is imperative to restart applications as little as possible when developing.

The following three sections will cover a few of the ways we have extended rapid turnaround to make our development environment more dynamic and responsive. The first section will cover how to configure rapid turnaround of frameworks when using the old `ProjectBuilderWO` (the development environment on Windows and when doing cross-platform development on OS X). The second section covers the open-source logging package log4j and some of the nifty ways it can be leveraged in a WebObjects application. The final section covers a neat base addition called a File Notification Center and how it can be used in the development process.

Developer Setup

Being properly set up for rapid turnaround development is essential to being a productive developer. The new Project Builder on OS X has made a number of great advancements in the area of rapid turnaround development. One of the nicest improvements is that you no longer need to perform a 'Make Install' of framework projects in order to make class file changes available to applications.

For those of you not using the new Project Builder (for example if you are still developing on an earlier version of WebObjects, need full cross-platform development support or are on the Windows platform), this next section is for you. If you are using the new Project Builder on OS X you can skip the next section, unless you wish to reminisce about the good old days of WebObjects 4.5 and ProjectBuilderWO.

Rapid Turnaround Development with ProjectBuilderWO

Before the days of WebObjects 5 and the new Project Builder, WebObjects frameworks needed to be installed after each compilation in order for the `MyFramework.framework` directory to appear in your framework search path (for example: `/Local/Library/Frameworks`). This was a huge pain, especially for large projects. For example, changing one line of code in a framework file required minutes worth of compilation time, and intensive resource copying.

The setup about to be described is somewhat complicated and should really only be attempted if you find that your development time is being wasted by repetitive installations of frameworks. The screenshots and scripts given overleaf are with respect to ProjectBuilderWO on OS X, although it is fairly simple to see what changes need to be made for Windows.

Chapter 15

The basic idea is pretty simple: augment the regular framework build process with an awk script (awk is a scripting language that can be executed by the build arguments of ProjectBuilderWO) that will place the built framework in a special place on a file system, then modify the dynamic linking of a WebObjects application at runtime to find the regularly built frameworks instead of the installed frameworks.

First things first: imagine you have a single framework, `MyFramework` and a single application that depends on that framework, `MyApplication`. In your home directory, create a folder named `roots`. Inside the `roots` directory add another directory: `objroots`. Next, after clicking on the build icon, copy the awk script below and paste it into the build arguments of the regular build target:

```
SYMROOT=$HOME/roots OBJROOT=$HOME/roots/objroots/`grep PROJECTNAME PB.project |
awk '{print substr($3,0,length($3)-1)}'` DSTROOT=$HOME/roots/dstroot "RC_CFLAGS=-
F$HOME/roots -O0 -L$HOME/roots" "EXT_LD_FLAGS=-F$HOME/roots" "WARNING_CFLAGS=-
Wmost -Wno-precomp" "LOCAL_DIR_INCLUDE_DIRECTIVE=-I. -F$HOME/roots"
OPTIMIZE_BUILD_CFLAGS=-O0 OTHER_CFLAGS=-I$HOME/roots
```

Note, it is not necessary to install an awk interpreter to execute the above awk script. In order to test that everything is set up properly, verify that when the framework is built, a `MyFramework.framework` appears in the `~/roots` directory.

Add this framework to the application `MyApplication` (you can navigate to the `~/roots` and select the framework). You will also need to add the `~/roots` path to `MyApplications` framework search path. As always, make sure that no other copies of the built framework are lingering about in `/Local/Library/Frameworks` or `/Network/Library/Frameworks`. WebObjects is truly amazing at being able to find stuff at runtime.

Building `MyApplication` should work just fine, but running the application will produce the error:

```
Running 'ERBuyer.woa'...
dyld: /Local/Users/max/dev/Source/Common/Applications/ERBuyer/ERBuyer.woa/ERBuyer
can't open library:
/Local/Library/Frameworks/ERBusinessLogic.framework/Versions/A/ERBusinessLogic (No
such file or directory, errno = 2)),
```

In other words, the executable can't find the framework. To change the dynamic linking of the application to find the built framework, open the run panel for `MyApplication` and switch to the environment variables. Here, add the environment variable DYLD_FRAMEWORK_PATH = /Users/<your user name>/roots. It should look like this when finished:

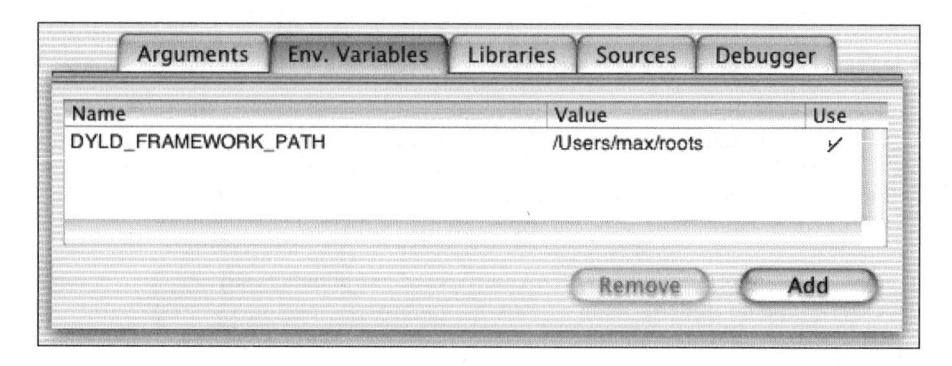

Name	Value	Use
DYLD_FRAMEWORK_PATH	/Users/max/roots	✓

The last touch is to make sure that both the framework and the application are in the global defaults `NSProjectSearch` path. If they are, then when starting the application (look at the monitor window) you should see a line similar to the following when `MyFramework` is linked in:

Found Framework MyFramework will locate resources in /Users/max/development/MyFramework

This way, when `WOComponents` or `DirectToWeb` rule files change in the framework, they will be reloaded in the same way they normally are for applications.

Log4j

One of the most important skills of developing complex applications is being able to quickly and accurately diagnose problems that crop up in the application at runtime. The usual approach to tracking down these types of runtime exceptions is either to fire up the old debugger or spray the suspected problem area with print line statements.

The problem with the debugger approach is that:

a. you need to have a good debugger (which WebObjects 4.5 and previous versions didn't really have in Java)

and more importantly (and this one doesn't go away):

b. setting breakpoints, tracking variables and stepping through code takes a fair amount of time

Another key problem with the debugger approach is that they are code centric. Most of the problems encountered when developing a complex database-driven application, center around the overall state of the object graph, which attempting to step through with a debugger can be very difficult. Furthermore, to enable a debugger's features you have to restart the application, which means you might lose a hard-to-reproduce situation.

There are some problems that really can only be tracked down by a good debugger (not usually having to do with your code at all). The other approach, adding a bunch of print lines, still means you have to restart the application, but now you also need to remember to comment out or remove spurious print lines before committing your code.

A better solution exists in log4j, an open-source Java logging package that is part of Apache's Jakarta project. log4j takes the approach that leaving in log statements is a good thing, especially if they can be turned on and off at runtime. Likewise, log4j also takes the approach that a log statement should not be restricted to just a `System.out.println` statement. Instead, the log statement is decoupled from any formatting and from the destination of where the log statement will be sent. To best see how the system is used, let's just look at some code log a few statements.

```
public static final
            Category cat = Category.getInstance("com.foo.MyCategory");

public void callingAllDevelopers() {
  cat.debug("This is a debugging statement.");
  cat.info("Thing is an info statement.");
  cat.warn("This is a warning statement.");
  cat.error("This is an error statement.");
  ...
}
```

The first line from the above code snippet demonstrates how a log4j logging Category is created. The first aspect to note is that Categories are hierarchical, meaning the `com.foo.MyCategory` is not an arbitrary name. Instead, it places the `MyCategory` Category under the `com` and `foo` Categories. This allows the `MyCategory` Category to inherit all of the logging characteristics from its parent Categories: `foo` and then `com`.

Apache's log4j also provides a priority level for each log statement to allow for finer-grained logging control. In the above code snippet you can see four of the most common priority levels (`DEBUG`, `INFO`, `WARN` and `ERROR`). The priority levels are important because these are what will determine if the logging statement will be logged.

For example if the Category `com` was set to the priority level `INFO`, then all of the statements except the `cat.debug` statement would be logged in the above method, `callingAllDevelopers()`. In this way log4j encourages the developer to group related logging categories in a hierarchical manner rather than inventing more logging priorities.

The real power is in log4j's ability to be configured and then reconfigured at runtime. The usual approach is to place all of your log4j configuration information in a Java properties or XML file. Let's look at a very simple log4j configuration file:

```
# log4j Configuration
#
# Set root category priority to DEBUG
#   also set its only appender to A1.log4j.rootCategory=DEBUG, A1

# A1 is set to be a ConsoleAppender. This outputs to
#   System.out.log4j.appender.A1=org.apache.log4j.ConsoleAppender

# A1 uses PatternLayout
log4j.appender.A1.layout=org.apache.log4j.PatternLayout
log4j.appender.A1.layout.ConversionPattern%d{MMM dd HH:mm:ss} %-5p %c - %m

# Base Category
log4j.category.com=INFO
# Tracking down a problem
log4j.category.com.foo.MyCategory=DEBUG
```

Log4j has three main components: categories, appenders, and layouts. These three types of components work together to enable developers to log messages according to message type and priority. They also control at runtime how these messages are formatted and where they are reported.

The first piece of jargon to get past is the notion of a log4j **appender**. An appender is where the log statement should be sent. In the above configuration we have configured the appender to be a `ConsoleAppender` because this is a developer system, and getting all of the log messages printed to the console makes sense.

However, once the application has been deployed, printing messages to the console is definitely not desirable. In this case you might choose to use one or more of the following:

- a `RollingFileAppender` to log messages to a file that rotates on a scheduled basis, an `SMTPAppender` to e-mail important log messages
- a `JMSAppender` to centralize all log messages via a JMS server
- an `NTEventLogAppender` to send messages to the event log if deployed on Windows

- a `JDBCAppender` to log messages to a database using JDBC
- NetStruxr's open-source `EREOFAppender` (found in `ERExtensions`) to log messages using EOF

Likewise Bill Bumgarner, co-founder of CodeFab, has created an open-source Mac OS X Cocoa application called Log4jMonitor that can be found at http://mosxland.sourcefourge.net.

Log4jMonitor includes an appender that appends log events to an NSText Cocoa widget. In this way the Log4jMonitor can be the target of one or many log4j enabled applications configured to log events to a SocketAppender. In this way you can remotely monitor logging events using a nice desktop application with a great looking Aqua interface.

One of the most important aspects to using multiple appenders in a system is setting the Threshold of the appender or the minimum priority level that this appender should log an event. For example, the configuration that NetStruxr has used successfully in deployment is to have the base Category, `er`, set to `INFO` and then have two appenders: a `RollingFileAppender` and an `EREOFAppender`.

The `RollingFileAppender` logs all the events of the system to a file specified in the configuration (for example `log4j.appender.A1.File=/tmp/MyApp.log4j`). Note that by setting the base priority to `INFO` this means that only those log events with priority `INFO` and above will generate a log event. The `EREOFAppender` has its threshold set to `WARN`. In this way when a warning or error message is generated on production, an entry will be created in a special logging table that is used to notify the developers of the problem.

The second piece of jargon is the notion of a log4j **layout**. A log4j layout is essentially specifying what other information to include in addition to the log message. For example, in the above configuration the `ConsoleAppender` has the layout set to a `PatternLayout` with a `ConversionPattern` of

```
%d{MMM dd HH:mm:ss} %-5p %c - %m.
```

What this means is that when the logging statement

```
cat.info("This is an info statement");
```

executes, what will get printed to the console will instead look like:

```
Aug 23 10:01:45 INFO com.foo.MyCategory - This is an info statement
```

In the above `ConversionPattern` `%d` specifies the date. The date format is specified in curly brackets. The `%-5p` specifies logging the priority of the log event and the `%m` is the log event message.

These are just three of some twenty to thirty conversion characters that can be specified to really beef up what your log events look like. Have a look at the Javadoc documentation for a complete breakdown of all the characters available in the `PatternLayout`. All of the documentation for log4j can be found at http://jakarta.apache.org/log4j/.

NetStruxr has extended the base `PatternLayout` (`ERPatternLayout` found in `ERExtensions`) to provide WebObjects-specific conversion characters for the WebObjects application name, application process id (WO 4.5 only), and a complete backtrace of the log event.

So, when every bit of information about a particular log event is required, say for warnings on production, the append is configured like so:

```
log4j.appender.MailMessage.Threshold=WARN
log4j.appender.MailMessage.layout=er.extensions.ERPatternLayout
log4j.appender.MailMessage.layout.ConversionPattern=%d{MMM dd HH:mm:ss} %$[%#] %-
5p %c %x - %m%n %@
```

An example from a warning for a simple `cat.warn` statement produces a formatted log event that looks like (which has been formatted for readability):

Aug 23 10:01:45 ERBuyer[4549] WARN er.webobjects.components.EditContactPopup
User: <BuyerUser: Super Cow 368>
  - Using EditContactPopup without specifing binding: companyContactsKey.

Defaulting to session.company.users.
  at EditContactPopup.availableUsers (EditContactPopup.java:51)
  at er.directtoweb.CustomEditComponent.appendToResponse
                          (CustomEditComponent.java:112)
  at er.directtoweb.ERTabInspectPage.appendToResponse
                          (ERTabInspectPage.java:49)

In addition to the `PatternLayout`, log4j provides an `HTMLLayout` and an `XMLLayout` for formatting log events that might be sent to either an `HTMLAppender` or `XMLAppender`.

The last part of log4j we should spend a bit of time on is: how do Categories inherit priorities from their parent. Recall the above configuration file had three priority entries, namely:

```
# Base Category
log4j.category.com=WARN
log4j.category.com.bar=INFO
# Tracking down a problem
log4j.category.com.foo.MyCategory=DEBUG
```

So now if we imagine in our application that we have this very contrived bit of code:

```
public static Category
      catHomePage = Category.getInstance("com.bar.HomePage");
public static
      Category catPageWrapper = Category.getInstance("com.PageWrapper");
public static
      Category catMyCategory = Category.getInstance("com.foo.MyCategory");

public void someMethod() {
  catHomePage.info("HomePage has is doing something.");
  catPageWrapper.info("PageWrapper is also doing something.");
  // Some important code...
  catMyCategory.debug("Starting delicate procedure.");
  // More real code...
  catMyCategory.warn("The user is null!");
}
```

Given the above configuration we would see the following output to the console:

Aug 23 10:01:45 INFO infocom.PageWrapper-PagerWrapper is also doing something.
Aug 23 10:01:47 DEBUG com.foo.MyCategory - Starting delicate procedure.
Aug 23 10:01:51 WARN com.foo.MyCategory - The user is null!

Note that because the Category `com.bar.HomePage` inherits from the `com` Category, which is set to priority `WARN`, the `catHomePage.info()` method does not generate a logging event that would be printed to the console. If now this simple application was put into production and configured:

```
# Base Category
log4j.category.com=WARN
```

the only message that would get logged to the appender is the `catMyCategory.warn()` message.

Runtime reconfiguration is not actually built into log4j, but adding this ability is quite straightforward. All of the code related to loading and reloading the log4j configuration file is in the ERLog4j Class in the ERExtensions framework. "Log4j" is a WebObjects framework developed by Netstruxr and is a wrapper framework for the log4j java Apache project.

The idea is pretty simple: if `WOCaching` is disabled (development mode), after every transaction check if the log4j configuration file has changed. If changes occurred, then reload the configuration file.

> *(Note that being notified when a file changes (a la `NSNotificationCenter` style) is actually covered in the next section entitled "File Notification Center.")*

Configuring and reconfiguring the Log4j system from a Java Properties file is pretty simple. Given the path to the configuration file, the code is simply:

```
Properties result = new Properties();
FileInputStream in = new FileInputStream(configurationFilePath);
result.load(in);
in.close();
PropertyConfigurator.configure(result);
```

So, how has NetStruxr exploited being able to change logging behavior at runtime? I will list just three examples from our open-source frameworks to demonstrate its power.

The first is the adaptor channel, which allows the developer to see all of the SQL that the application is producing. This can be a powerful tool for tracking down performance issues and database-related problems. The downside is that you usually have to wade through tens if not hundreds of pages of SQL statements before even getting to the page where the problem resides.

To solve this, NetStruxr added a Category `er.transaction.adaptor.ERAdaptorDebugEnabled` (`ERExtensions.java` in ERExtensions). When set to `DEBUG` all the SQL is output. Set it to `INFO`, and the SQL goes away.

A second feature is being able to find the inserted, updated and deleted objects when an `EOEditingContext` has `saveChanges()` called on it. NetStruxr has an editing context delegate (`EREditingContextDelegate` in ERExtensions) in place on every editing context that is created.

This delegate has implemented the method `editingContextWillSaveChanges()` which is called on the delegate before the `editingContext` pushes the changes to its `parentObjectStore`. The default `parentObjectStore` is an `EOObjectStoreCoordinator`, which pushes changes to the database). NetStruxr added a Category `er.transaction.delegate.EREditingContextDelegate`, which when set to the `DEBUG` priority will log all of the objects that have been inserted, updated and deleted.

Likewise, for the updated objects it will also log the updated values. Turning this category on and off at runtime can be an extremely efficient way of determining what is getting changed when saving an `EOEditingContext`.

The last example I will give is tracing rule firing in `DirectToWeb`. The most powerful aspect of `DirectToWeb` is the incredible defaulting ability of the rule system. Imagine the complexity of building the following logic in code: by default the `EOAttribute firstName` of a User will be displayed as "First Name", except in the `MyInternal` application where it will always be referred to as "User First Name" everywhere but the `pageConfiguration ListRealUsers` where it will be displayed as "Client First Name".

Providing for the above defaulting in code can make that code quite complex. With a rule system, however, the above could be expressed in three rules, namely:

```
(attribute.entity.name LIKE '*User') AND (propertyKey LIKE '*firstName')
Key: displayNameForPropertyKey
Priority: 10
Value: "First Name"

(attribute.entity.name LIKE '*InternalUser') AND (propertyKey LIKE '*firstName')
Key: displayNameForPropertyKey
Priority: 20
Value: "Internal First Name"

(pageConfiguration = 'ListRealUsers') AND propertyKey = 'firstName')
Key: displayNameForPropertyKey
Priority: 50
Value: "Client User Name"
```

With all of this power comes the problem of tracking down why a certain rule is not firing or resolving for a given `pageConfiguration`. Built into `DirectToWeb` is the default `D2WTraceRuleFiringEnabled`, which when enabled will display every rule as it fires. There are three problems with this.

The first problem is that only rules that need to be resolved are printed, rules that have already been cached will not print. This can become painfully obvious if you are tracking down why a rule isn't firing only to learn that a rule that fired and was cached five pages ago is getting reused on the current page.

The second problem is that the output displayed for a rule firing doesn't list the potential candidates, or to say this another way: What are all the possible rules that could be fired under the current situation? This is mainly useful for tracking down problems related to general rules having too high of a priority level and thus filtering out a more specific rule with a lower priority level.

The final problem with the plain vanilla `D2WTraceRuleFiringEnabled` is that when tracking down an issue, the developer is usually only interested in one right hand side key, say `componentName` or formatter. Listing all the rules makes finding the key you are interested in more work.

With these problems in mind NetStruxr used Log4j to create a rule tracing system that shows all the candidates when a rule fires and shows both cached and resolved rules. It can also be restricted to only the right hand side keys of interest and has one master Category, which controls whether any of the above should be done. This means that rule resolving in production is fast.

The master Category is `er.directtoweb.rules.ERD2WTraceRuleFiringEnabled`. If you set this to `DEBUG`, then Categories will be dynamically created following the format: `er.directtoweb.rules.<right hand side key>.{fire or cache}`.

In this way, if one wanted to trace the right hand side key `displayNameForProperty`, the configuration file would look like:

```
log4j.category.er.directtoweb.rules.ERD2WTraceRuleFiringEnabled=DEBUG
log4j.category.er.directtoweb.rules.displayNameForProperty=DEBUG
```

If you further only wanted to see the `displayNameForProperty` rules that are actually firing, the configuration would look like:

```
log4j.category.er.directtoweb.rules.displayNameForProperty.fire=DEBUG
```

All of the code for implementing the above logging behavior can be found in `ERD2WModel.java` in the `ERDirectToWeb` framework.

Another fringe benefit of moving to Log4j is that it promotes writing intelligent log statements that can be reused by others when tracking down issues that might come up at a later point.

File Notification Center

Another useful base level extension is the addition of a File Notification Center (`ERXFileNotificationCenter` found in `ERExtensions`).

The file notification center functions in a similar manner to the regular `NSNotificationCenter`. The exception to this is that instead of specifying a notification string, for example `ApplicationDidFinishLaunching`, the developer specifies the `File` object or the path of the file in the file system.

If you are unfamiliar with notifications and how they are used, read Apple's documentation on `NSNotification` and `NSNotificationCenter`. The one line explanation is that a notification is an inner-application (not intra-application like JMS) message that is posted when an event occurs. When the message gets posted, observers of that event are then given a chance to perform some actions in response to the event.

The real advantage of a notification is that the event and the response to the event are decoupled. In the case of a file notification center, the event is the file changing in the file system. All of the files registered with the file notification center are checked at the end of every request-response cycle for any changes, and the observers for the changed files are then given a chance to perform any actions in response to the changed file.

Because checking a bunch of files' last modification dates after every transaction is expensive, the file notification center is disabled when `WOCachingEnabled` is `true` by default. `WOCachingEnabled` equal to `true` usually indicates that the application is in deployment. The following code extract shows an example of how to register an observer for a file:

```
// Observer class
public static MyFileObserver {
  public void reloadFile() {
    // Reload the file and do something with it.
  }
}
```

Then to track when a `File` object (`myFile` for example) changes, the code would look like:

```
ERXFileNotificationCenter.defaultCenter(new MyFileObserver(),
                                        new NSSelector("reloadFile",
                                        new Class[0]),
                                        myFile);
```

Note that the WebObjects 4.5 Java 1.1 implementation of `ERXFileNotificationCenter` retains the observer object so that Java's garbage collector will not throw away the above observer. When the base frameworks are ported to WebObjects 5, `ERXFileNotificationCenter` will use a weak reference to the observer just like the `NSNotificationCenter`. This means that the observer will need to be retained by the object registering the observer.

This also means that the observer object will need to be removed as an observer from the notification center before it is finalized or risk a `NullPointerException` the next time a file changes.

So how has NetStruxr used the file notification center to increase developer productivity? There are a number of cases. The most obvious case has already been mentioned: tracking and then reloading log4j configuration files when they change has been a huge time saver.

Another case of improved productivity through the use of the file notification center is the hierarchal navigation system used in all NetStruxr applications. It is built dynamically at runtime from a number of property lists found in our frameworks and applications. These property lists contain navigation items where each item knows how to display itself (width, height, arrays of conditions to be satisfied to be displayed, actions when clicked, and so on) as well as its child navigation items.

Tweaking the navigation of the application can take a fair amount of time with every change requiring a restart of the application to see the results. Once retrofitted to use the file notification center, tweaking the navigation items (even removing and adding items) takes no more than a reload of the page to see the results.

Template Based Approach To Thrown Validation Exceptions

The last case we'll mention briefly is a template-based approach to model thrown validation exceptions; these are hard coded exceptions, such as, "The property firstName is not allowed to be NULL."

These types of exception message are not necessarily clear to users, so what every WebObjects developer ends up writing is a way to catch these model thrown exceptions and 'clean' them up so that they make sense to the user, for example an alternative to the message above might be: "Please provide a First Name."

This is more user friendly; however, a better implementation would be to specify outside the code the template to be used for a validation exception and be able to scope this template by `entity`, `propertyKey` and `target language` (such as English or French). NetStruxr has achieved this by building a validation exception factory. This factory automatically converts model thrown validation exceptions into the template-based version.

`ERXValidationFactory`, `ERXValidationException` and `EREntityClassDescription` are the relevant classes and are located in the EReXtensions Framework.

In this way, the applications don't have to worry about converting validation exceptions. Instead, `myValidationException.getMessage()` returns a user presentable exception message. At startup the validation factory loads a bunch of property lists from all of the frameworks as well as the application.

These property lists could even be localized. Changing a validation exception message no longer requires changing code. With the above validation factory it just requires changing a template file in a framework. Add in the file notification center and we have a way to modify validation messages at runtime.

DirectToWeb Template-Based Approach

Quick question: what is the most time consuming aspect of building a web application? If you have done this type of development before, you might have answered any one of the following: making the look of the site consistent, integrating pieces designed by graphic design artists or driving up your banner ad click through rate by hand...

When I started at NetStruxr, I thought that DirectToWeb was demo-ware, not what a real WebObjects developer would use to build an application. Now a year and a half later I wouldn't dream of using anything else. Have you ever heard the saying "If version one of an application ships thank marketing, if version two ships without a complete rewrite of the application from the ground up, thank engineering"?. Before NetStruxr I had definitely experienced the 'complete rewrite scenario', mainly due to all the changes that take place as an application matures.

When the application ships, it is usually obvious what could have been written differently had the requirements of the application been more clearly defined at the beginning of the development cycle.

Fortunately this hasn't been the case at NetStruxr at all, so far we have shipped two major releases and six minor releases and with every release the application from a developer's standpoint is tighter and better thought out. I would attribute this to DirectToWeb's encouragement to lay out an application according to the Model-View-Controller paradigm; DirectToWeb's notion of a view is the template.

The developer controls the layout with rules that determine which components to mix and match. This is opposed to the common WebObjects view approach, which is to place controller logic in a `WOComponent` and achieve a hybrid Control-View mix. Rule-based user interfaces are much easier to maintain.

In the following sections, two of the more interesting aspects of DirectToWeb are covered (from our perspective). The first section looks at adding new templates to handle subtasks and targets. The second section covers how to create a custom look for a DirectToWeb application, and then examines how to handle multiple DirectToWeb looks in the same application.

Template Extensions

Being able to extend and create new templates is another area where NetStruxr has really extended the base functionality of DirectToWeb. Take for example the DirectToWeb list page. Built into DirectToWeb is one list page for listing objects. Having only one list page available was just not adequate for NetStruxr's needs, so we built ten additional list page templates.

In the base `ERDirectToWeb` framework NetStruxr has added thirteen more templates in addition to extending the base DirectToWeb list template with `ERListPageTemplate` to date.

Chapter 15

To name a few:

- `ERGroupingListPageTemplate`
  displays lists grouped by a key and separated by a rule-specified grouping component
- `ERCalendarListPageTemplate`
  displays a list of `EnterpriseObjects` in a month calendar view
- `ERListXMLPageTemplate`
  reuses formatting display rules to produce XML
- `ERPickListPageTemplate`
  for selecting multiple objects with checkboxes

The notion of a subtask and a target was introduced to keep track of all of these templates without introducing direct dependencies between a page configuration and a template name. These were needed because the only way a page configuration would be able to use, say, the grouping list page, would be to specify `pageName = 'ERGroupingListPageTemplate'`.

Writing this rule, of course, always limits that `pageConfiguration` to using the template named `ERGroupingListPageTemplate`, which might not be what you always want as we'll show in the next section. So how is it possible to uniquely identify which template is needed for a given page configuration when you have fourteen list page templates to choose from?

The solution is to introduce a subtask and a target. The subtask is pretty simple; it serves to restrict the available templates. Possible sub-tasks include `calendar`, `group`, `compact`, `wizard`, and `tab`. The target is simply the destination of the output. The default target is html, but other possible choices are: print, XML and CSV.

Given a task, subtask, and target, the rule system is able to uniquely identify one template. For example, a given page configuration would require these three rules to identify the `ERGroupingListPageTemplate` as the template to use:

Lhs	Rhs Key	Rhs	Priority
(pageConfiguration = 'ListGroupUsersRestricted')	task	list	100
(pageConfiguration = 'ListGroupUsersRestricted')	subTask	group	100
(pageConfiguration = 'ListGroupUsersRestricted')	target	html	100

So how would the above resolve to the `ERGroupingListPageTemplate`? In the rule file of the `ERDirectToWeb` framework is this rule:

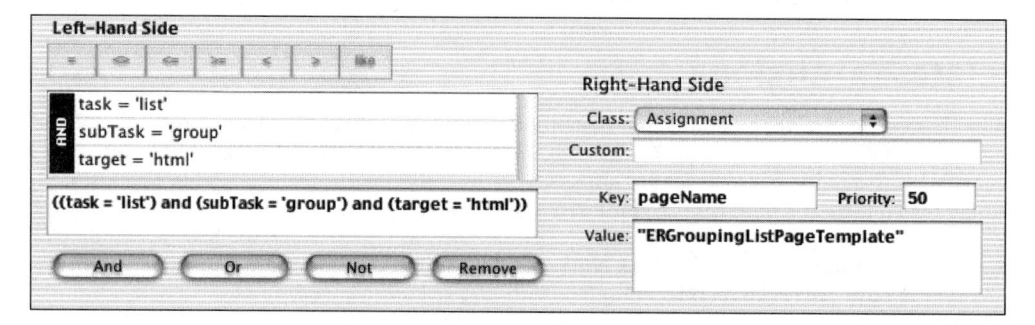

```
Left-Hand Side
    task = 'list'
AND subTask = 'group'
    target = 'html'

((task = 'list') and (subTask = 'group') and (target = 'html'))

Right-Hand Side
Class: Assignment
Custom:
Key: pageName            Priority: 50
Value: "ERGroupingListPageTemplate"
```

You might think that NetStruxr developers have to write a few more rules for every page configuration, but actually, a few more default rules will automatically resolve tasks and subtasks for 'well formed' page configuration names.

For example, the above named configuration `ListGroupUsersRestricted` actually didn't need to have any rules specified to generate the task, subtask and target rules. These base rules in the `ERDirectToWeb` rule file cover the above situation:

Lhs	Rhs Key	Rhs Value	Priority
(pageConfiguration like 'List*')	task	list	10
(pageConfiguration like 'ListGroup*')	subTask	group	20
true	target	html	10

Note that the `target = 'html'` above is the default behavior.

The list pages aren't the only places where NetStruxr has introduced new templates. In addition to extending the built-in query page with `ERQueryPageTemplate`, we have added an `ERQueryPageWithFetchSpecification` to use an `EOFetchSpecification` as the basis for the query.

In the areas of editing and inspecting, we have added a multiple step wizard template called `ERWizardCreationPageTemplate`, which is a much improved tab page. There are also many others including an XML target version for single object exporting and a compact template for embedded inspecting and editing.

NetStruxr has also extended the messaging aspect of DirectToWeb. Built into DirectToWeb are the `confirm` and `error` tasks. Each task has one corresponding template. NetStruxr needs a slightly more flexible messaging system so we introduced the concept of a `message` task with `error`, `confirm` and `question` subtasks. Each of these subtasks has a base NetStruxr template in the `ERDirectToWeb` framework.

By focusing on building reusable templates that do not have anything to do with NetStruxr-specific components or enterprise objects, we have been able to reuse code many times.

Skinnable Applications

Skinnable applications are those whose look we can completely change while keeping the same functionality. DirectToWeb itself already provides the concept of a dynamic appearance with three built-in looks that a developer can choose from when creating a DirectToWeb application using the Assistant.

If after reading the previous section the first thing you did was to grab a copy of `ERDirectToWeb` and open up one of the templates only to find that it has a very bare-bones look to it, you may start thinking to yourself that NetStruxr's applications look just like a stock DirectToWeb application.

This is far from the truth. NetStruxr's DirectToWeb applications have a significant ability to be customized, a feature that is not found in the `ERDirectToWeb` framework. So, why spend time creating the base level templates in the first place? Well, `ERDirectToWeb` is our testing bench with regard to templates.

We first make sure that they work correctly in the base form, that is, all the code that is required to make the template work its magic is in the Java file of the template class. Then, once we have the base template working correctly we subclass it in a look framework and make it appear consistent with the rest of the templates in that framework.

If you recall from the previous section's discussion of framework architecture, we noted that our 'skin' frameworks reside at the NetStruxr Components level. A given skin framework only contains subclasses of the base templates. These subclasses extend the base templates, and are polished with style elements, custom images, and reformatting in some cases.

We try not to place any code in these look frameworks because we want to keep all the logic at the base framework level. Likewise, we try not to introduce any dependencies between a skin framework and the applications or the base component frameworks. In this way, an application or framework does not become dependent upon a particular look and can thus have its skin swapped out, or even have multiple skin frameworks used in the same application.

Visually, the pieces fit together something like this:

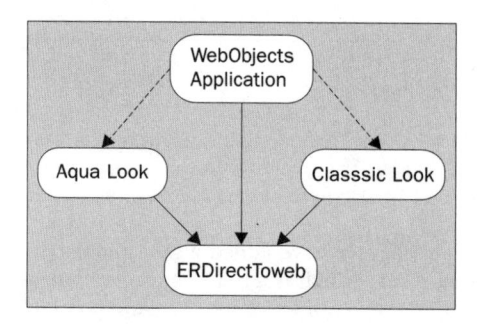

In the above diagram solid arrows indicate direct dependencies while the dotted lines represent that the framework has been linked into the application. So, how is it possible for an application's look to change just by linking in a different skin framework? To answer that question, we need to first understand exactly what is contained in a skin framework.

NetStruxr skin frameworks are composed of a style-sheet, a DirectToWeb rule file and a number of templates. The style sheet is a pretty obvious one; this is the style sheet that is used for the entire application when this look is active. The skin framework's rule file, more specifically the rules contained in the file, are actually what causes the look of the application to change. Recall from the previous section how the `ERDirectToWeb` framework rule file has a number of default rules of the form:

```
task = 'list' AND subTask = 'group' => pageName = 'ERGroupingListPageTemplate'
```

So, if we had created an `aqua` skin framework and we wanted the `aqua` subclass `ERGroupingListPageTemplateAqua` to be used instead of the default grouping list template, in every case when the `aqua` look should be active, we would add the following rule to the `aqua` look's rule file:

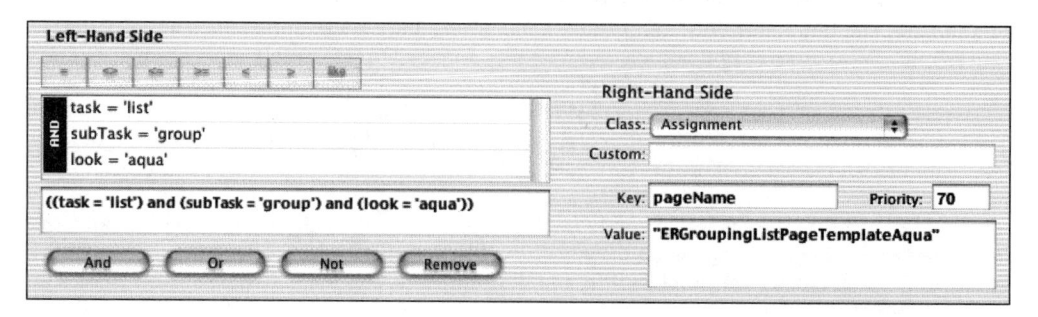

Note also that we have added the default rule `'look' => 'aqua'` so that when this framework is linked into an application it will set the look to be aqua.

So now we have the effect that without changing a line of code, the style-sheet of the application changes and all of the DirectToWeb pages that have aqua versions are used instead of the default templates in the base framework. It is also possible to link multiple skin frameworks into the same application, however when dealing with multiple looks in the same application you need to be able to have a way of determining which look should be active.

For example, let's say that we have linked two skin frameworks: `ERAquaLook` and `ERClassicLook` into an application. Both of these skin frameworks will load rules that in essence say 'I am the default look'. If left this way, the default rule with the highest priority will win out. If both rules are of equal priority, then one will be chosen at random. In either case the application would end up using only one look, possibly at random. To fix this let's imagine that we have a method from the application's session object that looks something like:

```
public String look() {
    return user().isOldSchoolUser() ? "classic" : "aqua";
}
```

Then, to have this method used instead of either one of the default rules, we could add the following rule at a higher priority level than either of the defaults:

Left-Hand Side	Right-Hand Side
= ⟺ ⇐ ≥ < > like	Class: Custom
	Custom: er.directtoweb.DelayedKeyValueAssignment
	Key: look Priority: 200
	Value: "session.look"
And Or Not Remove	

Note that the above rule uses a `DelayedKeyValueAssignment` (`DelayedKeyValueAssignment` is NetStruxr's class, even though it is not prefixed with 'ER') from the `er.directtoweb` package, not the default `KeyValueAssignment`.

The brief explanation is that NetStruxr has completely rewritten the rule-caching scheme to be faster and more efficient and has done away with the notion of significant keys. Because of this overhaul the original `KeyValueAssignment`'s return value will be cached. In the case of the `DelayedKeyValueAssignment` the rule is actually cached and not the result. In this way the key path entered, `session.look`, will be resolved every time the rule engine attempts to resolve the key 'look'.

Patterns and Techniques

This final section will cover several instructive techniques that we have used with great success at NetStruxr. The first part covers how to get more out of your exceptions. It covers a list of information that should be reported when an exception occurs that helps track down the original cause.

The second section shows how to implement in an elegant manner a `LoginRequiredDirectAction` class, which seamlessly handles logging a user into the system, if not already logged in, before completing the original direct action.

The final section shows how NetStruxr implemented a user preference system for DirectToWeb list pages that remembers the users preferred batch size and sort orderings for any given page.

Handling Exceptions

One of the most important deployment activities is monitoring and tracking down runtime exceptions that occur on the production systems. In this short section we are going to look at some ways to maximize the amount of useful information available when an exception occurs.

Usually, one of the first things any WebObjects developer learns is that it is very important to override the `handleException` method on `WOApplication` to provide a friendly exception page. The first thing to be careful of when overriding this method is to place any code occurring in this method in a `try...catch` block.

If for some reason the code throws a `NullPointerException`, the application dies. So let's look at a slightly trimmed-down handle exception method used in all of NetStruxr's applications.

```
public WOResponse handleException (Throwable exception, WOContext context) {

    NSMutableDictionary extraInfo = new NSMutableDictionary();
    if (context != null && context.page()!=null) {
```

We create a mutable dictionary to hold the extra information to include with the exception.

Let's look at the four possible pieces of information that might help track down the exception. The first is the URL of the `WORequest` with the host information trimmed off.

```
        extraInfo.setObjectForKey(context.page().toString(), "currentPage");
        extraInfo.setObjectForKey(context.request().uri(),"uri");
```

The URI can be particularly helpful when tracking down exceptions caused by direct actions, however the URI's of component actions which are generated by WebObjects normally don't provide very much information, except they can tell you which component on the page invoked the action that caused the exception.

To glean this nugget of information look for the last English-looking name in the URI and that will be the component that invoked the action, for example given the component action URI:

MyApp.woa/wo/HomePage0.9.8.3.4.2PageWrapper.0.2.3.4.4.8PickNewsStory.9.8.4.5

the action would have been invoked from the `PickNewsStory` component.

The `currentPage` is a pretty obvious example of useful information, but not to be overlooked. The next, `pageConfiguration`, is really only applicable to DirectToWeb applications. Because DirectToWeb is template-based this means that the same `WOComponent` or template will be used for many different configurations. Knowing which configuration an exception was thrown on can be a huge time saver in determining what is causing an exception related to a DirectToWeb page.

```
        if (context.page() instanceof D2WComponent) {
            D2WContext c = ((D2WComponent)context.page()).d2wContext();
```

```
        String pageConfiguration=(String)c.valueForKey("pageConfiguration");
        if (pageConfiguration != null) {
          extraInfo.setObjectForKey(pageConfiguration,"pageConfiguration");
        }
      }

      if (context.session()!= null && context.session().statistics()!= null) {
        extraInfo.setObjectForKey(s.statistics(), "previousPageList");
      }
    }
```

The last is the session's statistics store, which is an often forgotten means of determining which pages a user has already visited. The statistics method from `WOSession` will return an `NSArray` of the previous page names the user has visited. If just the name of the `WOComponent` isn't providing enough information about the page, for example if you are using DirectToWeb, then you can override the method `descriptionForResponse` and provide a more descriptive name for the component.

For example `ERD2WPage` from `ERDirectToWeb` is the superclass for most of NetStruxr's DirectToWeb templates. The `descriptionForResponse` method from this class looks like:

```
    public String descriptionForResponse(WOResponse r, WOContext c) {
      String descriptionForResponse =
                    (String)d2wContext().valueForKey("pageConfiguration");
      if (descriptionForResponse != null) {
        return descriptionForResponse;
      } else {
        return super.descriptionForResponse(aResponse, aContext);
      }
    }
```

The following lines of code report the exception in some fashion other than just printing it out. For example this method might send the exception as an e-mail:

```
      reportException(exception, extraInfo);
      WOResponse response = null;
      if (!erDebuggingEnabled() &&
          exception.toString().startsWith("EOGeneralAdaptorException:")) {
        response = handleGeneralAdaptorException(exception, context);
      }
```

If not in deployment then show default error page, otherwise show friendly error page:

```
      if(erDebuggingEnabled()) {
        return super.handleException(exception, context)
      } else {
        if(response != null) {
          return response;
        } else {
          return pageWithName("ERErrorPage",context).generateResponse());
        }
      }
    }
```

Notice from the above method the only methods that are NetStruxr specific are: `reportException`, `handleGeneralAdaptorException` and `erDebuggingEnabled`.

`reportException` is a general method for reporting exceptions, `handleGeneralAdaptorException` is a method that cleans up the `editingContext` so that future problems won't occur even if the user hits the back button, and the last method, `erDebuggingEnabled`, is nothing more than a flag denoting whether the application is in development or deployment mode.

Having a flag that is independent of `WOCachingEnabled` can sometimes be very helpful when tracking down issues with an application in production.

Tracking down obscure exceptions can be a huge waste of time. Gathering as much information as possible when the exception occurs can prevent dead ends and unnecessary speculation. At NetStruxr in addition to the above four items we throw all sorts of goodies into the extra information gathered about the exception, such as the current user, selected project and current navigation state, to name a few.

LoginRequiredDirectAction

The `LoginRequiredDirectAction` (a subclass of `WODirectAction`) is a very good and simple idea – any action in the direct action class `LoginRequiredDirectAction` will require that a user hitting that action be logged into the system before completing the action. NetStruxr makes heavy use of direct actions in all of the notification e-mails that are sent to users of the system. Every e-mail sent will usually contain between ten and fifteen hyperlinks ("Click here to see the project information" or "Click here to see more about this Lease Offer").

Multiply this by the two hundred e-mails that the system currently sends, and it is pretty easy to see that if all of those methods have to perform checks and return different pages, the experience for the user will not be consistent without a whole lot of work. Another great use of login required actions is when mixing public and private parts of sites where you really only want to prompt the user to log-in once.

We looked at a possible implementation of this in Chapter 7, however, let's look at a more involved example: the basic setup is very simple. The three pertinent class files are `LoginPage.java` (a subclass of `WOComponent`), `DirectAction.java` and `LoginRequiredDirectAction` (both subclasses of `WODirectAction`). Now let's assume that the Session has a method `user()` which will return the logged in user. Note, if `user()` returns `null`, then no one has logged in yet.

For this contrived example, let's imagine that an e-mail from a WebObjects-based system contains the following URL:

http://my.foo.com/Apps/WebObjects/MyApp.woa/wa/LoginRequiredDirectAction/superSecret?a=56&b=baby

What we would like to happen is that when a user clicks on the e-mail link they will be required to log-in before getting access to the direct action `superSecret`, however if they are already logged into the system and then click on the link they should not be required to log-in.

Let's start by looking at the first bit of code that will execute when the above action is clicked, namely the source to `LoginRequiredDirectAction.java`:

```java
    public class LoginRequiredDirectAction extends WODirectAction {
      public LoginRequiredDirectAction(WORequest r) {
        super(r);
      }

      public WOActionResults performActionNamed(String actionName) {

        WOActionResults result;
        if (((Session)session()).user() != null) {
          result = super.performActionNamed(actionName);
        } else {
          LoginPage p = (LoginPage)pageWithName("LoginPage");
          p.takeValueForKey( bindingsFromURI( request().uri() ) ), "rbindings");

          if(actionName != null) {
            p.takeValueForKey(getClass().getName()+"/"+actionName);
          } else {
            p.takeValueForKey(null, "raction");
          }
          result=p;
        }

        return result;
      }
```

The following action must have access to it restricted. Note that you will always have access to the sesssion's user and the form values:

```java
    public WOActionResults superSecretAction() {
      return pageWithName("SuperSecretPage");
    }

    public static String bindingsFromURI(String uri) {
      int index = uri.indexOf("?");

      if(index != -1) {
        return uri.substring(index+1);
      } else {
        return null;
      }
    }
  }
```

As you can see in the above class, all of the logic to determine if the user is logged into the system is in the `performActionMethod`. The default behavior of the `performActionMethod` in `WODirectAction` is simply to invoke that method on the current class. By overriding this method we can check if the user is logged in before the direct action is invoked.

This has the advantage that the `superSecretAction()` method does not have to perform any of the user checks (`user() == null` or does the request have a cookie for the user), instead it can assume that if it is being called, then the user is logged into the system.

Let's assume that the user who received the e-mail is not currently logged into the system when the hyperlink is clicked. In this case the `LoginPage` is returned with the current direct action being set the to the `raction` (redirect action) and the bindings associated with the action being set to the variable `rbindings`. The code for the `LoginPage` is quite simple:

```
public class LoginPage extends WOComponent {
  public String raction;
  public String rbindings;
  public String errorMessage;
  public String username;
  public String password;
}
```

The way this component works is that it has a `WOForm` with a `WOSubmitButton`, which is bound to a direct action named `login`. In addition to having a `WOTextField` for the user's username and password, the form has two `WOHiddenFields` that have `raction` and `rbinding` bound to them. In this way, the login page will never suffer session timeouts and the `raction` and `rbindings` will be sent with the username and password to the direct action when the user hits the '**Log me in**' submit button.

To see what happens after they hit the login button, let's look at the `loginAction()` in `DirectAction.java`. We begin by extracting the values from the query string:

```
public class DirectAction extends WODirectAction {

  public WOActionResults loginAction() {
    WOActionResults result = null;
    String username = (String)request().formValueForKey("username");
    String password = (String)request().formValueForKey("password");
    String raction = (String)request().formValueForKey("raction");
    String rbindings = (String)request().formValueForKey("rbindings");
    String errorMessage = null;
```

The login logic assumes that if the user is logged in to the system, `errorMessage` will be `null`. If so, (bad login, no password provided, account inactivated) then prompt user for correct information.

```
    if (errorMessage != null) {
      LoginPage p =(LoginPage)pageWithName("LoginPage");
      p.takeValueForKey(username,"username");
      p.takeValueForKey(password,"password");
      p.takeValueForKey(errorMessage,"errorMessage");

      if (raction != null) {
        p.takeValueForKey(raction, "raction");
        p.takeValueForKey(rbindings, "rbindings");
      }
      result = p;
```

If `raction` is not `null` then the page has a redirect. Redirect to the action:

```
    } else {
      if (raction != null) {
        result = redirectToActionWithQueryString(request(),
                                                 raction,
                                                 null,
                                                 rbindings);
```

otherwise just take the user to the home page:

```
      } else {
        result = pageWithName("Home");
      }
```

```
        }
        return result;
    }
```

The following utility method simply generates a `WODirect` with a given query string:

```
    public static WORedirect
                    redirectToActionWithQueryString(WORequest r,
                                                    String actionName,
                                                    NSDictionary bindings,
                                                    String queryString) {
        WOContext context = new WOContext(r);
        WORedirect page =(WORedirect)WOApplication.application()
                                    .pageWithName("WORedirect", context);

        String url = context.directActionURLForActionNamed(actionName,
                                                           bindings);

        if ((queryString != null) && (!queryString.equals(""))) {
          if(url.indexOf("?") == -1) {
            url += "?";
          } else {
            url +=   "&";
          }
          url += queryString;
        }

        page.setURL(url);
        return page;
    }
}
```

Notice that the above `loginAction` method really covers three cases. The first case is when the user botched the login process in some way, so the `LoginPage` is returned with a nice error message, as well as the `raction` and `rbindings` if present. The second case is when the user successfully logged into the system, and they don't have a redirect action (`raction` is `null`) so the page `Home` is returned.

This would be the normal case of logging into the system via a link from the public web site. The third and most interesting case is when the user has logged in and `raction` is not `null`, meaning the user needs to be redirected to the direct action identified by the `raction` variable.

Now recall the contrived example from above, at this point the variables `raction` and `rbindings` should be `LoginrequiredDirectAction/superSecret` and `a=42&b=baby`, respectively. Given this information, we use the static convenience method `redirectToActionWithQueryString` to generate a `WORedirect` to the `raction`, with the `rbindings` tacked onto the end.

When the `WORedirect` is returned, the result should be that the original direct action from the e-mail is again invoked on the WebObjects application. The main difference this time around is that the user is logged into the application so the `performActionMethod` in `LoginRequiredDirectAction` will simply call super's implementation, which will then call the method `superSecretAction`.

Direct actions can be a very powerful entrance point to any WebObjects application. At NetStruxr our users can view their e-mail notifications in either our online applications or via e-mail. We didn't want to have two duplicate notification bodies, one for the e-mail and one for the notification that appears on the user's homepage.

Instead, the above pattern was developed so that the same direct action would work from inside the application as just a regular direct action and from an e-mail as a direct action that would require the user to log in. The above pattern demonstrates an easy way to handle this problem in a simple and elegant manner.

User Preferences

In this final patterns and techniques section we are going to look at how NetStruxr implemented a User Preference system for DirectToWeb list pages that keeps track of preferences for each user of the system for:

- ❑ The preferred number of items to be displayed per page per DirectToWeb list page configuration
- ❑ The preferred sort orderings for each of these pages

This final topic should definitely be placed in the advanced category, so if everything doesn't quite fit together for you the first time through don't be discouraged, even those very familiar with WebObjects should get some mental stimulation out of what shall follow.

If you recall from the previous section on building an application using templates, one of the most powerful aspects is the notion of a named configuration, also called a page configuration. Each page configuration is nothing more than a dynamic name for the displayed page.

Thus for the user preference system we wish to store preferences for each user for each named list page configuration. In this section we will limit the scope to DirectToWeb list pages, but once the principle is in place it is easy to see how it can be used throughout an application.

The Goal

So let's break down the pieces, what is a DirectToWeb list page?

A `DirectToWeb` list page is really made up of two parts:

- ❑ the interaction with the rule system to display the objects
- ❑ a `WODisplayGroup` that manages all of the Enterprise Objects

It is the `WODisplayGroup` that we are interested in seeing. This is the object that does all of the hard work in terms of controlling the batch size, returning batches of objects, sorting the objects, and so on. The `WODisplayGroup` encompasses a lot of functionality that a beginning (and even advanced) developer usually ends up writing by accident.

Recall that a `WODisplayGroup` is the basic user interface manager for a WebObjects Application that accesses a database. It collects objects from an `EODataSource` (defined in `EOControl`), filters and sorts them, and maintains a selection in the filtered subset.

A `WODisplayGroup` has four main parts:

- ❑ a datasource
- ❑ an array of `EOSortOrderings`
- ❑ a batch size
- ❑ optionally an array of query qualifiers

This last portion is not of interest to us as we are only using the `WODisplayGroup` to list objects, not to fetch them.

Let's take a look at `WODisplayGroup`, spending a bit of time on each of the relevant parts above.

The datasource is probably the most confusing aspect of the `WODisplayGroup`. A datasource is nothing more than a means of abstracting the source of data. In the case of EOF all datasources extend the abstract class `EODataSource` that defines a number of methods to return Enterprise Objects. The two most common concrete `EODataSource` subclasses are `EOArrayDataSource` and `EODatabaseDataSource`.

The `EODatabaseDataSource` is composed of an entity name and an editing context. In this way an `EODatabaseDataSource` can handle qualifying enterprise objects of a particular entity. The other datasource is the `EOArrayDataSource` that is composed of nothing more than an array of enterprise objects. The `EOArrayDataSource` handles qualifying enterprise objects in the datasources array of objects. The `WODisplayGroup` defines both the accessor and mutator methods for the datasource, namely `datasource()` and `setDataSource()`.

The array of `EOSortOrderings` is pretty simple. An `EOSortOrdering` is nothing more than a key and the sort order (ascending or descending). For example if you wanted to construct an `EOSortOrdering` for the key `firstName` sorted ascending, the code would look like:

```
EOSortOrdering firstNameSort = new EOSortOrder("firstName",
                                       EOSortOrder.CompareAscending);
```

This sort ordering could then be used to sort a mutable array of `User` objects if they had `firstName` as an `EOAttribute`. The `WODisplayGroup` has an array of these sort orderings that it will apply to the objects returned from the datasource in the order in which the `EOSortOrders` appear in the array.

For example if a display group had an array containing two sort orderings, an ascending sort of the `firstName` key and an descending sort of the `lastModified` key, then the objects returned from the datasource would first be sorted ascending by the `firstName` attribute before being sorted descending by the `lastModified` attribute.

`WODisplayGroup` has two methods `setSortArderings()` and `sortOrderings()` for setting and getting the array of `EOSortOrderings` being used to sort the displayed objects. The batch size of the `WODisplayGroup` defines the number of objects to be returned when asking a `WODisplayGroup` for its `displayedObjects()` as opposed to the `allObjects()` method, which returns the entire data set.

Other useful methods on the `WODisplayGroup` related to batches are `setNumberOfObjectsPerBatch()` for setting the batch size, `batchCount()` returns the total number of batches and `currentBatchIndex()` and `setCurrentBatchIndex()` are useful for moving through the batches in any order.

So, now that we know how a `WODisplayGroup` can be useful when displaying a number of objects sorted in batches, how does the user interact with it in a DirectToWeb list page? To answer this let's look at a list page.

A DirectToWeb list page is composed of three parts:

- ❑ a navigation bar at the top for moving between batches of objects
- ❑ an array `displayPropertyKeys` that are usually attributes of the objects being displayed (`firstName`, `birthday`, and so on)
- ❑ the objects being displayed

The breakdown of the list page looks like this:

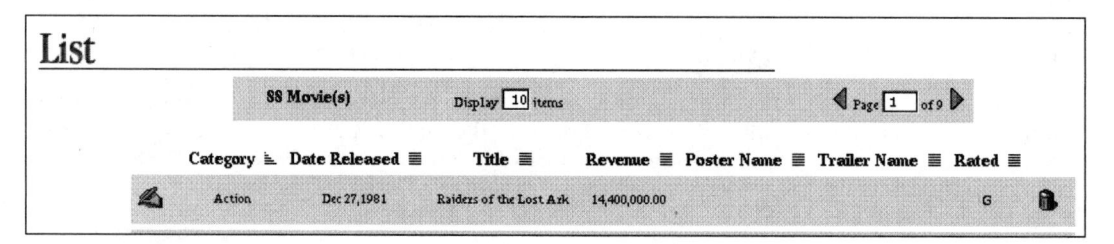

List

88 Movie(s)	Display 10 items				Page 1 of 9
Category ≜ Date Released ≣	Title ≣	Revenue ≣	Poster Name ≣	Trailer Name ≣	Rated ≣
Action Dec 27,1981	Raiders of the Lost Ark	14,400,000.00			G

Notice also that by each `propertyKey` being displayed is a little tornado image. This image is contained in the `WOSortOrder` component that when clicked will sort all of the objects either ascending or descending according to that attribute. The `WOSortOrder` achieves this sorting ability by adding, removing and modifying the `EOSortOrder` array of a `WODisplayGroup` that is passed to the `WOSortOrder` component via its bindings.

The component used to navigate between batches of displayed objects is called a `WOBatchNavigationBar`. The source for this component as well as the `WOSortOrder` can be found in the `JavaWOExtensions` framework that ships with WebObjects. The `WOBatchNavigationBar` is nothing more than a visual control for the batches of a `WODisplayGroup` that is passed in through its bindings.

For example look at the bindings on the hyperlinks around the `next` and `previous` triangles used to move back and forth between batches:

```
NextBatchLink: WOHyperlink {
   action = ^displayGroup.displayNextBatch;
}

PreviousBatchLink: WOHyperlink {
   action = ^displayGroup.displayPreviousBatch;
}
```

The Problems

We now know enough to build a user preference system for storing `WODisplayGroup` batch size and sort orderings on a per `pageConfiguration` basis. We basically have two paths to consider, the first is getting the preferences from the User to the `WODisplayGroup` and the second is propagating the changes made to the `WODisplayGroup` back to the User and ultimately the database. Since the second route is easier, let's look at the first one, how to get the User's preferences to the `WODisplayGroup`.

Getting the Preferences from the User To the WODisplayGroup

Let's first start with the DirectToWeb list page: `D2WListPage`, the superclass of all DirectToWeb list pages. The `D2WListPage` owns and configures the `WODisplayGroup`. Thus it would make sense to extend this page to understand the concept of `UserPreferences`. However, if you recall from the second section on framework architecture, NetStruxr's `ERDirectToWeb` framework shouldn't know anything about Users.

With this in mind let's instead just imagine that you can ask the all knowing `D2WContext` for the key `userPreferences` and if a rule is loaded that under the current conditions will fire, then it will return an object that implements the `NSKeyValueCoding` interface. Once we have an object that implements `KeyValueCoding`, we can ask it questions in the form of `valueForKey`.

So, let's define the questions related to `batchSize` as the key `batchSize.<current pageConfiguration>`, and the questions related to `sortOrdering` as `sortOrdering.<current pageConfiguration>`. So, what would all of this look like in code?

Let's take a look at a few methods from `ERListPage` – an extension of `D2WListPage` from `ERDirectToWeb`. The method to calculate the batch size is:

```java
    private Integer _batchSize = null;
    public int numberOfObjectsPerBatch() {
      if (_batchSize == null) {
        NSKeyValueCoding userPreferences =
                (NSKeyValueCoding)d2wContext().valueForKey("userPreferences");
        if (userPreferences!=null) {
          Number batchSizePref = (Number)userPreferences.valueForKey(
                            "batchSize."+d2wContext()
                                    .valueForKey("pageConfiguration"));

          if (batchSizePref!=null) {
            _batchSize = new Integer(batchSizePref.intValue());
          }
        }

        if (_batchSize == null) {
          _batchSize = new Integer(
                    (String) d2wContext().valueForKey("defaultBatchSize"));
          }
        }
        return _batchSize.intValue();
    }
```

The method to calculate the `EOSortOrderings` is:

```java
    public NSArray sortOrderings() {
       NSArray sortOrderings = null;
       NSKeyValueCoding userPreferences = null;

       userPrerernces =
                (NSKeyValueCoding)d2wContext().valueForKey("userPreferences");

       if (userPreferences!=null) {
           sortOrderings = (NSArray)userPreferences.valueForKey(
              "sortOrdering." + d2wContext().valueForKey("pageConfiguration"));
       }

       if (sortOrderings==null) {
         NSArray sortOrderingDefinition =
                    (NSArray)d2wContext().valueForKey("defaultSortOrdering");

          EOSortOrdering sortOrdering;
          if (sortOrderingDefinition!=null) {
            NSMutableArray so=new NSMutableArray();

            String key;
            NSSelector selectror;
```

```
              for (int i=0; i< sortOrderingDefinition.count();) {
                key = (String)sortOrderingDefinition.objectAtIndex(i++)
                selector = new NSSelector(
                          (String)sortOrderingDefinition.objectAtIndex(i++),
                          ERXConstant.ObjectClassArray
                     )

                sortOrdering = new EOSortOrdering(key, selector);

                so.addObject(sortOrdering);
              }
              sortOrderings = so;
            }
        }
        return sortOrderings;
    }
```

The last method of interest is making sure that the `WODisplayGroup` uses the above sort ordering and batch size. To do this we override the method `setLocalContext()` and perform the initialization of the `WODisplayGroup` at this point.

When using nested DirectToWeb configurations (a DirectToWeb list page inside a DirectToWeb tab page for example) the `WOSwitchComponents` used when determining which template to use, will cache and reuse WOComponents as long as you are on the same page. Thus the safe place to set up a `WODisplayGroup` is when a `D2WContext` is set on the page.

```
    private boolean _hasBeenInitialized = false;

    public void setLocalContext(D2WContext newValue) {
      super.setLocalContext(newValue);

      if (!_hasBeenInitialized) {
        NSArray sortOrderings = sortOrderings();
        if(sortOrderings!=null) {
          displayGroup().setSortOrderings(sortOrderings);
        } else {
          displayGroup().setSortOrderings(ERXConstant.EmptyArray);
        }

        displayGroup().setNumberOfObjectsPerBatch(numberOfObjectsPerBatch());
        displayGroup().fetch();
        displayGroup().updateDisplayedObjects();
        _hasBeenInitialized = true;
      }
    }
```

So now with the above three methods we can retrieve from the `D2WContext` an object that implements `KeyValueCoding` and get batch sizes and sort orderings for a given page configuration.

How do we put something into the `D2WContext` that will return an object that implements `KeyValueCoding` that holds the current User's preferences? The short answer is with a custom assignment and a rule.

The long answer is with this custom `Assignment` subclass:

```
package er.wo;

public class UserPreferencesAssignment extends Assignment {

  public UserPreferencesAssignment (EOKeyValueUnarchiver u) {
    super(u);
  }

  public UserPreferencesAssignment (String key, Object value) {
    super(key,value);
  }

  public Object fire(D2WContext c) {
    return User.userPreferences();
  }
}
```

And this rule added to the components rule file:

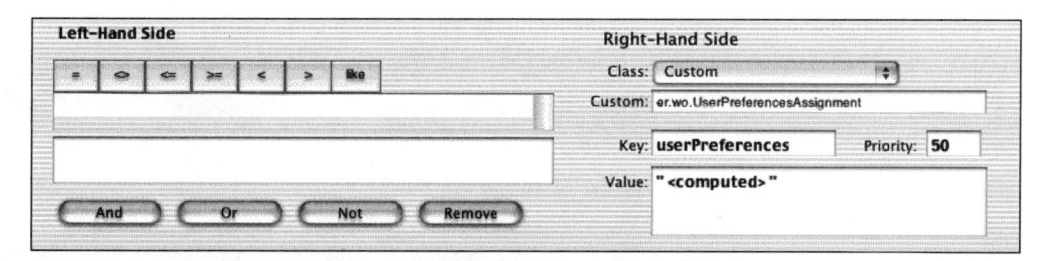

Left-Hand Side	Right-Hand Side
= ◇ ⇐ ≥ < > like	Class: Custom
	Custom: er.wo.UserPreferencesAssignment
	Key: userPreferences Priority: 50
	Value: " <computed> "
And Or Not Remove	

Note the above rule doesn't have any left hand side keys, meaning it will fire under all cases. For those unfamiliar with custom `Assignments`, they are simply a way of getting your own code to execute when a rule fires. The result of the rule firing will be cached for the life of the app so that, because the one rule added is not restricted, the object returned by the method `User.userPreferences()` will be cached and reused every time a DirectToWeb page asks its `D2WContext` for the key `userPreferences`.

Before looking at this method, let's first look at the storage and retrieval of a User's preferences. For storing the preferences let's create an `EOEntity` called `UserPreference` that will have a to-one relationship to a User. Conversely, a User will have many `UserPreferences`. This simple model will look like:

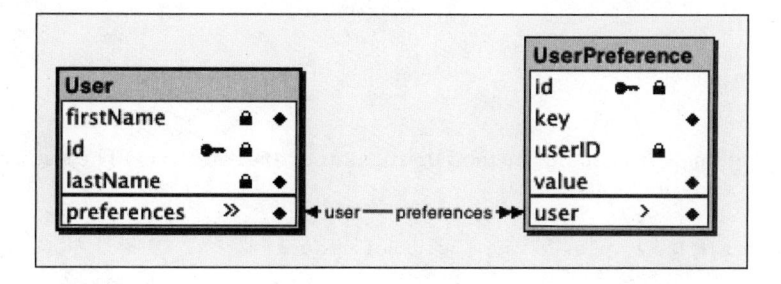

```
User                          UserPreference
firstName    🔒 ◆             id        ⊸ 🔒
id           ⊸ 🔒             key          ◆
lastName     🔒 ◆             userID    🔒
preferences  »  ◆  ← user ── preferences →  value        ◆
                                            user      >  ◆
```

Chapter 15

The `UserPreference` will have two class attributes, `key` and `value`, both `Strings` marked as non-locking to avoid `EOGeneralAdaptor` exceptions that might be caused by the same user having two browser windows open and changing the sort of the same list page (yes, this really did happen in a production environment) and the entity will be mapped to an `EOGenericRecord`. Likewise a User will have a `preferences()` accessor method that will return an `NSArray` of `UserPreference` objects.

Before continuing much further I would like to set up a little more structure. Because the business logic set of frameworks isn't aware of session objects it can sometimes be painful to know at the `EnterpriseObject` level whom the current actor is. To get around this issue at NetStruxr the notion of an actor at the business logic layer was introduced.

We'll show the full, multithreaded implementation of the actor at the business logic layer. For simplicity's sake, though, the rest of the user preference code assumes the application is in single-threaded mode. The actor methods in the `BusinessLogic` class are shown below.

```
    private static NSMutableDictionary
                              _actorsPerThread = new NSMutableDictionary();
    public synchronized static void setActor(User actor) {
      Object key = Thread.currentThread().getName();

      if (actor!=null) {
        _actorsPerThread.setObjectForKey(actor,key);
      } else {
        _actorsPerThread.removeObjectForKey(key);
      }
    }

    public synchronized static User actor() {
      Object key = Thread.currentThread().getName();

      return (User)_actorsPerThread.objectForKey(key);
    }
```

Then in the Session's `awake()` and `sleep()` methods the following must be added (assuming a `user()` method returns the current `user()`).

```
    public void awake() {
        super.awake();
        if (user()!=null) {
          BusinessLogic.setActor(user());
        }
    }
     public void sleep() {
        BusinessLogic.setActor(null);
        super.sleep();
     }
```

So now finally returning back to our method `User.userPreferences()`. The static method `userPreferences()` looks like:

```
    private static NSKeyValueCoding _userPreferences;

    public static NSKeyValueCoding userPreferences() {
      if (_userPreferences==null) {
```

```
      _userPreferences = new _UserPreferences();
    }
    return _userPreferences;
}
```

This of course leads to more questions, namely, what does the static inner class `_UserPreferences` look like? This class implements the logic for storing and retrieving user preferences for the current `BusinessLogic`'s actor via key value coding.

Let's look at this class a few methods at a time:

```
public static class _UserPreferences implements NSKeyValueCoding {

  private EOEditingContext _preferencesEditingContext;
  private EOEditingContext preferencesEditingContext() {
    if (_preferencesEditingContext==null) {
      _preferencesEditingContext=new EOEditingContext();
    }
    return _preferencesEditingContext;
  }

  public NSArray preferences() {
    User user = BusinessLogic.actor();

    if(user != null) {
      user = (User)EOUtilities.localInstanceOfObject(
                                 preferencesEditingContext(), user);
    } else {
      user = null;
    }

    if(user != null) {
      return user.preferences();
    } else {
      return ERXConstant.EmptyArray;
    }
  }
```

So far so good, all we have defined so far is an accessor method to return private `EOEditingContext` and a method to return an `NSArray` of preferences for the current actor.

```
  private EOEnterpriseObject preferenceRecordForKey(String key) {
    EOEnterpriseObject result=null;

    if (key!=null) {

      String prefkey = "";
      Enumeration e = preferences().objectEnumerator();
      EOEnterpriseObject pref = null;
      while(e.hasMoreElements ()) {
        pref = (EOEnterpriseObject)e.nextElement();
        prefKey = (String)pref.valueForKey("key");

        if ( prefKey!=null && prefKey.equals(key) ) {
          result = pref;
          break;
        }
      }
```

Chapter 15

```
    }
    return result;
}
```

The above method `preferenceRecordForKey` shows the implementation finding a `UserPreference` object for a given key. Recall from earlier, the batch size preference key looks like `batchSize.<page configuration>`.

```
public Object valueForKey(String key) {
  Object result=null;
  EOEnterpriseObject pref=preferenceRecordForKey(key);
  if (pref!=null)
    result = decodedValue((String)pref.valueForKey("value"));
    return result;
}

private final static String VALUE="_V";

public Object decodedValue(String encodedValue) {
  NSDictionary d = (NSDictionary)NSPropertyListSerialization
                        .propertyListFromString(encodedValue);
  EOKeyValueUnarchiver u = new EOKeyValueUnarchiver(d);
  return u.decodeObjectForKey(VALUE);
}
```

The above two methods show the implementation of the `valueForKey()` method of the `KeyValueCoding` interface. This is the method that is called when the DirectToWeb list page asks the `userPreferences` object for, say, `batchSize.ListMyUsers`. If you are unfamiliar with the `EOKeyValueUnarchiver` and `EOKeyValueArchiver` all you really need to know is that they are convenience objects useful when saving and re-hydrating an object to and from disk or database.

Note that in the case of the sort orders the object that will be returned is an `NSArray` of possibly multiple `EOSortOrders`. Let's also take a look at the `takeValueForKey` implementation, as we will soon need to be recording when a user changes their preferences.

```
public void takeValueForKey(Object value, String key) {
  if (preferencesEditingContext().hasChanges()) {
    preferencesEditingContext().revert();
  }

  EOEnterpriseObject pref=preferenceRecordForKey(key);

  User u = (User)EOUtilities.localInstanceOfObject(
                    preferencesEditingContext(),
                    BusinessLogic.actor()
            );

  if (pref!=null) {
    if(value!=null) {
      String  encodedValue=encodedValue(value);
      if(ERExtensions.safeDifferent(
              encodedValue,pref.valueForKey("value"))) {
        pref.takeValueForKey(encodedValue, "value");
      }
    } else {
        pref.removeObjectFromBothSidesOfRelationshipWithKey(u,"user");
    }
```

426

```
        } else if (value!=null) {
      User u = (User)EOUtilities.localInstanceOfObject(
                          preferencesEditingContext(),
                          BusinessLogic.actor());
      pref=ERUtilities.createEOLinkedToEO("Preference",
                                          preferencesEditingContext(),
                                          "preferences",
                                          u);
      pref.takeValueForKey(key,"key");
      pref.takeValueForKey(encodedValue(value),"value");
    }
    if(preferencesEditingContext().hasChanges()) {
      preferencesEditingContext().saveChanges();
    }
  }
}
public String encodedValue(Object value) {
  EOKeyValueArchiver archiver=new EOKeyValueArchiver();
  archiver.encodeObject(value,VALUE);
  return NSPropertyListSerialization.stringFromPropertyList(
                                          archiver.dictionary());
}
```

The above methods are almost the inverse of the `valueForKey()` methods with the added bonus of creating a preference if it doesn't already exist and saving the changes to the database. The methods `ERUtilities.createEOLinkedToEO` and `ERExtensions.safeDifferent` are both convenience methods from the `ERExtensions` framework that are pretty self-explanatory.

Propagating the Changes Made To the WODisplayGroup Back To the User

So now we can sit back and enjoy propagating a change in the sort ordering or batch size back to the `User.userPreferences()` object. To accomplish this we aren't going to simply make the `WOBatchNavigationBar` and `WOSortOrder` know about pushing changed values into an `NSKeyValueCoding` object from a `D2WContext`. Instead these elements will be extended to post `NSNotifications` when they change.

In this way at higher levels handlers can be set up to catch and save those changes. First the display element modifications: `WOSortOrder`'s `toggleClicked()` method is extended in `ERSortOrder` like so:

```
public final static String SortOrderingChanged = "SortOrderingChanged";
public WOComponent toggleClicked() {
  super.toggleClicked();
  D2WContext context=(D2WContext)valueForBinding("d2wContext");
  if (context != null) {
    NSNotificationCenter.defaultCenter().postNotification(
                          SortOrderingChanged,
                          displayGroup().sortOrderings(),
                          new NSDictionary(context, "d2wContext"));
  }
  return null;
}
```

Likewise `WOBatchNavigationBar`'s method `setNumberOfObjectsPerBatch` has been extended in `ERBatchNavigationBar`:

Chapter 15

```
    public final static String BatchSizeChanged = "BatchSizeChanged";
    public void setNumberOfObjectsPerBatch(Number newValue) {
      super.setNumberOfObjectsPerBatch(newValue);

      D2WContext context=(D2WContext)valueForBinding("d2wContext");

      if (context!=null && newValue != null) {
          NSNotificationCenter.defaultCenter().postNotification(
                              BatchSizeChanged,
                              new Integer(newValue.intValue()),
                              new NSDictionary(context,"d2wContext"));
        }
      }
    }
```

Both of the above components can be found in the ERExtensions framework. So if a notification is posted in the woods without a handler in place to catch it, was it really posted? The answer is yes, however we do need to put in some handlers to say that those notifications are caught.

To do this we return back to our User class and add the following UserPreferenceHandler static inner class:

```
  public static class _UserPreferenceHandler {

    public void handleBatchSizeChange(NSNotification n) {
      handleChange("batchSize", n);
    }

    public void handleSortOrderingChange(NSNotification n) {
      handleChange("sortOrdering", n);
    }

    public void handleChange(String prefName, NSNotification n) {
      if (BusinessLogic.actor() != null) {
        NSKeyValueCoding context = (NSKeyValueCoding)n.userInfo()
                                     .objectForKey("d2wContext");
        if (context!=null && context.valueForKey("pageConfiguration")!=null) {
          userPreferences().takeValueForKey(
                   n.object(),
                   prefName + "." +
                   (String)context.valueForKey("pageConfiguration"));
        }
      }
    }
  }
```

All this handler class does is propagate a notification object into the userPreferences() using takeValueForKey() for the given preference and page configuration. Now the last step is to register an instance of the UserPreferenceHandler for the notifications. This is easily done in the principle class of a components level framework.

The code for registering the handlers is:

```
User._UserPreferenceHandler uph = new User._UserPreferenceHandler();
ERRetainer.retain(uph);

Class[] notificationClassArray = new Class[] { NSNotification.class };
```

```
        NSSelector selector = null;

        selector = new NSSelector("handleSortOrderingChange",
                         notificationClassArray);
        NSNotificationCenter.defaultCenter().addObserver(
                        uph,
                        selector,
                        ERSortOrder.SortOrderingChanged,
                        null);

        selector = new NSSelector("handleBatchSizeChange",
                         notificationClassArray);
        NSNotificationCenter.defaultCenter().addObserver(uph,
                        selector,
                        ERBatchNavigationBar.BatchSizeChanged,
                        null);
```

Note that the static method `ERRetainer.retain` simply retains a reference to the object so that it will not be eligible for garbage collection.

What is particularly useful about this implementation is that the idea of the user's preferences is completely encapsulated in a nice object and the only interaction is via key value coding for pushing in or pulling out preferences. Likewise there aren't any restrictions as to what can and can't be pushed in as a preference. This makes the user's preferences completely transparent in many ways.

Summary

In this chapter, we looked at effective framework architecture in keeping with the Model – View – Controller paradigm for enabling maximum reusability. We discussed rapid turnaround development as a means for saving time and money in terms of developer resources.

We learned that log4j is an excellent time-saving tool for debugging and promotes writing intelligent log statements that can be reused by others when tracking down issues that might come up at a later point. We also extended `DirectToWeb` templates to create custom skin frameworks, which allowed us to 'skin' a WebObjects application.

Next, we implemented a login-required `WODirectAction` subclass, `LoginRequiredDirectAction`, which seamlessly handles logging a user into the system before completing the original direct action. Finally, we built a user preference system for DirectToWeb list pages that remembers the user's preferred batch size and sort orderings for any given page.

The only real conclusion that you can draw from NetStruxr's experience is: though some people may consider corporate real estate boring, WebObjects is powerful and DirectToWeb is very cool.

The hardest part for me in putting together the content for this case study was deciding what to leave out. I tried to choose topics that cover a broad spectrum of interests and experience levels. If you are new to WebObjects, I hope you have picked up a few new ideas and design patterns. If you are an old hat in the WebObjects world, I hope you also learned a few new things, and if nothing else enjoyed reading about a WebObjects success story.

A

The EOUtilities Class

The `EOUtilities` class is a very useful class. It exposes some very powerful functionality that can be used instead of writing a lot of code. It also does this at a lower level of EOF than most programmers work at. The first thing we need to do to use `EOUtilities` is add `EOAccess` to our class. The following statement goes near the top of the class definition after the package declaration, if present:

```
import com.webobjects.eoaccess;
```

Because `EOUtilites` operates at such a low EOF level, it does not have access to the default editing context. We must provide an editing context for each method when called, and decide which editing context to use. The easiest way to get an editing context is to grab the current user session's default editing context. For the examples below, the variable `'ec'` will represent such an editing context. Below is an example of how to grab the current session's editing context:

```
EOEditingContext ec = session().defaultEditingContext();
```

This code would be valid within a `WOComponent` sub-class where `this.session()` is defined as the current session.

`EOUtilities` is designed as a collection of static methods. This means that we never instantiate `EOUtilities`. The following statement can fetch an object from an Entity using the supplied editing context. We do not even need to know what the primary key attribute is, and the primary key attribute does not need to have accessors.

```
MyClass myObject = (MyClass) EOUtilities.objectWithPrimaryKeyValue(ec,
                                            "MyEntity",
                                            new Integer(99));
```

Appendix A

In this example the object with a primary key value of 99 is sought. If it is found, the object myObject will be populated. If more than one record is found, or if the entity has a compound primary key, an error occurs. If no objects are found, a null object is returned. In any case, the programmer should test the returned value before using it, and use try/catch blocks as part of good programming style.

Locking Editing Contexts

As with any EOF call, the programmer must be mindful of the current editing context. In WebObjects 5, the programmer is no longer shielded from locking warnings when they occur. These warnings are to remind the programmer that Java is by default multithreaded. To avoid locking warnings, be sure to lock and unlock an editing context before using it. If the current editing context is the session's default editing context, then this locking is already handled by WebObjects. The example below creates a new editing context for fetching an object, and then the editing context is locked before use, and unlocked after use.

```
EOEditingContext myNewEC = new EOEditingContext();
myNewEC.lock();
MyClass myObject = (MyClass) EOUtilities.objectWithPrimaryKeyValue(myNewEC,
                                                     "MyEntity",
                                                     new Integer(99));
myNewEC.unlock();
```

Remember that any relationships from this new object will cause locking warnings when they are touched. Also remember that locks are cumulative. If the same editing context is locked more than once, it will remain locked until it is unlocked that many times. This is especially tricky when dealing with loops for example, so avoid locking and unlocking within a loop.

Primary Keys

Primary keys are essential for database operations. They come in two forms: compound and simple. Compound primary keys are usually used in "join" tables used to link two other tables together in a many-to-many relationship. Primary keys are special attributes of an entity. In a good relational database design, the value of the primary key is meaningless – it simply identifies a unique object. As such it should never be set by the application. EOF should have free reign to set the primary key's value. Therefore, it follows that in the programmer's EOModel there should not be an accessor associated with this attribute. EOUtilities can then be used to retrieve the value of the primary key should it be needed.

Raw Rows

EOUtilites is where we would turn if you needed to implement a specific feature of the database that the adaptor was incapable of handling or handling efficiently. An example of this is if we wanted to count the number of records in the database. EOF can count records very easily by using the count() method on an NSArray of every object in the database. Of course this means that EOF would have to load every object in the database. Depending on the number of rows, this could take a while, and would certainly use a lot of RAM. The EOUtilities solution would be to write some raw SQL and send it off to the database and let the database do what it does best:

The EOUtilities Class

```
NSArray countArray = EOUtilites.rawRowsForSQL(ec,
                                              "myModel",
                     "select count(*) from myTable");
NSDictionary countDict = (NSDictionary) countArray.objectAtIndex(0);
Integer rowCount = Integer.valueOf(countDict.valueForKey("count"));
```

However, this must be done with great caution, because in doing this we are short-circuiting one of EOF's greatest strengths. EOF is designed to keep the programmer from having to write SQL. This is because the SQL we write may not work on a different database, as not all SQLs are created equal. This is especially true if we are taking advantage of a database vendor-specific feature or add-on. In these cases, we should review the vendor-specific `EOAdaptor` subclass to see if the functionality is already there. We should also consider using a Fetch Specification stored in the EOModel or a stored procedure stored in the database before resorting to raw SQL. If raw SQL must be used, then ideally we should query the EOModel and construct the SQL statement using information from the EOModel. We can query the EOModel for field names and ask the `EOAdaptor` for its operators in order to create a more generic and reusable code base.

Exceptions

The most common exception in `EOUtilities` is "More Than One" which is thrown by any of the "object..." methods that are expected to return exactly one object. Here's an example:

```
try {
  Movie movie = EOUtilities.objectMatchingKeyAndValue( myEC,
                                                       "Movie",
                                                       "title",
                                           "Star Wars" );
} catch (moreThanOneException moreE) {
  // handle the exception here
} catch (Exception e) {
  // Handle all other exceptions here
}
```

These calls do not throw an exception when they fail to retrieve a single object. The methods may return an empty object that the programmer must then test and deal with.

```
MyClass myObject = (MyClass) EOUtilities.objectWithPrimaryKeyValue(ec,
                                                                   "MyEntity",
                                                       new Integer(99));
System.out.println ("Primary Key = " + EOUtilities.primaryKeyForObject(ec,
                                                                       myObject));
```

The example above will always report "99" as the value of the primary key regardless of whether or not the record exists in the database. The programmer must test a fault or another not `null` attribute to be sure that the returned object is not a phantom.

Appendix A

Database Connections

During the development of an application, the database URL and other connection information may be stored in the EOModel for convenience. However, at application deployment time, the application may use a different database. This means that the database connection information in the EOModel must be edited every time a new build of the application is ready to be released to production. A better approach is to have the application dynamically set the connection information when it starts up. This information can be obtained from the environment or command-line parameters. It could even come from the user, when the user logs into the application through a standard login panel. This is especially important if the database is enforcing user-level security. `EOUtilities` has a method called `connectWithModelNamed()` that accepts a connection dictionary and sets up a connection to the database.

Useful EOUtilities Methods

In this section we will discuss many of the useful methods associated with `EOUtilities`.

Creating New EOs

The follow method can be used to create a new EO.

createAndInsertInstance()

```
public static com.webobjects.eocontrol.EOEnterpriseObject
    createAndInsertInstance(
    com.webobjects.eocontrol.EOEditingContext editingContext,
                                    String entityName)
```

The `createAndInsertInstance()` method accomplishes in one step the creation of a new EO of the class associated with the specified entity, and insertion of that object into the specified editing context. The returned object will be of class `EOEnterpriseObject`, but can be cast to the specific class type. In the example below, the editing context has already been defined as `myEC`.

```
Movie newMovie = (Movie) createAndInsertInstance(myEC, "Movie");
```

Fetching Multiple Objects

In this section we'll examine the methods available to us if we want to retrieve more than one object at once.

objectsWithQualifierFormat()

```
public static NSArray objectsWithQualifierFormat(
            com.webobjects.eocontrol.EOEditingContext editingContext,
                                    String entityName,
                                    String format,
                                    NSArray arguments)
```

The `objectsWithQualifierFormat()` method is used to fetch EOs from an entity using the supplied format string and arguments. The string is a valid SQL statement WHERE clause, substituting C formatting characters instead of values. For objects, use "%@" as the place holder, as shown in the example opposite:

The EOUtilities Class

```
NSMutableArray argArray = new NSMutableArray();
argArray.addObject("Star Wars");
String formatString = new String("title=%@");
NSArray results = EOUtilities.objectsWithQualifierFormat(myEC,
                                                formatString,
                                                argArray);
```

This method would be used when the arguments of the query are already in an ordered array. The order of the objects in the array must match the format string.

objectsMatchingKeyAndValue()

```
public static NSArray objectsMatchingKeyAndValue(
        com.webobjects.eocontrol.EOEditingContext editingContext,
                                            String entityName,
                                               String key,
                                               Object value)
```

The `objectsMatchingKeyAndValue()` method is used to fetch records from an entity using a single key and value as criteria. Use this method as a quick way to fetch all records matching one value in a field. In the example below we will fetch a list of all movies with an "R" rating:

```
NSArray results = EOUtilities.objectsMatchingKeyAndValue( myEC,
                                                "rated",
                                                "R" );
```

objectsMatchingValues()

```
public static NSArray objectsMatchingValues(
        com.webobjects.eocontrol.EOEditingContext editingContext,
                                            String entityName,
                                            NSDictionary values)
```

The `objectsMatchingValues()` method is used to fetch an array of EOs from an entity using the supplied dictionary of `values` as criteria. The criteria are used as `AND` qualifiers and all criteria must be met by the resultset. Therefore, we can use this method if there is more than one criterion to be satisfied. This method can also be used in conjunction with the `destinationKeyForSourceObject()` method to access keys that do not have accessor methods, as illustrated below:

```
Studio studio = (Studio) EOUtilities.objectMatchingKeyAndValue(myEC,
                                                "Studio",
                                                "name",
                                            "20th Century Fox");
NSDictionary studioForeignKey = EOUtilities.destinationKeyForSourceObject(
                                                myEC,
                                                studio,
                                                "movies");
NSArray results = EOUtilities.objectsMatchingValues( myEC,
                                                "Movie",
                                            studioForeignKey );
```

objectsOfClass()

```
public static NSArray objectsOfClass(
            com.webobjects.eocontrol.EOEditingContext editingContext,
                                        Class classObject)
```

The `objectsOfClass()` method is a quick way to get all of the EOs from an entity. This method is extremely useful for reference lookup tables, for example a list of states, where the entire list of data is needed. Unfortunately, the list usually will need to be sorted before use. This method will throw an exception if more than one entity exists for the class. In the example below, we fetch a list of all studios; this could be used in a pop-up list:

```
NSArray results = objectsOfClass(myEC,
                "webobjectsexamples.businesslogic.movies.server.Studio");
```

objectsForEntityNamed()

```
public static NSArray objectsForEntityNamed(
com.webobjects.eocontrol.EOEditingContext editingContext, String entityName)
```

The `objectsForEntityNamed()` method is an easy way to retrieve all the EOs from an entity, where we pass the method the editing context and the entity name.

objectsWithFetchSpecificationAndBindings()

```
public static NSArray objectsWithFetchSpecificationAndBindings(
            com.webobjects.eocontrol.EOEditingContext editingContext,
                                        String entityName,
                                        String fetchSpecName,
                                        NSDictionary bindings)
```

The `objectsWithFetchSpecificationAndBindings()` method is used to fetch an array of EOs resulting from the EOModel's fetch specification, with the name specified using the supplied dictionary of bindings. Here's an example of it being used:

```
NSDictionary bindingsDict = new NSMutableDictionary();
bindingsDict.setObjectForKey("20th Century Fox", "studio");
bindingsDict.setObjectForKey("Star", "title");
NSArray results = objectsWithFetchSpecificationAndBindings( myEC,
                                        "Movie",
                                        "QualifierVariable",
                                        bindingsDict );
```

Fetching Single Objects

The methods in this section are used to fetch exactly one record from the database and turn it into an object. These methods must be used very cautiously because they rely on the database design to enforce the uniqueness of the results. When in doubt, it is preferable to use one of the "Multiple Objects" methods from the previous section and simply count the results.

The EOUtilities Class

objectMatchingKeyAndValue()

```
public static com.webobjects.eocontrol.EOEnterpriseObject
        objectMatchingKeyAndValue(
        com.webobjects.eocontrol.EOEditingContext editingContext,
                                        String entityName,
                                            String key,
                                            Object value)
```

The `objectMatchingKeyAndValue()` method is used to fetch exactly one EO from an entity matching the criteria defined with one key and value. This method throws an exception if more than one object is found.

This method is helpful if the database has a unique index constraint on the field in question even though the field is not the primary key. The method can also be used where the normal result of such a fetch will be one record and the exceptional case can be handled as an error. However, this method should not be used to fetch using the primary key because there is another API for that purpose.

If no objects are found, it may return a phantom object. The returned object should be tested before use. In the example below the title should be unique, but since it is common for two movies to have the same name, the code needs to handle that eventuality and trap those errors. The `try/catch` statements should be implied in the block below to handle `MoreThanOneException` and `null` object results:

```
Movie movie = EOUtilities.objectMatchingKeyAndValue( myEC,
                                            "Movie",
                                            "title",
                                    "Star Wars" );
```

objectMatchingValues()

```
public static com.webobjects.eocontrol.EOEnterpriseObject
        objectMatchingValues(
        com.webobjects.eocontrol.EOEditingContext editingContext,
                                        String entityName,
                                    NSDictionary values)
```

The `objectMatchingValues()` method is used to fetch exactly one EO from an entity by using the dictionary of key value pairs as AND criteria. All of the criteria must be met. This method should be used when the database enforces a compound unique index on the fields in question and when the expected result is exactly one object. Any other result should be handled as an error. This method throws an exception if more than one object is found. If no objects are found, it may return a phantom object. The returned object should be tested before use; `try/catch` statements are implied in the example block below to handle `MoreThanOneException` and `null` object results.

```
NSMutableDictionary valueDict = new NSMutableDictionary();
valueDict.setObjectForKey("title", "Star Wars");
valueDict.setObjectForKey("rated", "PG");
Movie movie = EOUtilities.objectmatchingValues( myEC, "Movie", valueDict );
```

objectWithFetchSpecificationAndBindings()

```
public static com.webobjects.eocontrol.EOEnterpriseObject
        objectWithFetchSpecificationAndBindings(
        com.webobjects.eocontrol.EOEditingContext editingContext,
                                        String entityName,
                                    String fetchSpecName,
                                    NSDictionary bindings)
```

Appendix A

The `objectWithFetchSpecificationAndBindings()` method makes using EOModel-defined Fetch Specifications easy and returns exactly one EO by just supplying the entity, fetch specification and a dictionary of bindings. This method is just like the `objectsWithFetchSpecificationAndBindings()` method above except that it should only be used when the results should be exactly one record. Any other result will need to be handled as an error, and the method throws an exception if more than one object are found. As usual, if no objects are found, it may return a phantom object, and the returned object should be tested before use. Here's an example of it in use:

```
NSDictionary bindingsDict = new NSMutableDictionary();
bindingsDict.setObjectForKey("20th Century Fox", "studio");
bindingsDict.setObjectForKey("Star", "title");
Movie movie = (Movie) objectWithFetchSpecificationAndBindings( myEC,
                                                                "Movie",
                                                      "QualifierVariable",
                                                             bindingsDict);
```

objectWithPrimaryKey()

```
public static com.webobjects.eocontrol.EOEnterpriseObject
        objectWithPrimaryKey(
        com.webobjects.eocontrol.EOEditingContext editingContext,
                                      String entityName,
                           NSDictionary keyDictionary)
```

The `objectwithPrimaryKeyValue()` is used to fetch exactly one EO from an entity that matches the primary key dictionary supplied. Ideally the primary key of the entity should not have accessor methods defined. If primary keys are used in conjunction with directactions, then this is the ideal method to turn those direct action keys into objects. This method throws an exception if more than one object is found; if no objects are found, it may return a phantom object. As before, the returned object should be tested before use. In the example below, `request()` refers to the current request inside the `WODirectAction` class:

```
Number movieOID = Long.valueOf( request().formValueForKey("id") );
Movie movie = (Movie) EOUtilities.objectWithPrimaryKeyValue( myEC,
                                                              "Movie",
                                                         movieOID );
```

objectWithPrimaryKeyValue()

```
public static com.webobjects.eocontrol.EOEnterpriseObject
        objectWithPrimaryKeyValue(
        com.webobjects.eocontrol.EOEditingContext editingContext,
                                        String entityName,
                                            Object value)
```

This method performs exactly the same action as the `objectWithPrimaryKey()` method, except that the primary key value is supplied to the method instead of the primary key dictionary. Here's the equivalent of the previous example, but using the `objectWithPrimaryKeyValue()` method instead:

```
Number movieOID = Long.valueOf( request().formValueForKey("id") );
Movie movie = (Movie) EOUtilities.objectWithPrimaryKeyValue( myEC,
                                                              "Movie",
                                                         movieOID );
```

The EOUtilities Class

objectWithQualifierFormat()

```
public static com.webobjects.eocontrol.EOEnterpriseObject
objectWithQualifierFormat( com.webobjects.eocontrol.EOEditingContext
editingContext, String entityName, String format, NSArray arguments)
```

This is equivalent to the `objectsWithQualifierFormat()` method, but it returns a single EO. In the example of its use below, error checking is required as there is a high likelihood of having two movies with the same title:

```
NSMutableArray argArray = new NSMutableArray();
argArray.addObject("Star Wars");
String formatString = new String("title=%@");
Movie movie = EOUtilities.objectWithQualifierFormat(myEC,
                                    formatString,
                                        argArray);
```

Accessing Object Information

The following methods are used to access the object data.

destinationKeyForSourceObject()

```
public static NSDictionary destinationKeyForSourceObject(
            com.webobjects.eocontrol.EOEditingContext editingContext,
            com.webobjects.eocontrol.EOEnterpriseObject object,
            String relationshipName)
```

The `destinationKeyForSourceObject()` method is used to find the foreign key and value in a relationship defined in the model. The foreign key will be the related attribute in the related entity. Here's an example, where we fetch an object, get the foreign key and value from the `"movies"` relationship, and then obtain a resultset based upon this relationship:

```
Studio studio = (Studio) EOUtilities.objectMatchingKeyAndValue(myEC,
                                            "Studio",
                                            "name",
                                    "20th Century Fox");
NSDictionary studioForeignKey = EOUtilities.destinationKeyForSourceObject(
                                            myEC,
                                            studio,
                                            "movies");
NSArray results = EOUtilities.objectsMatchingValues( myEC,
                                            "Movie",
                                    studioForeignKey );
```

localInstanceOfObject()

```
public static com.webobjects.eocontrol.EOEnterpriseObject
    localInstanceOfObject(
        com.webobjects.eocontrol.EOEditingContext editingContext,
        com.webobjects.eocontrol.EOEnterpriseObject object)
```

Appendix A

The `localInstanceOfObject()` method is used to translate the supplied EO into the supplied editing context. This method is necessary to assure that the object is being used in the correct editing context; using an object in the wrong context puts the program at risk of locking errors and multi-threading problems. We should always bring an object into a local editing context before using it. Before using this object in the current session, we need to make a local instance of it. In the example below, assume that the method `topMovie()` is in the application class, and returns a `Movie` object:

```
Movie movie = EOUtilities.localInstanceOfObject( myEC,
              ((Application)WOApplication.application()).topMovie() );
```

localInstancesOfObjects()

```
public static NSArray localInstancesOfObjects(
         com.webobjects.eocontrol.EOEditingContext editingContext,
                                         NSArray objects)
```

This method has exactly the same functionality as `localInstanceOfObjects()` method except that it translates more than one EO into the editing context.

primaryKeyForObject()

```
public static NSDictionary primaryKeyForObject(
         com.webobjects.eocontrol.EOEditingContext editingContext,
         com.webobjects.eocontrol.EOEnterpriseObject object)
```

The `primaryKeyForObject()` method returns a dictionary containing one key value pair that is the primary key attribute and its value, even if the EOModel does not specify that the attribute has accessors. This is a very safe way to get the value of the primary key of an EO without defining accessors, which may cause problems if used incorrectly. The entity must have just one primary key, and if the entity has a compound primary key then an exception will be thrown. If no primary key can be found then an exception will be thrown. The example below could be used to get the primary key for the `movie` object:

```
NSDictionary keyDict = EOUtilities.primaryKeyForObject(
                                   movie.editingContext(),
                                                   movie)
Number oid = keyDict.objectForKey("movieID");
```

Dealing with Raw Rows

Raw rows are a way to deal with data that is not defined in the EOModel effectively. Raw rows can be used to get transient results that then can be thrown away, or transformed into real EOs.

executeStoredProcedureNamed()

```
public static NSDictionary executeStoredProcedureNamed(
         com.webobjects.eocontrol.EOEditingContext editingContext,
                                  String storedProcedureName,
                                        NSDictionary arguments)
```

The `executeStoredProcedureNamed()` method is used to run a stored procedure on the database server that does not actually return data. The returned dictionary contains return values such as number of rows updated, if the stored procedure returns any values at all. The format of the stored procedure is completely dependent on the database vendor. The example opposite is for Oracle.

Oracle Stored Procedure:

```
CREATE OR REPLACE PROCEDURE PROC1(
    X   IN    VARCHAR2,
    Y   OUT   VARCHAR2,
    Z   OUT   VARCHAR2) IS
BEGIN
    Y := X;
    Z := 'World';
END;
```

WebObjects:

```
NSDictionary argDict = new NSDictionary("Hello","There");
NSDictionary retDict  =  EOUtilities.executeStoredProcedureNamed(MyEC,
                                                          "proc1",
                                                          argDict );
dat1 = (String)retDict.valueForKey("y"); // "Hello"
dat2 = (String)retDict.valueForKey("z"); // "World"
```

objectFromRawRow()

```
public static com.webobjects.eocontrol.EOEnterpriseObject objectFromRawRow(
            com.webobjects.eocontrol.EOEditingContext editingContext,
                                       String entityName,
                                       NSDictionary row)
```

The `objectFromRawRow()` method is used to convert raw rows, once they have been fetched from the database using one of the other methods in this section, into EOs. The raw row must include the entity's primary key. This method actually fires a fault using `EOEditingContext`'s `faultForRawRow()` method. The example below assumes that `movieDict` has already been fetched from the database from the `Movie` table:

```
Movie movie = EOUtilities.objectFromRawRow( myEC, "Movie", movieDict );
```

rawRowsForSQL()

```
public static NSArray rawRowsForSQL(
           com.webobjects.eocontrol.EOEditingContext editingContext,
                                       String modelName,
                                       String sqlString)
```

The `rawRowsForSQL()` method is used to fetch the results of a query executed on the database using the supplied SQL statement. You should note that the syntax of the statement is not checked before it is sent to the database. The model name is used for database connectivity. The exact syntax of the SQL statement is tied to the target SQL database vendor; if the vendor changes the syntax of the SQL statement may need to change too.

The example overleaf is designed to work with OpenBase taking advantage of that vendor's indexing and searching ability. It assumes that the `Summary` field in the `Plot Summary` table has been indexed. In this example we want to count how many times the letter 'a' appears in each summary. The resulting raw row dictionaries will have two keys, `MOVIE_ID` and `HITS`:

Appendix A

```
String sqlText = new String("SELECT MOVIE_ID,
                        count(MOVIE_ID) AS HITS FROM PLOT_SUMMARY
                        WHERE SUMMARY LIKE \"*a*\"
                        GROUP BY MOVIE_ID");
NSArray results = EOUtilities.rawRowsForSQL( myEC, "PlotSummary", sqlText );
```

rawRowsForStoredProcedureNamed()

```
public static NSArray rawRowsForStoredProcedureNamed(
                com.webobjects.eocontrol.EOEditingContext editingContext,
                                String storedProcedureName,
                                NSDictionary arguments)
```

The `rawRowsForStoredProcedureNamed()` method is used to fetch the results of a stored procedure. The supplied dictionary of arguments is passed to the stored procedure as arguments. This method is very useful when a stored procedure returns a success or failure message. The example below gets raw rows from a stored procedure named `Proc1` but does not send any parameters:

```
NSArray results = EOUtilities.rawRowsForStoredProcedureNamed ( myEC,
                                                "Proc1",
                                        new NSDictionary() );
```

rawRowsMatchingKeyAndValue()

```
public static NSArray rawRowsMatchingKeyAndValue(
                com.webobjects.eocontrol.EOEditingContext editingContext,
                                String entityName,
                                String key,
                                Object value)
```

The `rawRowsMatchingKeyAndValue()` method is used to fetch raw row dictionaries from an entity when exactly one qualifier is specified using the supplied key and value.

```
NSArray results = EOUtilities.rawRowsMatchingKeyAndValue( myEC,
                                                "Movie",
                                                "title",
                                                "Star Wars" );
```

rawRowsMatchingValues()

```
public static NSArray rawRowsMatchingValues(
                com.webobjects.eocontrol.EOEditingContext editingContext,
                String entityName,
                NSDictionary values)
```

The `rawRowsMatchingValues()` method is used to fetch raw row dictionaries from an entity using a dictionary of key-value pairs as the qualifier. In other words, this is the raw row equivalent of `objectsMatchingValues()`. All elements in the dictionary are joined together using AND qualifiers such that all criteria must be met in the result set. Here's an example of the method being used:

```
NSMutableDictionary valueDict = new NSMutableDictionary();
valueDict.setObjectForKey("title", "Star Wars");
valueDict.setObjectForKey("rated", "PG");
NSArray results = EOUtilities.rawRowsMatchingValues( myEC,
                                                "Movie",
                                                valueDict );
```

rawRowsWithQualifierFormat()

```
public static NSArray rawRowsWithQualifierFormat(
            com.webobjects.eocontrol.EOEditingContext editingContext,
                                         String entityName,
                                            String format,
                                         NSArray arguments)
```

The `rawRowsWithQualifierFormat()` method is used to fetch raw row dictionaries from an entity, using a string qualifier and an array of values. Therefore, this is the raw row equivalent of `objectsWithQualifierFormat()`.

Accessing the EOF Stack

The methods in this section pertain to the actual connection to the database.

connectWithModelNamed()

```
public static void connectWithModelNamed(
            com.webobjects.eocontrol.EOEditingContext editingContext,
                                         String modelName,
                                         NSDictionary overrides)
```

The `connectWithModelNamed()` method facilitates logging into the database with credentials usually supplied by the user at runtime. This method throws an exception if the connection fails because of invalid username or password or another reason. Since the `.eomodeld` file is just a text file, it would be considered a security risk to store the password to the database in this file. Using this method allows the programmer to store that password in a safer place, such as a command line parameter. Here's a typical example:

```
NSMutableDictionary settingsToOverride = new NSMutableDictionary();
settingsToOverride.setObjectForKey("xxxxx", "userName");
settingsToOverride.setObjectForKey("xxxxx", "password");
EOUtilities.connectWithModelNamed(this.defaultEditingContext(),
                                        "WOMovies",
                                  settingsToOverride );
```

databaseContextForModelNamed()

```
public static EODatabaseContext databaseContextForModelNamed(
            com.webobjects.eocontrol.EOEditingContext editingContext,
                                         String modelName)
```

The `databaseContextForModelNamed()` is used to get the database context currently being used for the supplied model. Do not confuse database context with editing context. The example below shows how you can use the `EODatabaseContext` to get to the `EODatabase`.

```
EODatabaseContext aDatabaseContext =
                        EOUtilities.databaseContextForModelNamed(
                                                myEC,
                                                "WOMovies" );
EODatabase aDatabase = aDatabaseContext.database();
```

Appendix A

Accessing EOModel Information

The methods in this section are used to return an enterprise object entity object for a given object or name. Having access to an `EOEntity` object is useful for finding out other model information such as the table name from the database. This in turn could be used to generate raw SQL.

entityForClass()

```
public static EOEntity entityForClass(
            com.webobjects.eocontrol.EOEditingContext editingContext,
                                        Class classObject)
```

The `entityForClass()` method is used to get an `EOEntity` object from an EOModel in the current editing context, when the class specified is known. If the entity cannot be found or is not unique, then an exception is thrown. Here's an example:

```
EOEntity movieEntity = EOUtilities.entityForClass ( myEC,
            webobjectsexamples.businesslogic.movies.server.Studio );
```

entityForObject()

```
public static EOEntity entityForObject(
            com.webobjects.eocontrol.EOEditingContext editingContext,
            com.webobjects.eocontrol.EOEnterpriseObject object)
```

The `entityForObject()` method performs the same functionality as `entityForClass()`, except that an EO is supplied as argument instead of a class.

entityNamed()

```
public static EOEntity entityNamed(
            com.webobjects.eocontrol.EOEditingContext editingContext,
                                        String entityName)
```

The `entityNamed()` method is used to get an `EOEntity` object from an EOModel in the current editing context, when the entity name is known. The programmer needs to make sure that the entity name exists and is unique, or an exception will be thrown. Here's a typical example of how this method is used:

```
EOEntity movieEntity = EOUtilities.entityNamed( myEC, "Movie" );
```

modelGroup()

```
public static EOModelGroup modelGroup(com.webobjects.eocontrol.EOEditingContext
    editingContext)
```

The `modelGroup()` method is used to get an `EOModelGroup` object associated with the root object store (an `EOObjectStoreCoordinator`). From the model group a list of EOModels can be found. This is useful when the programmer wants to interrogate or change the EOModel directly. The example below gives you a list of all EOModels currently in the project:

```
EOModelGroup modelGroup = EOUtilities.entityForClass ( myEC );
NSArray models = modelGroup.models();
```

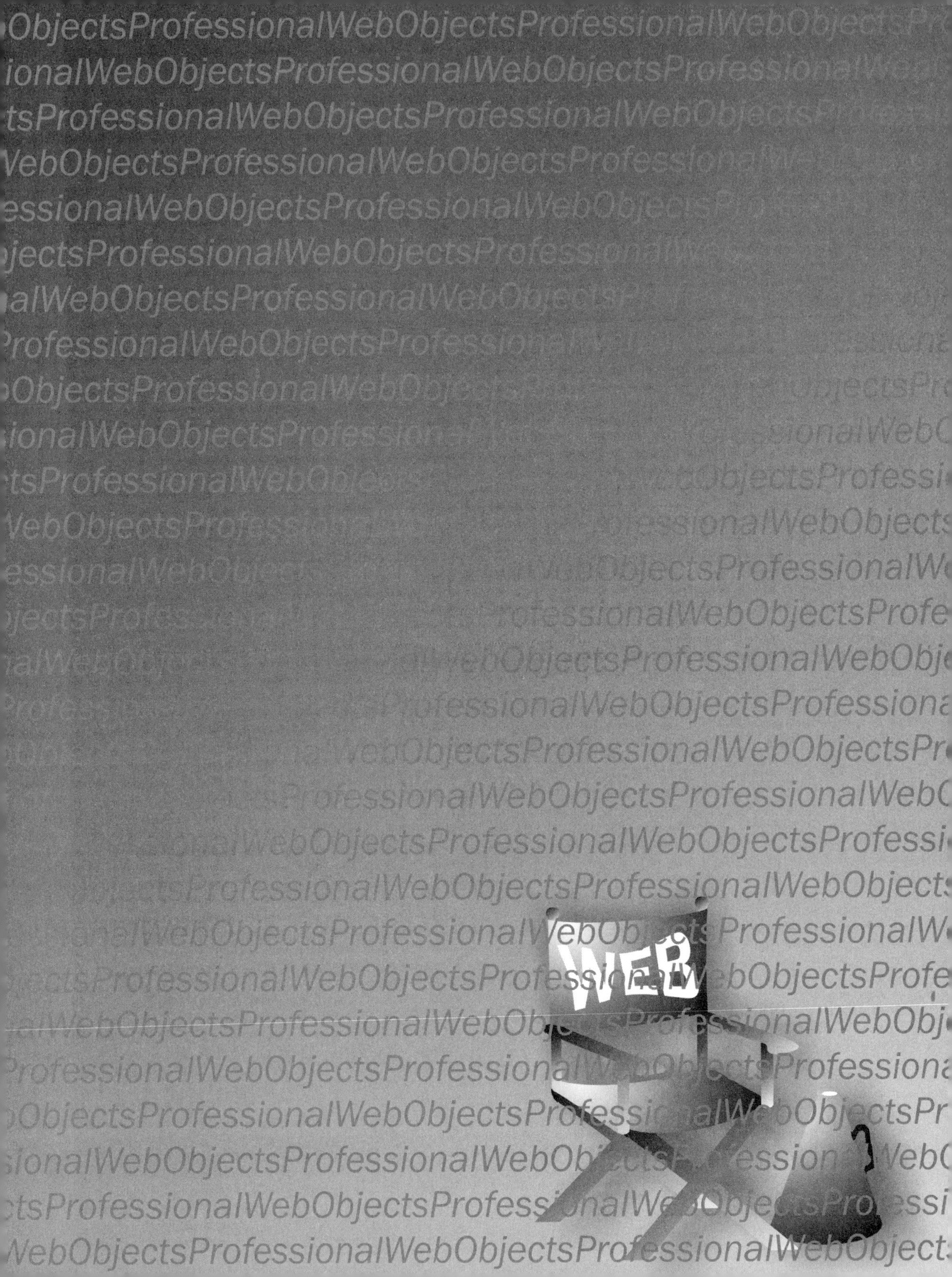
WEB

Index

A Guide to the Index

The index is arranged hierarchically, in alphabetical order, with symbols preceding the letter A. Most second-level entries and many third-level entries also occur as first-level entries. This is to ensure that users will find the information they require however they choose to search for it.

A

ACID (Atomicity, Consistency, Isolation, Durability) properties, transactions, 95
Action phase, request-response cycle, 86
   invokeAction() method, invoking, 86
   submitName() method, invoking, 86
actions, 50, 318
   as methods returning objects sent to user, 50, 322
   D2W embedded components, action binding rules, 309
   direct actions, adding to components, 173
      default history cache size, limited, 174
      direct action links, replacing hyperlinks with, 174
      example, 173
      not using direct actions, reasons for, 178
      static links, replacing hyperlinks with, 174
      URL connect modes, 376
      WODirectAction subclass, creating by WebObjects, 174
   JavaClient one week scenario example, 318
Adaptor, WebObjects, 15
adaptors, HTTP, 372
   API- & CGI-based, adaptor types, 373
      platforms supported, 374
      source code, 374
   configuration info, obtaining, 377
      available applications, 378
      sources, 377
         configuration file, 378
         Host List, 378
         Multicast request, 378
      ways of, 377
   configuring settings, 374
   functionality, deployment management, 372
      diagram, 373
      process flow, analyzing, 373
      request steps, 372
      WOAdaptor, connecting with, 373
adaptors, JDBC, 102
   ERAdaptorDebugEnabled Category, adaptor channel, 403
addToKey/removeFrom~() methods, KVC, 227
   to-many relationships, handling, 227
allObjects/displayed~() methods, WODisplayGroup class, 419
appenders, log4j, 400
   multiple appenders, setting Threshold level, 401
   NetStruxr example using log4j, 401
   printing log messages to console, alternatives to, 400
appendToResponse() method, WOApplication/~Element/~Session classes, 85, 180
   as a request-response method, overview, 85
      login application example, 87, 88, 89
      Response phase, invoking by, 86
   dynamic elements, implementing by, 83
Apple Developer Connection documentation tool, 28
applications, WebObjects
   as a NetStruxr framework basic level, 396
   building & installing, deployment management, 359
   D2W (Direct To Web), creating by, 254, 274
      generated components, overview, 267
   info types contained, 165
   locking, application-level, 246
   member variables as data storage locations, 351
   multiple application instances, running concurrently, 367, 369, 386
      cached instance info, not synchronized by default, 367
      number of instances, determining, 386
   non-D2W application example, designing own, 273
      Main, redesigning, 276
         <BODY> & <HTML> tags, removing, 276
         key, action & components, adding, 276
         submitName() method, modifying, 276
      PageWrapper, adding components to, 275
      PageWrapper, creating, 274
      PersonalizedGreeting, creating, 277
      Session.java, source code, 274
   skinnable applications, NetStruxr, 409
   WOAdaptor/~Application classes, WebObject Framework, 79
architecture, WebObjects, 15
   multi-tier, benefits, 16
      performance, 16
      scalability, 16
      security, 17
   overview, 17
      diagrams, 17
ArrayList class, java.util, 343
aspects, associations, 324
   directional, uni- & bi-, 324

Assignment class

Assignment class, 290
    effect example, D2W Rule System, 289
        DefaultAssignment class, 290
            instance methods, 291
    NetStruxr user preference example, 423
associations, 324
    as MVC Controllers, 324
    aspects, directional, 324
    JavaClient one day scenario example, 328
attribute key, D2WContext class, 286
attributes, 113
    accessing programmatically, 116
        methods, 116
    advanced properties, configuring
        Allow Null Value, 139
        Custom Formatting, 139
        Password class, 140
        Read Only, 138
    creating, e-commerce store application example, 113
        attribute inspector tool, EOModeler, 113
    EOEntity class, 22
    properties, 113
        Class, 115
        Column & Derived options, 114
        External Type, 114
        Internal Data Type, list of, 114
        Name, 113
        Primary Key, 115
        Used For Locking, 116
        Value Type, mapping used, 117
    prototypes, EOModeler, 118
Awake phase, request-response cycle, 86

B

batch faulting
    skipping EOFault creation, prefetching, 193
batchXXX() methods, WODisplayGroup class, 419
    NetStruxr user preference example, 427
binding, 50
    automatic bindings, pushing/pulling for components, 180
        pass-through bindings in stateless components, 182
        request methods, WebObjects, 180
    bindings, 63
        file changes, conditional coding, 67
    object browser example, WebObjects Builder, 50
        running, 54

C

caching, 194
    fetch specification, 194
    firing rules, D2W Rule System, 295
    JavaMonitor, 366
canAccessFieldsDirectly() method, NSKeyValueCoding interface, 217
categories, log4j, 402
    inheriting priorities from parent, mechanism, 402
    NetStruxr example using log4j, 402
collection classes/interfaces, java.util, 343
    ArrayList, 343
    HashMap, 343
component() method, WOContext class, 84

components, web, 153
    as a NetStruxr framework basic level, 396
    automatic bindings, example pushing/pulling, 180
        MenuBar.java, 182
        MenuElement.java, 181
        request methods, WebObjects, 180
        WROXComponent.java, 180
            getBindingList() method, 180
            reset() method, 181
    building components with components, example, 83, 165
    communication example, WebObjects Builder, 68
        new component, linking to, 69
            PersonalizedGreeting instance, creating, 70
            submitName() method, changing, 70
        project creation, steps, 69
    creating, 154
        examples, overview, 155
        web page structure, 154
    D2W (Direct To Web), generating using, 267
        D2W apps as components, elements, 252
    definition, 154
    direct actions, example adding, 173
        BookDisplay.java, 177
        BookDisplay.wod, appending URL query parameters, 175
        default history cache size, limited, 174
        direct action links, replacing hyperlinks with, 174
        MenuBar.wod, 177
        MyDirectAction.java, 175
        not using direct actions, reasons for, 178
        static links, replacing hyperlinks with, 174
        WODirectAction subclass, creating by WebObjects, 174
        WROXPage.java, 176
    finished WROXPage.java example, 185
        MenuBar.wod, 185
    login panel, example creating, 156
        LoginCheck.html, 161
            WOConditionals, adding, 161
        LoginCheck.java, 163
        LoginCheck.wod, 162
        LoginForm.html, 157
            bindings, creating, 158
        LoginForm.java, 159
            accessor/mutator methods, 159
            login() method, 160
        LoginForm.wod, 159
        Session.java, 160
        testing, Main.html/~.wod, 163
        user interface, design considerations, 156
    navigation bar, example creating, 165
        getArea/~Page() methods, WROXPage class, 166
        MenuBar.html, 169
        MenuBar.java, 171
        MenuBar.wod, 170
        MenuElement.html, 167
        MenuElement.java, 168
        MenuElement.wod, 168
        navigation menus, 165
        testing, 171
        WROXComponent.java, 166
        WROXPage.java, 166
    non-synchronizing, example creating, 184
        as stateless components, 179
        stateless components as non-synchronizing, 184
        WROXComponent.java, 185
    pass-through bindings in stateless components, example, 182
        MenuBar.wod, 183
        MenuElement.java, 182
        MenuElement.wod, 183

components, web (Cont'd)
  property-level components, D2W, 302
    custom, 302
  reasons for using, 155
  stateless, example creating, 178
    advantages, statelessness, 178
    as non-synchronizing components, 179
    limitations, statelessness, 179
    MenuElement.java, 179
      getColor() method, 179
    pass-through bindings, 182
conditional coding, 64
  isNameEntered() method example, 64
  generating stub using WebObjects Builder, 65
  templates & bindings, changing, 67
  WOConditionals, adding to HTML, 64, 65
    running example, 67
constants
  as data storage location, 354
    code assumptions implying constants, checking, 354
  data design principles, 338
constraints, databases
  validation, defying database rules, 237
context, 84
  D2WContext class, 283
  NetStruxr user preference example, 422
  WOContext class, WebObjects Framework, 84
cookies, 353
  creating cookie, 353
  limitations, 354
  saving & restoring session using cookies, 353
cookieWithName() method, WOCookie class, 353
CVS (Concurrent Versions System)
  RuleEditor and, exclusive-locking mechanism, 297

D

D2W (Direct To Web), 249
  application, creating, 254
    Mac OS X setup, 254
    Windows setup, 254
  architecture, 251
    D2W Factory, D2W class, 252
      Factory design pattern, using, 252
      Rule System, customizing using, 296
    DTW Context, D2WContext class, 252
    EOModel files, 253
    user.d2wmodel rule file, 253, 287
  benefits, D2W as RBRAD, 25
  components generated, example, 252, 267
    Main, 253, 257, 268, 276
      defaultPage() method, 258
      source code, 257
    MenuHeader, 253, 269, 273
      bindings, 270
      button displays, looks, 273
      methods, overriden, 271
      methods, returns, 271
      source code, 270
    PageWrapper, 253, 274, 275
  development optimization techniques, 309
    custom template components, creating framework for, 309
    EO business logic classes in a separate framework, 309
    reusable property-level components, using in shared framework, 309
    segmenting rules across multiple rule files, 309
    strict naming convention, adopting, 310
  embedded components, 306

interfaces, implementing by D2W pages, 262
JavaDirectToWeb/~DTWGeneration/~EOProject component frameworks, 250
looks, default types, 255
  basic, 255
  changing looks, 257
  neutral, 256
  WebObjects, 256
non-D2W application, designing, 273
overview, 249
  definition, 249
  documentation, 251
  reasons for using, 250
  when to use, 250
property-level components, 302
Rule System, 286
templates (tasks), 253, 259
  modifying using Web Assistant, 278
  pages corresponding to, factory methods creating, 260
tracing rule-firing, log4j & NetStruxr, 404
D2W pages, 260
  interfaces, implementing by, 262
  message pages, 266
    Error page, example creating, 267
    interfaces implementing, 266
  multiple object, 264
    interfaces implementing, 264
    List page, example creating, 264
    Query page, example creating, 265
      nextPage() method, 266
  single object, 262
    Edit page, example creating, 263
    interfaces implementing, 262
  types of, corresponding to templates, 260
    Confirm, 261
    Edit, 260
    EditRelationship, 261
    Error, 262
    Inspect, 260
    List, 260
    Page Configuration, 262
    Query, 260
    QueryAll, 261
    Select, 261
D2WContext class, 283
  keys, basic & derived, 285
    as Rule System significant keys, caching rule-firing, 295
    attribute, 286
    entity, 286
    pageConfiguration, 286
    propertyType/~KeyIsKeyPath, 285
    relationship, 286
    Rule System, determining key values, 286
    session, 286
    task, 285
  templates & rules, tying together, 283
    displayNameForProperty property, using, 285
    displayPropertyKeys key, binding list key to, 284
    dynamic elements using D2WContext in D2W templates, 284
    example, 284
    property-level components, using, 284
D2WEdit/~Inspect embedded components, 308
  example, 308
D2WList embedded component, 307
  example, 307
D2WQuery/~Select embedded components, 308

D2WTraceRuleFiringEnabled class

D2WTraceRuleFiringEnabled class, 404
   NetStruxr ERD2WTraceRuleFiringEnabled Category,
      overcoming limitations, 405
   tracing rule-firing, limitations, 404
Data Browser, EOModeler, 110
data design, 334
   class design, creating custom classes, 340
   constant & variable data, separating, 338
      constants, reasons for final declarations, 338
      editor vs. auditor, 339
      unchanged data items duration, 340
      variables, changing data, 339
   data types, understanding available, 341
   Java collections, ArrayList/HashMap classes, 343
      unsynchronized for multiple thread access, 343
   method design, get/set methods, 344
      clear method naming requirements, 344
      debugging advantages, 344
   model vocabulary, creating, 335
      advantages, 335
      related data items, 336
      term descriptions, containing, 335
      vague vocabulary, disadvantages, 336
   repeatability, design process, 334
   restrictions, data, 336
      access & modification rights, specifying, 336
      counts & existence, describing, 336
      permissible values, listing, 336
   use cases, 337
      covering all possibilities, 338
      describing, 337
      maintenance, 338
      writing story, 337
   WebObjects Foundation collections, 343
      NSArray/~MutableArray classes, 343
      NSDictionary/~MutableDictionary classes, 343
data storage, locations, 345
   application member variables, 351
      initializing sessions, 351
      loading data in application, 351
      other application subordinates needing data, problems with, 352
   constants, 354
      code assumptions implying constants, checking, 354
   cookies, 353
      creating cookie, 353
      limitations, 354
      saving & restoring session using, 353
   databases, 346
      access constraint violations, dealing with, 350
      accessibility, role-connected permissions, 349
      content independence, applying integrity constraints, 347
      databases as shared resources, 347
      databases with dependencies & synchronization, 348
      differentiated access levels, creating separate WebObjects apps for, 349
      fetch specification, string searches, 348
      fixed choice lists for searches, recommended, 349
      object-relational mapping, 346
      stored procedures, pros & cons, 347
      transactions, managing, 347
      unique item IDs, primary key values, 348
      WebObjects applications, not independent, 348
   Enterprise Objects, 351
   file system, 350
      file collections, specifying hierarchically in referencing data item, 351
   location choices, 346
      characteristics, 346

   sessions, 352
      expiration time, setting, 352
      logout functionality, providing, 352
      object references to sessions, caching risks, 353
   URLs/web pages, 350
data types, 341
   floating point, 341
      char type, holding Unicode-encoded character, 342
      money values, floating point inaccuracies, 342
   integer, 341
   internal, attribute properties, 114
      available, list of, 114
   Java 1.3.1 types, 341
data, managing, 333
   data design, 334
   data storage, locations, 345
   overview, customer order example, 333
   user interface design, 344
databases, 94
   accessibility, role-connected permissions, 349
      constraint violations, dealing with, 350
      differentiated access levels, creating separate WebObjects apps for, 349
   as data storage location, overview, 346
   as shared resources, 347
   column-level locking, 245
   constraints and validation, 237
   content independence, applying integrity constraints, 347
      databases with dependencies & synchronization, 348
      short column names, recommended, 348
      WebObjects applications, not independent, 348
   database schema, 94
      e-commerce store application example, 98
      normalization, 95
      primary/foreign keys, 94
      SQL statements & stored procedures, 95
   e-commerce store application example
      database setup, 101
   EOF advantages for, 19
   fetch specification, string searches, 348
   File System and, 94
   fixed choice lists for searches, recommended, 349
   JDBC
      application deployment, managing, 387
   JDBC, Java database connectivity, 102
   multiple databases, EOModeler accessing, 133
      distributed transactions, EOF not supporting, 133
        options avoiding limitation, 133
      EOModelGroup class, using, 133
   object-relational mapping, 346
   overview, 94
   runtime connection to, EOModeler example, 134
      changeDatabaseConnectionInfo() method, 135
      code listing, 134
   SQL scripts, generating by EOModeler, 130
      not for entities mapping to views/aliases, 131
      referential integrity constraint, generating, 131
   stored procedures, pros & cons, 347
   synchronizing model with content, EOModeler, 132
   transactions, 95, 347
      managing, 347
   unique item IDs, primary key values, 348
      separate display strings for each list item, 349
   WODisplayGroup database integration class, WebObjects Framework, 83
datasource/set~() methods, WODisplayGroup class, 419

e-commerce store application example

debugging
    JavaMonitor, 366, 370
DelayedKeyValueAssignment class, NetStruxr, 411
    skinnable applications, creating, 411
deployment, managing, 357
    adaptors, HTTP, 372
    application, building & installing, 359
        Build directory structure, 360
        deployment environment, transferring to, 361
        performance, monitoring, 361
        right platform, selecting, 360
    architecture, application types, 384
        large-sized, 385
        medium-sized, 385
        other scenarios, 386
        simple, 384
        small database-intensive, 385
    checklist, steps, 388
    database connections, JDBC drivers, 387
        classpath, setting, 387
        diagram, 387
        EOModels, pointing to correct database, 387
        index file, base configuration file, 388
        instance connections, 388
    deployment files, 379
        instance logfile, 381
        JavaConfig.plist, 380
        Licence.key, 382
        Makefiles, 381
        SiteConfig.xml, 381
        WebServerConfig.plist, 380
    development to deployment, 357
        licenses, comparing, 358
    frameworks, 382
    JavaMonitor, 361
    load balancing, 376
    multiple application instances, running concurrently, 367, 369, 386
        cached instance info, not synchronized by default, 367
        number of instances, determining, 386
    patches, installing, 359
    scaling applications, 386
    services, 383
    URL connect modes, 375
    web servers, 378
    WebObjects, installing for deployment, 358
    wotaskd daemon, 370
designing data, see data design.
Developer Help Center documentation tool, Mac OS X, 26
development tools, WebObjects, 31
    EOModeler, 31
    Project Builder, 32
    WebObjects Builder, 31
dictionaries, 221
    key-value coding, example using, 221
    NSKeyValueCoding interface, implementing, 221
Direct To Web, see D2W.
DirectAction container class, 35
    LoginRequiredDirectAction class example, NetStruxr, 414
    URL connect modes, 376
DirectToJavaClient, see JavaClient/DirectToJavaClient frameworks.
displayNameForProperty property, D2WContext class, 285
    custom property-level components, example, 305
    effect example, D2W Rule System, 291

displayPropertyKeys key, D2WContext class
    custom property-level components, example, 304
    embedded components, using by, 308
    example, 284
    pageConfiguration key, adding rule for by, 299
documentation tools, 26
    Apple Developer Connection, 28
    Developer Help Center, Mac OS X, 26
    JavaBrowser, 27
    WOInfoCenter, Windows, 27
drivers, JDBC, 102, 103
    application deployment, managing, 387
    downloading & installing, 103
        databases used, vendors, 103
        diagram, 104
        drivers types, 103
        target deployment platforms & JDKs, 103
        Windows, steps, 104
    types of, 102
dynamic elements
    D2WContext class, tying together templates & rules, 284
    main elements, WebObjects, 83
    WODynamicElement class, 83

E

e-commerce store application example, 97
    attribute properties, configuring advanced Password class, 140
    attributes, creating, 113
        attribute inspector tool, EOModeler, 113
        optimistic locking, using, 116
            steps, 116
        properties, list of, 113
        prototypes, creating, 118
    database schema, 98
        entities with attributes, list of, 99
        translating into EOModeler model, steps, 99
        UML class diagram, 98
    database setup, 101
        application development model, creating, 105
            URL, entering, 106
        JDBC drivers, adaptors & plugins, installing/configuring, 102
        OpenBase database, creating, 105
    entities, creating, 111
        adding to model, 117
        Address, 120
        Category, 117
        Customer, 119
        entity inspector tool, EOModeler, 112
        EOPrototypes, 118
        Item, 119
        LineItem, 121
        Name/Table ~/Class properties, 112
        Order, 120
        Payment, 121
    entity properties, configuring advanced, 136
    EO class generation, transforming model into Java code, 127
        Order class, 128
            accessor methods, 129
            toString() method, 129
        Password class, representing attributes, 140
    functions, creating, 149
        invoking in code, 149

451

e-commerce store application example (Cont'd)
  modeling existing database, 123
    building new model, 124
    New Model Wizard, using, 123
  relationship properties, configuring advanced, 140
    advanced relationship inspector tool, EOModeler, 140
  relationships, creating, 121
    adding to model, 122
    Name/Destination/Joins properties, 122
    one-to-one, 122
    relationship inspector tool, EOModeler, 122
  requirements, 97
  stored procedures, creating, 147
    adding to model, 147
    invoking in code, 148
editing context, see EOEditingContext class.
editingContextWillSaveChanges() method, EREditingContextDelegate Category, 403
elementID() method, WOContext class, 84
embedded components, D2W, 306
  action binding, rules for, 309
  D2WEmbeddedComponent class, extending, 307
  displayPropertyKeys, using, 308
  Rule System, supporting, 308
  types of, 306
    D2WEdit/~Inspect, example, 308
    D2WList, example, 307
    D2WQuery/~Select, 308
entities, 21, 96
  advanced properties, configuring, 136
    Batch Faulting Size, 137
    External Query, 136
    Options, 137
    Parent area, 138
    Qualifier, 137
  creating, e-commerce store application example, 111
    adding to model, 117
    entities with attributes, list of, 99
    entity inspector tool, EOModeler, 112
  EOModeler model creation process, overview, 96
  Main/Other/Enumeration entities, DirectToJavaClient, 330
  Name/Table ~/Class properties, 112
entity key, D2WContext class, 286
  pageConfiguration key, providing rules for by, 299
  Rule System example, 293
EO (Enterprise Objects)
  as data storage location, 351
EOAccess layer, EOF, 21
  EOEntity class, 21
  EOModel class, 22
EOAdaptorChannel class
  methods
    updateValuesInRowDescribedByQualifier(), 193
EOArrayDataSource/~DatabaseDataSource classes, 419
  as WODisplayGroup data sources, 419
EOAssociation class, 324
  EOTableColumnAssociation subclass, 324
EOComponentController/EOEntity~ classes, 331
  DirectToJavaClient framework, XML outputting as Controllers, 331
EOControl layer, EOF, 22
  EOCustomObject/~GenericRecord classes, 23
  EOEditingContext class, 22
  EOEnterpriseObject interface, 22
EOController class, 331
  EOComponentController/EOEntity~ subclasses, 331

EOCustomObject/~GenericRecord classes, 23, 234
  EOValidation interface, default implementation, 234
EODatabaseContext/~EditingContext classes
  pessimistic locking, using by, 243
EODisplayGroup class
  JavaClient one day scenario example, 328
  JavaClient one week scenario example, 322
  qualifyDataSource() method, 328
EODistribution/~Generation layers, 25
  intelligent object distribution, JavaClient, 25
  EODistribution and CORBA/RMI, comparing, 25
EODistribution/~Generation layers, EOF, 23
EOEditingContext class, 22, 190
  fetch specification example, creating manually, 200
  fetch specification example, creating using EOModeler, 209
  functionality, tracking object changes, 20, 190
    undo/redo object modifications, methods for, 191
EOEnterpriseObject interface, 22
EOEntity class, 21, 205
  attrributes & relationships, 22
  fetch specification example, creating using EOModeler, 205
  methods, 205
    fetchSpecificationNamed(), 205
EOF (Enterprise Objects Framework), 19, 190
  advantages of using, 19
    database independence, 19
    editing context, transaction management, 20
    maintainability, 19
    multiple database support, 20
    object faulting & uniquing, 20
    object inheritance support, 20
    primary/foreign key generation, automatic, 20
    referential integrity enforcement, 20
    reusability, 19
  EOEditingContext class, tracking changes, 190
    undo/redo object modifications, methods for, 191
  EOQualifier class, determining objects to be collected, 191
  layers & classes, 21
  layers, component classes
    EOAccess, 21
      EOAdaptor/~Database sub-layers, 21
    EOControl, 22
    EODistribution/~Generation, 23, 25
    EOInterface, 23
EOFault class
  batch faulting, skipping EOFault creation, 193
EOFetchSpecification class, 191
  fetch specification example, creating manually, 199
  fetch specification example, creating using EOModeler, 202
  functionality, fetch specification, 191
  methods
    fetchSpecificationWithQualifierBindings(), 205
  see also fetch specification.
EOInterface layer, EOF, 23
  HTML, Swing & Cocoa versions, 23
EOKeyValueCoding interface, 223
  DefaultImplementation inner class, 224
    accessing data, ways of, 224
    functionality, diagram, 225
  EOF KVC, implementing, 225
  special key-value coding, overview, 223
  storedValueForKey/takeStoredValueForKey() methods, 224
EOModel class, 22
  database connections, deployment management, 387

fetch specification

EOModeler, 96
  as WebObjects development tool, 31
  attribute properties, configuring advanced, 138
  e-commerce store application example, 97, 99
    application development model, creating, 105
    EO class generation, transforming model into Java code, 127
    translating database schema into EOModeler model, steps, 99
  entity properties, configuring advanced, 136
  EOGenericRecord class, default Enterprise Object, 128
  fetch specification example, creating manually, 195
  fetch specification example, creating using, 202
  functions, creating & adding to model, 149
  key-value coding example using dictionaries, 222
  model creation process, overview, 93, 96
    entities, 96
    files created, 97
    relationships, 96
  modeling existing database, 123
    building new model, 124
    New Model Wizard, using, 123
  multiple databases, accessing, 133
    distributed transactions, EOF not supporting, 133
      options avoiding limitation, 133
    EOModelGroup class, using, 133
  prototypes, 118
  purpose, database schema - Enterprise Objects mapping, 96
  relationship properties, configuring advanced, 140
    join table example, flattening many-to-many relationships, 142
  runtime database connection, example, 134
    changeDatabaseConnectionInfo() method, 135
    code listing, 134
  SQL scripts, generating, 130
    not for entities mapping to views/aliases, 131
    referential integrity constraint, generating, 131
  stored procedures, creating & adding to model, 147
  synchronizing model with database content, 132
  user interface, 108
    Data Browser, 110
    diagram/browser/table view modes, 108
    inspector tool, 110
    internal representation, viewing files, 111
  userInfo dictionary, 294
    adding key to, using D2W Rule System, 294
EOQualifier abstract class, 191
  D2W Rule System cause conditions, using by, 292
  fetch specification example, creating manually, 198
  functionality, determining objects to be collected, 191
    qualified fetching, fetch specification, 192
  JavaClient one day scenario example, 328
  qualifiers syntax, database-independent, 199
    qualifier operators, 292
  subclasses, 198
EOQualifierVariables class
  fetch specification example, creating manually, 199
EOSortOrdering class, 192, 419
  array of, WODisplayGroup class, 419
    EOSortOrderings calculation method, example, 421
    toggleClicked() method, example extending, 427
  fetch specification, 192
    in-memory ordering, 192
    ordering during initial fetch, 192
  fetch specification example, creating manually, 199
  methods, 192
    SortArrayUsingKeyOrderArray/Sorted~(), 192
    sortOrderingWithKey(), 192

EOTableColumnAssociation class, 324
EOUtilities class
  methods
    objectsMatchingValues(), 160
EOValidation interface, 233
  default implementation, 234
    EOCustomObject/~GenericRecord classes, using, 234
  NSValidation methods, triggering by own methods, 233
  special validation, overview, 233
  validateForInsert/~Delete/~Update/~Save() additional methods, 233
ERAdaptorDebugEnabled Category, NetStruxr, 403
  as adaptor channel for log4j, 403
ERD2WTraceRuleFiringEnabled Category, NetStruxr, 405
  D2WTraceRuleFiringEnabled class, limitations, 404
  NetStruxr example using log4j, 405
  tracing D2W rule-firing, log4j runtime behavior, 405
ERDirectToWeb framework, NetStruxr, 297
  caching rule-firing, D2W Rule System, 297
  new templates, adding to application, 407
EREditingContextDelegate Category, NetStruxr, 403
  editingContextWillSaveChanges() method, 403
  finding inserted/updated/deleted objects, log4j runtime logging, 403
ERGroupingListPageTemplate, NetStruxr, 408
  example using, 408
ERPatternLayout class, NetStruxr, 401
ERQueryPageTemplate, NetStruxr, 409
ERWizardCreationPageTemplate, NetStruxr, 409
ERXFileNotificationCenter class, NetStruxr, 405
  disabled when WOCachingEnabled is true by default, 405
  functionality, 405
  rapid turnaround development, advantages for, 406
  registering file observer & tracking file changes, example, 405
exceptions, handling
  NetStruxr, 412
    example, 413
    tracking down exceptions, info sources, 412
  validation, 235

F

Factory design pattern
  D2W class, using by, 252
fetch specification, 191
  creating manually, example, 194
  creating using EOModeler, example, 202
  database string searches, 348
  EOFetchSpecification class, using, 191
  in-memory ordering, EOSortOrdering class, 192
  key-value coding example using dictionaries, 222
  model-based, retrieving using EOEntity class, 205
    binding substitution values using NSDictionary, 205
    component, adding to sample application, 206
    key path, specifying, 205
  ordering during initial fetch, EOSortOrdering class, 192
  overview, 211
  performance improvement options, 193
    caching, 194
    prefetching, 193
    sharing, 194

fetch specification (Cont'd)
  qualified/unqualified fetching, EOQualifier class, 192
  raw rows, fetching, 193
    raw SQL, fetching, 193
  see also EOFetchSpecification class.
fetch specification example, creating manually, 194
  custom code, adding in Project Builder, 198
    editing context, creating, 200
    EOQualifier subclasses, using, 198
    sorting returned data, 199
    source code, 200
  finished application, 202
  requirements, gathering, 195
  user interface, creating in WebObjects Builder, 195
    component, using, 195
    conditionals, keys, message & tables, adding, 196
fetch specification example, creating using EOModeler, 202
  custom code, adding in Project Builder, 209
    fetch results, returning by editing context, 209
    fetch specification, getting, 209
    source code, 209
  finished application, 210
  model-based fetch specification, retrieving, 205
  requirements, gathering using EOModeler, 202
    placeholder, adding, 203
    sort ordering, setting, 204
    SQL tab, writing SQL/entering in raw SQL, 205
  user interface, creating in WebObjects Builder, 206
    component & hyperlink, adding, 206
    keys, adding, 207
    repetition, displaying search results, 207
    search page, designing, 206
    WOConditional, adding, 208
fetchSpecificationNamed() method, EOEntity class
  fetch specification example, creating using EOModeler, 205
fetchSpecificationWithQualifierBindings() method, EOFetchSpecification class, 205
file system
  as data storage location, 350
    file collections, specifying hierarchically in referencing data item, 351
  databases and, 94
floating point data types, 341
  base 2 to 10 conversion table, 341
  char type, holding Unicode-encoded character, 342
  money values, floating point inaccuracies, 342
    arbitrary precision arithmetic, solution limitations, 342
  normalized vs. non-normalized numbers, 342
foreign keys, databases, 94
  automatic generation, EOF, 20
formatters, 239
  validation, 239
Foundation Framework, classes, 78, 343
  NSArray/~MutableArray, 343
  NSDictionary/~MutableDictionary, 343
frameworks, 382
  Apple/third-party types, 382
  deployment, managing, 382
  installing, 382
functions
  creating, e-commerce store application example, 149
    invoking in code, 149

G

generateResponse() method, WOActionResponse class, 85
getAmount/set~() methods, KVC, 226
globalIDForRow() method, EOEntity class
  attributes, accessing programmatically, 116
GUI
  validation, 240

H

HashMap class, java.util, 343
HTML editor, WebObjects Builder, 45
  adding static element, example, 45
  Inspectors, modifying HTML elements, 46
    Dynamic, 55
    Generic, 47
    Static, 46
  Palette/Validation Warning/API Editor tools, 49
  path view, 49
  Reformat HTML, cleaning up HTML, 49
  source view, manually editing HTML, 48
hyperlinks
  configuring using WebObjects Builder s Inspectors, 71
  replacing with direct action links, components, 174
  replacing with static links, components, 174

I

IDE (Integrated Development Environment)
  Project Builder, external IDE support, 40
inspector tool, EOModeler, 110
  advanced relationship inspector, 140
  attribute inspector, 113
  entity inspector, 112
  relationship inspector, 122
Inspectors, WebObjects Builder s HTML editor, 46
  Dynamic, 55
  Generic, 47
  hyperlinks, configuring using, 71
  Static, 46
integrity constraints, databases, 347
  short column names, recommended, 348
interfaces, D2W pages, 262
  message pages, 266
    ConfirmPageInterface, 267
    ErrorPageInterface, 267
      example, 267
  multiple object pages, 264
    ListPageInterface, 264
      example, 264
    QueryPageInterface/QueryAllPage~, 265
      example, 265
    SelectPageInterface, 264
  single object pages, 262
    EditPageInterface/InspectPage~, 262
      example, 263
    EditRelationshipPageInterface, 262
intValue/float~() methods, KVC, 227
  type checking/conversion, 227

key-value coding (KVC)

invokeAction() method,
WOApplication/~Element/~Session
classes, 85, 180
  Action phase, invoking by, 86
  login application example, 87, 90
  WOActionResponse object, returning, 85

J

JavaBrowser class library browser, 27
  adding classes to, example, 27
  output, 28
JavaClient/DirectToJavaClient frameworks, 24, 313
  benefits, DirectToJavaClient as RBRAD, 25
  benefits, JavaClient, 24
    deployable as web/desktop app, 24
    intelligent object distribution, EODistribution layer, 25
    partitioned business logic, 25
    richer user interface, 24
  HTML outputting, JavaClient, 331
  Main/Other/Enumeration entities, DirectToJavaClient, 330
  one day scenario, application example, 326
    creating application, 326
    OrderLookupController.nib, analyzing, 328
      LineItem display group, associations & relationships, 328
      LoginName text field, EOQualifier bindings, 328
      Query button, EODisplayGroup bindings, 328
  one hour scenario, application example, 328
    Assistant menu, tabs, 330
      Entities, 330
      Miscellaneous/XML, 331
      Properties, 331
      Widgets/Window, 331
    creating application, 329
      UI modifications, 329
      UI, running changed, 330
  one week scenario, application example, 314
    creating application on Mac OS X, 314
    creating application on Windows, 314
    EODisplayGroups & associations, adding, 322
    files contained, overview, 315
    main window, creating, 315
      final look, 318
      table, adding, 317
      UI widget, adding, 316
    OrderLookupController.java, final version, 324
      prior changes, list of, 325
    outlets & actions, adding, 318
      functionality, outlets & actions, 322
      Lookup button, adding functionality to, 320
      OrderLookupController.java, modifying, 321
  XML outputting, DirectToJavaClient, 331
    as EOController subclasses, 331
JavaMonitor, 361
  application configuration options, 365
    AutoOpenInBrowser, 366
    AutoRecover, 366
    Caching Enabled, 366
    Debugging Enabled, 366
    LifeBeat Interval, 366
    Minimum Active Sessions, 366
    Output Path, 366
    Path, 365
  applications, adding, 364
    adding application instances, 367
    application configuration options, 365
    multiple application instances, running concurrently, 367, 369
  debugging, 370

  functionality, deployment management, 361
    diagram, 361
    running circumstances, 368
  host running wotaskd, setting up within Monitor, 363
    new entry in hosts listing, content, 364
  location, 362
  scheduling, 369
    application restart frequency, determining, 369
JavaScript
  validation, 238
    example, 238
JDBC (Java DataBase Connectivity), 102
  adaptors, 102
  application deployment, managing, 387
    classpath, setting, 387
    diagram, 387
    EOModels, pointing to correct database, 387
    index file, base configuration file, 388
    instance connections, 388
  drivers, 102, 103
    downloading & installing, 103
  e-commerce store application example, 102
  plugins, 107
jEdit Java IDE
  Project Builder, external IDE support, 40
joins
  join table example, flattening many-to-many relationships, 142

K

key/set~() methods, KVC, 226
keys, 50
  as instance variables/methods returning values, 50
  D2WContext basic & derived keys, 285
    as Rule System significant keys, caching rule-firing, 295
    attribute, 286
    entity, 286
    pageConfiguration, 286
    propertyType/~KeyIsKeyPath, 285
    relationship, 286
    Rule System, determining key values, 286
    session, 286
    task, 285
  overview, key-value coding, 215
key-value coding (KVC), 215
  benefits, 216
  dictionaries, example using, 221
    creating Main page, 223
    fetch specification, specifying in EOModeler, 222
    table, producing from fetch request, 222
  EOF KVC, implementing
    default, key/set~() accessors, 226
    EOEnterpriseObject interface, 22
    guidelines, 225
    handling to-many relationships, addToKey/removeFrom~() methods, 227
    own accessor methods, implementing, 226
    type coercion, getAmount/set~() methods, 226
  general, NSKeyValueCoding interface, 216
    classes, interfaces & constant, table of, 216
    DefaultImplementation inner class, 219
    dictionary holding store/retrieve values, example, 218
    NSKeyValueCodingAdditions interface, handling key paths, 220
    Utility inner class, generalizing KVC usage, 220
  keys, overview, 215

455

key-value coding (KVC) (Cont'd)
    NullValue inner class, handling null values, 228
    package access instance variables, using, 228
        options, 228
        ValueAccessor inner class, example adding to package, 228
    special, EOKeyValueCoding interface, 223
        classes & interfaces, list of, 224
        DefaultImplementation inner class, 224
        functionality, 223
    type checking/conversion, 227
        intValue/float~() methods, 227
    see also EOKeyValueCoding interface

L

layouts, log4j, 401
    ERPatternLayout class, NetStruxr, 401
    NetStruxr example using log4j, 401
like qualifier operator
    pageConfiguration key and, example, 299
        internal page, 300
        standard page, 300
lists, 72
    creating using WebObjects Builder, example, 72
        displaying lists, 73
            table cell, adding, 73
            WORepetition, formatting list in table, 73
        running, 74
        variables & methods, adding to session
            addUserName() method, 73
            Session class constructor, 72
            submitName() method, 73
    D2W list pages, component parts, 418, 419
load balancing, 376
    deployment, managing, 376
    Round Robin/Random/Load Average algorithms, 377
locking, 240
    application-level locking, 246
    column-level locking, 245
        example, 246
        pros & cons, 245
    optimistic, 241
    pessimistic locking, 242
        lock on demand, 244
        lock on select, 243
        lock on update, 244
lockObject() method
    pessimistic locking example, 245
log4j, Apache Jakarta, 399
    changing logging behavior at runtime, NetStruxr ways of, 403
    Log4jMonitor, 401
    main components, 400
        appenders, 400
        categories, 402
        layouts, 401
    NetStruxr example using, 399
        debugging, limitations, 399
    runtime logging reconfiguration, NetStruxr, 403
        example, 403

M

Makefiles, applications, 381
    list of, 381

methods
    creating using WebObjects Builder, example, 60
        submitName() method, source code, 62
        testing, 61
        WOForm, binding to WOTextField/WOString, 61
        WOForm, creating, 60
MVC (Model-View-Controller) pattern
    associations as MVC Controllers, 324

N

NetStruxr
    company history, 391
    corporate real estate case study, 393
        online corporate real estate, problems with, 391
        requirements & solution, 393
    DelayedKeyValueAssignment class, 411
    ERDirectToWeb framework, 297
    ERXFileNotificationCenter, file notification center, 405
        development advantages, 406
    exceptions, handling, 412
        example, 413
        pageConfiguration, tracking down exceptions, 412
        session's statistics store, tracking down exceptions, 413
        URI, tracking down exceptions, 412
    framework architecture, basic levels, 394
        advantages, 396
        Applications, 396
        Base Extensions, 396
        Business Logic, 396
        Components, 396
        diagram, 395
        reusability & flexibility in WebObjects development, 394
    log4j and, runtime logging reconfiguration, 403
        ERAdaptorDebugEnabled Category, adaptor channel, 403
        ERD2WTraceRuleFiringEnabled Category, tracing rule-firing, 404
        EREditingContextDelegate Category, finding inserted/updated/deleted objects, 403
    log4j example, 399
        appenders, configuring, 400
        categories, inheriting priorities from parent, 402
        debugging, limitations, 399
        layout, configuring, 401
            ERPatternLayout class, 401
        logging category, creating, 400
        priority levels, providing, 400
        runtime configuration file, 400
        tracing rule-firing, 404
    LoginRequiredDirectAction class example, 414
        DirectAction class, 416
            loginAction() method, 416
            redirectToActionWithQueryString() method, 417
            use cases, loginAction() method, 417
        LoginPage class, 415
        performActionNamed() method, 414
        superSecretAction() method, 415
    ProjectBuilderWO, example using, 397
        adding framework to application, 398
        correcting runtime error, 398
        running application, error thrown, 398
        single framework & depending application, creating, 398
    rapid turnaround development, 397
        developer setup, 397
        time-consuming development aspects, 407

NetStruxr (Cont'd)
  skin framework, creating, 409
    diagram, 410
    overview, 410
    stylesheet, D2W rule file & templates, component parts, 410
  template-based approach to thrown validation exceptions, 406
  templates (D2W tasks), adding new to application, 407
    ERGroupingListPageTemplate, 408
    ERQueryPageTemplate, 409
    ERWizardCreationPageTemplate, 409
    list of, 408
  user preference system, example implementing, 418
NetStruxr user preference system, example implementing, 418
  D2W list page, component parts, 418, 419
    WODisplayGroup class, overview, 418
  getting preferences from user to WODisplayGroup, 420
    actor methods, BusinessLogic class, 424
    adding rule to components rule file, 423
    awake/sleep() method modifications, Session class, 424
    ERListPage class, 421
      numberOfObjectsPerBatch() method, 421
      setLocalContext() method, 422
      sortOrderings() method, 421
    UserPreferences static inner class, 425
      preferenceRecordForKey() method, 425
      preferences/~EditingContext() methods, 425
      takeValueForKey/encodedValue() methods, 426
      valueForKey/decodedValue() methods, 426
    userPreferences() static method, User class, 424
    UserPreferencesAssignment class, 423
  propagating WODisplayGroup changes back to user, 427
    setNumberOfObjectsPerBatch() method, ERNavigationBar class, 427
    toggleClicked() method, ERSortOrder class, 427
    UserPreferenceHandler static inner class, 428
      registering handlers, source code, 428
  user preferences, storage & retrieval mechanism, 423
    User/~Preference classes, attributes & methods, 424
New Model Wizard, EOModeler, 123
  functionality, 123
    building model, 124
  starting, 123
nextPage() method, NextPageDelegate interface, 305
  functionality, 305
  interface implementation, example, 306
NextPageDelegate interface, 305
  creating class implementing, Select page example, 305
    deleteCustomer() method, 305
    nextPage() method, 306
  nextPage() method, 305
normalization, databases, 95
  NF (Normal Forms), 95
    example, 95
NSArray class, 343
  raw rows, fetching, 193
NSDictionary class, 343
  fetch specification example, creating using EOModeler, 205
  NSKeyValueCoding interface, implementing, 221
  raw rows, fetching, 193

NSKeyValueCoding abstract interface, 216
  DefaultImplementation inner class
    accessing property, ways of, 219
    example, 217
    functionality, diagram, 220
  general key-value coding, overview, 216
  methods, 217
    canAccessFieldsDirectly(), 217
    valueForKey/takeValueForKey(), setting/retrieving values, 217
  NSDictionary, implementing by, 221
  NullValue inner class, handling null values, 228
  package access instance variables, using, 228
    ValueAccessor inner class, example adding to package, 228
  Utility inner class, generalizing KVC usage, 220
NSKeyValueCodingAdditions interface
  key paths, handling, 220
NSMutableArray class, com.webobjects.foundation, 343
  list creation example, WebObjects Builder, 73
NSMutableDictionary class, 343
  fetch specification example, creating using EOModeler, 205
  methods
    setObjectForKey(), 160
NSValidation interface
  DefaultImplementation inner class, 230
    example, 230
  methods, implementing in custom code, 231
    example, 232
    tasks performed by methods, 232
    validateKey() method, Object argument, 231
  property validation, overview, 229
  Utility inner class, generalizing validation usage, 231
  validateValueForKey/~TakeValueForKeyPath() methods, 229
    EOValidation methods, triggering by, 233

O

object browser, WebObjects Builder, 50
  binding example, 50
    component displaying key value, creating, 52
    key & action, creating & binding to component, 53
    key, creating & binding to WOTextField, 51
    running, 54
    showTest() method, modifying, 54
    WOForm, adding to HTML, 50
    WOString/WOHyperlink, adding to new text, 53
    WOTextField/WOSubmitButton, adding to WOForm, 50
  binding keys/actions to WO HTML elements, 50
objectsMatchingValues() method, EOUtilities class, 160
  D2W components example, 259
  login panel example, components, 160
objectWithPrimaryKeyValue() method, EOUtilities class
  attributes, accessing programmatically, 116
OpenBase database server, 105
  e-commerce store application example, 105
    application development model, creating, 105
    OpenBaseManager, launching, 105

optimistic locking, 116, 241
  attribute properties, 116
  functionality, 241
    compound index of primary keys & attribute, creating, 242
    database triggers, modifying locking, 242
    multiple attributes, locking, 241
    single attribute, locking, 242
    unsuitable attributes for locking, 241
  snapshot & database data, comparing, 241
outlets, 318
  functionality, 322
  JavaClient one week scenario example, 318

P

package access instance variables
  key-value coding, using by, 228
pageConfiguration key, D2WContext class, 286, 298
  creating pages using, example, 298
  like qualifier operator and, example, 299
    internal page, 300
    standard page, 300
  NetStruxr, handling exceptions, 412
  page configurations, reasons for using, 298
  rule number reduction tips, 301
  Rule System example, 293
  setting up in RuleEditor, 299
    displayPropertyKeys key, adding rule for, 299
    field lengths, choosing, 299
    labels for attributes, choosing, 299
    task & entity keys, providing rules for, 299
pageWithName() method, WOComponent class, 78
performActionNamed() method, WODirectAction class, 175
performance
  multi-tier architecture, WebObjects, 16
permissions
  database accessibility, role-connected permissions, 349
pessimistic locking, 242
  limitations, 242
  lock on demand, 244
  lock on select, 243
    default update strategy, setting, 243
    EODatabaseContext/~EditingContext classes, using, 243
    locking specific objects for specific fetch, 243
  lock on update, 244
plugins, JDBC, 107
  e-commerce store application example, 108
  WebObjects plugins, 107
    custom, 107
    default, 107
prefetching, fetch specification, 193
  batch faulting, skipping EOFault creation, 193
primary keys, databases, 94
  as attribute property, 115
  automatic generation, EOF, 20
  Propagate Primary Key property, relationships, 141
  simple & compound, 94
Project Builder, 32
  accessing, 32
    Mac users, 32
    Windows users, 33
  as WebObjects development tool, 32

  changing preferences, mechanism for, 36
    Build tab, 37
    Editing tab, 37
    General tab, default, 36
    Syntax/Debugging tabs, 37
  directories/folders/files, project structure
    Application/Session/DirectAction, core WebObjects classes, 35
    Main folder files, Web Components directory, 35
    other folders, 36
  fetch specification example, creating manually, 198
  fetch specification example, creating using EOModeler, 209
  Hello World application example, creating, 37
    method returning date/time, adding, 38
    running, 39
    see also WebObjects Builder.
  Java IDE integration, 40
    external IDE support, 40
    Project Builder's code editing limitations, 40
  NetStruxr example using ProjectBuilderWO, 397
property-level components, D2W, 302
  custom, creating & using in D2W pages, 302
    displayPropertyKeys/~NameForProperty, configuring, 304
    source code, 303
  types of, 302
propertyType/~KeyIsKeyPath keys, D2WContext class, 285
prototypes, EOModeler, 118
  creating, e-commerce store application example, 118

Q

qualifiers, see EOQualifier.
qualifyDataSource() method, EODisplayGroup class
  JavaClient one day scenario example, 328

R

raw rows
  fetching, fetch specification, 193
  raw SQL, fetching, 193
RBRAD (Rules-Based Rapid Application Development), 25
  benefits, rules-based development, 25
    customized rules, 26
    intelligent default rules, 26
    rapid development cycle, 25
    UI generation, rules-based, 26
referential integrity constraints
  automatic enforcement, EOF, 20
  SQL scripts, generating by EOModeler, 131
relationship key, D2WContext class, 286
relationships, 96, 121
  advanced properties, configuring, 140
    advanced relationship inspector tool, EOModeler, 140
    Batch Faulting, 141
    Delete Rule/Nullify/Cascade/Deny/NoAction, 141
    join table example, flattening many-to-many relationships, 142
    Optionality, 140
    Owns Destination/Propagate Primary Key, 141
  creating, e-commerce store application example, 121
    relationship inspector tool, EOModeler, 122
  EOEntity class, 22
  EOModeler model creation process, overview, 96

stored procedures, databases

relationships (Cont'd)
  JavaClient one day scenario example, 328
  Name/Destination/Joins properties, 122
  one-to-many, key-value handling, 227
  one-to-one, 122
request-response cycle, 14, 84
  basic methods, WOApplication/~Element/~Session
    classes, 84
    appendToResponse(), 85
    invokeAction(), 85
    takeValuesFromRequest(), 85
  functionality, 14, 85
  login application example, 87
    basic methods, overriding & adding to files, 87
    running, 88
    submitName() method, 90
    URL, component parts, 90
  phases, 86
    Action, 86
    Awake, 86
    Response, 86
    Sleep, 87
    Sync, 86
  transactions as request-response cycle
    processing, 14
  WORequest/~Response classes, WebObjects
    Framework, 78
requests
  methods called by WebObjects, 180
Response phase, request-response cycle, 86
  appendToResponse() method, invoking, 86
Rule System, D2W, 286
  .d2wmodel rule filenames, 287
    user.d2wmodel/d2w.~ rule files,
      applications/frameworks, 287
  caching rule-firing, 295
    adding new significant key, 296
    ERDirectToWeb framework, NetStruxr, 297
    example, 295
    standard significant keys, using, 295
  cause & effect, rules, 288
    cause example, conditions, 291
      qualifiers, using, 292
      running, 292
      session rules, 294
      userInfo dictionary example, EOModeler, 294
    effect example, Assignment subclass, 289
      DefaultAssignment class, 290
  customizing D2W factory using, 296
  D2WContext keys, determining values of, 286
    D2WContext as Rule System's Gatekeeper, 293
    entity rule, 293
    look rule, 293
    pageName rule, 293
    providing rules for keys, 293
    task rule, 293
  overview, 286
  priority levels, 288
    candidate rules, choosing, 288
    if no candidates, exception thrown, 289
  RBRAD benefits, rules-based development, 25
  RuleEditor, functionality, 297
    committing changes to field, 298
    custom assignment packages, 297
    CVS and, exclusive-locking mechanism, 297
  stock quantity example, 287
  tracing rule-firing, log4j & NetStruxr, 404
    D2WTraceRuleFiringEnabled class, 404

S

scalability
  multi-tier architecture, WebObjects, 16
scheduling, JavaMonitor, 369
  application restart frequency, determining, 369
security
  database accessibility, role-connected
    permissions, 349
    constraint violations, dealing with, 350
    differentiated access levels, creating separate
      WebObjects apps for, 349
  multi-tier architecture, WebObjects, 17
services, 383
  deployment, managing, 383
  list of, Win 2k/Solaris/Mac OS X platforms, 383
Session class
  adding variables & methods to session, list creation
    example
    addUserName() method, 73
    class constructor, 72
    submitName() method, 73
  as a shell interacting with WOSession, example, 81
  sessions as data storage locations, 352
session key, D2WContext class, 286
  Rule System example, 294
sessions
  JavaMonitor, 366
  NetStruxr, handling exceptions, 413
  URL connect modes, 375
  see also Session class, WOSession class
**setNumberOfObjectsPerBatch() method,
  WOBatchNavigationBar class**
  NetStruxr user preference example, 427
setObjectForKey() method, NSMutableDictionary class
  login panel example, components, 160
setRefreshesRefetchedObjects() method
  pessimistic locking example, 243
setValueForBinding() method
  pushing bindings manually, components, 179
sharing
  fetch specification, 194
skin framework, NetStruxr, 409
  creating application, example, 411
  overview, 410
    diagram, 410
  stylesheet, D2W rule file & templates, component
    parts, 410
Sleep phase, request-response cycle, 87
**SortArrayUsingKeyOrderArray/Sorted~() methods,
  EOSortOrdering class, 192**
**sortOrderings/set~() methods, WODisplayGroup
  class, 419**
**sortOrderingWithKey() method, EOSortOrdering
  class, 192**
SQL statements, databases, 95
  example, 95
state
  stateless components, 178
    as non-synchronizing components, 179
    pass-through bindings in, 182
stored procedures, databases, 95, 147, 347
  creating, e-commerce store application example, 147
    adding to model, 147
    invoking in code, 148
  functionality, pros & cons, 347

459

storedValueForKey/takeStoredValueForKey() methods,
  EOKeyValueCoding interface, 224
storing data, see data storage, locations.
submitName() method, 86
  request-response cycle, invoking by, 86
    login application example, 90
Swing
  personalized application example using, variables, 56
Sync phase, request-response cycle, 86
  takeValuesFromRequest() method, invoking, 86
synchronization, databases, 132
  ArrayList/HashMap classes, unsynchronized for multiple thread access, 343
  cached multiple application instance info, not synchronized by default, 367
  databases with dependencies & synchronization, 348
  fixed choice lists for searches, recommended, 349
  stateless components, non-synchronizing, 179, 184
  synchronizing model with database content, EOModeler, 132
  unique item IDs, primary key values, 348
synchronizesVariablesWithBindings() method
  non-synchronizing components, example creating, 184

T

takeValuesFromRequest() method, 180
takeValuesFromRequest() method, WOApplication/~Element/~Session classes, 85
  as a request-response method, overview, 85
    login application example, 87, 89
    Sync phase, invoking by, 86
task key, D2WContext class, 285
  pageConfiguration key, providing rules for by, 299
  Rule System example, 293
tasks, D2W, see templates.
templates (tasks), D2W, 253, 259
  advantages, 253
  custom template, example creating/using, 280
  factory methods creating pages corresponding to, 260
    Confirm, 261
    Edit, 260
    EditRelationship, 261
    Error, 262
    Inspect, 260
    List, 260
    Page Configuration, 262
    Query, 260
    QueryAll, 261
    Select, 261
  functionality, 259
    9 templates (tasks) for each default look, 260
  interfaces, implementing by D2W pages, 262
  modifying using Web Assistant, 278
    Expert Mode, using, 279
    rule, adding/editing manually, 280
    rule, newly-added, 279
    saving changes, 279
  NetStruxr, adding new templates to application, 407
    ERGroupingListPageTemplate, 408
    ERQueryPageTemplate, 409
    ERWizardCreationPageTemplate, 409
    list of, 408
templates, HTML, 63
  file changes, conditional coding, 67

toggleClicked() method, WOSortOrder class
  NetStruxr user preference example, 427
transactions, 14, 95
  ACID properties, 95
  distributed transactions, EOF not supporting, 133
    options avoiding limitation, 133
  request-response cycle, steps, 14

U

updateValuesInRowDescribedByQualifier() method, EOAdaptorChannel class
  raw rows, fetching, 193
URL (Universal Resource Locators), 375
  appending URL query parameters to components, 175
  application connect modes, deployment management, 375
    deployed URL (post-logging into app, session-based), 375
    deployed URL (pre-logging into app), 375
    deployed URL (test instance), 376
    Direct Action URL, 376
    Direct-Connect, 375
  as data storage location, 350
  component parts, request-response example, 90
    CGI WebObjects Adaptor, 90
    context ID, 91
    request handler key, 90
    session ID, 91
    standard HTTP URI, 90
    WebObjects application, 90
use cases, data design, 337
  covering all possibilities, 338
  describing, 337
  maintenance, 338
  writing story, 337
user interface design, 344
  data model and, designing separately, 345
    potential problems, 345
  web browser as client interface, 345
user preferences, see NetStruxr user preference example.

V

validateForInsert/~Delete/~Update/~Save() methods, EOValidation interface, 233
  default implementation, 234
  functionality, 234
validateValueForKey/~TakeValueForKeyPath() methods, NSValidation interface, 229
  default implementation, 231
  EOValidation methods, triggering by, 233
  functionality, 230
validation, 229
  alternative strategies, 237
  database constraints, defying database rules, 237
  exceptions, handling, 235
    aggregating exceptions, custom coding, 236
    aggregating exceptions, EOValidate default implementation, 235
    user input exceptions, 235
    validation method exceptions, 235
  formatters, 239
  GUI, 240

validation (Cont'd)
　JavaScript, 238
　　example, 238
　property, NSValidation interface, 229
　　classes & interfaces, 229
　　DefaultImplementation inner class, 230
　　methods, implementing in custom code, 231
　　Utility inner class, generalizing validation usage, 231
　special, EOValidation interface, 233
　　default implementation, 234
　see also EOValidation interface
valueForBinding() method
　pulling bindings manually, components, 179
valueForKey() method, KeyValueCoding interface
　NetStruxr user preference example, 426
valueForKey/takeValueForKey() methods, NSKeyValueCoding interface, 217
variables, 56
　creating & reading from, example, 58
　　creating variable by editing source file, 58
　　creating variable using WebObjects Builder, 59
　data design principles, 339
　package access instance variables, KVC using, 228
　Swing personalized application example, 56
　　ActionListener-derived inner class, 57
　　constructor, 56
　　main() method, 57
　　running, 57
view modes, EOModeler, 108
　browser, 109
　diagram, 108
　table, 109

W

Web Assistant
　D2W templates (tasks), modifying, 278
　　Expert Mode, using, 279
　　rules, adding new, 279
　　saving changes, 279
web components, see components.
web pages
　as data storage location, 350
　WOElement/~Component/~DynamicElement classes, WebObjects Framework, 82
web servers, 378
　deployment, managing, 378
　WebServerResources directory, 379
　　split installations, 379
WebObjects Builder, 44
　as WebObjects development tool, 31, 56
　components communication example, 68
　　new component, linking to, 69
　　project creation, steps, 69
　conditional coding, 64
　　isNameEntered() method example, 65
　fetch specification example, creating manually, 195
　fetch specification example, creating using EOModeler, 206
　Hello World application example, creating, 37
　　HTML file, editing, 37
　　WOString placeholder, binding to date property, 39
　see also Project Builder.

　HTML editor, 45
　　Palette/Validation Warning/API Editor tools, 49
　　path view, 49
　　Reformat HTML, cleaning up HTML, 49
　　source view, manually editing HTML, 48
　　Static/Generic/Dynamic Inspectors, modifying HTML elements, 46, 55
　hyperlinks, configuring using Inspectors, 71
　launching, 44
　lists, example creating, 72
　　displaying lists, 73
　　running, 74
　methods, example creating, 60
　　submitName() method, source code, 62
　　testing, 61
　　WOForm, binding to WOTextField/WOString, 61
　　WOForm, creating, 60
　object browser, binding keys/actions to WO HTML elements, 50
　　binding example, 50
　variables, example creating, 59
WebObjects Framework, classes, 77
　database integration-level, 83
　　WODisplayGroup, 83
　overview, 78
　　client-WOSession-WOApplication interaction, diagram, 81
　page-level, 82
　　WOComponent, 82
　　WODynamicElement, 83
　　WOElement, 82
　request-level, 78
　　WOContext, 84
　　WOMessage, 79
　　WOResponse, 79
　server- & application-level, 79
　　WOAdaptor, 79
　　WOApplication, 80
　session-level, 80
　　WOSession, 81
willRead/~Change() methods, KVC, 226
WOActionResponse abstract class
　invokeAction() method, returning by, 85
WOAdaptor class, 79, 373
　HTTP adaptors, connecting with, 373
WOApplication class, 80
　member variables as data storage locations, 351
　　initializing sessions, 351
　　loading data in application, 351
　　other application subordinates needing data, problems with, 352
　methods, 84
　subclassing, example, 80
WOBatchNavigationBar class, 420
　as WODisplayGroup batch size control, 420
　　batch size calculation method, example, 421
　　setNumberOfObjectsPerBatch() method, example extending, 427
WOBuilder
　key-value coding example using dictionaries, 222
WOCachingEnabled class
　if true by default, then ERXFileNotificationCenter disabled, 405
WOCheckBox class
　D2W components example, 268
WOComponent class, 82
　containing other WOComponents, 83
　D2W apps as components, 252
　login panel example, components, 158
　methods, 84

461

WOComponentContent class, 162
  D2W components example, 272
  login panel example, components, 162
  navigation bar example, components, 167
  non-D2W application example, 275
WOConditional class, conditional coding, 64
  adding conditionals to HTML, 65
    running example, 67
  D2W components example, 269
  fetch specification example, creating manually, 196
  fetch specification example, creating using
    EOModeler, 208
  login panel example, components, 162
WOContext class, 84
  methods, 84
WOCookie class, 353
  as data storage location, 353
  methods, 353
WOCustomObject class
  JavaScript validation example, 238
WODirectAction class
  direct actions, adding to components, 174
  LoginRequiredDirectAction subclass example,
    NetStruxr, 414
  methods
    performActionNamed(), 175
WODisplayGroup class, 83, 418
  component parts, 418
    EOArrayDataSource/~DatabaseDataSource classes,
      data sources, 419
    EOSortOrderings, array of, 419
    WOBatchNavigationBar class, batch size
      control, 419, 420
  D2W list pages, component parts, 418, 419
  methods, 419
  NetStruxr user preference example, 420
    getting preferences from user to WODisplayGroup, 420
    propagating WODisplayGroup changes back to
      user, 427
WODynamicElement abstract class, 83
  methods, 84
WOElement abstract class, 82
  methods, 82, 84
WOExtensions framework, 83
WOForm class
  binding example, WebObjects Builder's object
    browser, 50
  login panel example, components, 158
  method creation example, WebObjects Builder, 60
  non-D2W application example, 276
WOGenericContainer class
  navigation bar example, components, 167
WOGenericElement class
  navigation bar example, components, 167
WOHyperlink class
  binding example, WebObjects Builder's object
    browser, 53
  configuring hyperlinks using WebObjects Builder s
    Inspectors, 71
  D2W components example, 270
  fetch specification example, creating manually, 196
  fetch specification example, creating using
    EOModeler, 206
  navigation bar example, components, 169
WOInfoCenter documentation tool, Windows, 27
WOJavaScript class, 239
  JavaScript validation example, 238

WOMessage class, 79
  WORequest/~Response classes, extending by, 79
WOPasswordField class
  D2W components example, 268
WORedirect class
  LoginRequiredDirectAction class example,
    NetStruxr, 417
WORepetition class, 73
  fetch specification example, creating manually, 196
  fetch specification example, creating using
    EOModeler, 206
  list creation example, WebObjects Builder, 73
  non-D2W application example, 275
WORequest class, 15, 79
  WOMessage, extending, 79
WOResponse class, 15, 79
  WOMessage, extending, 79
WOSession class, 81
  methods, 84
  Session class example, 81
  sessions as data storage locations, 352
    logout functionality, providing, 352
    object references to sessions, caching risks, 353
    session expiration time, setting, 352
WOString class
  binding example, WebObjects Builder's object
    browser, 53
  fetch specification example, creating manually, 196
  fetch specification example, creating using
    EOModeler, 207
  Hello World application example, creating, 39
  method creation example, WebObjects Builder, 61
  non-D2W application example, 275
WOSubmit class
  fetch specification example, creating manually, 195
  fetch specification example, creating using
    EOModeler, 206
WOSubmitButton class
  binding example, WebObjects Builder's object
    browser, 50
  D2W components example, 268
  login panel example, components, 158
  non-D2W application example, 276
  SAME AS WOSUBMIT!!!.
wotaskd daemon, 370
  configuration info, accessing, 371
    output, document entries, 372
  functionality, deployment management, 370
    diagram, 370
  host running wotaskd, setting up within Monitor, 363
  password protection, 372
WOTextField class
  binding example, WebObjects Builder's object
    browser, 50
  D2W components example, 268
  fetch specification example, creating manually, 195
  fetch specification example, creating using
    EOModeler, 206
  login panel example, components, 158
  method creation example, WebObjects Builder, 61
  non-D2W application example, 276

X

XML (eXtensible Markup Language)
  DirectToJavaClient framework, XML outputting, 331
    as EOController subclasses, 331

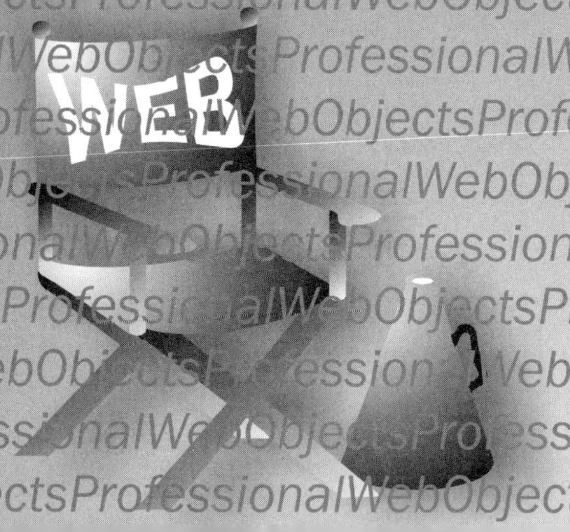
WEB

p2p.wrox.com
The programmer's resource centre

A unique free service from Wrox Press
with the aim of helping programmers to help each other

Wrox Press aims to provide timely and practical information to today's programmer. P2P is a list server offering a host of targeted mailing lists where you can share knowledge with your fellow programmers and find solutions to your problems. Whatever the level of your programming knowledge, and whatever technology you use, P2P can provide you with the information you need.

ASP — Support for beginners and professionals, including a resource page with hundreds of links, and a popular ASP+ mailing list.

DATABASES — For database programmers, offering support on SQL Server, mySQL, and Oracle.

MOBILE — Software development for the mobile market is growing rapidly. We provide lists for the several current standards, including WAP, WindowsCE, and Symbian.

JAVA — A complete set of Java lists, covering beginners, professionals, and server-side programmers (including JSP, servlets and EJBs)

.NET — Microsoft's new OS platform, covering topics such as ASP+, C#, and general .Net discussion.

VISUAL BASIC — Covers all aspects of VB programming, from programming Office macros to creating components for the .Net platform.

WEB DESIGN — As web page requirements become more complex, programmer sare taking a more important role in creating web sites. For these programmers, we offer lists covering technologies such as Flash, Coldfusion, and JavaScript.

XML — Covering all aspects of XML, including XSLT and schemas.

OPEN SOURCE — Many Open Source topics covered including PHP, Apache, Perl, Linux, Python and more.

FOREIGN LANGUAGE — Several lists dedicated to Spanish and German speaking programmers, categories include .Net, Java, XML, PHP and XML.

How To Subscribe

Simply visit the P2P site, at **http://p2p.wrox.com/**

Select the 'FAQ' option on the side menu bar for more information about the subscription process and our service.